Selected Studies
in Marriage and the Family

Selected Studies

in Marriage and the Family

THIRD EDITION

Edited by

Robert F. Winch

Northwestern University

Louis Wolf Goodman

Northwestern University

HOLT, RINEHART and WINSTON, INC.

*New York Chicago San Francisco Atlanta Dallas
Montreal Toronto London*

PREFACE

This third edition of *Selected Studies in Marriage and the Family* appears fifteen years after the first edition and six years after the second. Excluding the first chapter, there are 62 articles, 42 of which are new to this edition. Almost all of these new articles have appeared since the publication of the second edition in 1962. Stated differently, about one-fifth of the articles from the first edition and about one-third of those from the second are reprinted in this book.

Although the material has shifted greatly from one edition to another, the objective has remained constant—to present the sixty or so articles that can provide the most comprehensive statement of the sociology of marriage and the family and then to give coherence to the set of readings by organizing and introducing them. Another objective has been to try to make the analysis preponderantly general (that is, culture-free) but also to present some information about the family in the United States.

In the first chapter we summarize some of the elements of scientific procedure and relate them to problems involved in studying the family. Assuredly, as with other classes of phenomena, durable knowledge about the family can be achieved only through the use of scientific method. We hope that the first chapter will provide the reader with a set of criteria for judging the contributions in the rest of the book.

After Chapter 1, the organization of the book is rather similar to, but not identical with that of Robert F. Winch's *The Modern Family*. Chapters 2 and 5 consider the structure and functions of the family, Chapter 3 views these elements in the flux of time, and Chapter 4 considers the structural and functional diversity of the family in the United States.

The triadic family—father, mother, and child—involves two major dyads that are the foci of the remainder of the book. The relation of parent and child is the subject of Part II. The influence of the family on the child begins before birth, both with respect to the social position the child will come to occupy and with the behavioral dispositions the child will acquire, which we subsume under the rubrics of role and personality. Beyond this, there are papers concerned with the impact on the child of social structures—both societal and familial—and with the consequences of parental disciplinary practices and of parental values. Lest it be hastily assumed that the family's influence on the individual terminates with childhood, Part II continues its concern with the parent-child relationship from the offspring's coming to adulthood until the time when the parent has become aged and at times disengaged.

Part III considers the other major dyad—that of husband and wife. One paper takes up the gamut of possible ways in which mates may be selected, while another views the conditions under which mate-selection is so important to the family that they set up procedures of "love control." Factors that determine who marries whom in the United States and the nature of love, the elements of the marital relationship and the conditions under which it is dissolved constitute problems for analysis in this section. The book closes with a characterization of the role of the divorcee and an actuarial assessment of the success of remarriage.

Although the editors of this book have selected articles, arranged them, and written commentaries with the foregoing organization in mind, they are aware that other perspectives can be served with the same offerings. Other kinds of organizing themes would include: the natural history of the family,[1] the family studied cross-culturally,[2] the social psychology of the family,[3] the ethnology of the family,[4] the family as a study in role-contradictions (or marginality and alienation),[5] and ethnic families.[6]

The editors of the present volume wish to acknowledge their debt to Professors Robert McGinnis of Cornell University and Herbert R. Barringer of the University of Hawaii, who participated in the earlier editions and contributed to the format of those books.

R. F. W.

L. W. G.

May 1968
Evanston, Illinois

See articles in this volume by:

[1]Nimkoff-Middleton, Ogburn, Goode (on family in industrialization), and Blood.

[2]Fortes, Nimkoff-Middleton, Adams, Lewis, Barry et. al., Sweetser, Sugimoto, Vogel, and Freeman.

[3]Dyer, E. Maccoby, Lynn, Bandura et al., Baumrind, Brim, Kohn, Strodtbeck, and Cumming.

[4]Rainwater, Campisi, Leichter-Mitchell, Lewis, Scott, Sugimoto.

[5]Whyte, Komarovsky, Parsons, Cumming, Vogel, Freeman.

[6]Re the Jewish family in the United States—Leichter-Mitchell, Strodtbeck, Winch; on the Italian family in the United States—Campisi, Strodtbeck; on the Negro family in the United States—Heer, Rainwater.

CONTENTS

PART ONE

A General Sociology of the Family:
Methodology, Concepts, and Propositions

1

SCIENTIFIC METHOD AND THE STUDY OF THE FAMILY

Reports in this volume have been prepared by members of a curious breed—the social scientist. This breed is curious in that it attempts to focus a powerful mechanism, the scientific method, on the most mundane of matters, man's routine behavior. Why should the social scientist study who marries whom when we all may know that a man marries the first woman with whom he falls in love, whom he seeks to marry, and who accepts his offer?

This "simple truth" is of little interest to the social scientist. It is not a response to the kind of question asked by the researcher. In mate-selection, as with other topics, it is the scientist's task to identify the relevant variables, to determine the relationships among these variables, to weave these relationships into a theory, and then to assess the utility of that theory as an explanation of systematic observations of what actually occurs. Throughout this process the social scientist is seeking answers to questions like: What general principle will predict the kind of woman a specific man is likely to meet? What general principle will predict the one woman among those he meets with whom he is most likely to fall in love?

The term "science" will be discussed in some detail on the following pages. The important point to grasp at the outset is that science consists not of orderly sets of facts, not of established truth. Rather, science is a method, a procedure for arriving at reasonably adequate explanations of the various aspects of the state of nature; it does not arrive at unalterable statements of final truth. Science is a method, not fact. Social science, then, is the process of applying the method of science to the analysis of social behavior. In the present collection we consider the scientific analysis of marital and familial structures and functions.

Scientific study of marriage and the family has a single purpose: to acquire stable, systematic, unbiased knowledge about these phenomena. Although such knowledge can be used to reduce human grief, the main purpose of such studies, and of this collection, is not to promote human happiness and welfare, but to make this knowledge available for whosoever may find it useful.

This introductory chapter provides the reader with some standards by means of which each article in the book can be judged as to its scientific merit. Some of the articles may seem eloquent and others heavy with jargon such as "homogamy" and "complementariness." While treasuring literary style, the editors have given top priority to scientific merit.[1] For

[1] While deploring turgid and opaque writing in any context, the editors believe with Bertrand Russell that the language of daily life does not suffice for tech-

this reason the editors suggest to the reader that questions of the following order should guide his evaluation of each article:

1. What is asserted?
2. Can the truth of the assertion be tested by the scientific method?
3. Do the indexes selected by the author adequately reflect the original conceptual variables?
4. Does the author actually bring evidence to bear on the question so that a negative outcome is possible and, thus, does he test the assertion?
5. If a test is offered, is it sufficiently conclusive that the reader is justified in accepting the assertion as tentative truth and using it in his life as a guidepost?
6. Can the assertion be generalized so that it leads to predictions about a class of events?
7. Is the assertion linked to other assertions so as to form a theoretical web, or "nomological net" as it is sometimes called?

In this section we deal with two major topics: The nature of science and how social researchers utilize the scientific method to study marriage and the family. The purpose of this discussion is to give the reader a background that will help him answer the questions raised in the preceeding paragraphs.

Science may be regarded as a way of considering man's perceptions of the state of nature plus a method for organizing and understanding these perceptions. Man can never be certain that any of his perceptions are accurate reflections of the state of nature. Because of this, scientists can never be sure that any description of the state of nature[2] is correct. However, scientists do generate descriptions in which they are relatively and tentatively confident. These descriptions of the state of nature are accepted only after systematic comparison with all other descriptions which the researcher has at his disposal. Furthermore, a given description can be rejected whenever a new description is devised that is judged to be superior. The systematic comparison of competing descriptions (sometimes called theories) is part of the scientific method.

Although facts are highly useful, the ultimate goal of science is not the collecting and classifying of facts. This task is admirably accomplished by the compilers of almanacs. Rather, the objective of science is the development of a completely general and systematic set of theories from which hypotheses are deduced and verified, and in terms of which the structures and changes of animate and inanimate phenomena may be best explained.

The objective of the scientist is to obtain satisfactory answers to *how* questions: *How* do social phenomena come to appear as they do, and

---

nical discourse. Russell remarks that what he calls "the cult of 'common usage' " excuses ignorance of mathematics and other fields "in those who have had only a classical education." From Bertrand Russell, *Portraits from Memory and Other Essays*. New York: Simon and Schuster, Inc., 1956, p. 166. Relevant here is the discussion under "Utilizing the Scientific Outlook" near the end of this chapter.

[2] In this essay "description" includes studies of the type sometimes referred to as "analytical." See note 3.

how do they undergo the processes of change which characterize them? Before the scientist can ever learn how to ask the *how* questions properly, however, he must first ask and answer another set—the *what* questions. Before one can begin to explain *how* phenomena come to exist and change as they do, one must know of *what* they are structured, and with *what* speed these structures change. To phrase it differently, before a scientist tries to explain a phenomenon, he should have an accurate picture of that phenomenon. To put it more systematically, we can consider two types of investigation. The first focuses on a *property* such as income distribution in the United States or incidence of a particular disease. The second focuses on *relations* that explain how one property of a given population functions with respect to other properties in that population.[3]

The papers by Glick and Parke on the life cycle of the family and by Carter and Plateris on trends in divorce illustrate the focus on properties. Those by Brim on the association between sibling arrangement and sex-role socialization, and by Wolfe on the correlates of marital power exemplify studies of relations.

A study of a property provides information about the distribution of that property in some specified population, for example, the median age at first marriage for males in the United States during 1965 (the population is the United States during 1965; the property is the median age at marriage).

By linking two or more properties, a study of relations makes possible a better-than-chance prediction of one property given a value (or values) on one (or more) related properties. Thus Brim shows that there is tendency for a boy whose only sibling is an older sister to exhibit more girlish behavior than will a boy whose only sibling is an older brother (property 1, sex of older sibling, is related to property 2, sex-role learned by younger sibling).

There is one additional distinction which is useful to draw between types of scientific investigations. This concerns whether a study is theory-free or theory-bound.

In the sense of theory testing, the basis for this distinction is apparent. Studies of properties are theory-free. They do not test theories, rather each measures a single property. Studies of relations are theory-bound. Each tests a proposed relationship between two or more sets of properties (variables). In the next section we shall see that such a proposed relationship is known to scientists as a theory.

There is another sense in which scientific investigations may be theory-free or theory-bound. This concerns whether the study is or is not guided by a theory. Especially during the early development of a scientific field, investigations tend to be oriented toward the task of mapping a hitherto unknown domain. In this early stage there is little or no theory to guide studies. During this period researchers are looking for the major

---

[3] The distinction between these two types of investigation is sometimes referred to as that between descriptive and analytical studies. These terms, however, have created such dispute in their interpretation that we prefer to avoid them.

ariables and trying to get some understanding as to which variables co-vary with each other. Sometimes this early phase is spoken of as the "classificatory" stage of development. It is out of such work that the information is developed from which the important variables can be conceptualized and a beginning made in the construction of theory. As a field develops, more and more theory is available to guide studies, and studies become, in this sense, theory-bound. Both theory-free and theory-bound studies are essential to the development of science. However, it is interesting to note that theory-bound investigations generally do stand closer to the goals of science and thereby represent a more highly developed state of a discipline. On the other hand, theory-free investigations lay the necessary base for the more advanced undertakings.

The first step toward the construction of a "nomological net" or web of theory is the measurement of properties. The next step consists of linking these properties in a statement which describes the relations between them. A theoretical web is finally constructed when all relevant properties are linked by relational statements.

THEORY AND THE EVALUATION OF THEORY

A scientific theory is a statement of the way in which abstract variables are related to each other and from which verifiable hypotheses are deduced. Such a hypothesis asserts an expected relationship between the indexes of two or more abstract variables. The term "verifiable" has a special meaning for the scientist. It refers to the capacity of a theory to generate hypotheses that are not rejected when the relevant empirical data (observations of the state of nature) are collected in a properly designed study. To be scientifically proper, a design must provide the logical possibility that the data will lead to the rejection of the hypothesis, that is, to the conclusion that the data do not support the expected relationship between the indexes of the abstract variables.

Verifiability is not the only criterion for evaluating the usefulness of the explanations provided by a theory. Another standard is "comprehensiveness."[4] Comprehensiveness refers to the scope of the theory's explanation. The more *comprehensive* of two theories explains more aspects of the state of nature. The more *verifiable* of two theories can provide more evidence that it explains aspects of the state of nature accurately. The ideal theory facilitates the generation of accurate hypotheses about a wide slice of the state of nature. In his article in the present volume, Adams alleges that his conception of the family enables him to account for a greater range of behavior than have other theories, that it is more comprehensive in ex-

---

[4] The editors have used the terms "comprehensiveness" and "complexity" as attributes of theories. Both terms denote the range or coverage of phenomena in the theories. The difference is that comprehensiveness refers to the range of phenomena to be explained, the range of the dependent variable; complexity refers to the range of explanatory variables, the number of independent variables.

plaining the mother-child family rather than in regarding it theoretically as a deviant form.

These criteria for the evaluation of theories assert nothing about how a theory may be first suggested. A theory may be suggested by an insight, an intuition, a dream, or any other bit of experience. The suggesting of the theory is, however, only the first step. To satisfy the requisites of science, a theory must culminate in a statement from which testable hypotheses are deduced, tested, and then verified or rejected before we can judge whether the theory is scientifically useful. Thus the term "verifiable" in our definition of a scientific theory prevents us from regarding as scientific knowledge any theory based exclusively on insight, intuition or revelation, but allows us to use such experiences as a beginning point in the construction of a theory.

SINGLE-FACTOR AND MULTI-FACTOR THEORIES

With reasonable security we may generalize to all of social science the observation that no complete theory exists. Instead, we find theories that are in varying stages of development, that is, theories that contain statements of relations of varying degrees of comprehensiveness, verifiability, and complexity. The least complex of such theories may be labeled the "single-factor" theory. These theories attempt to explain variation in a class of phenomena in terms of the operation of a single variable. In other words, a single-factor study is a relational study, but one in which the investigation is confined to one relation. Bossard's analysis of mate-selection in terms of residential propinquity is illustrative of this type.[5]

From the work of Bossard and others who have studied the relation between mate-selection and race, then, we can predict that men tend to marry women who live near them rather than those whose residences are remote. But from studies based upon New Haven data we can also predict that men are more likely to marry women similar to themselves with respect to religion, ethnic grouping, social class, and age group than to marry women who differ from themselves in these social characteristics.[6] When we consider all of these factors together, we have a "multi-factor" theory, and we are able to go considerably farther toward the goal of predicting who marries whom than we could have be considering any one of these factors by itself. We can generalize from this example and say that as relevant factors are added to a theory (that is, as the theory is made more complex) the more complete will be the explanation. Moreover,

[5] James H. S. Bossard, "Residential Propinquity as a Factor in Marriage Selection," *American Journal of Sociology*, 1932, 38: 219–224.

[6] August B. Hollingshead, "Cultural Factors in the Selection of Marriage Mates," pp. 486–496 of this volume. To compare a simple theory with a more complex version, see the treatment by Katz and Hill of Bossard's theory of residential propinquity: Alvin M. Katz and Reuben Hill, "Residential Propinquity and Marital Selection: A Review of Theory, Method, and Fact," pp. 496–503 of this volume.

the fusing of these several correlates of mate-selection into the single concept, "the field of eligibles,"[7] illustrates both the shift to a higher level of
abstraction and how such a shift depends upon multi-factor theories.

Since the goal of science is to explain as much about a given phenomenon as is practically possible, one may wonder why all theories are not
considerably more complex. One important reason is that the more complex the theory, the more difficulty the researcher has in subjecting it to
empirical test and in using it for predictive purposes. With single-factor
hypotheses one may use simple techniques of analysis,[8] but with every
added factor the methods of testing hypotheses become more difficult
and tedious.[9]

While the articles in this volume contain conclusions, it must be
realized that these conclusions are far from complete. And, like the conclusions of all scientific fields, they are certainly not final. The present
status of the sociology of the family is indicated by the fact that some of
these papers are simply studies of properties and others are single-factor
theories. But a scientific discipline cannot reach maturity without first acquiring a fund of knowledge about properties and about simple relations
between pairs of properties.

THE PROCESS OF ABSTRACTION

Theories consist of statements of relations between sets of abstract
categories. Abstraction is a means of creating a class of phenomena by
taking account of the properties that observed objects have in common and
excluding from consideration the properties on which they show variety.
Quadrupeds constitute a class of animals having four legs; variation
among the beasts with respect to size, color of hair, and so forth, are ignored in the construction of this class. Abstraction is a process of selecting
aspects of the concrete world that are useful to look at and of excluding
those aspects thought to be irrelevant. The point of view and the purpose
of the observing scientist determines what is useful, as well as what is irrelevant. Let us take the notion of parenthood. If a biologist should study
parenthood, he might select from the very complicated set of attitudes,
experiences and relationships denoted by that term only those features
bearing on genetics and reproduction. An economist studying parenthood
might select only those aspects relevant to understanding changes and
rates of change in the demand for and consumption of goods and services.
A sociologist might select aspects concerning the socialization of the child
or its inheritance. All of these scientists would be abstracting. Each would
consider only those aspects of the complex reality he regards as relevant

[7] Thomas Ktsanes and Virginia Ktsanes, "The Theory of Complementary
Needs in Mate Selection," pp. 517–529 of this volume.

[8] Such as the *t* test and the zero-order r.

[9] The tedium of multivariate analysis has been markedly reduced by the development and availability of high-speed computers.

to his questions and would exclude from consideration phenomena that scientists with other questions might choose to study.

Each of these scientists would be selecting for study a different set of events, which might be called sociological, psychological, biological, or whatever. Sometimes these sets are spoken of as "levels," as the sociological, or the psychological level of abstraction. Social scientists often use the phrase "levels of abstraction" in another sense: to denote various levels of generality. In this usage the more general term "field of eligibles" is said to be at a higher level of abstraction than terms it subsumes such as "nearness of residence" and "similarity of religion."

From the scientific point of view the "real world" is a confusing scene filled with heterogeneous information. Abstraction enables the scientist to simplify the heterogeneity of the concrete world by excluding from his consideration data that are irrelevant to his purpose. For this reason the process of abstraction is a necessary step in the constructing and testing of theories.

Let us summarize the argument of this section. Sociological thinking (like thinking in other sciences) involves the abstracting process. By this term is meant that from the wholeness of his perceptions of the empirical world the sociologist selects only those properties he deems to be distinctively sociological and he excludes all other properties. Abstraction then, is the process through which the sociologist arrives at sociological concepts. Accordingly, as we shall see in the next section, when a sociologist theorizes, he is asserting relationships among conceptually defined variables and thus making use of the products of the abstracting process. To test empirically the relationships he believes prevail among concepts, he once again abstracts in selecting empirical indexes to represent these concepts as well as possible.

STATING THE THEORY AT THE CONCEPTUAL LEVEL

A concept is something that exists as an idea but not as a perception. Although any type of thought may be expressed conceptually, the word "concept" is most often used by social scientists to refer to a conceptually defined variable. In this essay our use of the word "concept" is not so restricted, but refers to any thought that is expressed as an idea. When theories begin to take form, they exist only as concepts in the mind of the theorist. An assertion of a relationship between conceptually defined variables is a conceptual proposition (or a proposition asserted at the conceptual level). A series of such propositions that can be related to each other (that are said to be compendent) constitutes a theory.

STATING THE THEORY AT THE OPERATIONAL (EMPIRICAL) LEVEL

Before a theory may be subjected to an empirical test, there must be some way of relating observations to the conceptual variables. To do this, a scientist creates an index (or operational definition) of each conceptual variable in the proposition to be tested. This step is accomplished by means of the logical processes called "index construction" and "deduction."[10]

The essence of deduction is "the derivation of conclusions *necessarily* involved in the premises."[11] To illustrate, if we set forth the premises (1) that all men are mortal and (2) that William Jones is a man, then we must conclude that Mr. Jones is mortal because this conclusion is a necessary consequence of the premises. Deductive logic is important to scientists because it is by means of deduction that they proceed from a theory stated at the conceptual level through index construction to concrete data.

The researcher uses deduction in the following manner. The first premise is a statement of a relationship among the conceptual variables. The second premise contains indexes of the conceptual variables in the first premise.[12] From these premises he deduces hypotheses that can be tested empirically. For example, if we wish to test Toby's idea that children's orientation to education is a function of class position,[13] we may state our premises in this manner: (1) Children's orientation to education is positively correlated with position in the class structure (the higher the child's social position, the more favorable his orientation to education is likely to be). (2a) School achievement, as measured by grade placement per age level is an index of orientation to education. (2b) Monthly rental value of home is an index of social class position. From these premises we hypothesize that school achievement is positively correlated with monthly rental value of home. Thus, by using school achievement and home rental value as indexes of the conceptual variables (orientation to education and class position, respectively) in the first premise, we are able to test the statement of relationship. The adequacy of our test depends in part upon the quality of the indexes, and in part upon the adequacy of the research design.

[10] For a discussion of deduction, see Morris R. Cohen and Ernest Nagel, *An Introduction to Logic and Scientific Method*. New York: Harcourt, Brace & World, Inc., 1934, especially chaps. 7 and 14. For a discussion of deductive reasoning and theory verification in sociology, see Hans L. Zetterberg, *On Theory and Verification in Sociology*. New York: Tressler, 1954.

[11] Cohen and Nagel, p. 273. (Italics in original.)

[12] A strict operationalist would label the second premise an "operational definition." For a discussion of operationalism, see Gustav Bergmann and Kenneth W. Spence, "Operationism and Theory Construction," in Melvin H. Marx, ed., *Psychological Theory*. New York: Crowell-Collier and Macmillan, Inc., 1951, pp. 54–66.

[13] Jackson Toby, "Orientation to Education as a Factor in the School Maladjustment of Lower-Class Children," pp. 339–348 of this volume.

COUNTING AND MEASUREMENT

Hypotheses concern characteristics of members of classes of phenomena. We speak of these classes of phenomena as populations (or universes) whether or not the units of observation are human beings. Verification involves counting and measuring. In the crudest case the scientist counts individuals to determine the number who do and who do not have a given characteristic. If the characteristic can be measured, the scientist will ordinarily prefer to measure the degree to which each individual possesses it.

Scientific measurement involves considerably more than Geiger counters and oscilloscopes. It may include any technique of recording the phenomenon in question with a minimum of fluctuation resulting from human idiosyncrasies. It may depend upon a multimillion dollar cyclotron or a man standing on a street corner counting passers-by. Following are criteria for assessing the worth of a scientific instrument (that is, for telling how good an index is): relevance, validity, and reliability. By relevance we mean an affirmative answer to the question, Does it measure what the scientist happens to be interested in? By validity we mean the degree to which it measures what it is supposed to measure. Reliability refers to the degree to which the instrument gives constant measurements of an unchanging entity on different occasions.

In a broad sense, measurement consists of transforming physical characteristics into numbers or, more properly, into numerals. In this sense, even the assignment of serial numbers to soldiers or to equipment constitutes measurement. Similarly, the transformation of academic classifications, freshman, sophomore, junior, senior, into the numerals 1, 2, 3, 4 respectively is a form of measurement.[14] The important point here is that such numerals should not be confused with real numbers for they do not necessarily have the algebraic properties of numbers. Addition, for example, is a property of numbers, but if we try to apply the arithmetic truth $1 + 1 = 2$ to the above illustrative measurement, we obtain the ridiculous proposition: "Two freshmen equal one sophomore." All too frequently social scientists fall into the trap of confusing numerals with numbers and incorrectly investing the former with mathematical properties of the latter. Whenever an investigator reports that he has added or multiplied scores of some sort, the reader should ask himself whether or not the operation is justified by the measurement that was used.

It is conventional to distinguish four types of scale for the measurement of an operational variable (or index): nominal, ordinal, interval, and ratio. A nominal scale is an unordered set of categories; with respect to the population under study the set of categories must be mutually exclusive and collectively exhaustive. An example of a nominal scale is a set of categories for classifying the religious affiliation of respondents in a

---

[14] The development of data-processing equipment and the punchcard with its numbered columns and rows has stimulated this kind of coding process whereby a numeral stands for a category.

survey in the United States, such as the following: Protestant, Catholic, Jewish, other, no religion, and declined-to-respond.

An ordinal scale is a nominal scale in which the categories have some "natural" or "inherent" order. Warner's categories of social class constitute an example: upper-upper, lower-upper, upper-middle, lower-middle, upper-lower and lower-lower. It would be quite as acceptable to reverse the order just shown, but any other order would seem absurd, and the reader would be disposed to comment that the order of the categories had been scrambled. Measurement for both the nominal and ordinal scales consists of determining to which category each individual under scrutiny belongs and then counting the number in each category after all have been so classified.

An interval scale involves the idea of a metric—a unit that is of the same size at any location along the dimension under consideration. For example, we assert that 37° F is as much higher than 33° F as 95° F is above 91° F.

A ratio scale is an interval scale plus the specification of an absolute zero point. Temperature when measured from absolute zero conforms to a ratio scale for only under this condition can a reading of, say, 100° be said to be twice as hot as a reading of 50°. In social science, income is the most obvious example of a ratio scale.[15]

SAMPLING IN STUDIES OF PROPERTIES

Studies of properties and studies of relations call for different approaches to the problem of sampling. Let us discuss first what is involved in the study of properties. We notice first that the end toward which such a study is aimed is to provide the number which completes such a statement as, "The crude birth rate of the United States in 1967 was _____ per 100 population," or, "The median age at first marriage for white males in the United States in 1967 was _____ years." Ideally the procedure for arriving at the answer to a question about some property would be to make an observation on every member of the referent population and then to compute the desired parameter (value for the population) by means of simple arithmetic.

Because of the expense involved it is usually impossible to count all the individuals in an entire population who do or do not have a characteristic, or to measure a characteristic for an entire population. The compromise of the scientist (both social and natural) is to draw a sample of the population which he tries to make as representative of the whole population as he can, that is, a sample in which the proportion of each of the

[15] To those who are interested in pursuing this topic we add the following comments. We may conceive of these four types of scale as constituting a hierarchy from nominal at the bottom through ordinal and interval to ratio at the top. This hierarchy means that each scale (a) contains more information than the one below it and (b) permits more arithmetical and statistical operations than those below it.

constituent segments, strata, and so forth, is the same as in the population. Since "even a large sample confined to a portion of the population is devoid of information about the excluded portions,"[16] and since the purpose of this kind of investigation is to arrive at a statement about the entire population, representativeness of the sample is very important. With a representative sample the scientist is able to make an estimate of the value in the population of the property in which he is interested, or more technically, he is able to estimate the parameter of that property in the population. If, as is usually the case, the scientist also wishes to calculate the probability that his estimate deviates by any given amount from the true value, he must also sample randomly. In its most elementary form, labeled *simple* random sampling, the process consists of selecting a sample of size n (where n is a positive integer) in such a fashion that any such sample of size n is just as likely—but no liklier—to be chosen than any other sample of size n.[17] Random sampling also assures a degree of representativeness of the sample, although this method does not maximize representativeness.

SAMPLING IN STUDIES OF RELATIONS

The purpose of studies of relations is to find the nature of the relation, if any, between two or more variables. It frequently happens that the scrutiny of a relation or the test of a hypothesis is best carried out with something other than a representative sample. In the study by Strodtbeck,[18] for example, there was interest in the relation between orientation to achievement in adolescent boys on the one hand and ethnicity on the other. If Strodtbeck had sampled the population of his city representatively, he probably would not have obtained a large enough sample of the ethnic groups he intended to compare to make his comparison representative of these groups. Furthermore, with a representative sample, the Jews would have been largely in the middle class and the Italians more heavily distributed in the lower class. For this reason social class would have become confounded with ethnicity. Because he wanted to test a hypothesis about relations between specific variables, he had to sample in a way that would clearly separate the effects of these two variables. Therefore, Strodtbeck "held constant" the variable social class and drew samples of equal

[16] G. W. Snedecor, *Statistical Methods*, 4th ed. Ames, Iowa: Collegiate Press, Inc., 1946, p. 460.

[17] The emphasis on the representativeness of the sample should not be construed as implying approval of the so-called "quota" sample. For a detailed but elementary discussion of sampling procedures in social research, see Leslie Kish, "Selection of the Sample," in Leon Festinger and Daniel Katz, eds., *Research Methods in the Behavioral Sciences.* New York: Holt, Rinehart and Winston, Inc., 1953, chap. 5.

[18] Fred L. Strodtbeck, "Family Interaction, Values, and Achievement," pp. 364–380 of this volume.

numbers of middle-class Jews and Italians and of lower-class Jews and Italians. This procedure allowed him to examine the relationship between ethnicity and orientation to achievement (the two variables he hoped to relate), and to exclude from analysis the effect of social class upon orientation to achievement.

As with studies of properties, it is important to note that randomness of sampling is essential within the categories to be compared if the investigator expects to rely upon statistical analysis to make probabilistic inferences about the truth or falsity of the relationships in the population sampled. To this end, Strodtbeck drew random samples of the four categories described above.

DESIGN OF RESEARCH: THE "CLASSICAL" EXPERIMENT

From the discussion to follow we shall see that the conclusions which we may draw from a piece of research are determined in part by the way in which the study is set up or, to use the more technical term, are dependent in part on the "design" of the research. Although it is frequently impossible to use such a rigorous and ideal design in social research, we shall first consider a classical design of experiment. Then we shall note the ways in which certain practicable designs diverge from the ideal and with what logical consequences.

The simplest design that contains the essentials of the experimental method is as follows: A random sample is divided into two groups (or subsamples), one called the "experimental" group, and the other the "control" group. At this stage the two groups should be as much alike as possible in all relevant respects. If the assignment of individuals from the original sample to the two subsamples is done in a random manner, then the experimental and control groups should be representative samples of the population.[19]

After the two groups have been formed, every individual in each group is measured with respect to the index of the variable under study, or a count is made in each group to determine how many individuals possess or lack the attribute in question.

Next the experimental group—but not the control group—is subjected to a certain controlled condition (sometimes called "treatment"). After the experimental group has undergone the treatment, measures are obtained from both groups with respect to the variable about which the experimenter is concerned.

We now have two measurements (before and after treatment) on each of the two groups (experimental and control). Concerning these four

---

[19] While random assignment to the two groups is probably the usual procedure, if conditions are favorable, the matched-pair method is more efficient. For a discussion of the effects of random assignment of subjects, see Robert McGinnis, "Randomization and Inference in Sociological Research," *American Sociological Review*, 1958, 23: 408–414.

measurements the researcher sets up what he calls "null hypotheses." A null hypothesis asserts that the obtained difference is *no greater than might reasonably have occurred by chance alone.*[20]

The researcher sets up two null hypotheses. The first of these is employed in a comparison of the experimental-before and control-before measurements. The samples of these groups should have been so drawn that the null hypothesis is sustained.[21] If the null hypothesis is upheld in this first comparison, a second null hypothesis is asserted. It states that there is no difference between the experimental-after and control-after groups. If the null hypothesis is also sustained here, we can infer that the experimental treatment has not resulted in a measureable effect. If it is rejected, we have evidence that the treatment caused the experimental group to change in a measureable way.

Now let us summarize in schematic form this discussion of what we shall call the "fourfold" or "four-cell" design:

1. A random sample of some specified population is drawn.

2. By random assignment or some other procedure, the sample is divided into two subsamples, called "the experimental group" and "the control group."

3. Every individual in each group is measured with respect to the index of the variable under study. Or if the variable is an attribute, frequencies of "present" and "absent" are counted. The counts or measurements are entered in the "experimental-before" and "control-before" cells of the fourfold table in Figure 1 [page 16].

4. The two groups are compared with respect to the distribution of the variable measured or counted. Since the two groups are intended to be alike at this stage, it is expected that the differences between them as revealed by the measure will be no greater than might reasonably be expected that the null hypothesis will be accepted.

5. The experimental group is subjected to some controlled condition, stimulus, or treatment. The control group does not have this experience.

6. Every individual in both groups is again measured with respect to the index of the variable under study. The counts or measurements are entered in the "experimental-after" and "control-after" cells of the fourfold table in Figure 1.

7. Again the two groups are compared with respect to the distribution of the variable measured or counted. Since this comparison is made after

---

[20] Strictly speaking, a null hypothesis asserts that the two subsamples being considered, only one of which has been subjected to an experimental treatment, differ so little with respect to the measured variable that the probability is acceptably high that they could have been drawn from a single population; that is, a null hypothesis implies that the experimental treatment has had no measurable effect.

[21] It will be recalled that under the ideal procedure no treatment has yet been administered and that individuals from a randomly drawn sample have been randomly assigned to the experimental and control subsamples. Accordingly, it is reasonable for the experimenter to expect that the first null hypothesis will be sustained.

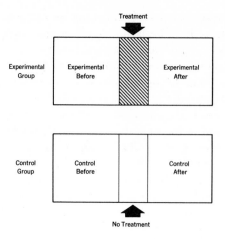

FIG. 1.   Schematic diagram of four-cell experimental design

the treatment and since the two groups were alike before treatment, a greater than chance difference at this point (a rejection of the null hypothesis) is interpreted as an effect of the treatment.[22]

STATISTICAL ASSESSMENT OF RESULTS OF THE "CLASSICAL" EXPERIMENT

Implied in the discussion of single-factor and multi-factor theories is the point that, because our theories are mostly simple, or "weak," our explanations are limited. By a weak theory we refer to a theory whose predictions, though more often right than wrong, are still frequently wrong.[23] In a discipline characterized by weak theory the results of research are frequently ambiguous. It is necessary, therefore, to use statistical analysis to determine whether or not the results deviate enough from a chance outcome to be regarded as consonant with the prediction of the theory.

To determine the probability that an observed difference might have arisen by chance alone, or, as statisticians say, to measure the significance of the difference, statistical techniques such as chi-square (χ^2), the criti-

[22] The term "experiment" has been used by various writers with a variety of denotations. The editors of this volume regard the following as necessary conditions for a study to be judged an "experiment": experimental and control groups, controlled treatment or stimulus, and observations made both before and after treatment. Accordingly, the fourfold design is the simplest prototype of what we call the "experimental method."

[23] We may phrase this point in the language of correlation analysis. Theories in social science frequently lead to correlations no greater than .4. This may be phrased that such a theory "explains" 16 per cent $(.4)^2 \times 100$ of the variance in the dependent variable and leaves 84 percent $(100 - 16)$ "unexplained."

cal ratio, and the *t* test are applied. When an author uses the expression "P<.05," he is telling us that, for a sample of the size used, a difference as great as that obtained could have occurred by chance alone less than 5 times out of 100.[24] This knowledge makes us reasonably certain that the difference is not a chance occurrence, but the evidence would be more compelling if P < .01 or if P < .001. These symbols tell us that if the null hypothesis is correct, a difference as large as that observed would not be expected to occur as often as once in 100 or 1000 trials respectively. Such a result, which is said to be "statistically significant" at the ".01" or ".001 level," is fairly convincing evidence that the null hypothesis is false and that instead there is a real difference between the population characteristics under investigation.

INTERPRETATION OF RESULTS OF THE "CLASSICAL" EXPERIMENT

If the results of a research are statistically significant,[25] and in the direction hypothesized, they are interpreted as supporting the hypothesis. Then the researcher tentatively concludes (draws the generalization) that whenever a representative sample of the population studied is subjected to the same treatment under the same conditions, the result will be approximately the same. This conclusion must, of course, be qualified by the fact that, no matter how small the likelihood, the possibility always exists that the result might have occurred by chance.

[24] A critical ratio of 1.96 is always significant at the .05 level, and a critical ratio of 2.58 is always significant at the .01 level. The significance of an obtained *t* or chi-square, however, varies with the degrees of freedom involved. Tables of areas of the normal curve (for interpretation of the critical ratio), of *t*, and of chi-square are available in Herbert Arkin and Raymond R. Colton, *Tables for Statisticians.* New York: Barnes & Noble, Inc., 1950. Discussion of the application of such tests to social data is presented in standard statistical texts, including Hubert M. Blalock, Jr., *Social Statistics.* New York: McGraw-Hill, Inc., 1960. The symbol "P" above stands for "probability."

[25] What constitutes statistical significance is largely a matter of convention in the various disciplines. In fields where it is difficult to produce significant results, scientists are frequently satisfied if the probability that an observed result might have arisen by chance is no more than 1 in 20; in other disciplines 1 in 100 or 1 in 1000 may be the minimum chance probability for a result to be regarded as significant. What the statistician refers to as type II error (or β error) enters into the choice of significance level. Type II error is the error of the acceptance of an hypothesis when it is false; type I error (or α error) is the rejection of an hypothesis when it is true. A .01 significance level implies that, on the average, for each 100 samples drawn from a population in which the null hypothesis is true, one (type I) error will be made, and the null hypothesis will be rejected. Because of the reciprocal relationship between type I error and type II error it is not necessarily sound scientific judgement to minimize type I error.

Such a generalization is founded on one of the assumptions basic to science: that *there is uniformity in nature,* or in other words, that what results today from a particular combination of elements under specified circumstances will result tomorrow from an identical combination of elements under duplicated circumstances. The assumption can never be demonstrated with any finality, either logically or empirically. Since scientists do seem capable of making better than chance predictions of some kinds of future events, however, the assumption is pragmatically tenable. We must point out that an act of faith is involved in the scientist's assumption of uniformity in nature.

APPROXIMATIONS TO THE "CLASSICAL" EXPERIMENT

Although the "classical" experimental design described above leads to "stronger" conclusions than do some other designs about to be considered, there are still other designs that have additional advantages.[26] As we shall see, however, there are many problems in social science (as there are in natural science) where the utilization of this design is impossible. Accordingly research designs have been established that constitute approximations to the "classical" design. In the following example we can readily note the difficulty of applying the fourfold experimental design to sociological problems. Let us assume that we wish to test the hypothesis that nonmobile couples are less likely to be divorced than couples whose socioeconomic status is changed. In this case the treatment would consist of manipulating the families' social mobility. Since it is at least conceivable that the direction of mobility would make a difference, we would need two experimental groups—one which we would move upward and the other downward. Our control group would be permitted no mobility in either direction. We would have to keep our families under these conditions for a "reasonable" period, in this kind of problem probably no less than ten years. And for the same period we would have to maintain very strict control over the activities of all the families in our sample—both experimental and control. Naturally it is difficult to obtain random samples willing to undergo such experimental treatment over such a prolonged period. This difficulty has led sociologists to seek other designs of research that are less onerous to their subjects and still yield scientifically useful information.

Such an approximation appears in the study by Kohn,[27] where parents are categorized according to their social class. Logically, this design is roughly comparable to the use of only the experimental-after and control-after cells in the fourfold table. It is immaterial how we make the assignment; thus we may speak of middle-class parents as comprising the

[26] Donald T. Campbell, "Factors Relevant to the Validity of Experiments in Social Settings," *Psychological Bulletin,* 1957, 54: 297–312.

[27] See Melvin L. Kohn, "Social Class and Parental Values," pp. 349–363 of this volume.

experimental group and working-class parents as the control group or the other way about. The important departure from the "classical" design is that both "before" cells are missing. A research in which the "before" cells are missing but in which there are two or more "after" cells is sometimes spoken of as a "correlational" study; the coordinate adjective for a study using the full fourfold design is "experimental."

With designs in which the "before" cells are missing we can never be certain whether the obtained differences result from the supposedly differentiating factor (for example, sex of sibling) or are more meaningfully associated with some other factor or factors for which the sample was not controlled (for example, physical condition of infant at birth). The fourfold method with its random assignment of subjects to control and experimental groups gives us the assurance, telling us that the groups were alike before the treatment was administered. [28]

Because of the frequency of its appearance in the literature of social science, we should also mention what we may call the "clinical" design or method. This method involves taking from the two "after" cells individuals who show the effect, and then trying to ascertain the nature of the treatment to which they have been subjected. To illustrate this method let us assume that a psychiatrist examines a number of juvenile delinquents in a child guidance clinic and observes what appears to be a high incidence of broken homes among them. From these observations he concludes that juvenile delinquency is a consequence of broken homes.

Now let us examine what he has done. He has seen an aggregate of subjects who are probably not a random sample of any population. These subjects have in common a characteristic, delinquency, which the psychiatrist regards as the effect of the treatment of broken homes. Note that under the conditions specified he has no nondelinquent subjects. For

[28] This set of considerations has led Selvin to take the extreme position that tests of significance are therefore useless and meaningless in correlational studies. (See Hanan C. Selvin, "A Critique of Tests of Significance in Survey Research," *American Sociological Review*, 1957, 22: 519–527.) It is the editors' position (a) that in the absence of the complete fourfold design it is frequently scientifically useful and statistically legitimate to determine whether or not a "real" difference exists (that is, to determine whether or not it is "significant" at some specified level), (b) that to turn up a significant difference is not equivalent to demonstrating causation because without the fourfold design the probability rises sharply that one or more uncontrolled variables are influencing the result, (c) that the researcher would be well advised to search for such a variable or variables by gathering data on them and performing relevant analyses, and (d) that the researcher must be more cautious in interpreting results from a correlational study than from an experimental study. With respect to point (c), see Paul F. Lazarsfeld, "Interpretation of Statistical Relations as a Research Scientist," in Paul F. Lazarsfeld and Morris Rosenberg, eds., *The Language of Social Research*. New York: The Free Press, 1955, pp. 115–125; Herbert Hyman, *Survey Designs and Analysis*. New York: The Free Press, 1955, chap. 7; and Hubert M. Blalock, Jr., *Causal Inferences in Nonexperimental Research*. Chapel Hill: University of North Carolina Press, 1961.

this reason he has no way to determine whether the proportion having been subjected to the treatment (broken homes) is greater among those who do, or among those who do not show the effect (delinquency). He is assuming the proportion of broken homes to be greater among the delinquents; his data cannot certify this to be true.

In other words, the clinical method has its own logical limitations in addition to those associated with correlational studies. We have already noted that when a study involves only the two "after" cells, it is never possible to conclude that the observed difference between those two cells is a consequence of the variable (or treatment) under study and of that variable only. The additional limitation resulting from the clinical method is that the researcher has no way of knowing how great a difference he should try to explain, or, indeed whether or not the difference which he is trying to explain exists.

Before concluding our remarks about the clinical method, let us note one further way in which it is frequently used. This is the single case. In some fields it is not unusual to find articles in which some general proposition is advanced, the evidence for which is from a single case. To continue with our example of the preceding paragraphs, we would have an illustration of this procedure if the psychiatrist had seen just one delinquent child, had discovered that this child came from a broken home, and then had presented this finding as a generally valid proposition.

What may we say about the logical status of this kind of evidence? We may note that all the logical limitations of the clinical method are of course still operative and that one more has been added. This limitation results from the fact that with only one case the investigator does not know if the treatment which he has identified as causative is common to, or occurs with high incidence among, individuals showing the experimental effect. To refer to our example again, simply because he had seen one delinquent who came from a broken home, the psychiatrist would be completely unjustified in concluding that all, most, or many delinquents came from broken homes.

It is commonplace that it is extremely hazardous to generalize from a single case. From this analysis, we can see that the hazard consists in all the limitations of the two-cell design, plus the additional limitations of the clinical design, plus the lack of evidence that the treatment observed occurs with any appreciable frequency among individuals manifesting the experimental effect.

HYPOTHESIS-GENERATING DESIGNS

Our consideration of designs of research has been from the standpoint of studying relations among variables. When we view as our objective the testing of hypotheses, it is clear that, of the designs we have discussed, the four-cell experimental method is best. If, however, our objective is the generation of new hypotheses, there is much to be said for the other methods, especially the clinical method. For example, when it is at all empirical, the Freudian literature consists almost entirely of clinical designs, frequently with but a single case. While the foregoing logical analysis shows that such studies can never be conclusive in establishing hypotheses, the Freudian literature has been remarkably fruitful as a source of new hypotheses. The clinical type of study has great value in the generation of hypotheses because, although it may involve only one or a very few cases, the cases are generally studied in great detail. Since such a study frequently portrays its cases through time, moreover, it gives the reader a description of a hypothesized process.[29] An ethnographic description of a single culture, it should be added, is logically a clinical design based on a single case.[30] Although such studies can never establish propositions that are generally valid in any crosscultural sense, they have provided social scientists with many ideas for hypotheses. Finally, we may note that the single case may be presented to facilitate communication, that is, to *illustrate* (but of course not to prove) a proposition. This is the purpose of the case presented by Ktsanes and Ktsanes.[31]

UTILIZING THE SCIENTIFIC OUTLOOK

Before proceeding further, the reader should be cautioned about a possible difficulty which he may experience in undertaking to apply the findings of scientific research. Because the language of science and the language of everyday life do not stand in a one-to-one relationship, one can be misled by a direct translation. Human thought, including that of the scientist, is no more profound nor precise than the language used for expressing it. To facilitate communication and to refine his abstractions the scientist develops a language which, while borrowing terminology from the language of common sense, strips this conventional terminology of its ambiguity, or "surplus meaning". The concepts of scientists are, so to speak, skeletons of the concepts of common sense.

The conversations of common sense, on the other hand, usually proceed on the assumption that A knows what B means by a particular term, though neither may be quite sure. For example, the concept "love" can take on a variety of meanings. One cannot always be certain whether it refers to sexual desire, infatuation, brotherly love, "mature" love, or any other of a number of distinctions commonly made. In "The Theory of Complementary Needs in Mate-Selection," on p. 520, Winch offers a

---

[29] Of course the presence of information about change implies observations distributed through time, and, in turn, this suggests a clinical method involving the two experimental cells wherein the researcher is seeking, without the benefit of control cells, to infer the nature of the treatment.

[30] When describing a culture, the anthropologist is concerned with a single case (the culture in question) despite the possibility that thousands or even millions of individuals may participate in that culture.

[31] Ktsanes and Ktsanes.

scientific definition of this same concept. Is this what we mean in every-day conversation? Probably not, for Winch has sought to abstract the con-cept to the point where surplus meaning and the ambiguity of the above terms are minimized. Since in interpersonal interaction a less abstract and more connotative concept is more likely to be used, one should not at-tempt to apply scientific propositions to one's personal problems or affairs without carefully examining the definitions involved in these propositions. The layman tends to think of his problems in the language of common sense, and this form of discourse is somewhat remote from the abstractions of science. Certainly these remarks do not imply that everyday problems are not "real" problems, nor that scientific propositions are of no practical use. Rather it *is* implied that care should be exercised to avoid confusing the two realms of discourse.

We have just concluded a discussion on the use of scientific method in social research. Our purpose has been to provide the reader with some means of evaluating the papers to follow. We, the editors, regard these articles as being among the best studies of marriage and the family. In view of the scientific immaturity of social science generally, however, the reader need not be surprised in discovering that few of these studies em-ploy the fourfold experimental design and that many of them will prove vulnerable to criticism from the standpoint of ideal scientific procedure. As a consequence of the foregoing discussion, we hope that the reader will keep in mind the questions listed on page 4 to guide his evaluation of each article. Such questions are in order with respect to each article in the book. For that matter, such questions are in order whenever someone asserts: "The truth is that. . . ."

2

STRUCTURE AND FUNCTION: THEIR ANALYTICAL UTILITY IN THE SOCIOLOGY OF THE FAMILY

The study of any subject matter is usually guided by a central set of notions that gives that study form and direction. There are a number of such sets available to the sociologist of marriage and the family,[1] but the one that has had the greatest impact to date may be labeled "the structural-functional" approach.

The main purpose of this chapter and the three which follow is to familiarize the student with the three concepts that are most central to the structural-functional approach: structure, function, and role.

Chapter two deals with the concepts "structure" and "function." A social structure is "a social system viewed as a network of social roles and positions."[2] By describing different types of social structures in primitive and modern societies, Meyer Fortes shows how the seemingly exotic behaviors of different cultures can be made comparable and understandable. His discussion sheds light on the salience of familial structures in primitive society.

The utility of the notion "function" is described by Robert F. Winch, who presents the formulation that certain functions must be fulfilled for a society to continue in being. He then goes on to discuss functions which may be fulfilled by the family.

Using cross-cultural data M. F. Nimkoff and Russell Middleton demonstrate that a society's familial structure tends to be related to its subsistance pattern and to the amount and kind of familial property in that society. What these authors call the independent family system (which is apparently the same as what others call the isolated nuclear family) tends to predominate in hunting and gathering societies. On the other hand, the extended family tends to be associated with agricultural societies and with those having a secure food supply and/or a system of social stratification; the extended family is adapted to the control of some kinds of property.

[1]For a discussion of various approaches to the study of the family see *Handbook of Marriage and the Family*, Harold T. Christensen ed. Chicago: Rand McNally & Company, 1964.

[2]Robert F. Winch, *The Modern Family*. New York: Holt, Rinehart and Winston, Inc., 1963, p. 10.

The proposition that the (triadic) nuclear family is the irreducible unit in familial organization is challenged by Richard N. Adams, who asserts that the elementary unit is the dyad. The nuclear family, he says, consists of three dyads: maternal (mother and her child or children), paternal (father and children), and conjugal (man and woman, whether or not married). Adams criticizes Murdock's and Talcott Parsons' functional interpretation of the family on the ground that they claim that the functions in question are fulfilled only by the family. (Winch's formulation makes the locus of the fulfillment of functions a question to be answered in the ethnography of each society.)

Primitive Kinship *

Meyer Fortes

Ministers, political orators and editorial writers are apt to tell us that the family is the keystone of society. From the biological point of view it would indeed seem to be the ultimate social institution. The conjugal family—husband and wife and their children—gives social expression to the function of human reproduction. Early travelers from our civilization were sometimes shocked because they could find no obvious counterpart of our family among primitive peoples. When they found large communal households, inhabited by men, women and children having the most bizarre and sometimes downright indecent relationships to one another (in the terminology of our family), they took this as conclusive evidence that these cultures were barbaric.

We have come to know primitive peoples at closer range in recent years. What they have taught us has radically

°Reprinted with permission from Meyer Fortes, "Primitive Kinship," Scientific American, 1959, 200: 147–158. Copyright © (1959) by Scientific American, Inc. All rights reserved.

altered our judgment of their family organizations and given us an humbler understanding of our own. Primitive family types vary in their constitution, but they are always precisely structured institutions, embracing the primary loyalty and life activity of their large memberships and enduring from generation to generation. The exact prescription of relationships among members gives each individual a significantly defined connection to a wide circle of his kin. To the individual member, the family's property is the source of livelihodd, its ancestors are his gods, its elders his government and its young men his defense and his support in old age. In simpler cultures (e.g., the Australian aborigines) family and society are actually coterminous: all men are either kinsmen or potential enemies.

We, in contrast, are primarily citizens, not kinsmen. The family is organized anew with each marriage. It must share our allegiance with the many competing claims of our society: the loyalties we owe to the institutions that employ us, to our professional organizations, to political parties, to community and nation. A family of such reduced status and scope is, as a matter of fact, distinctly out of the ordinary as families go. The Hebrew families of the Bible and the Roman *gens* more closely resemble the extended family systems of contemporary primitive cultures than they do our own. Of all the primitive societies I know, the one that most closely resembles ours in isolating the conjugal family as the basic social unit is the Iban, a tribe of head-hunters in North Borneo. The vocabulary we employ to describe our kin—our uncles, aunts and cousins—beyond the immediate conjugal family fails to suggest the compelling ties that bind the kinship of peoples other than those of modern European and American civilization. Students of primitive kinship systems have found that they employ a terminology wholly unlike our own: the "classificatory" system, which groups relatives by status rather than sorting out their genetic interrelationships. It appears that all kinship systems obey certain universal principles governing the separation, inner unity and orderly sequence of generations. Viewed from the vantage point of such understanding, our family appears to be the much-curtailed form of a once far more elaborate and comprehensive organization.

Two "facts of life" necessarily provide the basis of every family: the fact of sexual intercourse is institutionalized in marriage; the fact of parturition is institutionalized in parenthood. Societies differ greatly, however, in which of these institutions they select as the more important. Our society selects marriage: the result is the conjugal family, centered upon a single marital relationship and the children it produces. Most human societies, however, rate parenthood above marriage. This results in the consanguineal family, centered upon a single line of descent.

Biologically our lineal inheritance derives equally from both sides of the family according to Mendelian law. Societies that prize lineage, however, restrict social inheritance either to the maternal or the paternal line. The social heritage—that is, property, citizenship, office, rank—passes either through the father or through the mother. "Patrilineal" descent (father to son) was the rule in ancient Rome, China and Israel, and occurs in many primitive societies. "Matrilineal" descent (mother's brother to sister's son) is common in Asia, Africa, Oceania and aboriginal America.

THE MATRILINEALLY STRUCTURED FAMILY

One matrilineal society that flourishes today is the ancient, wealthy and artistic kingdom of Ashanti in Ghana, West Africa. While European mores have made some inroads among the Ashanti, back-country Ashanti villages still keep to their strictly matrilineal ways. Let us consider how such a society works.

First of all, let us note that a matrilineal society is not a matriarchal society: it is not ruled by women. So far as I know there is not, nor has there ever been, such a thing as a genuine matriarchal government. In every preliterate society men, not women, hold the political, legal and economic power; the women usually remain legal minors all their lives, subject to the authority of their menfolk. Primitive peoples usually understand quite well why men, not women, must be the rulers. The women, they say, are incapacitated for

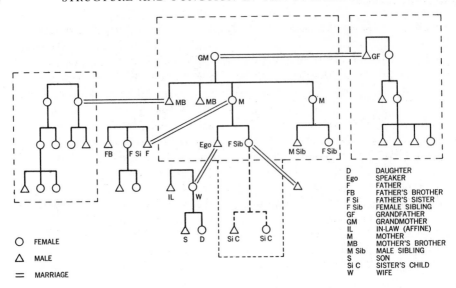

CHART 1   Ashanti Matrilineal Family

warfare and the affairs of state by the necessity of bearing and rearing children. Many peoples, including the Ashanti, believe that women are magically dangerous to men during menstruation and after childbirth.

In describing the Ashanti kinship system I am going to use common English terms (like "aunt" and "cousin") rather than attempt to translate the native terminology. The typical Ashanti household consists of an old woman, her daughters, their children and one or two of her sons. The old woman, the daughters and the sons are all married, but where are their spouses? We can suppose that all of these people are on good terms with their husbands and wives; nevertheless they do not form part of the same household with them, because they do not belong to the same clan. The spouses all live nearby, in households belonging to their own clans. The legal head of the household is one of the old woman's sons; he inherited his role from his mother's brother, not his father; he will pass it on to his sister's son, not his own [see Chart 2 on page 27].

Among the Ashanti marriage is governed by strict moral, legal and religious rules. Yet it is clear that the Ashanti find the fact of descent much more important than the fact of marriage. That is why the households are formed by mothers and children rather than by husbands and wives. The lineage group to which the old woman and her children belong is united by the bond of common descent from an ancestress of perhaps the 10th generation before that of the youngest members. Through this ancestress the group traces its descent from an even more remote mythological ancestress: the progenitor of their clan, one of the eight clans into which the Ashanti people is divided.

It is considered a sin and a crime for members of the same Ashanti lineage to have sexual relations; by this token they must look for spouses of independent descent, that is, of a different clan. Since husband and wife commonly reside in separate households, they must live near each other if they are to have a normal marital relationship. More than 80 per cent of all

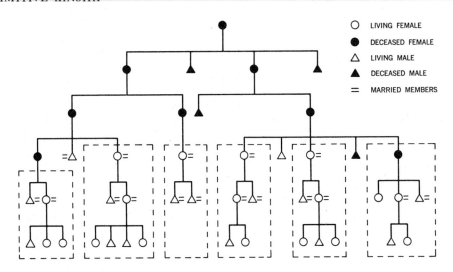

○	LIVING FEMALE
●	DECEASED FEMALE
△	LIVING MALE
▲	DECEASED MALE
=	MARRIED MEMBERS

CHART 2   Ashanti Lineage

marriages occur within the village community. Usually, therefore, one or two lineages of each of the eight clans is found in a village of average size.

The Ashanti rule of matrilineal descent has implications that reach far beyond the domestic household. Every Ashanti is by birth a citizen of the chiefdom to which his maternal lineage belongs. A man or woman can build a house freely on any vacant site in this chiefdom, and can farm any piece of unclaimed soil in the lands it owns. An individual has no such rights in any other chiefdom. By the rule of matrilineal descent, a man can will no property to his own children; they belong to another household and another clan: his wife's. A man's heirs and successors are his sisters' sons. On his death his property and any position of hereditary rank he may hold pass automatically to his oldest nephew. If he wishes his own sons and daughters to benefit from his property, he must be content to make them gifts during his lifetime. They can accept his gifts only with the consent of his matrilineal heirs and of the elders in his lineage group. In the A-

shanti tradition the individual comes under the authority of the mother's brother, not the father. It is the mother's brother whose consent is legally essential for a girl or boy to marry; he is also responsible for any costs that arise from divorce or other suits against them.

How do marriage and parenthood work out in such a system of kinship rules? It is undeniable that the Ashanti have delicate problems of marital adjustment. Both husband and wife must reach a compromise between their primary loyalties to matrilineal kin and their attachment to each other and to their children. When a man marries, he acquires legal rights to his wife's marital fidelity and to domestic services such as the regular provision of his meals. If a wife commits adultery, her husband can claim damages from the other man and apologies and a gift of placation from the wife, even if, as often happens, he does not divorce her. He can and will insist on divorce if his wife neglects her household duties or refuses to sleep with him. The husband is in turn obliged to provide food,

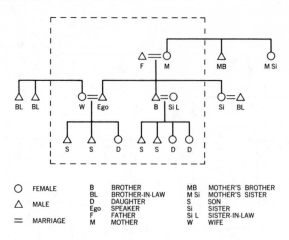

○	FEMALE	B	BROTHER	MB	MOTHER'S BROTHER
		BL	BROTHER-IN-LAW	M Si	MOTHER'S SISTER
△	MALE	D	DAUGHTER	S	SON
		Ego	SPEAKER	Si	SISTER
		F	FATHER	Si L	SISTER-IN-LAW
=	MARRIAGE	M	MOTHER	W	WIFE

CHART 3   Tallensi Patrilineal Family

clothing and general care for his wife and children. If he fails in these duties, his wife can divorce him. In fact, divorce is very common among the A-shanti. Usually it is free of acrimony, for it does not involve the splitting of a household.

What an Ashanti man does not acquire by marriage is rights over his wife's reproductive powers, that is, over the children she bears him. These belong to her lineage, as opposed to his. An Ashanti man cannot demand help from his sons, for example in farming or in the payment of a debt, as he can from his sisters' sons. He can punish his nephew, but not his sons. He can order his nieces to marry a man of his choice, but not his daughter.

THE PATRILINEALLY STRUCTURED FAMILY

At the opposite extreme from the Ashanti are the Tallensi, who live nearby in Ghana's remote northern uplands. The Tallensi kinship and marriage system is the mirror image of that of the Ashanti. The Tallensi household is not matrilineal but patrilineal; it consists of a group of men, usually a man and his

sons and grandsons, together with their wives and unmarried daughters. The men of this household and others in the immediate neighborhood all share the same patrilineal descent, which they can trace back in the male line to a single male ancestor (see Chart 4 on page 29]. Tallensi men share their land, are equally eligible for family offices and join in the worship of ancestral spirits. Like the Ashanti, the Tallensi are "exogamous"; their children must marry members of clans other than their own. Among the Tallensi, however, a woman joins her husband's household on marriage, because he has rights not only to her domestic services and marital fidelity, but also to her children. This is crucial distinction between matrilineal and patrilineal systems.

THE BILATERALLY STRUCTURED FAMILY

Our Western way of reckoning kinship is neither matrilineal nor patrilineal. Rather, it is "bilateral" [see Chart 5 on page 29]. That is, we consider our mothers' kin to be as closely related to us as our fathers'. Nowadays we follow the same etiquette with both maternal

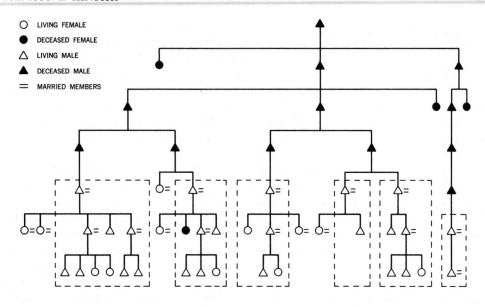

CHART 4 Tallensi Lineage

and paternal relatives. Our terminology distinctly reflects the equality of our conjugal family system. Since we rate the conjugal (husband-wife) over the lineal (parent-child) bond, the paternal or maternal orientation of the lineage becomes a matter of indifference. In naming our spouses' relatives we assimilate them to our own: a mother-in-law is a kind of mother, a brother-in law is a kind of brother, and we treat them accordingly.

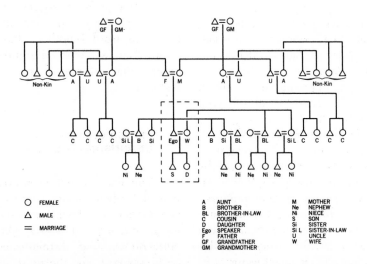

CHART 5 Modern European Family

KINSHIP TERMINOLOGY

Our kinship terminology, like that of the Eskimos and a few other peoples, follows the so-called descriptive system. We have separate labels for each category of our kin, according to their generation, their sex and their linkage to us by descent or marriage. We distinguish our parents ("father" and "mother") from their male siblings ("uncles") and their female siblings ("aunts"). We have different appellations for our own siblings ("brother," "sister") and for our aunts' and uncles' children ("cousins").

Most primitive peoples use the entirely different labels of the classificatory system. This system often strikes Westerners as odd, although it is widespread among the peoples of mankind. Its principle is that in each generation all relatives of the same sex are addressed in the same way, no matter how remote the relationship. A sister and a female first- or second-cousin are all called "sister"; a father, an uncle and more distant male collaterals of their generation are called "father." A woman addresses her nieces and nephews, as well as her own offspring, as "my children." The nieces and nephews, as well as her own children, call her "mother." The Tallensi, the Swazi of South Africa and many other societies even use words for "father" with a feminine suffix added, to designate the sisters of all the men they address as "father." A Swazi calls his mother's brother a "male mother."

This terminology was recognized for the first time nearly a century ago by a great U. S. anthropologist, Lewis H. Morgan. His *Systems of Consanguinity and Affinity of the Human Family*, published in 1871, founded the modern study of kinship systems. Morgan and his followers believed that classificatory terminology had survived from an extremely primitive stage of social organization, in which a group of sisters would mate promiscuously with a group of brothers and would rear the offspring in common.

By now Morgan's theory of "group marriage" has been completely discredited. Modern anthropology has discovered far more cogent reasons for the existence of classificatory terminology. If a man calls all the male relatives of his generation "brother," it is not because at some remote period the promiscuity of the elder generation made it impossible to tell one's brother from one's cousin. The reason is that such generalized terminology expresses the deep sense of corporate unity in the extended family. A child in such a family knows very well which of the women of the household is his physiological mother. Like children anywhere in the world, he will love his real mother as he loves none of her sisters or female cousins. Yet in the joint family those sisters and cousins share his mother's duties to him, and he must observe the same code of politeness with each of them. If his real mother should die, another of the women he calls "mother" will replace her. The classificatory terminology binds together groups that share status and responsibilities. To people like the Ashanti and Tallensi the word "mother" has a social rather than a biological significance: it defines one rank in a complex family system.

PRINCIPLES OF KINSHIP

The need to define relationships is crucial in every society, and all kinship systems have evolved in response to this need. We are indebted to A. R. Radcliffe-Brown, the distinguished British anthropologist, for the most satisfactory statement of the underlying principles.

The first of these establishes a clear demarcation between successive generations. The elders are not only physiological progenitors of their young; they also protect and nurture them throughout childhood and provide their first training in the crafts, customs and morals of the tribe. This all-important relationship requires not only love on the part of the parents but also respect on the part of the children. Parental authority is incompatible with complete intimacy. Most societies banish everything sexual from the parent-and-child relationship; the universal taboo on incest between parent and child epitomizes the cleavage between elder and younger generations. Many societies enforce certain "avoidances" that help to maintain social distance between generations. The Tallensi, for example, forbid an eldest son to eat from his father's dish. Some central African tribes carry avoidance to extremes. One tribe, the Nyakyusa, requires fathers and children to live in separate villages. In the matrilineal Ashanti society, on the other hand, it is the uncle to whom children show respect (or at least resentful submission). Ashanti fathers are not figures of authority to their children and need not keep aloof from them. Indeed, the father's lack of authority over his children is compensated for by warm bonds of trust and affection.

Radcliffe-Brown's second principle is the so-called sibling rule of unity and loyalty among the members of a single generation. The unity among siblings (meaning cousins as well as brothers and sisters) is the converse of the first principle of separation between each generation of siblings and the next. Internally, of course, each generation is differentiated by sex and order of birth. Yet the rule generally prevails that siblings share all things on equal terms. Frequently the sibling principle is generalized to include all tribesmen of the same genera-

tion. In East and West Africa this is institutionalized in the so-called age-grade system. The pastoral Masai, for example, initiate youths into their lowest "grade" of junior warriors every seven years, two successive grades forming a "generation set." Members of a set are classificatory brothers to each other and are classificatory fathers to the next set. Cattle-keeping and warfare are the tasks of the junior sets, while government is the prerogative of the senior sets.

The third principle of kinship, according to Radcliffe-Brown's scheme, accounts for the orderly succession of the distinct sibling groups in time: this is the rule of "filiation." Most societies, as we have seen, stress this rule more strongly than we do. Filiation is usually traced on strictly matrilineal or patrilineal lines. Occasionally the two modes are combined. In some African tribes the individual inherits land and political offices from his father, and livestock and religious-cult memberships from his mother. The bond of common filiation forms social groups that reach beyond the single household in time as well as space. These groups are often called clans. Frequently they are exogamous; as among the Ashanti and Tallensi, their members may not marry one another but must seek mates from other clans. This establishes "affinal" (in-law) relationships between clans and binds them into a still larger unit: the tribe.

THE FUTURE OF KINSHIP-BASED SOCIETIES

What happens to kinship-based societies when industry, a money economy and Western education impinge on them? Recent investigation shows an increasing breakdown of both patrilineal and matrilineal family systems under such conditions. In their place bilateral systems similar to our own become established. The reasons are obvious. Industry and commerce require the individual to earn wages and to enter legal contracts not as a member of a family but on his own. Western law and education emphasize the responsibilities of individual citizenship and parenthood, as opposed to group citizenship and collective responsibility of kinfolk to children.

In his legal and economic roles the individual separates from his kin group. The family constituted by marriage becomes his primary concern. In Africa and elsewhere, as people become industrialized, we are witnessing processes of social evolution analogous to those that shaped the much more limited institution that we call the family.

Basic Societal Functions *

Robert F. Winch

Various writers have begun their theorizing about the nature of society by asserting that certain things must be done in order for the society to continue in being.[1] These "things" have been called "functional prerequisites of societal survival and continuity"[2] and "functional requisites."[3] On the ground that it seems to communicate more easily, this writer prefers the term *basic societal functions*, or *basic functions* for short.

It seems as though each sociologist who has thought about basic societal functions has come up with his own list. The anarchy is more apparent than real,

however, since the diversity is more in phrasing than in meaning. In the writer's list, which follows, no claim is made for originality of content; rather, the effort has been to capture the essence of the basic functions about which there seems to be general consensus and to phrase these functions as simply as possible. Thus it seems to the writer that the following functions must be carried out in order for a society to remain in being:

1. Replacements for dying members of the society must be provided.

2. Goods and services must be produced and distributed for the support of the society.

3. There must be provision for accommodating conflicts and maintaining order, internally and externally.

4. Human replacements must be trained to become participating members of the society.

5. There must be procedures for dealing with emotional crises, for harmonizing the goals for individuals with the values of the society, and for maintaining a sense of purpose.

In other words, every known human society has some organized way of carrying

*Adapted from Robert F. Winch, The Modern Family. New York: Holt, Rinehart and Winston, Inc., 1963, pp. 7, 14–17.

[1] W. G. Sumner and A. G. Keller, *The Science of Society* (4 vols.; New Haven, Conn.: Yale University Press, 1927); J. W. Bennett and M. M. Tumin, *Social Life* (New York: Knopf, 1948); M. J. Levy, Jr., *The Structure of Society* (Princeton, N. J.: Princeton University Press, 1952).

[2] John W. Bennett and Melvin M. Tumin, *Social Life*, New York, Knopf, 1948, p. 42.

[3] M. J. Levy, Jr. *The Structure of Society*, Princeton, N.J., Princeton University Press, 1952, p. 62.

out the above functions. For this reason we think of these functions as universal, as being basic societal functions.

FUNCTION AS A JANUS-FACED CONCEPT[4]

It was remarked above that functions were activities which had to be carried on if the society was to survive. With a somewhat different meaning however the term *function* has been used to denote services that the family or other agency provides for individuals. This points up an ambiguity in the literature to which Homans has referred: that on the one hand function refers to consequences of activities that contribute to the survival of the society, and on the other to outcomes of activities that meet the needs of individuals. (It is hardly necessary to emphasize that not all activities will promote *both* societal survival *and* individual welfare. Thus defensive war may be necessary for the society's survival while still being fatal to numerous individuals.) Homans observed that two eminent anthropologists have taken opposite sides in their emphasis on this question: Radcliffe-Brown has emphasized function as related to group survival, whereas Malinowski has emphasized the gratification of the needs of individuals.[5]

In the writer's judgment it is fruitless to debate whether Malinowski or Radcliffe-Brown was right. Both asked cogent questions, and it would be folly not to continue asking these questions. It seems useful to incorporate both views and to propose that the analysis of functions be consistently Januslike in that an effort should be made to describe and to explain their two distinguishable aspects: the individual-oriented and the society-oriented. This seems the obvious locus in which to observe the interlocking of the theories of social psychology and of sociology, respectively.[6]

FUNCTIONS, CORE RELATIONSHIPS, AND STRUCTURES

If we can agree that any ongoing society must provide for what we have called the five basic societal functions and if we can visualize these functions as the consequences of social interaction (of what else could they be consequences?), then it makes sense to assume that for each function there will be in all societies some characteristic interaction between two or more individuals whose roles are differentiated with respect to the function under consideration. When there is a characteristic relationship between two or more differentiated roles in the carrying out of a basic societal function, let us speak of it as a *core relationship*. Then it is useful to think of *basic societal structures* (or *institutional structures*) as elaborations of core relationships.

Now let us apply our concepts of core relationship and basic societal struc-

---

[4] *Janus:* A Roman deity thought to preside "over doors and gates and over beginnings and endings, commonly represented with two faces in opposite directions."—*The American College Dictionary.* In the present context the emphasis is not on the connotation of deceit but on the two points of view with respect to function—that of society and that of the individual.

[5] George C. Homans, *The Human Group* (New York: Harcourt, 1950), p. 268.

[6] Related to the individual- and society-oriented aspects of function is Pareto's conception of utility to the individual and utility to the community. Cf. Vilfredo Pareto, *The Mind and Society* (New York: Harcourt, 1935) Vol. IV, chap. 12, esp. p. 1461.

ture to the five basic societal functions postulated above. Let us begin with the first function. The replacement of members can occur through birth or through recruitment from some other society. It seems obvious that throughout history most replacements have been of the former kind. Virtually without exception the only institutionalized setting for human reproduction is the marital relationship. Thus the core relationship for the function of replacement is husband-wife-offspring, or, stating the relationship from the viewpoint of the last-mentioned, father-mother-child.[7] Irrespective of the phrasing, this triad of positions constitutes the nuclear family. Then we may view the extended family as an elaboration of the nuclear family, and family (or familial structure), which refers to both nuclear and extended forms, is the basic societal structure corresponding to the basic societal function of replacement.

With respect to goods and services it seems useful to try to capture the relevant variation by positing one core relationship with respect to production—worker-manager—and a second bearing on the distributive aspect—producer-consumer. Of course in modern mass societies the economic function is elaborated into a commercial-industrial complex (or economic structure) with thousands of occupations.

Let us speak of the maintenance of order and the accommodation of conflicts as the political function. A corresponding core relationship of official-constituent could include both the

policeman on the beat with his concern for the footpad and the latter's quarry, and also the judge listening to two disputants. The corresponding political structure includes not only elected and appointed public officials and civil servants, but party workers and member, lobbyists and "influence-peddlers," and members of the general public viewed as actual or potential voters.

Let us refer to the training of replacements as the function of socialization-education, let us use that phrase with a wide denotation so that it includes not only what the infant learns from his mother about the emotional content of the mother-child relationship[8] and what the army recruit learns from the rifle instructor on the firing range but also what the older worker learns from his elders about how to occupy his time after retirement. Here the core relationship seems without question to be teacher-pupil. The educational structure includes schools (both public and private) from the prenursery to the post-doctoral levels, the in-service training of trade unions and of corporations, the formal instruction of the lecture hall, and the informal tuition of a boy teaching his younger brother to spit through his teeth.

Every society needs some procedure whereby individually conceived goals are brought into some sort of harmony, or accommodation at least, with the goals the group must subscribe to if the group is to persist. It is usual for such goals of the group to be imbedded in the society's theology. Furthermore, there must be some patterned ways of explaining and responding to recurring crises—flood,

---

[7] It is obvious that both of these phrasings refer to the same triad of positions. The difference in phrasing points up the fact that we lack terms to denote familial positions and must refer to them in terms of composites of roles (or role-sets), e.g., husband-father and wife-mother.

[8] Here we distinguish between the content of what is learned and the emotional gratification or reward which may accompany learning.

drought, pestilence, death. Frequently explanations for the inexplicable appear in theology, and patterned responses for recurring crises appear in religious ritual. Let us use the term *religious function* to denote the consequences we have just noted. The core relationship is *priest-parishioner*. The *religious structure* may be conceived as including not only religious functionaries and devout believers but also those who perform the religious function in what we customarily think of as nonreligious settings. In other words, aspects of the religious function, as it has been specified above, may be carried out in secular occupational roles. Examples are the producers of consumers' goods, their advertising agencies and television networks, all of which contribute to the integration of goals; the scientists who push back the frontier of the unexplained; the social agencies and psychiatrists who deal with crises of various kinds.

Types of Family and Types of Economy *

M. F. Nimkoff and Russell Middleton

The simplest type of family is a unit consisting of a married man and woman with their offspring, the type familiar to us in the West. Because the accent is on the husband-wife relationship, it has been referred to as the *conjugal* family. It has also been called the *nuclear* family, being the basic unit of all more complex forms.

A more complex family form may be produced by uniting two or more nuclear families through a common husband or wife, as in polygyny or polyandry, respectively; Murdock has designated such families *compound* families. A different type of family can be produced by uniting families of individuals between whom there is a blood tie, that is, either siblings or parents and children. Thus, two or more brothers with their wives and offspring may form a corporate unit. Or the family may comprise the father, mother, their unmarried children, and their married sons or daughters, their spouses and children. Because the emphasis here is on the blood ties, these have been designated *consanguine*. They vary in size, from the largest (normally comprising the families of procreation of at least two siblings or cousins in each of at least two adjacent generations) to those of intermediate size (normally consisting of the families of procreation of only one individual in the senior generation but of at least two individuals in the next generation) to those of smallest size (usually consisting of only two related families of procreation, other than polygamous unions, of adjacent generations). Murdock calls these *extended* families, *lineal* families, and *stem* families, respectively. But since he describes lineal families as "small extended families," and stem families as "minimal extended families," in the present study we combine all three into the single category, *extended* family. These we contrast with *independent* families, defined as familial groups which do not normally include more than one nuclear or polygamous family. A family system is independent if the head of a family of procreation is neither subject to the

°*Adapted from* The American Journal of Sociology, 1960,66: 215–225, *by permission of* The University of Chicago Press.

authority of any of his relatives nor economically dependent upon them.

It is assumed, here, that the family is a function of the social order, which is a complex of religious, political, economic, aesthetic, and other activity. In this paper we examine the relationship between the family and economy and, specifically consider the subsistence patterns associated with the two basic family types, the independent and the extended. Such an examination, it is hoped, will shed light on social conditions associated with them and, therefore, on some of the factors that give rise to them.

The statistical data are from a "World Ethnographic Sample," selected by Murdock, covering 565 cultures said to be representative of the entire known range of cultural variation.[1] Data on subsistence patterns are available for all the cultures, but data as to family type are not reported for 16 societies, leaving a sample of 549 societies for purposes of this study.

The societies are classified by Murdock according to major types of food-getting activities: agriculture; animal husbandry; fishing, shellfishing, and marine hunting; and hunting and gathering. Each activity is rated as dominant, codominant, important, unimportant, or

[1] George Peter Murdock, "World Ethnographic Sample," *American Anthropologist*, XX, No. 4 (August, 1957), 664–87. The original data are revised in accordance with a list of additions and corrections issued by Murdock in mimeographed form on October 14, 1957. Two other corrections have been made for this study: The Chenchu appear to have an independent rather than an extended family system, and the Timbira have a subsistence pattern which is predominantly agricultural, hunting and gathering being important and fishing and animal husbandry absent or unimportant. The Timbira were earlier classified as a solely hunting and gathering people.

TABLE 1   Subsistence patterns of societies in the sample

Subsistence Pattern	No. of Societies	Percentage of Total
Agriculture dominant	341	62.1
Animal husbandry dominant	42	7.6
Fishing, shellfishing, and marine hunting dominant	40	7.3
Hunting and gathering dominant	72	13.1
Agriculture and animal husbandry codominant	18	3.3
Agriculture and fishing codominant	18	3.3
Agriculture and hunting-gathering codominant	3	0.5
Animal husbandry and fishing codominant	1	0.2
Fishing and hunting-gathering codominant	14	2.6
Total	549	100.0

absent. The 549 societies in the sample are distributed among these subsistence patterns as shown in Table 1. Of the 549 societies, 301 or 54.8 per cent are characterized by the extended family system and 248 or 45.2 per cent by the independent family system.

SUBSISTENCE PATTERNS AND TYPE OF FAMILY

Information regarding family type as related to subsistence pattern is presented in Table 2. The null hypothesis was tested that the type of family system is independent of variations in the subsistence pattern. A chi-square value was computed from a 6×2 table. The eleven subsistence-pattern categories of Table 2 were reduced to six and placed in rank order according to their theoretical productivity and stability. The resulting categories were as follows: (1) agriculture and animal husbandry codominant; (2) agriculture dominant or codominant with

TABLE 2   Family type and subsistence pattern

| | Family Type | | | |
| | INDEPENDENT | | EXTENDED | |
Subsistence Pattern	N	Per Cent	N	Per Cent
Agriculture and animal husbandry codominant	2	11.1	16	88.9
Agriculture and fishing codominant	4	22.2	14	77.8
Agriculture and hunting codominant	1	33.3	2	66.7
Fishing dominant	15	37.5	25	62.5
Agriculture dominant, animal husbandry important	72	39.8	109	60.2
Agriculture dominant, animal husbandry absent or unimportant	73	45.6	87	54.4
Animal husbandry dominant or codominant with fishing	21	48.8	22	51.2
Fishing and hunting codominant	7	50.0	7	50.0
Hunting and gathering dominant; agriculture or animal husbandry important	10	55.6	8	44.4
Hunting and gathering dominant; fishing important; agriculture, or animal husbandry absent or unimportant	22	73.3	8	26.7
Hunting and gathering dominant; agriculture, animal husbandry, and fishing absent or unimportant	20	83.3	4	16.7

other subsistence patterns; (3) fishing or animal husbandry dominant or codominant with hunting and gathering; and (4)–(6) identical with the last three categories of Table 2. The computation yielded a chi-square value of 35.01, which, with five degrees of freedom, is significant beyond the .001 level. Consequently, the null hypothesis was rejected, and it appears that there is a rough relationship between the type of family system and the subsistence pattern ordered according to productivity and stability.

Table 2 shows that (1) the independent family is most common in "pure" hunting and gathering cultures, that is, those in which hunting and gathering are dominant and other subsistence patterns either absent or unimportant; (2) the independent family is more common than is the extended family in "mixed" hunting and gathering cultures (those in which hunting and gathering are dominant but in which one of the other subsistence patterns is important). (3) The extended family and the independent family occur with equal or about equal frequency in societies where fishing and hunting are codominant or where animal husbandry is either dominant or codominant with fishing; (4) the extended family is the prevailing type in societies where fishing is dominant; (5) the extended family is the prevailing type in all classes of society in which agriculture is dominant. (6) The extended family is more common in societies where agriculture is codominant with one of the other subsistence types than it is in societies with agriculture dominant. (7) The greatest frequency of the extended family occurs in societies with agriculture and animal husbandry codominant.

SOCIETAL FUNCTIONS AND FAMILY TYPE

How is the association of the independent family with hunting culture, and the extended family with dominantly fishing or agricultural society, to be accounted for?

The advantages of the extended family have been admirably set forth by Linton, who, however, minimizes the disadvantages almost to the point of neglect.[2] The extended family capitalizes the asexual associations of siblings; the independent family capitalizes the sexual attraction between adults. The paramount advantages of the extended family are economic. The efficiency of the household is not impaired by the removal of both son and daughter at marriage as it is in the individual family system. In the latter a husband and wife must start married life with little experience and limited resources, whereas the parental household is a going concern. In the extended family the members have the advantage of long association and familiarity with one another—circumstances useful in economic co-operation. There is more security, too, for the individual in the extended family in times of economic deprivation and other crises. Thus death or divorce is not so serious as in the conjugal family, for the removal of one parent from the home does not deprive the children of association with other adults of the same sex as the missing one. There is also a possible social or recreational advantage in the more ample fellowship of the extended family. Although some nuclear families are larger than some extended families, on the average in any society extended families are likely to be larger.

When a sample of persons in Pakistan was asked what they considered to be the advantages of the joint family, they mentioned chiefly economy in expenses, security against illness and other calamities, and the fun of living in a big family.[3] When asked what they regarded as the disadvantages, they said only that the joint family may foster idleness and discourage initiative. Other critics of the joint family mention the possibility of friction between father and son, brother and brother, mother-in-law and daughter-in-law; the fact that leadership is based on age, not necessarily on ability; and the lack of privacy, especially between husband and wife.

These observations indicate that the ties that bind the members of the extended family may be weakened by tensions that threaten the integration of the group. The desire for economic independence and the desire for privacy, among other things, may dispose the young adults to establish independent households. On the other hand, where the interpersonal relationships are pleasant, the sentiment regarding blood ties makes the extended family popular.

A point worth noting is that either type of family can perform the major functions required of it by society. Legitimate reproduction is performed solely by the conjugal units, whether organized independently or as part of an extended family unit; its frequency, however, may be affected by the presence or absence of the extended family. Rearing the young, especially the very young, is mainly a function of the nuclear family, whether organized separately or not. But, in the extended family, relatives give the parents much assistance with the socialization of their children. In a society with independent families the responsibility for child nurture resting on the parents is correspondingly greater, except in a society like the United States with a highly developed auxiliary structure for formal education.

[2] Ralph Linton, *The Study of Man* (New York: Appleton-Century Co., 1936), chap. x.

[3] A. F. A. Husain, *Human and Social Impact of Technological Change in Pakistan*, a report on a survey conducted by the University of Dacca and published with the assistance of UNESCO, Vol. I (Pakistan: Geoffrey Cumberlege, Oxford University Press, 1956), 77–78.

FOOD SUPPLY AND FAMILY TYPE

Since the frequency of different family types varies with type of economy, we look to the economic situation for clues as to what favors the one type or the other. Three economic factors seem especially relevant: the size of the food supply, the degree of spatial mobility involved in subsistence activities, and the kind and amount of family property.

In general, the size of family seems to be a function of the food supply. Since the supply of food is usually less stable and abundant in hunting than in agricultural societies, hunting does not encourage the extended family as much as does agriculture. Hunters generally cannot feed the members of the extended family so well, or so advantageously utilize their labor, as can agriculturalists.

This general point has been explored previously by Steward, who stresses the importance of the size and composition of the family as adjustive factors in the exploitation of the environment.[4] When game and wild plants are limited and dispersed, the members of a hunting or gathering society will generally scatter to achieve their optimal exploitation. Steward sees the existence of the independent family in hunting societies as one aspect of the low population densities generally associated with hunting. Among the Western Shoshone, who are primarily gatherers of wild vegetable foods and lower forms of animal life, the fragmented family, he argues, is closely determined by their subsistence patterns. Participation of many persons in seed- and root-gathering generally not only fails to increase the per capita harvest but decreases it.

The nature of the subsistence pattern and food supply may also have a more indirect relation to type of family. Barry, Child, and Bacon maintain that in societies that store food before using it the child-rearing patterns differ from those in societies which consume food as soon as it is procured.[5] In societies which lack techniques for preserving and storing food a greater emphasis is placed on self-reliance and training in achievement than in societies with a high accumulation of food resources. The resulting personality type might thus be more congenial to the independent family system, which provides greater scope for the expression of individualism and independence.

The production of household arts is generally more highly developed under agriculture than hunting. Thus the handicrafts provide in the former instance a greater market for labor and so encourage the extended family.

SPATIAL MOBILITY AND FAMILY TYPE

The nomadic nature of hunting also militates against the large extended family, as suggested by the folk saying that he travels farthest who travels alone. Murdock provides information on the settlement patterns of the societies in the ethnographic sample, and it is possible to examine the relationship of family type to the local degree of spatial mobility. As is shown in Table 3, the extended family system is found least often among purely nomadic or migratory bands and is most common among sedentary peoples with a

---

[4] Julian H. Steward, *Theory of Culture Change: The Methodology of Multilinear Evolution* (Urbana: University of Illinois Press, 1955).

[5] H. Barry, I. L. Child, and M. K. Bacon, "Relation of Child Training to Subsistence Economy," *American Anthropologist*, January, 1959, pp. 414–63.

TABLE 3 Societies with extended family systems by degree of spatial mobility

Degree of Spatial Mobility	No. of Societies	Per Cent
Nomadic or migratory	61	27.9
Seminomadic (nomadic only during certain seasons of the year)	78	51.3
Sedentary	410	60.0

$$\chi^2 = 22.75; \text{ d.f.} = 2; P < .001.$$

fixed residence. Semi-nomadic societies, whose people lead a migratory life only during certain seasons of the year, are intermediate with regard to the frequency of the extended type of family.

It must be recognized, however, that mobility patterns do not consitute an independent variable; rather, they tend to be an integral part of the general pattern of subsistence. There are relatively few agricultural societies which are nomadic or seminomadic, and few societies in which animal husbandry or hunting and gathering are dominant that are sedentary. Thus, when general subsistence patterns are partialed out in the analysis, there is no significant relationship between mobility and family type. It is only in the case of fishing societies that the migratory pattern is not determined largely by the general nature of the subsistence activity. Of the 53 societies in which fishing is dominant or codominant with hunting and gathering, 28 are nomadic or seminomadic, and 25 are sedentary. The extended family is present in 80 per cent of the sedentary fishing societies but in only 39.3 per cent of the nomadic or seminomadic fishing societies. This, in itself, may be taken as further evidence that the extended family system is dependent upon a more plentiful and stable food supply, for a sedentary fishing economy is possible only where fish occur in relative abundance.

PROPERTY AND FAMILY TYPE

Among hunters, private property is recognized in certain privileges, such as names, songs, dances, emblems, religious objects and rituals, and memberships in sodalities. Property of this kind may be transmitted through the family line but would not seem to influence greatly the type of family. In the case of movable property, individual rights are generally recognized, but, again among hunters, the amount of movable property is usually not great. Ownership of livestock intensifies the idea of individual ownership and helps to buttress the extended family, which occurs more often among herders than among hunters.

The concept of the ownership of land appears to have a considerable bearing on type of family. Hunters probably seldom have a notion of ownership of land, although rights to the use of an area for hunting purposes are common. These rights are usually tribal or communal in scope, rarely individual or familial.[6] Mobility makes individual or family ownership difficult. For herders, land is meaningful mainly as pasturage, and, if it is scarce, notions of individual or family property in it may develop. But land acquires special significance where, as in

[6] Robert H. Lowie, *Social Organization* (New York: Rinehart & Co., 1948), p. 140.

stable agriculture, the group remains rooted to it over a long time, unlike the situation in shifting cultivation, where it is difficult to develop the idea of permanent ownership.

Among stable agriculturalists, ownership of land is a highly important source of pride, prestige, and power. The family becomes attached to the land, well adapted to working it, and reluctant to divide it. If division results in many small pieces, each member of the family owning and working his own piece, the system becomes relatively unproductive. There is a disposition under the circumstances to hold the family land intact and to add to it if possible. In highly developed form, as in classical Japan, this practice leads to the idea that the current generation is only the custodian and the family head only the trustee of the estate.

The disposition to hold the family land intact and to increase it if possible was seen in pre-Communist China, where surveys in certain regions showed a correlation between size of farm and size of family.[7] It appears that the family tries to stretch itself by adding new members in order to cultivate more land. The family can increase its size by reproduction, by adoption, and/or by adding relatives, via extended family.

Supporting evidence of the relationship between amount of property and type of family is provided by India, where the frequency of the joint family is positively correlated with caste positions.[8] The upper castes, which own more property—especially land—than the lower, have more joint families, whereas the

---

[7] John L. Buck, *Chinese Farm Economy* (Chicago: University of Chicago Press, 1930), p. 334.

[8] Oscar Lewis, *Village Life in Northern India* (Urbana: University of Illinois Press, 1958), p. 17, Table 5.

TABLE 4 Societies with extended family systems by degree of social stratification

Degree of Social Stratification	No. of Societies	Per Cent
Little or none*	173	37.0
Moderate†	44	54.5
Considerable‡	295	64.1
$\chi^2 = 32.19$; d.f. $= 2$; $P < .001$.		

* No slavery; little or no other stratification.
† No slavery, but wealth distinctions of importance, based on possessions or distribution of property, without definite crystallization into hereditary social classes.
‡ Slavery and/or relatively great stratification among free men.

very poor out-castes have the largest proportion of independent families.

STRATIFICATION AND FAMILY TYPE

The relationship of property to family type can be tested by additional data from Murdock's world ethnographic sample. It is assumed that societies with appreciable stratification will generally have more family wealth than those with little or no stratification. The null hypothesis was tested that the type of family system is independent of the degree of stratification of societies (Table 4). The chi-square value was significant beyond the .001 level, and the null hypothesis was rejected. Thus, it appears that the greater the degree of social stratification, the greater is the tendency for the extended rather than the independent family system to become established.

Even when the subsistence pattern is partialed out as a factor, there continues to be a striking difference between those societies with a relatively little and those with a relatively great degree of social stratification (Table 5). The hypothesis that a greater proportion of societies with relatively great stratification have extended family systems than socie-

TABLE 5 Societies with extended family systems, by subsistence pattern and social stratification

	Great Stratification		*Little Stratification*	
SUBSISTENCE PATTERN	N	PER CENT OF TOTAL	N	PER CENT OF TOTAL
Agriculture dominant or codominant*	274	62.8	90	51.1
Animal husbandry dominant or codominant with fishing or hunting and gathering*	29	62.1	14	28.6
Fishing dominant or codominant with hunting and gathering†	31	83.9	20	20.0
Hunting and gathering dominant*	16	50.0	57	22.8

* Difference between societies with little stratification and societies with great stratification in the presence of the extended family system significant beyond the .05 level, one-tailed test.
† Difference significant beyond the .001 level.

TABLE 6 Hunting and gathering societies with extended family systems

Subsistence Pattern	*Society and Location*
I. Hunting and gathering dominant; agriculture or animal husbandry important	Kiowa—American Plains Comanche—American Plains Blackfoot (Siksika)—American Plains Cheyenne—American Plains Western Apache—American Southwest Motilon (Iroka)—Venezuela Siriono—Interior Amazonia Caduveo—Gran Chaco
II. Hunting and gathering dominant; fishing important; agriculture or animal husbandry absent or unimportant	Pomo (Clear Lake)—California Shasta (Eastern)—California Yana—California Wappo—California Hukundika—American Great Basin and Plateau Lengua—Gran Chaco Yukaghir—Arctic Asia Tiwi—Australia Vedda—Ceylon
III. Hunting and gathering dominant; agriculture, animal husbandy, and fishing absent or unimportant	Maidu (Mountain)—California Chiricahua Apache—American Southwest Bororo—Mato Grosso Dorobo—Upper Nile

ties with little stratification was tested for each of the four groups of subsistence patterns by computing chi-square values corrected for continuity from 2 × 2 contingency tables. The chi-square values were significant with a one-tailed test beyond the .05 level for three of the groups of subsistence patterns and beyond the .001 level for the group of societies in which fishing is dominant or codominant with hunting and gathering. We may conclude, then, that there is a tendency for more highly stratified societies to have an extended family system, even when the subsistence level is held constant through partialing techniques.

MODERN INDUSTRIAL SOCIETY

The world ethnographic sample which furnishes the statistical data for this study includes only a very few cases of industrial society. The subsistence base of an industrial society is, of course, mainly agriculture, although herding and fishing may be important. But a significant characteristic of industrial society is the relatively small percentage of the population engaged in agriculture: in the United States in 1950 only 12 per cent of the total active population were engaged in agricultural occupations. In England and Wales in 1951 the corresponding figure was 5 per cent—the lowest in the world.[9]

The censuses which have been taken in industrial societies give us data for families, by households. In the United States in 1956, 96.7 per cent of all married couples maintained separate dwelling places.[10] While it is possible for extended families to exist with separate dwellings for the component conjugal units, nevertheless the family in most industrial societies is in fact, as field studies indicate, organized along independent, not extended lines.

The association of the independent family with industrial society is usually accounted for mainly by characteristics of industry itself. One is the small demand for family labor. Unlike the situation in simpler economies, employment in industrial society is provided by non-family agencies on the basis of individual competence, not family membership. Payment is in money, which is individualizing in its effects, whereas earlier labor was unpaid family labor, unifying in its influence. The modern industrial scene is also characterized by high rates of physical mobility, which separates the members of families and makes interaction more difficult.

The modern industrial society, with its small independent family, is then like the simpler hunting and gathering society and, in part, apparently for some of the same reasons, namely, limited need for family labor and physical mobility.[11] The hunter is mobile because he pursues the game: the industrial worker, the job.

Property is more highly developed in modern industrial society than in the earlier agricultural society, but property is mainly in money, individually acquired, not in family-owned land.

To sum up, the independent family is associated with hunting and the extended family with agriculture. Family type is influenced by type of subsistence through the food supply, demand for family labor, physical mobility, and property. The food supply, the demand for family labor, and property are more highly developed in agricultural than in hunting societies.

These findings are generalizations based on many societies. In a given society the causative situation may be highly complex, and various factors, some of which have been identified, may offset the influence of the type of subsistence. The reliability of the findings depends, of course, upon the accuracy of classification of the family and subsistence patterns of the 549 cultures which form the basis of this study.

[9] *Yearbook of Food and Agriculture Production, 1957*, Vol. II (Rome: Food and Agriculture Organization, 1958).

[10] *Statistical Abstract of the United States* (Washington, D.C.: Government Printing Office, 1957), p. 46.

[11] A notable exception is highly industrialized Japan, where virtually all men and women marry and live in a consanguineously related household (Irene Taeuber, *The Population of Japan* [Princeton, N.J.: Princeton University Press, 1958]). It is reported, however, that a person entering employment in a Japanese factory tends to make it a lifelong commitment. (James G. Abegglen, *The Japanese Factory: Aspects of Its Social Organization* [Glencoe, Ill.: Free Press, 1958]).

An Inquiry into the Nature of the Family

Richard N. Adams

Literature on the human family appearing during the past decade has taken a decided swing away from the earlier simple classificatory goals of identifying lineality, locality, descent groups, and formal kin structures. The new direction as has been noted by many persons active in the movement, has been towards examining the phenomenon within wider dimensions. No longer, for example, is it possible to speak simply and securely of matrilocality or of patrilocality without extensive and adequate analysis of the precise configurations standing behind the activities of the members of the particular society concerned (Fortes 1949; Goodenough 1956). In a very real sense many of the formerly analytic terms have become heuristic and descriptive.

With respect to the form of the nuclear family, however, there has been little evidence of increased interest in fundamentals. Concern here is as ancient as any in the field of social organization, but treatments of it continue to be predominantly expressions of profound convictions, buttressed by more or less convincing logical arguments stemming from a variety of theoretical premises. A recent example of this may be found in Weston LaBarre's *The Human Animal* (1954), an absorbing and provocative though unconvincing argument for the absolute

necessity and inevitability of a continuing nuclear family. A more rigorous argument with the same conclusion but based on different kinds of evidence is contained in G. P. Murdock's *Social Structure* (1949). Murdock claims, on the basis of an examination of 250 societies, that there are no cases where the nuclear family is not the fundamental unit or cell upon which all further familial and kin elaborations are based. Both before and after Murdock's study, exceptions to this picture were cited, specifically the Nayar of Malabar (Linton 1936; Gough 1952; Cappannari 1953), but in principle Murdock's judgment has met with general approval. Even an examination of the *kibbutz* led Spiro (1954) to conclude that whereas the *kibbutz* may have eliminated the nuclear family, it did so only through converting the entire community into a single large *gemeinschaft*.

The purpose of the present essay is to question whether some arguments in support of this general view are satisfactory and to do so through a review of selected cases in which the nuclear family is manifestly only one type of basic form. This is in accord with, but varies in focus from, the interest expressed by Marion Levy (1955) when he asked whether the nuclear family was "institutionalized" in all societies. Levy pointed out that even though the statuses of father, mother, spouse, sister, and brother may be present, they may not function as a nuclear family unit. He gave as an example the case of the traditional Chinese family. In the present paper the position is taken that social organization is flex-

°*Adapted from Richard N. Adams, "An Inquiry into the Nature of the Family," in Gertrude Dole and Robert L. Carneiro eds., Essays in the Science of Culture: In Honor of Leslie A. White, pp. 30–49, Copyright © 1960, Thomas Y. Crowell Company.*

ible enough to permit different forms of the family to exist simultaneously. These different forms may not even take care of the same general functional needs of the total society, and in many cases certain of the standard nuclear family statuses (that is, mother-wife, father-husband, unmarried children) may not function at all. So far as present evidence indicates, there is no question but that these statuses are present in the society; rather it is a question of how they are filled and how they function. The flexibility of social organization permitting the appearance of different family forms rests on the fact that there are more elemental forms of the family than the nuclear, and that different forms may function in relation to different aspects or characteristics of the total social structure.

The cases to be discussed are taken from contemporary Central and South America. We are intentionally treating only this material (and omitting the Nayar and similar cases) because it better illuminates the propositions we wish to explore. Studies in Latin America have increasingly indicated that while most contemporary family systems of that region reckon descent bilaterally, there are many instances where family forms other than the nuclear are operative. The nuclear family is generally replaced in these circumstances by a group based on what we will call the maternal dyad, a residential unit composed of a mother and one or more children. As is the case in many nuclear family residences, these dyad households may also have a variety of other members present, both kin and non-kin.

Our interest will focus on two dyad forms: the maternal dyad, just described; and an adult dyad, composed of a man and woman, which we shall clumsily call the sexual or conjugal dyad. This dyad may be based simply on the sexual act, or

may be further sanctioned by marriage. There is a third dyad, the paternal (composed of father and one or more children) which we will not treat here. It is with no intent of minimizing the importance of this dyad in the world at large that it is minimized here, but simply because it does not appear in significant numbers apart from the nuclear family in our data.[1] The identification of the maternal dyad, as distinct from the nuclear family, is made on the basis of the fact that there is no husband-father regularly resident. The cases used here are based on a distinction made between households with a woman head and those with a man head. This identification in terms of the sex of household heads stems from the nature of census data from which much of the information is derived. While having both theoretical and practical disadvantages, it serves sufficiently well for present purposes. The presence of woman-headed households (in these bilateral societies) is being used here as an index to the prevalence of the maternal dyad family form, and man-headed households as an index to the prevalence of the nuclear family form. While some woman-headed households are doubtless due to widowhood, the percentage of widows seldom exceeds 5 per cent of the women in the society, and, of course, many widows are not heads of households. While some man-headed households may be paternal dyads and not nuclear families, the number is not signi-

---

[1] It would perhaps be well to note at this point that not only the paternal dyad, but many other forms both of family elements and artificial or pseudo-kin relationships are pertinent to the discussion as it progresses. In the interests of brevity, I am raising these principles for discussion, and am intentionally not pursuing here all the lines of exploration they suggest.

ficant in all cases where specific information is available.

SOME CASES FROM LATIN AMERICA

In his recent monograph on the community of Villa Recôncavo, Bahia, Brazil, Harry W. Hutchinson (1957) defines an entire social class segment of his community in terms of the fact that it is composed of woman-headed households. Ninety (31 per cent) of the 290 households in the community were reported to be of this type in the 1950 census. Although Hutchinson says (1957:151) that, "The composition of these households almost defies classification," he promptly notes that 55 of them (19 per cent of the total number of families, and 61 per cent of the 90) are "composed of mothers and children, with the addition in some cases of relatives and an *agregado* as well as boarders." The other households in this class, Hutchinson describes as "left overs" from other families or marital unions. Although Hutchinson evidently feels that these families offer the scientist nothing but confusion, the fact that they were sufficiently distinct to move him to the extreme of categorizing them as an entirely separate "social class," and the fact that they do manifest a considerable consistency with respect to the presence of the dyad family indicate that they do not defy classification.

The Services, in their report on Tobatí, Paraguay (1954), indicate that what they call "incomplete" families form a prominent part of the community. Of a total of 292 families, only 133 (45.5 per cent) are complete nuclear families (with or without additional members); of the remainder, 113 (38.8 per cent of the total) are woman-headed households. This detailed report gives a somewhat higher woman-headed household rate than Emma Reh's earlier study (1947) of the Paraguayan community of Piribebuy where she estimated that 60 per cent of the families were complete and 33 per cent were headed by women. Since there are almost as many woman-headed households as man-headed households in Tobatí, there is little doubt that the maternal dyad is the basis of a highly significant portion of the household units.

Although national statistics for Brazil and Paraguay were not available to the writer, there is evidence from other areas that the presence of maternal dyad families is not a matter of limited or local significance. In Central America, 1950 census data are available for four countries concerning the relative number of families recorded as having women as heads of households:

Country	Number of Families	Per cent of Families with Woman Heads
Guatemala	561,944	16.8
El Salvador	366,199	25.5
Nicaragua	175,462	26.0
Costa Rica	143,167	17.2

Within this general picture for Central America, there is great variation both with respect to area and to ethnic types. Ethnically, there is a marked difference between Guatemalan departments (a department is equivalent to a U.S. state) where the population is heavily Mayan Indian, and departments occupied predominantly by Spanish Americans, called Ladinos. In the predominantly Indian departments (so classified because 70 per cent or more of their population was registered as Indian in the 1950 census) the total percentage of families with women as heads runs between 10 per cent and 20 per cent. Only two of the seven departments of this type had percentages greater than 15 per cent. Outside these departments, the percentage ran as high as 35 per cent. While the woman-headed household rate of the Ladino population is generally higher than that of the Indians, there is also a pronounced difference from one region to another within the Ladino area. In El Salvador a block of six departments (out of a total of thirteen) has percentages between 25 per cent and 30 per cent, while three Pacific coastal departments of Nicaragua run over 30 per cent. Although lack of data from Honduras (Honduras census data on heads of household were not tabulated by sex) makes a large blank in the Central American picture, the material from the aforementioned four countries makes it perfectly evident that woman-headed families are a widespread and common form in Ladino society. There is evidence from one area, El Salvador, that there is also a significant difference between urban and rural populations in this respect. (Urban is defined in the Salvadorean census as pertaining to a municipal or district capital town; the population outside of these towns is rural.) While only 20.3 per cent of the Salvadorean rural families have women heads, 34.7 per cent of the urban families are of this type.[2]

The presence, then, of woman heads of households in Central America is not a confused and random situation but is definitely associated with the Ladino population, is concentrated in certain regions, and is probably more commonly associated with town dwellers than with rural populations (Adams 1957).

Another region from which there has been an increasing number of reports of dyad families is the Caribbean and the Guianas. Of the studies that have appeared in recent years one in particular has addressed itself to this issue and should concern us here. Raymond T. Smith (1956) studied three Negro towns in British Guiana in which the percentage of woman heads of households was as follows:

Town	Number of Households	Per cent of Households with Woman Heads
August Town	275	37.1
Perseverance	103	16.5
Better Hope	71	29.2

Many accounts of West Indian societies have indicated the presence of these families (as in the work of Herskovits, Campbell, Simey, and Henriquez) but for present purposes we will restrict ourselves to the work of Smith.

These cases from Paraguay, Brazil, Central America, and British Guiana give ample evidence that in contemporary populations with bilateral descent systems woman-headed households are quite common. We infer, especially from those cases which have been described in some detail, that this is an index to an almost equally high incidence of families that have the maternal dyad as their basic unit.

THE UNIVERSAL FUNCTIONS APPROACH

The problem now is to arrive at a theoretical framework that will make these data intelligible. As literature on the family is extensive, we will restrict

[2] While this urban-rural comparison superficially compares with the material cited by Franklin Frazier for Negro families of the United States, caution should be observed since the Salvador data do not make the same distinctions between "owners" and "tenants" and, more important, between "rural farm" and "rural nonfarm," as Frazier makes. See Frazier (1939: 570–1).

ourselves to a limited number of theories concerning the status of the nuclear family. The writers of particular interest to us here are Murdock, Parsons, and R. T. Smith.

Murdock's Multiple-Function Approach

Murdock's major reasons for seeing the nuclear family as a universal and inevitable phenomenon are that it was present in all the societies in his original sample for *Social Structure* (1949), and that logically is seemed to him that the family fulfilled a number of functions better than any other conceivable agency. The four functions he regards as primary (although he would doubtless allow others for any specific society) are "fundamental to human social life—the sexual, the economic, the reproductive, and the educational." Murdock is quite explicit in saying that "Agencies or relationships outside of the family may, to be sure, share in the fulfillment of any of these functions, but they never supplant the family" (1949:10). The immediate issue that arises from Murdock's propositions is whether in fact other agencies have not frequently taken over the functions that he regards as being uniquely served by the nuclear family. In reading Murdock, one gathers that he is referring not only to the presence of a nuclear family in all societies, but also to its pervasiveness among household groups in all societies. The implication is that its absence is considered by him to be an abnormal situation. When he says that "no society . . . has succeeded in finding an adequate substitute for the nuclear family, to which it might transfer these functions," one cannot help concluding that almost everyone in all societies must therefore rely on the nuclear family to fulfill these functions.

The cases cited earlier make it clear that large segments of some contemporary societies do not have functioning nuclear families, and that the nonnuclear family segments cannot fruitfully be cast aside as "abnormal" or "disorganized," but are regular, viable, family units in a regular, functioning society. With respect to the four functions listed by Murdock, we simply find that other social agents do in fact take over the functions for extended periods; precisely who may do it varies from one society to another. The educational function may be taken care of by the mother, other relatives, chums, schools, and so on. The rationale that a male child must have a resident father in order to learn to be a man does not hold in fact. The economic function may be handled by the mother and the children as they grow older; to this can be added grandparents, brothers, and other relatives who help either regularly or periodically. And, of course, the sexual function is handled well by other married men, boarders, visitors, friends, and so forth. The reproductive function does not need the father's presence; a midwife is more useful. While there is no denying the social necessity of the functions that Murdock has delineated, there is evidence that some families can achieve them without the presence of someone identified as a "father-husband."

Parsons' Dual-Function Approach

In a recent collection of papers Talcott Parsons (1955) has expressed the opinion that the multiple-functions approach is not adequate to explain the basic necessity of the nuclear family. In its place, he offers another functional explanation. There are, he feels, two functions, and two functions only, that are necessary everywhere and account for the universal presence of the nuclear family. One of these concerns, which Murdock calls the "educational," is namely the necessity of providing socialization of the child. The other (not on Murdock's list, but again he probably would not deny its potential importance) consists of the constant development and balancing of the adult personality which is achieved because of the constant interaction between spouses. Parsons singles out this second function as being of particular importance in explaining the restrengthening of the American (U.S.A.) nuclear family today.

Since Parsons proposes these two functions as being essential everywhere, any documented instance in which they are not operative should be sufficient to cast doubt on his thesis. Such an instance is provided by R. T. Smith's detailed study of the British Guiana Negro family. While Smith would hold that the nuclear family does have universality in the sense that all the statuses therein are recognized, he makes it clear in his study that some households remain with women as heads for extended periods, often for the greater part of the adult life of the woman concerned. He adds, furthermore, that even when men are attached to the household, it is precisely during this period that the "men spend a considerable amount of time working away from home and they do not take any significant part in the daily life of the household . . . There are no tasks allotted to a man in his role as husband-father beyond seeing that the house is kept in good repair, and providing food and clothing for his spouse and the children" (1956:112–113). The function of socio-psychological integration assigned by Parsons to the husband-wife relationship would have considerable difficulty operating if the husband were absent most of the time. The specific functions that Smith assigns to the husband-father are economic. Parsons' argument for the universality of the nuclear family is basically no stronger than that of Murdock since the functions delineated by both can be taken care of by other agents

in the society, or by other members of the family.

The fundamental weakness in Murdock's and Parsons' points of view is that they take functions that may be "imperatives," "universal functions," or "basic prerequisites" for a society, and try to correlate them with functions that are fulfilled by the nuclear family. Since it is mistakenly believed that the nuclear family form is found everywhere, that is, a universal, it must therefore be correlated with some universal requirement of human society. It is correct that there are social prerequisites, and that the nuclear family has numerous functions; but to correlate the two is a deduction that is not empirically supported.

A STRUCTURAL APPROACH

Another approach to the problem of the significance of the woman-headed household and maternal-dyad families is taken up in Smith's study (n.d.). Following the lead of his mentor, Meyer Fortes, Smith regards the family as something to be studied empirically and within a temporal as well as spatial framework (Fortes 1949) and not a hard-shelled cell that forms the building unit of all kin-based social structure. Unlike Murdock and Parsons, Smith has approached the family from the point of view of the ethnographer and not the ethnologist or comparative sociologist, and studied a society where the dyad family and woman-headed households are normal. Much of Smith's work is of interest, but we will concentrate here on some major propositions referring to the woman-headed households.

Smith reports that the woman-headed household in British Guiana Negro society almost always goes through a stage during which there is a man attached to it.[3] A family starts in a nuclear form, and later develops into the maternal dyad form when the man leaves. Smith goes on to propose that there is a basic "matri-focal" quality in the familial relations so that it is relatively easy for a family to be reduced to the maternal dyad type; the husband-wife relationship and the father-child relationship are much less important than is the mother-child relationship. The weak character of the husband-father role is related to a situation in the general social structure in British Guiana. General social status is conferred through ascribed membership in an ethnic-class group. The specific occupation of the husband, in the lower class, confers no prestige, and hence the children have nothing to gain from their fathers in this matter. This is made more obvious by comparing the lower class Negroes with members of the higher class. In the latter, the occupation of the father is of importance for the general social status of the entire family, and the father is considered an indispensable part of the family. Smith correlates the presence of the woman-headed household with a social status system in which the father can achieve no superior status.

---

[3] This temporal difference was also noted in a survey of El Salvador in terms of residence pattern: "even though the patterned residence at the time of marriage or beginning to live together may be neo-local, the subsequent departure of the man of the family leaves it a domestic establishment based on the fact that the woman lives there. It is, if you like, matrilocality by-default." And further: "The solidarity of the Salvadorean nuclear family was reported in some places (Texistepeque and Chinameca) to be increased after the birth of children. This does not, however, seem to hold in all cases in view of the numerous cases in which the woman has retained her children and the man has gone elsewhere" (Adams 1957: 460–461).

Smith's work provides an important structural analysis of the significance of the woman-headed household and shows that the maternal dyad can and does exist effectively in spite of the theoretical positions of Murdock and Parsons. Parsons, who had access to Smith's study prior to the preparation of his own paper, failed to see the full implications of the Guiana material (Parsons 1955:13f.). The fact that the Guiana family may include a man long enough to get a household institutionalized in the local society and to undertake the procreation of children, does not mean that the man is present to fulfill either of the functions that Parsons tries to hold as being "root functions" that "must be found wherever there is a family or kinship system at all. . . ."

THE ELEMENTAL FAMILY UNITS: DYADS AND NUCLEUS

In rejecting the propositions advanced by Parsons and Murdock in favor of a structural approach, their position concerning the elemental importance of the nuclear family is also cast into doubt. If "functions" do not explain the absence of the nuclear family in some situations, they can hardly be called upon to support the claim of universality for that form. No matter how fruitful this position has been in reference to other problems in social structure, we must seek an alternative view here.

The nuclear family comprises three sets of relationship that are identifiable as dyads. There is the relationship based on coitus between a man and a woman, and which may be identified as the sexual dyad until or unless it is recognized as a marital union, in which case it becomes a conjugal dyad. There is second, the maternal dyad, composed of mother and child, that presumably begins at the time of conception but is not of great social significance as a dyad until parturition. And third, there is the paternal dyad, between father and child, that is identified specifically because of the relationship established by the sexual or conjugal dyad. Both the sexual and conjugal dyad, on the one hand, and the maternal on the other, have clear cut correlates in biological activity. The paternal does not. So no matter what importance it may hold in a given society, at the present level of analysis it must be looked upon as a dyadic relationship of a different order; it exists not by virtue of a biological correlate, but by virtue of other dyads. Once given these dyads (all three, the sexual-conjugal, maternal, and paternal) there are important economic functions that may be assigned them. Infant dependency through nursing is, after all, an economic relationship as well as a biological one. But the economic cooperation and interdependency that may be assigned beyond this level is clearly a socially defined activity with no immediate biological correlates.

If we reject the idea that the nuclear family is the fundamental "atom" in the social "molecule," or the irreducible unit of human kin organization, and take initially the two dyads with biological correlates as two distinct components which must each be present at certain times, but not necessarily always or simultaneously, we will be approaching a view of the elements of social organization which is less biased by contemporary social system philosophy. If we allow that the nuclear family is not the minimum model for the building of subsequent structures, then we can see that it is basically, as Lowie partially suggested (1948:215), an unstable combination of two simpler elements, each of which is also unstable and temporal. This allows us to look at more complex forms without the bias of assuming the nuclear family always to be present, and to seek excuses for its absence.

There is a significance to be attached to the nuclear as well as the dyad forms, but it is distinctive. The conjugal or sexual dyad is particularly significant because it is the reproductive unit of the society; the maternal dyad is the temporal link between successive generations of adult dyads. While theoretically the two kinds of dyads can operate independently at all times, the society would be a sadly disjointed affair were they to do so. Their combination into a nuclear family provides generational relationships for all concerned. Since such combinations can be short-lived activity for the individuals involved, and actually may occupy only a limited time, most people are theoretically available most of the time to focus on the dyadic relationships.

The reason that human societies have supported the nuclear family in such abundance can be found at the level of social analysis. Like all animals, human beings live not only in families, but in larger aggregates which, following general usage, can generically be called *communities*. A community cannot maintain stability and continuity solely with such unstable and temporal forms as dyads for elemental units. Seen from this point of view, the nuclear family becomes one combination that, if on nothing more than a random basis, must inevitably occur from time to time. It is the simplest way of joining the two dyads. Since the mother is the only adult in the maternal dyad, and the wife is the only female in the sexual dyad, they can be jointed most readily by identifying the wife with the mother. Once this identification is made, the nuclear unit is created and can fulfill many potential functions. But while its occurrence is inevitable, its continuation is by no means inevitable because each of the dyads alone can also fulfill some functions, and there are, in addition, presumably other societal agents that can also fulfill them. The nuclear family therefore becomes only *one of the ways* the community maintains itself. For some functions and under some circumstances, individuals may be effective agents; for others the elemental dyads are more efficient; for yet others the nuclear family may serve, and still others find other kinds of groups more useful. There are, in short, *alternative* ways in which the basic kin units can be used and combined for continued maintenance of the community.

The social universals of human society are not, then, as has been held by many students, the nuclear family and the community, but rather the community and the two dyads. The nuclear family is, in a sense, a structural by-product of the nature of the dyads, but one which is almost inevitable, even if for the briefest period. However, beyond these, the dyads may be subject to a variety of combinations to further the continuity of the community. The case described by Spiro (1954) as existing in the *kibbutz*, and the details of the woman-headed households of the British Guiana Negroes described by Smith should not be interpreted as being exceptions to a principle of nuclear family universality, but as positive illustrations of how dyads may and do operate outside of the nuclear family.

Before turning to the final points of the paper, we should deal briefly with other possible dyadic forms. Two candidates for basic forms are the paternal and sibling dyads. The appearance of a paternal dyad, as was mentioned earlier, is a result of the joining of the maternal and sexual dyads in the easiest way they can be joined. It is a logical derivative, a potential focus of social emphasis and available for further combinations itself. The sibling dyad is logically somewhat similar, being a derivative of the joining of two maternal dyads through the presence of a common mother. Again, once created it serves as a potential focus of emphasis and

can combine with other dyads. While logically other dyads can be derived through further combinations, it is not within the scope of this essay to take the next step, and begin a logical and exhaustive construction of the possible combinations and derivative combinations of dyads, triads, quadics, and so on. It seems reasonable, however, to assume that such an analysis would lead us far in the creation of models of social structure, and offer insight into the actual forms that kin groups take in human society.[4]

It should not be thought that the concept of the dyad in social structure has gone unnoticed in social anthropology. Its significance, however, has usually been in descriptive terms rather than as an analytical tool. A. R. Radcliffe-Brown, certainly a pioneer in structural studies, pointed out on a number of occasions that the basic elements of social structure were dyadic:

> I regard as a part of the social structure all social relations of person to person. For example, the kinship structure of any society consists of a number of such dyadic relations, as between a father and son, or a mother's brother and his sister's son. In an Australian tribe the whole social structure is based on a network of such relations of person to person, established through genealogical connections (1952a:191; see also 1952b:52–53).

But Radcliffe-Brown's view was somewhat different from that proposed here, as he also held that, "The unit of structure from which a kinship system is built up is the group which I call an 'elementary family,' consisting of a man and his wife and their child or children, whether they are living together or not" (1952b:51). The nuclear family, as a constellation of statuses, served as the cen-

[4]Analysis based on triadic and quadic relations has already been started in communications research.

tral block although, unlike Murdock and Parsons, Radcliffe-Brown did not hold that this unit must everywhere exist.

While Radcliffe-Brown saw in the "elementary family" three kinds of social relationships, "that between parent and child, that between children of the same parents (siblings), and that between husband and wife as parents of the same child or children" (1952b:51), he did not expressly project these as potential analytical units that could themselves be examined apart from the nuclear family context and considered as distinctive building blocks. On the other hand, Radcliffe-Brown did, in his principles of "the unity of the sibling group" and "the unity of the lineage," recognize the theoretical significance of a society's placing emphasis upon a given set of relationships that, in terms of the present discussion, we would see as a "sibling dyad" and either the maternal or paternal dyad. He did not carry it farther at the time of the essay in question to include the husband-wife dyad as also being a potential center of emphasis, nor did he distinguish between other maternal and paternal relations.

THE WOMAN-HEADED HOUSEHOLD AND THE TOTAL SOCIETY

The thesis presented by Smith concerning the reasons for the appearance of the woman-headed household provides an analysis that on the surface fits well into the present argument. Over a single life cycle of Guiana Negroes the sexual or conjugal dyad tends to come into play strongly only at limited periods—for procreation and for support of the woman with infant. As a woman becomes free of dependent infants, the conjugal relation can and often does disappear or change its character. This dyad is weak because the members are part of an ethnically distinct, lower class community in which there is no status differentiation possible between males, and hence, little that one man can offer a family or son over what another can offer. According to this analysis we would expect to find similar developments in other similar situations. However, the data from Latin America do not support the extension of the analysis. Three examples will indicate the nature of the variations.

The first involves a comparison of the Guatemalan Indians and neighboring Ladinos. The former have predominantly nuclear families while the latter have a significantly high proportion of woman-headed households. The populations involved hold comparable positions within the total social structure, but the Indians in particular are similar to the Guiana Negroes in being a lower class ethnic group within which the status of the father does not necessarily give status to the son. There is some variation in this matter, and a situation comparable to that of the Guiana Negroes is to be found less among the more traditional Indians than among the more acculturated ones. Among both Indians and Ladinos some segments of the population work on plantations, some live in independent villages, and some are part-time subsistence farmers and part time laborers. Both have the same general concept of land tenure, and both live within the same general national context. But, it will be remembered, in the predominantly Indian departments the percentage of households with women as heads is considerably lower than that of the Ladino departments.

Although Indians and Ladinos live under similar conditions, the Ladino family is much closer to the model Smith sets up for the British Guiana Negroes than is the Mayan Indian family. The difference lies in what Smith has referred to in the Guiana situation as the "marginal nature of the husband-father role" that gives rise to a "matrifocal system of domestic relations and household groupings." Shifting the theoretical focus from the structure of the family to the values associated with it is in one sense a shorthand method of indicating that somewhere the structure, in spite of overtly similar conditions, is different. Thus, presumably the Indians have within the structure of their total community certain features which stress the father-husband role, but they are not necessarily the same features whose absence causes the weak role in the Guiana Negro situation.

Smith reports another case in a later paper (n.d.) in which he says that the East Indian residents of British Guiana (like the Guatemalan Mayan Indians) have retained a strong father-husband role in spite of the similarity to the Negroes in their general circumstances. "Quite apart from their historical derivation the ideal patterns of [East] Indian culture and family life have themselves become an object of value in distinguishing Indians from their nearest neighbors in the ethnic status system, the Negroes." If Smith is interpreting his Guiana data and I my Guatemalan material correctly, the reasons behind women-headed households among the Guiana Negroes are relative to the structure of the particular society. Values associated with one phase or aspect of the social structural system may in fact conflict with or contradict values stemming from or associated with other aspects. Thus in many Guatemalan Indian stiuations, where the population works on coffee plantations, the nuclear family is not sustained through variable social status derived from the father, but is important economically. During the five or six months of harvest, the wife also brings in a significant income through picking coffee. This means that a man with a wife has access to a larger income than one without a wife.

Societies, in which families exist, offer many faces, and the form a specific family takes must integrate with as much of the total system as possible. Total systems are complex and seldom completely self-integrated, so some aspects will be more significant for the family form of some parts of the population, while other aspects prove to be more important for others. There is thus room for variation in the form a family may take simply because different families may be answering to different structural features.

The last case involves the Guiana Negroes and the Ladinos themselves, both societies in which two distinctive forms of the family appear within similar total structural situations Smith reported, and the censuses for Central America show, that within these populations there are variations in the degree to which the woman-headed household occurs. If Smith's argument with respect to the relation between the dyadic Negro household and the total system is valid, we must then account for the presence of some continuous nuclear families. The answer here is probably the same as that just discussed. Within the total structure, there is room for variation, and we must assume that in spite of the structural features appearing to be the same, we are not identifying those features which the different family forms are answering to.

The evidence from the present cases does not provide us with a clear enough picture to delineate with precision why some families go one way and some go another. It is here that we must rest our case simply by preferring to place our confidence in the structural approach to solve the issue as over and against the "universal functions" preferred by other writers. We need to seek out facts pertaining to a number of situations:

1. We need to delineate the types of structural aspects which can differ-

entially affect family forms within a single class or ethnic societal group, or both.

2. Given this, we need then to establish the principles which will hold for such relationships within any society.

SUMMARY AND CONCLUSIONS

The preceding discussion has been exploratory, working on the hypothesis-building level. The following summary remarks are made in the light of the same approach.

1. The concept of "functions" as being activities necessary to the maintenance of the species, society, or individual personality is one which is not satisfactory to explain the various forms that the family may have in a given society. The economic, sexual, reproductive, and educational functions as outlined by Murdock, or the socialization and adult-personality-maintaining functions of Parsons may be taken care of by the nuclear family under some circumstances and not under others. We cannot agree with Parsons that there are "root functions" everywhere associated with the nuclear family. If there are such things, they would probably be better identified in terms of the community and the dyads. The search for universal functions has unfortunately become an activity not unlike the continuing search for human instincts: it is not that there are none, but that it is misleading unless it is correlated with structure.

2. A theoretical analysis of the human family must not start with the assumption that the nuclear family is a basic cell or atom, but rather that there are two distinct dyadic relations that go into the formation of the nuclear family as well as into other family forms.

While the concept of the nuclear family is doubtless useful for many kinds of social analysis, the fact that it fails in analyzing some family forms means we must look further. A full understanding of family form requires an analysis beginning with dyads. With this kind of approach, it may well prove that the nuclear family has not had the extensive ramifications which have been attributed to it heretofore. By adding other dyads, we are in a position to re-analyze kin and family structure as well as to pursue more analytically the nature of intrafamilial and other interpersonal relationships. It has been recognized that the nuclear family, as found among apes and men, is essentially a very primitive form. It is not surprising to find that man's culture elaborates on the dyadic possibilities of the family, and produces forms intricate and fantastic.

3. Smith's work among the British Guiana Negroes gives us a most important insight into the structural correlates of the woman-headed household in that society. It leads us to the next step, which is to seek the structural correlates which will explain why woman-headed households sometimes appear and sometimes do not within apparently a single structural system. One step in this explanation is to have recourse to the theoretical position that the other aspects of the total social structure may be working adversely to those which are producing a nuclear or a dyadic emphasis. The emphasis thus placed, however, must have structural correlates, even if they are merely reflective of some structural aspect that is about to disappear. In this case we need more research into the exact nature of form and structure relationships, both in a synchronic and a diachronic context.

4. The final general position to be derived from the preceding discussion

is that it is neither necessary nor valid to attempt to find a single normal structural form for the family within a society. That there *may* be only one is possible; but the assumption that there *can* be only one is unfruitful. The conviction that there is only one right way is older than social science, but it continues to make itself felt today. Many sociologists and anthropologists have regarded the woman-headed household as an abnormal, incomplete, or disorganized form of the family. This has contributed to the argument that the nuclear family is an indispensable, basic, stable, family type, and that its absence must therefore represent a breakdown. If we accept the notion, however, that the basic relational elements of the family are dyadic, and that the nuclear family is a more complex arrangement but one which is probably even less significant temporally than its dyad components, then we are in a position to see women-headed households as alternative or secondary norms rather than forms of disorganization. The assertion that the nuclear family successfully fulfills certain functions is perfectly valid. But the reverse assertion that other social forms can never suitably fulfill these functions is both empirically and theoretically invalid.

The denial of this reverse assertion is also important for our approach to other cultural forms. The search for a fundamental cell or building block of kin organization leads not only to a misplaced emphasis on the nuclear family, but towards a biased approach in the study of the entire family system. As Goodenough (1956) has pointed out with respect to residence, there are ethnographic ways of seeing things, and there are ethnological ways of seeing the same things. Just as the desire to discover cross-cultural regularities has led to forcing an ethnological straight jacket on a society's residence rules, so it has led to misleading assumptions concerning the identification of the nuclear family as the minimum structural form of family organization. If we look into other aspects of culture, it seems likely that we should assume that all cultural forms are alternatives (in the Lintonian sense) until a given form can be demonstrated to be universal by the ethnographers. To assume that a form, because it is a variant, is abnormal, is to evade the task before us. The first job of science is, after all, to study what *is*, not what might, or could, or should be.

Bibliography

ADAMS, RICHARD N. 1957 "Culture Surveys of Panama—Nicaragua—Guatemala—El Salvador—Honduras." *Panamerican Sanitary Bureau, Scientific Publications,* 33.

CAPPANNARI, STEPHEN C. 1953 "Marriage in Malabar," *Southwestern Journal of Anthropology,* 9:263–267.

FORTES, MEYER 1949 "Time and Social Structure: An Ashanti Cast Study." In *Social Structure; Studies Presented to A. R. Radcliffe-Brown,* ed. by Meyer Fortes, pp. 54–84. Oxford, Clarendon Press.

FRAZIER, E. FRANKLIN 1939 *The Negro Family in the United States.* Chicago, The University of Chicago Press.

GOODENOUGH, WARD H. 1956 "Residence Rules." *Southwestern Journal of Anthropology*, 12:22–37.

GOUGH, E. KATHLEEN 1952 "Changing Kinship Usages in the Setting of Political and Economic Change among the Nayar of Malabar." *Journal of the Royal Anthropological Institute*, 82:71–88.

HUTCHINSON, HARRY WILLIAM 1957 *Village and Plantation Life in Northeastern Brazil.* The American Ethnological Society. Seattle, University of Washington Press.

LaBARRE, WESTON 1954 *The Human Animal.* Chicago, The University of Chicago Press.

LÉVI-STRAUSS, CLAUDE 1956 "The Family." In *Man, Culture, and Society*, ed. by H. L. Shapiro, pp. 261–285. New York, Oxford University Press.

LEVY, MARION J., JR. 1955 "Some Questions about Parsons' Treatment of the Incest Problem." *The British Journal of Sociology*, 6:277–285.

LINTON, RALPH 1936 *The Study of Man.* New York, D. Appleton-Century Company, Inc.

LOWIE, ROBERT H. 1948 *Social Organization.* New York, Rinehart & Company.

MURDOCK, GEORGE P. 1949 *Social Structure.* New York, The Macmillan Company.

PARSONS, TALCOTT 1955 "The American Family: Its Relations to Personality and to the Social Structure." In *Family, Socialization and Interaction Process*, by Talcott Parsons and Robert F. Bales, pp. 3–33. Glencoe, The Free Press.

RADCLIFFE-BROWN, A. R. 1952a "On Social Structure." In *Structure and Function in Primitive Society*, pp. 188–204. Glencoe, The Free Press. 1952b "The Study of Kinship Systems." In *Structure and Function in Primitive Society*, pp. 49–89. Glencoe, The Free Press.

REH, EMMA 1946 *Paraguayan Rural Life.* Washington, D.C., Institute of Inter-American Affairs.

SERVICE, ELMAN R., and HELEN S. SERVICE 1954 *Tobatí: Paraguayan Town.* Chicago, The University of Chicago Press.

SMITH, RAYMOND T. 1956 *The Negro Family in British Guiana: Family Structure and Social Status in the Villlages.* London, Routledge and Kegan Paul. n.d. "Family Structure and Plantation Systems in the New World." Paper presented at the Seminar on Plantation Systems of the New World, San Juan, Puerto Rico, 1957.

SPIRO, MELFORD E. 1954 "Is the Family Universal?" *American Anthropologist*, 56:839–846.

3

SOCIAL CHANGE AND THE FAMILY

The three articles in this chapter agree that the family has been changing. As he surveys the American nuclear family, William F. Ogburn finds that with the exception of "the affectional function" the family has been losing functions. (In a later chapter Robert O. Blood[1] argues that the American nuclear family has been acquiring new functions as it has been losing its traditional functions.)

William J. Goode challenges the formulation that the shift from the extended to the nuclear family awaits the onset of industrialization, and argues that the family affects the course of change. However, he simultaneously recognizes that extra-familial changes can affect familial functioning. Goode specifies the types of changes that industrialization is working on the family, and then he indicates how the family might be best organized to facilitate the industrializing process.

In the final article of this chapter, Winch and Rae Lesser Blumberg attempt to dispel some of the ambiguity which has surrounded the discussion of the family and social change. Their paper has two points of emphasis: It indicates the central problems of conceptualization and operationalization which have consistently muddled the handling of this topic. They develop an argument about the relation between societal complexity and familial organization.

[1] Robert O. Blood, Jr., "Impact of Urbanization on American Family Structure and Functioning," pp. 554–562 of this volume.

The Changing Functions of the Family *

William F. Ogburn

The dilemma of the modern family is due to its loss of function. Throughout the period of written history the family has been the major social institution. Indeed, in the long period of prehistory, as well as in historical times, the family has been a larger social institution than it is in the Twentieth Century in the United States and western Europe.

°Adapted from William F. Ogburn, "The Changing Family," The Family, 1938, 19: 139–43.

THE CHANGING FUNCTIONS OF THE FAMILY

Prior to modern times the power and prestige of the family was due to seven functions it performed:

Foremost was the economic function. The family was the factory of the time. It was a self-sufficient unit, or nearly so. The members of the family consumed only what they produced. Hence money, banks, stores, factories were not needed. A wife was a business partner, a good foreman, or competent worker.

As a result of this economic function the family became a center of prestige and gave status to its members, its second function. A member of a family was less an individual and more a member of a family. It was the family name that was important, rather than the first name. Most families stayed for generations on the same pieces of land in or near a small community and hence had an opportunity to establish reputations. It was important to marry into the right family, as well as to marry the individual. The family name was a badge and had to be guarded at all cost and at all times.

The nature of the household economy was such as to make the home the center for education, not only of the infant and child or pre-school age, but also the youth for his vocational education, physical education, domestic science, and so on. The higher education was often obtained by employing a tutor who lived with the family.

A fourth function was that of protecting the members. The husband protected the wife by virtue of his physical prowess, a protection now furnished by the police. The elders found a place readily in the household of the child to spend the twilight of their lives. Children were an old age insurance.

The family exercised a religious function, also, as evidenced by grace at meals, family prayers, and the reading together of passages in the Bible. Husbands and wives were supposed to be members of the same church.

Recreation in those days was not a function of industry; that is, it was not commercialized. There was some community recreation but it was often at the homestead of some family. Recreation centers outside the home were few.

A final function was that of providing affection between mates and the procreation of children.

These seven functions—economic, status giving, educational, religious, recreational protective, and affectional —may be thought of as bonds that tied the members of a family together. If one asks why do the various members of the family stay together instead of each going his way, the answer is that they are tied together by these functions. If they didn't exist, it is not easy to see that there would be any family.

The dilemma of the modern family is caused by the loss of many of these functions in recent times. The economic function has gone to the factory, store, office, and restaurant, leaving little of economic activity to the family of the city apartment. About half of education has been transferred to the schools, where the teacher is a part-time or substitute parent. Recreation is found in moving pictures, parks, city streets, clubs, with bridge and radio at home. Religion doesn't seem to make as much difference in family matters as formerly, grace at meals and family prayers are rare. As to protection, the child is protected at home, but the state helps also with its child labor laws and reform schools. The police and social legislation indicate how the protective function has been transferred to the state, as has the educational function. Family status has been lost in marked degree along with these other functions in an age of mobility and large cities. It is the individual that has become more important and the family less so. On the other hand the family still remains the center of the affectional life and is the only recognized place for producing children.

From this survey it may be seen that at least six of the seven family functions have been reduced as family activities in recent times, and it may be claimed that only one remains as vigorous and extensive as in prior eras.[1]

The loss of these functions from the family institution does not mean that they have been lost to society. They have not disappeared from society as they have from the family. Rather they have been transferred from the family to other institutions, schools, factories, stores, clubs, commissions, and so on. What is the family's loss is the gain of the state and of industry.

One other point may be noted as to these changes in the family. Their causes can be traced largely to the inventions using steam as power. The old

family existed with the handicrafts in the city and with subsistence farming in the country. Steam power made possible cities, factories, modern transportation, mass production, and specialization, which are part of the process of the transference of functions away from the family.

There are a number of consequences of the uses of this power. One is the increase in separation and divorce. A sample of the census of 1930, weighted slightly in favor of cities, showed about one in ten families broken by separation, annulment, or divorce. It is well known that one in every five or six marriages contracted will end in a divorce court.[2] The reason is clear. The bonds that hold married couples together are weaker and fewer. Hence husbands and wives fall apart. Women can get jobs outside the home, and men can get meals and mending done elsewhere. The one function remaining more or less as strong as formerly, the affectional tie, however, is not as strong alone as the seven ties together. The affectional bond snaps and there follows separation and divorce.

The situation is affected not only by steam but by one other invention, the contraceptive. It seems that this invention increases the amount of marriage and promotes early marriage, rather than the contrary as is sometimes claimed. But it would also tend to result in more families without children. Divorce is many times as frequent among couples without children as with them.

Another consequence of the transfer of functions from the family is the decline of the authority of the family.

---

[1] ". . . it may be said that the affectional function is still centered in the family circle and that no evidence is recorded of any extensive transfer elsewhere. The evidence of increased separations and divorces does not prove that husbands and wives now find marriage less agreeable than their ancestors did. It may mean only that certain functions and traditions which once operated to hold even an inharmonious family together have now weakened or disappeared. . . . The future stability of the family will depend . . . [largely] . . . on the strength of the affectional bonds." William F. Ogburn, "The Family and Its Functions" in *Recent Social Trends*, McGraw-Hill, 1933, pp. 663, 708—Eds.

[2] For more recent figures concerning divorce, see pp. 609–614—Eds.

There are no longer families that dominate societies as was once the case. Much greater authority rests with state and industry. So also authority in the family declines. The husband's authority over the wife is not what it used to be. The state challenges the authority of the parent over the child, for instance, as to its education and as to its labor. The child grows up accustomed to authorities, many of them elsewhere than at home. The respect which a child has for its parents rests more upon their personalities than upon authorities they possess. So the respect one member has for another is not bolstered up by powers and sanctions. So if the respect is not based upon personality it is not likely to exist.

Another result of the shift of functions from the family to other institutions is the change in the nature of marriage. Marriage was at one time a semi-business proposition, which parents and elders realized fully and the young people realized in part. The young man looked for a good homemaker, who was diligent, thrifty, and capable. It was worth while for a young woman to have a reputation among the neighbors in this regard. The young man was certainly expected to be a good provider, to come from a good family, and to have status. If either had property, that was an item of consideration. Under this framework there was a chance for some romance, unless the marriage was arranged by the parents and unless dowries were of overshadowing importance. Marriage was viewed as an institution, a business. On the other hand, romantic love alone was another thing. It came and went. You were in love today but not tomorrow. It was not considered a phenomenon stable enough upon which to erect a business, to raise and rear a family.

There must be something else, efficiency and ability.

With the shift of functions away from the family, romantic love has taken over marriage, aided by moving pictures and the pulp magazines. Whether the wife is a good cook is a secondary consideration. It is not necessary that she be a good seamstress any more than she needs to know how to spin and weave. Hence, there are more hasty marriages. It has become necessary for states to pass laws requiring a certain amount of time to elapse between the purchase of a license and marriage.

Another result of the decline of the family functions is the conflict between the new conditions of family life and the old attitudes surviving from an earlier type of family life. Thus the older philosophy said that woman's place was the home. True enough it was when she made soap, wove cloth, and prepared medicine from herbs. But the maxim is not so clear for women with no children living at home. . . . Often these women live in small apartments quite unsuitable for economic activity. Besides, one in every 8 or 9 married women helps out the family income by drawing wages for work done outside the home. Many men feel it reflects on them to have their wives work for wages. Others feel that they are head of the house, a position that had more significance under the household economy. The conflict is apparent in the case of girls, who do not know whether to prepare for marriage or for jobs. It is not only difficult to do both, but there is also a psychological conflict between the new economic freedom of self-support and the lifelong devotion to husband, children, and home.

One effect of the invention of the contraceptive has been a loss of a family function rather than a transfer of that function to another social institution. I refer to childbearing. No other social institution produces children and illegitimacy is probably on the decline. Thus, at the time when the American colonies won their independence from Great Britain, 10 wives bore 78 children; one hundred and fifty years later 10 wives bear only 23 children. The cost of rearing a child, especially in the city, is great today. Not many fathers could provide opportunities for education and health to seven or eight children, especially when the law forces the family to care for them until they are almost twenty years of age. Fewer children mean, then, more advantages and opportunities, and no doubt better food, less illness, and superior physical well being.

But the gain on the psychological side is not so clear. The only child and the oldest child are a much larger percentage of all children now than formerly. They receive relatively more attention than middle children. They are with adults more. These conditions cause more geniuses but also more failures. They are said to be more narcissistic and exhibitionistic. It is claimed by psychoanalysts that neurotics are drawn proportionately more from the only, oldest, and youngest children. Indulgent parents are more likely to "spoil" an only child than those of a large brood. Anxious mothers are more likely to inculcate anxiety in an oldest child than in a middle child. Such problem children in youth are a responsibility of the family and school in wealthy neighborhoods. But in poor neighborhoods, where mothers work away from home and where the streets are the playground, such problem children become a responsibility of the state, for their gang life leads to delinquencies of various kinds that may bring them up against the law.

The problem of the family rearing of children in a modern city is due in part to the survival of the older attitudes which are in a practical way incompatible with modern urban conditions, and to the absence of a definite pattern of guidance in a changing society for parents whose intelligence quotients may not be very high. No ethic has as yet risen to take the place of the one followed in the Victorian era.

Not all the difficulty is due to conditions within the family. The conditions outside the family make successful family life difficult. For the family does not exist in a vacuum, as the saying goes, but is a part of society. The inventions which have so changed the institution of the family have also changed society. These changes in society that impinge on the family, often with disastrous effects, may be summarized by the word heterogeneity. There are in a modern city many groups to which the members of a family belong. Formerly they were members of the church, and of perhaps two or three clubs. Now the men of the family belong to a business group, to a church, to a union or trade association, and to some clubs. The wife may belong to a business group, a card club, a church, a social club. The children belong to a school group, perhaps a play group, and perhaps a club.

The meaning of these various memberships lies in the important role the group plays in shaping one's conduct. We conform to the folkways and mores that are set by the group. We become like the group within which we live. We cannot long resist the pressure of Main Street. A man does not rise much above the level of the group in which he lives, nor does he fall much below this level. Our self is really what the group influences make it. Hence, personality is a social product.

Now in modern times the group influences that determine the character of the members of the family do not flow from the family alone, or from just one group. The members of the family belong to many groups, each one having its own folkways and social evaluations. The boys' gang has a set of standards different from those of the school children, or of the family, or the church. Often these values conflict. Pavlov is said to have produced a neurosis in a dog. He did it by conditioning the dog to respond positively to a great circle of light thrown on a screen. The same dog was conditioned to respond negatively to a great ellipse of light thrown on the same screen at another time. Then when the great experimenter changed the light from a circle and an ellipse to a midway type of figure, the dog did not know what to do, and broke down in a fit of trembling. The conflicting values and standards of the different societies, business associations, churches, athletic groups, and pleasure groups may produce somewhat similar conflicts.

There is a competition with the family by other groups for the control over its members. The family no longer holds sway. The nature of family life is such that it is necessarily important, but it often breaks down under the competition with other groups. Parents thus lose control over their children, husbands and wives lose influence with each other.

This situation is affected by one other condition, namely, city life. When the village is small, consisting of a few hundred persons, and there is little travel and communication with the outside, everyone knows everything about everybody else. Life is in a goldfish bowl. The result is a homogeneity. The set of values for a particular club or association perforce conforms to a general village pattern.

But under city life, the members of the different groups do not know one another. They often come from different neighborhoods, one may never see another member of a club except when the club meets. Hence, city life presents isolation and heterogeneity. In addition communication from the outside world brings—via magazine, radio, and moving picture—the folkways of other places and other lands. The result is an individualization of the members of the family. The individual no longer has his moral problems solved for him by the family group. The heterogeneity of society and the rapidity of social change make impossible specific formulae which tell one what to do in different situations. Right and wrong have to be figured out by the individual, which calls for a high I.Q. and some ability to think in an emotional situation.

Such are some of the consequences following from the loss of functions by the family due to modern invention.

The Role of the Family in Industrialization *

William J. Goode

(1) Our epoch is unique in many ways, but none is more striking than this, that almost all the societies of the world have become afflicted with an ultimately transforming desire to improve their economic well-being, to become industrialized. Many analysts of the past assumed that these influences always created the same results, that societies undergoing improvements in technology went through the same phases of social development. Recent scientific materials have given us a fund of descriptions of social changes which for the first time will permit a serious testing of that general proposition. Certainly, at present, no one has precisely stated or proved any set of determinate relations between industrialization and variations in family systems. If industrialization were, as is often assumed, always the causal variable, and the family the dependent one, then such determinate relations would presumably be known already.

TRAITS OF THE CONJUGAL FAMILY SYSTEM

(2) But if such relations are not systematically known, at least one major generalization has long been clear from the data, that when industrialization takes place, a strong movement toward a conjugal type of family also occurs, i.e., a system whose focus is on the husband-wife tie, and in which the nuclear family is relatively independent of other kinfolk. This is the system typical of the urban industrialized Western World, although it is also found among some societies with a low technology, such as the Eskimo. Its main characteristics are the following:

(a) The extended or joint family pattern becomes rare, and corporate kin structures disappear.

(b) A relatively free choice of spouse is possible, based on love, and an independent household is set up.

(c) Dowry and bride price disappear.

(d) Marriages between kin become less common.

(e) Authority of the parent over the child, and of husband over the wife, diminishes.

(f) Equality between the sexes is greater; the legal system moves toward equality of inheritance among all children.

It should be emphasized, that these propositions are phrased in comparative terms. In no family system is there absolute equality between the sexes; men dominate in all of them. Freedom of mate choice exists in no system. Even in the most industrialized regions of the West, the married couple maintains many ties with their extended kin.

°Adapted from Social Problems of Development, Vol. 7 of the United States papers prepared for the United Nations Conference in 1963 on the Application of Science and Technology for the benefit of the less developed areas, pp. 32–38, United States Government Printing Office, n. d.

3. Indeed, even theoretically is seems unlikely that a family system could evolve that would be absolutely independent. The destruction of kin ties with secondary kin would violate the kin relations within the core of the nuclear family; e.g., to cast off one's father-in-law completely is to risk alienating one's wife; to deny a kin tie with aunt or uncle is to annoy or hurt one's father or mother. Even the statement on divorce must be comparative. Although many Western family analysts have deplored the destruction of the older family system, the diminution of the patriarch's authority, and the rising tide of divorce, in the past other systems have had as high a rate of divorce.

IDEOLOGY OF THE CONJUGAL FAMILY SYSTEM

4. This system has its attackers and defenders, but in contrast to the older, more restrictive family systems in both non-Communist and Communist countries, it is generally viewed as giving freedom. It permits marriage by personal choice, as against the fiat of family elders, and thus helps to erode ancient class barriers. It denies the validity of male privilege and allows the woman some scope for personal development. Indeed, the ideology of the conjugal family has generally entered a country before any substantial industrializing has taken place, and has the same effect as the equally radical ideology of economic progress by which so many countries have recently come to guide their decisions. Both ideologies, it should be noted, are shared and promulgated by the Communist and non-Communist countries.

5. Indeed, the ideology which stresses industrial expansion and the material goods it brings and the ideology that urges freedom from old restrictions in family life, are closely tied. They are likely to enter in a less developed country at about the same time. Their connections can be seen in the apparent harmonies between the conjugal system and the needs of an industrial system. The rough empirical observation that whenever a country moves toward industrialization its family system begins also to move toward some type of conjugal system suggests that in important ways a family system may hinder or facilitate industrialization. Revolutionary regimes typically create legislation, governing areas of family life, suggesting that they understand how the older system hampered industrial growth.

STRUCTURAL "FIT" BETWEEN INDUSTRIALISM AND THE CONJUGAL SYSTEM

6. The major structural ways in which a conjugal system is useful to an industrialized system are the following:

(a) Since couples are free to set up their households independently, they may move physically to wherever the demands of the industrial system call them.

(b) The individual with talent can move upward occupationally, without having obligation to all of his extended family.

(c) Industrial decisions can be made without interference by the larger kin structure.

(d) The young man who must make decisions in his job need no longer be subject to the traditional thinking of family elders.

(e) Hiring and promotion are based on merit, and less on family connections.

(f) The system can use the talents of women, without needing the permission of husbands or fathers.

(g) An industrial system, based as it is on impersonal individual achievement, creates much psychological tension; the conjugal system lays great stress on individual, emotional ties within the family, and especially on the emotional solace which its members give to one another. The family therefore becomes the place where the emotional imbalance of industrial participation is redressed somewhat.

7. The West was the first great area to become industrialized, and its family patterns have been different from those of Arabic Islam, China, Japan, and India for well over 1,000 years, in ways that made industrialization easier. Without tracing out their consequences in detail, let us simply note some of these differences:

(a) No corporate kin groups existed in the West, such as genuine lineages.

(b) The eldest male was not necessarily the head of the great extended kin.

8. For example, the Puritans of 17th-century New England placed greater emphasis on love between husband and wife, self-reliance at early ages, the individual's responsibility for his own actions (and thus, a lesser control by family elders), a refusal to accept the traditional restrictions of the stratification system, and a greater freedom to choose one's own spouse. These shifts constituted real steps toward the conjugal system of the present day, and thus facilitated the movement of human energies into industrialization.

9. The crucial importance of family patterns in facilitating or hindering industrialization can be seen in the instructive differences between China and Japan but space prevents analysis at this point.

PERSISTENCE OF FAMILY ORGANIZATION

10. A major worldwide revolution in family patterns is occurring, a movement toward some kind of conjugal system. However, since each family pattern was very different from others at the beginning, it follows that many specific rates of change in family traits may proceed at different speeds and even in different directions, though going toward a similar type of system. For example, divorce and illegitimacy rates have dropped steadily in Japan; divorce rates in the West have risen, but have dropped in certain segments of Arabic Islam. Ages at marriage have risen in Japan, Arabic Islam, and India, but have lowered in the West.

11. Consequently, even when one deplores the human losses inevitable in any great alterations of social values and behavior, we must not suppose that what we observe is simply family disorganization. Rather, one form of organization is being transformed into another type. The major functions of the family remain the same, and continue as a foundation of the larger societal structure:

(a) Biological reproduction and maintenance.

(b) Status placement.

(c) Socialization.

(d) Social control.

(e) Emotional maintenance, or the psychodynamic input-output balance of emotional security in the individual.

GUIDELINES FOR FAMILY REORGANIZATION

12. Therefore, if—as we insist—the individual and the society cannot operate adequately unless some kind of family system continues to be effective,

several guidelines begin to be visible, which are useful in formulating policy for countries which seek industrial development.

13. First, like other social institutions or smaller social subsystems in the larger society, the family serves the individual and the society, but it also has needs of its own that cannot be ignored.

14. Second, if a considerable input of planned behavioral and ideological energy must be put into the system to change it, alterations must not be allowed to proceed at random. The family system can be changed by massive attack, but it may become disorganized unless its own foundations are kept intact.

15. Third, these facts mean that if no attention is paid to family needs, the central aim of industrialization will also be frustrated. Industrialization as a goal cannot be the sole focus. It must be part of a larger plan or reorganization. To pour all energy into industrialization will actually hinder its maximum development, because of the drag created by the malfunctioning of other institutions such as the family. Only recently in the southern United States, in Puerto Rico, and in a handful of Latin American countries has enough reorganization of the family and of its relation to the larger society taken place to permit a freeing of industrializing potential.

16. Finally, since all change, like all action, must ultimately be carried out by individuals, some alteration in their life situation must be created. Mere exhortation, coercion, or mass measures are not sufficient in the area of the family. An illustrative contrast is afforded by the quick drop in mortality when a clean water supply is introduced, even without changing individual habits, as against the apparently great difficulty of introducing contraceptives, which must be decided upon and used individually.

17. This last point can be fruitfully examined in more detail by means of modern role theory. In familial as in other areas of social behavior, the individual constantly moves through a sequence of decisions and actions by a process of what may be called "role bargaining." In any role relationship, each individual expects another person to act in certain ways, in that he predicts with some accuracy how the other will behave, and also judges that performance ethically, morally, esthetically, or in other evaluative ways. Both parties in a role relationship, then, have such mutual expectations: the mother and the son, husband and wife, or chieftain and follower. If one fails to perform correctly, the other will probably not change his expectations, but will try to make him behave better, by punishment, cajoling, promises of rewards, or by himself failing to carry-out the other's expectations. If the son is disobedient, the father may punish or may withdraw some of his contributions to the role relationship, but he is less likely simply to stop expecting obedience.

18. Of course, if one person is wealthier, more powerful or persuasive, or has less interest in continuing the relationship, he may be able to demand more or contribute less to the relationship. However, what prevents such relationships from degenerating into crass calculations of material benefit, or into crude exploitations of the less fortunate, is that all individual role relations are embedded in complex networks of other role systems. That is, many people, who may be called here "third parties," are also interested in, say, the performances of mother and son toward one another—e.g., the other siblings in the family, the father, other more distant relatives,

neighborhood families, and even the corner policeman. Consequently, the terms of contribution and counterpayment in most role bargains are kept within the limits set by a larger group of people, whose actions and values would be hurt or hampered if each set of individuals were allowed to make their own bargains without outside controls.

19. The ideology of the conjugal family offers much freedom of choice, and therefore appeals especially to the young, to women, and to the educated. No system guarantees family harmony to its participants, and therefore all family systems are under some strains—indeed, one fruitful way of analyzing them is to consider them as networks of role relations held together by strains and counterstrains. However, those with power do not relinquish it gladly, so that planned change must often support those who have little power, in order to change the terms of existing role bargains.

CONTROL OVER THE FLOW OF TALENT: THE PROBLEM OF CLASS

20. A primary process for the facilitation of industrialization must be the increased flow of talent and creative ideas into positions where problems are to be solved. Unfortunately, no family system—and I do not exclude Communist systems—supports the occupational placement of men and women solely on the basis of merit. Rather, the keystone of all stratification systems is the family, which holds them intact. Plato's solution for this situation was the elimination of the family as Athens knew it. Short of this solution, whose cost in energy might well defeat the goal of industrialization, what can be done?

21. The answer must lie in restricting the number of jobs and opportunities which are under the control of family elders. Its importance may be seen in an interesting paradox. Theoretical formulations suggest that a conjugal system is more in harmony with the needs of industrialization than many other family systems, but the families that are most successful in the present industrial pattern, i.e., the middle and upper class strata, in fact have more frequent communication and exchanges with extended kin, control more effectively the dating and other premarital behavior of their children, grant less freedom in choice of mate, and have a lower divorce rate; i.e., follow the conjugal pattern less than do the lower class strata. Moreover, this relationship seems to have been observable in Western society for centuries. The crucial class difference is that in most epochs it is the upper strata that control the jobs whenever the economy of polity expands, because they have created the jobs. In the 11th and 12th centuries, when the Church expanded greatly through the creation of numerous nunneries, monasteries, and churches, the elite was instrumental in that expansion, and could demand family obedience in exchange for opening such opportunities to its sons. The economic and political opportunities of colonial conquest were also in the hands of the elite, who decided on and led that expansion. Simply put, elders in lower strata families cannot successfully attempt to force their youngsters to conform to all family ideals, because the new opportunities are not under their control. By contrast, in most periods of economic or political expansion, the family elders of the elite could maintain the kin network, because those who rebelled might lose their political, economic, and social positions.

22. Can anything be done? Al-

though genuine revolutions do remove from high position many of the elite, after the new system has emerged and the turmoil has subsided, their sons are still likely to enjoy a statistically greater chance of advancement than do sons of the former peasants. In any event, most newly industrializing nations have not undergone a genuine revolution. Moreover, it is possible that such nations, which have a shortage of well-trained people, may find really creative talents as well as leadership potential in the sons of the elite, so that forbidding them advancement would actually hamper the country's development.

23. What is crucial, however, is not the class origin of the new generation, but whether their family and kin groups can still control their placement. To the extent that this power has been removed from family loci, the young need no longer conform to their wishes, in family, economic, or political decisions. The strength of the elite class depends on the control over the young within its individual families, and this control depends in turn on their resources in role bargaining with their young. In turn, the removal of this vital element in role bargaining ultimately reduces the effectiveness of such elite class controls.

24. It follows that any country seeking to develop industrially must spend some of its energies in combating nepotism. Of course, those who hire as well as those who obtain jobs nepotically can at times assert that the appointment was a good one, but nepotism removes the individual from the free market of achievement, from universal standards of evaluation, and perpetuates the older family customs that hinder industrialization, by making the younger person dependent on the family for his advancement.

THE UTILIZATION OF WOMEN

25. A similar principle operates in a related area, the utilization of women. In all societies women have worked. Industrialism, however, is the first type of society to permit women to advance on their own merits. Even in societies that gave great freedom to women, such as late Imperial Rome, women were given no such opportunity. More important, what jobs they got were dependent on the decisions of their husbands or fathers, so that they could never obtain an independent base from which to negotiate a better role bargain with men. Consequently, they could not move toward political equality, or substantial rights in family decisions.

26. The utilization of women can free half of the talent in the country, for the growth and enrichment of the country. This shift in family patterns is especially difficult, since women are untrained and their men object to the personal freedom which women demand, once they begin to obtain jobs and to work independently of family controls in the hands of males. Here again, it is striking that in industrialized countries, a higher percentage of women in the lower social strata are in the labor force than of those in the upper strata, where male authority is greater. Men especially object to women working because this puts them in the position of losing the ego-satisfaction they obtained from the social subordination of women. And, in no country have men been willing to accept the jobs traditionally given over to women, such as housekeeping, caring for children, and so on. Indeed, it can be supposed that one of the unanticipated advantages of the Chinese commune system was that the traditional home services such as food preparation, laun-

dry, and child care were still given to women, and men continued to obtain these services. As a consequence, the Chinese male's objection to equalitarianism—which has of course continued in the face of official pressures—was not intensified by their being forced to do "women's work." However, one anticipated byproduct of the commune was the freeing of women's abilities for the furtherance of industrial development, and by comparison with the very strong repression of Chinese women in the past, their progress has been considerable. What is analytically important, however, is that this could be accomplished only to the extent that obtaining jobs and promotions began to be based on the individual merit of the woman, not on the decision of her male kin. Thereby, the control of kin is reduced, and the flow of talent is made easier. This movement has been minuscule in Japan, where there continues to be an enormous wastage of skill among the women, especially at the middle and upper occupational levels from which they are almost barred. . . .

Societal Complexity and Familial Organization [*]

Robert F. Winch and Rae Lesser Blumberg

Introduction

In his book World Revolution and Family Patterns,[1] William J. Goode has concluded that as the nations of the world become industrialized and urbanized, their familial systems are converging on what he calls the conjugal family system. With this book Goode has achieved a synthesis of a generation of sociological dialogue about the direction of trends in familial organization.

The round of thesis might be entitled "the withering away of the family." An early salvo in this round was fired by Wirth, who viewed the city as freeing the individual from the "kinship group characteristic of the country." Seeing a similar process but evaluating it more dourly was Zimmerman, for whom the contemporaneous American family was "atomistic," meaning that it exerted minimum influence over the behavior of the individual. To Parsons the emerging familial form was isolated and nuclear, although the precise meaning of the former adjective has been variously interpreted. Linton concurred by remarking the "extreme degeneration" of the extended family, "the increasing anonymity of individuals and conjugal family groups," and the decrease of sanctions to prevent marital dissolutions.[2]

[2] Louis Wirth, "Urbanism as a Way of Life," American Journal of Sociology, 1938, 44: 1–24; Carle C. Zimmerman, Family and Civilization. New York: Harper & Row, Publishers, 1947; Talcott Parsons, "The Social Structure of the Family," in Ruth Nanda Anshen ed., The Family: Its Function and Destiny. New York: Harper & Row, Publishers, 1949, pp. 173–201; and Ralph Linton, "The Natural History of the Family,"

[*] This article was written specifically for this volume.

[1] William J. Goode, World Revolution and Family Patterns. New York: The Free Press, 1963.

Antithesis was the product of a set of revisionists employing a generally more limited—but empirically based—frame of reference: Sussman, Greer, Sharp and Axelrod, Bell and Boat, Townsend, Young and Willmott, Firth and Djamour, Litwak, Haller, Key, Mitchell, Rogers and Leichter, and Leichter and Mitchell.[3] These investi-

gators emphasized the extent to which U. S. and British urban families of the working and middle classes were *not* isolated. On the contrary, they found that these families, although nuclear, engaged in considerable interaction with other related nuclear families, and that this interaction not only constituted a considerable proportion of the off-the-job social life of the family members but also provided instrumental aid in illness and other episodes of need and crisis.

Actually, the revisionists never did join issues with Wirth, Zimmerman, Parsons, or Linton, who seemed to be asserting or implying that the family—generally the urban middle-class family of the United States—was less enmeshed in a network of the extended family than was the familial form from which it was evolving, be that a rural (perhaps peasant) family or, in the case of Zimmerman, the tribal family of Homeric Greece. What the revisionists actually refuted was something the former authors never asserted—although their imprecise diction may have justified the interpretation—that the urban nuclear family was *absolutely* isolated from kinsmen.

Goode then provided the synthesis by integrating the foregoing cross-currents into a cogent formulation. Noting the diversity of familial types in

in Anshen, pp. 18–38. See also Talcott Parsons and Robert F. Bales, *Family, Socialization and Interaction Process.* New York: The Free Press, 1955.

[3] Marvin B. Sussman, "The Help Pattern in the Middle Class Family," *American Sociological Review,* 1953, 18: 22–28, and later articles; Scott Greer, "Urbanism Reconsidered," *American Sociological Review,* 1956, 21: 22–25; Harry Sharp and Morris Axelrod, "Mutual Aid among Relatives in an Urban Population," in Ronald Freedman *et al.* eds., *Principles of Sociology.* New York: Holt, Rinehart and Winston, Inc., 1956, pp. 433–439; Wendell Bell and Marion D. Boat, "Urban Neighborhoods and Informal Social Relations," *American Journal of Sociology,* 1957, 62: 391–398; Peter Townsend, *The Family Life of Older People: An Inquiry in East London.* London: Routledge & Kegan Paul Ltd., 1957; Michael Young and Peter Willmott, *Family and Kinship in East London.* New York: The Free Press, 1957; Raymond Firth and Judith Djamour, "Kinship in South Borough," in Raymond Firth ed., *Two Studies of Kinship in London.* London: Athlone Press, University of London, 1956; Eugene Litwak, "Occupational Mobility and Extended Family Cohesion," *American Sociological Review,* 1960, 25: 9–21; A. O. Haller, "The Urban Family," *American Journal of Sociology,* 1961, 66: 621–622; William H. Key, "Rural-Urban Differences and the Family," *Sociological Quarterly,* 1961, 2: 49–56; William E. Mitchell, "Descent Groups among New York City Jews," *Jewish Journal of Sociology,* 1961, 3: 121–128; Candace L. Rogers and Hope J. Leichter, "Laterality and Conflict in Kinship Ties," in William J. Goode ed., *Readings on the Family and Society.* Engle-

wood Cliffs, N. J.: Prentice-Hall, Inc., 1964, pp. 213–218; Hope Jensen Leichter and William E. Mitchell, *Kinship and Casework.* New York: Russell Sage Foundation, 1967. Much of this literature has been summarized in: Marvin B. Sussman and Lee Burchinal, "Kin Family Network: Unheralded Structure in Current Conceptualizations of Family Functioning" and "Parental Aid to Married Children: Implications for Family Functioning," *Marriage and Family Living,* 1962, 24: 231–240 and 320–332, respectively.

traditional societies—patrilineal or matrilineal or other, polygamous or monogamous, extended or not—Goode proposed that coordinate with the trend of societies toward modernization, industrialization, and urbanization, there is a convergence of these diverse traditional familial forms onto what he calls the "conjugal family."[4]

It is our judgment that Goode's thesis is an insightful conclusion drawn from fragmentary and intransigent data. The next step in constructing the sociology of the family, we believe, should be to pose and to try to answer two important questions.

1. *Under which conditions does the nuclear family occur?* Goode notes that the conjugal family is found in technologically simple societies, such as the Eskimo, as well as in urban, industrial Western ones. But by defining the conjugal family in terms of the fading away of a series of preexisting familial prerogatives,[5] Goode places the conju-

gal family of primitive societies beyond the reach of his conceptual framework. Accordingly he cannot address the general question of the occurrence of the small family—whether it be called the nuclear or the conjugal family.

2. *Under which conditions and in which respects does the nuclear family vary in societies where it is embedded in the social and cultural pattern?* Goode explores only one factor, socioeconomic status, as a source of variation in familism *within* societies. Otherwise he tends to present conjugal familism as an ideal type—a virtually undifferentiated end-state. On the *Day of Convergence*, it would seem, all families will have become non-isolated nuclear units.

In this paper we propose to build upon Goode's formulation so as to make

---

[4] The term "nuclear family" refers to an adult man and woman and their minor children, if any. To us it carries no connotation as to whether there are active and functional relationships with kinsmen. To Goode, on the other hand, the term implies an absence of such ties, and accordingly he uses the term "conjugal family" to refer to the same group—the adult couple and their children—plus the connotation of interaction with kinsmen. That is, Goode's formulation takes account of the revisionists' reports that the nuclear families they observe tend to have kinship ties. As Goode uses it, the term "conjugal family" is the same as Litwak's "modified extended family" and our "non-isolated nuclear family."

[5] Goode has defined conjugal familism in a variety of ways, all having to do with the increasing focus on the nuclear family as most, but not all, ties and interdependencies with kinfolk fall by the wayside. The following list gives the best description of

what he considers the main characteristics of the conjugal family system:

(a) The extended family pattern becomes rare, and corporate kin structures disappear.

(b) A relatively free choice of spouse is possible, based on love, and an independent household is set up.

(c) Dowry and bride-price disappear.

(d) Marriages between kin become less common.

(e) Authority of the parent over the child, and of the husband over the wife, diminishes.

(f) Equality between the sexes is greater; the legal system moves toward equality of inheritance among all children.

See William J. Goode, "The Role of the Family in Industrialization," *Social Problems of Development and Urbanization*, vol. vii, United States Papers Prepared for the United Nations Conference on the Application of Science and Technology for the Benefit of the Less Developed Areas, Washington, D.C., Agency for International Development (no date), p. 32.

possible at least a preliminary examination of these two important questions.

To explore the first question, we suggest replacing Goode's term "world revolution" with the concept we shall call "societal complexity." This shift in concept removes the necessity of concentrating almost exclusively on the world's headlong rush into industrialization, urbanization, and modernization, for the substitution permits the ahistorical ordering of all known human societies along a dimension representing degree of organizational complexity, structural differentiation, and technological "development." The immediate benefit is that we are able to scrutinize the entire spectrum of societies from simple to complex and then to hypothesize that societal complexity is curvilinearly related to nuclear familism.[6]

To explore the second question, no change of terminology is needed. Instead, we propose that the dimensions of familism in developing and developed societies be made the subject of empirical inquiry rather than a deductive typological conclusion. For example, in contrast to the single nuclear family form implied by Goode's hypothesis of convergence, we shall consider evidence from one highly developed country, the United States, to the effect that at least three types of family can be distinguished. Similarly, this approach permits the incorporation of findings suggesting that degree of familism in industrial societies is a function of a variety of other variables beyond variation in social class, especially migration and ethnicity.[7]

SOME OBSERVATIONS ON GOODE'S STUDY

By using a wide range of data Goode has corrected some of the more fanciful errors of his predecessors in the "thesis round." For example, in noting that the Eskimo as well as industrial societies have a small-family pattern Goode has dispelled the myth that all non-modern societies have elaborate kinship systems. He points out that the masses of even the most prototypically traditional societies have lived in small, conjugal households—a consequence of the poverty and high mortality rates suffered by the masses in such societies.[8] Goode also emphasizes that in both traditional and modern societies the greatest degree of extended familism is encountered among the higher socioeconomic strata. (In this connection, the contribution of Sjoberg as another puncturer of myths deserves mention. He writes that the extended family oc-

---

6 Marsh cites the work of Forde, Fortes and Kirchhoff in support of there being a curvilinear relationship between societal complexity and familial organization. See Robert M. Marsh, *Comparative Sociology: A Codification of Cross-Societal Analysis.* New York: Harcourt, Brace & World, Inc., 1967, p. 73.

7 Robert F. Winch, Scott Greer, and Rae Lesser Blumberg, "Ethnicity and Extended Familism in an Upper-Middle-Class Suburb," *American Sociological Review,* 1967, 32: 265–272 and Robert F. Winch and Scott Greer, "Urbanism, Ethnicity, and Extended Familism," *Journal of Marriage and the Family,* 1968, 30: 40–45.

8 See also Marion J. Levy, Jr., "Aspects of the Analysis of Family Structure," in Ansley J. Coale, Lloyd A. Fallers, Marion J. Levy, Jr., David M. Schneider and Silvan S. Tomkins, *Aspects of the Analysis of Family Structure.* Princeton, N.J.: Princeton University Press, 1956, pp. 1–63; and Thomas K. Burch, "The Size and Structure of Families: A Comparative Analysis of Census Data," *American Sociological Review,* 1967, 32: 347–363.

cupying a house bursting with kin has *not* been, in Wirth's phrase, "the kinship group characteristic of the country," but a phenomenon of the elite in traditional societies, and the *urban* elite at that.[9])

OUR THESIS

We have asserted that Goode's framework of "world revolution" has led to a penetrating hypothesis of the convergence of diverse familial patterns onto what he calls the conjugal form. We shall undertake to give further development to this idea. To account for all the available evidence—including some presented by Goode—it seems advisable to conceptualize a dimension of societal complexity. For the moment we shall regard this term as a primitive and define it in a subsequent section. If we think of societies arrayed along this dimension from the very simplest at the left end to the most highly developed at the right, we find that Goode has concentrated on the right side, that is, on that part of the continuum ranging from relatively complex traditional societies to highly complex industrial, urban societies. It is over this range that Goode finds a convergence of diverse traditional family forms onto the modern conjugal family.

We have posed two questions that lead into terrain beyond that mapped by Goode's hypothesis of convergence: (1) under which conditions does nuclear familism (or the pattern of the small family) occur, and (2) under which conditions

does nuclear familism vary within societies?

To analyze question (1) we shall define and discuss societal complexity as well as familial structure and familial functions. Before undertaking the analysis it is advisable for us to indicate that although we shall speak of independent and dependent variables, we do not believe that there exists among the variables we shall consider any invariant causal sequence. Goode has argued too forcefully on the negative side for unidirectional causation to be credible in the present state of our knowledge. We shall consider the intriguing study by Nimkoff and Middleton, which not only supports the curvilinear hypothesis but also seems to specify conditions under which the small-family pattern arises.

With respect to question (2) we shall relate the findings of Nimkoff and Middleton to findings that American family patterns covary with migration, rural-urban residence, ethnicity, and occupation. Finally we shall probe more deeply into variation in familism within relatively complex societies by considering the triangular relationships between "female power," "familial complexity" and some of the intrasocietal variables that covary with familial complexity such as socioeconomic status.

SOME REMARKS ON ONE DEPENDENT VARIABLE: FAMILIAL STRUCTURE

It is our view that the literature on the sociology of the family suffers from the failure to make one important distinction—that between household and family.[10] Taking account of the fact that

[9] Gideon Sjoberg, *The Pre-Industrial City.* New York: The Free Press, 1960, p. 158; See also Sidney M. Greenfield, "Industrialization and the Family in Sociological Theory," *American Journal of Sociology,* 1961, 67: 312–322.

[10] One of the few writers to emphasize this distinction is Paul Bohannan, *Social Anthropology.* New York: Holt, Rinehart & Winston, Inc., 1963.

household refers to people living together whether related or not, and family refers to relatives whether or not living together, we shall speak of the domestic family when we wish to denote related persons living together. With this distinction in mind let us consider some definitions.

Social system: a social group with two or more differentiated social positions; the positions of a social system and the relationships among them specify its structure.

Social position: "a location in a social structure which is associated with a set of social norms." [11]

Family: a social system whose structure is specified by familial positions and whose basic societal function is replacement.

Nuclear family: a social system consisting of the three following familial positions: husband-father, wife-mother, and offspring-sibling, in which the last mentioned is an unmarried minor.

It should be noted that:

(a) there may be more than one incumbent of each position, that is, there may be a polyandrous nuclear family (more than one incumbent in the position of husband-father), a polygynous nuclear family (more than one incumbent in the position of wife-mother),[12] and of course

a nuclear family including two or more children;

(b) where these positions are considered two at a time and with respect to the connecting relationship (for example, the marital relationship of husband and wife), we speak of a dyad of the nuclear family;[13]

(c) there are exactly three dyads in the nuclear family— husband-wife, mother-offspring, and father-offspring; of course we could mention more if we were to distinguish more positions, such as brother, sister, older brother, younger sister, senior wife, and so forth.

Incomplete nuclear family: a social system including incumbents in only one or two of the three nuclear positions. Among the types of incomplete nuclear family are:

(a) a mother and her child(ren),

(b) a marital couple with no children, and

(c) a set of siblings.

Ill.: Rand McNally & Company, 1964, pp. 462–500, especially p. 467. The above set of definitions is phrased with a view to facilitating theorizing; granting a certain arbitrary quality in their phrasing, we have no disposition to quarrel with anyone who chooses, for example, to define his terms so that a polygynous family turns out to be extended rather than nuclear.

[13] Richard Adams makes a forceful and persuasive argument that it is more useful to conceptualize the dyad (rather than the nuclear family) as the basic structural building block of human kin organization. Therefore, dyadic families, such as the one consisting of the mother and her child(ren), are not viewed as abnormal by this structural approach. Richard N. Adams, "An Inquiry into the Nature of the Family," in Gertrude Dole and Robert L. Carniero eds., *Essays in Science of Culture in Honor of Leslie A. White.* New York: Thomas Y. Crowell Company, 1960, pp. 30–49.

[11] Frederick L. Bates, "Position, Role, and Status: A Reformulation of Concepts," *Social Forces,* 1956, 34: 313–321.

[12] Not all theorists of the family are disposed to regard polygamous families as nuclear. For example, see Bohannan, *Social Anthropology,* who treats them with extended families. On the other hand, Zelditch speaks of polygamous families as "compound nuclear families." See Morris Zelditch, Jr., "Cross-Cultural Analyses of Family Structure," in Harold T. Christensen ed. *Handbook of Marriage and the Family.* Skokie,

Of course a social system consisting of one or more incumbents in each of the three nuclear positions may be spoken of as a "complete nuclear family."

Extended family: a social system consisting of two or more familial positions, at least one dyad of which is *not* a nuclear dyad. An example would be a complete nuclear family plus the paternal uncle of the husband-father. Inclusion in the system of the father of the husband-father would also constitute an extended family since the definition of the nuclear family limits the generations to two—one adult and one minor. It should be noted that:

(a) unlike the nuclear family, the extended family does not have a fixed number of specifiable positions;

(b) the extended family must include at least one non-nuclear dyad; and

(c) of course a system involving two or more related nuclear families is an extended family.

Domestic family: a set of persons related to each other by blood, marriage, or adoption, and residing in a common dwelling unit. As defined, "domestic" is a purely ecological term and denotes no systemic relationship among family members, whereas the terms "nuclear" and "extended" are purely systemic and denote no ecological relationship among the members. Of course we may combine ecological and systemic adjectives to make such a phrase as "complete nuclear domestic family."

SOME REMARKS ON ANOTHER DEPENDENT VARIABLE: FAMILIAL FUNCTIONS

Many writers have proposed activities that members of an autonomous and independent social system must carry out in order to assure the survival of that system. Under the rubric of basic societal functions, Winch has proposed the following five categories of activities as constituting such a set: reproductive, economic, political, socializing-educational, and religious.[14] In general these activities may be carried on in a variety of structural contexts. (Of course the reproductive function is an exception since its legitimate fulfillment is the monopoly of the nuclear family.) Thus in a subsistence economy it is frequently the case that the family—extended or nuclear—is the unit of production, of distribution, and of consumption; in such a setting the economy is not differentiated from the family. In highly developed societies we are accustomed to the presence of a variety of economically specialized organizations that may be viewed at the analytic level as collectively comprising a specialized economic structure of the society.

Very simple, undifferentiated societies tend to be organized on the basis of kinship.[15] This means that the family has not only the function of reproduction but also the other four mentioned above, with the consequence that the head of a family is not only a progenitor but also an economic leader, political leader, teacher, and priest.

Because of its basic societal function —reproduction—and its structure, Winch reasons that the family, especially the nuclear family, has two derived functions. From its function of providing human replacements comes the necessity to provide each new arrival with an identity and a position in the society. For this he proposes the phrase "position-conferring" function. Because the family, and again especially the nuclear family, is a relatively small and usually solidary group, it

[14] Robert F. Winch, *The Modern Family,* rev. ed. New York: Holt, Rinehart & Winston, Inc., 1963, chap. 1.

[15] Meyer Fortes, "Primitive Kinship," *Scientific American,* 1959, 200: 147–158.

frequently also has the function of constituting an emotional haven—a site for the mutual enjoyment of personal and collective triumphs and the assuaging of emotional bruises. For this function Winch proposes the term "emotional gratification."

Homans has noted that the term function has been used in two quite different senses. First, the term has been used to refer to consequences of activities that contribute to the survival of social systems as systems, and second, to consequences of activities that meet the needs of individuals.[16] Winch has attempted to integrate both of these uses into a single Janus-faced concept of function as both system-serving and individual-serving.[17]

With respect to the individual-serving aspects of functions, it can be argued that the consequences of functions can be viewed as resources, that these resources—when cathected—become rewards, and hence that one who exercises control over resources has the potential capability to influence the behavior of others.[18]

Cutting across the group-serving versus individual-serving distinction is the question as to whether each function is more instrumental or more expressive. Since some conceptual utility of this distinction will presently be suggested, we propose the schema below:

EXTENDED FAMILISM: A FUNCTIONAL VARIABLE

A social system is understood to have a structure and functions. To the degree that it is completely functional, it is an autonomous and independent social system. Since systems vary in this regard, it is useful to conceptualize a gradient of functionality ranging from those functions carried out by such a self-sufficient social system to a state of complete functionlessness, at which point the system ceases to exist. In particular, it is useful to think of extended families in this way since they differ considerably from each other in functionality. Moreover, a single family may vary in functionality overtime. These considerations lead to the following definition:

Extended familism: the gradient of functionality of the kin network as reckoned from a single nuclear family.

From time to time we may use the phrase "extended familism" to emphasize

---

[16] George C. Homans, *The Human Group.* New York: Harcourt, Brace & World, Inc., 1950, p. 268.

[17] Winch, pp. 14–15.

[18] Robert F. Winch, *Identification and Its Familial Determinants.* Indianapolis: The Bobbs-Merrill Company, Inc., 1962.

	Functions that are primarily	
	INSTRUMENTAL	EXPRESSIVE
Basic Societal Functions	Reproductive Economic Political *Educational	Religious *Socializing
Derived Familial Functions	Position-conferring	Emotionally gratifying

* Here the socializing-educational function is divided into components proposed to be primarily instrumental and primarily expressive.

the functionality of the extended kin net-work or the phrase "nuclear familism" to emphasize the relative absence of the functionality of the extended kin network.

SOME DIFFICULTIES IN CONCEPTUALIZING THE INDEPENDENT VARIABLE

The "world revolution" remarked by Goode involves industrialization, urban-ization, social change, modernization, Westernization, and decolonialization. Even though each of these concepts is at least partially independent of the others at both the empirical and analytical levels and even though each has its distinct bibliography, still many writers subsume most or all of the processes named under one or another of these terms. This state of affairs has had two consequences. First, each concept tends in use to become a catch-all. Second, attempts to define such terms precisely give rise to outcries that the resulting formulation is time-bound or culture-bound or otherwise unsuitable.

In view of the foregoing, it is not sur-prising that there is little consensus about how to measure the "world revolution." One school sees the heart of the matter in the degree to which non-human power has superseded human power, and some of its members accordingly adopt as their index the number of kilowatt hours consumed per capita per annum. But to students of urbanization who must incorporate into their conceptual framework the cases of Thebes and Timbuktu as well as Tokyo, the world did not begin with Thomas Alva Edison.

Shevky and Bell have offered the concept of the "scale of the society" as a way of thinking about our independent variable.[19] To the anthropologically ori-

ented formulation of the Wilsons,[20] from whom they got the term, Shevky and Bell added the ideas of Colin Clark on the shifts from primary to secondary to terti-ary industry and some of the concepts underlying Wirth's view of urbanism: size, density and heterogeneity.[21] Through an analysis to ascertain under-lying dimensions of U.S. census data and the construction of some indexes, Shevky and Bell sought to build a logical bridge between readily available data and the concepts of Wirth, Clark, and the Wil-sons. Despite the underlying concept of a continuum of societal scale, however, the operations of social area analysis seem to be mainly appropriate for the urban pop-ulations of societies at the extreme indus-trial end of the scale of complexity.[22]

---

plication and Computational Procedures. Stanford, Conn.: Stanford University Press, 1955.

[20] Godfrey and Monica Wilson, The Analysis of Social Change: Based on Obser-vations in Central Africa. Cambridge: Cam-bridge University Press, 1945.

[21] Wirth, pp. 1–24.

[22] Some critics have charged that the Shevky-Bell method of social area analysis is not applicable beyond the cities of the United States, but such a verdict may be too harsh. After some modifications in his analysis Mc-Elrath was able to use the method in a study of areas of Rome. See Dennis C. McElrath, "The Social Areas of Rome," American So-ciological Review, 1962, 27: 376–391. A sub-sequent effort to apply the technique in Niger, however, has encountered much more difficulty since the three settlements studied there barely registered as "urban" on scales designed for more complex societies. See Leo F. Van Hoey, Emergent Urbanization: Im-plications and Theory of Social Scale Verified in Niger, West Africa, unpublished doctoral dissertation, Northwestern University, 1966. Recent efforts to focus on nations rather than cities have resulted in additional measures, such as the "relative external dependence index" based upon the ratio of the value of a

[19] Eshref Shevky and Wendell Bell, Social Area Analysis: Theory, Illustrative Ap-

In the face of all the diffuseness of concepts and dissensus about measurement there does seem to be agreement on a vaguely conceived but generally accepted set of changes that transform tribal, or traditional, societies to whatever it is we are trying to denote when we talk of "developed societies." The idea that societies develop from simple to complex states has been recognized for some time. Herbert Spencer's formulation of societal evolution is one example; others are the polar ideal types of Tönnies (*Gemeinschaft-Gesellschaft*) and Durkheim (*solidarité mécanique-solidarité organique*) as well as Redfield's more recent idea of the folk-urban continuum.[23] Attempts to operationalize a continuum of societal complexity can be traced back to Hobhouse, Wheeler and Ginsberg in 1915 and the more recent efforts of Naroll and of Freeman and Winch in 1956 and 1957 re-

spectively.[24] Naroll constructed his "social development index" from data on 30 preliterate societies, and Freeman and Winch used a sample of 48 societies to establish a scale of societal complexity up to the emergence of written language.

SOCIETAL COMPLEXITY AND SOCIETAL DIFFERENTIATION: STATIC AND DYNAMIC CANDIDATES FOR THE INDEPENDENT VARIABLE

Until we are better able to comprehend exactly what societal development and its various partial synonyms denote, we believe it is prudent to move along to what seems to be the most relevant and most immediate consequence of that process—societal complexity, and its dynamic counterpart, societal differentiation.[25]

Implied in the concept of societal complexity is a model of social change. Social organization—whether a society or a business—becomes more complex by growing from a simple, homogeneous system to one that is differentiated and includes specialized subsystems. Central to the process by which a simple society

---

country's imports to the square of the distance from the point of importation. See Jack P. Gibbs and Walter T. Martin, "Urbanization, Technology, and the Division of Labor: International Patterns," *American Sociological Review*, 1962, 27: 667–677. Finally, it is important to note that not all efforts in this direction have been made by sociologists and anthropologists. For an effort by a geographer to measure societal complexity by considering distribution of cities by size and geographic interdependence, see Brian Berry, "City-Size Distribution and Economic Development," *Economic Development and Cultural Change*, 1961, 9: 573–588.

[23] Herbert Spencer, *The Principles of Sociology*, New York, Appleton-Century-Crofts, 1910; Ferdinand Tönnies, *Fundamental Concepts in Society*, translated by Charles P. Loomis, ed. New York: American Book Company 1940; Emile Durkheim, *The Division of Labor in Society*, translated by George Simpson. New York: Crowell-Collier and Macmillan, Inc., 1933; Robert Redfield, "The Folk Society," *American Journal of Sociology*, 1947, 52: 293–308.

[24] L. T. Hobhouse, G. C. Wheeler and M. Ginsberg, *The Material Culture and Social Institutions of the Simpler Peoples*. London: Chapman & Hall, Ltd., 1915; Raoul Naroll, "A Preliminary Index of Social Development," *American Anthropologist*, 1956, 58: 687–713; Linton C. Freeman and Robert F. Winch, "Societal Complexity: An Empirical Test of a Typology of Societies," *American Journal of Sociology*, 1957, 62: 461–466.

[25] Some might argue that societal differentiation is synonymous with the developmental process rather than a consequence thereof. To us the equivalence is not complete in that differentiation neither denotes nor connotes a cause of differentiation, whereas industrialization, and so forth do suggest states of affairs that eventuate in differentiation.

develops is the fact that at the concrete level the number of (differentiated) social positions in the society increases.[26] For example, at the simplest level a boy's father would serve also as his priest, teacher, and so forth. As specialized occupations of priest and teacher arise in such a society, as these new social positions develop, the boy comes to attend to three different persons instead of one. And of course in highly developed societies the number of occupations runs into the thousands. This process is spoken of as societal differentiation; its product, or static counterpart, is known as societal complexity. When conceived as broadly as possible, division of labor seems to be equivalent to societal complexity.

Evidence from the left side of the continuum of societal complexity converges on the finding that differentiation from the very simple folk society occurs in a more or less patterned sequence. In their sample drawn from the Cross-cultural Survey and the Human Relations Area Files, Freeman and Winch found that emergence of the occupations of priest and teacher seems generally to occur after the development of a money economy and a recognizable government but before the emergence of bureaucrats or of a written language.[27]

There is no need to conclude that a social system will always change in the direction of greater complexity. When the process becomes clearly understood, it seems likely that the explanation will assert that one necessary condition for societal differentiation to occur is an increase in resources. For example, a surplus must be available to support a priest or a teacher. On the other hand, when resources become scarce, as in a disaster, the complexity of the social system affected can be expected to diminish.

THE NIMKOFF-MIDDLETON STUDY[28]

Now let us consider the perspective of societal complexity and see how it contributes to the analysis of (1) the emergence of either the nuclear or the extended familial system and (2) sources of variation in familism within societies.

Using evidence overwhelmingly drawn from the "simpler" (or left) side of the continuum of societal complexity, Nimkoff and Middleton have tested the hypothesis of a correlation between type of subsistence pattern and type of familial system. The evidence is drawn from the 549 of the 565 cultures in Murdock's "World Ethnographic Sample" (WES) that could be coded on these two variables.[29] Coding for type of subsistence

---

[26] Thus it is assumed that at the concrete level there are more social positions in an industrial society (with its thousands of occupations) than in a society with sedentary agriculture, and in the latter than in a hunting-gathering society. At the analytic level, however, the number of social positions is constant for all societies irrespective of level of complexity; for the number is determined by a constant set of societal functions postulated to provide the dynamic of every society.

[27] Freeman and Winch, pp. 461–466. Subsequently Freeman improved on the technique of Freeman and Winch, and Tatje and Naroll improved on that of Naroll. Tatje and Freeman's ranked societies very simi-

and Naroll then reported that their procedure larly with respect to complexity; the Spearman correlation was + .87. See Linton C. Freeman, *An Empirical Test of Folk-Urbanism*, unpublished doctoral dissertation, Northwestern University, 1957; Terrence A. Tatje and Raoul Naroll, "Two Measures of Social Complexity: An Empirical Comparison," unpublished manuscript, no date.

[28] M. F. Nimkoff and Russell Middleton, "Types of Family and Types of Economy," *American Journal of Sociology*, 1960, 66: 215–225. See pp. 80–83 in this volume.

[29] George Peter Murdock, "World Ethnographic Sample," *American Anthropologist*, 1957, 59: 664–687.

was with respect to Murdock's categories as to the presence or absence, and the importance of, such subsistence activities as hunting and gathering, fishing, animal husbandry and agriculture. Type of familial system was dichotomized into independent[30] and extended.

A relationship emerged: peoples at the least complex level of subsistence—hunting and gathering—almost without exception have independent familial systems, whereas extended familism was almost universally encountered among societies on a more complex level of subsistence—sedentary agriculture with part-time herding.

Continuing their secondary analysis, Nimkoff and Middleton isolated four factors that appear to influence type of familial system through their association with type of subsistence: (1) abundance and stability of the food supply; (2) degree of demand for the family as a unit of labor; (3) the amount of geographic mobility involved in subsistence activities, and (4) the amount and nature of property. The first of these factors can be considered to be the most important in the sense that the only deviant cases of extended familism among hunting and gathering peoples occurred among those whose food supplies were unusually plentiful and regular for that type of subsistence, and also in the sense that, statis-

tically speaking, food supply "explained" the correlations between the other three factors and type of familism. In short, a relatively ample and regular food supply, high use of the family as a laboring unit, low necessity for geographic mobility with respect to subsistence, and strongly developed concepts of property (especially land) as owned collectively rather than individually were associated with the maximum probability of extended familism, and of course the reverse conditions were associated with familism of the independent-conjugal-nuclear type.

One other factor emerged as important: in societies complex enough to have stratification (which presupposes an assured food supply and the concept of property), this factor was positively correlated with extended familism even when type of subsistence was held constant.[31]

Having concluded that type of subsistence, type of familial property and degree of stratification are related to type of familial system among the simpler societies in the WES, Nimkoff and Middleton extrapolated beyond their data and proposed that some of the same relationships should hold among the modern industrial societies. In the latter type of society there are a low demand for the family as the unit of labor (since individuals are hired for cash on achievement criteria) and a high degree of geographic mobility in the pursuit of subsistence (the hunter pursues his game; the industrial worker or bureaucrat, his job). To be sure, the concept of property is more highly developed among the modern practitioners of nuclear familism, but Nimkoff and Middleton suggested that the shift from both or either group-owned land to land individually acquired or to disposable

---

[30] Nimkoff and Middleton define families as independent if they "do not normally include more than one nuclear or polygamous family . . . [and] . . . if the head of a family of procreation is neither subject to the authority of any of his relatives nor economically dependent upon them," p. 215. Although the terms are not identical, it appears that for the discussion of their study, we may regard the independent family of Nimkoff and Middleton to be equivalent to our nuclear family (whether isolated or not) and to Goode's conjugal family, as well as to Litwak's modified extended family.

[31] Nimkoff and Middleton, p. 220 and tables 4 and 5.

cash makes for the easier emergence of nuclear familism.

From these considerations it seems to follow that there is a curvilinear relationship between societal complexity (as measured by type of subsistence) and familial complexity, as follows: at the simplest level of subsistence (hunting and gathering) there is a nuclear family system; at the intermediate level of subsistence (sedentary agriculture and herding) there is an extended family system; and with the industrial type of economy there is a nuclear family system.

Although the results of Nimkoff and Middleton are highly suggestive and theoretically plausible, it is premature to conclude that they have isolated the "conditions under which" the nuclear familial system emerges. Their method does not yield a causal chain, and the data themselves must be scrutinized for sources of bias.[32]

As we have noted, the Nimkoff-Middleton study is based upon data drawn from ethnographies concerning 549 of the 565 societies in Murdock's WES. Most of the other studies of societal complexity that have been cited here are based on the WES or an early version of the WES (both or either the Cross-cultural Survey or the Human Relations Area Files) or on some modification of one of these data-banks. Since this remark can be applied to the studies by Naroll, Freeman-Winch, Freeman, and Tatje-Naroll, it follows that these studies have a consider-

able number of societies and ethnographic sources in common. For this reason it is necessary to conclude that these different studies can not be regarded as independent studies of the same or similar hypotheses. Rather similarities of results between studies can be thought of as registering alternate-forms of reliability in the sense of measuring degree of equivalence of variations on a basically common technique.

Another important qualification to keep in mind in interpreting these results is that these studies of societal complexity have been secondary analyses. That is, the social scientists who have performed these studies have been using data that were not gathered for this purpose, nor indeed were the data coded with this purpose in mind. Of course all data must be coded before quantitative analysis can be undertaken. The difficulty with secondary analysis is that the user of the data often does not know the rules that were followed in coding the data; hence he cannot know which information has been included and which excluded. With respect to the WES, however, the situation is unusually good since Murdock has specified in considerable detail a set of 15 variables that have been coded and since Sawyer and LeVine have factor-analyzed intercorrelations among these variables. Of the nine factors extracted by Sawyer and LeVine, the first four were Murdock's "basic types of economy": agriculture, animal husbandry, fishing, and hunting and gathering. The next four factors related to variations in the familial system: nuclear family household, patrilineality, matrilineality, and cross-cousin marriage. The final factor was that of social stratification.[33]

---

[32] The reader is reminded that although we have spoken of societal complexity as our independent variable and familial complexity as our dependent variable, we have disavowed any claim for an invariant or unidirectional relationship between the two. As Goode has shown, the family is not merely a passive entitey acted upon by the forces of industrialization; feedbacks are numerous and complex, see note 5.

[33] Jack Sawyer and Robert LeVine, "Cultural Dimensions: A Factor Analysis of the World Ethnographic Sample," *American Anthropologist*, 1966, 68: 708–731. Mur-

The results of the Sawyer-LeVine study do not indicate that there is anything spurious about the correlations reported by Nimkoff-Middleton. What these results do indicate, however, is that since other information was not included, it was not possible to find any other type of correlation, for example, that the nature of the value-system or of the religious organization might have any influence either on the level of subsistence or on familial complexity.

A final comment on the methodology of our problem is that the measures of societal complexity based on the WES or some derivative of it cover mainly the left side and not the full range of complexity. With such a measure, therefore, it is not possible to test a general hypothesis about societal complexity.[34]

THE WINCH-GREER-BLUMBERG STUDIES

In presenting the findings of these studies, we are addressing our second question, which concerns the factors involved in *intra*societal variation in nuclear familism. In this discussion we shall confine our attention to one advanced, industrial society—the United States.[35] We shall present evidence relating to the dimensions of ethnicity, migration, and rural-urban residence, as well as socioeconomic status.

In a sample drawn from an upper-middle-class suburb of Chicago, ethnicity (as indexed by religious preference) was found to be the strongest predictor of the degree of extended familism: Jews had more kin in the Chicago area, they interacted with more of their kin and did so more frequently, and they exchanged more goods and services with their relatives (that is, had more functional interaction with them) than did the Catholics and Protestants. Because all of the respondents in this study lived in two adjacent census tracts in a single suburb, there was little variation in socioeconomic status. Although migration correlated considerably with familism (non-migrants were most familistic) and although Jews were much less likely to be migrants than were Catholics or Protestants, still Jews were more familistic than the others when migratory status was held constant.[36]

In a somewhat parallel study using a probability sample of the state of Wiscon-

---

dock's criteria for including societies in his sample were: for each of his 60 cultural subareas, the largest society; the ethnographically best described societies; the societies constituting examples of each basic type of economy (noted above—the most complex is plow agriculture!), and of each major rule of descent (matrilineal, patrilineal, double, or bilateral) represented in the area; the societies representing each linguistic stock or major subfamily found in the area; and other area societies representing distinctive cultures, p. 667. It is evident that such selection criteria will grossly underrepresent modern nations, and this is indeed what occurs in the WES.

[34] Marsh has advanced the cause by proposing a four-component measure consisting of two components that measure variation among simpler societies and two components that measure variation among developed societies, p. 35. It would be advisable to add a third pair of components to measure variation in such a way as to overlap the ranges covered by the other four.

[35] It is not clear at which point along the dimension of complexity a society becomes differentiated enough to have two or more types of familial organization. The limiting factor in this discussion is the lack of comparable data on the family systems of other societies.

[36] Winch, Greer, and Blumberg, pp. 265–272.

sin, ethnicity, migration, and residence (rural versus urban) all had some predictive power with respect to extended familism. Catholics and Lutherans were more familistic than "other Protestants," but the degree of correlation was considerably less than in the suburban study, and it disappeared when one or both spouses were migrants. In general, socioeconomic status proved to be a very weak predictor of extended familism, but one index of it —occupation of the husband—was about as strong as ethnicity. And as with ethnicity, controlling for migratory status wiped out the relationship between occupation and familism except among migrant couples.[37]

Some parallels can be drawn between the variables proving significant in the foregoing two studies and the four factors that emerged in the Nimkoff-Middleton analysis of the simpler societies of the WES:

1. *Migration* emerged in all of these studies: the degree of extended familism was lower among those who were geographically mobile. Nimkoff and Middleton report that for the simpler societies, mobility was completely related to type of economy. Technical difficulties have prevented our making a parallel determination for the two American studies.

2. *Property in the form of land* was associated with extended familism among the societies of the WES. In Wisconsin the degree of extended familism was higher among rural than among urban nuclear families. Although we do not have data on this point, it seems plausible that land ownership might be more common among rural than urban residents.

3. *Family as a unit of labor* correlated with extended familism in the Nimkoff-Middleton study. In the suburban study it was discovered that those families

wherein the father had ever been associated in a family business were likely to be high in extended familism. It would seem that the rural families of Wisconsin—at least to the extent that they are farmers— would also make some use of their families as workers, and it will be recalled that the rural families were more extended-familistic on the average than were the urban families. It is consistent with this presentation that among farm families and among those where the head had been in a family business, the high scores on extended familism were especially high on functionality—their exchange of goods and services with kinfolk.

Toward the simpler end of the scale of societal complexity, it appears that the factors just noted—spatial immobility, collectively owned property, and family labor—are indicative of the higher level of subsistence (plow agriculture) rather than the lower (hunting and gathering). At the more complex end of the scale, it seems that we have found some segments of the population (namely Jews) that show these traits considerably more than others (namely "other Protestants") and also show the greatest degree of extended familism.

Now have we any grounds for believing that these Midwesterners who happen to be from different ethnic categories are at different points along the continuum of societal complexity? Or must we ascribe these ethnic differences to the "black box" of culture? One of the most intriguing aspects of the Nimkoff-Middleton analysis is the manner in which they relate all the factors correlated with familism to their measure of societal complexity. Let us see if we can perform a parallel operation with ethnicity.

Even though ethnic heterogeneity is not a necessary concomitant of a high degree of societal complexity—witness Scandinavia—it tends to increase positive-

[37] Winch and Greer,

ly with complexity. (Note its frequent use as an index of urbanism.) But not all the diverse ethnic categories found in a complex society have originated there. In this fact lies the relation between ethnicity and complexity. Each ethnic category enters the scene from some particular niche with respect to complexity. For each ethnic category the question to be asked is: were they formerly hunters, peasants, cash-crop farmers, tradesmen, or bureaucrats?

With respect to migrants to the United States, it should not seem strange that Polish Jews, who were shopkeepers well acquainted with the ways of a money-economy and the necessity of literacy, should advance faster than Polish Catholics who were peasants and migrated to the United States at the same time. If it is true that the level of familism is currently higher among Polish Jews than among Polish Catholics, this may at first seem puzzling since it might be expected that the immigrant Catholic peasants originally had the extended family systems typical of sedentary agriculturists. But as Pius Okigbo documents with reference to West Africa, where control over land is the basis of familial authority, the extended family structure can be severely upset by the loss or economic eclipse of this authority.[38] It is easier for an immigrant trader than an immigrant peasant to reestablish himself in his old subsistence pursuit so as to provide continuing opportunities for family members. The immigrant entrepreneur is more likely to retain more of the family organization built up around his traditional mode of subsistence than is the peasant who left the authority basis of his family system

behind in the "ould sod." This reasoning suggests two hypotheses:

1. The amount of change in the familial system of incoming ethnic categories is positively related to the amount of change in type of subsistence.

2. The rate of advancement of incoming ethnic categories is positively related to the complexity level of their original type of subsistence.

From this reasoning it follows that, with number of generations since migration held constant, even (and perhaps especially) when socio-economic status is controlled, we should expect categories of peasant origin to show less extended familism than categories of trade origin. (It should be noted that exceptions to these predictions are made for people of peasant origin who become farmers in this country.) To the extent that Greeks, Armenians, Lebanese, Syrians, and so forth resemble the Jews in coming from a trade-based type of subsistence (that is, level of societal complexity) and are able to move into trade in their new environment, their rate of socioeconomic advance and maintenance of networks of extended kin should outstrip contemporaneous cohorts of peasant origin. We should expect the Greeks to be like the Jews in having relatively high proportions of veterans of family businesses, lower proportions in the nomadic bureaucratic occupations, and highly functional rather than merely large kin networks.

To this point our assertions have concerned members of ethnic categories arriving in this country at roughly the same time. The crest of the wave of Jewish immigration arrived at least a quarter of a century after the peak of Christian migration from Europe.[39] The Christians'

---

[38] Pius Okigbo, "Social Consequences of Economic Development in West Africa," *Annals of the American Academy of Political and Social Science*, 1956, 305: 125–133.

[39] Modal years for numbers of migrants from Great Britain, Ireland, Scandinavia, and Germany were in the latter half of the nine-

greater time in this country has allowed more opportunity to disperse, and hence we should expect them to have fewer extended kin nearby.

SOCIETAL COMPLEXITY, FAMILIAL COMPLEXITY, AND FEMALE POWER

We have proposed that the relation between societal complexity and familial complexity (or extended familism) is curvilinear. That is, if we should plot scale of societal complexity on an abscissa and degree of extended familism on an ordinate, the resulting curve would have a tail at either end of the distribution and an intermediate hump. Accordingly, highly developed societies would be registering relatively low extended familism. One element in the decline in extended familism in complex societies is frequently a reduction in economic functionality. Since so much of the male's daily activity is instrumental (especially economic) in nature, men tend to lose interest in the family when it ceases to function as an economic organization. We should not be surprised to find, then, that as instrumental functions decline within the family, the maintenance of kin ties becomes a feminine task.

Because of the biological fact that only women bear and nurse children, there is a tendency for societies to define the duties of women as less mobile, as pertaining more to home and hearth,[40] and

thus it seems plausible that in the more highly developed societies there should be less differentiation among women than among men. As the occupations of men become more diverse, they cease to have as much in common as before, and here we can see one basis for kin-keeping to become a woman's activity. If Parsons and Bales are right in linking instrumental roles to men and expressive roles to women,[41] and if, as seems to be the case from the evidence on the sequences of societal differentiation, instrumental functions tend to leave the family at a faster rate than do expressive functions, this would be another pressure for women to take over the kin-keeping activities.

These theoretical deductions are consistent with Clignet's observation that in contemporary Africa, as in other parts of the world, the less functional kin affiliations are, "the more familial ties will be maintained by women rather than by men." Clignet goes on to remark that "the severance of such ties is usually more threatening for the former than for the latter."[42] In the context of intergenerational solidarity Sweetser has studied the same phenomenon, and she concludes:

"Intergenerational solidarity follows the line of male succession in instrumental tasks; when the latter disappears, matrilineal solidarity between generations becomes the rule. We have a society in which kin can rarely be of use to men in their daily business, while kin can be of considerable use to women in their daily business."[43]

---

teenth century; for Italy, Poland, and the U.S.S.R. and Baltic States were in the first quarter of the twentieth century. U. S. Bureau of the Census, *Historical Statistics of the United States, Colonial Times to 1957*, Washington, 1960, pp. 56–57.

[40] Robert F. Winch, *The Modern Family*, rev. ed. New York: Holt, Rinehart & Winston, Inc., 1963, chap. 12.

[41] Parsons and Bales, p. 23.

[42] Remi Clignet, "Urbanization and Family Structure in the Ivory Coast," *Comparative Studies in Society and History*, 1966, 8: 395–401. Quotations are from p. 399.

[43] Dorrian Apple Sweetser, "The Effect of Industrialization on Intergenerational Solidarity," *Rural Sociology*, 1966, 31: 156–170. Quotation is from p. 169.

Among the simplest societies one may speak of the median instrumental functionality of women; among the most complex societies there is of course much differentiation, and hence one should relate the instrumental functionality of women to such variables as social class, rural versus urban residence, employment outside the home, and so forth. When several of these many factors making for differentiation act in combination, the effect may be even more pronounced. Accordingly, it is not surprising that the extreme case of female familial power appears to occur most strikingly within societies in the upper rather than the lower sectors of the continuum of societal complexity. Let us proceed from this reasoning in an attempt to illuminate the "matrifocal family."

this mother-child incomplete nuclear family is also common among certain sectors of the lower classes in many Latin American and Caribbean countries,[45] and far from rare among urban, lower-class whites in the United States.

Furthermore, despite the fact that the Caribbean islanders, British Guianians and Americans most likely to live in such families are black, an explanation based on ethnicity, "West African origins" or caste is inadequate. For in Guatemala, female-headed families are more common among Spanish-American *Ladinos* than among Mayan Indians, the local lower-class ethnic group; and in the U. S. itself, while 47 percent of urban Negro families with incomes under $3,000 are headed by females, so are 38 percent of their white counterparts.[46]

THE MOTHER-CHILD INCOMPLETE NUCLEAR FAMILY

Recently—since the cauldron containing the long-simmering American problems of poverty, discrimination and race reached a raging boil in the sixties, and particularly since the publication of the document popularly known as "the Moynihan Report"[44] —one type of family has been hotly discussed and frequently bemoaned in the United States. This type of family consists of a woman and her children with no permanently resident husband-father; it may include other members, particularly the maternal grandmother of the children. Its current notoriety stems from the fact that in this country it occurs in greatest proportion among urban, lower-class Negroes. But

[44] Office of Policy Planning and Research, United States Department of Labor, *The Negro Family: The Case for National Action*, Washington, 1965.

[45] Adams gives statistics on the occurrence of female-headed households in Guatemala, El Salvador, Nicaragua and Costa Rica; and presents findings from Brazil and Paraguay. He also discusses Raymond T. Smith's investigations of mother-headed families in British Guiana. Some sources on the occurrence of this type of family in the Caribbean are as follows: Judith Blake, *Family Structure in Jamaica*. New York: The Free Press, 1961; J. Mayone Stycos and Kurt W. Back, *The Control of Human Fertility in Jamaica*. Ithaca, N. Y.: Cornell University Press, 1964; F. M. Henriques, *Family and Colour in Jamaica*. London: Eyre and Spottiswoode, 1953; T. S. Simey, *Welfare and Planning in the West Indies*. Oxford: Clarendon Press, 1946; and Raymond T. Smith, "Culture and Social Structure in The Caribbean," *Comparative Studies in Society and History*. Vol. VI, The Hague, The Netherlands, October 1963, pp. 24–46.

[46] Adams, p. 34 and Lee Rainwater, "Crucible of Identity: The Negro Lower-Class Family," *Daedalus*, 1965, 95: 172–216, p. 181. In order to put U. S. mother-centered familism in perspective, let us present the

What is needed is the delineation of the structural features common to all of these instances of mother-centered families. As Adams points out, given the evidence that large segments of some contemporary societies manifest this type of family, it is better sociology to regard it as one among a set of family types, each of which calls for explanation, than to regard it as "abnormal" or "disorganized" and thereby to relegate it to "social pathology."[47] Accordingly, after discussing some of the dimensions of the mother-child dyadic family among U. S. Negroes, we shall seek to extract those factors apparently making for its appearance in other settings as well.

The one factor that seems to impress observers of the black ghetto scene as most critical is the economic status of the

complete table from which the Negro-white statistic was taken:

Proportion of female heads for families with children by race, income and urban-rural categories

	Rural	Urban	Total
	PER CENT	PER CENT	PER CENT
Negroes			
under $3000	18	47	36
$3000 and over	5	8	7
Total	14	23	21
White			
under $3000	12	38	22
$3000 and over	2	4	3
Total	4	7	6

Source: U. S. Census: 1960, PC (1) D. U. S. Volume, Table 225; State Volume, Table 140.

More recently, the U. S. Bureau of the Census informs us that in 1966, 31 percent of the Negro households were headed by women with no husbands present; the corresponding figure for white households was 19 percent. Among the Negro female heads of households, 40 percent were either divorced or separated, whereas for white the figure was 21 percent (U. S. Bureau of the Census, *Current Population Reports—Population Characteristics*, Series P–20, No. 164, April 12, 1967).

47 Adams, p. 36. As mentioned, Adams regards the dyad as the basic structural building block of the family. See note 13.

average lower-class man: low, marginal, and insecure. It is a commonplace that, relatively speaking, Negro women have been much better off with the opportunity for regular, even though poorly paid, employment. Failing that, they have experienced easier access to public assistance for their families.

Less well known, however, are the following two relevant empirical generalizations:

1. Marital stability tends to be greater in the more economically advantaged strata of societies.[48]

2. The higher the economic level of the family, the greater on the average is the marital dominance of the husband.[49]

Given that the Negro lower-class male is at the bottom of the economic spectrum in American society, the second proposition above predicts that he will frequently exhibit minimum—probably negative—marital dominance,[50] and this is what we find. Ethnographic accounts of

48 William J. Goode, "A Cross Cultural Analysis of Divorce Rates," *International Social Science Journal*, 1962, 14: 527–538.

49 Robert O. Blood, Jr., and Donald M. Wolfe, *Husbands and Wives: The Dynamics of Married Living*. New York: The Free Press, 1960, chap. 2. Although Yugoslav and Greek studies have shown a contrary relationship—the higher the status of the husband, the lower his marital authority—the present writers surmise that this finding may be a result of recent migration from rural areas and thus be a transitory vestige of peasant culture. See *Olivera Buric and Andjelka Zecevic, "Family Authority, Marital Satisfaction, and the Social Network in Yugoslavia," and Constantina Safilios-Rothschild, "A Comparison of Power Structure and Marital Satisfaction in Urban Greek and French Families," Journal of Marriage and the Family*, 1967, 29: 325–336 and 345–352, respectively.

50 Joan Aldous, "The Restoration of the Lower Class Male as Household Head: Support for the Moynihan Thesis," paper presented before the American Sociological Association, 1967.

what we find.   Ethnographic accounts of Negro life in the slums indicate that many of the women tend to show very little respect for Negro men. During periods of unemployment, moreover, a husband is frequently treated by his wife as having no claim upon her loyalty, her company, or indeed even the use of their common facilities.[51] Not only is the woman responsible for running the household but frequently for providing its stable economic support.

Relatively speaking, then, the role-performance of the ghetto black woman is often markedly more competent than is the man's. In the sense that the woman keeps the family running and the man is supererogatory, there is a functional basis for female dominance, low respect for males, and fragile marriages.

MATRILINEAL EXTENSION OF THE MOTHER-CHILD INCOMPLETE NUCLEAR FAMILY INTO A PARTICULAR FORM OF EXTENDED FAMILY

Ethnographic accounts of the lower-class urban black family indicate that frequently (but we cannot be sure just how frequently) the maternal grandmother socializes and nurtures her grandchildren and runs the house while the young mother provides the funds through her employment. It appears that such a three-generational matrilineal family is not uncommon, whether or not they all live in a common dwelling unit.

Ethnographies such as Rainwater's give some indication as to the way in which boys and girls are prepared for this kind of family. In the black ghettos it appears that neither boys nor girls develop very high expectations of marriage —either with respect to its stability or the gratifications to be derived from it. From the middle-class point of view another element in underplaying marriage is that it seems not to have much significance as a *rite de passage* to mark the achievement of adult status. Rather it appears that for the girl adulthood comes upon her becoming a mother for the first time, and for the boy when he has fathered his first child. When a girl becomes premaritally pregnant, it is frequently assumed that she will stay at home and that her mother (or parents if she also has a resident father) will assume responsibility for her child. Rainwater further reports that at this time it is typical for the girl's mother to care for the child and for the girl to become more active socially with her peer group and more active sexually as well.[52]

To the writers' knowledge it is not possible from presently available data to tell whether or not the mother-child family of black ghetto usually includes the maternal grandmother. The reason is that the data of the U. S. Bureau of the Census do not shed light directly on familial structure. If a maternal grandmother lives in the next apartment to her daughter and the latter's children, the grandmother is not a part of the mother-child family in the bookkeeping of the Census, no matter how active the grandmother may be in keeping the family running. What is critical here is that members of a family living in two or more separate dwelling units may interact with each other in a sufficiently functional manner to constitute a single familial social system, and yet such a family would not be recorded as such by the Census.

Nevertheless, with respect to the three-generational households actually counted by the Census, they are reported as being twice as common among nonwhites as among whites—9.2 percent versus 4.5 percent—in husband-wife households, and three times as common among nonwhites—3.1 percent versus 1.0 percent—in other than husband-wife house-

51 Rainwater, pp. 172–216.

52 Rainwater, pp. 172–216.

holds.[53] It must be emphasized that even should there exist an equal number of three-generational families who happen *not* to reside in the same household, this would not raise the percentage of matriarchal families to anything approaching a norm among either blacks or whites.

COMMON ELEMENTS UNDERLYING MOTHER-CHILD INCOMPLETE NUCLEAR FAMILIES

1. *Poverty.* In all the societies where mother-centered families have been documented, they are apparently most characteristic of the lower class.

2. *Class-related marital characteristics.* In general, we know that:

a. Women who have worked outside the home tend to have more domestic power than those who haven't.[54]

b. Lower-class women are more likely to be in the labor force; the difference is especially pronounced when there are small children at home.[55]

c. As mentioned above, a study based on data from Detroit reports that the lower the economic level of the family, the less on the average is the marital dominance of the husband.

d. Also as noted, marital stability in a number of societies is inversely related to socioeconomic status.

3. *Subsistence-complexity factors.* Poverty is not enough. Some lower-class

groups seem virtually "immune" to this form of the family, while among others it is rampant:

a. We have noted that the mother-child dyadic family is more common among poor *urban* Americans than among poor *rural* Americans. Its higher association with urban populations is also documented by Adams for Central America.[56]

b. Where the family is the unit of labor, mother-centered families are infrequent.

c. Where the individual is the unit of labor, mother-centered families are most likely where the woman is less economically marginal than the man. As discussed above, Negro males of the urban lower class are most likely to fall into this unenviable situation in the U. S. But again let us stress that this factor is not unique to American ghettos. Indeed, the generally vulnerable position of the male entering the industrial economy at its bottom level has been noted by many writers. For example, Smelser, in his analysis of the Industrial Revolution and family disorganization in England, has pointed out that at certain stages wives and children were more likely to be steadily employed than adult males.[57]

[53] *U. S. Census of Population: 1960.* Final Report PC (2)-4A. Table 17.

[54] Wolfe, pp. 99–117.

[55] When there are children under six present, and women in general register their lowest level of labor force participation, a full 28.3 percent of the wives of men earning less that $2,000 per year are in the labor force, while only 6.2 percent of women whose husbands earn from $7,000 to $9,999 work. U. S. Bureau of the Census, *Current Population Reports—Labor Force*, Series P-50, No. 87, January 1959, Table F, p. 5.

[56] Adams, p. 34.

[57] Smelser mentions the introduction of the power loom, which demanded young persons and women, but very few adult males, to give one such instance. Of interest is the following table introduced by Smelser as evidence: "In [one] factory, I found the number of hands 245, of whom were—

Females above 18 years of age	129
Females under 18	38
Males above 18	42
Males under 18	36

which is about the average of other establishments of this nature." *Parliamentary Papers*, 1840, Hand-loom Weavers, p. 607, in Neil J. Smelser, *Social Change in the Industrial Revolution*. Chicago: University of Chicago Press, 1959, p. 200.

4. *Biological factors*. Everywhere, the biological tie is closer between mother and child than between father and child.

As we try to integrate these considerations, the following picture emerges: In more complex societies the family tends to show a relatively low degree of extended familism. More analytically, the family has simple organization and a low level of instrumental functionality. As instrumental functionality has been leaving the family, it has become less vital, less rewarding and less interesting to men; they have a smaller stake in it. At the lower-class level, husbands tend to have the least domestic power relative to their wives. At this level again, in the urban setting, men show the highest proportions of being economically more marginal than wives. For these reasons there is little to bind such a man to such a woman. Since the mother-child tie is stronger than the father-child bond, it is the biologically given, the mother-child dyad, that survives while the marital tie has little payoff for either spouse and is correspondingly fragile. Thus, under the conditions we have enumerated, we encounter the maximum incidence of the lowest existing level of family structure, and the apogee of "female power."

THREE FAMILIAL TYPES IN THE UNITED STATES

Focusing now on the U. S., we find we have described three types of family that may be found in this country. Of course these types are not clearly set off from each other, but rather they will be found to blur into each other. Moreover, no claim is made that these three exhaust the set of familial types in American society. With these qualifications the three

familial types that have been considered are as follows:

1. *A nuclear family embedded in a network of extended kin*. Among the segments of population considered, this type seems to be more characteristic of Jews than of the others. If the presence of 12 or more households of extended kin in the metropolitan area be used as a criterion of "high" extended familism, our sample of suburban Jews showed 78 percent of its households having high extended familism, compared with 35 percent for Catholics and 14 percent for Protestants.

2. *An isolated nuclear family*. This type occurs most frequently among white Protestants although within this category it accounts for probably no more than one out of every four families (28 percent in the suburban sample and 22 percent in the "other Protestant" category of the Wisconsin sample reported no kin in the locality). Our data do not reveal the frequency of this type among Negroes.

3. *A mother-child nuclear family, sometimes with matrilineal extension*. It appears that this form is more widely known among poor urban blacks than in other segments of American society although even there it is not clear that it is a majority pattern. As has been pointed out, it is not clear in which proportion of poor Negro urban families with a female head the maternal grandmother is actually a functioning member. Moreoever, although this type is proportionately most frequent among the poor black urban segment of the population, it does appear of course in other segments as well.

Are there other types? There may be; we cannot be sure. The dimensions of analysis used here are two: (a) completeness versus incompleteness of the nuclear family, and (b) isolation of the nuclear family versus extended familism. It would appear that the Italian-American family as described by Campisi[58] would fit into our type 1 (along with the Jews). But it is conceivable that we could use other variables (including complexity-subsistence factors) for the analysis and emerge with different types. This is clearly a matter for further research.

But more importantly, it should be cross-cultural research. In this manner, complexity factors could be related to more precise studies of variations in familial structure and function, opening up an important new dimension for sociological investigation.

SUMMARY

Goode's formulation that around the world societies are developing small-family systems has inspired us to question the prospect that there is a single emerging familial form and to look for correlates of familial variation. To do this, we have proposed that the independent variable be conceptualized as societal complexity and that (although we are not the first to remark it) familial complexity is a curvilinear function of societal complexity. Very simple and very developed societies show the pattern of the nuclear family, whereas societies of intermediate complexity show the pattern of the extended family. From intersocietal data it appears that the existence of the extended family is associated with a reliable food supply, a demand for the family as a unit of labor, little geographic mobility in subsistence

activities, and the collective (familial) ownership of land. It is important to remember that the data supporting these relationships—those of the World Ethnographic Sample—have been shorn of information about institutional contexts other than family and economy, and accordingly cannot show other societal structures covarying with type of family.

Using two dimensions of analysis—degree of isolation of the nuclear family, and its completeness versus incompleteness—we have proposed the existence of three familial types in the United States: isolated nuclear, non-isolated nuclear, and mother-child nuclear (sometimes with matrilineal extension). It was found that degree of isolation varied with migration, socioeconomic status, urban versus rural residence and ethnicity. With respect to ethnicity, the Protestants showed the greatest, and the Jews the least proportions of isolated families, and it was proposed that familial types of ethnic categories varied with their level of societal complexity at the time of their entry into a society and with the amount of change in their type of subsistence. The mother-child incomplete nuclear family—found in highest proportion in the black urban ghetto—is associated with poverty, greater economic marginality of the man than of the woman, and low instrumental functionality of the nuclear family as a unit.

On the basis of published studies and our own work we have extended Goode's synthesis both intersocietally and intrasocietally. As with his work, however, our paper has had to rely upon fragmentary data, and hence there is an urgent need for research to give greater empirical support to these propositions.

[58] Paul J. Campisi, "The Italian Family in the United States," *American Journal of Sociology*, 1948, 53: 443–449.

4

THE DIVERSITY OF THE AMERICAN FAMILY

A moment's reflection reminds us of the variety of ways in which families are constituted in the United States. Ethnic traditions, religious preference, racial ascription, socioeconomic status, and many other factors all contribute to the kind of family each of us experiences. Rather than collect thumbnail sketches of a multitude of family types, we have chosen to present four articles which will remind the reader of the richness in the American family.

Beginning with a description of the family the Italian immigrant brings with him, Paul Campisi shows how the style of family life changes as the succeeding generations become increasingly assimilated into the American way of life, and the conflicts and accommodations which are part of the making of this intergenerational change.

Lee Rainwater describes the lot of the Negro lower-class family. He shows that the family is the hub around which life in the Negro ghetto revolves and that phenomena like the high birth rate, the family matriarch, and gang behavior may be viewed as functional adaptations to a situation prescribed by racial and socioeconomic status. Rainwater feels that the situation he describes demands a remedy. The last pages of the article contain his proposals.

The third article deals with a perennial issue in the sociology of the family: should the American nuclear family be regarded as isolated or as involved in a network of kin? Robert F. Winch proposes a dimension with isolation at one end and extended familism at the other. With his associates he has worked out four indexes of this variable. With these indexes it is possible to measure the isolation of the nuclear family. The analysis also shows how diversity in the nuclear family with respect to isolation-extended-familism covaries with urbanism-ruralism, migration, and ethnicity.

The measures used by Winch show Jews as manifesting a relatively high degree of extended familism. Through their account of family life among first- and second-generation Jews in New York City, Hope Jensen Leichter and William E. Mitchell give substance to the more familistic end of the dimension of isolation-extended familism.

The Italian Family in the United States *

Paul J. Campisi

The changes in the Italian family in America can be visualized in terms of a continuum which ranges from an unacculturated Old World type to a highly acculturated and urbanized American type of family. This transformation can be understood by an analysis of three types of families which have characterized Italian family living in America: the Old World peasant Italian family which existed at the time of the mass migration from Italy (1890–1910) and which can be placed at the unacculturated end of the continuum; the first-generation Italian family in America, which at the beginning of contact with American culture was much like the first but which changed and continues to change increasingly so that it occupies a position somewhere between the two extremes; and, finally, the second-generation Italian family which represents a cross-fertilization of the first-generation Italian family and the American contemporary urban family, with the trend being in the direction of the American type. Consequently, the position this family assumes is near the American-urban end of the continuum.

Since there are significant differences between the northern Italian and southern Italian families and since there are even greater differences between peasant, middle-class, and upper-class families, it seems expedient to single out one type of family for discussion and analysis, namely, the southern Italian peasant family. During the period of mass migration from Italy the bulk of the immigrants were from southern Italy (including Sicily).[1] These immigrants came mostly from small-village backgrounds as peasant farmers, peasant workers, or simple artisans, and as such they brought with them a southern Italian folk-peasant culture. It is this type of background which the majority of Italian families in America have today.[2]

This paper cannot possibly present an adequate analysis of all the important changes observed in the Italian family. Therefore, a simple tabular form (see Table 1) is used to display the most important details.

[1] During the decade of 1900–1910, of the 2,045,877 Italians who came to America, the majority were from southern Italy.

[2] The observations in this paper are based on the literature in the field, on my own specific research in America on the acculturation of Italians, and, finally, on personal impressions and conclusions as a participant observer. A visit to southern Italy and Sicily three years ago gave me an opportunity to come in contact with the Old World peasant-type family. While this type of family has changed considerably from the time of the mass migration to America, enough structural and functional family lags exist to make the reconstruction of it in this paper reasonably valid.

° Adapted from Paul J. Campisi, "Ethnic Family Patterns: The Italian Family in the United States," The American Journal of Sociology, 1948, 53: 443–449, by permission of The University of Chicago Press.

THE SOUTHERN ITALIAN PEASANT FAMILY IN AMERICA

At the time of the great population movement from Italy to America, beginning at the end of the nineteenth century, the southern Italian peasant family was a folk societal family. One of the chief characteristics of the folk society is that its culture is highly integrated, the separate parts forming a strongly geared and functionally meaningful whole.[3] This intimate interconnection between the various parts of a folk culture indicates that it would be artificial and fruitless to attempt to isolate, even for the sake of study and analysis, any one part, such as the family, and to proceed to discuss that as a discrete and distinct entity. All the characteristics of the Old World Italian peasant family are intimately tied in with such institutions and practices as religion, the planting and gathering of food, the celebrations of feasts and holidays, the education of the children, the treatment of the sick, the protection of the person, and with all other aspects of small-village folk culture. In the final analysis Old World peasant-family life meant small-village life, and the two were inseparable aspects of a coercive folk-peasant culture. This fact sharply distinguishes the Old World peasant family from the first- and second-generation families in America.

THE FIRST-GENERATION SOUTHERN ITALIAN PEASANT FAMILY IN AMERICA

By the first-generation Italian family is simply meant that organization of parents and offspring wherein both parents

[3]See Robert Redfield, "The Folk Society," *American Journal of Sociology*, LII, 1947, 293–308.

are of foreign birth and wherein an attempt is made to perpetuate an Italian way of life in the transplanted household. This is a family in transition, still struggling against great odds to keep alive those customs and traditions which were sacred in the Old World culture. As a result of many internal and external pressures which have cut it off from its Old World foundations, the first-generation family is marked by considerable confusion, conflict, and disorganization. The uncertain and precarious position of the first-generation Italian family today is further aggravated by the loss of that strong family and community culture which had been such an indispensable part of the Old World peasant family. It is this loss in the first-generation family which pushes it away from the unacculturated end of the continuum to a position somewhere in the middle.[4]

THE SECOND-GENERATION SOUTHERN ITALIAN FAMILY IN AMERICA

This refers to that organization of parents and offspring wherein both the parents are native American-born but have foreign-born parents who attempted to transmit to them an Italian way of live in the original first-generation family in America.

Among the significant characteristics of this type of family is the orientation which the American-born parents make to the American culture. This adjustment tends to take three forms. One is that of complete abandonment of the Old World way of life. The individual changes his

[4]For an excellent analysis of the importance of a strong family and community culture see Margaret Park Redfield, "The American Family: Consensus and Freedom," pp. 23–37 above.

Italian name, moves away from the Italian neighborhood and in some cases from the community, and has little to do with his foreign-born parents and relatives.[5] The ideal is to become acculturated in as short a time as possible. This type of second-generation Italian generally passes for an American family and is rare. A second form of second-generation Italian family is a marginal one. In this type there is a seriously felt need to become Americanized and hence to shape the structure and functions of the family in accordance with the contemporary urban American type of family. The parental way of life is not wholly repudiated, although there is some degree of rejection. This family is likely to move out of the Italian neighborhood and to communicate less and less with first-generation Italians, but the bond with the first-generation family is not broken completely. Intimate communication is maintained with the parental household, and the relationships with the parents as well as with immigrant relatives are affectionate and understanding. A third form which the second-generation family takes is of orientation inward toward an Italian way of life. This type of family generally prefers to remain in the Italian neighborhood, close to the parental home. Its interaction with the non-Italian world is at a minimum, and its interests are tied up with those of the Italian community. Of the three, the second type is the most representative second-generation Italian family in America. This is the family depicted in Table 1.

Table 1 reveals the movement of the first- and second-generation Italian families away from the Old World peasant pattern and toward the contemporary

5 See Carlo Sforza, *The Real Italians*, New York, Columbia University Press, 1942, for an interesting account of Italian-Americans who change their names.

American family type. In this persistent and continuous process of acculturation there are three stages: (1) the initial-contact stage, (2) the conflict stage, and (3) the accommodation stage.

THE INITIAL-CONTACT STAGE

In the first decade of Italian living in America the structure of the Old World family is still fairly well intact, but pressures from within and outside the family are beginning to crack, albeit imperceptibly, the Old World peasant pattern. Producing this incipient distortion are the following: the very act of physical separation from the parental family and village culture; the necessity to work and operate with a somewhat strange and foreign body of household tools, equipment, gadgets, furniture, cooking utensils, and other physical objects, in addition to making an adjustment to a different physical environment, including climate, urban ecological conditions, and tenement living arrangements; the birth of children and the increasing contact with American medical practices regarding child care; the necessity to work for wages at unfamiliar tasks, a new experience for the peasant farmer; the attendance of Italian children in American parochial and public schools; the informal interaction of the children with the settlement house, the church associations, the neighborhood clubs, the neighborhood gang, and other organizations; the continuing residence in America and increasing period of isolation from the Old World; the acceptance of work by the housewife outside the home for wages; the increasing recognition by both parents and children that the Italian way of life in the American community means low status, social and economic discrimination, and prejudice; and the increasing pressure by American legal, educational, political, and economic

TABLE 1 Differences between the Southern Italian peasant family in Italy and the first- and second-generation Italian family in America

Southern Italian Peasant Family in Italy	First-Generation Southern Italian Family in America	Second-Generation Southern Italian Family in America
A. GENERAL CHARACTERISTICS		
1. Patriarchal	Fictitiously patriarchal	Tends to be democratic
2. Folk-peasant	Quasi-urban	Urban and modern
3. Well integrated	Disorganized and in conflict	Variable, depending on the particular family situation
4. Stationary	Mobile	High degree of mobility
5. Active community life	Inactive in the American community but somewhat active in the Italian neighborhood	Inactive in the Italian neighborhood, but increasingly active in American community
6. Emphasis on the sacred	Emphasis on the sacred is weakened	Emphasis on the secular
7. Home and land owned by family	In the small city the home may be owned, but in a large city the home is usually a flat or an apartment	Ownership of home is an ideal, but many are satisfied with flat
8. Strong family and community culture	Family culture in conflict	Weakened family culture reflecting vague American situation
9. Sharing of common goals	No sharing of common goals	No sharing of common goals
10. Children live for the parents	Children live for themselves	Parents live for the children
11. Children are an economic asset	Children are an economic asset for few working years only and may be an economic liability	Children are an economic liability
12. Many family celebrations of special feasts, holidays, etc.	Few family celebrations of feasts and holidays	Christmas only family affair, with Thanksgiving being variable
13. Culture is transmitted only by the family	Italian culture is transmitted only by family, but American culture is transmitted by American institutions other than the family	American culture is transmitted by the family and by other American institutions
14. Strong in-group solidarity	Weakened in-group solidarity	Little in-group solidarity
15. Many functions: economic, recreational, religious, social affectional, and protective	Functions include semi-recreational, social, and affectional	Functions reduced to affectional, in the main
B. SIZE		
1. Large-family system	Believe in a large-family system but cannot achieve it because of migration	Small-family system
2. Many children (10 is not unusual)	Fair number of children (10 is unusual)	Few children (10 is rare)
3. Extended kinship to godparents	Extended kinship, but godparent relationship is weakened	No extended kinship to godparents

TABLE 1 (Continued)

Southern Italian Peasant Family in Italy	First-Generation Southern Italian Family in America	Second-Generation Southern Italian Family in America
C. ROLES AND STATUSES		
1. Father has highest status	Father loses high status, or it is fictitiously maintained	Father shares high status with mother and children; slight patriarchal survival
2. Primogeniture: eldest son has high status	Rule of primogeniture is variable; success more important than position	No primogeniture; all children tend to have equal status
3. Mother center of domestic life only and must not work for wages	Mother center of domestic life but may work for wages and belong to some clubs	Mother acknowledges domestic duties but reserves time for much social life and may work for wages
4. Father can punish children severely	Father has learned that American law forbids this	Father has learned it is poor psychology to do so
5. Family regards itself as having high status and role in the community	Family does not have high status and role in the American community but may have it in the Italian colony	Family struggles for high status and role in the American community and tends to reject high status and role in the Italian community
6. Women are educated for marriage only	Women receive some formal education as well as family education for marriage	Emphasis is on general education with reference to personality development rather than to future marriage
7. The individual is subordinate to the family	Rights of the individual increasingly recognized	The family is subordinate to the individual
8. Daughter-in-law is subservient to the husband's family	Daughter-in-law is in conflict with husband's family	Daughter-in-law is more or less independent of husband's family
9. Son is expected to work hard and contribute to family income	Son is expected to work hard and contribute to family income, but this is a seldom-realized goal	Son is expected to do well in school and need not contribute to family income
D. INTERPERSONAL RELATIONS		
1. Husband and wife must not show affection in the family or in public	Husband and wife are not demonstrative in public or in the family but tolerate it in their married children	Husband and wife may be demonstrative in the family and in public
2. Boys are superior to girls	Boys are regarded a superior to girls	Boys tend to be regarded as superior to girls, but girls have high status also
3. Father is consciously feared, respected, and imitated	Father is not consciously feared or imitated but is respected	Father is not consciously feared. He may be imitated and may be admired
4. Great love for mother	Great love for mother but much ambivalence from cultural tensions	Love for mother is shared with father

TABLE 1 (Continued)

Southern Italian Peasant Family in Italy First-Generation	First-Generation Southern Italian Family in America	Second-Generation Southern Italian Family in America
5. Baby indulgently treated by all	Baby indulgently treated by all	Baby indulgently treated by all with increasing concern regarding sanitation, discipline, and sibling rivalry

E. MARRIAGE

1. Marriage in early teens	Marriage in late teens or early twenties	Marriage in early or middle twenties
2. Selection of mate by parents	Selection of mate by individual with parental consent	Selection of mate by individual regardless of parental consent
3. Must marry someone from the same village	This is an ideal, but marriage with someone from same region (i.e, province) is tolerated; very reluctant permission granted to marry outside nationality; no permission for marriage outside religion	Increasing number of marriages outside nationality and outside religion
4. Dowry rights	No dowry	No dowry
5. Marriage always involves a religious ceremony	Marriage almost always involves both a religious and a secular ceremony	Marriage usually involves both, but there is an increasing number of marriages without benefit of religious ceremony

F. BIRTH AND CHILD CARE

1. Many magical and superstitious beliefs in connection with pregnancy	Many survivals of old beliefs and superstitions	Few magical and superstitious notions in connection with pregnancy
2. Delivery takes place in a special confinement room in the home; midwife assists	Delivery takes place generally in a hospital; family doctor displaces midwife	Delivery takes place almost always in a hospital; specialist, obstetrician, or general practitioner assists
3. Child illnesses are treated by folk remedies; local physician only in emergencies or crises	Child illnesses are treated partially by folk remedies but mostly by the family doctor	Child illnesses are treated by a pediatrician; much use of latest developments in medicine (vaccines, etc.)
4. Child is breast-fed either by the mother or by a wet nurse; weaning takes place at about end of 2d or 3d year by camouflaging the breasts	Child is breast-fed if possible; if not, it is bottle-fed; same practice with variations regarding weaning	Child is bottle-fed as soon as possible; breast-feeding is rare; no weaning problems
5. No birth control	Some birth control	Birth control is the rule

TABLE 1 (Continued)

Southern Italian Peasant Family in Italy	First-Generation Southern Italian Family in America	Second-Generation Southern Italian Family in America
G. SEX ATTITUDES		
1. Child is allowed to go naked about the house up to the age of 5 or 6; after this there is rigid enforcement of the rule of modesty	Variable, depending on the individual family's situation	This is variable, depending on the individual family; development of modesty is much earlier than in Old World peasant family
2. Sex matters are not discussed in family	Sex matters are not discussed in family	Sex matters increasingly discussed in family but not as freely as in "old American family
3. Adultery is severely punished by the man's taking matters into his own hands	Adultery results in divorce or separation	Adultery may result in divorce or separation
4. Chastity rule rigidly enforced by chaperonage; lack of it is ground for immediate separation on wedding night	Attempts to chaperon fail, but chastity is an expectation; lack of it is grounds for separation, but there are few cases of this kind in America	No chaperonage; chastity is expected, but lack of it may be reluctantly tolerated
5. No premarital kissing and petting are allowed	No premarital kissing and petting are allowed openly	Premarital kissing and petting are allowed openly
6. Boys and girls attend separate schools	Schools are coeducational	Schools are coeducational
H. DIVORCE AND SEPARATION		
1. No divorce allowed	No divorce allowed, but some do divorce	Religion forbids it, but it is practiced
2. Desertion is rare	Desertion is rare	Desertion is rare
I. PSYCHOLOGICAL ASPECTS		
1. Fosters security in the individual	Fosters conflict in the individual	Fosters security with some conflict lags
2. The family provides a specific way of life; hence, there is little personal disorganization	Famly is in conflict, hence cannot provide a specific way of life; yields marginal American-Italian way of life	Family reflects confused American situation, does not give individual a specific way of life, but marginality is weakened
3. Recreation is within family	Recreation is both with and outside the family	Recreation is in the main outside the family, this is variable, depending on individual family situation

institutions for the Americanization of the foreigner.

Nonetheless, the first-generation Italian family in this phase is a highly integrated one, as in the Old World. The demands of the American community are not seriously felt in the insulated Italian colony, and the children are too young seriously to articulate their newly acquired needs and wishes. The Italian family is stabilized by the strong drive to return to Italy.

THE CONFLICT STAGE

In this period the first-generation family experiences its most profound changes and is finally wrenched from its Old World foundation. It is now chiefly characterized by the conflict between two ways of life, the one American and the other Italian, and by the incompatibility of parents and children. This phase begins roughly during the second decade of living in America—specifically, when the children unhesitatingly express their acquired American expectations and attempt to transmit them in the family situation and when the parents in turn attempt to reinforce the pattern of the Old World peasant family. Conflicting definitions of various family situations threaten to destroy whatever stability the family had maintained through the first period. This is the period of great frustration and of misunderstanding between parents and children. In this undeclared state of war between two ways of life it is the parents who have the most to lose, for their complete acceptance of the American way of living means the destruction of the Old World ideal.

The first-generation Italian family is also constantly made to feel the force of external pressures coming from outside the Italian colony. It is inevitable that the family structure should crumble under the incessant hammering. Not able to draw upon a complete culture and social system to support its position, the family pattern, already weakened, now begins to change radically: the father loses his importance, the daughters acquire unheard-of independence; in short, the children press down upon the first-generation family an American way of life.

ACCOMMODATION STAGE

This period begins with the realization by parents and children that the continuation of hostility, misunderstanding, and contraventive behavior can result only in complete deterioration of the family. The ambivalent attitude of the children toward the parents, of great affection, on the one hand, and hostility, on the other, now tends to be replaced by a more tolerant disposition. This stage begins when the offspring reach adulthood and marry and establish households of their own, for by this time the control by the parents is greatly lessened.

Among the many factors which operate to bring about a new stability in the family are the realization on the part of the parents that life in America is to be permanent; the adult age of the offspring; the almost complete dependence of the parents on the offspring, including use of the children as informants, interpreters, guides, and translators of the American world; recognition on the part of the parents that social and economic success can come to the offspring only as they become more and more like "old" Americans; the conscious and unconscious acculturation of the parents themselves with a consequent minimizing of many potential conflicts; the long period of isolation from the Old World which makes the small-village culture and peasant family seem less real; the decision by the parents to sacrifice certain aspects of the Old

World family for the sake of retaining the affection of the children; the acknowledgment by the children that the first-generation family is a truncated one and that complete repudiation of the parents would leave them completely isolated; the success of the first-generation family in instilling in the offspring respect and affection for the parents; and the gradual understanding by the children that successful interaction with the American world is possible by accepting marginal roles and that complete denial of the Old World family is unnecessary.

The accommodation between parents and offspring permits the second-generation Italians to orientate themselves increasingly toward an American way of life. The second-generation household, therefore, tends to pattern itself after the contemporary urban American family. Considerable intermarriage, the advanced age of the parents, the loosening of ties with the Italian neighborhood, and the development of intimate relationships with non-Italians make the transition of the second-generation family comparatively easy.

Crucible of Identity: *The Negro Lower-Class Family* *

Lee Rainwater

The study deals with the residents of the Pruitt-Igoe housing projects in St. Louis. Some 10,000 people live in these projects which comprise forty-three eleven-story buildings near the downtown area of St. Louis. Over half of the households have female heads, and for over half of the households the principal income comes from public assistance of one kind or another. The research has been in the field for a little over two years. It is a broad community study which thus far has relied principally on methods of participant observation and open-ended interviewing. Data on families come from repeated interviews and observations with a small group of families. The field workers are identified as graduate students at Washington University who have no connection with the housing authority or other officials, but are simply interested in

learning about how families in the project live. This very intensive study of families yields a wealth of information (over 10,000 pages of interview and observation reports) which obviously cannot be analyzed within the limits of one article. In this article I have limited myself to outlining a typical family stage sequence and discussing some of the psychosocial implications of growing up in families characterized by this sequence. In addition, I have tried to limit myself to findings which other literature on Negro family life suggests are not limited to the residents of the housing projects we are studying. . . .

THE FUNCTIONAL AUTONOMY OF THE NEGRO FAMILY   .

At the center of the matrix of Negro institutional life lies the family. It is in the family that individuals are trained for participation in the culture and find per-

°*Adapted from* Daedalus, 1965, 95: pp. 172–216 *by permission of the American Academy of Arts and Sciences.*

sonal and group identity and continuity. The "freedom" allowed by white society is greatest here, and this freedom has been used to create an institutional variant more distinctive perhaps to the Negro subculture than any other. (Much of the content of Negro art and entertainment derives exactly from the distinctive characteristics of Negro family life.) At each stage in the Negro's experience of American life—slavery, segregation, *de facto* ghettoization—whites have found it less necessary to interfere in the relations between the sexes and between parents and children than in other areas of the Negro's existence. His adaptations in this area, therefore, have been less constrained by whites than in many other areas.

Now that the larger society is becoming increasingly committed to integrating Negroes into the main stream of American life, however, we can expect increasing constraint (benevolent as it may be) to be placed on the autonomy of the Negro family system.[1] These constraints will be designed to pull the Negroes into meaningful integration with the larger society, to give up ways which are inimical to successful performance in the larger society, and to adopt new ways that are functional in that society. The strategic questions of the civil rights movement and of the war on poverty are ones that have to do with how one provides functional equivalents for the existing subculture before the capacity to make a life within its confines is destroyed.

The history of the Negro family has been ably documented by historians and sociologists.[2] In slavery, conjugal and family ties were reluctantly and ambivalently recognized by the slave holders, were often violated by them, but proved necessary to the slave system. This necessity stemmed both from the profitable offspring of slave sexual unions and the necessity for their nurture, and from the fact that the slaves' efforts to sustain patterns of sexual and parental relations mollified the men and women whose labor could not simply be commanded. From nature's promptings, the thinning memories of African heritage, and the example and guilt-ridden permission of the slave holders, slaves constructed a partial family system and sets of relations that generated conjugal and familial sentiments. The slaveholder's recognition in advertisements for runaway slaves of marital and family sentiments as motivations for absconding provides one indication that strong family ties were possible, though perhaps not common, in the slave quarter. The mother-centered family with its emphasis on the primacy of the mother-child relation and only tenuous ties to a man, then, is the legacy of adaptations worked out by Negroes during slavery.

After emancipation this family design often also served well to cope with the social disorganization of Negro life in the late nineteenth century. Matrifocal families, ambivalence about the desirability of marriage, ready acceptance of illegitimacy, all sustained some kind of family life in situations which often made it difficult to maintain a full nuclear family. Yet in the hundred years since emancipation, Negroes in rural areas have been able to maintain full nuclear families almost as well as similarly situated whites.

[1] For example, the lead sentence in a *St. Louis Post Dispatch* article of July 20, 1965, begins "A White House study group is laying the ground work for an attempt to better the structure of the Negro family."

[2] See Kenneth Stampp, *The Peculiar Institution* (New York, 1956); John Hope Franklin, *From Slavery to Freedom* (New York, 1956); Frank Tannenbaum, *Slave and Citizen* (New York, 1946); E. Franklin Frazier, *The Negro Family in the United States* (Chicago, 1939); and Melville J. Herskovits, *The Myth of the Negro Past* (New York, 1941).

As we will see, it is the move to the city that results in the very high proportion of mother-headed households. In the rural system the man continues to have important functions; it is difficult for a woman to make a crop by herself, or even with the help of other women. In the city, however, the woman can earn wages just as a man can, and she can receive welfare payments more easily than he can. In rural areas, although there may be high illegitimacy rates and high rates of marital disruption, men and women have an interest in getting together, families are headed by a husband-wife pair much more often than in the city. That pair may be much less stable than in the more prosperous segments of Negro and white communities but it is more likely to exist among rural Negroes than among urban ones.

The matrifocal character of the Negro lower-class family in the United States has much in common with Caribbean Negro family patterns; research in both areas has done a great deal to increase our understanding of the Negro situation. However, there are important differences in the family forms of the two areas.[3] The

impact of white European family models has been much greater in the United States than in the Caribbean both because of the relative population proportions of white and colored peoples and because equalitarian values in the United States have had a great impact on Negroes even when they have not on whites. The typical Caribbean mating pattern is that women go through several visiting and common-law unions but eventually marry; that is they marry legally only relatively late in their sexual lives. The Caribbean marriage is the crowning of a sexual and procreative career; it is considered a serious and difficult step.

In the United States, in contrast, Negroes marry at only a slightly lower rate and slightly higher age than whites.[4] Most Negro women marry relatively early in their careers; marriage is not regarded as the same kind of crowning choice and achievement that it is in the Caribbean. For lower-class Negroes in the United States marriage ceremonies are rather informal affairs. In the Caribbean, marriage is regarded as quite costly because of the feasting which goes along with it; ideally it is performed in church.

In the United States, unlike the Caribbean, early marriage confers a kind of permanent respectable status upon a woman which she can use to deny any subsequent accusations of immorality or promiscuity once the marriage is broken and she becomes sexually involved in visiting or common-law relations. The relevant effective status for many Negro women is that of "having been married" rather than "being married"; having the right to be called "Mrs." rather than currently being Mrs. Someone-in-Particular.

[3] See Raymond T. Smith, *The Negro Family in British Guiana* (New York, 1956); J. Mayone Stycos and Kurt W. Back, *The Control of Human Fertility in Jamaica* (Ithaca, N. Y., 1964); F. M. Henriques, *Family and Colour in Jamaica* (London, 1953); Judith Blake, *Family Structure in Jamaica* (Glencoe, Ill., 1961); and Raymond T. Smith, "Culture and Social Structure in The Caribbean," *Comparative Studies in Society and History*, Vol. VI (The Hague, The Netherlands, October 1963), pp. 24–46. For a broader comparative discussion of the matrifocal family see Peter Kunstadter, "A Survey of the Consanguine or Matrifocal Family," *American Anthropologist*, Vol. 65, No. 1 (February 1963), pp. 56–66; and Ruth M. Boyer, "The Matrifocal Family Among the Mescalero: Additional Data," *American Anthropologist*, Vol. 66, No. 3 (June 1964), pp. 593–602.

[4] Paul C. Glick, *American Families* (New York, 1957), pp. 133 ff.

TABLE 1 Proportion of female heads for families with children by race, income, and urban-rural categories

	Rural	Urban	Total
	PER CENT	PER CENT	PER CENT
Negroes			
under $3000	18	47	36
$3000 and over	5	8	7
Total	14	23	21
White			
under $3000	12	38	22
$3000 and over	2	4	3
Total	4	7	6

SOURCE: U. S. Census: 1960, PC (1) D. U. S. Volume. Table 225; State Volume, Table 140.

For Negro lower-class women, then, first marriage has the same kind of importance as having a first child. Both indicate that the girl has become a woman but neither one that this is the last such activity in which she will engage. It seems very likely that only a minority of Negro women in the urban slum go through their child-rearing years with only one man around the house.

Among the Negro urban poor, then, a great many women have the experience of heading a family for part of their mature lives, and a great many children spend some part of their formative years in a household without a father-mother pair. From Table 1 we see that in 1960, forty-seven per cent of the Negro poor urban families with children had a female head. Unfortunately cumulative statistics are hard to come by; but, given this very high level for a cross-sectional sample (and taking into account the fact that the median age of the children in these families is about six years), it seems very likely that as many as two-thirds of Negro urban poor children will not live in families headed by a man and a woman throughout the first eighteen years of their lives.

One of the other distinctive characteristics of Negro families, both poor and not so poor, is the fact that Negro households have a much higher proportion of relatives outside the mother-father-children triangle than is the case with whites. For example, in St. Louis Negro families average 0.8 other relatives per household compared to only 0.4 for white families. In the case of the more prosperous Negro families this is likely to mean that an older relative lives in the home providing baby-sitting services while both the husband and wife work and thus further their climb toward stable working- or middle-class status. In the poor Negro families it is much more likely that the household is headed by an older relative who brings under her wings a daughter and that daughter's children. It is important to note that the three-generation household with the grandmother at the head exists only when there is no husband present. Thus, despite the high proportion of female-headed households in this group and despite the high proportion of households that contain other relatives, we find that almost all married couples in the St. Louis Negro slum community have their own household. In other words, when a couple marries it establishes its own household; when that couple breaks up the mother either maintains that household or moves back to her parents or grandparents.

Finally we should note that Negro

slum families have more children than do either white slum families or stable working- and middle-class Negro families. Mobile Negro families limit their fertility sharply in the interest of bringing the advantages of mobility more fully to the few children that they do have. Since the Negro slum family is both more likely to have the father absent and more likely to have more children in the family, the mother has a more demanding task with fewer resources at her disposal. When we examine the patterns of life of the stem family we shall see that even the presence of several mothers does not necessarily lighten the work load for the principal mother in charge.

THE FORMATION AND MAINTENANCE OF FAMILIES

We will outline below the several stages and forms of Negro lower-class family life. At many points these family forms and the interpersonal relations that exist within them will be seen to have characteristics in common with the life styles of white lower-class families.[5] At

[5] For discussions of white lower-class families, see Lee Rainwater, Richard P. Coleman, and Gerald Handel, *Workingman's Wife* (New York, 1959); Lee Rainwater, *Family Design* (Chicago, 1964); Herbert Gans, *The Urban Villagers* (New York, 1962); Albert K. Cohen and Harold M. Hodges, "Characteristics of the Lower-Blue-Collar-Class," *Social Problems*, Vol. 10, No. 4 (Spring 1963), pp. 303–334; S. M. Miller, "The American Lower Classes: A Typological Approach," in Arthur B. Shostak and William Gomberg, *Blue Collar World* (Englewood Cliffs, N. J., 1964); and Mirra Komarovsky, *Blue Collar Marriage* (New York, 1964). Discussions of Negro slum life can be found in St. Clair Drake and Horace R. Cayton, *Black Metropolis* (New York, 1962), and Kenneth B. Clark, *Dark Ghetto* (New York, 1965); and of Negro community life in

other points there are differences, or the Negro pattern will be seen to be more sharply divergent from the family life of stable working- and middle-class couples.

It is important to recognize that lower-class Negroes know that their particular family forms are different from those of the rest of the society and that, though they often see these forms as representing the only ways of behaving given their circumstances, they also think of the more stable family forms of the working class as more desirable. That is, lower-class Negroes know what the "normal American family" is supposed to be like, and they consider a stable family-centered way of life superior to the conjugal and familial situations in which they often find themselves. Their conceptions of the good American life include the notion of a father-husband who functions as an adequate provider and interested member of the family, a hard working home-bound mother who is concerned about her children's welfare and her husband's needs, and children who look up to their parents and perform well in school and other outside places to reflect credit on their families. This image of what family life can be like is very real from time to time as lower-class men and women grow up and move through adulthood. Many of them make efforts to establish such families but find it impossible to do so either because of the direct impact of economic disabilities or because they are not able to sustain in their day-to-day lives the ideals which they hold.[6] While

small-town and rural settings in Allison Davis, Burleigh B. Gardner, and Mary Gardner, *Deep South* (Chicago, 1944), and Hylan Lewis, *Blackways of Kent* (Chapel Hill, N. C., 1955).

[6] For general discussions of the extent to which lower-class people hold the values of the larger society, see Albert K. Cohen, *Delinquent Boys* (New York, 1955); Hyman

these ideals do serve as a meaningful guide to lower-class couples who are mobile out of the group, for a great many others the existence of such ideas about normal family life represents a recurrent source of stress within families as individuals become aware that they are failing to measure up to the ideals, or as others within the family and outside it use the ideals as an aggressive weapon for criticizing each other's performance. It is not at all uncommon for husbands or wives or children to try to hold others in the family to the norms of stable family life while they themselves engage in behaviors which violate these norms. The effect of such criticism in the end is to deepen commitment to the deviant sexual and parental norms of a slum subculture. Unless they are careful, social workers and other professionals exacerbate the tendency to use the norms of "American family life" as weapons by supporting these norms in situations where they are in reality unsupportable, thus aggravating the sense of failing and being failed by others which is chronic for lower-class people.

Going Together

The initial steps toward mating and family formation in the Negro slum take place in a context of highly developed boys' and girls' peer groups. Adolescents tend to become deeply involved in their peer-group societies beginning as early as the age of twelve or thirteen and continue to be involved after first pregnancies and first marriages. Boys and girls are heavily committed both to their same sex peer groups and to the activities that those groups carry out. While classical gang activity does not necessarily characterize Negro slum communities everywhere, loosely-knit peer-groups do.

The world of the Negro slum is wide open to exploration by adolescent boys and girls: "Negro communities provide a flow of common experience in which young people and their elders share, and out of which delinquent behavior emerges almost imperceptibly."[7] More than is possible in white slum communities, Negro adolescents have an opportunity to interact with adults in various "high life" activities; their behavior more often represents an identification with the behavior of adults than an attempt to set up group standards and activities that differ from those of adults.

Boys and young men participating in the street system of peer-group activity are much caught up in games of furthering and enhancing their status as significant persons. These games are played out in small and large gatherings through various kinds of verbal contests that go under the names of "sounding," "signifying," and "working game." Very much a part of a boy's or man's status in this group is his ability to win women. The man who has several women "up tight," who is successful in "pimping off" women for sexual favors and material benefits, is much admired. In sharp contrast to white lower-class groups, there is little tendency for males to separate girls into "good" and "bad" categories.[8] Observations of

---

Rodman, "The Lower Class Value Stretch," *Social Forces*, Vol. 42, No. 2 (December 1963), pp. 205 ff; and William L. Yancey, "The Culture of Poverty: Not So Much Parsimony," unpublished manuscript, Social Science Institute, Washington University.

[7] James F. Short, Jr., and Fred L. Strodtbeck, *Group Process and Gang Delinquency* (Chicago, 1965), p. 114. Chapter V (pages 102–115) of this book contains a very useful discussion of differences between white and Negro lower-class communities.

[8] Discussions of white lower-class attitudes toward sex may be found in Arnold W. Green, "The Cult of Personality and Sexual

groups of Negro youths suggest that girls and women are much more readily referred to as "that bitch" or "that whore" than they are by their names, and this seems to be a universal tendency carrying no connotation that "that bitch" is morally inferior to or different from other women. Thus, all women are essentially the same, all women are legitimate targets, and no girl or woman is expected to be virginal except for reason of lack of opportunity or immaturity. From their participation in the peer group and according to standards legitimated by the total Negro slum culture, Negro boys and young men are propelled in the direction of girls to test their "strength" as seducers. They are mercilessly rated by both their peers and the opposite sex in their ability to "talk" to girls; a young man will go to great lengths to avoid the reputation of having a "weak" line.[9]

The girls share these definitions of the nature of heterosexual relations; they take for granted that almost any male they deal with will try to seduce them and that given sufficient inducement (social not monetary) they may wish to go along with his line. Although girls have a great deal of ambivalence about participating in sexual relations, this ambivalence is minimally moral and has much more to do

with a desire not to be taken advantage of or get in trouble. Girls develop defenses against the exploitative orientations of men by devaluing the significance of sexual relations ("he really didn't do anything bad to me"), and as time goes on by developing their own appreciation of the intrinsic rewards of sexual intercourse.

The informal social relations of slum Negroes begin in adolescence to be highly sexualized. Although parents have many qualms about boys and, particularly, girls entering into this system, they seldom feel there is much they can do to prevent their children's sexual involvement. They usually confine themselves to counseling somewhat hopelessly against girls becoming pregnant or boys being forced into situations where they might have to marry a girl they do not want to marry.

Girls are propelled toward boys and men in order to demonstrate their maturity and attractiveness; in the process they are constantly exposed to pressures for seduction, to boys "rapping" to them. An active girl will "go with" quite a number of boys, but she will generally try to restrict the number with whom she has intercourse to the few to whom she is attracted or (as happens not infrequently) to those whose threats of physical violence she cannot avoid. For their part, the boys move rapidly from girl to girl seeking to have intercourse with as many as they can and thus build up their "reps." The activity of seduction is itself highly cathected; there is gratification in simply "talking to" a girl as long as the boy can feel that he has acquitted himself well.

At sixteen Joan Bemias enjoys spending time with three or four very close girl friends. She tells us they follow this routine when the girls want to go out and none of the boys they have been seeing lately is available: "Every time we get ready to go someplace we look through all the telephone numbers of boys we'd have and we call them and talk so sweet

---

Relations," *Psychiatry*, Vol. 4 (1941), pp. 343–348; William F. Whyte, "A Slum Sex Code," *American Journal of Sociology*, Vol. 49, No. 1 (July 1943), pp. 24–31; and Lee Rainwater, "Marital Sexuality in Four Cultures of Poverty," *Journal of Marriage and the Family*, Vol. 26, No. 4 (November 1964), pp. 457–466.

[9]See Boone Hammond, "The Contest System: A Survival Technique," Master's Honors paper, Washington University, 1965. See also Ira L. Reiss, "Premarital Sexual Permissiveness Among Negroes and Whites," *American Sociological Review*, Vol. 29, No. 5 (October 1964), pp. 688–698.

to them that they'd come on around. All of them had cars you see. (I: What do you do to keep all these fellows interested?) Well nothing. We don't have to make love with all of them. Let's see, Joe, J. B., Albert, and Paul, out of all of them I've been going out with I've only had sex with four boys, that's all." She goes on to say that she and her girl friends resist boys by being unresponsive to their lines and by breaking off relations with them on the ground that they're going out with other girls. It is also clear from her comments that the girl friends support each other in resisting the boys when they are out together in groups.

Joan has had a relationship with a boy which has lasted six months, but she has managed to hold the frequency of intercourse down to four times. Initially she managed to hold this particular boy off for a month but eventually gave in.

Becoming Pregnant

It is clear that the contest elements in relationships between men and women continue even in relationships that become quite steady. Despite the girls' ambivalence about sexual relations and their manifold efforts to reduce its frequency, the operation of chance often eventuates in their becoming pregnant.[10] This was the case with Joan. With this we reach the second stage in the formation of families, that of premarital pregnancy. (We are outlining an ideal-typical sequence and not, of course, implying that all girls in the Negro slum culture become pregnant before they marry but only that a great many of them do.)

Joan was caught despite the fact that she was considerably more sophisticated about contraception than most girls or young women in the group (her mother had both instructed her in contraceptive

techniques and constantly warned her to take precautions). No one was particularly surprised at her pregnancy although she, her boy friend, her mother, and others regarded it as unfortunate. For girls in the Negro slum, pregnancy before marriage is expected in much the same way that parents expect their children to catch mumps or chicken pox; if they are lucky it will not happen but if it happens people are not too surprised and everyone knows what to do about it. It was quickly decided that Joan and the baby would stay at home. It seems clear from the preparations that Joan's mother is making that she expects to have the main responsibility for caring for the infant. Joan seems quite indifferent to the baby; she shows little interest in mothering the child although she is not particularly adverse to the idea so long as the baby does not interfere too much with her continued participation in her peer group.

Establishing who the father is under these circumstances seems to be important and confers a kind of legitimacy on the birth; not to know who one's father is, on the other hand, seems the ultimate in illegitimacy. Actually Joan had a choice in the imputation of fatherhood; she chose J. B. because he is older than she, and because she may marry him if he can get a divorce from his wife. She could have chosen Paul (with whom she had also had intercourse at about the time she became pregnant), but she would have done this reluctantly since Paul is a year younger than she and somehow this does not seem fitting.

In general, when a girl becomes pregnant while still living at home it seems taken for granted that she will continue to live there and that her parents will take a major responsibility for rearing the children. Since there are usually siblings who can help out and even siblings who will be playmates for the child, the addition of a third generation to the household does

[10] See the discussion of aleatory processes leading to premarital fatherhood in Short and Strodtbeck, *op. cit.*, pp. 44–45.

not seem to place a great stress on relationships within the family. It seems common for the first pregnancy to have a liberating influence on the mother once the child is born in that she becomes socially and sexually more active than she was before. She no longer has to be concerned with preserving her status as a single girl. Since her mother is usually willing to take care of the child for a few years, the unwed mother has an opportunity to go out with girl friends and with men and thus become more deeply involved in the peer-group society of her culture. As she has more children and perhaps marries she will find it necessary to settle down and spend more time around the house fulfilling the functions of a mother herself.

It would seem that for girls pregnancy is the real measure of maturity, the dividing line between adolescence and womanhood. Perhaps because of this, as well as because of the ready resources for child care, girls in the Negro slum community show much less concern about pregnancy than do girls in the white lower-class community and are less motivated to marry the fathers of their children. When a girl becomes pregnant the question of marriage certainly arises and is considered, but the girl often decides that she would rather not marry the man either because she does not want to settle down yet or because she does not think he would make a good husband.

It is in the easy attitudes toward premarital pregnancy that the matrifocal character of the Negro lower-class family appears most clearly. In order to have and raise a family it is simply not necessary, though it may be desirable, to have a man around the house. While the AFDC program may make it easier to maintain such attitudes in the urban situation, this pattern existed long before the program was initiated and continues in families where support comes from other sources.

Finally it should be noted that fathering a child similarly confers maturity on boys and young men although perhaps it is less salient for them. If the boy has any interest in the girl he will tend to feel that the fact that he has impregnated her gives him an additional claim on her. He will be stricter in seeking to enforce his exclusive rights over her (though not exclusive loyalty to her). This exclusive right does not mean that he expects to marry her but only that there is a new and special bond between them. If the girl is not willing to accept such claims she may find it necessary to break off the relationship rather than tolerate the man's jealousy. Since others in the peer group have a vested interest in not allowing a couple to be too loyal to each other they go out of their way to question and challenge each partner about the loyalty of the other, thus contributing to the deterioration of the relationship. This same kind of questioning and challenging continues if the couple marries and represents one source of the instability of the marital relationship.

Getting Married

As noted earlier, despite the high degree of premarital sexual activity and the rather high proportion of premarital pregnancies, most lower-class Negro men and women eventually do marry and stay together for a shorter or longer period of time. Marriage is an intimidating prospect and is approached ambivalently by both parties. For the girl it means giving up a familiar and comfortable home that, unlike some other lower-class subcultures, places few real restrictions on her behavior. (While marriage can appear to be an escape from interpersonal difficulties at home, these difficulties seldom seem to revolve around effective restrictions placed on her behavior by her parents.) The girl also has good reason to be suspicious of the likelihood that men will be able to perform stably in the role of husband and provider; she is reluctant to be tied down by a man who will not prove to be worth it.

From the man's point of view the fickleness of women makes marriage problematic. It is one thing to have a girl friend step out on you, but it is quite another to have a wife do so. Whereas premarital sexual relations and fatherhood carry almost no connotation of responsibility for the welfare of the partner, marriage is supposed to mean that a man behaves more responsibly, becoming a provider for his wife and children even though he may not be expected to give up all the gratifications of participation in the street system.

For all of these reasons both boys and girls tend to have rather negative views of marriage as well as a low expectation that marriage will prove a stable and gratifying existence. When marriage does take place it tends to represent a tentative commitment on the part of both parties with a strong tendency to seek greater commitment on the part of the partner than on one's own part. Marriage is regarded as a fragile arrangement held together primarily by affectional ties rather than instrumental concerns.

In general, as in white lower-class groups, the decision to marry seems to be taken rather impulsively.[11] Since everyone knows that sooner or later he will get married, in spite of the fact that he may not be sanguine about the prospect, Negro lower-class men and women are alert for clues that the time has arrived. The time may arrive because of a pregnancy in

a steady relationship that seems gratifying to both partners, or as a way of getting out of what seems to be an awkward situation, or as a self-indulgence during periods when a boy and girl are feeling very sorry for themselves. Thus, one girl tells us that when she marries her husband will cook all of her meals for her and she will not have any housework; another girl says that when she marries it will be to a man who has plenty of money and will have to take her out often and really show her a good time.

Boys see in marriage the possibility of regular sexual intercourse without having to fight for it, or a girl safe from venereal disease, or a relationship to a nurturant figure who will fulfill the functions of a mother. For boys, marriage can also be a way of asserting their independence from the peer group if its demands become burdensome. In this case the young man seeks to have the best of both worlds.[12]

Marriage as a way out of an unpleasant situation can be seen in the case of one of our informants, Janet Cowan:

> Janet has been going with two men, one of them married and the other single. The married man's wife took exception to their relationship and killed her husband. Within a week Janet and her single boy friend, Howard, were married. One way out of the turmoil the murder of her married boy friend stimulated (they lived in the same building) was to choose marriage as a way of "settling down." However, after marrying the new couple seemed to have little idea how to set themselves up as a family. Janet was reluctant to leave her parents' home because her parents cared for her two illegitimate children. Howard was unemployed and therefore unacceptable in his parent-in-law's home, nor were his own parents willing to have his wife move in with them. Howard was also reluctant to give up another girl friend in an-

[11] Rainwater, *And the Poor Get Children*, *op. cit.*, pp. 61–63. See also, Carlfred B. Broderick, "Social Heterosexual Development Among Urban Negroes and Whites," *Journal of Marriage and the Family*, Vol. 27 (May 1965), pp. 200–212. Broderick finds that although white boys and girls, and Negro girls become more interested in marriage as they get older, Negro boys become *less* interested in late adolescence than they were as preadolescents.

[12] Walter Miller, "The Corner Gang Boys Get Married," *Trans-action*, Vol. 1, No. 1 (November 1963), pp. 10–12.

other part of town. Although both he and his wife maintained that it was all right for a couple to step out on each other so long as the other partner did not know about it, they were both jealous if they suspected anything of this kind. In the end they gave up on the idea of marriage and went their separate ways.

In general, then, the movement toward marriage is an uncertain and tentative one. Once the couple does settle down together in a household of their own, they have the problem of working out a mutually acceptable organization of rights and duties, expectations and performances, that will meet their needs.

Husband-wife Relations

Characteristic of both the Negro and white lower class is a high degree of conjugal role segregation.[13] That is, husbands and wives tend to think of themselves as having very separate kinds of functioning in the instrumental organization of family life, and also as pursuing recreational and outside interests separately. The husband is expected to be a provider; he resists assuming functions around the home so long as he feels he is doing his proper job of bringing home a pay check. He feels he has the right to indulge himself in little ways if he is successful at this task. The wife is expected to care for the home and children and make her husband feel welcome and comfortable. Much that is distinctive to Negro family life stems from the fact that husbands often are not stable providers. Even when a particular man is, his wife's conception of men in general is such that she is pessimistic about the likelihood that he will continue to do well in this area. A great many Negro wives work to supplement the family income. When this is so the separate incomes earned by husband and wife tend to be treated not as "family" income but

as the individual property of the two persons involved. If their wives work, husbands are likely to feel that they are entitled to retain a larger share of the income they provide; the wives, in turn, feel that the husbands have no right to benefit from the purchases they make out of their own money. There is, then, "my money" and "your money." In this situation the husband may come to feel that the wife should support the children out of her income and the he can retain all of his income for himself.

While white lower-class wives often are very much intimidated by their husbands, Negro lower-class wives come to feel that they have a right to give as good as they get. If the husband indulges himself, they have the right to indulge themselves. If the husband steps out on his wife, she has the right to step out on him. The commitment of husbands and wives to each other seems often a highly instrumental one after the "honeymoon" period. Many wives feel they owe the husband nothing once he fails to perform his provider role. If the husband is unemployed the wife increasingly refuses to perform her usual duties for him. For example one woman, after mentioning that her husband had cooked four eggs for himself, commented, "I cook for him when he's working but right now he's unemployed; he can cook for himself." It is important, however, to understand that the man's status in the home depends not so much on whether he is working as on whether he brings money into the home. Thus, in several of the families we have studied in which the husband receives disability payments his status is as well-recognized as in families in which the husband is working.[14]

[13] Rainwater, *Family Design, op. cit.*, pp. 28–60.

[14] Yancey, *op. cit.* The effects of unemployment on the family have been discussed by E. Wright Bakke, *Citizens Without Work* (New Haven, Conn., 1940); Mirra Komarovsky, *The Unemployed Man and His Family*

Because of the high degree of conjugal role segregation, both white and Negro lower-class families tend to be matrifocal in comparison to middle-class families. They are matrifocal in the sense that the wife makes most of the decisions that keep the family going and has the greatest sense of responsibility to the family. In white as well as in Negro lower-class families women tend to look to their female relatives for support and counsel, and to treat their husbands as essentially uninterested in the day-to-day problems of family living.15 In the Negro lower-class family these tendencies are all considerably exaggerated so that the matrifocality is much clearer than in white lower-class families.

The fact that both sexes in the Negro slum culture have equal right to the various satisfactions of life (earning an income, sex, drinking, and peer-group activity which conflicts with family responsibilities) means that there is less pretense to patriarchal authority in the Negro than in the white lower class. Since men find the overt debasement of their status very threatening, the Negro family is much more vulnerable to disruption when men are temporarily unable to perform their provider roles. Also, when men are unemployed the temptations for them to engage in street adventures which repercuss on the marital relationship are much greater. This fact is well-recognized by

Negro lower-class wives; they often seem as concerned about what their unemployed husbands will do instead of working as they are about the fact that the husband is no longer bringing money into the home.

It is tempting to cope with the likelihood of disloyalty by denying the usual norms of fidelity, by maintaining instead that extra-marital affairs are acceptable as long as they do not interfere with family functioning. Quite a few informants tell us this, but we have yet to observe a situation in which a couple maintains a stable relationship under these circumstances without a great deal of conflict. Thus one woman in her forties who has been married for many years and has four children first outlined this deviant norm and then illustrated how it did not work out:

> My husband and I, we go out alone and sometimes stay all night. But when I get back my husband doesn't ask me a thing and I don't ask him anything. . . . A couple of years ago I suspected he was going out on me. One day I came home and my daughter was here. I told her to tell me when he left the house. I went into the bedroom and got into bed and then I heard him come in. He left in about ten minutes and my daughter came in and told me he was gone. I got out of bed and put on my clothes and started following him. Soon I saw him walking with a young girl and I began walking after them. They were just laughing and joking right out loud right on the sidewalk. He was carrying a large package of hers. I walked up behind them until I was about a yard from them. I had a large dirk which I opened and had decided to take one long slash across the both of them. Just when I decided to swing at them I lost my balance—I have a bad hip. Anyway, I didn't cut them because I lost my balance. Then I called his name and he turned around and stared at me. He didn't move at all. He was shaking all over. That girl just ran away from us. He still had her package so the next day she called on the telephone and said she

(New York, 1960); and Earl L. Koos, *Families in Trouble* (New York, 1946). What seems distinctive to the Negro slum culture is the short time lapse between the husband's loss of a job and his wife's considering him superfluous.

15 See particularly Komarovsky's discussion of "barriers to marital communications" (Chapter 7) and "confidants outside of marriage" (Chapter 9), in *Blue Collar Marriage, op. cit.*

wanted to come pick it up. My husband washed his face, brushed his teeth, took out his false tooth and started scrubbing it and put on a clean shirt and everything, just for her. We went downstairs together and gave her the package and she left.

So you see my husband does run around on me and it seems like he does it a lot. The thing about it is he's just getting too old to be pulling that kind of stuff. If a young man does it then that's not so bad—but an old man, he just looks foolish. One of these days he'll catch me but I'll just tell him, "Buddy you owe me one," and that'll be all there is to it. He hasn't caught me yet though.

In this case, as in others, the wife is not able to leave well enough alone; her jealousy forces her to a confrontation. Actually seeing her husband with another woman stimulates her to violence.

With couples who have managed to stay married for a good many years, these peccadillos are tolerable although they generate a great deal of conflict in the marital relationship. At earlier ages the partners are likely to be both prouder and less innured to the hopelessness of maintaining stable relationships; outside involvements are therefore much more likely to be disruptive of the marriage.

Marital breakup

The precipitating causes of marital disruption seem to fall mainly into economic or sexual categories. As noted, the husband has little credit with his wife to tide him over periods of unemployment. Wives seem very willing to withdraw commitment from husbands who are not bringing money into the house. They take the point of view that he has no right to take up space around the house, to use its facilities, or to demand loyalty from her. Even where the wife is not inclined to press these claims, the husband tends to be touchy because he knows that such definitions are usual in his group, and he

may, therefore, prove difficult for even a well-meaning wife to deal with. As noted above, if husbands do not work they tend to play around. Since they continue to maintain some contact with their peer groups, whenever they have time on their hands they move back into the world of the street system and are likely to get involved in activities which pose a threat to their family relalionships.

Drink is a great enemy of the lower-class housewife, both white and Negro. Lower-class wives fear their husband's drinking because it costs money, because the husband may become violent and take out his frustrations on his wife, and because drinking may lead to sexual involvements with other women.[16]

The combination of economic problems and sexual difficulties can be seen in the case of the following couple in their early twenties:

When the field worker first came to know them, the Wilsons seemed to be working hard to establish a stable family life. The couple had been married about three years and had a two-year-old son. Their apartment was very sparsely furnished but also very clean. Within six weeks the couple had acquired several rooms of inexpensive furniture and obviously had gone to a great deal of effort to make a liveable home. Husband and wife worked on different shifts so that the husband could take care of the child while the wife worked. They looked forward to saving enough money to move out of the housing project into a more desirable neighborhood. Six weeks later, however, the husband had lost his job. He and his wife were in great conflict. She made him feel unwelcome at home and he strongly suspected her of going out with other men. A short time later they had separated. It is impossible to disentangle the various factors involved in this separation

---

[16] Rainwater, *Family Design, op. cit.,* pp. 305–308.

into a sequence of cause and effect, but we can see something of the impact of the total complex.

First Mr. Wilson loses his job: "I went to work one day and the man told me that I would have to work until 1:00. I asked him if there would be any extra pay for working overtime and he said no. I asked him why and he said, 'If you don't like it you can kiss my ass.' He said that to me. I said, 'Why do I have to do all that?' He said, 'Because I said so.' I wanted to jam (fight) him but I said to myself I don't want to be that ignorant, I don't want to be as ignorant as he is, so I just cut out and left. Later his father called me (it was a family firm) and asked why I left and I told him. He said, 'If you don't want to go along with my son then you're fired.' I said O.K. They had another Negro man come in to help me part time before they fired me. I think they were trying to have him work full time because he worked for them before. He has seven kids and he takes their shit."

The field worker observed that things were not as hard as they could be because his wife had a job, to which he replied, "Yeah, I know, that's just where the trouble is. My wife has become independent since she began working. If I don't get a job pretty soon I'll go crazy. We have a lot of little arguments about nothing since she got so independent." He went on to say that his wife had become a completely different person recently; she was hard to talk to because she felt that now that she was working and he was not there was nothing that he could tell her. On her last pay day his wife did not return home for three days; when she did she had only seven cents left from her pay check. He said that he loved his wife very much and had begged her to quit fooling around. He is pretty sure that she is having an affair with the man with whom she rides to work. To make matters worse his wife's sister counsels her that she does not have to stay home with him as long as he is out of work. Finally the wife moved most of their furniture out of the apartment so that he came home to find an empty apartment. He moved back to his parents' home (also in the housing project).

One interesting effect of this experience was the radical change in the husband's attitudes toward race relations. When he and his wife were doing well together and had hopes of moving up in the world he was quite critical of Negroes; "Our people are not ready for integration in many cases because they really don't know how to act. You figure if our people don't want to be bothered with whites then why in hell should the white man want to be bothered with them. There are some of us who are ready; there are others who aren't quite ready yet so I don't see why they're doing all of this hollering." A scarce eight months later he addressed white people as he spoke for two hours into a tape recorder, "If we're willing to be with you, why aren't you willing to be with us? Do our color make us look dirty and low down and cheap? Or do you know the real meaning of 'nigger'? Anyone can be a nigger, white, colored, orange or any other color. It's something that you labeled us with. You put us away like you put a can away on the shelf with a label on it. The can is marked 'Poison: stay away from it.' You want us to help build your country but you don't want us to live in it. . . . You give me respect; I'll give you respect. If you threaten to take my life, I'll take yours and believe me I know how to take a life. We do believe that man was put here to live together as human beings; not one that's superior and the one that's a dog, but as human beings. And if you don't want to live this way then you become the dog and we'll become the human beings. There's too much corruption, too much hate, too much one individual trying to step on another. If we don't get together in a hurry we will destroy each other." It was clear from what the respondent said that he had been much influenced by Black Muslim philosophy, yet again and again in his comments one can see the displacement into a public, race relations dialogue of the sense of rage, frustration and victimization that he had experienced in his ill-fated marriage.[17]

Finally, it should be noted that migration plays a part in marital disruption. Sometimes marriages do not break up in the dramatic way described above but rather simply become increasingly unsatisfactory to one or both partners. In such a situation the temptation to move to another city, from South to North, or North to West, is great. Several wives told us that their first marriages were broken when they moved with their children to the North and their husbands stayed behind.

> "After we couldn't get along I left the farm and came here and stayed away three or four days. I didn't come here to stay. I came to visit but I liked it and so I said, 'I'm gonna leave!' He said, 'I'll be glad if you do.' Well, maybe he didn't mean it but I thought he did. . . . I miss him sometimes, you know. I think about him I guess. But just in a small way. That's what I can't understand about life sometimes; you know—how people can go on like that and still break up and meet somebody else. Why couldn't—oh, I don't know!"

The gains and losses in marriage and in the post-marital state often seem quite comparable. Once they have had the experience of marriage, many women in the Negro slum culture see little to recommend it in the future, important as the first marriage may have been in establishing their maturity and respectability.

The House of Mothers

As we have seen, perhaps a majority of mothers in the Negro slum community

17 For a discussion of the relationship between Black Nationalist ideology and the Negro struggle to achieve a sense of valid personal identity, see Howard Brotz, *The Black Jews of Harlem* (New York, 1963), and E. U. Essien-Udom, *Black Nationalism: A Search for Identity in America* (Chicago, 1962).

spend at least part of their mature life as mothers heading a family. The Negro mother may be a working mother or she may be an AFDC mother, but in either case she has the problems of maintaining a household, socializing her children, and achieving for herself some sense of membership in relations with other women and with men. As is apparent from the earlier discussion, she often receives her training in how to run such a household by observing her own mother manage without a husband. Similarly she often learns how to run a three-generation household because she herself brought a third generation into her home with her first, premarital, pregnancy.

Because men are not expected to be much help around the house, having to be head of the household is not particularly intimidating to the Negro mother if she can feel some security about income. She knows it is a hard, hopeless, and often thankless task, but she also knows that it is possible. The maternal household in the slum is generally run with a minimum of organization. The children quickly learn to fend for themselves, to go to the store, to make small purchases, to bring change home, to watch after themselves when the mother has to be out of the home, to amuse themselves, to set their own schedules of sleeping, eating, and going to school. Housekeeping practices may be poor, furniture takes a terrific beating from the children, and emergencies constantly arise. The Negro mother in this situation copes by not setting too high standards for herself, by letting things take their course. Life is most difficult when there are babies and preschool children around because then the mother is confined to the home. If she is a grandmother and the children are her daughter's, she is often confined since it is taken as a matter of course that the mother has the right to continue her outside activities and that the grandmother has the duty to be responsible for the child.

In this culture there is little of the sense of the awesome responsibility of caring for children that is characteristic of the working and middle class. There is not the deep psychological involvement with babies which has been observed with the working-class mother.[18] The baby's needs are cared for on a catch-as-catch-can basis. If there are other children around and they happen to like babies, the baby can be over-stimulated; if this is not the case, the baby is left alone a good deal of the time. As quickly as he can move around he learns to fend for himself.

The three-generation maternal household is a busy place. In contrast to working- and middle-class homes it tends to be open to the world, with many non-family members coming in and out at all times as the children are visited by friends, the teenagers by their boy friends and girl friends, the mother by her friends and perhaps an occasional boy friend, and the grandmother by fewer friends but still by an occasional boy friend.

The openness of the household is, among other things, a reflection of the mother's sense of impotence in the face of the street system. Negro lower-class mothers often indicate that they try very hard to keep their young children at home and away from the streets; they often seem to make the children virtual prisoners in the home. As the children grow and go to school they inevitably do become involved in peer-group activities. The mother gradually gives up, feeling that once the child is lost to this pernicious outside world there is little she can do to continue to control him and direct his development. She will try to limit the types of activities that go on in the home and to re-strict the kinds of friends that her children can bring into the home, but even this she must give up as time goes on, as the children become older and less attentive to her direction.

The grandmothers in their late forties, fifties, and sixties tend increasingly to stay at home. The home becomes a kind of court at which other family members gather and to which they bring their friends for sociability, and as a by-product provide amusement and entertainment for the mother. A grandmother may provide a home for her daughters, their children, and sometimes their children's children, and yet receive very little in a material way from them; but one of the things she does receive is a sense of human involvement, a sense that although life may have passed her by she is not completely isolated from it.

The lack of control that mothers have over much that goes on in their households is most dramatically apparent in the fact that their older children seem to have the right to come home at any time once they have moved and to stay in the home without contributing to its maintenance. Though the mother may be resentful about being taken advantage of, she does not feel she can turn her children away. For example, sixty-five-year-old Mrs. Washington plays hostess for weeks or months at a time to her forty-year-old daughter and her small children, and to her twenty-three-year-old granddaughter and her children. When these daughters come home with their families the grandmother is expected to take care of the young children and must argue with her daughter and granddaughter to receive contributions to the daily household ration of food and liquor. Or, a twenty-year-old son comes home from the Air Force and feels he has the right to live at home without working and to run up an eighty-dollar long-distance telephone bill.

---

[18] Rainwater, Coleman, and Handel, *op. cit.*, pp. 88–102.

Even aged parents living alone in small apartments sometimes acknowledge such obligations to their children or grandchildren. Again, the only clear return they receive for their hospitality is the reduction of isolation that comes from having people around and interesting activity going on. When in the Washington home the daughter and granddaughter and their children move in with the grandmother, or when they come to visit for shorter periods of time, the occasion has a party atmosphere. The women sit around talking and reminiscing. Though boy friends may be present, they take little part; instead they sit passively, enjoying the stories and drinking along with the women. It would seem that in this kind of party activity the women are defined as the stars. Grandmother, daughter, and granddaughter in turn take the center of the stage telling a story from the family's past, talking about a particularly interesting night out on the town or just making some general observation about life. In the course of these events a good deal of liquor is consumed. In such a household as this little attention is paid to the children since the competition by adults for attention is stiff.

Boy Friends, Not Husbands

It is with an understanding of the problems of isolation which older mothers have that we can obtain the best insight into the role and function of boy friends in the maternal household. The older mothers, surrounded by their own children and grandchildren, are not able to move freely in the outside world, to participate in the high life which they enjoyed when younger and more foot-loose. They are disillusioned with marriage as providing any more secure economic base than they can achieve on their own. They see marriage as involving just another responsibility without a concomitant reward

—"It's the greatest thing in the world to come home in the afternoon and not have some curly headed twot in the house yellin' at me and askin' me where supper is, where I've been, what I've been doin', and who I've been seein'." In this situation the woman is tempted to form relationships with men that are not so demanding as marriage but still provide companionship and an opportunity for occasional sexual gratification.

There seem to be two kinds of boy friends. Some boy friends "pimp" off mothers; they extract payment in food or money for their companionship. This leads to the custom sometimes called "Mother's Day," the tenth of the month when the AFDC checks come.[19] On this day one can observe an influx of men into the neighborhood, and much partying. But there is another kind of boy friend, perhaps more numerous than the first, who instead of being paid for his services pays for the right to be a pseudo family member. He may be the father of one of the woman's children and for this reason makes a steady contribution to the family's support, or he may simply be a man whose company the mother enjoys and who makes reasonable gifts to the family for the time he spends with them (and perhaps implicitly for the sexual favors he receives). While the boy friend does not assume fatherly authority within the family, he often is known and liked by the children. The older children appreciate the meaningfulness of their mother's relationship with him—one girl said of her mother's boy friend:

"We don't none of us (the children) want her to marry again. It's all right if she wants to live by herself and have a boy

19 Cf. Michael Schwartz and George Henderson, "The Culture of Unemployment: Some Notes on Negro Children," in Schostak and Gomborg, op. cit.

friend. It's not because we're afraid we're going to have some more sisters and brothers, which it wouldn't make us much difference, but I think she be too old."

Even when the boy friend contributes ten or twenty dollars a month to the family he is in a certain sense getting a bargain. If he is a well-accepted boy friend he spends considerable time around the house, has a chance to relax in an atmosphere less competitive than that of his peer group, is fed and cared for by the woman, yet has no responsibilities which he cannot renounce when he wishes. When women have stable relationships of this kind with boy friends they often consider marrying them but are reluctant to take such a step. Even the well-liked boy friend has some shortcomings—one woman said of her boy friend:

> "Well he works; I know that. He seems to be a nice person, kind hearted. He believes in survival for me and my family. He don't much mind sharing with my youngsters. If I ask him for a helping hand he don't seem to mind that. The only part I dislike is his drinking."

The woman in this situation has worked out a reasonably stable adaptation to the problems of her life; she is fearful of upsetting this adaptation by marrying again. It seems easier to take the "sweet" part of the relationship with a man without the complexities that marriage might involve.

It is in the light of this pattern of women living in families and men living by themselves in rooming houses, odd rooms, here and there, that we can understand Daniel Patrick Moynihan's observation that during their mature years men simply disappear; that is, that census data show a very high sex ratio of women to men.[20] In St. Louis, starting at the age range twenty to twenty-four there are only seventy-two men for every one hundred women. This ratio does not climb to ninety until the age range fifty to fifty-four. Men often do not have real homes; they move about from one household where they have kinship or sexual ties to another; they live in flop houses and rooming houses; they spend time in institutions. They are not household members in the only "homes" that they have —the homes of their mothers and of their girl friends.

It is in this kind of world that boys and girls in the Negro slum community learn their sex roles. It is not just, or even mainly, that fathers are often absent but that the male role models around boys are ones which emphasize expressive, affectional techniques for making one's way in the world. The female role models available to girls emphasize an exaggerated self-sufficiency (fom the point of view of the middle class) and the danger of allowing oneself to be dependent on men for anything that is crucial. By the time she is mature, the woman learns that she is most secure when she herself manages the family affairs and when she dominates her men. The man learns that he exposes himself to the least risk of failure when he does not assume a husband's and father's responsibilities but instead counts on his ability to court women and to ingratiate himself with them.

IDENTITY PROCESSES IN THE FAMILY

Up to this point we have been examining the sequential development of family stages in the Negro slum community, paying only incidental attention to the psychological responses family members make to these social forms and not concerning ourselves with the effect the family forms have on the psychosocial de-

[20] Daniel Patrick Moynihan, "Employment, Income, and the Ordeal of the Negro Family," *Daedalus* (Fall 1965), pp. 760–61.

velopment of the children who grow up in them. Now we want to examine the effect that growing up in this kind of a system has in terms of socialization and personality development.

Household groups function for cultures in carrying out the initial phases of socialization and personality formation. It is in the family that the child learns the most primitive categories of existence and experience, and that he develops his most deeply held beliefs about the world and about himself.[21] From the child's point of view, the household *is* the world; his experiences as he moves out of it into the larger world are always interpreted in terms of his particular experience within the home. The painful experiences which a child in the Negro slum culture has are, therefore, interpreted as in some sense a reflection of this family world. The impact of the system of victimization is transmitted through the family; the child cannot be expected to have the sophistication an outside observer has for seeing exactly where the villains are. From the child's point of view, if he is hungry it is his parents' fault; if he experiences frustrations in the streets or in the school it is his parents' fault; if that world seems incomprehensible to him it is his parents' fault; if people are aggressive or destructive toward each other it is his parents' fault, not

that of a system of race relations. In another culture this might not be the case; if a subculture could exist which provided comfort and security within its limited world and the individual experienced frustration only when he moved out into the larger society, the family might not be thought so much to blame. The effect of the caste system, however, is to bring home through a chain of cause and effect all of the victimization processes, and to bring them home in such a way that it is often very difficult even for adults in the system to see the connection between the pain they feel at the moment and the structured patterns of the caste system.

Let us take as a central question that of identity formation within the Negro slum family. We are concerned with the question of who the individual believes himself to be and to be becoming. For Erikson, identity means a sense of continuity and social sameness which bridges what the individual "*was* as a child and what he is *about to become* and also reconciles his *conception of himself* and his community's recognition of him." Thus identity is a "self-realization coupled with a mutual recognition."[22] In the early childhood years identity is family-bound since the child's identity is his identity *vis-à-vis* other members of the family. Later he incorporates into his sense of who he is and is becoming his experiences outside the family, but always influenced by the interpretations and evaluations of those experiences that the family gives. As the child tries on identities, *announces* them, the family sits as judge of his pretensions. Family members are both the most important judges and the most critical ones, since who he is allowed to become affects them in their

[21] Talcott Parsons concludes his discussion of child socialization, the development of an "internalized family system" and internalized role differentiation by observing, "The internalization of the family collectivity as an object and its values should not be lost sight of. This is crucial with respect to . . . the assumption of representative roles outside the family on behalf of it. Here it is the child's family membership which is decisive, and thus his acting in a role in terms of its values for 'such as he.' " Talcott Parsons and Robert F. Bales, *Family, Socialization and Interaction Process* (Glencoe, Ill., 1955), p. 113.

[22] Erik H. Erikson, "Identity and the Life Cycle," *Psychological Issues*, Vol. 1, No. 1 (1959).

own identity strivings more crucially than it affects anyone else. The child seeks a sense of valid identity, a sense of being a particular person with a satisfactory degree of congruence between who he feels he is, who he announces himself to be, and where he feels his society places him.[23] He is uncomfortable when he experiences disjunction between his own needs and the kinds of needs legitimated by those around him, or when he feels a disjunction between his sense of himself and the image of himself that others play back to him.[24]

"Tell It Like It Is"

When families become involved in important quarrels the psychosocial underpinnings of family life are laid bare. One such quarrel in a family we have been studying brings together in one place many of the themes that seem to dominate identity problems in Negro slum culture. The incident illustrates in a particularly forceful and dramatic way family processes which our field work, and some other contemporary studies of slum family life, suggests unfold more

[23] For discussion of the dynamics of the individual's *announcements* and the society's *placements* in the formation of identity, see Gregory Stone, "Appearance and the Self," in Arnold Rose, *Human Behavior in Social Process* (Boston, 1962), pp. 86–118.

[24] The importance of identity for social behavior is discussed in detail in Ward Goodenough, *Cooperation and Change* (New York, 1963), pp. 176–251, and in Lee Rainwater, "Work and Identity in the Lower Class," in Sam H. Warner, Jr., *Planning for the Quality of Urban Life* (Cambridge, Mass., forthcoming). The images of self and of other family members is a crucial variable in Hess and Handel's psychosocial analysis of family life; see Robert D. Hess and Gerald Handel, *Family Worlds* (Chicago, 1959), especially pp. 6–11.

subtly in a great many families at the lower-class level. The family involved, the Johnsons, is certainly not the most disorganized one we have studied; in some respects their way of life represents a realistic adaptation to the hard living of a family nineteen years on AFDC with a monthly income of $202 for nine people. The two oldest daughters, Mary Jane (eighteen years old) and Esther (sixteen) are pregnant; Mary Jane has one illegitimate child. The adolescent sons, Bob and Richard, are much involved in the social and sexual activities of their peer group. The three other children, ranging in age from twelve to fourteen, are apparently also moving into this kind of peer-group society.

When the argument started Bob and Esther were alone in the apartment with Mary Jane's baby. Esther took exception to Bob's playing with the baby because she had been left in charge; the argument quickly progressed to a fight in which Bob cuffed Esther around, and she tried to cut him with a knife. The police were called and subdued Bob with their nightsticks. At this point the rest of the family and the field worker arrived. As the argument continued, these themes relevant to the analysis which follows appeared:

1) The sisters said that Bob was not their brother (he is a half-brother to Esther, and Mary Jane's full brother). Indeed, they said their mother "didn't have no husband. These kids don't even know who their daddies are." The mother defended herself by saying that she had one legal husband, and one common-law husband, no more.

2) The sisters said that their fathers had never done anything for them, nor had their mother. She retorted that she had raised them "to the age of womanhood" and now would care for their babies.

3) Esther continued to threaten to cut Bob if she got a chance (a month later they fought again, and she did cut Bob, who required twenty-one stitches).

4) The sisters accused their mother of favoring their lazy brothers and asked her to put them out of the house. She retorted that the girls were as lazy, that they made no contribution to maintaining the household, could not get their boy friends to marry them or support their children, that all the support came from her AFDC check. Mary Jane retorted that "the baby has a check of her own."

5) The girls threatened to leave the house if their mother refused to put their brothers out. They said they could force their boy friends to support them by taking them to court, and Esther threatened to cut her boy friend's throat if he did not co-operate.

6) Mrs. Johnson said the girls could leave if they wished but that she would keep their babies; "I'll not have it, not knowing who's taking care of them."

7) When her thirteen-year-old sister laughed at all of this, Esther told her not to laugh because she, too, would be pregnant within a year.

8) When Bob laughed, Esther attacked him and his brother by saying that both were not man enough to make babies, as she and her sister had been able to do.

9) As the field worker left, Mrs. Johnson sought his sympathy. "You see, Joe, how hard it is for me to bring up a family. . . . They sit around and talk to me like I'm some kind of a dog and not their mother."

10) Finally, it is important to note for the analysis which follows that the following labels—"black-assed," "black bastard," "bitch," and other profane terms—were liberally used by Esther and Mary Jane, and rather less liberally by their mother, to refer to each other, to the girls' boy friends, to Bob, and to the thirteen-year-old daughter.

Several of the themes outlined previously appear forcefully in the course of this argument. In the last year and a half the mother has become a grandmother and expects shortly to add two more grandchildren to her household. She takes it for granted that it is her responsibility to care for the grandchildren and that she has the right to decide what will be done with the children since her own daughters are not fully responsible. She makes this very clear to them when they threaten to move out, a threat which they do not really wish to make good nor could they if they wished to.

However, only as an act of will is Mrs. Johnson able to make this a family. She must constantly cope with the tendency of her adolescent children to disrupt the family group and to deny that they are in fact a family—"He ain't no brother of mine"; "The baby has a check of her own." Though we do not know exactly what processes communicate these facts to the children it is clear that in growing up they have learned to regard themselves as not fully part of a solidary collectivity. During the quarrel this message was reinforced for the twelve-, thirteen-, and fourteen-year-old daughters by the four-way argument among their older sisters, older brother, and their mother.

The argument represents vicious unmasking of the individual members' pretenses to being competent individuals.[25] The efforts of the two girls to present themselves as masters of their own fate are unmasked by the mother. The girls in turn unmask the pretensions of the mother and of their two brothers. When the thirteen-year-old daughter expresses some amusement they turn on her, telling her that it won't be long before she too becomes pregnant. Each member of the family in turn is told that he can expect to

[25] See the discussion of "masking" and "unmasking" in relation to disorganization and re-equilibration in families by John P. Spiegel, "The Resolution of Role Conflict within the Family," in Norman W. Bell and Ezra F. Vogel, A Modern Introduction to the Family (Glencoe, Ill., 1960), pp. 375–377.

be no more than a victim of his world, but that this is somehow inevitably his own fault.

In this argument masculinity is consistently demeaned. Bob has no right to play with his niece, the boys are not really masculine because at fifteen and sixteen years they have yet to father children, their own fathers were no goods who failed to do anything for their family. These notions probably come originally from the mother, who enjoys recounting the story of having her common-law husband imprisoned for nonsupport, but this comes back to haunt her as her daughters accuse her of being no better than they in ability to force support and nurturance from a man. In contrast, the girls came off somewhat better than the boys, although they must accept the label of stupid girls because they have similarly failed and inconveniently become pregnant in the first place. At least they can and have had children and therefore have some meaningful connection with the ongoing substance of life. There is something important and dramatic in which they participate, while the boys, despite their sexual activity, "can't get no babies."

In most societies, as children grow and are formed by their elders into suitable members of the society they gain increasingly a sense of competence and ability to master the behavioral environment their particular world presents. But in Negro slum culture growing up involves and ever-increasing appreciation of one's shortcomings, of the impossibility of finding a self-sufficient and gratifying way of living.[26] It is in the family first and most devastatingly that one learns these lessons. As the child's sense of frustration

builds he too can strike out and unmask the pretensions of others. The result is a peculiar strength and a pervasive weakness. The strength involves the ability to tolerate and defend against degrading verbal and physical aggressions from others and not to give up completely. The weakness involves the inability to embark hopefully on any course of action that might make things better, particularly action which involves cooperating and trusting attitudes toward others. Family members become potential enemies to each other, as the frequency of observing the police being called in to settle family quarrels brings home all too dramatically.

The conceptions parents have of their children are such that they are constantly alert as the child matures to evidence that he is as bad as everyone else. That is, in lower-class culture human nature is conceived of as essentially bad, destructive, immoral.[27] This is the nature of things. Therefore any one child must be inherently bad unless his parents are very lucky indeed. If the mother can keep the child insulated from the outside world, she feels she may be able to prevent his inherent badness from coming out. She feels that once he is let out into the larger world the badness will come to the fore since that is his nature. This means that in identity development of the child he is constantly exposed to identity labeling by his parents as a bad person. Since as he grows up he does not experience his world as particularly gratifying, it is very easy

---

[26] See the discussion of self-identity and self-esteem in Thomas F. Pettigrew, *A Profile of the Negro American* (Princeton, N. J., 1964), pp. 6–11.

[27] Rainwater, Coleman, and Handel, *op. cit.*, pp. 44–51. See also the discussion of the greater level of "anomie" and mistrust among lower-class people in Ephriam Mizruchi, *Success and Opportunity* (New York, 1954). Unpublished research by the author indicates that for one urban lower-class sample (Chicago) Negroes scored about 50 per cent higher on Srole's anomie scale than did comparable whites.

for him to conclude that this lack of gratification is due to the fact that something
is wrong with him. This, in turn, can
readily be assimilated to the definitions of
being a bad person offered him by those
with whom he lives.[28] In this way the Negro slum child learns his culture's conception of being-in-the-world, a conception
that emphasizes inherent evil in a chaotic,
hostile, destructive world. . . .

Remedies

Finally, it is clear that we, no less
than the inhabitants of the ghetto, are not
masters of their fate because we are not
masters of our own total society. Despite
the battles with poverty on many fronts
we can find little evidence to sustain our
hope of winning the war given current
programs and strategies.

The question of strategy is particularly crucial when one moves from an examination of destructive cultural and interaction patterns in Negro families to the
question of how these families might
achieve a more stable and gratifying life.
It is tempting to see the family as the
main villain of the piece, and to seek to
develop programs which attack directly
this family pathology. Should we not have
extensive programs of family therapy,
family counseling, family-life education,
and the like? Is this not the prerequisite to
enabling slum Negro families to take advantage of other opportunities? Yet, how
pale such efforts seem compared to the
deep-seated problems of self-image and
family process described above. Can an
army of social workers undo the damage of
three hundred years by talking and listening without massive changes in the social

[28] For a discussion of the child's propensity from a very early age for speculation and
developing explanations, see William V. Sil-
verberg, *Childhood Experience and Personal
Destiny* (New York, 1953), pp. 81 ff.

and economic situations of the families
with whom they are to deal? And, if such
changes take place, will the social-worker
army be needed?

If we are right that present Negro
family patterns have been created as adaptations to a particular socioeconomic situation, it would make more sense to change
that socioeconomic stiuation and then depend upon the people involved to make
new adaptations as time goes on. If Negro providers have steady jobs and decent
incomes, if Negro children have some
realistic expectation of moving toward
such a goal, if slum Negroes come to feel
that they have the chance to affect their
own futures and to receive respect from
those around them, then (and only then)
the destructive patterns described are
likely to change. The change, though
slow and uneven from individual to individual, will in a certain sense be automa-
tic because it will represent an adaptation
to changed socio-economic circumstances
which have direct and highly valued implications for the person.

It is possible to think of three kinds of
extra-family change that are required if
family patterns are to change; these are
outlined in the chart on page 125 as pairs
of current deprivations and needed remedies. Unless the major effort is to provide these kinds of remedies, there is a
very real danger that programs to "better the structure of the Negro family" by
direct intervention will serve the un-
intended functions of distracting the
country from the pressing needs for
socioeconomic reform and providing an
alibi for the failure to embark on the
basic institutional changes that are
needed to do anything about abolishing
both white and Negro poverty. It would
be sad, indeed, if, after the Negro revolt
brought to national prominence the
continuing problem of poverty, our ex-
pertise about Negro slum culture served
to deflect the national impluse into symp-

Deprivation effect of caste victimization	Needed remedy
I. Poverty	Employment income for men; income maintenance for mothers
II. Trained incapacity to function in a bureaucratized and industrialized world	Meaningful education of the next generation
III. Powerlessness and stigmatization	Organizational participation for aggressive pursuit of Negroes' self-interest
	Strong sanctions against callous or indifferent service to slum Negroes
	Pride in group identity, Negro *and* American

tom-treatment rather than basic reform. If that happens, social scientists will have served those they study poorly indeed.

Let us consider each of the needed remedies in terms of its probable impact on the family. First, the problem of poverty: employed men are less likely to leave their families than are unemployed men, and when they do stay they are more likely to have the respect of their wives and children. A program whose sole effect would be to employ at reasonable wages slum men for work using the skills they now have would do more than any other possible program to stabilize slum family life. But the wages must be high enough to enable the man to maintain his self-respect as a provider, and stable enough to make it worthwhile to change the nature of his adaptation to his world (no one-year emergency programs will do). Once men learn that work pays off it would be possible to recruit men for part-time retraining for more highly skilled jobs, but the initial emphasis must be on the provision of full-time, permanent unskilled jobs. Obviously it will be easier to do this in the context of full employment and a tight labor market.[29]

[29] This line of argument concerning the employment problems of Negroes, and poverty war strategy more generally, is developed with great cogency by James Tobin, "On Improving the Economic Status of the

For at least a generation, however, there will continue to be a large number of female-headed households. Given the demands of socializing a new generation for non-slum living, it is probably uneconomical to encourage mothers to work. Rather, income maintenance programs must be increased to realistic levels, and mothers must be recognized as doing socially useful work for which they are paid rather than as "feeding at the public trough." The bureaucratic morass which currently hampers flexible strategies of combining employment income and welfare payments to make ends meet must also be modified if young workers are not to be pushed prematurely out of the home.

Education has the second priority. (It is second only because without stable family income arrangements the school system must work against the tremendous resistance of competing life-style adaptations to poverty and economic insecurity.) As Kenneth Clark has argued so effectively, slum schools now function more to stultify and discourage slum children than

Negro," *Daedalus* (Fall 1965), and previously by Gunnar Myrdal, in his *Challenge to Affluence* (New York, 1963), and Orville R. Gursslin and Jack L. Roach, in their "Some Issues in Training the Employed," *Social Problems*, Vol. 12, No. 1 (Summer 1964), pp. 68–77.

to stimulate and train them. The capacity of educators to alibi their lack of commitment to their charges is protean. The making of a different kind of generation must be taken by educators as a stimulating and worthwhile challenge. Once the goal has been accepted they must be given the resources with which to achieve it and the flexibility necessary to experiment with different approaches to accomplish the goal. Education must be broadly conceived to include much more than classroom work, and probably more than a nine-months schedule.[30]

If slum children can come to see the schools as representing a really likely avenue of escape from their difficult situation (even before adolescence they know it is the only *possible* escape) then their commitment to school activities will feed back into their families in a positive way. The parents will feel proud rather than ashamed, and they will feel less need to damn the child as a way to avoid blaming themselves for his failure. The sense of positive family identity will be enriched as the child becomes an attractive object, an ego resource, to his parents. Because he himself feels more competent, he will see them as less depriving and weak. If children's greater commitment to school begins to reduce their involvement in destructive or aimless peer-group activities this too will repercuss positively on the family situation since parents will worry less about their children's involvement in an immoral outside world, and be less inclined to deal with them in harsh, rejecting, or indifferent ways.

Cross-cutting the deprivations of poverty and trained incapacity is the fact of powerlessness and stigmatization. Slum people know that they have little ability

to protect themselves and to force recognition of their abstract rights. They know that they are looked down on and scapegoated. They are always vulnerable to the slights, insults, and indifference of the white and Negro functionaries with whom they deal—policemen, social workers, school teachers, landlords, employers, retailers, janitors. To come into contact with others carries the constant danger of moral attack and insult.[31] If processes of status degradation within families are to be interrupted, then they must be interrupted on the outside first.

One way out of the situation of impotence and dammed-up in-group aggression is the organization of meaningful protest against the larger society. Such protest can and will take many forms, not always so neat and rational as the outsider might hope. But, coupled with, and supporting, current programs of economic and educational change, involvement of slum Negroes in organizational activity can do a great deal to build a sense of pride and potency. While only a very small minority of slum Negroes can be expected to participate personally in such movements, the vicarious involvement of the majority can have important effects on their sense of self-respect and worth.

Some of the needed changes probably can be made from the top, by decision in Washington, with minimal effective organization within the slum; but others can come only in response to aggressive pressure on the part of the victims themselves. This is probably particularly true of the entrenched tendency of service personnel to enhance their own sense of self and to indulge their middle-class *resentment* by stigmatizing and

---

[30] See Chapter 6 (pages 111–153) of Kenneth Clark, *op. cit.*, for a discussion of the destructive effects of ghetto schools on their students.

[31] See the discussion of "moral danger" in Lee Rainwater, "Fear and the House-as-Haven in the Lower Class," *Journal of the American Institute of Planners*, February 1966 (in press).

exploiting those they serve. Only effective protest can change endemic patterns of police harassment and brutality, or teachers' indifference and insults, or butchers' heavy thumbs, or indifferent street cleaning and garbage disposal. And the goal of the protest must be to make this kind of insult to the humanity of the slum-dweller too expensive for the perpetrator to afford; it must cost him election defeats, suspensions without pay, job dismissals, license revocations, fines, and the like.

To the extent that the slum dweller avoids stigmatization in the outside world, he will feel more fully a person within the family and better able to function constructively within it since he will not be tempted to make up deficits in self-esteem in ways that are destructive of family solidarity. The "me" of personal identity and the multiple "we" of family, Negro, and American identity are all inextricably linked; a healthier experience of identity in any one sector will repercuss on all the others.

Some Observations on Extended Familism in the United States *

Robert F. Winch

SOME WRITERS WHO HAVE REPRESENTED THE AMERICAN FAMILY TO BE BOTH ISOLATED AND NUCLEAR

Over the past generation there has been considerable diversity in the writings of American sociologists as to whether the American family is characteristically of the isolated nuclear form or whether it is typically involved in interaction with a network of kin. Among American sociologists there are three whose writings have been interpreted as expressing the former view: Carle C. Zimmerman, Louis Wirth, and Talcott Parsons.

The locus of power, authority and influence was the focus of Zimmerman's analysis of the family. As he viewed the classical Athenian and Roman and the modern Western civilizations, he found that he could distinguish three types of familial organization. "Atomistic" is the

rubric Zimmerman applied to the type exerting the least control over the behavior of its members.[1] He found the American family to have been generally atomistic since early in the nineteenth century.

Wirth's view of the urban family was a corollary of his view of the urban way of life. To him, social relationships in the city were impersonal, superficial, transitory, segmental, anonymous, and even anomic. In the city, he said, the

[1] Zimmerman's other two types are the "trustee" and the "domestic." The former is the type of "maximum strength," having power to the point of controlling the life and death of its members. The latter is the type of "medium strength," viewed by Zimmerman as the most common type in the world. Sec. Carle C. Zimmerman, *Family and Civilization.* New York: Harper & Row, Publishers, 1947.

* *This article was written specifically for this volume*

bonds of kinship were weak, and the individual members were thus free "from the large kinship group characteristic of the country . . . [to] pursue their own diverging interests in their vocational, educational, religious, recreational, and political life."[2]

Parsons speaks of the American family as "an open, multilineal, conjugal system . . . made up exclusively of interlocking conjugal families."[3] The fact that this system lacks "any structural bias in favor of solidarity with the ascendant and descendant families in any one line of descent has enormously increased the structural isolation of the individual conjugal family." Also relevant is his observation that the American "isolated nuclear family" has become almost completely functionless on the macroscopic level and, for its members, retains only the functions of the socialization of children and the stabilization of adult personalities.[4]

SOME WRITERS WHO HAVE REPRESENTED THE AMERICAN FAMILY AS PARTICIPATING ACTIVELY IN A KIN NETWORK

After the past three writers had painted a picture of the American family as very limited in function and weak in influence, nuclear in form and isolated from kinsmen, there came a spate of studies purporting to challenge some of these formulations. Dotson found that among the urban working class there was little participation in voluntary organizations but that family and kinship provided companionship and recreation.[5] Greer found that about three-quarters of his Los Angeles respondents were visiting kinsmen at least as often as once a month, and he concluded that the interaction of urban residents with their kinsmen constituted "the most important social relations for all types of urban populations."[6] Litwak found that about one-third of his sample of Buffalo housewives reported having received visits from kinsmen as often as once a week, and he went on to posit what he called the "modified extended family," which he said:

> . . . differs from the "classical extended" family in that it does not demand geographical propinquity, occupational involvement, or nepotism, nor does it have an hierarchical authority structure. On the other hand, it differs from the isolated nuclear family structure in that it does provide significant and continuing aid to the nuclear family. The modified extended family consists of a series of nuclear families bound together on an equalitarian basis, with a strong emphasis on these extended family bonds as an end value.[7]

[2] Louis Wirth, "Urbanism as a Way of Life," *American Journal of Sociology,* 1938, 44: 1–24; reprinted in Paul K. Hatt and Albert J. Reiss, Jr. eds., *Reader in Urban Sociology.* New York: The Free Press, 1951, pp. 32–49. See especially pp. 40 and 46.

[3] Talcott Parsons, "The Social Structure of the Family," in Ruth Nanda Anshen ed., *The Family: Its Function and Destiny.* New York: Harper & Row, Publishers, 1949, pp. 173–201, especially pp. 174, 175 and 180.

[4] Talcott Parsons and Robert F. Bales, *Family, Socialization and Interaction Process.* New York: The Free Press, 1955, pp. 16–17.

[5] Floyd Dotson, "Patterns of Voluntary Association among Urban Working-Class Families," *American Sociological Review,* 1951, 16: 687–693.

[6] Scott Greer, "Urbanism Reconsidered: A Comparative Study of Local Areas in a Metropolis," *American Sociological Review,* 1956, 21, 19–25. Scott Greer, "Individual Participation in Mass Society," in Roland Young ed., *Approaches to the Study of Politics.* Evanston, Ill.: Northwestern University Press, 1958, pp. 329–342, especially p. 330.

[7] Eugene Litwak, "Occupational Mobility and Extended Family Cohesion," *Amer-*

It is difficult to tell from Litwak's writing just how widespread he believes the modified extended family to be in American society and whether or not he believes it to be largely concentrated in specific socioeconomic strata, occupations, or other categories, and thus far he has not presented data on this point.

Sussman found that the overwhelming majority of urban families he studied engaged in some form of mutual aid with their parents and that the maintenance of intergenerational continuity was greater when marriages were culturally homogamous.[8] Finally, the Detroit Area Study of the University of Michigan discovered that only 11 percent of the families in their Detroit sample had no households of kin in that metropolitan area. The authors stated that most respondents reported having engaged in some mutual aid with relatives, and they concluded:

> The "typical" Detroiter is very much a member of an extended family group . . . There is little doubt that the kin group is continuing to play an important part in the life of the metropolitan family.[9]

These findings have been interpreted as more or less direct refutation of the earlier formulations of Zimmerman, Wirth, and Parsons. Perhaps the most emphatic statement comes from

one sociologist quoting another as saying, "The isolated nuclear family is a myth. This has already been conclusively demonstrated. It does not merit any further attention of the field, and I, for one, refuse to waste any more time even discussing it."[10]

DIFFICULTIES INVOLVED IN TESTING THE FORMULATIONS OF THE EARLIER WRITERS

How can it happen, one might ask, that in a relatively short time—a decade or two at the most—opinion can shift from one belief to its polar opposite about a state of affairs that exists under our eyes —the nature of the family in American cities? Where such radical shifts occur, one ready inference is that there may be poor science.

As we try to assess the American family in the light of the conflicting views portrayed above, it becomes advisable to state as clearly as possible what the issues are—what was claimed by the earlier writers and the nature of the evidence viewed as refutation.

Since the range over which Zimmerman seeks to generalize is the complete sweep of Western civilization starting with the Greeks of Homeric times, his standard of a strong family system comes from early Athens and early Rome, and his data are historical. Except for the highland clans of the Appalachian and Ozark Mountains, Zimmerman asserts that from the founding of America as a white society its family has been atomistic. It is clear that the authors of the more

---

ican Sociological Review, 1960, 25: 9–21. It would seem as apt to use the term "nonisolated nuclear family" to refer to this pattern.

[8] Marvin B. Sussman, "The Isolated Nuclear Family: Fact or Fiction," Social Problems, 1959, 6: 333–340; and "Family Continuity: Selective Factors Which Affect Relationships between Families at Generational Levels," Marriage and Family Living, 1954, 16: 112–120.

[9] Survey Research Center, A Social Profile of Detroit: 1955. Ann Arbor, Mich.: Institute for Social Research, 1956, chaps. 4–5; quotation is from p. 26.

[10] Irving Rosow, "Intergenerational Relationships: Problems and Proposals," in Ethel Shanas and Gordon F. Streib, Social Structure and the Family: Generational Relations. Englewood Cliffs, N.J.: Prentice-Hall, Inc., 1965, pp. 341–378; quotation is from p. 341.

recent studies have made no effort to compare their observations with such historically remote forms. Hence the recent studies have not joined issues with Zimmerman.

To Wirth the city was a lonely, if fascinating, scene. Not only was the urbanite cut off from kinsmen but from diffuse social contact generally. The categorical nexus of money had replaced the sympathetic nexus of kinship. It should be noted that this was one of a multitude of more or less contemporaneous formulations of the same general idea in which urban life was presented as ideal—typically opposite from rural or tribal life.[11] Illustrations of such pairs of terms are folk-urban, *Gemeinschaft-Gesellschaft*, sacred-secular, and diffuseness-specificity.

If we were to interpret the ideal type as a proposition about reality, we might hypothesize that:

(a) all rural (or tribal) residents live in households of extended families and have warm, diffuse relationships with all their kinsmen, whereas

(b) no urban resident lives in a household with any extended kinsman or has a warm, diffuse relationship with any of his kinsmen.

Given this extreme phrasing, a single negative case would suffice to falsify either hypothesis. We know of course that ideal types are intended to be exaggerations of reality, but it seems possible that some of the critics of the isolated nuclear family had in mind such a hypothesis as (b) when giving expression to their refutation. After all this has been remarked, however, it is necessary to conclude that Wirth's manner of thought and style of writing were such as to produce virtually no researchable and hence falsifiable propositions.

[11] And the American urban family from what Goode has called "the classical family of Western nostalgia." William J. Goode, *After Divorce*. New York: The Free Press, 1956, p. 3.

The above paragraph on Parsons' views shows his reasoning that the American kinship system produces the isolated nuclear family, but that passage does not provide defining characteristics that would make possible some estimation as to the prevalence of such a familial form. Elsewhere Parsons has provided more operational language. Commenting that the isolation of the nuclear family does *not* imply a break in the relations of the spouses with their families of orientation, Parsons explains that to him this isolation does mean that (1) the nuclear family "normally" has its own household "not shared with members of the family of orientation of either spouse" and (2) that typically the household is economically independent of any other household.[12]

What evidence can be marshalled to show whether or not American families are isolated in the sense that Parsons uses that term? The statistic relevant to Parsons' condition (1) above is the percentage of married couples who have their own households and have no relatives other than their children in the household. According to the U.S. Bureau of the Census, 97.2 percent of all married couples had their own households in 1959,[13] and in 1960 only one in ten husband-wife households contained relatives other than their own children.[14] For an overwhelming majority of the American population, then, Parsons' condition (1) is empirically confirmed.

Parsons' condition (2) concerns the economic independence of the household. There do not appear to be any

[12] Parsons and Bales, pp. 10–11.

[13] U.S. Bureau of the Census, *Current Population Reports—Population Characteristics*, Series P-20, No. 100, April 13, 1960, Table 2, p. 9.

[14] U.S. Bureau of the Census, *United States Census of Population: 1960*, Final Report PC(2)–4A, Washington, U.S. Government Printing Office, 1963, Table 17.

satisfactory data on this point. There are some studies of seeming relevance. For example, there are two local studies using urban samples in which a majority of the respondents reported giving and/or receiving financial aid to or from kinsmen.[15] Although these reports did not show the phrasing of their questions, it appears that a family was listed as receiving financial aid from a kinsman if this had happened only once. Although it is possible that some may interpret such data as refuting Parsons' position with respect to his condition (2), it seems evident that these data are not directly relevant since Parsons is apparently referring to an enduring state of affairs rather than to non-recurring financial aid given in an emergency.

Concerning Parsons' views on the isolated nuclear family, then, it appears that the revisionists have not contested his assertions about the American family system being open, multilineal, and conjugal. With respect to Parsons' two operational criteria for the isolated nuclear family, it turns out that his first criterion—separate households—is clearly substantiated, that no data have appeared to test the second—economic independence of households—and that the data of the revisionists do not bear very directly on either of these two criteria.

In summary, the formulations of Zimmerman and Wirth are not researchable with respect to whether or not the American nuclear family is isolated. Parsons has suggested two criteria for isolation, but it is possible to allege, as Litwak has done, that a family could be isolated

by Parsons' two criteria and still not "really" be isolated.

EXTENDED FAMILISM AND ISOLATION: SOME PROPOSED MEASURES

At this juncture we may ask whether or not the criteria of Parsons constitute the most meaningful way either to conceptualize or to operationalize isolation as this term pertains to the nuclear family. The literature on the aged[16] has brought out that not only do aged people like to live in their own households apart from their children, but also that they like to have their separate households located near those of their children. That is, they like to maintain a good deal of autonomy and independence and still be able to have the company and emotional support of their offspring as well as their help when it is needed. For this reason, the separateness of households is not an adequate measure of isolation,[17] and it seems advisable to devise some other measures that can be used to measure the isolation of the nuclear family. Since isolation constitutes only one end of each measure, the term "extended familism" will be introduced to designate the conceptual significance of the other end. Let us consider some relevant indexes and data.

[15] Marvin B. Sussman, "The Isolated Nuclear Family: Fact or Fiction," *Social Problems*, 1959, 6, 333–340; and Reuben Hill, "The Three Generation Research Design: A Method for Studying Family and Social Change," paper presented before The Ninth International Seminar on Family Research in Tokyo, September 1965.

[16] See, for example, Peter Townsend, *The Family Life of Old People: An Inquiry in East London*. London: Routledge & Kegan Paul Ltd., 1957; Michael Young and Hildred Geertz, "Old Age in London and San Francisco," *British Journal of Sociology*, 1961, 12: 124–141.

[17] And whereas programs of social security do serve to reduce the economic dependence of aged people, they continue to need other kinds of assistance and emotional support.

**Extensity of Presence
of Households of Kin**

The first condition that would make a nuclear family isolated, we may suggest, is that it has no kinsmen in the local community.[18] We may count the number of kinsmen a family has in the community or—what turns out to be easier and probably both more valid and more reliable—the number of households of kin it has in the community. We may think of those with no household of local kin as being in this sense totally isolated.[19] We may think of those with relatively few households of kin as relatively isolated. We may think of those with relatively many households of kin in the area as relatively familistic. We may speak of this variable as extensity of presence of households of kin in the local community.

**Intensity of Presence
of Households of Kin**

Another way to look at how isolated or non-isolated a nuclear family may be is to examine the degrees of kinship represented among the households of their kin in the local community. Let us speak of all those members of a person's family of orientation (parents and siblings) plus those of his family of procreation (spouse and offspring) as his nuclear kin. Let us speak of all his other kin except those to whom he is related through

18 The referent of community may be specified by the researcher or left to be defined by the respondent. In the suburban study referred to below the former procedure was used, and the specification was to the metropolitan area of Chicago. In the statewide study of Wisconsin the referent was defined by the respondent.

19 Of course this is not complete Litwakian isolation since one might still have contact by mail or by long distance telephone with relatives who would come to one's aid in a time of need.   .

his spouse as his extended kin.[20] If he has households of both nuclear and extended kin in the local area, he is less isolated familistically than if he has members of only one of these categories or none at all. Then we shall speak of the least isolated (or most extended-familistic) nuclear family as one wherein both the husband and the wife have households of both nuclear and extended kin in the community. Again nuclear families having no households of kin locally would be the most isolated, and nuclear families having some but not all four[21] of the categories of kin would be in an intermediate degree of isolation. This measure we speak of as intensity of presence of households of kin in the local community.

Interaction With Households of Kin

Extended familism and its opposite, isolation, may be thought of as involving a third measure—regular interaction with households of kin. How often the interaction must be in order to be considered regular is of course an arbitrary matter. Similarly it is arbitrary whether or not the researcher defines interaction to include mail and telephone contacts as well as face-to-face encounters. Here the measure may be specified as the number of households of kin interacted with regularly (once a month or more, say) by some member of one's own household. This measure may be called interaction with households of kin.[22]

20 That is, all of ego's non-nuclear kin to whom the first link of kinship, as we trace from ego, is consanguineal.

21 Husband's nuclear, husband's extended, wife's nuclear, and wife's extended.

22 Of course, depending on one's purpose, one may wish to limit the contacts to local kin or one may prefer to define interaction to include contacts with kin wherever they may be. The latter procedure, to be used

Functionality of Interaction with Kin

A fourth measure of extended familism-isolation concerns the instrumental value of interaction with kinsmen. To measure this we may ask how many times a householder names some relative outside his own household when asked a battery of questions about both or either of the following: from whom or to whom he receives or gives various services—borrowing or lending money, babysitting, getting a job, borrowing or lending equipment, buying at discount, taking children for overnight, and so forth. This measure is called functionality of interaction with (local) kinsmen. [23]

With each of these four measures it is possible to look at the family descriptively—to see what proportion of families may be considered as isolated. Also it becomes possible to see whether or not, as the early writers seemed to believe, the urban American family is more isolated than the rural. Furthermore, it is possible to see a correlation between extended familism and ethnicity and to suggest notions as to what process may underlie the correlation.

---

below, is the emphasis in Litwak's "modified extended family." See p. 128 above.

Because the time available for an interview in the Wisconsin study was much shorter than in the suburban study, it was necessary to introduce some shortcuts in the Wisconsin interview. Whereas the suburban study provided a credible basis for tallying the actual number of households of kin interacted with, the only credible basis for summing interaction in the abridged Wisconsin interview was by the number of categories (from 0 to 6) of kin households: respondent's siblings, respondent's parents, respondent's other kin, and then the same three categories of respondent's spouse's kin.

[23] As with interaction, the researcher's purpose may lead to his including non-local kinsmen. See note 22.

SOME DATA ON ISOLATION-EXTENDED FAMILISM

In the fall of 1964 a survey was based on a state-wide probability sample in Wisconsin. Among the responses were data on the four measures of isolation-extended familism presented in the preceding section. For each measure it seems appropriate to regard as isolated the proportion of respondents who have given the "none" response: the 14 percent who have no household of kin present in the community, [24] the 8 percent who have no interaction with kin, and the 13 percent who have no functional interaction with their kin. We may view these percentages as estimates of the proportion of families in Wisconsin that may be viewed as isolated in terms of the various measures. Perhaps we should reverse the emphasis and note that from 86 to 92 percent of the nuclear families were nonisolated, depending on the measure used.

The lack of a precisely specified, clearly observable and consensually meaningful standard of either isolation or nonisolation has made it difficult to test the formulations of Wirth and Parsons that the American nuclear urban family is isolated. [25] The same difficulty appears in the writings of the revisionists who deny that isolation. To remedy this unsatisfactory state of affairs, let us com-

[24] Since the same proportion report "none" on both extensity and intensity of presence, only one percentage for presence is reported here. The result is that the number of measures of isolation collapses to three. It is at the other—or extended familism—end of the scale that we have four meaningful measures.

[25] Of course Parsons' condition (1)—separate households—is precisely specified and clearly observable, but its meaning is simply that America has a nuclear family system or, more precisely, a nuclear family residential

TABLE 1 Percentage distribution of respondents by ecological type and by level of extended familism, for four measures of extended familism

MEASURE AND LEVEL OF EXTENDED FAMILISM	Ecology*				
	METRO-POLITAN	OTHER	RURAL	TOTAL	GAMMA
Extensity of Presence[a]	N=115	N=286	N=112	N=513	
None	17.4	14.0	10.7	14.0	
Some	40.0	48.6	38.4	44.4	.10
High	42.6	37.4	50.9	41.5	
Intensity of Presence[b]	N=115	N=286	N=112	N=513	
None	17.4	14.0	10.7	14.0	
Some	60.9	64.0	64.3	63.4	.09
High	21.7	22.0	25.0	22.6	
Interaction[c]	N=115	N=286	N=112	N=513	
None	7.8	7.7	7.1	7.6	
Some	55.7	49.7	35.7	48.0	.20**
High	36.5	42.7	57.1	44.4	
Functionality[d]	N=115	N=286	N=112	N=513	
None	20.0	12.6	7.1	13.1	
Some	59.1	52.8	47.3	53.0	.30**
High	20.9	34.6	45.5	33.9	

[a]*Extensity of presence* refers to the number of households of kin in the community: "some" = 1–8; "high" = 9+.

[b]*Intensity of presence* refers to the degree of kin present in the community; a nuclear kinsman is a member of the respondent's family of orientation or of procreation; "none" means neither the respondent nor spouse reports any household of kin in the community; "high" means both respondent and spouse report having households of both nuclear and extended kin in the community; "some" signifies the presence of kin but not satisfying the conditions of the "high" category.

[c]*Interaction* refers to the number of categories of households of kin with which some member of the respondent's household has been in contact (face-to-face, phone or mail) at least monthly; "some" = 1–3; "high" = 4+ .6.

[d]*Functionality* refers to the number of categories of service either given and/or received from some kinsman; "some" = 1–2; "high" = 3+.

*The three ecological types are: Metropolitan: Milwaukee, Madison, West Allis and Wauwatosa; Rural: unincorporated territory outside any SMSA; Other: residual territory—small cities, suburbs, etc.

**The gammas so marked as significant at the .01 level; the others are not significant at the .05 level. Although the data in this and subsequent tables are reported as percentages, the measures of association and tests of significance have been conducted on the frequencies.

pare the family in urban Wisconsin with the family in rural parts of that state. If Wirth and Parsons are correct, we

system. There is nothing about the concept of the nuclear family system that indicates the degree to which related nuclear families may be isolated from each other. Parsons' condition (2)—economic independence—is potentially both precisely specified and clearly observable, but its meaning, like that of Parsons' condition (1), has been challenged by Litwak in the latter's formulation of the "modified extended family."

should expect to find a greater proportion of isolated families in urban areas than in rural. Whether or not the revisionists would deny this is not evident from their writings.

It will be seen in the first row of each of the four parts of Table 1 that there is a rather slight urban-rural gradient such that respondents in metropolitan areas are more isolated than those in rural areas.[26] Most of the rural-urban

[26] Only with respect to interaction and

variation in extended familism is due to migration as is seen in the facts that: (a) both spouses were migrants in 94 percent of the couples having no household of kin in the community, and (b) where neither spouse was a migrant, the correlation between ruralism-urbanism and extended familism disappeared.

Thus the data are consistent with the proposition that to a small degree the proportion of nuclear families that are isolated is greater in the city than in the countryside, and this difference appears to be largely the consequence of migration. The proportion isolated in the suburbs and small cities is intermediate between the urban and rural proportions.

ETHNICITY AND EXTENDED FAMILISM

There is a bit of folk wisdom to the effect that the disposition to interact with relatives is not spread uniformly through the United States but that some categories of people are more prone to such behavior than are others. For example, the legendary man-in-the-street may be heard to remark that members of one ethnic category or another—and of course they vary from one man-in-the-street to the next—are especially likely to associate with their relatives.

Data relevant to such folk wisdom have been gathered in two settings—the statewide sample in Wisconsin referred to above, and a sample in an upper-middle-class suburb of Chicago. The suburban sample was about 50 percent Jewish, 30 percent Protestant, and 20 percent Catholic. (An ethnic category is an aggregate of people sharing, and therefore participating in, a common

culture. Since our interest is in culture rather than attitudes toward or beliefs about a supernatural being, this variable is being called ethnicity rather than religion.)

The prediction of one school of men-in-the-street was confirmed by the finding that with respect to all four measures of extended familism the Jewish aggregate showed the highest degree of extended familism. The Protestants were lowest on all four measures. Although they were intermediate between Jews and Protestants on all four measures, the Catholics resembled the Jews more on the functionality of interaction, and otherwise they resembled the Protestants more than they did the Jews. [27]

The Wisconsin sample provided desirable heterogeneity with respect to socioeconomic level and residential area but proved unfortunately homogeneous with respect to ethnicity. The outcome was that there were too few Jews for statistical analysis; similarly, the number of Negroes was too small to allow them to be treated as a separate category for statistical analysis. Accordingly, both Negroes and Jews were removed from the sample, and the analysis was carried out on white Christians. Catholics constituted a little over a third of the sample, and more than half of the rest proved to be Lutherans. Accordingly, the categorization used was: Catholic, Lutheran, and other Protestant.

In the Wisconsin study three of the four measures of extended familism correlated significantly with ethnicity: the Catholics had more households of kin than the "other" Protestants (gamma for extensity = .26, for intensity = .25), and they had regular contact with more cate-

functionality, however, is there enough variation in the bivariate distributions for the hypothesis of chance to be rejected at the .05 level of probability.

[27] Robert F. Winch, Scott Greer, and Rae Lesser Blumberg, "Ethnicity and Extended Familism in an Upper-Middle-Class Suburb," *American Sociological Review*, 1967, 32: 265–272.

gories of kin (gamma for interaction = .17), but there was no difference with respect to functionality (gamma = .02). The Lutherans turned out to be just about as familistic as the Catholics, which means more familistic than the other Protestants.[28]

The finding that Jews were more familistic than Christians with respect to the four measures of extended familism mentioned above stimulated a quest for an explanation. It was proposed that occupation and migration might be intervening variables. The steps in the reasoning ran as follows:

1. Because of prejudice and discrimination Jews are differentially distributed in the occupational system—overrepresented in the free professions, small businesses and sales, and underrepresented in bureaucratic occupations, especially in the giant corporations. Such data as are available seem to confirm this point.[29]

2. The types of occupation in which the Jews are overrepresented are less likely than the bureaucratic occupations to require moving about the country.

3. Since migration lowers the probability that an individual will have households of kinsmen living in the

same community, then if Jews are less migratory than Christians, as reasoned in step 2, it should eventuate that on the average Jews would have more kinsmen living near them.

Thus the reasoning accounts for the greater extended familism of the Jews on the basis of an inferred greater availability of kinsmen in the community.

It will be recalled that there were enough Jews for statistical analysis only in the suburban sample. As would be expected, this sample was fairly homogeneous with respect to socioeconomic level. Beacuse of difficulty in classifying occupations in a manner relevant to step 1, this step was collapsed with step 2, and an empirical check was made on the chain of reasoning by noting the intercorrelations of ethnicity, migration, and extended familism. It turned out (a) that the Jews were less migratory than the Christians, and (b) the less migratory households reported greater familism than the more migratory. So far the data support the hypothesis. If the explanation is correct, however, the correlation between ethnicity and familism should drop sharply when level of migration is held constant, and this did not happen. Despite migratory status, the Jews were more familistic than the others. The statistical analysis led to the conclusion that *the Jews* were not more familistic because they were less migratory but they *were less migratory because they were more familistic than the Christians.*[30]

In the Wisconsin data there is a correlation between ethnicity and migration—the "other" Protestants being more migratory than the Lutherans and the Catholics. Also the less migratory are more familistic in Wisconsin. In Wisconsin, however, it turns out that among the less migratory, especially among couples of low socioeconomic status, there is

[28] Robert F. Winch and Scott Greer, "Urbanism, Ethnicity and Extended Familism," *Journal of Marriage and the Family*, 1968, 30, 40–45. In the suburban study with the Jews present, however, the correlations between ethnicity and the four measures of extended familism were much higher: .81, .68, .74, and .29 respectively.

[29] Donald J. Bogue, *The Population of the United States*. New York: The Free Press, 1959, table 23–12, p. 703; Benjamin R. Epstein and Arnold Forster, *Some of My Best Friends . . . .* New York: Farrar, Straus & Giroux, Inc., 1962, chaps. 13–16, especially pp. 207 and 225; Nathan Glazer and Daniel Patrick Moynihan, *Beyond the Melting Pot: The Negroes, Puerto Ricans, Jews, Italians, and Irish of New York City.* Cambridge, Mass.: M.I.T. Press, 1959, pp. 143–155.

[30] Winch, Greer and Blumberg, p. 275.

little difference in familism, but among the more migratory, especially among those of high socioeconomic status, the Catholics and Lutherans are more familistic than the "other" Protestants.

Considering the two studies together, we may view the results as suggesting that there may be three patterns of relationship between migration and extended familism.[31] Of the ethnic categories considered, Protestants other than Lutherans seem most likely to move from their birthplaces and least likely to move into communities where they have relatives. One might conjecture that the "other" Protestant, being moved typically by his company, may live in several small cities in a particular sales region, then move from one regional office to another, and finally to the home office. Lutherans, Catholics, and Jews are less likely to move, and when they do, are more likely to move where they have relatives.

Before they migrate, there is not much difference in extended familism among the three Christian categories, but, irrespective of whether we are considering migrants or non-migrants, Christians as a category are less familistic than Jews. The fact that migration accounts for much of the variation in familism among the Christian categories but *not* for the variation between Christians and Jews leaves us with the residual interpretation that perhaps the unique history of the Jews—diaspora, prejudice, discrimination, pogroms—have fostered a cultural conviction as to the survival-value of in-group attitudes and behaviors while designating the family as the prime in-group.

SUMMARY, INTERPRETATION, AND CONCLUSIONS

From the 1930s into the 1950s various sociologists have described the American family system in somewhat various ways but all more or less consistent with the formulation of the isolated nuclear family.[32] The familial form they were describing was that of the urban middle class.

Viewing this form over a historical perspective of twenty-five hundred years, Zimmerman found that American nuclear families were not organized into extended systems and that kinsmen outside the American nuclear family had no control over those within it. These defining characteristics of what he called the "atomistic" family Zimmerman saw as elements in the decay of civilizations. Although it was not a defining characteristic, Zimmerman stated that another property of the atomistic family was a low birth rate.

Like Zimmerman, Wirth remarked on the disappearance of control by kinsmen. He saw the thinning of familial relationships as part of the urban mode of interaction, and he seemed to use the city center as his prototypic scene of urban interaction. He was in agreement with Zimmerman about the direction of change although he certainly was not nearly as distressed about that change. He differed from Zimmerman in the norms by which he judged the American family; he did not use as this standard

---

[31] Although the corresponding questionnaire items in the two studies are not sufficiently similar for the demonstration to be made in tabular form, the order of ethnicity from most familistic and least migratory to least familistic and most migratory is: Jews, Catholics, Lutherans, "other" Protestants.

[32] The actual dates of the writings cited are from 1938 (Wirth's "Urbanism") to 1955 (Parsons-Bales' *Family*). In somewhat the same tradition is Ogburn's analysis of the loss of familial functions in the American family published in *Recent Social Trends* in 1933.

the extended family of early Athens or early Rome but apparently something more like the ideal-typical folk society of Tönnies or of Redfield.

Parsons attributed prime responsibility for the isolation of the American nuclear family to the way in which Americans classify their kin, and specifically to their impartiality between the agnatic (male) and uterine (female) descent groups. He provided two operational handles for the problem of evaluating the degree of isolation of the American family—neolocality of residence, and financial independence of the household.

The revisionists of the idea that the American family was typically the isolated nuclear family found that:

i. urban people reported a great deal of interaction with kin,

ii. urban people, especially of the working class, reported that visiting with kin constituted a major form of recreation, and

iii. the majority of urban people reported having engaged in some form of mutual aid with kinsmen.

Data from the U.S. Bureau of the Census have been presented here to show that:

iv. Parsons was largely right in asserting that the American family was "isolated" in the sense of "normally" having its own household "not shared with members of the family of orientation of either spouse."

Unfortunately it was not possible to find data relevant to Parsons' second condition—that the households are mutually independent in an economic sense.

On the other hand, the position has been taken that there are other more meaningful ways of conceptualizing and operationalizing isolation of the nuclear family. This paper has undertaken to define the concept of extended familism in terms of several indexes: number of households of kin in the community (extensity of presence), number of households of certain classes of kin (intensity), interaction with households of kin, and functionality of that interaction.

Data from a study of suburban households and from a state-wide sample revealed that:

v. most people in both studies report that they have households of kin in their community, that they interact with their kin, and that the interaction has at least some degree of functionality.

It was suggested that one way to interpret the formulations of the earlier writers was to the effect that rural people should prove more familistic than urban people. It was found that:

vi. although rural people do not have significantly more households of kin in the community (on the average), they do have a bit more (and significantly more) interaction with their kin and functional interaction with them (Wisconsin data).

The last conclusion from the two sets of data is that:

vii. as defined, extended familism varies with ethnicity, Jews being the most familistic of the ethnic categories studied, and "other" Protestants being the least.

Migration appears to account for the differences in familism among categories of Christians but not for the difference between Christians and Jews. Here the cause may be found in the long history of persecution and segregation of the Jews and a firmly learned conviction as to the protective value of kinsmen.

Jewish Extended Familism *

by Hope Jensen Leichter and William E. Mitchell

. . . The Jewish Family Service of New York is a family counseling agency, primarily serving the Jewish community of New York City, although not entirely restricted to Jewish families . . .

The clients studied came from the regular casework offices of the agency. For life-cycle contrast, certain clients in the special Service to the Aged of the agency were also studied . . .

SOCIOCULTURAL BACKGROUND OF CLIENT FAMILIES

Stage of Life Cycle

The client families were married couples, mainly with children still living at home. For 87 per cent the current marriage was their only one. Relatively few were young couples; only 3 per cent of the husbands and wives were twenty-

* *Adapted from* Kinship and Casework. *New York: Russell Sage Foundation, 1967, pp. 39–125*

five years old or younger. Relatively few were elderly; only 8 per cent of the husbands and wives were fifty-six or older. The largest group, 45 per cent, were between thirty-six and forty-five; 19 per cent were between twenty-six and thirty-five; 25 per cent were between forty-six and fifty-five. All but 4 per cent of the families had children. Of those having children, 86 per cent had one, two, or three children at home. All the children were under six in only 13 per cent of the families with children, and in only 8 per cent all were over eighteen. Thus in most families the children ranged from early school age through high school age. Eighty-two per cent of the parents of husbands and wives were living. . .

As Table 1 indicates, the majority of the client sample is drawn from the children of immigrants.

Sufficient information exists to classify 172 client husbands' present or most recent main occupation according to the United States census categories. . . . (see Table 2.)

TABLE 1 Birthplace of clients and their parents

	Husbands	Wives	Clients' Fathers	Clients' Mothers
	(Percentages)			
United States	76	80	8	13
Europe	22	18	91	85
Elsewhere	2	2	1	2
Total	100	100	100	100
	(186)	(209)	(378)	(388)

In Tables 1 and 2 the figures in parentheses indicate the number of cases on which the percentages are based.

TABLE 2 Census classification of client husbands' jobs

	Per Cent	
	WHITE COLLAR	
Professional, technical	16	
Managerial, proprietor	17	59
Clerical and sales	26	
	BLUE COLLAR	
Craftsmen, foremen	16	
Operatives	17	41
Service and labor	8	
Total	100	
	(172)	

THE KINSHIP VALUES OF CLIENT FAMILIES

The Content of Kinship Values

Residence

Combined households are definitely not an ideal, but geographic proximity to kin is of value for many. A fair number agreed that "*It is usually nice for a young married couple to live near their parents.*" Even those who thought that the nuclear family should function as an independent unit felt, from the parents' point of view that children should live near their parents, because seeing their children as adults is one of the rights and joys of being a parent:

> I would like them to be somewhere in the vicinity . . . but out of town I would say definitely no . . . this is your life. As parents, you have brought up your children. You want to see the fruit of your labor, it's the development of your own . . . Now they are married, you want to see their houses . . .

Obligations for interaction

Despite dim views about the prospects of combined households, strong values support obligations to interact with kin. These obligations are reflected in the idea that geographic proximity to kin is desirable and are also expressed more generally. Cutting oneself off from kin is considered reprehensible and self-

ish, and those who attempt to reduce contacts with kin may be severely sanctioned. The majority agreed, for example, that "*It's selfish for someone to cut himself off from his relatives.*" Someone who cuts himself off from his kin would be "antisocial . . ."

Kin and nonkin institutions

At the same time, economic relationships with kin are expected to be fraught with conflict. Most clients disagreed with the idea that "*If you have to borrow money, it's better to do it from a relative than a bank . . .*"

Nevertheless, the problems of such borrowing were mentioned frequently. If difficulties in repaying debts should arise, emotional involvements would only complicate them, with the possibility that the relationships of relatives might be broken up . . .

Boundaries of kin knowledge

Figure 1 contains two genealogies that were obtained in interviews with one family. The data on the husband's kin were given by the husband, and those on the wife's kin were given by the wife. The total number of individuals recognized as kin by this family is 587, clearly a very large figure. Moreover, even a genealogy as extensive as this is not necessarily complete, since the criteria for recognizing an individual as a kin are variable . . .

By comparison with data from other studies, the number of kin known by these client families is large. Compared with one study conducted in London, the total number of recognized kin for these client families is larger.[1] The client genealogies, however, tend to show greater lateral extension and less generation depth. The size of the clients' network of known kin is also large by comparison with the study made among Vassar undergraduates, but again clients tend to have information on fewer generations than the Vassar students.[2] By comparison with still another study, the client sample is less able to trace lineal ancestry . . .[3]

Boundaries of kin interaction

It is evident from the data on the number of individuals recognized as kin, the number of kin seen only at big family gatherings, and the number seen more often than at big family gatherings that most of the client families have large kin networks. Data on cognatic kin obtained through the questionnaire procedure indicate that only 11 per cent of the families had 15 or fewer kin that were effective, while 59 per cent listed from 16 to 45 kin, and 20 per cent listed from 46 to

[1] Firth, Raymond W., ed., *Two Studies of Kinship in London*. London: The Athlone Press, 1956.

[2] Codere, Helen, "A Genealogical Study of Kinship in the United States," *Psychiatry*, February, 1955, 18: 65–79.

[3] Young, Michael, and Hildred Geertz, "Old Age in London and San Francisco: Some Families Compared," *The British Journal of Sociology*, June, 1961, 12: 124–141.
In considering the "less generation depth" of these respondents it is relevant that migration was common in the parental generation and that the migration of the parents must have lowered the probability that the clients would have known their grandparents or other relatives of the grandparents' generation.—Eds.

60 kin. Nine per cent of the families listed 61 or more kin. Thus most families have a large number of cognatic kin with whom they maintain some degree of effective social interaction. The actual number of kin is undoubtedly larger than that represented merely by the categories of cognatic kin included in the questionnaire . . .

Defining network boundaries

But the basis for selecting kin with whom to interact is not always clear to all involved because it varies with the activity, and because the genealogical relationship between kin depends on the perspective of each individual. Considerable ambiguity and a basis for conflict result.[4] Even with kin such as parents and siblings, who are closest genealogically, the decision of inclusion and exclusion may be a problem from the perspective of a spouse or someone slightly more distant. The shifting and uncertain criteria for defining boundaries of the kin network are clear in explanations of which kin were included at particular events.

A description of which kin one woman invited to her daughter's engagement party reveals several implicit criteria. The bridegroom had three siblings, all of whom had to be included because of the principle of genealogical equivalence. On the other hand, the grandfather of the bridegroom and the mother's sister were included not by virtue of genealogical closeness alone, but because they lived with kin who were closer genealogically. A principle of representativeness, or balancing the various sides of the family, also operated; but this prin-

[4] Leichter, Hope J., and William E. Mitchell, "Feuds and Fissions Within the Conjugal Kindred," paper read at the Annual Meeting of the American Anthropological Association, Minneapolis, November, 1960.

HUSBAND'S KIN

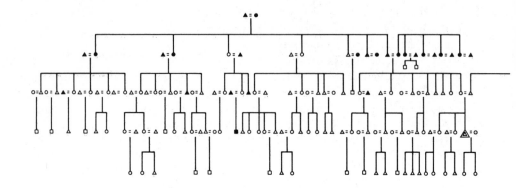

WIFE'S KIN

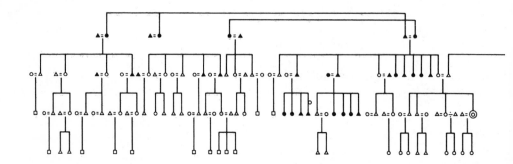

△ MALE LIVING   = MARITAL TIE

▲ MALE DECEASED   ÷ DIVORCE

○ FEMALE LIVING | PARENT·CHILD TIE

● FEMALE DECEASED   − SIBLING TIE

□ SEX NOT SPECIFIED BY CLIENT

HUSBAND'S KIN continued on following page.

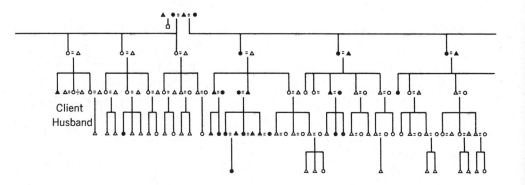

Client
Husband

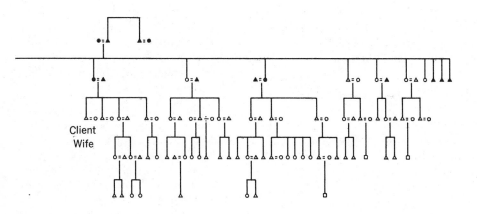

Client
Wife

HUSBAND'S KIN (continued)

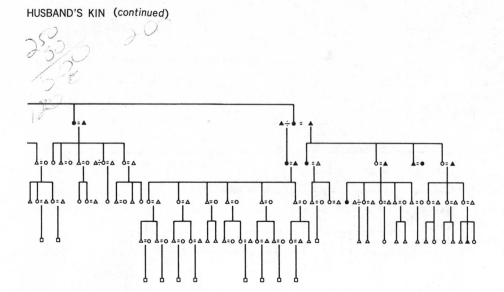

ciple was complicated by the lack of geographic proximity of the client's brothers. Therefore, a principle of substitution was employed; the client's uncle and his wife, who were in geographic proximity, were substituted for her brothers, not on the basis of genealogical closeness, but in order to maintain balance. The number of kin in the same genealogical position is also relevant; all the husband's kin were included since there were not many. Finally, the physical facilities influenced the limits of the total number who could be included. As she explained:

> I made a dinner, and, of course, it had to be completely kosher. I had service for 12, but we were 18. We managed, you know; God bless the salad plates.

When the boundaries of the network are fluid, varying with the individual perspective and the occasion, and when so many criteria are employed in deciding where to draw the lines for a specific event, it is not surprising that all parties do not always see the criteria in the same light. As one woman explained, no matter what you do, "You insult somebody anyhow." The intensity of emotion attached to boundary definitions is great, since basic ties of kinship are expressed in each event in which an individual is included or excluded; in addition, these events are often public. In the following description about participation in a wedding, the woman felt that a high moral prerogative was attached to the principle of "genealogical equivalence" and was deeply offended at its violation:

> There are only three grandchildren in the family . . . two granddaughters walked [in the wedding procession] . . . and my daughter didn't . . . No one else was taken out . . . my daughter was most certainly insulted and hurt. . . . Everyone walked up to me and said, "How come Shirley wasn't in the ceremony?" and I said, "Well, she just doesn't rate" and I was very angry about it.

The definitions of boundaries in a group and network differ in a significant way. In a group the boundaries are the same regardless of the particular individual member who is the reference point; individuals are members by virtue of their relationship to the social unit, not just to each other. In a network the boundaries are different from the perspective of each individual; the individuals that are considered kin by one person are not necessarily the same as those considered kin by close relatives of this person, even though they have certain kin in common. Kin within a network do not necessarily have any significant relationship to each other except that they are both related to the specific individual who was the reference point. The only individuals in a society who can have the same network of kin are unmarried siblings. Husbands and wives may come to be incorporated in each other's kin networks, but they bring to the family different perspectives on the issue of who are kin.

The boundaries of the network also differ according to the criteria employed and according to activities: the network may include all those whom the individual is able to name as kin or all those living within a given geographic area, but these kin may be different from those with whom the family exchanges economic services. For every kinship event decisions must be made about who is and who is not to be included as a kin. Thus considerable energy is expended in the process of boundary definition, and inconsistent definitions among kin easily cause conflict.

Despite the elusive nature of the boundaries of the kin network and the incumbent problems, most of the client families can be considered to have large kin networks by almost any of the varying criteria that can be employed. Most have information about a large number of kin, more than has been found in other urban groups. Their genealogies are characterized by a high degree of lateral extension and comparatively little generation depth. In addition, some degree of interaction is maintained with a high proportion of the recognized living kin. Most interaction and closest ties of sentiment are with kin who are closest genealogically but the urban environment by no means restricts all forms of effective social interaction to this narrow genealogical range. On the contrary, the genealogical extension of effective and familiar kin is great for most families. Thus, in fact, as well as in values, clients have an extensive kin network . . .

THE OMNIPRESENCE OF KIN: PROXIMITY AND COMMUNICATION

Geographic Proximity

Kin in the New York City area

None of the research families was completely without kin in the area that they defined as New York City; all mentioned one or more blood kin, implying that all of the families have at least one kin family within the area.

Most families have many more kin in the New York City area. Eighty-six per cent of the research families had 16 or more, and 54 per cent had 31 or more blood kin within the New York City area; many of these kin were married and had families . . .

Kin within walking distance

Distinctions intermediate between the New York City area and walking distance exist. For example, borough demarcations may seem like "a different country." Parts of Long Island were often described as far away, and it is not clear how often this was considered to be within the New York City area. But walking distance was a particularly crucial cutoff. Having kin within walking distance implies that contacts are possible without prearrangement. In such cases kin often meet in the street or are frequently brought together by religious practice. One woman explained about her grandfather:

He went to a synagogue on our street, and he always came to our house on the way, to have coffee my mother had for him.

Living within walking distance makes possible some degree of overlap of household activities, such as joint shopping and exchange of many other services . . .

A high proportion of the client families, 53 per cent, have at least one or more kin households within walking distance. Nearly a quarter had two or three kin households within walking distance; and a few, 6 per cent, had more than three households within walking distance. For some families having kin within walking distance is clearly the result of a conscious decision to live near kin. One woman who lived in a middle-income housing project hoped very much to obtain an apartment in the same project for her mother and father.. She did not wish to have them in the same building because this would give the children too much chance for going to her mother's; however, she did wish to have them in the project where her mother could be within easy reach. She said her mother "is really very anxious to come . . . they will be living with school things and the things that children do. I'll be in and out of her house to see if she needs anything." In this case the elderly parents clearly preferred to live near kin, even though it meant that the husband would have to commute some distance to his work. Thus values of geographic proximity to kin are supported by behavior.

Kin in the same building

Living in the same building with kin constitutes a further degree of geographic proximity that exists for at least some of the client families, 13 per cent of whom have one or more kin households in the same building . . .

Kin in the same household

Living in combined households with kin is clearly not valued by most clients.

At present only 8 per cent of the client families are living in the same household with kin. Most of these do so because kin have moved in with them. However, when examining past residence with kin, the picture is different, providing a clear indication of the importance of looking at family patterns in terms of particular stages of the life cycle. Sixty-one per cent of the client families have had at some time some form of combined household with kin, in contrast to values about combined households.

Combined households with kin occur in a variety of ways. The client families may have moved in with kin, generally with their parents; or kin, usually their elderly parents, may have moved in with the client family. Different reasons predominate for the two forms of combined households. For client stays in the home of kin the most frequent reason given by clients was lack of housing, accounting for 42 per cent. Kin living in the client's home occurred most frequently because of illness, pregnancy, old age, or incapacity, which accounted for 41 per cent of the stays, compared with only 19 per cent of the times when the client stayed in the home of kin. Financial problems and unemployment were most often given as reasons for the clients staying in the homes of their relatives. Military service was another reason given more frequently for staying in the home of kin than for having kin in the client's home. These differences in part reflect the stage of the life cycle in which these two types of residence are most likely to occur . . .

Communication with Kin

In any society a variety of modes of communication are possible. The forms of communication vary with other characteristics of the society, but particularly with its technology. In most primitive societies communication is face to face.

In an industrial society, however, other forms of communication are available.

The telephone is a most important technological invention in our society. Although obvious, its significance has not been fully recognized in theories about society and has not been amply studied. The use of the telephone not only mitigates against diminished contact through distance, it may actually intensify contacts. It makes it necessary to examine geographic proximity of kin in a different light. In an urban area like New York City, the telephone is available at almost all times and places. Within an urban area, particularly within the area of local telephone calls, kin are accessible for interaction, even if they live at some distance, for example, in another borough . . .

Communication by telephone

Kinship values clearly entail the obligation to maintain contact with kin by telephone as well as other means. The telephone is the most readily available mode of contact with kin, and there are definite expectations that it should be used. Failing to communicate by telephone is as much a breach of kinship obligations as any other failure to interact.

The general importance of telephone contact among kin is indicated by the fact that 95 per cent of the client wives maintained telephone contact with kin; of these, 47 per cent listed one or more relatives with whom they talked at least once a day . . . wives are to some extent delegated the task of "representing" the family in kin contacts . . . Women talk with kin more often than men; almost all wives communicate with kin by telephone but fewer husbands do. Only 70 per cent of the husbands indicate that they have some contact with relatives as compared with 95 per cent of the wives

THE BINDING POWER OF ASSISTANCE AND RECIPROCITY

Assistance is a crucial factor binding kin relationships. Economic aid and the gamut of major and minor services—baby sitting, shopping assistance, giving information, help with household repairs, helping with household tasks during illness—are but a few of the main forms of assistance that are regularly exchanged between client families and their kin. Assistance in the form of emotional support is also crucial, but here we will first examine what may be termed instrumental assistance; that is, concrete acts that are directed to carrying out specific tasks. As will be seen, the exchange of instrumental assistance is intimately bound up with emotional ties; instrumental assistance may be symbolic of emotional support. Like other areas of kin relationships, exchange of assistance is interpersonal; it is governed by fundamental and powerful norms about obligations between kin. Severe sanctions may be imposed for failing to live up to these obligations.

In practice, almost all of the client families have relied on kin for assistance. The importance of assistance among kin is reflected in actual behavior as well as in values. Although the specific forms of assistance vary considerably from family to family, related in part to different needs at different life-cycle states, some form of assistance was received from kin in almost all families; 95 per cent of the client families had received services and/ or monetary aid from kin. As shown in the analysis of kinship values, there are strong obligations to assist kin . . .

Alternative Sources of Assistance for the Nuclear Family

Kin are the closest, most intimate part of the social network of most of the clients, having the greatest access to their lives. It is natural to turn to kin unless there are circumstances that make it preferable to turn elsewhere. There were several areas where families more frequently turn to other sources than to kin.

First, there is a tendency to turn to external institutions if the particular type of aid can be obtained better through a specialized institution than through kin. For example, in assistance in getting jobs, kin often do give information, but unions and placement agencies have wider sources of information.

Child-rearing advice is another area in which more families indicated that they turned to sources other than to kin. The immigrant status of their parents and generational differences in values about child rearing create problems in relying on parents. However, interviews indicate that frequently relatives give "a lot of advice even though it's not asked for"; kin feel it is their right and duty to offer child-rearing advice so that there is no need to seek advice. Nonetheless, most families indicated that if they were seeking advice they would turn to other sources. The most frequently checked source was books. No one indicated that he relied on a social worker . . .

Reciprocity in Assistance Among Kin

Instrumental assistance reinforces emotional ties among kin, particularly since assistance among kin is reciprocal. Just as the families we have interviewed rely on kin, so do other families in their kin network. In other words, kin are interdependent for instrumental assistance; reciprocity is basic to interdependence.

Reciprocity in exchanges among kin was clear in questionnaire data. Not only had 95 per cent of the families received some form of economic or service assistance from kin, but 94 per cent of the families had also given some kind of instrumental assistance to kin. No one family necessarily gives and receives the same amount, or gives and receives the same things from the same people. But as a group, families are both giving aid to and receiving aid from kin . . . One may reciprocate for one form of assistance through giving a very different kind . . .

When reciprocity is not in kind, a system of exchange cannot operate unless there are values that make it possible to reckon the equivalence of various kinds of assistance. Complex scales for determining equivalence in exchanges among kin clearly exist and are a vital concern for the clients. The following statement measures equivalence in gift-giving on a number of dimensions:

> We had a catered affair. . . . We had 42 pounds of fish, we had chopped herring and pickled herring. . . . It was really very nice . . . and my sister gave him $25. . . . This was five and a half years after her friend's son was bar mitzvahed. . . . And she gave him the *same*. . . . Just for a sandwich thing. . . . Not even a sandwich . . . tidbits at somebody's house. . . . $25 to a stranger whom you don't know. . . . And she gave her own nephew $25 at this kind of an affair. . . . It hurts me deeply. . . . It rankles.

Several variables enter this calculation; first, the style and expense of the particular form of entertainment; second, the kin or nonkin form of relationship; and third, the monetary value of the gift. The exchange was entirely monetary, but an equal amount of money did not mean equivalence in the overall balance considering all criteria. . . .

In assistance, as well as in the extent of geographic proximity and communication, and the extensiveness of kin ties, almost all client families are deeply involved with their kin.

5

FAMILIAL STRUCTURE VIEWED AS ROLES

"Role" is a concept that complements the previously introduced concepts of "structure" and "function." One writer has provided a useful definition of role as "a part of a social position consisting of a more or less integrated or related sub-set of social norms which is distinguishable from other [sub-sets] of norms forming the same position."[1] Accordingly, the concept of role facilitates the analysis of positions in social systems. Using marital roles as his context, William G. Dyer discusses roles and the positions they comprise from the standpoint of norms, expectations and sanctions, and he suggests how the concept of role can be used in analyzing marital conflict and finding adjustive possibilities.

In a colorful description of life in a Mexican village Oscar Lewis discusses the most important familial roles, the relationships connecting them, and the particular way in which these elements of familial structure interact to fulfill basic societal functions.

The third selection shows the changing role patterns which characterize American families as the spouses progress from marriage to old age. With the arrival of their first child, the young couple adopt the roles of parents. With the passage of time and the ultimate marriage of their last-born, the content of these roles shifts. Moreover, the timing of these shifts is also subject to variation. This is shown by Paul C. Glick and Robert Parke, Jr., as they bring the resources of the U.S. Bureau of the Census to bear on the task of describing the life cycle of the nuclear family in the United States.[2]

The description of "roles" is especially useful for showing how two spheres of life impinge upon each other. Myriad occupational, religious, sex, and political behaviors must be brought into focus if one wants to understand the significance of familial life for the individual.

In the final selections of this chapter William H. Whyte describes the situation of the "company wife" and Mirra Komarovsky depicts the "woman-student." These articles demonstrate that roles are not played out in isolation. Both papers stress the conflict and strain that can result from the conflicting demands of familial and extra-familial role expecta-

[1] Frederick L. Bates, "Position, Role, and Status: A Reformulation of Concepts," *Social Forces*, 1956, 34: 313–321. Quotation is from p. 314. On the general topic of roles see also Bruce J. Biddle and Edwin J. Thomas, *Role Theory: Concepts and Research*. New York: John Wiley & Sons, Inc., 1966.

[2] The life cycle of both the nuclear and the extended families in Japan are subjected to similar analysis in Kiyomi Morioka, "Life Cycle Patterns in Japan, China, and the United States," paper presented at the Sixth World Congress of Sociology, Evian, France, 1966.

tions. Komarovsky enhances our understanding of the "woman" by also showing her as a "student." By describing the wife of a businessman as a "company wife," Whyte helps us appreciate her role as "family wife."

Analyzing Marital Adjustment Using Role Theory[*]

William G. Dyer

. . . Role theory allows us to understand the forms of adjustment that [a newly married couple] in their new roles usually need to make relative to each other. Following are the major factors to be considered in marital adjustment using role analysis as the basic framework:[1]

1. NORMATIVE ORIENTATIONS

The way one behaves in his role in a social situation depends in large measure on his understanding of the cultural norms, or standards of behavior that direct and orient his thinking about the situation. The new husband and wife have learned over a period of years as a result of experience in their own and other families, and what they have read, seen or heard, what constitutes their basic attitudes about family life. Some of these understandings will be mutually agreeable since they have been reared in a common culture and these norms will be shared. Generally the couple will

agree that the marriage should be monogamous, a ceremony should be performed before a legal official, and a number of other norms concerning marriage common in American culture. The indications are that the shared norms are becoming established around patterns of equality with some significant exceptions.[2]

However, the husband and wife through socialization and experience in non-shared social systems may be oriented to normative systems that may be conflicting or at least foreign to the new marriage partner. Nye and Mac-Dougal suggest that each family builds its own sub-culture; thus, the new husband and wife, coming from different family sub-cultures are oriented to a certain set of different normative patterns.[3] Since the new husband and wife are still an important, if not a central part of their parents' family system there will still be some internal and external pres-

[*]Adapted from Journal of Marriage and the Family, 1962, 24: 371–375.

[1]For a more extensive treatment of these elements, see Theodore M. Newcomb, Social Psychology. New York: Dryden Press, 1950. Chaps. 8, 9, 13, 14 & 15.

[2]William G. Dyer, "The Institutionalization of Equalitarian Family Norms," Marriage and Family Living, 20, No. 1 (February, 1958), pp. 53–58.

[3]Ivan Nye and Evelyn MacDougal, "Do Families Have Subcultures?" Sociology and Social Research, 44 (May-June, 1960).

sures to conform to the norms of their particular family of orientation. When we consider that the husband and wife may also be oriented to different religious, social, regional, and political social systems or sub-cultures, it is apparent there is a great possibility that the new husband and wife may be directed by non-shared normative patterns. Since conflicts, disagreements, or misunderstandings may arise out of behavior directed by these non-shared norms, adjustments of these disparate normative orientations is important in marital adjustment.

The situation of adjustment is further complicated when we consider that in addition to the possibility that the new husband and wife are oriented and directed by non-shared normative systems, they may also have certain personal, idiosyncratic beliefs and practices. These behaviors are not normative in the sense they are not a part of a shared system of cultural or sub-cultural patterns. They represent the individual reactions and responses that have become more or less habitual with the person. Each person has his own individual components in the way he dresses, keeps house, reacts to tension, etc. Where these individual reactions irritate, conflict with or otherwise disturb the marital partner, some adjustment is necessary.

2. POSITION-ROLE

Stemming from the norms held by the persons involved, each of the marriage partners comes into the new relationship with certain ideas as to how he or she should behave as a husband or wife. These perceptions of one's role in the new family are often not explicitly stated or understood by the person. . . .

One's role differs from one's norms or personal preferences as shown by this example: It may be agreed that it is part of the wife's role to prepare meals, but disagreements may occur as to what kind of meals should be prepared, how they are served, etc. In this case there is role agreement, but disparity comes either from behaviors that arise out of different sub-culture norms or differnt personal preferences. In a sense the role represents a general set of norms within which are also found a cluster of more specific normative and personal elements.

. . . Position is never divorced from role and the major problems of position differences come as one performs his role in terms of his perception of his position. If a husband feels his position has higher status, he usually transfers these feelings into his role performance. If he is the higher status figure, then he often thinks he should make the final decisions, give the orders, demand favors, etc.

3. ROLE EXPECTATIONS

Not only does each marriage partner enter marriage with certain ideas as to how he should behave in his new position, but each has also certain expectations as to how the other person should behave in his (the other's) role. Role expectations, then, are the ways one person feels the other should behave.[4] In terms of the new marriage relationship, the new husband has some ideas as to how he should behave as a husband (his role) and he also has some idea as to how his wife should behave in her role (his role expectations of his wife). Conversely the wife has some definition of her role and certain expectations of her husband's role.

[4] See Talcott Parsons, *The Social System*. Glencoe: Free Press, 1951, p. 38.

One problem in the matter of role behavior is focused in the question of role definitions vs. role performance. There is often a difference between what is agreed on as to what one should do and what one *actually* does. A husband and wife could both agree that it is part of the husband's role to plan and carry out the recreational activities of the growing boys in the family. In actuality the husband does not do this. It could be maintained that the husband's role is what he actually does in his position, but the expectations of the wife appear, at least at first in the marriage, to be derived from the definition of behavior that is agreed on between them.

In marriage each partner probably starts out with certain expectations as to how husbands or wives in general ought to behave and these generalized expectations are applied to the specific behavior of the other partner. Later, part of the expectations may be altered to include the specialized expectation of specific role elements derived out of their experience together. For example, at first a wife may expect her husband to be a general handyman around the house (derived from her generalized expectations) and is disappointed when he prefers to golf. Later an agreement may be reached that he must at least mow the lawn, wash the car, and replace used light bulbs. If the husband does no 'handyman" type jobs at all he is violating a generalized expectation. If he fails to take out the garbage he is not meeting a specifically agreed on expectation.

It should be pointed out that each partner usually has not only expectations of *what* should be done by the other but also *how* the particular function should be carried out. The wife may not only expect her husband to share in the household tasks but to do it in a cooperative, pleasant manner. Her expectations can be violated should he not perform the task or if he does it in a surly, unpleasant way.

A. R. Mangus in his article on mental health in the family, using a theoretical orientation very similar to the one used here,[5] points out that expectations may also be centered around a conception of the marriage partner as a total personality. Each partner usually has not only expectations of what and how the other person should behave in his role, but also how the other person should be as a person. Conflicts may come when one's self perception does not agree with the perception of the marriage partner. The husband may see himself as efficient, helpful, friendly while his wife sees him as stingy, suspicious and overbearing. If the wife expects her husband to be a certain kind of personality his behavior, manifesting symptoms of a contrary type, will elicit negative reactions from her. The problem is intensified when he cannot understand why she sees him this way because he sees himself so differently.

An important part of this analysis is to try to see expectations as attached to specific role functions rather than becoming generalized around the total person, this may distort her perceptions of him in all his role performances. Under these circumstances, adjustment in the sense to be described below may be difficult to achieve for it is uncertain that the change of role performance on the part of the husband will alter her perceptions of him as a total person although it may be argued that alterations in role performance may be the most effective way for the wife to develop a new conception of her husband.

[5] A. R. Mangus, "Family Impacts on Mental Health," *Marriage and Family Living*, 19 (August, 1957), pp. 256–62.

4. SANCTIONS

Sanctions are the rewards or punishments administered by one person to another to the degree the other person meets or fails to meet his role expectations. In the family situation, if the husband's performance in his role meets the wife's role expectations, she will generally apply positive sanctions or rewards such as praise, affection, good will, etc. If his role performance violates her expectations she will often apply negative sanctions—tears, quarreling, or withdrawal of affection.

It is generally the case, that human interactions move along most smoothly if the following conditions exist: (1) if the parties interacting have a high level of agreement of norms and personal preferences, (2) if the parties involved agree as to the role definitions and role expectations of each other, (3) if the role performance of one is in agreement with the role expectations of the other and positive sanctions are the end result of the interaction.

MARRIAGE ADJUSTMENT

Using the above conceptual scheme, we may now consider marriage adjustment:

A. Points of Conflict

Conflicts in the marriage situation may arise at the following places in terms of the above schema:

1. If the norms and personal preferences of the husband are in conflict with those of the wife.

2. If the role performance of the husband does not agree with the role expectations of the wife.

3. If the role performance of the wife does not agree with the role expectations of the husband.

In each of the above cases dissatisfaction with the marriage relationship may occur with a resulting application of negative sanction. Negative sanctions may be directly or indirectly applied, or these feelings of dissatisfaction may be repressed or directed towards someone or something else. The frustration-aggression hypothesis could be applied here as each of these points of conflict could be sources of frustration.[6]

B. Possible Methods of Adjustment

In each of the above conflict situations, there are certain kinds of adjustments available:

1. In conflict point one, the couple needs to clarify to each other their norms or personal preferences so that each knows exactly the point of view of the other. This of necessity involves mature and extensive communication. To the degree the disparity between norms is translated into role performance the following adjustments would be more applicable.

2. In conflict situations two and three, the possibility of adjustment are the same:

a. The husband (or wife) can change his role performance completely to meet the role expectations of his partner.

b. The husband (or wife) can change his role expectations completely to coincide with the role performance of the partner.

c. There can be a mutual adjustment, each partner altering some. The husband (or wife) can alter his role to a degree and the partner alters his role expectations to a similar degree so that role performance and role expectations are

[6] John Dollard, et al. *Frustration and Aggression*. New Haven: Yale University Press, 1939.

compatible. In each of the above cases the end result is an agreement between role performance and role expectations.

3. There is also another type of adjustment possible. In some cases the couple might recognize a disparity between role performance and role expectations or between norms and also acknowledge that change is difficult or impossible and could "agree to disagree." In such cases the one partner recognizes and respects the position of the other without accepting or adjusting to it. This pattern of "agreeing to disagree" is not adjustment in the same

sense as the others listed above. The "adjustment" comes from both partners agreeing that a certain area is "out of bounds" as far as the application of sanctions is concerned. There is not change in behavior but some change in expectations in that each now expects certain areas not to be raised as issues and that no sanctions will be applied over these "out of bound" issues. This type of adjustment may be possible in certain areas of married life but some areas may be too vital to the relationship not to have reached one of the other types of adjustment. . . .

Familial Roles in Tepoztlán *

Oscar Lewis

Tepoztlán is a family-centered community. The biological family, the predominant type, consists of parents and unmarried children and constitutes the basic production unit of the village. Families in Tepoztlán are strong and cohesive, held together by traditional bonds of loyalty, common economic strivings, mutual dependence, the prospect of inheritance, and, finally, the absence of any other social group to which the individual can turn. Cooperation within the immediate family is essential, for without a family the individual stands unprotected and isolated, a prey to every form of aggression, exploitation, and humiliation known in Tepoztlán. It is within the small biological family that Tepoztecans seek personal security.

The extended family provides some additional security, particularly in times of emergency. It is characterized by a

°Adapted with permission from Oscar Lewis, Tepoztlán: Village in Mexico. New York: Holt, Rinehart and Winston, Inc., 1960, pp. 54–68.

limited reciprocity of cooperation which includes borrowing and labor exchange. No institutionalized day-to-day cooperative endeavors exist between families, related or unrelated, however, and as a rule little aid is given or received. Visiting among relatives is surprisingly infrequent; it is limited to such special occasions as the annual barrio fiesta, illnesses, births, weddings, and deaths.

Over 70 percent of the 662 village housesites are occupied by the simple biological family, only 16 percent by multiple families. Most of the latter consist of parents living with their unmarried children and also with a married son and his family. There are some cases of a married daughter living with her parents and of married siblings sharing a common housesite. The number of persons per housesite ranges from 1 (45 cases, mainly widows or widowers) to 17 (1 case), with smaller households more numerous than larger ones. Most housesites hold a single house, although some have two, three, or four.

Several factors reveal a patriarchal emphasis in family organization: a principle of male superiority (husband over wife, brothers over sisters), a strong preference for patrilocal residence, and patrilineal descent. Tepoztecans are deprecatory of matrilocal residence, saying that when a young man goes to live with his wife's family after marriage "He was given away like a dog" or "He went as a male daughter-in-law." Nevertheless, over 20 percent of all married couples showed matrilocal residence. Most of the husbands in these cases were poor young men, either orphans or men who had married much older women or women of higher social and economic status. Each person in the village is known by the surnames of both his father and mother, but the latter is always given last and with successive generations is eliminated.

The nature of interpersonal relations within the family may perhaps best be understood if we examine them as they occur between husbands and wives, parents and children, among siblings, with the extended family, and with *compadres*.

HUSBANDS AND WIVES

According to the ideal culture pattern for husband-wife relations in Tepoztlán, the husband is authoritarian and patriarchal; he is master of the household and enjoys the highest status in it. He is responsible for the support of the family and for the behavior of its members, and he makes all major decisions. It is his prerogative to be given obedience, respect and service by his wife and children. The wife is expected to be submissive, faithful, and devoted to her husband, and to ask for his advice and permission before venturing on any but the most minor enterprises. She should be industrious and manage to save money no matter how small her husband's income. She should not be critical or jealous of her husband's activities outside the home nor even show any curiosity about them.

In most homes there is outward compliance to the ideal pattern, but few husbands are the dominant figures they seek to be and few wives are completely submissive. Many marriages reveal conflict on the question of authority and the roles of the spouses. The most even-tempered marriages are those which follow a middle course: the wife does little to challenge the authority of her husband and the husband is not too overbearing toward his wife.

Conflicts of this kind between husbands and wives are fostered by a basic discrepancy between actual roles and ideal roles in the organization of the family. Even though the wife is subordinate to her husband, it is she who has the central role within the house. She is responsible for planning, organizing, and managing the household, and for the training and care of the children. The husband traditionally turns over all his earnings to her. She is thus in a position to do a great deal of spending, borrowing, and paying back in secret, particularly since in most cases the husband does not interfere with her handling of the money so long as she gives some to him whenever he asks for it. The "good" wife should not refuse her husband's requests for money; if she does she may receive a scolding or a beating. The wife is free to sell small quantities of the family corn or her own chickens and eggs. She is supposed to obtain her husband's permission before going to a doctor or a *cuarndero*, [native healer] visiting, or buying or selling in quantity, but the husband's frequent absences permit her to do many of these things without his knowledge.

The husband's actual participation in family and household affairs is minimal. His work is outside the home. The division of labor is clear-cut; except for emergencies and for such jobs as hauling water and repairing the house, the husband does not concern himself with the house or the children. The men are gone a good part of the day, sometimes for several days at a time depending on their work and the season of the year. In the past, Tepoztecan men worked in distant mines or on haciendas, and were absent from the village for long periods; before the Revolution, large numbers of men worked on nearby haciendas and returned home only once every two weeks. At present, about 150 men work on haciendas for from four to six months during the dry season, making visits to their homes once a week. With the husband away, the wife not only is head of the family but sometimes also has to support herself and the children.

Even more important perhaps than a husband's absence from his home are his behavior and attitude when he is at home. He avoids intimacy with the members of his family with the purpose of gaining respect from them. He holds himself aloof from the petty details of the household and expects to be undisturbed by complaints, requests, or noise. Unless he is told otherwise, he assumes that the home situation is as he wants it. Since wives are held accountable for everything that happens in the home, they tend to withhold information which might bring them disapproval or punishment. Thus, the loftiness of the husband's position tends to separate him from the very persons he is trying to control and inadvertently to give his wife and children the freedom he does not wish them to have.

In many homes the husband's sense of security is a function of the extent to which he can control his wife and children or make them fear him. Wife beating, more common in the past than now but still widespread, is resorted to for offenses that range from not having a good meal ready on time to suspicion of adultery. A jealous wife or a wife who objects to her husband's activities or judgment may also receive a beating. Wives are not expected to offer any resistance to the punishment. Wife beating is a recognized legal offense in the village but few wives report their husbands to the local authorities.

Tepoztecan women readily express hostility toward men and often characterize all men as "bad." Self-pity and a sense of martyrdom are common among married women, many of whom break down and cry when telling their life stories. As they grow older they often become more self-assertive and oppose their husband's attempts to limit their freedom and their business ventures. They begin to show preference for work outside the home and to feel deprived when they are tied down by housework and children. The present trend in the village is for the younger women and even the unmarried girls to take on the more independent attitudes of the older women.

Women are more in conflict with traditional ways than are the men. Their standards of behavior for themselves and their husbands are changing; they veer between the old ideal roles and new needs and experiences. They readily admit to the superiority of men and tend to admire a man who is *macho* or manly, yet they describe the "good" husband as one who is not dominating but relatively passive. They also tend to regard the very submissive wife more as a fool than as an ideal. Apparently the women do not feel inadequate when they do not achieve the ideal of feminine behavior; indeed, they seem to feel pride rather than guilt in self-assertion.

Husbands often find themselves in a defensive position. They must conserve the old order of things if they are to maintain their control in the home, but the changes within the village in the past twenty years or so make this objective difficult. Such technological advances as the corn mills, the road, and the bus service to Cuernavaca have affected the women more than the men. An increasing number of the more ambitious married women now raise animals, or grow fruit on a larger scale, or sell family produce at the Tepoztlán and Cuernavaca markets. The more capable women are able to help their husbands substantially, in fact, without exception, every man who has prospered since the Revolution has done so with the help of his wife. Most men balk at permitting their wives to sell at the Cuernavaca market, however, despite the fact that the extra money would be welcome. In the past, this type of work was carried on exclusively by widows or women who "had no man to control them," and many of them were promiscuous and had little status. The fear of giving his wife more freedom and the subsequent threat to his role as provider are factors which prevent most men from allowing their wives to earn as much as they might.

Most young husbands are equally unprepared to give their brides of one or two years the freedom and authority they need to assume the responsibility for running independent households. In the past, when young wives lived with their mothers-in-law often for many years, their husbands had little difficulty in controlling them and felt correspondingly more secure. The men are unanimous in believing that women must be kept under strict surveillance if their good behavior is to be assured. Wives are generally forbidden to have female friends, for their husbands see such friends as potential go-betweens for the wife and a lover. Most women discontinue all friendships when they marry, and men may drop their own friends after marriage for fear that an intimacy might develop between the wife and the friend. The majority of husbands are suspicious of any activities that take the wife out of the home. A young wife will often prefer to ask a neighbor or a relative to buy things for her rather than risk her husband's anger or village gossip by going to the market alone. Some young wives now do go out alone but they are considered suspect.

In sexual relations as in social relations, the Tepoztecan husband is expected to take the initiative and his wife to submit to his demands. It is believed that women have less *naturaleza*—that is, that they are sexually weaker than men. Husbands do not expect their wives to be sexually demanding or passionate, nor do they consider these traits desirable in a wife. Women who "need" men are referred to as *loca* (crazy) and are thought to be in an abnormal condition which may have been brought about by black magic. Respectable women properly express negative attitudes toward sex and do so forcefully. Some husbands deliberately refrain from arousing their wives sexually, as it is assumed that a passive or frigid wife will be more faithful. In general, sexual play is a technique men reserve for the seduction of other women.

The husbands' concern about the faithfulness of their wives generally lessens after several years of marriage. As the children get older and can help the mother and as the needs of the growing family increase, however, women frequently demand freedom for carrying on economic ventures. Since such activity necessitates their leaving the house more often, tension and suspicion are again awakened in the husband. Men feel most secure when their wives are pregnant or have an infant to care for; thus to have one child follow close upon another is a desirable state of affairs from the men's viewpoint.

Promiscuous sexual activity is a male prerogative in Tepoztlán, and the men feel under pressure to prove their manliness by having many "affairs." Usually they have extramarital relations with widows or unmarried women, less frequently with married women. Men now go to houses of prostitution in Cuernavaca, and venereal disease is becoming more common in the village. Although male adultery is considered undesirable behavior, it is nevertheless thought to be "natural" and a good wife is not supposed to be disturbed by it. Many women are resentful, however, especially if money is involved, and some openly quarrel with their husband and also withhold money from him. Interference by wives in such matters enrages the men and often results in wife beating.

Drunkenness is not as common in Tepoztlán as it is in surrounding villages or in other parts of Mexico, and it is more strongly disapproved of. Most men drink a small amount of alcohol regularly, but extensive drinking is limited to Sundays, fiestas, or formal occasions. Drinking is nevertheless an important emotional outlet for Tepoztecan men; they drink to get over *muina* or anger after a quarrel at home, to work up courage to punish a wife, to seduce a woman, or to fight with an enemy. Sometimes when the men come home drunk they are aggressive and beat their wives; at other times "because they lack judgment" they are affectionate and kiss and fondle the members of their family. Many wives resent their husband's drunken bouts both because of the probable violence and because of the money involved; only the most aggressive, however, try to break their husband of the habit.

Tepoztecans believe that wives who have suffered beatings or other harsh treatment may take revenge through sorcery, and Tepoztecan men are alert to this possibility. The most commonly feared type of sorcery is a potion made from a well-known herb called *toloache*, secretly dropped into a man's coffee or any other drink. This herb is said to contain a drug that will affect the brain if taken in large doses. In Tepoztlán it is also believed that it will make a man *tonto*—that is, stupid or

foolish and easily managed—and that an extra large dose will make him an idiot. The most important symptom to Tepoztecans is that the drugged man can no longer control his wife but is dominated by her. The man's mother or sister may attempt to cure him by secretly putting a counter-potion into his coffee. It is interesting to note that there is not a single known case of *toloache* given by a man to a woman.

PARENTS AND CHILDREN

Tepoztecan children are brought up to obey their elders and to submit to the will of their mother and father as long as they live under their parents' roof. From infancy on, they are encouraged to be passive and unobtrusive; older children are expected to be self-controlled and helpful. Great emphasis is placed on "good" behavior in children, for it is feared that a child improperly raised will not grow up to be a good worker and will get into trouble. Such a son or daughter is a cause for shame to his parents in the eyes of the community.

The mother is expected to teach the children good habits and to see to their religious training. As far as the children are concerned, family life revolves primarily around the mother. At an early age they learn not to expect to be held by their father or to have much physical contact with him. In many homes the father rules the children through the mother who then becomes the mediator between father and children, relaying requests, instructions, and warnings. The father expects the mother to help maintain his position of respect in the home, and in this most women comply. Children are repeatedly warned by relatives and other adults that the father must be respected. Most children are subdued and inhibited in the presence of their father and remain so well into adulthood. They are less consistent in their behavior toward their mother, thus reflecting her own varying attitudes, for she is at the same time punishing and protective, authoritative and submissive, serving and demanding.

Popular stereotypes in the village depict fathers as "hard" by nature and the mother as "soft." It is thought natural that a mother feels closer to her children than does the father; a mother who abandons her children is considered abnormal or *machorra* (like a man). When a man deserts his children—a more common occurrence—it is disapproved of but not considered a sign of abnormality. Again, the death of a mother is recognized as more disruptive to the household than the death of a father.

According to village culture patterns a mother has more ways of showing affection to her children than a father. She may kiss, fondle, or carry a nursing child as much as she wishes, and if a child is the youngest she may continue this behavior until he is five. She may also express affection through giving food, sewing clothes, nursing illness, and other attentions. Mothers often protect their children by not telling the father of misdeeds or by attempting to stop the father from punishing a child. Such interventions and deceptions are infuriating to the father, but they are nevertheless thought to be "natural" in a mother. In contrast to the mother, a father is limited in his ability to be demonstratively affectionate with his children. Traditionally, a father expresses his affection by buying a child little gifts, giving him pennies, or taking him to the fields or to a fiesta. When a child is ill, the father shows his concern chiefly by agreeing to call in a *curandero*.

Our data show a wide variation in the form and severity of punishments meted out to children. This situation stems from the varying amount of help needed from children in the home and from the differential treatment given boys and girls, older and younger children, and a favorite child. A Tepoztecan child is always punished for flouting the authority of his parents and for unwillingness to work. Other types of misbehavior—grumbling or quarrelsomeness, for example—are not so consistently punished.

Most parents believe in early punishment and begin at about the time the child starts to walk. Infants may be slapped for crying too much, although this is uncommon. Some children receive their first severe beating at three or four years of age, but it is between five and twelve that children are most frequently and harshly punished. After twelve years, punishment is reserved for the most serious offenses. The father inflicts the most severe punishments but the mother punishes more often. Mothers tend to punish daughters more than sons; fathers punish sons more than daughters.

Severe punishment is traditional in Tepoztlán. Some adults in the village remember such punishments as hanging a child in a net over a smoky fire of chile seeds; partial asphyxiation and an illness that lasted for days was the result. (This practice is reminiscent of an ancient Aztec punishment which placed rebellious subjects in a room filled with the fumes of burning chile seeds.) Similarly, a child formerly was punished for breaking a dish by scraping his arms with a piece of the dish until blood was drawn. It is significant of changing attitudes in the village that some of the old practices which had a strong magical component and were not necessarily performed in a spirit of cruelty are today interpreted as cruel. Yet even today beatings with a stick or a rope are not uncommonly given by fathers. Mothers more often hit with their hands, pinch, kick, or throw small stones at offending youngsters. On the whole, Tepoztecans agree that punishment has become less severe and that there is greater toleration toward children's faults. This is particularly true among the more permissive and better-educated younger generation.

Fear is one of the most important means by which Tepoztecan parents control their children. Mothers threaten to desert their children, playing on their fear of being orphans or of having to live with a stepmother. In the days when few visitors or tourists came to the village, children were told that if they were naughty they would be carried off by a stranger who would make them into soap. In the more isolated villages children still run to hide when they see an unfamiliar person. Many mothers and grandmothers tell young children stories of owls and coyotes that come out at night to eat bad children, and of bats and opossums that drink blood. Children who lie or disobey are warned that they will turn into devils and burn in hell. When children cry they may be told the story of Cahuasohuantun who eats the intestines of such children.

Lying and deception play a large part in parent-child relationships. Parents and other adults use deception as another means of controlling children; Tepoztecans actually would be at a loss in raising their children if they were without it. The use of little lies is so common as to be taken for granted, and children early become accustomed to it. Mothers, particularly, tend to make and break promises easily and to trick their children into doing as they wish. The effort of parents to keep their children "innocent," or, as they say, "to keep their eyes from being opened," makes deception necessary. Children, in turn, lie to escape punishment and to assert their own wishes. Moreover, the many restrictions placed upon children encourage lying; there is for example, much deception involved in courtship. Parents show little moral indignation about lying on the part of their children. They do not punish the lie so

much as the misdeed the lie was meant to hide; likewise, a parent or child caught in a lie is ashamed rather of being caught than of having lied.

The frequent use of deception causes some mutual distrust between parents and children. The children seldom confide in their parents, and early stop going to them for help with their troubles or for information. The parents on their part do not encourage the asking of questions, particularly about sex. Absurd or teasing answers are often given to children's questions.

The father assumes an important role in the life of a son when the boy is old enough to go to the fields. Most boys enjoy working in the fields with their father and look forward to it with great pleasure. Fathers are proud to take their young sons to the fields for the first time and frequently show great patience in teaching them. But even when father and sons go to the fields together day after day, there is no weakening of the respect relationship. The father maintains the role of teacher and when he speaks it is to advise. Talk between them about intimate subjects, the telling of jokes, or discussion of women all are strictly taboo, even after the sons are married.

Regardless of age or marital status a son is subject to his father's authority as long as he lives with his father. He receives no recompense other than his support and care and whatever spending money he can manage to procure. Some fathers are generous with sons who do a man's work; others continue to treat them as children. In the past, comparatively few unmarried sons left home to seek work elsewhere; even young men who were acutely dissatisfied with their home situation were reluctant to strike out for themselves. A certain apprehension of the outside world still holds sons at home— fears of falling ill among strangers, of having to do menial work, of not having the family to support them in case of trouble, of not being properly respected by others. Moreover, many boys feel bound to their mothers. Still another factor that prevents sons from leaving home is their economic dependence on their parents and a desire for their share of the inheritance. The dependence is, of course, mutual. Fathers are eager to have their sons at home to help support the family, and in most homes grown sons who work enjoy much the same service and care that the father receives.

Although fathers say they prefer sons to daughters, they not uncommonly show a mild favoritism toward a daughter. Relations between a father and a grown daughter are formal and distant, however, and physical contact is avoided. Kissing and embracing have strong incestuous connotations for both. Even young girls are extremely shy in the presence of their fathers and some married women say they are embarrassed at being seen by their father when they are pregnant. Fathers expect their daughters to be virgins when they marry. Any violation of this moral law is a blot on the father's and on the family's honor and incurs severe punishment.

Mothers more than fathers tend to have favorites among their children; usually they favor boys over girls and small children over grown children. Many mothers try to protect their sons if they think the father works them too hard, but only an occasional mother will interfere in the boy's behalf. It is common for a mother to be indulgent with her youngest child; she may nurse him and sleep with him much longer than the usual period. The indulgence of the youngest child is often in sharp contrast with the treatment of the older children, but generally speaking mothers give partial treatment to all children under five. The small children are given more food and toys and are taken to fiestas and on trips. Although dif-

ferential treatment of children according to sex and age is "accepted" as natural by Tepoztecan parents, there is evidence that habitual or gross displays of favoritism are resented by the other siblings. The resentment finds expression in surreptitious quarreling and fighting, in irritability, in unwillingness to share possessions, and in avoidance of one another.

From early childhood, boys are permitted more freedom of movement and of expression and more leisure for play than girls. The oldest son enjoys a particularly favored position. He receives more care and attention than subsequent sons, and his is often the only birthday other than the father's to be celebrated with a fiesta. But mothers sometimes have difficulty controlling the oldest son, for the boy may imitate his father in demanding service from the women of the family and in giving orders to the younger siblings. If the father dies, the oldest son is expected to take the father's place and to support his mother, brothers, and sisters. An extended struggle for authority as head of the family sometimes ensues between mother and son. Quarrels between mother and son about the inheritance also are apt to arise. Widows who inherit their husband's property have an advantage in the matter of maintaining authority and usually they keep the property until their death lest they lose all control over their sons.

Relations between mothers and daughters are usually very close. As the mother teaches the girl household skills and as they work side by side in the home, the daughter comes to identify with the mother and assume her role. A daughter's attitudes toward work, toward bearing children, and toward men and marriage are strongly influenced by her mother. The custom of having daughters work in the home is a deeply ingrained one, and a girl at home is at the complete disposal of her mother. With few exceptions mothers use their daughters very early for all types of errands and chores. Mothers tend to resent the fact that school takes the girls away from home for the major part of the day, and most parents remove their daughters from school as soon as they can. The majority of girls attend school only through the third grade or until they are eleven. Many mothers exploit their daughters, particularly the oldest, and some girls marry to escape the hard work at home. An occasional mother, however, identifies with her daughter and fulfills her own desire for schooling by allowing the girl to complete elementary school.

A mother is responsible for the chastity and reputation of her grown daughters. To many mothers this translates into a need to spy on them, to chaperone them, and to put pressure on them to conform. If a mother learns that a daughter has a *novio* [sweetheart], she may beat the girl herself rather than inform the father. If, however, a daughter becomes pregnant before marriage, the mother will usually be less harsh and more forgiving than the father. Respect relations between a mother and a daughter forbid them to speak of intimate subjects although not to the same extent as father-daughter relations. Mothers usually do not give their daughters information about menstruation nor discuss the body or any aspect of sexual relations with them. Nor do girls tell their mothers when they first menstruate or ask for information concerning pregnancy, birth, or marriage. When a mother learns that a daughter has begun to menstruate or is pregnant, however, she will offer advice. Mother-daughter relations are considerably weakened when a girl marries, particularly if the girl lives with her mother-in-law. If she leaves her mother-in-law to establish a home of her own, close relations with her mother are usually resumed. Women do not expect financial help from their married daughters but many do receive such help with

or without the knowledge of their sons-in-law.

SIBLINGS

Sibling solidarity is an ideal which parents hold before their children and to which lip-service is constantly given. In childhood, siblings are constant companions, sharing the same friends and the same games. The older children take care of the younger and are held responsible for their safety and well-being but they may not discipline them or exercise much authority over them. If a younger child cries or complains to the parents, the older child is scolded or punished. As a result, older children rarely run to their mothers with complaints or appeals for justice but younger children frequently do so. In the school, however, older children vent their aggression upon younger ones to such an extent that parents are reluctant to send small children to kindergarten.

The oldest sister in particular has the role of caring for the younger siblings and often shows maternal affection toward them; a newly-weaned child may sleep with her for several years. Some older daughters are now rejecting this role, however; they prefer to go to school and tend to be resentful if they cannot. The oldest brother has preferred status and can demand respect and obedience from younger siblings even though the parents try to frustrate his efforts in this direction unless or until he is an adult. The general pattern of male dominance, learned by boys from their fathers, is first put into practice in their relationships with their sisters. As soon as a girl is old enough to do housework, the brother begins to demand service from her just as his father does from his mother. A sister is expected to wash, iron, and mend her brother's clothes, prepare and serve his food, and so forth. Like their father, boys have a lively concern about their sister's "honor" and will beat her if they discover she has a *novio*.

Siblings of the same sex tend to associate with each other. Brothers work in the fields together, share confidences, and if there is no great age difference between them, share the same friends. This pattern is even stronger among sisters. Grown brothers and sisters, however, do not attend fiestas or other public affairs together, do not have mutual friends, and are reserved toward one another in public.

Many brothers and sisters, of course have warm relationships throughout their lives, but in many families sibling relations are poor. Among infants and young children, sibling rivalry and jealousy are so common that parents think them natural and take them for granted. Children are not prepared for the arrival of a new sibling and the pregnancy and birth are kept secret from them. An illness (called *chipilez*) that occurs in infancy is attributed to the child's jealousy of a new sibling. Even before the next baby is born, an illness in a nursing child or in a child being weaned is ascribed to jealousy. It is believed that infants "sense" when another child is expected and that the illness is caused by the fact that they are now "carrying the weight of the baby." Although death from *chipilez* is not infrequent, most children recover a few months after the new baby is born, since then, it is said, "the weight is lifted." If a child continues to cry for his mother and to show hostility to the new baby, he may be sent to live with his grandmother either temporarily or for as long as several years. Temper tantrums, common in the next-to-the-youngest child, also may be stopped in this way. Sometimes a youngest child is the butt of older siblings and for his own protection may be sent to live with his grandmother. The importance of the grandmother as a mother substitute is generally recognized in the village; the child who does not have a grandmother is considered unfortunate.

After marriage a number of factors weaken ties between siblings. Each brother or sister sets up an independent household, often widely separated, and in Tepoztlán practically no institutionalized forms of cooperation exist between married brothers and sisters. As we have seen earlier, only fourteen cases of married siblings living together on a single housesite were noted. Married sisters soon identify with their husband's interests. Moreover, since a married woman is under the authority of her husband, she is no longer free to visit her brothers at will. Brothers are more free to visit, but often there are strained relations between in-laws.

Again, favoritism on the part of the parents toward one or two married children may cause friction among adult siblings. For example, parents may show marked preference for a daughter's children or help a favored married daughter or son more than their other children. Division of inheritance also leads to quarrels among siblings; parents tend to leave more property to sons than to daughters, more to an older son, or to a favorite.

THE EXTENDED FAMILY

During the time a married couple lives with the husband's parents, they have little contact with the wife's family. When they live alone, ties with the wife's family become closer and often supersede those with the husband's family. In any case, however, the closest kinship tie is with the grandmother, whether on the paternal or the maternal side. The importance of the grandmother, especially as a mother substitute, has already been pointed out.

Aunts, particularly maternal aunts,

frequently have an affectionate relationship with nieces and nephews and in emergencies may act as mother substitutes. A boy who has eloped often brings his sweetheart to live with a favorite aunt. Uncles have a respect relationship with their nieces and nephews which may also be an affectionate one. Many children have a favorite uncle who singles them out for an occasional gift or favor. Work exchange between uncles and nephews occurs more often than between married siblings, but quarrels also are apt to occur, particularly over inheritance. After a man's death, a brother will sometimes claim a portion of the property from the widow, especially if her children are still small.

Cousins often have a relationship that resembles that of brother and sister. Parents encourage their children to play with their cousins, especially if they are neighbors; often a person's best and only friends turn out to be one or two favorite cousins. Cousin marriage is forbidden although some cases have occurred.

IN-LAWS

Because of patrilocal residence, the mother-in-law and daughter-in-law relationship is the most important of all in-law relationships. When a young bride goes to live with her husband's family, she is expected to take the role of a grown daughter and give her parents-in-law the same respect and obedience she gave her own parents. The mother-in-law assigns her work to her; generally it consists of the most burdensome tasks—grinding corn, making tortillas, and washing and ironing clothes for the entire family. In the past, when girls married at twelve or thirteen, they were unskilled and the mother-in-law taught them housework. The mother-in-law for her part must look

after her daughter-in-law when she gives birth and must chaperone the daughter-in-law and see to it that she remains a faithful wife. Many jokes depict the mother-in-law as a "policeman."

Although many mothers-in-law and daughters-in-law manage to get along fairly well, the relationship is a charged one and is recognized as such by Tepoztecans. Both women approach it with apprehension. Girls hear their mothers and other married women say that the daughter-in-law is the mother-in-law's "slave." They are afraid that they will not be able to please their mother-in-law and that they will feel like an outsider in a strange house. The mother-in-law fears that the girl her son brings home will be lazy, just another mouth to feed, or that she will be critical of the way the family lives.

Often the fears are justified and quarrels are the result. Perhaps this is even more true today than in the past because of the different standards of dress, cleanliness, and personal freedom held by younger and older women. Increasingly, the way out of an unpleasant situation for both is to separate the households. If the wife cannot persuade her husband to move and if her situation becomes intolerable, she returns to her parents' home. It is believed in the village that many marriages have been broken because the mother-in-law and daughter-in-law could not get on together. Father-in-law and daughter-in-law relations are similar to father-daughter relations but even more reserved.

Relations between the wife's parents and their son-in-law depend more on personal factors than on formal obligations, with exception of the usual respect obligations. In the past, the son-in-law was required to provide his father-in-law with wood and water for two years as part of the bride price. Now any work done by the son-in-law is voluntary and usually is limited to times when the father-in-law is ill or in need. If the mother-in-law is widowed and has property, the son-in-law may help her farm; if she has no means of support, a good son-in-law may help support her or invite her to live in his home.

Tepoztecan men are wary of their mothers-in-law. They think of her as a meddlesome, trouble-making figure and prefer to keep the relationship a distant one. Actually, most mothers urge their married daughters to try to please their husbands and to bear up under domestic difficulties. Fathers are more apt than mothers to feel a personal affront if their daughter is ill-treated by a son-in-law.

Relations between sisters-in-law and brothers-in-law are not formalized and depend largely on personal factors. Sisters-in-law, whether the wives of two brothers or the husband's wife and sister, are thrown together more often than brothers-in-law. In some families the wives of brothers compete for the esteem of the mother-in-law and carry tales about each other to her. Quarrels over inheritance involve the sisters-in-law as much as the siblings.

GODPARENTS, GODCHILDREN, AND CO-PARENTS

The system of *compadrazgo* establishes two sets of formal relationships between nonrelatives: the one is between "spiritual" godparents (*padrinos*) and their godchildren (*ahijados*); the other a relationship known as *compadres* or co-parents, is between the parents and the godparents. The general purpose of godparents is to provide security for the godchild. The godparents are in effect an additional set of parents who will act as guardians and sponsors of the godchild, care for him in emergencies, and adopt him if he is orphaned. In Tepoztlán, however, the relationship between *compadres* is much more functional and important than that between the godparent and godchild.

Godparents address their godchildren in the familiar *tu* and are addressed by the respectful *Usted*. Traditionally the godchild kissed the godparent's hand at each meeting, but this is no longer common. The godparent usually gives the child a few centavos when they meet, but many children actually never receive anything from their *padrinos*. *Compadres* address each other with the respectful *Usted;* theirs is a reciprocal respect relationship and in this lies its strength, for such a relationship is highly desirable to Tepoztecans. By respect, Tepoztecans mean a recognition of high and equal status and the avoidance of intimacy or undue familiarity. The latter includes joking and discussing sex or any other subjects of a personal nature. Compadres also may not drink together. They do often exchange favors, and borrowing between them is probably more frequent than between kin. At the death of one *compadre* the other is supposed to contribute toward the funeral expenses. *Compadres* invite each other to barrio fiestas and treat each other with special deference. Tepoztecans prefer *compadres* who are neither neighbors nor relatives; most *compadres* come from other barrios.

The three most important types of godparents in Tepoztlán are those of baptism, confirmation, and marriage. Reliable persons are sought as godparents of baptism. The husband's parents usually select the godparents of baptism for the first child, but as the couple grows older the husband may make the selection and often friendship rather than higher economic status dictates his choice. The godparents of baptism are obliged to assist at the baptism, to buy the infant's clothing for the occasion, and to pay the priest's fee. They also accompany the mother and child to the *sacamisa*, or first

Mass, forty days after the birth. If the child dies, the godparents arrange for the wake, dress the body for burial, and contribute to the funeral expenses. An important obligation of godparents is to urge their *compadres* to send the child to school when the time comes. If the child needs punishing, the parents may ask the godparents to scold him. The godparents of confirmation are usually selected by the godparents of baptism; occasionally the latter accept both roles. The godparents of marriage assist at the wedding and act as mediators if the couple later quarrels or separates.

One of the distinctive aspects of the *compadre* system in the village, and in fact in Mexico as a whole, is the way in which it has been extended far beyond the original Catholic forms. In most of Spain, only two or three types of godparents, popularly those of baptism, communion and confirmation, are known. In Tepoztlán, in addition to the three above, there are the following: godparents of *miscoton* (a Nahuatl term which refers to a small sweater which the godparent puts on the child to protect him from illness); of *medida* or *listón* (these terms refer to a small piece of ribbon, blessed by the priest, which is placed on a sick child as a charm); of *evangelio* (a woman of "bad"

reputation is asked to become godmother to a sick child and to pray in the church for his recovery); of *scapulary;* of the Child Jesus; and so on. The godparent system has been extended to secular activities as well. At soccer and basketball games each team has its godmother who dresses in white, carries flowers, acts as the sponsor, and hands out prizes to the winners. At social dances godmothers act as chaperones.

Social, economic, and political factors may enter into the operation of the *compadre* system. Poor families look for better-to-do godparents for their children. Similarly it is thought desirable to have a *compadre* from the city, for it is assumed that a city family can be of greater help in time of need. The more godchildren a man has, the more *compadres* and the wider circle of persons who can be counted on for favors. For this reason anyone who aspires to a position of leadership in the village must have many godchildren. There is some feeling against using the *compadre* system in this fashion, however, and some villagers consider having many *compadres* as a burden. In this case they try to limit their *compadre* relations by asking one or two families to serve as godparents for several children.

New Approaches in Studying the Life Cycle of the Family *

Paul C. Glick and Robert Parke, Jr.

The life cycle of the family has been widely accepted as a framework for the study of the conjugal family.[1] This orientation provides a means for analyzing the changes which take place in the composition and economic characteristics of fami-

°*Adapted and reprinted from* Demography, 1965, 2: 187–202.

[1]Among the pioneers in using the concept of the life cycle of the family were the rural sociologists. See especially Charles P. Loomis and C. Horace Hamilton, "Family Life Cycle Analysis," *Social Forces,* XV (De-

lies from marriage through childrearing, children leaving home, the "empty nest" period, and the final dissolution of the family. Over the decades for which data are available, marked changes have been observed in the age at marriage, in the size of completed family, and in life expectancy, and these changes have modified the characteristic ages at which husbands and wives reach the several stages of the family life cycle.

This paper features revised and updated estimates of the trends in the family life cycle stages during the twentieth century, based on the latest available survey data and on revised techniques for estimating the intervals between the stages. It also presents new data, based on the 1960 Census, on the typical patterns of change in family composition and economic characteristics from the beginning to the end of the cycle . . .[2]

STAGES OF THE FAMILY LIFE CYCLE

Marriage and Childbearing

Survey data on marriage and childbearing histories obtained in the Census Bureau's *Current Population Survey* in 1959 provide the best recently available basis known to the authors for calculating median ages of women at first marriage, birth of the first child, and birth of the last child for women who have passed, or nearly passed, through the childbearing ages. These data, together with other family life cycle measures, are shown in Table 1 [p. 169] and Tables 2 and 3 [p. 171].

The estimates of typical ages for the family life cycle stages are presented here for birth cohorts of women (women born in a given period), whereas earlier estimates were prepared for a given calendar year. The availability of data on age at marriage and age at birth of first and last child for birth cohorts of women made it natural to seek ways to cast figures on the later stages of the family life cycle in the same terms. In addition, the use of birth cohorts was chosen because it eliminated

---

cember, 1936), pp. 225–31. Earlier writings by Paul C. Glick on this subject include "The Family Cycle," *American Sociological Review*, XII, No. 2 (April, 1947), pp. 164–74; "The Life Cycle of the Family," *Marriage and Family Living*, XVIII, No. 1 (February, 1955), pp. 3–9; and *American Families* (New York: John Wiley & Sons, 1957), chaps. iii–v.

See also Paul C. Glick, David M. Heer, and John C. Beresford, "Family Formation and Family Composition: Trends and Prospects," in Marvin B. Sussman (ed.), *Sourcebook in Marriage and the Family* (Boston: Houghton Mifflin Company, 1963), pp. 37–10. A comprehensive treatment of the subject is found in Evelyn M. Duvall, *Family Development* (2d ed.; New York: J. B. Lippincott Co., 1962). See also Roy H. Rodgers and Reuben Hill, "The Developmental Approach," in *Handbook of Marriage and the Family*, ed. Harold Christensen (Chicago: Rand McNally & Co., 1964), chap. v; Lowry Nelson, *Rural Sociology* (2d ed.; New York: American Book Co., 1955), pp. 307–12; and Andrew Collver, "The Family Cycle in India and the United States," *American Sociological Review*, XXVIII, (February, 1963), pp. 86–96.

[2] The chief sources of data used in this paper are as follows: U.S. Bureau of the Census, *U.S. Census of Population; 1960; Detailed Characteristics, United States Summary*, Final Report PC(1)-1D, Tables 177–82 and 224; *Families*, Final Report PC(2)-4A, Tables 4–6, 9, 13, 15, 46, and 58; *Persons by Family Characteristics*, Final Report PC(1)-4B, Tables 4, 5, 10, 12, and 24; and *Sources and Structure of Family Income*, Final Report PC(2)-4C, Table 1; also U.S. Bureau of the Census, "Marriage, Fertility, and Childspacing: August 1959," *Current Population Reports*, Series P-20, No. 108, Tables 5–8, 13, 16, 17, and 23.

certain conceptual problems in the preparation of measures for a calendar year. The calendar year approach probably is satisfactory where patterns of marriage, childbearing, and survivorship are stable. Where, as in recent American history, these patterns have altered substantially, the meaning of intervals calculated from available calendar year data is open to question.

For example, the women who married in the 1940's did so at a median age about one year older than the women who married in the 1950's. This difference is reflected in ages at completion of childbearing. A majority of the women who married in the 1940's completed childbearing in the 1950's, and this fact is reflected in the data presented here. A presentation organized in terms of calendar years, as in the earlier studies, would relate age at marriage in the 1950's to age at completion of childbearing in the 1950's, a period with a quite different pattern of age at marriage than the 1940's.

The trend in the median age of women at first marriage shown in Table 1 was downward from 21.6 years for women born from 1880 to 1889 to 21.1 years for women born from 1900 to 1909, after which it rose to 21.7 years for women born from 1910 to 1919, most of whom were first married in the depression of the 1930's. Thereafter it declined, and projections based on the partial experience of the women born from 1930 to 1939 indicate an ultimate median age at first marriage of 19.9 years for this cohort.

Figures for men are not available on a basis comparable with those for women in Table 1, but estimates based on census figures indicate that the long-term decline in age at first marriage has been greater for men than for women. For males, the median age at first marriage was 26.1 years in 1890 but dropped 3.3 years to a median of 22.8 by 1960. For females the 1890 figure was 22.0 years, as compared

with a 1960 figure of 20.3 years, a drop of only 1.7 years.[3]

The trend in the median spacing of the first child is as follows . . .

Year of First Marriage	Median Years Marriage to Birth of First Child
1900–09	1.5
1910–19	1.4
1920–29	1.5
1930–39	1.7
1940–49	1.6
1950–59	1.3

. . . The figure for marriages in the 1950's is projected from incomplete experience.

The figures on median age of mother at birth of last child, shown in Figure 1 and Table 1, show a major decline in age at completion of childbearing, followed by a partial reversal. For the oldest cohort shown, the median age of mother at completion of childbearing was 32.9 years. The figure declines to 30.4 years for mothers born from 1900 to 1909 and subsequently rose to 31.5 years for mothers born from 1910 to 1919, paralleling the increase in median ages at marriage and birth of first child for this cohort. This increase appears to have been a temporary phenomenon, attributable to the particular experience of this cohort, most of whose marriages occurred in the depression years of the 1930's.

The median age at completion of childbearing for younger cohorts is necessarily unknown. However, the projected figure (based on partial childbearing histories) for the women born from 1920 to 1929 indicate that, on the average, these women will have their last child at some time during the twelve-month period when the woman is thirty years old. If this projection proves to be fairly accurate,

[3]U.S. Bureau of the Census, "Marital Status and Family Status: March 1962," *Current Population Reports*, Series P-20, No. 122, Table C.

TABLE 1   Median age of women at selected stages of the family life cycle, for women born from 1880 to 1939, by year of birth

Subject	Year of birth (birth cohort) of women					
	1880 to 1889	1890 to 1899	1900 to 1909	1910 to 1919	1920 to 1929	1930 to 1939
First marriage	21.6	21.4	21.1	21.7	20.8[1]	19.9[1]
Birth of first child	22.9	22.9	22.6	23.7	23.0[2]	21.5[2]
Birth of last child	32.9	31.1	30.4	31.5	30.0-31.0[3]	(NA)
First marriage of last child [4]	56.2	53.5	51.9	53.0	51.5-52.5	(NA)
Death of one spouse: For all couples [5]	57.0	59.4	62.3	63.7	64.4	64.4
For couples surviving to first marriage of last child [6]	69.2	63.1	67.8	68.2	67.2-68.2	(NA)

[1] Projected from partial experience on assumption that 96 percent of the cohort will ultimately marry.

[2] Projected from partial experience on assumption that 90 percent of all women in the cohort (including single) will ultimately become mothers.

[3] Projected as follows: Assuming that 48 percent of all women in this cohort (including single) will ultimately have a third child, partial experience to date indicates an ultimate median age of women at birth of the third child of 28.1 years. The median age of mothers in the cohort of 1900-09 and 1910-19 at birth of their last child of any order exceeded the median age at birth of their third child by an average of 2.4 years. This figure added to 28.1 gives 30.5 years, the center of the projection range shown.

[4] Assumes woman has last child at median age for cohort and last child marries at estimated median age at first marriage for children (see text).

[5] Assumes wife first married at median age for cohort to husband 3 years older.

[6] Measure applies to couples surviving jointly to median age of women at marriage of last child.

this group of women will complete childbearing at a younger median age than did the women born in the preceding decade.

The difference between the figures for median age at completion of childbearing and median age at first marriage provides a good index, if not an exact measure, of the median number of years from first marriage to completion of childbearing (Table 2).[4] This series follows a

[4] Figures based on a differencing of median ages at first marriage and completion of childbearing compare favorably with median intervals from first marriage to completion of childbearing from the 1959 survey for marriage cohorts of women that correspond in an approximate fashion to the birth cohorts of 1880–89 to 1910–19:

pattern of decline and partial recovery that is roughly parallel to the trend in completed family size. The 1959 survey, together with a projection for the youngest cohort shown, yields the figures shown in the accompanying tabulation for average number of children per woman ever

Marriage Cohort	Median Interval (Year)
1900-09	11.6
1910-19	9.1
1920-29	8.1
1930-39	9.1

The movement of both series is similar, but the range of variation between the highest and lowest level is greater when marriage cohorts are used.

married by the end of the childbearing period.

Year of Birth of Woman	Completed Fertility
1880-89	3.4
1890-99	2.8
1900-09	2.5
1910-19	2.5
1920-29	3.1

The relatively sharp increase in the fertility of the youngest cohort is not accompanied by any correspondingly sharp increase in the average interval from marriage to completion of childbearing projected for this cohort. This pattern may reflect, in part, a reduction in the average spacing interval per child, as compared with the cohort ten years older. It remains to be seen how figures on family size projected for even younger cohorts will affect the interval to completion of childbearing. Even assuming some shortening of the average spacing interval per child, it seems unlikely that the family size of 3.4 to 3.7 children per woman ever married projected for the women born in the 1940's can be achieved without lengthening the average period of childbearing and (barring unforseen declines in marriage age) increasing the average age at completion of childbearing.

Although the presentation thus far has concentrated on median ages at first marriage and at childbearing, both marriage and childbearing are subject to ranges of variation as shown in Figure 2 and Table 3. A conspicuous narrowing is apparent for the youngest two cohorts in the range between the first and third quartiles of age at first marriage; one-half the first marriages occur between these ages. The interquartile range was stable at a little over 6.0 years for the oldest four cohorts but narrowed to 4.7 years for the women born from 1920 to 1929 and to 4.0 years for those born from 1930 to 1939. It remains to be seen whether this increas-

ing homogeneity with regard to marriage patterns will be reflected in greater homogeneity with regard to age at completion of childbearing. The data show relatively minor fluctuations in the interquartile range for age at birth of last child, but these data do not include the young cohorts who have not yet completed childbearing, among whom the greatest change may be expected in the future.

Some women, of course, bear no children. The general trend in childlessness for the cohorts shown in this paper has been downward. About 23 percent of all women (including single) in the cohort of 1880–89 bore no children. The figure rose slightly to 26 percent for the women born from 1900 to 1909 and has been consistently downward since then. Projections for the women now in the middle of their childbearing indicate that they may complete childbearing with as few as 10 percent childless.

Children Leaving Home

The marriage of the last child in the family typically brings the number of members back down to the original couple, on the likely assumption that both the husband and wife have survived and are living together. Because of the variations in ages at marriage, size of family, spacing of children, and the spacing of the children's marriages, there can, of course, be a rather broad range of the ages of parents when their last child leaves home. Consequently, the data in Table 1 for age of the mother when her last child marries and the associated number of years from the mother's marriage to that of her last child (Table 2) are more of an abstraction than the values given for marriage and childbearing. The values for ages when the last child leaves home are actually illustrative figures that apply to mothers who had their last child

TABLE 2 Median number of years between selected events in the family life cycle, for women born from 1880 to 1939, by year of birth of woman

Subject	Year of birth (birth cohort) of woman					
	1880 to 1889	1890 to 1899	1900 to 1909	1910 to 1919	1920 to 1929	1930 to 1939
For all couples.						
First marriage to birth of last child	11.3	9.7	9.3	9.8	9.2-10.2	(NA)*
First marriage to death of one spouse	35.4	38.0	41.2	42.0	43.6	44.5
For couples surviving to marriage of last child:						
First marriage of couple to marriage of last child	43.6	32.1	30.8	31.3	30.7-31.7	(NA)
First marriage of last child to death of one spouse	13.0	14.6	15.9	15.2	15.2-16.2	(NA)

SOURCE: Same calculations as Table 1.

* (NA) Not available.

TABLE 3 Quartiles of age of women at first marriage and age of mothers at birth of last child, for women born from 1880 to 1939, by year of birth of woman

Subject	Year of birth (birth cohort) of women					
	1880 to 1889	1890 to 1899	1900 to 1909	1910 to 1919	1920 to 1929	1930 to 1939
Age at first marriage[1]						
First quartile	18.9	18.9	18.5	18.8	18.7	18.1
Second quartile (median)	21.6	21.4	21.1	21.7	20.8	19.9
Third quartile	25.2	25.1	24.8	25.2	23.4	22.1
Interquartile range, year	6.3	6.2	6.3	6.4	4.7	4.0
Age at birth of last child						
First quartile	27.4	26.4	25.2	26.6	(NA)*	(NA)
Second quartile (median)	32.9	31.1	30.4	31.5	30.0-31.0	(NA)
Third quartile	38.2	36.1	36.1	36.0	(NA)	(NA)
Interquartile range, year	10.8	9.7	10.9	9.4	(NA)	(NA)

SOURCE: Derived from U.S. Bureau of the Census, Current Population Reports, Series P-20, No. 108.

* (NA) Not available.

[1] Data for cohorts of 1920-1929 and 1930-1939 projected from partial experience on assumption that 96 percent of women will ultimately marry.

at the median age for the cohort and whose last child first married at the estimated median age for children.[5]

[5] The median age of the last child at first marriage was assumed to be the median age at first marriage of women born thirty years after the cohort in question, plus an allowance for the difference between the median age at first marriage for females and that for all children. The following example of the calculation of median age of mother at marriage of the last child relates to the women born from 1890 to 1899:

Women born from 1920 to 1929 may be about fifty-two years old, on the average, when their last child marries. The corresponding age was about fifty-six years for the oldest cohort shown. The currently younger age of the parents when their children leave home reflects the combined effect of several factors. The effect of the declining age at first marriage is the most obvious. There is also some evidence that the women who were in the midst of childbearing at the time of this writing were spacing their children more closely than their predecessors. In addition, the trend in average family size, which has been downward for most of the cohorts shown, has tended to reduce the age of mothers when the last child leaves home. However, anticipated future increases in family size may very well result in some increase in this age.

Dissolution of the Family

Improving survivorship has resulted in revolutionary changes in the average duration of married life, and this factor, together with changes in patterns of marriage and childbearing, has resulted in some lengthening of married life after the last child leaves home.

Two measures of survivorship are shown in Figure 1 and Table 1. Both measures describe the age of the wife at the death of one spouse; that is, at her death or that of her husband, whichever

Median age of mother at birth of last child, cohort of 1890–99	31.1
Median age at first marriage, cohort of 1920–29	20.8
Allowance for difference between median age at first marriage for females and that for all children	1.6
Median age at marriage of last child	53.5

The median age at first marriage for cohort of 1930–39 was used in estimating the median for children of the cohorts of 1900–1909 to 1920–29.

comes first. (These measures assume that the marriage is not previously broken by divorce or annulment.) Median age of wife at the death of one spouse *for all couples* is an illustrative figure that applies to married couples in which the wife was first married at the median age for the cohort, shown in Table 1. The measure reflects mortality rates for all ages following first marriage. Median age of wife at the death of one spouse *for couples surviving to first marriage of last child* is an illustrative figure that applies to couples surviving jointly to the estimated median age of women at the marriage of the last child. This measure reflects mortality rates only for the ages of the couple after the last child marries.

In this century there has been an increase of nine years in the average number of years that husband and wife live together, according to the figures on median years between marriage and the death of one spouse for all couples shown in Table 2. In the oldest group of women, the median of 35.4 years of married life for all couples was only slightly greater than the median interval of 34.6 years for surviving couples between their marriage and the marriage of their last child. In the oldest group, in other words, only about one-half of all couples survived to the median age at which the surviving couples saw their last child married. The effect of the increase in survivorship has been to increase greatly the proportion of couples enjoying many years of married life after the last child leaves home.

Despite this fact, the average number of child-free years during middle age has increased only moderately for couples who survive jointly to the time when their last child marries. Under current conditions, a couple has perhaps sixteen more years together after the last child marries, as compared with thirteen years for the oldest cohort shown. The corresponding age of wife at dissolution of the couple through death has not shown a comparable rise—in fact, it is level or declining slightly, as shown by the top line of Figure 1 and by Table 1. This interesting result is a consequence of the decline in the median age of the mother when her last child marries.

The approach employed here is not amenable to calculation of median ages at widowhood and still less to calculation of median duration of widowhood before death. . . . A computation of Meyers,[6] using life tables for 1949–51, shows that 65.3 percent of brides eventually become widows at an average age of 61.2 years and that these widows have an average (mean) period of widowhood before death of 18.7 years. The corresponding figure for the period of widowerhood, in the event that the husband survives, was 14.2 years.

Summary of Findings on Life Cycle Stages

Changes during the twentieth century in age at marriage, size of completed family, spacing of children, and life expectancy have had substantial effects on the life cycle of the average family. The youngest women for whom data are available compare as follows, on the average, with women who are forty to sixty years older: The youngest women marry one to two years younger and complete their childbearing two to three years younger; their age at the marriage of their last child is four to five years younger, and their length of married life is about nine years longer. As a consequence of the generally upward trend in fertility during the last two decades, present indications point to a return by women now in the midst of childbearing to an average family size not

[6]Robert J. Myers, "Statistical Measures in the Marital Life Cycles of Men and Women," *International Population Conference: 1959* (Vienna: Christopher Reisser's Sons), pp. 229–33.

far from that of two generations ago but with the children spaced somewhat closer together.

Labor Force Participation of Wife

Many of the family life cycle patterns, especially well exemplified by the labor force participation of the wife, occur in the form of a modified bell-shaped curve. The changing proportion of wives who are the labor force, shown in Figure 1,[7] deviates from the bell shape in the early years of marriage, when a larger proportion of wives is employed than a few years later when more of them are preoccupied with the rearing of children.

The basic similarity of the pattern when measured by two different methods is also illustrated by the labor force participation data in Figure 1.[8] Thus, regardless of whether the cycle is based on age of the husband or on number of years since the first marriage of the husband, essentially the same conclusion would be drawn about the characteristic rhythm of the labor force participation of wives outside the home. Yet there are some minor differences between the two curves, particularly for the younger families, which can be readily explained as an indication that labor force participation of young wives is somewhat more closely related to duration of marriage than to age of the husband.[9]

[7]Based on U.S. Bureau of the Census, *Families*, Tables 11 and 46.

[8]A third method of describing the family life cycle is used in Fig. 5.

[9]In plotting the two curves in Fig. 3, where the units of measurement of the independent variables are not the same, the distances on the horizontal axis were determined by the percent of all husband-wife families which were in the specified age group or marriage-duration group. Thus, the points were plotted at the midpoints of the cumulative percentages of cases in the specified

Establishing a Home

The index chosen for demonstrating the gradual process of establishing a more or less permanent home is the proportion of husband-wife families which were living in the same house in both 1955 and 1960 (Figure 2).[10] As the age of the husband increased, the proportion of families in the same house rose continuously, with no decline at the upper ages. Specifically,

need and willingness of young than older families to resettle. The circled values shown in the graph demonstrate that extremely small proportions of young husbands who had been married during the five years before the 1960 Census were still in the same house in which they had lived five years earlier—regardless of their ages in 1960.

Curves of increase in home ownership with advancing age of husband and

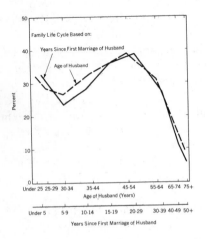

FIG. 1. Percent of husband-wife families with wife in labor force (United States, 1960)

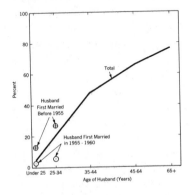

FIG. 2. Percent of husband-wife families with husband in same house 1955 and 1960 (United States, 1960)

only about 21 percent of the husbands 25–34 years old in 1960 were still living in the same home as five years earlier, whereas about 76 percent of those 65 and over remained in the same home. These figures provide a measure of the greater

groups. The same procedure was followed in all subsequent groups for uniformity of presentation. John B. Lansing and Leslie Kish use this procedure in comparing different measures of the life cycles of the family in their article, "Family Life Cycle as an Independent Variable," *American Sociological Review*, (1957) XXII, pp. 512–19.

[10] Based on U.S. Bureau of the Census, *Families*, Table 58.

with higher durations of marriage, not shown here, closely resemble the curve of residence in same house shown in Figure 4. In 1960, about one in every five of the couples married less than two years who had established a home also owned their home. This proportion rose to two in every five couples married two to four years, nearly three in every five married five to nine years, and nearly three out of every four married twenty years or more. All but 13 percent of the married couples in 1960 who had been married less than a year had established a separate home (that is, a home which was not maintained by relatives or nonrelatives). Corresponding proportions for those married one, two, three or four, five to nine, and ten years or more were 9, 6, 4, 2, and 1 percent, respectively.[11]

Rearing Children

During the first twenty-five years of married life, more than one-half of the husband-wife families have young children in the home (Figure 3).[12] Of those married less than five years in 1960, two-thirds had one or more children. The peak of childrearing is between five and twenty years after marriage, when about 85 percent of the husband-wife families in 1960 had some sons or daughters under eighteen at home. Thereafter the proportion with children still in the parental home drops off sharply.

Nonwhite families differ considerably from white families in the proportion with young children at home during the middle and late phases of the family life cycle. At the peak of the childbearing period, about 10 percent fewer of the nonwhite than of the white husband-wife families in 1960 had any sons or daughters under eighteen living with them. This fact is a reflection in part of the higher proportion of childlessness among nonwhite families. However, about twice as large a proportion of nonwhite than white husband-wife families with the husband married thirty to forty years still had some of their young children at home. This, in turn, reflects the fact that a higher proportion of nonwhite mothers continue to bear children into the upper portion of the reproductive period and to have larger families.

[11] See U.S. Bureau of the Census, *Families*, Tables 5 and 15, and *Persons by Family Characteristics*, Table 24.

[12] Based on U.S. Bureau of the Census, *Families*, Table 9.

Earning a Living

The curve of average family income from all sources rises as the husband-wife family proceeds through its life cycle, reaches a peak when the husband is between 45 and 55 years of age, falls gradually, and then falls more abruptly until it reaches a point during the advanced years that is below the level for the young family (Figure 4).[13] The same generalization applies when average family income is measured in terms of either the mean or the median. The difference between the two measures is slight for young families —among whom there are relatively few really high incomes—but the ratio of mean income to median income rises as the husband grows older until the mean is over half again as high as the median for families with the husband 75 years old and over. For most of the families with the husband at the upper ages, family income consists increasingly of money obtained from sources other than employment.

Income per family member is, in some respects, a better indicator of the changing economic well-being of the family at successive stages of the family life cycle than is income per family. As shown in Figure 6, income per family member rises very little during the period when the family is expanding in size, though income per family tends to rise more than one-half during the same period. Then, as family size contracts while family income remains at or near its peak, income per family member rises until it reaches its peak when the husband is 55–64 years old.[14]

[13] Based on U.S. Bureau of the Census, *Detailed Characteristics, United States Summary*, Table 224; *Families*, Tables 4 and 13; *Persons by Family Characteristics*, Tables 5 and 12; and *Sources and Structures of Family Income*, Table 1.

[14] As indicated above, income per family reaches its peak when the husband is 45–

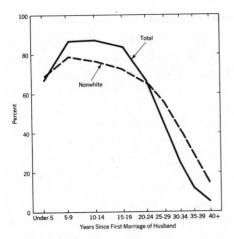

FIG. 3. Percent of husband-wife families with own children under 18 years old (United States, 1960)

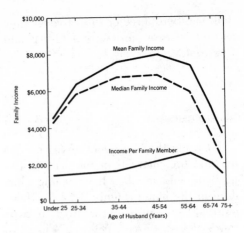

FIG. 4. Mean and median family income and income per family member, for husband-wife families (United States, 1960)

The wide range in economic well-being of families in the upper as compared with the lower income strata during successive family life cycle stages and the differences in age of husband at the time of peak family income are portrayed vividly in Figure 5.[15] Median family income for husband-wife families according to the 1960 Census was just under $6,000, whereas the lowest tenth of families had less than $2,000 income and the top tenth had more than $12,000. Where the husband was under 35, upper income families tended to fare better economically if there were no children in the home, perhaps as a consequence in part at least of the greater freedom of childless wives than

mothers to work outside the home; yet young lower income families did not show a similar pattern, perhaps in part because childless wives in impoverished homes may have great difficulty finding employment. As may have been expected,

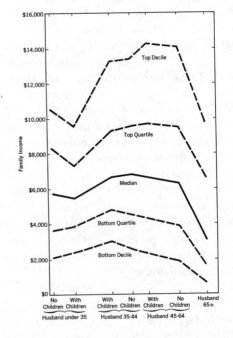

54, on the average. Thereafter it declines as the husband grows older. Mean income per family member of the oldest age group of husbands is virtually the same as that for the youngest. If income per family member were computed from the median rather than the mean, it would be only about two-thirds as large for the oldest as the youngest husbands.

[15] Based on same sources as Fig. 4. Lansing and Kish, op. cit., used a method similar to that shown here as their preferred method of describing the stages of the life cycle of the family.

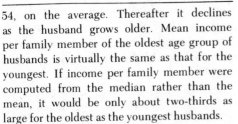

FIG. 5. Dispersion of family income, for husband-wife families (United States, 1960)

the period of peak family income occurred later in the family life cycle for upper strata than for the lower. This fact evidently reflects the tendency for the incomes of white-collar workers to decline little, if any, before retirement and for that of manual workers to reach a peak around age 40 and then to decline. It may also reflect differences in the employability and earnings of the wives in the upper and lower strata of the population.

Summary of Findings on Social and Economic Characteristics

During recent years the proportion of wives in the labor force declines from about one-third for those in the first five years of marriage to one-fourth for those married five to nine years, then rises to about two-fifths for those married about twenty-five years (about the time their children are leaving home). Seven out of eight couples who are in their first year of marriage have set up homes apart from relatives; after ten years all but 1 percent have separate homes. A plateau of child-bearing occurs between five and twenty years after marriage, when about 85 percent of the couples have some of their children in their home. Peak family income is found on the average among families with the husband 45–54 years old. Families in the lower economic strata are more likely to reach a peak of family income when the husband is around 40, but the corresponding age of husband for the upper strata tends to come much later. Because size of family usually declines at a faster rate than family income during the later stages of the family life cycle, the high point in income per family member is reached when the husband is 55–64 years old, on the average—about ten years after the peak in income per family. . . .

The Wife Problem*

William H. Whyte, Jr.

Over the last few decades American corporations have been evolving a pattern of social community able to provide their members with more and more of their basic social wants. Yet, the corporation now concedes, one of the principal members of its community remains officially almost unnoticed—to wit, the Wife. For the good of the corporation, many executives believe, it is time the matter was remedied. "We control a man's environment in business and we lose it entirely when he crosses the threshold of his home," one executive says mournfully. "Management, therefore, has a challenge

°Adapted from Life, January 7, 1952, 32–48.

and an obligation to deliberately plan and create a favorable, constructive attitude on the part of the wife that will liberate her husband's total energies for the job." Others, though they might not put it quite so baldly, agree that the step is logical.

Just how to do this is a problem that has many a management understandably baffled. On one very basic matter, however, management is not in the slightest baffled. It knows exactly what kind of wife it wants. With a remarkable uniformity of phrasing, corporation officials all over the country sketch the ideal. In her simplest terms she is a wife who (1) is highly adaptable, (2) is highly gregarious,

(3) realizes her husband belongs to the corporation.

Are the corporation specifications presumptuous? It would appear not. The fact is that this kind of wife is precisely what our schools and colleges—and U.S. society in general—seem to be giving the corporation.

Let us define terms: we are discussing the wives of the coming generation of management, whose husbands are between 25 and 40, and in junior or middle echelons of management or with logical aspirations of getting there. There is, of course, no sharp dividing line between age groups, but among older executives there is a strong feeling that this younger generation of wives is the most cooperative the corporation has ever enlisted. "Somehow," says one executive, "they seem to give us so much less trouble than the older ones." "Either the girls are better or the men are marrying better," says another. "But whatever it is with these people, *they get along.*"

THE NEGATIVE ROLE

Perhaps it is merely that this generation of wives has not yet grown older and more cantankerous. Perhaps. But there is evidence that this group-mindedness is the result of a shift in values more profound than one might suppose. The change is by no means peculiar to the corporation wife but by the nature of her job she may be the outstanding manifestation of it. And a preview, perhaps, of what is to come.

First, how do the wives conceive their own role? Critical literature has been answering the question rather forcefully, with the result that many Americans (and practically all Europeans) assume that the wife of the American businessman not only is the power behind the scenes but wants to become more so.

The picture needs considerable revision. For the striking thing that emerges from wives' comments is the negativeness of the role they sketch. As they explain it, the good wife is good by *not* doing things— by *not* complaining when her husband works late; by *not* fussing when a transfer is coming up; by *not* engaging in any controversial activity. Moreover, they agree heartily that a good wife can't help a husband as much as a bad wife can hurt one. And the bad wife, clearly, is one who obtrudes too much, whether as a "meddler," a "climber," a "fixer" or, simply, someone who "pushes" her man around.

Resolutely antifeminist, the executive wife conceives her role to be that of a "stabilizer"—the keeper of the retreat, the one who rests and rejuvenates the man for the next day's battle.

This stabilizing calls for more than good homemaking and training the kids not to bother daddy before dinner. Above all, wives emphasize, they have to be good listeners. They describe the job somewhat wryly. They must be "sounding boards," "refueling stations," "wailing walls." But they speak without resentment. Nurturing the male ego, they seem to feel, is not only a pretty good fulfillment of their own ego but a form of therapy made increasingly necessary by the corporation way of life. Management psychologists couldn't agree more. "Most top executives are very lonely people," as one puts it. "The greatest thing a man's wife can do is to let him unburden the worries he can't confess to in the office."

A SOCIAL OPERATOR

In addition to listening she can do some judicious talking. If she is careful about it she can be a valuable publicity agent for the husband. "In a subtle way," says one executive, "they put in a plug for the husband. They tell things he wouldn't dare tell for fear of seeming immodest." In simialr fashion they can humanize him if he's a boss. "About the time I get fed up with the bastard," says a junior executive, "here I am, going over to dinner at his house. And she's so nice. She jokes about him, kids him to his face. I figure he can't be so bad after all."

Low-key "stabilizing," then, the wife sees as her main task. There is another aspect to her role, however, and it is considerably less passive. For the good corporation wife must also be a social operator, and when husbands and wives sketch out the personal characteristics of the ideal wife it is the equipment for this role that comes first to their minds. What they ask for, more than any other quality, is gregariousness, or a reasonable facsimile. Here are some of the ways in which they spell it out.

EXECUTIVE: "She should do enough reading to be a good conversationalist. . . . Even if she doesn't like opera she should know something about it so if the conversation goes that way she can hold her own. She has to be able to go with you if you're going to make a speech or get an award, and not be ill at ease."

EXECUTIVE: "The hallmark of the good wife is the ability to put people at their ease."

WIFE: "The most important thing for an executive's wife is to know everybody's name and something about their family so you can talk to them—also, you've got to be able to put people at their ease."

EXECUTIVE: "Keeping herself so she is comfortable with people on the boss's level is important. I don't think reading and music and that kind of stuff are vital."

EXECUTIVE: "The kind you want is the kind that can have people drop in any time and make a good show of it even if the baby's diapers are lying around."

WIFE: "It's a very worthwhile bunch we have here. Edith Sampson down on Follansbee Road is sort of the intellectual type, but most of the gang are real people."

For the corporation wife, in short, being "sociable" is as important as stabilizing. Like the army wife, an analogy she detests, she must be a highly adaptable "mixer." In fact, she needs to be even more adaptable than the army wife, for the social conditions she meets are more varied. One year she may be a member of a company community, another year a branch manager's wife, expected to integrate with the local community—or, in some cases, to become a civic leader, and frequently, as the wife of the company representative, to provide a way station on the route of touring company brass.

"IT MAKES ME LAUGH"

As a rule, she is inextricably bound up in the corporation "family," often so much so that her entire behavior—including what and where she drinks—is subtly conditioned by the corporation. "It makes me laugh," says one wife in an eastern city dominated by one corporation. "If we were the kind to follow the Pattern, I'll tell you just what we would do. First, in a couple of years, we'd move out of Ferncrest Village (it's really pretty tacky there, you know). We wouldn't go straight to Eastmere Hills—that would look pushy at this stage of the game; we'd go to the hilly section off Scrubbs Mill Pike. About that time, we'd change from Christ Church to St. Edwards, and we'd start going to the Fortnightlys—it would be a different group entirely. Then, about 10 years later, we'd finally build in Eastmere Hills." It makes her laugh, she says, because that would be the signal to everybody that she had become a wife of the top-brass bracket. Which she probably will.

Few wives are as articulate as that on the social role, but intuitively they are generally superb at it; their antennae are sensitive, and they know the rules of the game by heart. Second nature to the seasoned wife, for example, are the following:

> Don't talk shop gossip with the Girls, particularly those who have husbands in the same department.
>
> Don't invite superiors in rank; let them make the first bid.
>
> Don't turn up at the office unless you absolutely have to.
>
> Don't get too chummy with the wives of associates 'your husband might soon pass on the way up.
>
> Don't be disagreeable to any company people you meet. You never know . . .
>
> Be attractive. There is a strong correlation between executive success and the wife's appearance. Particularly so in the case of the sales wife.
>
> Be a phone pal of your husband's secretary.
>
> Never—repeat, never—get tight at a company party (it may go down in a dossier).

One rule transcends all others: *Don't be too good.* Keeping up with the Joneses is still important. But where in pushier and more primitive times it implied going substantially ahead of the Joneses, today keeping up means just that: keeping up. One can move ahead, yes—but slightly, and the timing must be exquisite. Whatever the move, it must never be openly invidious.

Perhaps it is for this reason that, when it comes to buying an auto, the Buick is so much preferred: it envelops the whole executive spectrum and the jump from a Special to a Super, and from a Super to a Roadmaster, can be handled with tact.[1] Not always, though. In one

[1] The present equivalents of yesteryear's ranks shows a reach for the exotic. Special has become Le Sabre; Super is now Electra; and Roadmaster is Electra 225—Eds.

eastern steel town, where cars have always been the accepted symbol of rank, the chairman of the board has a Cadillac— certainly a high enough ceiling. The president, however, has taken to buying Buick Supers, with the result that people in the upper brackets are chafing because it would be unseemly to go higher. Except for the chairman, accordingly, only the local tradespeople drive Cadillacs and Roadmasters.

The good corporation wife, the rules continue, does not make friends uncomfortable by clothes too blatantly chic, by references to illustrious forebears or by excessive good breeding. And she avoids intellectual pretensions like the plague.

Are these rules of the game merely the old fact of conformity? In part, yes. But something new has been added. What was once a fact has now become a philosophy. Today's young couples not only concede their group-mindedness; they are outspokenly in favor of it. They blend with the group not because they fear to do otherwise but because they approve of it.

While few young wives are aware of the sacrifice involved, the role of the boss's wife is one that they very much covet. In talking about the qualities of the ideal wife—a subject they evidently had thought over long and often—they were at no loss. In one third of the cases the American woman's favorite cliché "gracious" came instantly to them, and in nearly all the others the descriptions spelled out the same thing. Theirs is a sort of First Lady ideal, a woman who takes things as they come with grace and poise, and a measure of *noblesse oblige;* in short, the perfect boss's wife. But how near do they come to the ideal?

WHAT A WIFE FACES

What, for example, of the listening job that wives take such pride in? How well can they listen? Consensus of a cross section of U.S. executives: not very well. ("And for God's sake, don't quote me.") There are excuses aplenty. "If he has had a rough day," says one wife, "I don't want to hear about it. He'd only get mad and say things the children shouldn't hear." The husband, however, may be the one chiefly to blame. He asks for active, intelligent listening, yet seldom wants advice ("Women just don't understand").

And how well does she handle the special social problem? In advancing the husband in the office, the corporation is quite likely to advance him socially as well. There is no easy out for the couple in such cases, and for the wife the inward tug of war between the social *status quo* and the prospect of advancement can be extremely poignant. "I must have made some terrible mistakes," laments one wife now in mid-passage. "I love people and I've made many intimate friends in the company, but since Charlie got his new job it's just been hell on us. He has so much control over their lives, and it's all gotten so complicated."

The fact that the office can spell sanctuary for the husband does not go unresented. Perhaps this is why the Christmas office party provkes such surprisingly bitter, if concealed, feeling from many wives. It dramatizes the wife's exclusion. Here, on this appointed day, is the world she can never share, and for all her brave little chuckles at the standing jokes of the office gang, she comes face to face with the fact. That is, if she's allowed to attend.

Burning though this exclusion may be to the wives, it is a topic they dislike intensely to talk about or to think about. And for them, indeed, the waters may well be better left muddy: to peer too deeply is to uncover an underlying point even more provoking. Where, the awful question comes up, does the man find his major satisfactions?

A common feminine observation is that a man's major satisfactions come from the home. If he's happy there, he can be happy in his work, and vice versa. The belief is probably necessary. Is it correct as well?

Item: As management psychologists note, the average executive shows a remarkable ability to repress his home worries while on the job; rarely, however, can he shut out office worries at home.

Item: The reaction to this Hobson's-choice question: "If you had to make the choice, which would you take: an increasingly satisfying work life and a proportionately souring home life—or the opposite?" The answers would surprise wives. "This business of doing it all for the family," as one husband confesses, "it's just a rationalization. If I got a windfall today I'd still knock myself out."

"Man's love is of man's life a thing apart," Byron once observed. " 'Tis woman's whole existence." So, for all the group integration and communication skills she can muster, it will probably remain.

The schism between Home and Office has been even more accentuated recently. Thanks, in part, to the way the tax structure has accumulated, the corporation now provides the man with a higher standard of living in his work than in his home—and, it might be added, a higher one than his wife enjoys. From 9 to 5 he may be a minor satrap, guiding the destiny of thousands, waited on by secretaries and subordinates; back in his servantless home he washes the dishes. Nor is it merely the fact of his satrapy; the corporation virtually rigs it so that he can have more fun away from home.

The expense account has become a way of life. There is not only travel. There are also luncheon clubs, company retreats, special conventions, parties and perquisites, and, though the wife may be thrown an occasional convention as a crumb, the expense-account world rarely encompasses her. It is primarily a man's word—and if the man is at a low salary, he is likely to find the pattern of life at 7118 Crestmere Road dull in comparison.

"The company has spoiled Jim terribly," says one wife. "Even when he was only earning $7,500 a year he used to be sent to Washington all the time. He'd go down in a Pullman drawing room and as J. R. Robinson of the General Company, take a two-room suite. Then he used to be asked by some of the company officers to a hunting and fishing lodge that the company kept in the north woods. When he went to New York, he'd entertain at 21, the Barberry Room and the Chambord. Me, meanwhile, I'd be eating a 30¢ hamburger and, when we went away together on vacation, we would have to go in our beat-up old car or borrow my sister's husband's. This taste of high life gives some of these characters delusions of grandeur. Small wonder that they get to fidgeting after they have been home a couple of weeks."

"What the hell can you say?" says one executive. "Here I am eating high off the hog, meeting interesting people, while Jo is slaving back home. I get a big bang out of all this, but I also have a sort of guilty feeling, so I say to her, 'Gee, honey, I hate all this traveling, but I just have to do it.' " Of the wives *Fortune* interviewed, many mentioned, commiseratingly, how their husbands looked forward to coming home, how awful it was sleeping in hotel beds, rattling around on trains and eating bum food.

There are some things, however, that cannot be explained away. For more than sirloins and drawing rooms are at issue; over the long pull this disparity aggravates perhaps the most subtle problem of marriage: equality of growth. If marriage, as Sociologist Everett Hughes puts it, is a

"mutual mobility bet," for whom are the cards stacked?

Growth can mean many things. To the younger generation of executives it seems to mean an increasing ability to handle and mix with people. And the terms are the same for the wife. "The wife who is not very sociable," goes a highly typical male observation, "might not affect the husband directly, but she can hurt him just the same. A lot of business is done weekends. If she doesn't go for this, her lack of growth can hold the man back." "I have seen it happen so many times," says another executive sadly. "He marries the kid sweetheart, the girl next door or a girl from the jerkwater college he went to. They start off with a lot in common. Then he starts going up. Fifteen years later he is a different guy entirely. But she's stayed home, literally and figuratively." Even the old idea of a wife as a sort of culture carrier is virtually dead; she is still expected to read and things like that, but for functional reasons. "Sure I want her to read good books and magazines," as one executive puts it. "I don't want her to make a fool of herself in conversation."

Fundamentally, of course, the problem goes back to whom the executive chooses in the first place. Is the moral that he should marry a girl "superior" to him? Thanks to the commonly accepted saw that a woman can pull a man up, but not vice versa, there are many who think he should. ("My best executives," remarks one boss, "are the ones who 'outmarried' themselves.") But the pitfalls are many. Her qualities may drive the man to preoccupation with office prestige in order to prove himself to her; furthermore, unless she is excellent at hiding her superiority—or lets it rest fallow—she can hurt his chances in a close "family" community. The Bryn Mawr accent can be absolute death for a career in some Midwestern corporations.

What kind of background for the woman, then, is the optimum? A serious career can be dismissed easily; there is almost universal agreement among wives, husbands and corporations on this score. Work before marriage, however, is generally approved. "I feel the fact that I worked before marriage," says one wife, "is a help. I know what goes on in an office and can understand what Charles is up against."

College? Here is the *summum bonum*. There are some obvious reasons; because virtually all executives now go to college, the couple in such cases starts off with shared values. But corporation people mention a reverse factor almost as much. It is not so important for the wife, they say, to have gone to college, but it is very important not to have *not* gone to college. If she hasn't, corporation people warn, she is prey to an inferiority complex that makes it difficult for her to achieve real poise. Some corporations, accordingly, make it their business to find out whether or not the wife has a degree.

More and more corporations these days are interviewing the wife before hiring an executive, and some are not uninterested in fiancées. There are many holdouts ("This railroad picks its executives and lets its executives pick their wives and so far it's been okay"), but roughly half of the companies on which *Fortune* has data have made wife-screening a regular practice and many of the others seem about ready to do so. And the look-see is not academic. About 20 per cent of its otherwise acceptable trainee applicants, one large company estimates, are turned down because of their wives.

Ordinarily, the screening is accomplished via "informal" social visits. Many executives, for example, make it a point to call on the wife in her own home. Louis Ruthenburg, board chairman of Servel (which never hires an executive without a look at the wife), likes to recall how one college president used to insist on eating breakfast with a candidate's family; the wife who didn't fix her husband a good breakfast, he used to say, wasn't a good risk. To help them spot such key indicators many executives rely heavily on their own wives. "My wife is very, very keen on this," says one president. "She can spot things I might miss. And if the gal isn't up to par with her, it's no go."

HOW TO SCREEN A WIFE

But the initial screening is only the beginning of the corporation's interest. In one way or another the corporation manages to keep an eye on the wife, and more and more the surveillance is deliberately planned. At the Container Corp. of America, for example, it is the duty of all vice presidents to get acquainted with their subordinates' wives, and on their travels they are expected to meet the wives of executives in the field. Thus, when a man's name comes up for promotion the company has the answers to these questions: What is the health of the family? What is their attitude toward parenthood? How does the wife run her home? Does she dress with taste?

The effect of all this surveillance on the husband's career is substantial. In the home office of an insurance company, to cite one not untypical example, the president is now sidetracking one of his top men in favor of a less able one; the former's wife "has absolutely no sense of public relations." In another company a very promising executive's career is being similarly checked; his wife, the boss explains, is "negative in her attitude toward the company. She feels that business is her husband's life and no part of hers." Wives who have donated income of their own to raise the family living standard may also call down sanctions on the husband. Says one president, "When a man buys a home he can't afford on his salary alone, we either question his judgment or feel that the wife wears the pants." In either case his career is not likely to profit.

So with alcohol. The little woman who gets tipsy in front of the boss is not quite the joke her celebration in cartoon and anecdote would indicate; indeed, it is almost frightening to find out to what degree executive futures have been irretrievably influenced by that fourth Martini. And it need happen only once. Recently, the president of a large utility felt it necessary to revise his former estimate of two executives. At the last company dinner their wives drank too many glasses of champagne. "They disported themselves," he says regretfully, "with utter lack of propriety."

Interestingly, divorce rarely disqualifies a man. Because of the phenomenon of the outgrown wife, the regret of most companies is tempered by the thought that the executive's next, and presumably more mobile, wife will be better for all concerned; one company, as a matter of fact, has a policy of sending executives away on extended trips if they need separating from nagging or retrograde wives.

One company has arranged for the team of consulting psychologists it retains to help out in delicate situations (currently they are making progress with an alcoholic wife). In most cases, however, the salvage task is up to the top man himself. "A lot of the 'company business' that presidents do," says one of them, "covers this sort of work. Take a situation I've got to wrestle with now. In one of our branch plants the wives of two vice presidents have started a feud. The men get along fine, but one of the wives is a real troublemaker. So I guess it's up to me to take a trip halfway across the continent—for other reasons, of course—and try and see what I can do about it."

Important as the wife-screening process may be, most executives realize that it is, at best, only a negative measure. For even with the most cooperative wives there can be much misunderstanding over such topics as travel and long hours. Therefore it is the company's duty, they argue, to *sell* the wife on the corporation's point of view. The result is an increasing use of such media as films, brochures and special mailings to drive home, in effect, the idea that the corporation isn't stealing her husband from her.

But something far more important is being brewed for the wife. It is not enough, in the view of many companies, that she merely be "sold" on the company; she should, they believe, now be integrated *into* it. "When a man comes to work for us," says William Given, chairman, American Brake Shoe Co., "we think of the company as employing the family, for it will be supporting the entire family, not merely the breadwinner." "The days of the strictly home wife," says a bank president, "are gone. She has become indispensable to our entire scheme of business." Among U.S. corporations, easily the most conspicuous and successful example of this kind of integration has been Thomas J. Watson's International Business Machines Corp. "Our wives," Watson explains, "are all part of the business. We started with just a few hundred people in 1914 and decided that no matter how large we grew we would carry it on in the family spirit. We always refer to our people as the 'I.B.M. Family' and we mean the wives and children as well as the men."

As a result the company can correctly claim that it makes available "complete social satisfactions." For $1 a year I.B.M. people enjoy a country club with swimming pool, bowling, 18-hole golf course, softball, tennis, picnics, and parties of all kinds. Even the children are integrated. At the age of 3 they may be enrolled in a special children's club, and at 8 go on to become junior members of the big club.

In keeping with the family spirit Mrs. Watson, a very gracious, modest woman, sets an example for other wives. "She's made my work play," her husband explains. "She has a great gift for human relations. I confer with her about personnel because she knows all the people. She has met them at luncheons where we hold a regular receiving line, and every year she goes to the 100-Percenter Club meetings." In addition to this, Mrs. Watson travels with her husband all over the world and keeps in touch with I.B.M. people; last year she traveled 38,046 miles and met 11,845 I.B.M. men and their wives.

Social integration, however, does not mean that the corporation necessarily *likes* the wife. A great many, as we have seen, do. But in some cases the corporation welcomes her largely as a means of defending itself against her. Amiable as it may be about it, the corporation is aware that the relationship is still triangular—or, to put it another way, if you can't beat 'em, join 'em. "Successes here," says one official, "are guys who eat and sleep the company. If a man's first interest is his wife and family, more power to him—but we don't want him." "We've got quite an equity in the man," another explains, "and it's only prudence to protect it by bringing the wife into the picture."

In fairness to the corporation wife, she must be recompensed somehow for the amount of time the company demands from her husband. Companies recognize the fact and are consequently more and more providing social facilities— from ladies' nights to special clubs—to hypo the sense of identification.

One corporation has gone considerably further. Via the wife of the heir apparent to the presidency, there has been set up, in effect, a finishing school so that the wives can be brought up to the same high standards. As soon as the husband reaches the $8,000-to-$10,000 bracket the wife becomes eligible for the grooming. It is all done very subtly: the group leader drops helpful advice on which are the preferred shops, where to dine, what to wear when doing it and, somewhat like a good cruise director, has a way of introducing newcomers to congenial people. "Her supervision is so clever and indirect," says one wife, "that the other wives appreciate it probably."

When the corporation turns to the Sales Wife, its attention becomes even more intense. As an economic lever on the salesman, companies have learned, there is no stimulus quite so effective as the wife, if properly handled. Some sales executives make a habit of writing provocative letters to the wife, reminding her of the sales-contest prizes her husband could win for her and how he is doing at the moment (not so well as he should be).

As an extra employee, the wife's potential is so great that with some concerns the "husband and wife team" is not only desirable but mandatory. And the wife is not always merely the junior member. "Wives can do a lot on their own," explains the president of a large paper-box company. "A lot of important business connections have grown from friendships between our wives and wives of executives of other companies. One of our executives' wives recently was down at Miami for two weeks, and a friendship she struck up with a woman there resulted in a big order from an account we hadn't been able to crack in 15 years."

Insurance companies, among the first to exploit this "team" potential, bear down heavily on the theme through a constant stream of literature addressed to wives. Through magazine articles penned by veteran wives they are told of the psychological requirements ("Earl Made a Believer of Me," Mrs. Earl Benton explains to wives in a typical article).

The question of integration is by no means simple. What we have been talking about so far is the kind of integration de-liberately planned by companies. But there is another kind. Quite beyond the immediate control of the corporation there are forces at work to draw the bonds between wife and corporation even tighter.

Paradoxically, perhaps the greatest of these is the very decentralization of in-dustry. Thanks to this growing trend, it is now a commonplace that the road to advancement is through transfer to the different seats of the corporation empire.

With their talent for adaptability, the younger generation of wives is in most re-spects well prepared for this new way of life. Most accept it philosophically, and a good many actually prefer it to staying put in one place. "Any time the curtains get dirty," says one wife, "I'm ready to move. I enjoy meeting new people and seeing new places. And it's kind of a vacation sometimes."

There are, nevertheless, some very real tensions produced. And for no one more than the wife. It is she, who has only one life in contrast to her husband's two, who is called upon to do most of the adjusting. The move at once breaks up most of her community friendships, sev-ers her local business relationships with the bank and the stores, takes her from the house and the garden on which she worked so long, and if the move takes her to a large city it probably drops her living standards also.

But it is the effect on the children that concerns wives most. While the children are very young, most wives agree, the effect is not harmful; they make and forget friends easily. As they reach junior-high age, however, a transfer can become a crisis. Recalls one wife: "Every time my daughter made a place for her-self at school with the other kids, we'd move, and she'd spend the next year try-ing to break in at another school. Last year, when she was a senior in high school, she had a nervous breakdown. She was sure she was an outsider." The effect is not often this drastic but, while most children sweat out their adjustment with-out overt pain, the process is one parents find vicariously wrenching. One executive who recently changed to a nontransfer-ring company has no trouble recalling the exact moment of his decision. One night at dinner his little boy turned to him. "Daddy," he said, "where do you really live?"

While constant transfer exposes the couple to many environments, it is, never-theless, one of the most powerful of all the forces for integration. Because moving makes their other roots so shallow and transitory, the couple instinctively clings all the harder to the corporation.

What are the wife's basic unadjusted feelings about all this? The answer is clear: she likes the way of life. To picture her as a helpless sort of being pushed around by the corporation would be to at-tribute to her a sense of plight she does not feel; she must be considered not only an object of the integration but a force for it in her own right. She has become such an ally of the corporation, in fact, that on several matters it would almost appear that she and the corporation are ganging up on the husband.

Whatever else she may think of the corporation, on three main points she and her sisters agree:

The corporation means opportunity

The big company, wives explain, plays fair. "We went over all the pros and cons of bigness before Jim joined Du Pont," says one wife, "and we've never regretted joining. The bigness holds out a challenge for you."

The corporation means benefits

"Eastman Kodak has wonderful good-will policies," a wife explains. "I used to have to attend to all the home details like insurance and bills. Now the company has someone who does those things for you—they even plan vacations for you."

The corporation means security

"Some companies may pay more at the start, but employment is not so secure. Here they never fire anybody, they just transfer you to another department."

Few wives go on to articulate their image of "the Company." But there is an image, nonetheless, that of a beneficent "system," at once impersonal and warm—in a nice kind of way, Big Brother.

There is, of course, another side to the picture. Many companies that have extensive wife programs do not attempt social integration, and some not only look on the wife—to borrow one executive's explanation—as none of their damn business, but take active steps to see that she *doesn't* get close to them. A sampling of executive views—oil company: "We are just as happy if we never see her at all." Tool company: "If wives get too close to management they always get too status-minded. That means trouble." Motor company: "Wives' activities are their own business. What do some of these companies want for their $10,000? Slavery too?"

IN PRAISE OF THE ORNERY WIFE [2]

Having concluded the report, we find that some second thoughts are in order—one being a fleeting wish that we had never brought the subject up; too many wives read it.

But the news is out, and if it is even a half-way accurate representation of what is in store for the coming generation of management, it gives us the heebie jeebies. The picture that emerges, in

[2] Reprinted from *Fortune*, November, 1951.

brief, is that of a society in which the individualist, rugged or otherwise, seems to be out, definitely. What the modern corporation wants is "group integration"; to them, the "good" wife is the wife who subordinates her own character and her aspirations to the smooth functioning of the system; the wife, in short, who "adapts." And a small, but growing number of companies are taking active measures to bring the personal lives of their members within the corporation's domain.

This kind of thing is disturbing enough. But what is much more disturbing is the wife's reaction to it. For the fact is that the group-life is precisely what she seems to *like*. Getting along with people, she indicates—in a hundred different ways—has become more than mere expediency; it has become a dedicated purpose.

This devotion to group values is by no means peculiar to the corporation way of life; it shows there more, perhaps, but it does not stem from it. Some corporations, to be sure, have been giving it a powerful assist, but the basic forces behind "social integration" are far more universal. The wives who join the corporation come already equipped with an amenable philosophy. And in this, they are not only the reflector of the values of a whole generation, but the tutors of another, a preview perhaps, of what is to come.

By all indications, the philosophy they embrace is growing steadily in appeal. And if one word could define a philosophy, "adapt" would be it. Already, thanks in part to the growing impact of "social engineering" (a phenomenon *Fortune* will examine more closely in a future issue), "adapt" has been so well articulated and so intricately rationalized that its value as a guide to conduct is no longer questioned.

Which is just the trouble.

The many virtues of adaptability, certainly, need no defense. But how much more are we to adapt? There is no ceiling in sight for the word. Indeed, it is becoming, in itself and without any qualification, an almost obsessive watchword. Whatever the circumstances, the good scout *adapts*. As The First Rule of "The Mental Hygiene Creed" (from the pamphlet, "The Doctor's Wife") typically enjoins: "I shall adapt to life, immediately, completely, and gracefully."

This is fatuous advice. "Adapt" is a meaningless word unless it is considered in relation to what one is supposed to be adapting to—and that tacit "life" needs lots of defining. To illustrate: there are a good many case histories at hand in which the husband has given up a job at a new post because his wife did not take to the community. Was she wrong? In the new lexicon of values, yes; as the obeisance paid "adapt" indicates, it is the environment that should be the constant; the individual, the variable. But might not she have been right after all? Some towns *are* stifling and backward, and one can adapt to them only by demeaning oneself. Should she, then, adapt? And if so, why?

Not only is the individual demeaned, but society as well. The status quo is institutionalized; the person who adapts can adapt only to something already existent. By extension, therefore, the advice implies that our creative capital is complete, and that we may live happily on the interest by merely refining and perfecting what we already have.

True, the very process of adapting may itself be dynamic. Many of our old notions of individual creativity are more sentimental than accurate; in "the well-adjusted group," as the social scientists have demonstrated, there is a total far above the sum of the individuals, and we have yet to exploit its full potential. With considerable persuasiveness, some go on to argue that the sheer working together by an increasingly group-minded people will furnish all the creative power society needs.

Just possibly, however, they may be wrong. We will go part way with their thesis; it is undeniably true that you don't have to be an s.o.b. to be creative. It is equally true, however, that a real advance in any field inevitably involves a conflict with the environment. And unless people temper their worship of environment, they may well evolve a society so well adjusted that no one would be able—or willing—to give it the sort of hotfoot it regularly needs. We would all be too busy participating and lubricating and integrating and communicating.

Several months ago a top official of one of the most group-integrating of corporations fell to musing over the death of a fellow official and his wife. It made him think a bit, he told one of his associates, of the drift of the company's personnel policy. "You know, they were terrifically stimulating people," he said. "They were the last *characters* I ever knew."

"I wonder," he added, thoughtfully, "whether we'll ever get any more."

It's not a trivial question.

Cultural Contradictions and Sex Roles*

Mirra Komarovsky

Profound changes in the role of women during the past century have been accompanied by innumerable contradictions and inconsistencies. With our rapidly changing and highly differentiated culture, with migrations and multiplied social contacts, the stage is set for myriads of combinations of incongruous elements. Cultural norms are often functionally unsuited to the social situations to which they apply. Thus, they may deter an individual from a course of action which would serve his own, and society's, interests best. Or, if behavior contrary to the norm is engaged in, the individual may suffer from guilt over violating mores which no longer serve any socially useful end. Sometimes culturally defined roles are adhered to in the face of new conditions without a conscious realization of the discrepancies involved. The reciprocal actions dictated by the roles may be at variance with those demanded by the actual situation. This may result in an imbalance of privileges and obligations[1] or in some frustration of basic interests.

Again, problems arise because changes in the mode of life have created new situations which have not as yet been defined by culture. Individuals left thus without social guidance tend to act in terms of egotistic or "short-run hedonistic" motives which at times defeat their own long-term interests or create conflict with others. The precise obligation of a gainfully employed wife toward the support of the family is one such undefined situation.

Finally, a third mode of discrepancy arises in the existence of incompatible cultural definitions of the same social situation, such as the clash of "old-fashioned" and "radical" mores, of religion and law, of norms of economic and familial institutions.

The problems raised by these discrepancies are social problems in the sense that they engender mental conflict or social conflict or otherwise frustrate some basic interest of large segments of the population.

This article sets forth in detail the nature of certain incompatible sex roles imposed by our society upon the college woman. It is based on data collected in 1942 and 1943. Members of an undergraduate course on the family were asked for two successive years to submit autobiographical documents focused on the topic; 73 were collected. In addition, 80 interviews, lasting about an hour each, were conducted with every member of a course in social psychology of the same institution—making a total of 153 documents ranging from a minimum of five to a maximum of thirty typewritten pages.

The generalization emerging from these documents is the existence of serious contradictions between two roles present in the social environment of the college

*Adapted from The American Journal of Sociology, 1946, 52: 184–89, by permission of The University of Chicago Press.

[1] Clifford Kirkpatrick, "The Measurement of Ethical Inconsistency in Marriage," International Journal of Ethics, XLVI (1936), 444–60.

woman. The goals set by each role are mutually exclusive, and the fundamental personality traits each evokes are at points diametrically opposed, so that what are assets for one become liabilities for the other, and the full realization of one role threatens defeat in the other.

One of these roles may be termed the "feminine" role. While there are a number of permissive variants of the feminine role for women of college age (the "good sport," the "glamour girl," the "young lady," the domestic "home girl," etc.) they have a common core of attributes defining the proper attitudes to men, family, work, love, etc., and a set of personality traits often described with reference to the male sex role as "not as dominant, or aggressive as men" or "more emotional, sympathetic."

The other and more recent role is, in a sense, no *sex* role at all, because it partly obliterates the differentiation in sex. It demands of the woman much the same virtues, patterns of behavior, and attitude that it does of the men of a corresponding age. We shall refer to this as the "modern" role.

Both roles are present in the social environment of these women throughout their lives, though, as the precise content of each sex role varies with age, so does the nature of their clashes change from one stage to another. In the period under discussion the conflict between the two roles apparently centers about academic work, social life, vocational plans, excellence in specific fields of endeavor, and a number of personality traits.

One manifestation of the problem is in the inconsistency of the goals set for the girl by her family.

Forty, or 26 per cent, of the respondents expressed some grievance against their families for failure to confront them with clear-cut and consistent goals. The majority, 74 per cent, denied having had such experiences. One student writes:

How am I to pursue any course single-mindedly when some way along the line a person I respect is sure to say, "You are on the wrong track and are wasting your time." Uncle John telephones every Sunday morning. His first question is: "Did you go out last night?" He would think me a "grind" if I were to stay home Saturday night to finish a term paper. My father expects me to get an "A" in every subject and is disappointed by a "B." He says I have plenty of time for social life. Mother says, "That 'A' in Philosophy is very nice dear. But please don't become so deep that no man will be good enough for you." And, finally, Aunt Mary's line is careers for women. "Prepare yourself for some profession. This is the only way to insure yourself independence and an interesting life. You have plenty of time to marry." . . .

A student reminisces:

All through high school my family urged me to work hard because they wished me to enter a first-rate college. At the same time they were always raving about a girl schoolmate who lived next door to us. How pretty and sweet she was, how popular, and what taste in clothes! Couldn't I also pay more attention to my appearance and to social life? They were overlooking the fact that this carefree friend of mine had little time left for school work and had failed several subjects. It seemed that my family has expected me to become Eve Curie and Hedy Lamar wrapped up in one.

Another comments:

My mother thinks that it is very nice to be smart in college but only if it doesn't take too much effort. She always tells me not to be too intellectual on dates, to be clever in a light sort of way. My father, on the other hand, wants me to study law. He thinks that if I applied myself I could make an excellent lawyer and keeps telling me that I am better fitted for this profession than my brother.

Another writes:

One of my two brothers writes: "Cover up that high forehead and act a little dumb once in a while"; while the other always urges upon me the importance of rigorous scholarship.

The students testified to a certain bewilderment and confusion caused by the failure on the part of the family to smooth the passage from one role to another, especially when the roles involved were contradictory. It seemed to some of them that they had awakened one morning to find their world upside down: what had hitherto evoked praise and rewards from relatives, now suddenly aroused censure. A student recollects:

I could match my older brother in skating, sledding, riflery, ball, and many of the other games we played. He enjoyed teaching me and took great pride in my accomplishments. Then one day it all changed. He must have suddenly become conscious of the fact that girls ought to be feminine. I was walking with him, proud to be able to make long strides and keep up with his long-legged steps when he turned to me in annoyance, "Can't you walk like a lady?" I still remember feeling hurt and bewildered by his scorn, when I had been led to expect approval. . . .

The final excerpt illustrates both the sudden transition of roles and the ambiguity of standards:

I major in English composition. This is not a completely "approved" field for girls so I usually just say "English." An English Literature major is quite liked and approved by boys. Somehow it is lumped with all the other arts and even has a little glamour. But a composition major is a girl to beware of because she supposedly will notice all your grammar mistakes, look at your letters too critically, and consider your ordinary speech and conversation as too crude.

I also work for a big metropolitan daily as a correspondent in the city room. I am well liked there and may possibly stay as a reporter after graduation in February. I have had several spreads [stories running to more than eight or ten inches of space], and this is considered pretty good for a college correspondent. Naturally, I was elated and pleased at such breaks, and as far as the city room is concerned I'm off to a very good start on a career that is hard for a man to achieve and even harder for a woman. General reporting is still a man's work in the opinion of most people. I have a lot of acclaim but also criticism, and I find it confusing and difficult to be praised for being clever and working hard and then, when my efforts promise to be successful, to be condemned and criticized for being unfeminine and ambitious.

Here are a few of these reactions:

My father: "I don't like this newspaper setup at all. The people you meet are making you less interested in marriage than ever. You're getting too educated and intellectual to be attractive to men."

My mother: "I don't like your attitude toward people. The paper is making you too analytical and calculating. Above all, you shouldn't sacrifice your education and career for marriage."

A lieutenant with two years of college: "It pleased me greatly to hear about your news assignment—good girl."

A Navy pilot with one year of college: "Undoubtedly, I'm old-fashioned, but I could never expect or feel right about a girl giving up a very promising or interesting future to hang around waiting for me to finish college. Nevertheless, congratulations on your job on the paper. Where in the world do you get that wonderful energy? Anyway I know you were thrilled at getting it and feel very glad for you. I've an idea that it means the same to you as that letter saying 'report for active duty' meant to me."

A graduate metallurgist now a private in the Army: "It was good to hear that you got that break with the paper. I am sure that talent will prove itself and that you will go far. But not too far, as I don't think you should become a career woman. You'll get repressed and not be interested enough in having fun if you keep after that career."

A lieutenant with a year and a half of

college: "All this career business is non-sense. A woman belongs in the home and absolutely no place else. My wife will have to stay home. That should keep her happy. Men are just superior in everything and women have no right to expect to compete with them. They should do just what will keep their husbands happy."

A graduate engineer—my fiancé: "Go right ahead and get as far as you can in your field. I am glad you are ambitious and clever, and I'm as anxious to see you happily successful as I am myself. It is a shame to let all those brains go to waste over just dusting and washing dishes. I think the usual home life and children are small sacrifices to make if a career will keep you happy. But I'd rather see you in radio because I am a bit wary of the effect upon our marriage of the way of life you will have around the newspaper."

Sixty-one, or 40 per cent, of the students indicated that they have occasionally "played dumb" on dates, that is, concealed some academic honor, pretended ignorance of some subject, or allowed the man the last word in an intellectual discussion. Among these were women who "threw games" and in general played down certain skills in obedience to the unwritten law that men must possess these skills to a superior degree. At the same time, in other areas of life, social pressures were being exerted upon these women to "play to win," to compete to the utmost of their abilities for intellectual distinction and academic honors. One student writes:

I was glad to transfer to a women's college. The two years at the co-ed university produced a constant strain. I am a good student; my family expects me to get good marks. At the same time I am normal enough to want to be invited to the Saturday night dance. Well, everyone knew that on that campus a reputation of a "brain" killed a girl socially. I was always fearful lest I say too much in class or answer a question which the boys I dated couldn't answer.

Here are some significant remarks made from the interviews:

When a girl asks me what marks I got last semester I answer, "Not so good—only one 'A'." When a boy asks the same question, I say very brightly with a note of surprise, "Imagine, I got an 'A'!"

I am engaged to a southern boy who doesn't think too much of the woman's intellect. In spite of myself, I play up to his theories because the less one knows and does, the more he does for you and thinks you "cute" into the bargain. . . . I allow him to explain things to me in great detail and to treat me as a child in financial matters.

One of the nicest techniques is to spell long words incorrectly once in a while. My boyfriend seems to get a great kick out of it and writes back, "Honey, you certainly don't know how to spell."

When my date said that he considers Ravel's *Bolero* the greatest piece of music ever written, I changed the subject because I knew I would talk down to him.

A boy advised me not to tell of my proficiency in math and not to talk of my plans to study medicine unless I knew my date well.

My fiancé didn't go to college. I intend to finish college and work hard at it, but in talking to him I make college appear a kind of a game. . . .

It embarrassed me that my "steady" in high school got worse marks than I. A boy should naturally do better in school. I would never tell him my marks and would often ask him to help me with my homework.

Mother used to tell me to lay off the brains on dates because glasses make me look too intellectual anyhow. . . .

How to do the job and remain popular was a tough task. If you worked your best, the boys resented the competition; if you acted feminine, they complained that you were clumsy. . . .

On dates I always go through the "I-don't-care-anything-you-want-to-do" routine. It gets monotonous but boys fear girls who make decisions. They think such girls would make nagging wives.

I am a natural leader and, when in the company of girls, usually take the lead. That is why I am so active in college activities. But I know that men fear bossy women, and I always have to watch myself on dates not to assume the "executive" role. Once a boy walking to the theater with me took the wrong street. I knew a short cut but kept quiet.

I let my fiancé make most of the decisions when we are out. It annoys me, but he prefers it.

I sometimes "play dumb" on dates, but it leaves a bad taste. The emotions are complicated. Part of me enjoys "putting something over" on the unsuspecting male. But this sense of superiority over him is mixed with feeling of guilt for my hypocrisy. Toward the "date" I feel some contempt because he is "taken in" by my technique, or if I like the boy, a kind of a maternal condescension. At times I resent him! Why isn't he my superior in all ways in which a man should excel so that I could be my natural self? What am I doing here with him, anyhow? Slumming?

And the funny part of it is that the man, I think, is not always so unsuspecting. He may sense the truth and become uneasy in the relation. "Where do I stand? Is she laughing up her sleeve or did she mean this praise? Was she really impressed with that little speech of mine or did she only pretend to know nothing about politics?" And once or twice I felt that the joke was on me: the boy saw through my wiles and felt contempt for me for stooping to such tricks.

Another aspect of the problem is the conflict between the psychogenetic personality of the girl and the cultural role foisted upon her by the milieu.[2] At times it is the girl with "masculine" interests and personality traits who chafes under the pressure to conform to the "feminine" pattern. At other times it is the family and the college who thrusts upon the reluctant girl the "modern" role.

[2] Margaret Mead, *Sex and Temperament in Three Primitive Societies*, New York, Morrow & Co., 1935.

While, historically, the "modern" role is the most recent one, ontogenetically it is the one emphasized earlier in the education of the college girl, if these 153 documents are representative. Society confronts the girl with powerful challenges and strong pressure to excel in certain competitive lines of endeavor and to develop certain techniques of adaptations very similar to those expected of her brothers. But, then, quite suddenly as it appears to these girls, the very success in meeting these challenges begins to cause anxiety. It is precisely those most successful in the earlier role who are now penalized.

It is not only the passage from age to age but the moving to another region or type of campus which may create for the girl similar problems. The precise content of sex roles, or, to put it in another way, the degree of their differentiation, varies with regional class, nativity, and other subcultures.

Whenever individuals show differences in response to some social situation, as have our 153 respondents, the question naturally arises as to the causes. It will be remembered that 40 per cent admitted some difficulties in personal relations with men due to conflicting sex roles but that 60 per cent said that they had no such problems. Inconsistency of parental expectations troubled 26 per cent of the students.

To account for individual differences would require another study, involving a classification of personalities in relation to the peculiar social environments of each. Generally speaking, it would seem that it is the girl with a "middle-of-the-road personality" who is most happily adjusted to the present historical moment. She is not a perfect incarnation of either role but is flexible enough to play both. She is a girl who is intelligent enough to do well in school but not so brilliant as to "get all 'A's' "; informed and alert but not consumed by an intellectual passion; capable but not talented in areas relatively new to women; able to stand on her own feet and to earn a living but not so good a living as to compete with men; capable of doing some job well (in case she does not marry or, otherwise, has to work) but not so identified with a profession as to need it for her happiness.

A search for less immediate causes of individual reactions would lead us further back to the study of genesis of the personality differences found relevant to the problem. One of the clues will cer-tainly be provided by the relation of the child to the parent of the same and of the opposite sex. This relation affects the con-ception of self and the inclination for a particular sex role.

The problems set forth in this article will persist, in the opinion of the writer, until the adult sex roles of women are re-defined in greater harmony with the socioeconomic and ideological character of modern society.[3] Until then neither the formal education nor the unverbalized sex roles of the adolescent woman can be cleared of intrinsic contradictions.

[3] See excellent discussions in Talcott Par-sons, "Age and Sex in the Social Structure of the United States," *American Sociological Review*, VII (1942), 604–16, and in the same issue, Ralph Linton, "Age and Sex Cate-gories," pp. 589–603, and Leonard S. Cot-trell, Jr., "The Adjustment of the Individual to His Age and Sex Roles," pp. 617–20.

PART TWO

The Parent-Child Relationship

6

THE POSITION-CONFERRING FUNCTION

As we have seen, a *social position* is a normatively differentiated location in a social system. Now we may add that a *status* is a position invidiously regarded. By virtue of being born into one family rather than into another, a person acquires a particular set of social positions and social statuses. These characteristics with which one is born and over which one has no control we speak of as "ascribed," as distinguished from those the person earns, which we call "achieved."

In the first selection of this chapter Robert F. Winch summarizes the means by which and the range over which positions are conferred by husbands on wives and by parents on children.

Illegitimacy may be viewed as a state of affairs wherein a child is born with no family to confer a position on him. Helen Martz reports data, fragmentary though they are, on illegitimacy in the United States over a quarter of a century, and seeks to correct some misinterpretations.

William J. Goode puts the notion of position-conferring in a broader context. He begins by evaluating the normative implications of legitimacy and illegitimacy both for the child and the parent. It becomes clear that status is not only conferred upon children by their parents, but that, as their lives develop, children have the opportunity to improve or diminish the status of their family as a whole. This selection concludes with a discussion of the efficacy of the family in determining positions of individuals in a stratification system.

How the Family Confers Positions *

Robert F. Winch

Position conferring refers to the assigning to an individual of a (social) position in some social structure. To call the function "status conferring" is to emphasize the social evaluation of the position conferred. A person is said to have as many

°*Adapted from Robert F. Winch, The Modern Family, New York, Holt, Rinehart, and Winston, Inc., 1963, pp. 281–283 and chapter 10.*

social positions as there are social systems in which he holds membership. A "family-oriented" position locates a person in the familial system, i.e., in his relations with occupants of other positions in the family. "Society-oriented" positions relate him through his memberships in other social systems to occupants of other positions in those systems. For example, when a given man, who is "husband-father" in his familial system, leaves home for the factory, he becomes a "worker" in relation to his "foreman." At school the boy, who is "son-brother" in his familial system, becomes "pupil" in relation to the "teacher." "Ascribed" positions and statuses are inherited; "achieved" positions and statuses are won.

Illegitimacy is a lack of a social position. A legitimate child is born into a family, and in all societies the family confers social positions upon its young. In American society, race, ethnoreligious identification, and socioeconomic status are involved in such ascription.

There are two aspects of the process by which the family confers social positions upon its young: providing locations for them in extrafamilial social systems, and transmitting the appropriate subculture.

By being located in a particular kind of community and at a particular level in the status system a family influences the probability that its sons will finish high school, attend and finish college, enter a manual or nonmanual occupation, and the rate at which they will move upward in the status system. (And since we shall see in Chapter 10 that women tend to marry at around their parents' status levels, families influence their daughters' social statuses as well.) Of course the outcome for any given young man is the resultant of a large number of influences, including his own intelligence, energy, and special aptitudes. The focus of interest here is on what generally happens, what is the tendency, what is the outcome for the average person in such and such a situation. The theme is forcefully summarized in the formulation that a person's life chances are critically influenced by the social position ascribed to him by his family, and that his life chances include "everything from the chance to stay alive during the first year after birth to the chance to view fine arts, the chance to remain healthy and grow tall, and if sick to get well again quickly, the chance to avoid becoming a juvenile delinquent—and very crucially, the chance to complete an intermediary or higher educational grade."[1]

Through exposing the child to a set of experiences both within and outside the home, the family creates a situation in which the child learns behaviors and attitudes and acquires the values and modes of perception more or less appropriate to the social positions the family confers upon him.

The more permanent the positions and statuses conferred by the family in any given society, the less is the opportunity that society provides for achieving positions and statuses. In this country the socioeconomic is one of the most emphasized of the achievable statuses. With certain exceptions, most particularly at the higher socioeconomic levels, the ultimate determinant of this kind of status in American society is the occupational system (and thus the economic structure). And of course marriage provides another avenue of vertical mobility, especially for women.

As young people leave school to get jobs and/or to marry, the educational system integrates them into the economic and/or familial systems. It does this through introducing students to employers, providing references to employers, and so on, on the one hand, while on the other not only does it provide a congenial locale for the marriage market, it is so organized as to foster the meeting and interaction of young people entering the marriage market.

With respect to the position-conferring function in America it seems correct

[1] Hans Gerth and C. Wright Mills, *Character and Social Structure* (New York: Harcourt, 1953), p. 313.

to conclude that the usual sequence is as follows: The child acquires from the family an ascribed socioeconomic status, one aspect of which is that the family determines the schools the child attends and to some degree the kind of reception the child gets at these schools. When the child emerges some years later as an adolescent or young adult, the school places its assessment on him as an applicant in the labor market (and in a sense in the marriage market as well). Both the reputation of the school and of the individual within the school influences the position (and status) at which the young person enters the occupational system and the familial system. Thus at first the family and later the school and finally the occupational system are largely responsible for fulfilling the position-conferring function.

With certain exceptions a woman loses many of her statuses on marrying, and for those she loses she takes over the corresponding statuses of her husband. The status-bearing link between the occupational structure and the family is the person or persons who are employed. Usually this is the husband-father, and therefore in the American family it is usual for the husband-father to confer statuses, including socioeconomic, on the wife-mother and the children.

Extent of Illegitimacy in the United States*

Helen E. Martz

The most inclusive figures on the incidence of illegitimacy are birth statistics collected by the National Vital Statistics Division (NVSD), Public Health Service, Deaprtment of Health, Education, and Welfare. Data on illegitimacy are based on information from the 34 States and the District of Columbia which require reporting of this information. Statistics for the Nation include estimates for the 16 States not reporting on illegitimacy (Table 1).

NVSD releases note that the estimated as well as reported figures cannot be considered complete since:

°*Adapted from* Health, Education, and Welfare Indicators, *September, 1963, Bureau of Family Services, Welfare Administration.*

1. births to married women are frequently not reported as illegitimate even though the husband is not the father of the child;

2. illegitimacy may be concealed through a falsified birth record;

3. the legal definition of illegitimacy varies between States; and

4. some illegitimate births may not be registered at all.

A decision to conceal an illegitimate birth is likely to be conditioned by attitudes in the mother's social group towards her and her illegitimate child, and by her ability, economic or otherwise, to go to another community before the birth of the child. Underregistration may be appreciably greater in illegitimate than in legitimate births, in illegitimate births to

TABLE 1   Estimated illegitimate live births

Year	Number of Births (000's)			Illegitimacy Ratio[1]		
	TOTAL	WHITE	NONWHITE	TOTAL	WHITE	NONWHITE
1940	89.5	40.3	49.2	37.9	19.5	168.3
1945	117.4	56.4	60.9	42.9	23.6	179.3
1950	141.6	53.5	88.1	39.8	17.5	179.6
1955	183.3	64.2	119.2	45.3	18.6	202.4
1960	224.3	82.5	141.8	52.7	22.9	215.8
1963[2]	259.4			63.3		

SOURCE: U. S. Department of Health, Education, and Welfare; Public Health Service, National Vital Statistics Division; annual *Vital Statistics of the United States*: [1]per 1,000 total live births. [2]Figures by color are not available for this year.

older rather than to younger mothers, and in illegitimate births to white rather than to nonwhite mothers.

Despite cautionary statements about the limitations of the national data and the fact that improved reporting of all births may in itself account for part of the reported rise in illegitimacy, these data are sometimes used without appropriate qualifications and are subject to different interpretations. Examples follow:

1. The estimated *total number of illegitimate births* increased from 89,500 in 1940 to 240,200 in 1961. But total live births also increased during this period from 2,360,000 to 4,268,000. Illegitimate births constituted 5.6 percent of the total live births in 1961 (1 in 19) as compared with 3.8 percent in 1940 (1 in 26). The gradual rise in this proportion, indicates that the problem is not one of sudden crisis but the continuing incidence of a long-term trend.

2. Twenty-two percent of all nonwhite babies were born out of wedlock in 1961 compared with 2.5 percent of all white babies. The number of *illegitimate nonwhite births* since 1940 has increasingly exceeded that for *white births;* in 1961, 62 percent of all illegitimate births were nonwhite compared with 55 percent in 1940 (Chart 3). But these facts taken alone can be misleading.

For example, since 1956, the annual rate of increase of white illegitimate babies has been greater than for nonwhite illegitimate babies. In 1961, an estimated 8,600 more white babies than in 1960 were born out of wedlock as compared to 7,300 more nonwhite babies. The 1960–1961 nonwhite increase was 5 percent whereas the white increase was twice as great— over 10 percent.

Also, there is a disproportionate number of nonwhites in the lower social and economic groups, where most reported illegitimacies occur. A substantial number of nonwhites live in poverty or deprivation, and cannot afford abortions or private medical and personal care which may involve a greater possibility of concealment of illegitimacy. Recent evidence points to a *higher incidence of illegitimacy for both white and nonwhite in very poor communities*, and to a lower incidence for both nonwhite and white in middle-class communities.

3. Forty-one percent of all illegitimate children were born to *teen-age mothers* (under 20 years of age). This teen-age group is the largest group in the total unmarried female population of child-bearing age (55 percent in 1961). Yet the illegitimacy rate (the number of illegitimate births per 1,000 unmarried women) is highest among women between 25 and 29 years of age, rather than among teen-agers. While the teen-age illegitimacy rate rose from 8.4 per thousand unmarried women in 1940 to 16 in

TABLE 2   Illegitimacy rates by age of mother (births per 1,000 unmarried women)

Year	Number (thousands)	Rates per 1,000 unmarried women by age of mother						
		15-44	15-19	20-24	25-29	30-34	35-39	40 plus
1940	89.5	7.1	7.4	9.5	7.2	5.1	3.4	1.2
1945	117.4	10.1	9.5	15.3	12.1	7.1	4.1	1.6
1950	141.6	14.1	12.6	21.3	19.9	13.3	7.2	2.0
1955	183.3	19.3	15.0	33.7	32.1	22.2	10.7	2.7
1960	224.3	21.6	15.7	40.3	42.0	27.5	13.9	3.6
1963	259.4	22.5	15.3	39.9	49.4	33.7	16.1	4.3

SOURCE: U. S. Department of Health, Education, and Welfare; Public Health Service, National Vital Statistics Division; annual *Vital Statistics of the United States.* [1]Rates by age of mother not available.

1961, the rate for currently unmarried women aged 25–29 rose from 8.5 in 1940 to 45 in 1961 (Table 2). The proportion of women who are separated and divorced in the childbearing age group 25–44 has been rising. (See "Trends in Divorce and Family Disruption," *Health Education, and Welfare Indicators*, September 1963). Although there have been increases in the number and proportion of teen-age girls (15 to 19 years of age) in the total child population, in recent years there has been a slight decrease in the percentage of all unmarried mothers who were teen-agers. This, of course, in no way lessens the seriousness of the special problems posed by teen-age unwed mothers.

4. While concern is expressed over the number of illegitimate children born to the same mother, for nearly half (48 percent) of the unmarried women who had a child in 1960, it was their first child. *Illegitimacy decreases with the number of children borne.* Only 18 percent of all reported illegitimate births represented a second child, 11 percent a third child, 7 percent a fourth child, and 3 percent a seventh child. Even for those who reported more than one birth, not all previous deliveries occurred out of wedlock . . .

Legitimacy, Illegitimacy, and the Family *

by William J. Goode

LEGITIMACY
AND ROLE OBLIGATIONS

. . . the human community and its culture have come to depend on the effectiveness of socialization—i.e., how well the child acquires the values, attitudes, or behaviors of his community and family . . .

. . . increasing dependence on socialization required the human community to control more fully the choice of

*Adapted from William J. Goode, The Family, Englewood Cliffs, N.J.: Prentice-Hall, Inc., 1965, pp. 19–24, 80–86.

mate as well as the subsequent family behavior of the couple. One form this control took was the disapproval of casual sexual unions which created a child without a family unit responsible for it. Those who established such a unit would have to be either mature enough to support themselves and their children, or be linked with another family unit such as an extended household, which contained enough adults to care for the next generation of children. . .

Thus legitimacy—and *therefore* illegitimacy—is a fundamental characteristic of the human family, shared by no other animal grouping, and is a central concept for understanding family behavior. It is for these reasons that we now consider various of its aspects.

By determining the social placement of the child, the rules of legitimacy help to define the role obligations of adults to the child. The infant is a symbol of many important role relations among adults. It indicates an intimacy between parents, and its existence makes continuing demands on a network of adults. These adults, in turn, make demands on one another because of the child. If the child has no acknowledged father, or the "wrong" father, these obligations are ambiguous or unmet, or run counter to already established duties. The already married father of an illegitimate child cannot take care of it without failing to some extent in his obligations to his own family, even if he is wealthy. The child whose parents are not married does not belong to the father's family, and neither the father nor his family needs to meet more than minimal legal obligations to the child. The child's position is ambiguous, and its socialization experience is likely to be inadequate. In short, it is the consequences for adults, for the society, more than for the child, which the rules against illegitimacy are supposed to prevent. For these reasons, illegitimacy is more of a

scandal than premarital sexual intercourse, even when the latter is also disapproved. Every society controls to some extent who may mate with whom, and disapproves of bearing children casually or as the accidental result of a sexual encounter. Far more control is exerted over who may produce children than over who may "date" whom. . .

SOCIAL NORMS DEFINING TYPES OF ILLEGITIMACY

Davis has . . . outlined the major structural forms of illegitimacy—that is, the five rules of childbirth, which, if violated, make the child illegitimate. The first rule is that the child should be born *after* marriage. The union may be one of many promiscuous relations, or may instead be that of an engaged couple. The second rule forbids adulterous procreation. In such a case of illegitimacy, the man may be married, or the woman, or both, thus creating three sub-types of adulterous illegitimacy.

Third, a rule of incest may be violated, and an illegitimate child may be born from the union of mother-son, father-daughter, or brother-sister. Another broad rule forbids childbirth to a man and woman of different castes. Finally, a rule of much narrower application prohibits childbirth to those who are required to be celibate, such as priests[1] . . .

Marriage can "solve" the problem of illegitimacy of only the first of Davis' types—when two unmarried people produce offspring. In all the other forms, the statuses of the individuals forbid marriage as a solution. It is also evident that there is less social disapproval of the first form than of the others. Moreover, disapproval is still less intense if a marriage

[1] Kingsley Davis, "The Forms of Illegitimacy," *Social Forces* (1939), 18:77–89.

is *likely* to occur, as would be true of a betrothed couple. These facts suggest that as a next step in analyzing the relation of the family to the society we might consider (1) a wider range of illegitimacy types, and (2) the *degree* of social disapproval. Even the first form mentioned above has a very different meaning in the Caribbean countries, where a high percentage of the population may live together in a consensual union and have children before marriage, or break up the union without marrying. Most of the countries in that region have illegitimacy rates of 30 per cent or more, and in several (e.g., Grenada, Jamaica, the Dominican Republic) the rate is over 60 per cent. Obviously, if a large segment or a majority of the population begin their lives as illegitimates, this status cannot carry so great a stigma as in our own society, where the rate is about 5 per cent.

Similarly, in a period of social disorganization, such as during a protracted revolution, social controls may weaken. Then the rate of illegitimacy may rise, and social disapproval will diminish. The *forms* of illegitimacy would be the same, but their social meaning would be different. In a society with clear lines of demarcation between classes and with strong barriers against social mobility, as in seventeenth-century France, a nobleman might have children by his mistress. Only rarely were such fathers able or willing to obtain noble rank for their illegitimate offspring, but neither did these offspring necessarily take a lowly position in the society. Their fathers could and sometimes did protect and help them . . .

. . . disapproval seems to be correlated roughly with the amount of disruption created by the illegitimacy, but disapproval also varies, depending both on who the offending parties are and who judges them. The upper social strata do not disapprove much of the illegitimacy occurring among the lower classes, but disapprove intensely if one of the offending parties is an upper-class woman, and still more strongly if her liaison is with a lower-class man. By contrast, in the last instance, no doubt lower-class men would feel little moral disapproval of *him* (but some envy), and considerable disapproval of *her*.

The most intense disapproval is directed against incestuous illegitimacy. First of all, it violates the incest taboos found universally in every society, according to which sexual relations are forbidden among members of the nuclear family except for husband and wife. These rules have several results or functions. They force the young in each generation to leave the nuclear family in order to find mates. Thereby, the society is made more cohesive, for many links are forged between families that might otherwise turn inward on themselves. The idiosyncrasies or innovations of a given family are ironed out or distributed more widely within the family. Sexual competition is eliminated from the nuclear family, which might otherwise split it open. Thus, we see again that rules of legitimacy are central in the relations of the family with the larger social structure.

A child of an incestuous union creates a special problem of social placement, because its status is so confused, as is that of its parents. If the child is born to a union between daughter and father, then its mother is also its sister. Its father is married to its grandmother, and its father is simultaneously its grandfather. Its brother (half-brother) is also its uncle (i.e., the brother of its mother). Similar status discrepancies arise if the child is the offspring of a brother-sister union, or a mother-son union. Obviously a marriage will not "solve" these problems, but only exacerbate them. Such marriages are forbidden, and in any event would not iron out the status discrepancies of the family members.

If a central element in understanding illegitimacy is the placement of the child, it follows that lower-caste or lower-class illegitimacy is of less concern to the society than is illegitimacy in other social strata. Lineage and family honor are much less a focus of attention in the lower social strata. There is usually no property to inherit, and thus none to protect by making certain that the proper families are united. The families of the young man and woman lose less rank if an illegitimate child is born. Moreover, lower-strata families control their young less strictly than do the upper. One consequence is that the illegitimacy rate is higher toward the lower social strata . . .

SOCIAL STATUS AND THE FAMILY

Man is an *evaluating* animal. He ranks not only things and activities but also people. One of the results of this evaluative process is the division of societies into classes or levels, such that people in a given class are ranked similarly; but the levels themselves are arranged in a hierarchical order. Which criteria are more or less important for placing people in classes will vary from society to society: courage and skill in war, technical knowledge, literary and humanistic learning, saintliness, or financial success. Stratification systems may also be compared by using several variables, such as the criteria for class placement, how difficult it is to move from class to class, how distinct the classes are, how socially distant the top classes are from the bottom, or how the total population is distributed among the classes.

It is the *family*, not merely the individual, that is ranked in the class structure. The family is the keystone of the stratification system, the social mechanism by which it is maintained. In the interaction of individuals at different class levels, both distance and equality can be observed. The southern plantation owner may talk intimately with one of his tenant farmers, and even share a cup of coffee with him at a local diner, but might not invite him to dinner in a restaurant. He would be still less likely to invite his tenant to a *family* dinner. Marriage, as the linking of two families, is the most complete expression of class equality . . .

Let us . . . [examine] . . . some of the relations between class position and family variables.

1. In Western countries the age of men at marriage rises with class position.

2. Generally, however, the nobility of Western countries married at younger ages than did other classes.

3. In Western countries, and perhaps generally where there is no frontier land available, farmers marry later than other groups.

4. Toward the upper social strata, young people are granted less freedom of mate choice.

5. When cross-class marriages occur, the woman is more likely than the man to marry upward.

6. In the West the birth rate increases as we approach the lower classes. However, *within* each social ranking or stratum, families with higher income have more children. And very likely in most societies the upper stratum had a higher birth rate, before the introduction of effective contraceptives.

7. Engagement or betrothal is longer toward the upper strata.

8. Where there is a bride price or a dowry system, the economic exchanges between the bride's family and the groom's family are more likely to approach equality toward the upper strata than toward the lower strata.

9. If polygamy is practiced, it is the men of high social or economic position who are more likely to have more than one wife.

10. In the West it is likely that the frequency of sexual intercourse is higher among couples toward the lower strata.

11. When contraceptives are introduced, the upper social strata are more likely to begin using them than are the lower social strata.

12. In the West premarital sexual intercourse begins at an earlier age among men in the lower social strata.

13. In the West extramarital sexual intercourse increases in frequency with increasing age among men in the upper strata, but decreases among men in the lower social strata.

14. The authority of elders and of men is higher toward the upper social strata.

15. The kinship network is more extended toward the upper strata.

16. In the United States upper-class mothers are more likely than middle-class women to justify their demands on children by asserting their authority; middle-class mothers are more likely to appeal to a general moral principle or to a rule originating outside the family circle itself.

17. In the United States middle-class families rear their children more permissivlely than do lower-class families, but demand higher achievement in the areas of skill, knowledge, and initiative.

18. The divorce rate is higher toward the lower social strata.

This list is not meant to be complete, and not all these relationships have been definitely proved. Even more important, we cannot explain why or how all the results occur. Such a summary does point out some significant regularities, however, and serves as a point of reference for analyzing the more general processes of interaction between stratification and the family . . .

. . . upper-class families in all stratification systems are engaged in a ceaseless struggle to maintain their position, by controlling access to opportunities, preventing acceptance, and by forcing their children to hew to upper-class standards. Since in fact the standards are higher toward the upper strata, the family must expend more energy and resources in dealing with these problems, or eventually lose its position. At the same time, these families have some chance at success, since the amount of resources available for these tasks rises with class position. The upper-class family can hire far more personnel for training its children, far more supervisors to see to it that they do not stray from the prescribed paths.

In addition, upper-class families can control the futures of their children more effectively, since the rebel upper-class child has more to lose than does the rebel lower-class child. In most societies the upper-class family head has been able to invoke both his own power and that of the law to stop a disapproved marriage, and can force some obedience because of his ability to dispense wealth or occupational opportunities. This *differential* control is the key to the resistance of the socially advantaged families to the erosive influence of the industrial system . . . The apparent stability of great families is an illusion; few retain their positions over many generations. . . . various studies of mobility under several Chinese dynasties show that over one third of the elite in any generation were from non-elite families.[2] An inquiry into the 1547 noble Swedish families that were listed in 1626 showed that 84 per cent had been wiped out by the third generation, or were surviving because of the marriage of a daughter. Only 2 families out of this large group survived for 9 generations. The upper class in the United States has

[2] Robert M. Marsh, in *The Mandarins* (Glencoe, Ill.: The Free Press, 1961), presents his own research and summarizes prior work on mobility.

been similarly unstable. Research into the continuity of English nobility from the mid-1600's to the mid-1900's also discloses a high rate of turnover.[3]

It should be kept in mind that upper-strata families are vying not only with upwardly moving lower-strata families, but also with *one another*. A family whose fertility is low may die out, but families with excessive fertility may be unable to provide for all their members and have to watch some of their kin sink to lesser positions in the society. Economic or governmental expansion, war and colonial growth, may take care of some of them . . .

---

[3] Bernard Barber, *Social Stratification,* pp. 423–427; see also the discussion of mobility in France in the work by Elinor G. Barber, already cited.

7

THE REPRODUCTIVE FUNCTION

The family's distinctive function, replacement of dying members of the society through sexual reproduction, shows enormous variation from one society to another. To explain such variation social scientists use the concept "demographic transition." Prototypically a society begins the demographic transition as an "underdeveloped" country with a high birth rate and a high death rate. When technological advances improve sanitation, medical care, and the supply and distribution of food, the death rate starts down. The immediate effect is that the population begins to grow rapidly, even "explosively." Subsequently the birth rate begins to decline, and growth levels off, becoming somewhat stable as the society's age structure becomes balanced. All selections in this chapter deal with the demographic transition—the first theoretically, and the others describing the demographic picture in countries at different stages in the transition.

Kingsley Davis and Judith Blake present a conceptualization of eleven variables that collectively account for variation in reproductive patterns. Their presentation facilitates an understanding of the methods of fertility regulation available to societies at different points on the demographic transition.

J. Mayone Stycos' study of family size in Peru shows a nation on the verge of lowering its fertility rate. Stycos suggests that the Peruvian fertility rate will not decline substantially until there is public discussion of contraceptive techniques and desired size of families. His findings indicate that women of the upper social classes want more children than do women of the lower classes, that the latter want fewer children than they have, and that they overestimate the number of children desired by other women.

Freedman, Takeshita, and Sun describe family planning in Taiwan, a country in which the fertility rate has begun to fall. Their discussion provides insight into the kinds of social development that bring about the demographic transition and into differences in responsiveness of segments of the population.

The third stage of the demographic transition is somewhat problematic. It is usually understood to be a period of equilibrium as the society's age structure becomes balanced and its rate of growth becomes stabilized. In the United States, however, the second stage of the transition came to an end toward the close of the first quarter of the present century, but the rate of growth has not yet become stabilized. Arthur Campbell describes trends of fertility in the United States. His discussion points to reasons for short-term instability in the fertility rate and offers evidence of the beginning of a long-term leveling trend. The effective use of contraceptive techniques is the critical factor for entering the final stage of the transition. Campbell gives evidence that this practice is widespread in the United

States and concludes by describing the process couples go through in planning their families.

Social Structure and Fertility: An Analytic Framework*

Kingsley Davis
Judith Blake

A striking feature of underdeveloped areas is that virtually all of them exhibit a much higher fertility than do urban-industrial societies. This well-documented but insufficiently analyzed fact is known to be connected with profound differences in social organization as between the two types of society, and is, therefore significant for the comparative sociology of reproduction. The clarity and importance of the contrast, however, should not be allowed to obscure the equally important fact that underdeveloped areas themselves differ markedly in social organization, and that these differences appear to bring about variations in fertility. Though the demographic statistics of backward regions have generally been so poor as to place in doubt the validity of reported differences, there are cases in which the evidence is reliable (e.g., as between Puerto Rico and Jamaica, or Arab Palestine and Ceylon). Of equal interest are the cases in which societies with differing social organization have the same level of fertility, for they may reach this common result by quite different institutional mechanisms. All told, ample opportunity exists for the comparative analysis of social structure as it affects fertility. In view of the bearing of future population trends on economic development, the pursuit of such analysis has a practical as well as a theoretical significance.

*Adapted from Economic Development and Cultural Change, 1956, 4: 211–235, with permission of The University of Chicago Press.

The present paper represents an attempt to set forth and utilize and analytical framwork for the comparative sociology of fertility. It first presents a classification of the intermediate variables through which any social factors influencing the level of fertility must operate. It next tries to show, in broad outline, how some types and elements of social organization, acting through these variables, appear to enhance or depress societal fertility. Our hope is that as more sociological and demographic information becomes available, the theories advanced can be refined further and tested empirically.

THE INTERMEDIATE VARIABLES

The process of reproduction involves three necessary steps sufficiently obvious to be generally recognized in human culture: (1) intercourse, (2) conception, and (3) gestation and parturition.[1] In analyzing cultural influences on fertility, one may well start with the factors directly connected with these three steps. Such factors would be those through which, and only through which, cultural condi-

[1] Although the physiologist sees more steps in the process, these can all be subsumed under the three headings given here. We are concerned only with the steps in reproduction as they may be socially recognized and utilized.

tions *can* affect fertility. For this reason, by way of convenience, they can be called the "intermediate variables" and can be presented schematically as follows:

I. *Factors Affecting Exposure to Intercourse ("Intercourse Variables").*

A. Those governing the formation and dissolution of unions in the reproductive period.[2]

1. Age of entry into sexual unions.

2. Permanent celibacy: proportion of women never entering sexual unions.

3. Amount of reproductive period spent after or between unions.

a. When unions are broken by divorce, separation, or desertion.

b. When unions are broken by death of husband.

B. Those governing the exposure to intercourse within unions.

4. Voluntary abstinence.

5. Involuntary abstinence (from im-

potence, illness, unavoidable but temporary separations).

6. Coital frequency (excluding periods of abstinence).

II. *Factors Affecting Exposure to Conception ("Conception Variables").*

7. Fecundity or infecundity, as affected by involuntary causes.

8. Use or non-use of contraception.

a. By mechanical and chemical means.

b. By other means.[3]

9. Fecundity or infecundity, as affected by voluntary causes (sterilization, subincision, medical treatment, etc.).

III. *Factors Affecting Gestation and Successful Parturition ("Gestation Variables").*

10. Foetal mortality from involuntary causes.

11. Foetal mortality from voluntary causes.

It is clear than *any* cultural factor that affects fertility must do so in some way classifiable under one or another of our eleven intermediate variables.[4] Hence the latter provide a framwork in terms of which the relevance of cultural factors to fertility can be judged. In fact, attempts to explain causal relationships' between institutions and fertility without such a framework have led to inconclu-

---

[2] Since sexual intercourse is not confined to wedlock, the term "sexual union" seems preferable to "marriage". A union is here defined as any heterosexual relationship in which either actual intercourse occurs or orgasm is produced for at least the male partner. Every society has a type of union (marriage) in which reproduction is expected, approved, and even enjoined. At the same time every society runs the risk of unions in which reproduction is condemned, either because they lack the legal form of marriage or because they violate one or more institutional taboos (adultery, incest, caste, or class endogamy, etc.—see K. Davis, "The Forms of Illegitimacy", *Social Forces*, Vol. 18, October 1939, pp. 77–89). Between the fully approved and the strongly proscribed unions, there may be other types which have a lesser grade than marriage but in which reproduction normally occurs. Such unions may be frequent, in some cases representing the majority of reproductive unions. Any satisfactory sociological analysis of reproduction must keep straight the different types of unions.

[3] Means of contraception other than mechanical and chemical include the "rhythm" method (which can also be classed as voluntary abstinence), withdrawal, simulated intercourse without penetration, various "perversions", etc.

[4] The reader will note that our list of variables does not include infanticide or child care. The reason for this omission is that our analysis is focused on factors affecting fertility strictly defined. Infanticide does, of course, affect family size and natural increase and may serve as an alternative to factors affecting fertility. It is therefore discussed briefly at a later point.

sive and confused writing on the subject.[5] The cultural factors, or "conditioning variables," are presumably many, and no effort is made here to classify them; but the "intermediate variables" offer a means of approach to selecting and analyzing these factors.

It is also clear that *each* of the eleven variables may have a negative (minus) or a positive (plus) effect on fertility. If by examining all societies we could find the range of influence of a given variable, any effect more negative than the midpoint of this range would be on the minus side, and any influence more positive would be on the plus side. If, for example, a society uses contraception successfully, it has a *minus* value with respect to variable number 8; if it uses *no* contraception, it has a plus value on this variable. The value of each variable refers to how it affects fertility in each case; so a positive use of something (e.g., contraception, abortion, abstinence) may mean that it has a "minus" fertility-value.

One cannot say, as is frequently implied in the literature, that some of these variables are affecting fertility in one society but not in another. *All* of the variables are present in *every* society. This is because, as mentioned before, each one *is* a variable—it can operate either to reduce or to enhance fertility. If abortion is *not* practiced, the fertility-value of vari-

able number 11 is "plus". In other words, the absence of a specific practice does not imply "no influence" on fertility, because this very absence is a form of influence. It follows that the position of any society, if stated at all, must be stated on all eleven variables.

Societies differing in their social organization do not necessarily have different fertility-values with respect to all the variables. On some of the variables they may exhibit quite similar values. A nomadic tribe may have the same age at marriage as a settled agrarian village; a primitive group may practice the same rate of abortion as an industrial society. Two contrasting societies are not likely, however, to manifest similar values for all the variables; they are not likely to do this even when their general fertility level is practically the same. The actual birth rate depends on the net balance of the values of all the variables. Though societies which generate a high fertility tend to be predominantly on the plus side, no society has the highest plus value on all eleven variables; and societies with low fertility turn out to be amazingly positive on a number of them.

It should, of course, be mentioned that cultural influences affecting our eleven variables do not necessarily represent rational attempts to govern fertility. Many fertility consequences stemming from socio-cultural conditions (especially in underdeveloped regions) are byproducts, being unanticipated and unrealized by members of the society. Surely by now social scientists know that they cannot confine their attention only to rational actions or treat nonrational actions as somehow defying systematic analysis. The requirements of a given society can be met just as well, and just as ill, by an unintentional level of fertility as by an intentional one.

---

[5] For instance, Frank Lorimer, *Culture and Human Fertility*, Paris, 1954, by failing to make clear the ways in which fertility *can* be affected, gives in some ways a confused picture of how it *is* affected. The reader may wish to compare our framework with a half-page outline of direct and indirect factors affecting fertility given by Raymond Pearl at the end of an article on "Biological Factors in Fertility," *Annals of the American Academy of Political and Social Science*, Vol. 188, November 1936, p. 24.

INSTITUTIONAL PATTERNS AND THE INTERMEDIATE VARIABLES: A PRELIMINARY ANALYSIS

From the standpoint of comparative sociology, an important question is how the fertility-values of our intermediate variables distribute themselves in different kinds of societies. A preliminary generalization is that underdeveloped societies tend to have high fertility-values for numbers 1, 2, 8, and 9 on the list; they *may* have high values for 3a, 3b, and 10; and they often have *low* values for 4 and 11. As for the remaining variables—5, 6, and 7—it is hard to prove that there are any consistent differences between pre-industrial and industrial societies. If this generalization is roughly accurate, then it becomes meaningful to re-group the eleven variables as follows:

THE INTERMEDIATE VARIABLES ACCORDING TO THEIR VALUES IN PRE-INDUSTRIAL SOCIETIES

Usually High Values

1. Age of entry into unions.
2. Permanent celibacy.
8. Contraception.
9. Sterilization, etc.

Usually Low Values

4. Voluntary abstinence.
10. Foetal mortality—involuntary

High or Low Values

3a. Time between unstable unions.
3b. Post-widowhood celibacy.
11. Foetal mortality—voluntary.

Indeterminate

5. Involuntary abstinence.

6. Frequency of coitus.
7. Involuntary sterility.

[After a detailed analysis of how each of these factors may affect fertility in both industrial and nonindustrial societies. The authors then proceed to the following conclusion.]

CONCLUSION: THE GENERAL PATTERN

Any analysis of institutional factors in fertility must first explain the well known fact that underdeveloped societies in general have a higher rate of reproduction than industrial societies. The explanation, in brief, is that the pre-industrial peoples, in the face of high mortality, have had to develop an institutional organization which would give them sufficient reproduction to survive. However, analysis at this level does not carry us very far. In order to study the effects of institutional factors, one needs to break down the reproductive process itself so as to distinguish clearly the various mechanisms through which, and only through which, any social factor *can* influence fertility. In trying to do this, we have found eleven "intermediate variables". When analysis is made along those lines, it can be seen that the generally high fertility of underdeveloped areas does not mean that these areas encourage high fertility in every respect. As we have seen, they do not have high plus values on *all* the intermediate variables. Why, then, do they have low values in some respects and not in others?

It is possible to discern a systematic difference between underdeveloped and developed societies with reference to the eleven variables. In general, the pre-industrial societies have high fertility-values for those variables farthest removed from the actual moment of parturition and which, therefore, imply an overall outlook favorable to fertility. To a much greater degree than industrial societies, they tend to encourage early exposure to intercourse—exhibiting a far younger age at marriage and a higher proportion married.

> ". . . between each sex act", and that for Chagga men "intercourse ten times in a single night is not unusual". Nothing is said about how these bizarre statistics are gathered, or about what age groups in the population are being considered. The authors say simply, "it is reported that", or "it is not unusual that", etc. Such reports are all the more questionable since societies apparently with a similar level of living are said to have extremely different figures—some at "once a week" or "once or twice a week"—without any explanation of why they should be so low and others fifteen or twenty times as high. (*Op. cit.*, pp. 78–79.)

They thus lose little potential fertility by delaying or avoiding the formation of unions. After unions have been formed, these societies tend to enjoin more abstinence than industrial societies do (and therefore have lower values on variable number 4), but such "sexual fasting" arises from religious and magical motives rather than as a deliberate fertility control measure, and it does not appear to be great enough to have a substantial negative effect on fertility.

Underdeveloped societies also have high fertility-values for the conception variables. They practice little contraception and virtually no sterilization. Consequently, the tendency is to *postpone* the issue of controlling pregnancy until a later point in the reproductive process, which means that when a couple wishes to avoid children, those methods nearest the point of parturition—abortion and infanticide—are employed. These have the advantage, in societies living close to privation, of being nearer to the actual moment when the child must be supported.

Industrial societies, on the other hand, exhibit low fertility-values for those variables involving the early stages of the reproductive process, especially age at marriage, proportion married, and contraception; and they manifest high fertility-values for the variables in the later stages, especially infanticide. It follows that for many of the variables the two types of society exhibit opposite values. This is true for age of entry into unions, permanent celibacy, voluntary abstinence, contraception, and (if included as a variable) infanticide. It is not *necessarily* true of the time spent between or after unions, of sterilization, or of abortion; and it, of course, is not true of those variables characterized as "indeterminate"—involuntary abstinence, frequency of coitus, or involuntary infecundity. But the general contrast is sufficiently clear to require explanation.

A key to the position of the industrial societies lies in the fact that, as compared to pre-industrial cultures, they have achieved their lower reproduction, not by acquiring low fertility-values for *all* the intermediate variables, but by singling out particular ones as the means to that result. They took those means of reducing fertility which involved the least institutional organization and re-organization and which involved the least human cost. In the secular decline of the birth rate they relied more heavily on the mere postponement of marriage than on non-marriage. They relied less on abstinence, which makes heavy demands on the individual, and more on contraception and abortion, which do not. They dropped infanticide altogether and, in the later stages, tended to reduce abortion. In other words, they have undertaken to lower fertility, not primarily by extending further the negative effect of the variables by which fertility was lowered in the pre-industrial stage, but by using readily available institutional mechanisms with respect to marriage and by employing the possibilities of their advanced technology for conception control. Marital postponement was easily extended in the early and middle stages of industrialization because the basis for it already existed in Western society and because contraception and relatively safe abortion freed those who married late from the necessity of pre-marital celibacy. Gradually, in the late stages of industrial development, contraception has gained such predominance that it has made low fertility-values on the other variables (including abortion and late marriage) unnecessary.

Social Class and Preferred Family Size in Peru[*]

J. Mayone Stycos

Until recently it was generally believed that the uneducated masses in underdeveloped areas desired large families. However, studies in a wide variety of countries within the past decade reveal that most lower-class women would prefer to have only three or four children, though they in fact have more. The older error of inferring attitudes from behavior has been replaced by what may be excessive optimism about the motivation of lower-class women to limit the size of their families.

The present investigation was designed, in part, to ascertain the existence and significance of differential family size preferences among various social classes in a Latin American country. In 1960 and 1961, with the financial assistance of the Population Council and the collaboration of the Peruvian School of Social Work, about 2,000 currently mated women in the city of Lima, Peru, and several hundred women in the highland town of Huaylas were administered a questionnaire on fer-

tility and attitudes toward fertility. [1] Interviewers were instructed to categorize the respondent's social class in one of four ranked groups (from A, highest, through D, lowest), depending on a list of criteria provided by a Peruvian commercial research firm. Although the judgments were largely subjective, differences among the classes in education, expenditure, occupational distribution, etc., are marked. These subjectively determined categories will be used throughout the present analysis. Data on Huaylas occasionally will be introduced for contrast with Lima, but the small number of cases and skewed distribution of social class there prevent detailed breakdowns.

Table 1 shows the distribution of responses to the question, "If you were to live your life over, how many children

[*]Adapted from The American Journal of Sociology, 1965, 70: 651–658, with permission of the University of Chicago Press.

[1]Since no census had been taken in Peru since 1940, 100 blocks were chosen at random from recent maps of Lima, and twenty currently mated women between the ages of 20–44 were selected systematically from each block, yielding a total of about 2,000 interviews. For contrast with the capital city, the highland town of Huaylas was chosen; and 344 women, representing the total eligible population who could be contacted, were interviewed. For further detail concerning sampling and interviewing see J. Mayone Stycos, "Female Employment and Fertility in Lima, Peru," *Milbank Memorial Fund Quarterly*, January, 1965.

would you like to have in all?" Means are also given for responses to the question, "How many children would you like your daughter to have?" As might be expected, Huaylas stands out in the number of children considered ideal, with a quarter of the women wanting seven or more, and with a mean desired number of five. Within Lima, however, we see a *direct* relation between class and preferred number. Despite the fact that there is also a direct relation between preferred number and actual number of living children, standardizing for the number of children does not diminish the differences between classes in the desired number of children. A similar relation prevails with respect to the number desired for one's daughter. No less than 46 per cent of the women in the lowest class would like their daughters to have two or fewer children, whereas only 9 per cent of the upper class women prefer such a small number of children for their daughters.

Since lower-class women want fewer than the upper class but in fact have more, it is not surprising to find that a third of the lower-class women have already exceeded the number they consider ideal, as contrasted with only 12 per cent of the upper class. If the respondents are consistent, we would then expect that the lower class would be less interested in having more children than they now have. This turns out to be true, as measured by a direct question on whether or not additional children are desired (Table 2). At every parity from one to six or more living children, the lower-class women are less likely to want additional children. Even when age and parity are simultaneously controlled, the class difference holds up in most instances. It is also of interest that age and parity are independently related to the desire for more children, controlling class. A similar pattern holds for the median preferred number of children (not shown), except that the relation to age is no longer a consistent one. In short, we find a persistent tendency for lower-class women to prefer fewer children than upper-class women.

This finding, while contrary to popular stereotypes about the lower classes in Peru, is entirely plausible. Urban

TABLE 1   Number of children preferred, by social class and residence

No. of Children	Lima				Huaylas
	CLASS A	CLASS B	CLASS C	CLASS D	
0-2	8	17	29	31	22
3	17	18	13	15	11
4	37	30	24	18	12
5–6	26	24	22	21	21
7+	7	6	8	9	12
All God sends	4	3	3	4	13
No answer	1	2	1	2	9
Total	100	100	100	100	100
Mean no. preferred*	4.6	4.3	4.1	4.0	5.1
Mean no. preferred, standardized for no. of living children†	4.7	4.4	4.0	4.0	5.1
Median no. preferred for daughter	4.1	4.0	3.3	3.2	3.6
No. of cases	(253)	(490)	(757)	(495)	(344)

* Eight or more preferred children scored as 9; "all God sends" scored as 10.
† Standardized by the distribution of living children for the entire Lima sample.

TABLE 2 Desire for more children, by social class, age of mother, and number of living children, Lima

Age of Mother	Per Cent Who Want No More Children		Bases for Percentages	
	CLASSES			
	A, B	C, D	A, B	C, D
0–1 living children:				
20–29	2	14	123	155
30–34	7	21	28	34
35+	31	29	32	38
2–3 living children:				
20–29	15	32	114	260
30–34	30	33	96	99
35+	50	54	137	93
4+ living children:				
20–29	40	58	20	140
30–34	36	54	55	166
35+	62	73	138	265

lower-class aspirations for education and material acquisitions may not differ greatly from those of the upper classes, but their ability to achieve them is far less. Thus, 98 per cent of classes A and B said they wanted, and 96 per cent said they expected, their youngest female child to have a secondary-school or university education. Class C has about the same desire (93 per cent), but their expectation drops off sharply to 71 per cent. In Class D the discrepancy is even larger: 71 per cent desire secondary-school ecucation but only 48 per cent expect it.[2] (In Huaylas, aspirations and expectations come together at a *low* level—15 per cent and 12 per cent.) The gap between desired and *achieved* education for children is doubtless even greater. In such a situation, children are a greater disadvantage to the lower than to the upper classes.

While this may be so objectively, what evidence do we have that it is so perceived by the lower classes? To what extent are the class differences in desired family size due to the perception of the *economic* disadvantages of children? To answer this question we asked whether having an additional child would affect the family's economic situation, and if not, whether having three more would affect it. The same type of question was asked with respect to the effect an additional child would have on the respondent's health. ("Do you believe that having one more child would harm, improve, or not affect your health?")

For present purposes, the significant finding is that there is a marked difference between classes with respect to the question on economic impact but not with respect to health. When child parity is introduced, lower-class women with less than two children are more likely than upper-class women to indicate that an additional child would affect their health adversely. But for two children or more, there is no difference between the classes. On the other hand, for the effect on the economic condition of the family, at each parity from two to three times as high a proportion of lower-class as upper-class women answered the question affirmatively.[3]

[2] Figures for male children are virtually identical.

[3] Only 14 per cent of upper-class women with two living children think an additional

Table 3 gives a more comprehensive summary of the responses to the economic question by combining information referring to both one more and three more children.

At each child parity the economic sensitivity of lower classes to additional children is higher than that of the upper classes. Moreover, while the sensitivity increases with a fair degree of regularity as parity increases among lower-class women, the trend is less clear for upper-class women; those with six or more children are no more sensitive than those with two. In short, differences revealed between social classes in desired numbers of children are consistent with differences in concern over the *economic* impact of additional children.

But to what extent does the perception of economic and health disadvantages of additional children predict the actual desire for more children? People might believe children a financial and health disadvantage and still desire more because of other advantages. Or they might feel no economic or health disadvantages and still want no more children. Table 4 shows that there is indeed a relation. If an additional child is felt to harm both the economic and health situation, then in nine out of ten instances in Lima the woman will want no more children. However, the absence of such feelings does not guarantee that a woman desires more children; half of those who feel no economic or health disadvantages still do not want any more children. Put another way, 46 per cent of those not wanting more children feel that neither their

child would affect their economic situation, and this figure does not vary as the number of children increases. On the other hand, 23 per cent of the lower-class women with two living children report that an additional child would affect their economic situation, and the proportion increases steadily to 39 per cent of those with six or more children.

TABLE 3   Mean economic sensitivity score, by number of living children and social class,* Lima

Living Children	Classes A–B	Classes C–D
0	1.6	2.2
1	1.9	2.6
2	2.4	2.7
3	2.3	2.9
4	2.4	2.9
5	2.5	2.8
6+	2.1	3.0

* Respondents were scored from one to four depending on combinations of responses: 1 = neither one nor three more children would affect the economic situation; 2 = three more children would affect it a little; 3 = three more children would affect it a lot; 4 = one more child would affect the economic situation.

TABLE 4   Per cent who want no more children, by opinion about impact of an additional child on health and economic situation, Lima

Economic Situation	Health Would Be Harmed	Health Would Not Be Harmed
Would be harmed	90	73
Would not be harmed	64	48

health nor economic situation would be affected by having an additional child. This might suggest that motivations other than these are of considerable importance, for example, the amount of energy required to rear children, or a sense of inappropriateness about having "too many" children. Since 95 per cent and 61 per cent of the two upper classes but less than 5 per cent of the lower classes have servants, it is clear that the former are far less concerned with energy loss due to additional children than are the lower classes.

We have seen that women in the lower classes want fewer children than the upper classes, but in fact have more. There is of course, a long and complex chain between felt desire for a particular number of children and its achievement, and we obviously cannot expect to discover all the intervening mechanisms in this particular analysis. However, the attitudes toward numbers of children that we have been discussing can be of various kinds. For example, when a middle-class American woman says she wants no more children or that an additional child would cause economic difficulties, the likelihood is that she has given the matter a good deal of thought, has discussed it with her husband, knows what to do about it, and knows what her friends are doing about it, etc. We believe that the same statement from a lower-class Peruvian woman does not generally imply any of these things, and may imply only a *latent* interest in controlling family size which at the moment of the interview may represent little more than wishful thinking.

Several types of data support this conclusion. Thus, when women are asked, "Have you ever thought about the number of children that you would like to have, or haven't you thought about it?" the proportion who answer positively drops markedly with social class: 73 per cent in the top class, 62 per cent in class B, 42 per cent in class C, and 35 per cent in the lowest class. In Huaylas the comparable figures are 23 per cent and 16 per cent for the upper and lower classes. Moreover, among those who have thought about it, lower-class women are much less likely than upper-class women to have discussed it with their husbands, the percentage dropping from 87 in class A to 57 in class D and 49 in Huaylas.[4]

[4] This does not impede women from specifying their husbands' desires. For example, in the lowest class, despite the fact that only a fifth of the women have ever discussed the number of children they and their spouses want, 93 per cent answered a question asking how many more children the husband wanted.

Notwithstanding the fact that lower-class women readily responded to our questions on desired numbers of children and wanted fewer children than upper-class women, only a minority say they have ever thought about it or discussed it with their husbands. Moreover, in Lima the more children a woman has the less likely she is to report ever having thought about it. Both class and parity independently affect the relation, so that as many as 90 per cent of the class A women with one birth or none, but only 29 per cent of the class D women with five or more births ever thought about the number of children they wanted. While it might be thought that the parity relation in fact conceals a relation with age, Table 5 shows that in most instances women under 30 are no more likely to have thought about it than women 35 and over. Class and parity, however, still maintain their relation to thought about ideal size.

Since we did not collect data on contraceptive practices, we cannot test the most plausible hypothesis: that those who think about family size are more likely to attempt to control it.[5] Of special interest here, however, is the fact that unlike our previous attitude-items on family size, thought and discussion about family size show a positive relation to social class and a negative relation to fertility.

Thus we noted that desire for more children decreased and sensitivity to the economic implications of additional children increased with greater number of children, but thought about the matter diminishes. In fact, there is no relation between expressed attitude toward the number of children and whether or not

[5] This proved to be the case in Puerto Rico and Israel. See R. Hill, J. M. Stycos, and K. W. Back, *The Family and Population Control* (Chapel Hill: University of North Carolina Press, 1959), pp. 317–18; and Bachi and Matras, *op. cit.*, p. 48.

TABLE 5   Per cent who have ever thought about number of children wanted, by social class, number of living children, and age of mother, Lima

Age of Mother	No. of Living Children		
	0–1	2–3	4+
Classes A and B:			
20–29	79	71	65
30–34	86	69	56
35+	77	64	49
Classes C and D:			
20–29	56	40	33
30–34	41	44	34
35+	47	54	29

the matter has been discussed or thought about (Table 6).

The fact that most lower-class women have not thought about family size and that there is no relation between desire for few children and thought or discussion about it leads to questions concerning the meaning of expressed attitudes on family size. The consistent preference among the lower classes for smaller families regardless of the measure utilized and regardless of age or parity suggests that the responses are not random. However, we believe that, because the degree of factual information about fertility and birth control is so limited and distorted for the lower classes, attitudes favorable to the small family remain in a latent stage, perhaps largely unrealized by the respondent until articulated to an interviewer.

Such topics are not discussed in the mass media in Peru nor are they a part of public health services. Since the lower classes have little access to private physicians or scientific literature, we wished to assess their knowledge of general facts concerning fertility and mortality. As we can see from Table 7, it is clear that most lower-class women in Lima do recognize the existence of differential fertility in Peru—that rural and poor women have more children than do urban and rich

women. Most of the Huaylas women, on the other hand, are ignorant of differential fertility and of changes in fertility and mortality. In Lima, with the exception of differential fertility, there are signigicant proportions misperceiving important social facts, and this misperception is inversely related to social class. Thus, as we move toward the lower class, increasing proportions believe there has been no change in fertility in the past generation; and of those who do see a change, over a third of the lower-class women believe fertility has *increased*. It might be thought that this is the result of perceptions of reduced infant mortality which make contemporary families seem larger. However, we see that lower-class women are also less likely to believe there has been a change in mortality, and, among those who do, over half of the two lower classes believe there has been an increase in mortality.[6] Moreover, those who say fertility has increased are somewhat less likely to say that mortality has declined.

Another interesting finding is that lower-class women believe the average woman bears ten or eleven children. In our own sample, currently married women aged 40–44 in the lowest-class group had an average of 7.2 live births. Census data for 1940 recorded only 6.1 live births for mothers 40–44 living outside the Lima-Callao area. Thus, lower-class women are greatly overestimating the fertility of the average woman.

Finally, lower-class women are less likely than upper-class women to believe other women desire the same number of children as they themselves do. Of those who see a difference, the lower classes are much more likely to think other women

[6]According to pre-test data, this is because they feel that the air, food, and life in general were more healthy in the "good old days."

TABLE 6   Attitudes toward family size by previous thought and discussion, Classes C and D,* Lima

	Per Cent		
	THREE MORE CHIDREN WOULD NOT AFFECT ECONOMIC SITUATION	THREE MORE CHILDREN WOULD NOT AFFECT HEALTH	0-3 CHILDREN PREFERRED
Discussed number desired	17	40	42
Thought about but didn't discuss number desired	15	36	42
Have not though about number desired	18	38	45

* The same absence of relation exists among the two upper classes.

TABLE 7   Perceptions concerning fertility and mortality

	Lima				Huaylas
	CLASS A	CLASS B	CLASS C	CLASS D	
Per cent who say poor have more children than rich*	75	88	94	89	29
Per cent who say rural women have more children than urban†	90	92	82	74	21
Per cent who see no generational change in fertility‡	16	11	22	36	64
Per cent of remainder who believe fertility has increased‡	5	7	18	38	47
Per cent who see no generational change in mortality§	19	18	22	29	66
Per cent of remainder who believe mortality has increased§	20	37	56	59	30
Median births by age 55 attributed to other women‖	6.5	8.2	10	11.4	10.1
Per cent who believe other women want same number of children as respondent#	53	47	37	37	51
Per cent of remainder who believe other women want more children than respondent#	14	20	34	35	54

* Do rich women have more children, fewer children, or the same number of children as poor women?

† Do women from the country have more, fewer, or the same number of children as women from Lima?

‡ In your parents' generation, did women have more, fewer, or the same number of births as nowadays?

§ In your parents' generation, did more, fewer, or the same number of children die as nowadays?

‖ How many births have most women had by the time they are 55 years old?

Do other women want to have more, fewer, or the same number of children as you?

want *more* children than they. Thus lower-class women are more likely to believe that other women want more children and have more children than they do.

CONCLUSIONS

We initially raised questions about lower-class motivation with respect to family size. It was found that lower-class Lima women desire fewer children and are more sensitive to the economic implications of additional children than are upper-class women with the same number of children. Moreover, in absolute terms, preferred family size is moderate; half of the women want no additional children after they have had two.

Further questions were raised about the significance of verbal statements of preference in a social context where the topic is not generally a public one and where the society does not support in a normative or technological sense the realization of such ideas and preferences. It was found that only a minority of lower-class women report they had ever thought about the number of children they desired, and even fewer had ever discussed it with their husbands. The preference for only a few children is probably a latent one which is brought out by the interviewer's questions but which seems to have little significance for behavior.

In the absence of a social context in which information on family size and family-size goals is shared, a number of erroneous beliefs are current which fur-

ther serve to inactivate small-family preferences. Lower-class women greatly overestimate the average fertility of other women, suggesting that they must think of their own fertility as quite low. Similarly, much more so than is true for women in the upper classes, they believe other women desire more children than they do. They are also much more likely to believe that both fertility and mortality have increased since their parents' generation. Lower-class women are, however, generally aware that differential fertility exists between social classes and residential groups. Most of the generalizations hold in an even more exaggerated form for the rural women.

The implications for applied programs are that, while lower-class urban women do not have to be convinced of the general desirability of having a moderate number of children, they need to have their latent inclinations activated by shifting discussion of the whole matter into socially approved channels. In addition to technological information, they must learn that other women want small families, that their own fertility is not lower than that of others, and that mortality as well as fertility has declined. Most of all, they must be encouraged to think about and articulate private opinions about family size until public opinion is created. A program that emphasizes not the creation of new goals but the social implementation of latent ones should have unusual appeal in urban Latin American societies that are typically conservative about public programs of fertility control.

Fertility and Family Planning in Taiwan:
A Case Study of the Demographic Transition*

Ronald Freedman, John Y. Takeshita, and T. H. Sun

Profound social changes probably are involved in that stage of the demographic transition in which mortality already has fallen to low levels and fertility has just begun to fall. We have an excellent opportunity to study such a period of change in Taiwan, where mortality is low and fertility has just begun to fall and is likely to decline further.

While many Western countries have passed through this stage, the description of the process and how various population strata are affected by it is largely speculative. This is one of many areas in the social sciences in which many believe that they know the facts but hard evidence is actually very scarce. In the case of Taiwan, we have good sources of data. The official population register for the whole island is unusually good for a society of this type. In addition, we now have for Taichung, Taiwan's provincial capital and fourth largest city, a large body of sample survey data for a probability sample of about 2,500 married women 20–39 years old. These are unique data for a Chinese, and in some respects for any, high-fertility population.

Low mortality and a significant amount of social and economic development probably are preconditions for a significant fall in fertility. If so, these preconditions are realized in Taiwan.[1]

Mortality has been low for some time. The great majority of children now survive to become adults so that it is no longer necessary to have a large number of babies to have three or four survive to adulthood. This was recognized as a fact by 75 per cent of the respondents in our survey. It is likely that increasing numbers of living children produce an increasing pressure not only on limited housing but also on all kinds of physical and social arrangements developed in a period when higher mortality restricted family size.

There has been considerable social and economic development in Taiwan since the war, in some areas continuing progress begun under the Japanese. Table 1 shows some of the changes between 1952 and 1961 on a number of significant measures of development and modernization. From these and other measures, it can be shown that Taiwan now is considerably in advance of the average level for developing high-fertility countries. Taiwan is ready for a fertility decline if its relatively high levels of the following indexes are relevant: urbanization, non-agricultural employment, highly productive agriculture oriented to a market, education, literacy, circulation of mass media, internal written communications. Taken

*Adapted from The American Journal of Sociology, 1964, 70: 16–27, with permission of The University of Chicago Press.

[1] Cf. R. Freedman, J. Y. Peng, J. Y. Takeshita, and T. H. Sun, "Fertility Trends in Taiwan: Tradition and Change," *Population Studies*, XVI (March, 1963), 219–36.

together, these various indexes indicate involvement of the population in a system of social interactions transcending traditional local and familial units.

Whatever the cause, it is clear that a decline in fertility is underway. Fertility has decreased all over the island each year since 1958, as has been shown in detail elsewhere.[2] The fertility changes from 1958 to 1962 are as follows:[3]

	Percentage Change 1958–62
Total fertility rate	−11
General fertility rate	− 5
Age specific birth rates:	
15–19	+ 5
20–24	+ 3
25–29	+ 3
30–34	−16
35–39	−27
40–44	−28
45–49	−28

The pattern of decline by age is especially significant. It shows increasingly marked declines for women at ages over 30 but no significant decline in the younger ages. This is exactly what would be expected if many women wanted a moderate number of living children, had them by age 30, and then tried to limit family size in some way. There is fragmentary evidence for the existence of such a pattern at the beginning of the fertility decline in a number of Western countries. Such a pattern of behavior is confirmed directly in data from a sample survey in Taichung, a city with a population of over 300,000 . . .

We discuss first what [our] survey data show about fertility values and family limitation in the child-bearing population as a whole. Then we consider how

²*Ibid.*
³These data are from the population register and were kindly provided by the Department of Civil Affairs, Province of Taiwan.

such fertility values and behavior vary in relation to indexes of modernization.

FERTILITY ATTITUDES AND FAMILY PLANNING

The Taichung survey data show that (1) there is strong consensus that a moderate number of sons and children is desirable; (2) a large proportion of wives has the desired number of living sons and children by their early thirties; (3) the overwhelming majority approves of the idea of family planning; and (4) a significant minority does something about limiting the number of their children when their goals for family size are attained.

Very few of the wives want very large families or feel that it is all up to fate (see Table 2). To be childless is considered a tragedy, one child definitely is not enough, and few mothers are satisfied with two. But the modal numbers desired are three and four—not six or more. In Tables 2 and 3 there are comparisons of the distributions of numbers of living children and of children wanted. Clearly, by the time women are in their thirties, the proportion who have five or more children alive is much greater than the proportion who want that many. The proportion of wives who want no more children rises sharply with the number of living children, and among those with six living children a majority would prefer fewer (Table 3).

In Taiwan, as in many high-fertility countries, it is regarded as very important to have one and preferably two sons. Ninety-two per cent of the wives in the survey regarded it as important for a family to have a male heir. The modal ideal of this population is a family with three or four children including two sons. But under current mortality and fertility these traditional values about sons are achieved relatively early in life. The proportion with two or more living sons rises from 17

TABLE 1 Trends in some indexes of social development for Taiwan (1952-61)

Year	Percentage Living in Five Largest Cities	Percentage over 12 Literate		Percentage over 12 Completed Primary Education		Percentage over 12 with Education beyond Primary School		Per 1,000 Circulation of Daily Newspapers†	Per Capita Postings of Domestic Mails per Year†	Percentage Male Labor Force over 12 in Non-Agricultural Occupations‡
		M	F	M	F	M	F			
1952	18	N.a.	N.a.	53§	28§	17	7	28	8	44
1958	20	60	40	60	35	23	10	43	31	49
1961	21	63	44	63	40	26	12	49||	33#	52

* Unless otherwise noted, all data are from the publications of the Department of Civil Affairs, Province of Taiwan, and are based on the register of population.

† Data from United Nations *Statistical Yearbook*.

‡ Excludes students, those engaged in "household management," and those listed as having no occupation.

§ For 1952 it was neccesary to assume that only persons over 12 had completed primary school.

|| For 1959.

For 1960.

TABLE 2 Number of children wife wants and number she has living, for wives 30-34 and 35-39 years old*

Age	No. Children Wife Wants or Has							
	0	1	2	3	4	5	6 OR MORE	UP TO GOD, FATE, ETC.
30–34 (N=741)								
Per cent who want	–	1	7	23	38	20	9	2
Per cent who have	3	5	8	21	27	21	15	–
35–39 (N=619)								
Per cent who want	–	1	7	19	40	18	11	4
Per cent who have	3	6	5	13	18	23	32	–

* All data in this and the following tables are from the sample surveys in Taichung described above.

TABLE 3 Proportion of wives age (30-39) who have
number of children they want, or prefer fewer
or more, to number of living children*

No. of Living Children	Per Cent			N
	PREFERS FEWER CHILDREN	HAS NO. SHE WANTS	PREFERS MORE CHILDREN	
0			100	36
1			99	72
2		24	76	91
3	5	49	46	226
4	14	62	24	304
5	47	41	12	292
6 or more	74	21	5	256

* For respondents giving definite response. Excludes those
giving answers like "up to God," "up to nature," etc., or no
answer.

per cent at age 20–24 to 68 per cent at age 30–34 and 74 per cent at age 35–39. Sixty per cent have at least one son at age 20–24, and 92 per cent have at least one son by age 35–39. In short, by the time women are in their early thirties, and often earlier, they have alive the children and the sons they want. Those with larger numbers of sons do not regard themselves as especially fortunate. In fact, the great majority of those with more than three sons are willing to say that they would have preferred fewer (see Table 4). Only 18 per cent of those with two sons and 2 per cent of those with three sons wanted more.

The moderate number of sons and children wanted in Taichung now does not necessarily represent a change from fifty or a hundred years ago. At that time a much larger number of births was needed to provide the smaller number of living children and sons probably regarded as essential then, as now. It may well be that the apparent stress in the culture at that time on unlimited fertility was a way of guaranteeing the essential minimum living number.

Since so many couples are having the children and sons they want relatively early in marriage it is not too surprising

that the great majority (92 per cent) of the wives in Taichung approve of the idea of doing something to limit family size. The proportion of couples who in fact have done something to limit family size increases sharply as the number of children wanted is attained and then exceeded (Table 5). For example, among women in their thirties with three or more children, a majority report some limiting practice if the number of living children they have exceeds the number wanted. This is in contrast to many reports that many women in other developing, high-fertility areas would prefer to have fewer than the large number they have borne but relatively few have done anything about it.[4]

Thirty-two per cent of all women had used a family-limiting procedure, that is, sterilization, induced abortion, or contraception. The proportion rises to 47 per cent among women in their thirties

[4]This pattern is reported in studies in India, Pakistan, Puerto Rico, Jamaica, and elsewhere. In contrast to India and Pakistan, Taiwan has much lower mortality and is more developed in terms of criteria like literacy, urbanization, etc. But it is not clear why it should differ from Puerto Rico, for example.

with at least three living children. As we shall see later, the proportion is as high as 79 per cent among better-educated couples with at least three children and two living sons.

Although 24 per cent of the couples had used contraception at some time, only 17 per cent reported current use at the time of the survey. Contraceptive practice is still in many cases intermittent, relatively ineffective, based on inadequate information, and often initiated only after the couple has more children than are wanted. Otherwise fertility would be lower than it is. Under these circumstances it is not surprising that many couples resort to limiting practices they consider undesirable. Although the

TABLE 4 Comparison of number of sons wife considers ideal for herself with number she has

No. of Living Sons	Ideal No. Less Than Has	No. Has Is Ideal	Ideal No. Greater Than Has	No Definite Ideal No. Given	N
0			94	6	549
1		11	82	7	743
2	2	75	18	5	792
3	39	55	2	4	389
4	73	22	1	4	169
5 or more	83	9	1	7	70

TABLE 5 Proportion who have practiced any form of family limitation*

No. Living Children	No. Preferred†	Wife's Age: 20–29		Wife's Age: 30–39	
		PERCENTAGE WHO HAVE DONE SOMETHING TO LIMIT FAMILY SIZE	NO. OF COUPLES	PERCENTAGE WHO HAVE DONE SOMETHING TO LIMIT FAMILY SIZE	NO. OF COUPLES
0	More than 0	4	126	6	36
1	More than 1	9	310	33	72
2	2	42	26	69	22
	More than 2	15	325	18	69
3	Less than 3	33	3	82	11
	3	47	88	59	111
	More than 3	11	178	31	104
4	Less than 4	47	15	80	44
	4	37	95	55	188
	More than 4	19	52	25	72
5	Less than 5	47	30	57	136
	5	43	21	44	121
	More than 5	12	8	17	35
6	Less than 6	22	13	51	189
	6	0	2	23	55
	More than 6	0	1	0	12

* Includes sterilization, induced abortion, and contraception.

† Excludes 84 cases giving answers like "up to God," "up to nature," etc., and 17 giving no answer.

overwhelming majority expressed disapproval of abortion and although induced abortions are illegal, 11 per cent of all wives and 15 per cent of those 35–39 reported at least one induced abortion. Eight per cent of all wives and 16 per cent of those 35–39 reported that they or their husbands had been sterilized. Induced abortion apparently is not regarded by many as an adequate single solution to the problem of family limitation, since 82 per cent of those who had had at least one induced abortion either were subsequently sterilized or also made use of contraception. Kingsley Davis has recently supported the thesis that induced abortion is used widely to solve the problem of too many living children during this stage of the demographic transition.[5] As we shall see below those who used this method exclusively are concentrated in the least modernized sectors of the population.

The prevalence of sterilization as a form of family limitation is probably related to the relatively good supply of medical personnel and facilities in Taiwan in general and in Taichung in particular.

A large part of the population is becoming aware of the prevalence of family-limitation practices. Whether or not the perceptions are correct, they probably provide social support for individual action in adopting such practices. In answer to the question: "How many people in Taiwan do you think are doing something to keep from getting pregnant too often or from having more children than they want?" 44 per cent said "many"; 20 per cent said "some"; 2 per cent said "none"; and 21 per cent said that they did not know.

[5] Kingsley Davis, "The Theory of Change and Response in Modern Demographic History," *Population Index*, XXIX (October, 1963), 345–66.

MODERNIZATION AND FERTILITY DIFFERENTIALS

Which groups or strata in Taichung have lowest fertility and lead the way in adopting family limitation? We can show by various other criteria that such modern fertility behavior is most characteristic of population groups in the most modernized sector. But first let us specify that in characterizing groups as having modern fertility behavior we mean that: they want the fewest children; more of those they have survive; they are more likely to do something to limit family size; and, if they resort to induced abortion, they are also likely to use contraception or to follow abortion with sterilization. The net result is lower fertility. We shall refer to this complex of fertility norms and behaviors as "the low-fertility complex."

Which groups are characterized by the low-fertility complex? As an initial summary we can say that it is most characteristic of:

The better-educated and those who read the mass media

Those with no farm experience, especially migrants from large cities to Taichung

Those who own more modern objects of consumption

Those who are less favorable to traditional Chinese family values

Those living in nuclear rather than stem or joint families

Those who work in an impersonal setting as employees of non-relatives

Those who have received information about family planning from multiple sources.

The use of *some* form of family limitation is more consistently related to the indexes of modernization than any *one* of the three major types of limitation considered or the measures of actual or desired fertility. We interpret this to mean that those with more modern characteris-

TABLE 6 Measures of actual and desired fertility, survival rates for children, proportions using various types of family limitation, by various indexes of modernization for wives 35-39 years old

Indexes of Modernization	No. of Couples	Mean No. of Live Births	Mean No. of Living Children	Survival Rate for Children	Mean No. of Children Wife Wants	Percentage Using STERILIZATION	ABORTION	CONTRACEPTION	ANY OF THREE	Percentage of Those with Abortion Never Using Other Methods
A. Wife's education:										
None	238	5.7	4.9	0.86	4.4	10	8	13	26	35
Primary, not graduated	42	5.2	4.7	.90	4.2	26	17	19	48	*
Primary, graduated	187	5.3	4.8	.90	4.2	18	18	32	51	9
Junior level, or senior, not graduated	77	4.5	4.1	.91	3.6	22	17	42	66	5
Graduate, senior level or more	75	3.6	3.4	.94	3.3	21	28	53	76	5
B. Wife's frequency of newspaper reading:										
Cannot read†	263	5.8	5.0	.86	4.5	11	8	18	31	24
Never, but can read	71	5.8	5.1	.89	4.2	16	17	13	34	33
Occasional	66	5.0	4.6	.92	4.1	24	26	33	61	12
Once a week	33	4.7	4.2	.89	3.8	21	21	27	48	*
3 or 4 times a week	41	3.6	3.3	.92	3.6	12	7	37	49	*
Every day	141	4.2	3.9	.93	3.6	21	23	48	71	9
C. No. of modern objects owned:‡										
0 or 1	48	6.4	5.2	.82	4.9	0	10	19	25	*
2	72	5.6	4.8	.85	4.4	7	10	14	22	*
3	87	5.6	4.7	.85	4.2	10	9	18	31	25
4	84	5.3	4.9	.93	4.2	20	14	14	36	8
5	95	4.6	4.1	.89	4.0	17	14	24	43	15
6	140	4.7	4.4	.92	3.9	21	16	39	63	14
7 or more	93	4.7	4.3	.92	3.9	25	29	48	75	7

TABLE 6—Continued

Indexes of Modernization	No. of Couples	Mean No. of Live Births	Mean No. of Living Children	Survival Rate for Children	Mean No. of Children Wife Wants	Percentage Using				Percentage of Those with Abortion Never Using Other Methods
						STERILIZATION	ABORTION	CONTRACEPTION	ANY OF THREE	
D. Household income:										
Under 1,000 NT	61	5.3	4.6	.87	4.3	7	3	15	23	*
1,000–1,499 NT	109	5.2	4.6	.89	4.0	16	9	23	40	20
1,500–1,999 NT	52	4.7	4.3	.92	3.9	25	25	38	64	0
2,000 or more	80	4.9	4.5	.92	4.1	15	13	35	68	0
E. Current farm status:										
Farm owner or tenant	56	6.1	5.4	.88	4.6	11	7	16	29	25
Not a farmer	263	4.8	4.3	.90	4.0	17	14	32	49	5
F. Couple's rural background:										
Both have rural background	355	5.4	4.8	.88	4.2	14	16	24	40	16
Only wife	71	5.1	4.4	.87	3.9	14	13	32	51	*
Only husband	70	4.5	4.1	.93	3.6	21	11	37	58	*
Neither	108	4.8	4.3	.90	4.1	22	16	30	53	6
G. Wife's community background:										
Taichung all life:										
No rural background	17	4.4	3.9	.90	4.2	16	5	21	37	*
Some rural background	66	5.8	5.0	.86	4.4	13	13	21	35	11
Migrant to Taichung, not rural:										
From city	34	3.5	3.4	.96	3.3	26	10	36	62	*
From small town	33	5.6	5.0	0.90	4.3	14	14	29	43	*
Migrant to Taichung, at least some rural background, covering most life:										

TABLE 6—Continued

Indexes of Modernization	No. of Couples	Mean No. of Live Births	Mean No. of Living Children	Survival Rate for Children	Mean No. of Children Wife Wants	Percentage Using				Percentage of Those with Abortion Never Using Other Methods
						STERILIZATION	ABORTION	CONTRACEPTION	ANY OF THREE	
Neither before nor after marriage	52	4.1	3.7	0.89	3.6	11	13	40	53	*
Before marriage only	76	5.1	4.6	.91	4.1	17	16	28	47	8
Both before and after marriage	32	6.1	5.6	.91	4.6	3	3	12	15	*
H. Type of family:										
Joint	27	5.2	4.8	.93	4.4	7	:	15	22	*
Stem	117	5.4	4.8	.88	4.3	19	13	20	40	14
Nuclear	475	5.1	4.5	.89	4.0	16	16	30	49	15
I. Wife's attitude toward living with children and support from them:										
Most traditional (1)	385	5.5	4.8	.87	4.1	12	11	23	37	21
(2)	89	4.7	4.3	.92	4.0	21	18	28	53	19
(3)	76	4.5	4.1	.92	3.5	26	13	33	59	0
(4)	27	4.1	3.9	.95	3.4	18	41	44	70	18
Least traditional (5)	39	4.7	4.4	.94	3.5	20	33	54	74	0
J. Husband's employment status:§										
Farmer	97	6.3	5.5	.87	4.8	9	10	16	28	21
Self-employed (non-professional)	153	5.8	5.0	.86	4.4	14	14	21	39	24
Family or relative's business	13	5.2	5.0	.96	4.1	31	8	15	46	*
Employed by others	341	4.6	4.1	.88	3.8	18	16	34	34	11

TABLE 6—Continued

Indexes of Modernization	No. of Couples	Mean No. of Live Births	Mean No. of Living Children	Survival Rate for Children	Mean No. of Children Wife Wants	Percentage Using				Percentage of Those with Abortion Never Using Other Methods
						STERILIZATION	ABORTION	CONTRACEPTION	ANY OF THREE	
K. Frequency of discussion of birth control:										
Never	232	5.0	4.4	.88	4.2	6	4	11	18	30
Once in a while	123	5.0	4.5	.90	4.1	32	20	34	68	12
Sometimes	160	5.3	4.6	.87	4.1	16	17	38	56	11
Often	104	5.5	5.0	.91	4.0	20	32	40	65	15
L. Wife's exposure to birth control information:										
None	185	5.2	4.7	.89	4.2	17	9	20	38	12
One source	97	4.8	4.3	.90	4.0	16	14	34	52	7
Two sources	31	4.5	4.0	0.90	3.6	6	39	68	74	0

* Base less than 10.

† Cannot read either Chinese or Japanese.

‡ The objects are: bicycle, radio with record-player, radio, electric fan, sewing machine, electric iron, clock or watch, electric cooking pan, motor-cycle.

§ Excludes eight self-employed professionals and six in partnerships.

tics try various methods to limit family size, but their practice of these methods frequently is either so late or so ineffective that it does not limit fertility to the desired level, although it does have the effect of producing a rather consistent fertility differential. That the practice of family limitation is still ineffective is indicated by the fact that for women age 35–39 the number of children born or living is higher than desired for almost every category of each of the thirteen social and economic characteristics considered. This is true despite the fact that in some of the advanced categories more than 75 per cent use some method, including sterilization for as much as 25 per cent of the wives in some subcategories. Modern family planning, if practiced, is begun late. Seventy-one per cent of those who have used contraception did not begin until after at least four pregnancies, and more than half waited until after five or more pregnancies. It would appear that we have here the demographic stage at which there is a groping for effective ways to achieve the desired family size. Those with the more modern characteristics do succeed in reducing family size to a greater degree than others but still not to the level they desire.

These rather sweeping generalizations summarize a large body of data. In Table 6 a series of modernization variables are shown, in relation to a standard set of dependent fertility variables, for wives 35–39 years old in the Taichung survey. By this age almost all the marriages have lasted long enough for differentials to be apparent and for discrepancies between desired and actual fertility to have developed. In general, the relationships shown illustratively in these tables for wives 35–39 years old also appear in less pronounced and consistent form for women at younger ages (20–24, 25–29, 30–34).

EDUCATION AND THE MASS MEDIA

Education and reading of the mass media may be particularly strategic in the development process and in fertility decline.[6] As Table 6 (Panels A and B) indicates, there is a strong relation between the low-fertility complex and either increasing education or frequency of reading newspapers. In Table 6 we show how the practice of family limitation is related to educational level for those who have at least three living children and two living sons—the numbers that would satisfy most couples. Again there is a very strong relationship of education to this part of the low-fertility complex. However, it is noteworthy that with the attainment of three children and two sons a substantial minority of even those with no education try to limit family size.

The use of each of the three major family limitation methods increases with education, but the increase is especially marked for contraception and sterilization—and this is true for most of the modernization indexes considered. Although many of the better-educated have induced abortions, they are less likely than the less educated to have restricted their practice of family planning to abortion. As the last column in Table 6 indicates, the proportion of those with an abortion who have never used another method decreases sharply with education. The relationship is similar for most other indexes of modernization. Sterilization is also associated with education and readership (as with most other modernization indexes). This is probably in large part an economic matter. The cost of sterilization makes this method less accessible to lower-status groups.

[6] R. Freedman, "Norms for Family Size in Underdeveloped Areas," *Proceedings of the Royal Society, B,* Vol. 159, 220–45, 1963.

CONSUMPTION OF MODERN OBJECTS

The respondents were asked whether the household owned any of nine modern objects of consumption (identified in Table 6, Panel C). The number of such objects owned may be treated as a rough index of the involvement of the household in a market economy transcending the local and familial. It is also a rough index of the attainment of a modern standard of living. This index is more closely and consistently related to the low-fertility complex than is household income (Table 6, Panel D). Apparently the amount of cash income is less important than how it is spent in placing the family in the modernizing sector. A sterilizing operation may be akin to a modern object of consumption. The proportion sterilized increases monotonically with the number of objects owned and reaches 25 per cent for wives 35–39 years old owning seven or more objects of this kind. As there is no such close relationship with income, it would appear that getting a sterilizing operation depends not only on whether the money is available but on whether there is a modern orientation to consumption. The relationship may be reciprocal. Sterilization may be one way to increase the probability that money to buy modern objects of consumption will be available.

RURAL BACKGROUND

Like most large cities in the developing countries, Taichung is populated largely by migrants from farms and villages. Even among the young couples sampled in our study, 80 per cent reported that one or both spouses had lived or were currently living on a farm. Taichung includes in its official boundaries a large

suburban farm area, and 18 per cent of the husbands in the study were farm owners or tenants (as a principal occupation).

Being a farmer in Taichung is associated with high fertility values and behavior—even though the suburban farmers of Taichung are closely linked to an urban market and institutions (Table 6, Panel E). Further, if both husband and wife have ever lived on a farm, fertility values are also high (Table 6, Panel F). Apparently the wife's farm background is more important than the husband's. Both migration status and farm-urban background affect fertility and family planning (Table 6, Panel G). Low fertility values are most characteristic of migrants to Taichung from other large cities. They are least characteristic of migrants to Taichung if the wife has spent most of her life both before and after marriage on a farm. More farm background or coming from smaller town is associated with higher fertility values within each of three migration classes: those living in Taichung all their lives, migrants to Taichung with no farm background, and migrants with a farm background.

The effect of rural background may be attributed largely to less education. Educational differences remain large when rural background is controlled, but rural background is of much lesser significance once education is controlled (results in unpublished tables).

FAMILY STRUCTURE

Living in a nuclear family rather than in a stem or joint family is linked to lower fertility values (Table 6, Panel H). . . . those in the nuclear units have made use of some method of family limitation twice as often as those in joint families. These facts are particularly significant since changes in family structure undoubtedly are an important cause and consequence of any major fertility decline.

Nuclear families in the younger ages are not so distinctively modern in fertility values when compared to stem or joint families. Probably this is due to the fact that the nuclear units do not always represent the most modern sector of the population in these younger ages. Many young couples begin their married life with the parents of the husband, and then those who are most modern in their attitudes are likely to begin a separate household later when they can. There is in fact a rather sharp increase in the proportion living in a nuclear unit as the age of the wife increases. Levy, Lang, and others[7] have made a convincing case for the propostion that even long before the war on the mainland the joint family was probably a normative ideal rather than an actual living situation for most Chinese at any one time. The nuclear family was probably most common in the lower-status groups because high mortality made the necessary personnel unavailable for an extended family form and because the poorer groups did not have the resources to support a larger unit. A pilot study in 1961[8] found precisely this situation prevailing in Taichung. The nuclear family was most common in the lowest status and least modern strata, in part (but not entirely) because mortality was highest in these groups. It is, therefore, all the more striking that we still find nuclear families generally to have the most modern fertility values and behaviors. It appears likely that further research will show that living in a nuclear unit may re-

[7] Olga Lang, *Chinese Family and Society* (New Haven, Conn.: Yale University Press, 1950); Marion Levy, *The Family Revolution in Modern China* (Cambridge, Mass.: Harvard University Press, 1949).

[8] Unpublished seminar paper by Solomon Chu, University of Michigan, Spring, 1963.

sult *either* from traditional structural features of low economic status or in quite a different way from the modernizing aspects of high status. Thus, living in a nuclear family is most likely to represent a desire to live in this way among high-status families and a necessity among those with lower status.

TRADITIONAL FAMILY ATTITUDES

Holding the most traditional Chinese attitudes about certain other aspects of family life is associated with the less modern fertility and family-planning values. Couples are classified in Table 6 (Panel I) in terms of the wife's answer to questions about whether or not she expected to live with her sons when they were grown up or to be supported by them if she did not live with them. A large majority of the wives answered "definitely yes" to both questions. This traditional majority was characterized by the highest desired and actual fertility and the lowest survival rate, by the least use of each type of family limitation, but by the greatest reliance on abortion alone when it was used. Lesser degrees of traditionalism are not clearly differentiated with respect to actual or desired fertility, but the use of family limitation does increase as traditionalism decreases. However, the barrier of traditional attitudes to the use of family limitation should not be exaggerated. After all, even in the group expressing the most traditional attitudes, 37 per cent had tried some form of family limitation by age 35–39.

EMPLOYMENT STATUS

The employment situation of the husband is another basis for classifying the family's degree of dependence on the more modern sector of the economy. Those who work for their relatives or in a family business exemplify the traditional work situation where kinship and economic systems are interwoven. The self-employed not in professional and technical occupations are also usually in the more traditional sector. They are mainly small shopkeepers or operate small businesses in which they rely on the help of the family members; in many cases the family lives on the business premises. Those employed by non-relatives are more likely to be working in the modern type of impersonal work relationship.

The data (Table 6, Panel J) confirm expectations that the more modern employment situation is related to the low-fertility complex and the traditional work situation to higher fertility values.

COMMUNICATION
ABOUT FAMILY LIMITATION

Those who adopt low fertility values are likely to be in a communication network in which the lower fertility values are supported either directly or indirectly. Higher education and mass media are likely to have such indirect effects. But respondents were also asked about specific direct communications about birth control from various sources (newspapers, radio, meetings of organizations). As Table 6 (Panel K) indicates, those who reported one or two such sources of information were much more likely to have low fertility values than those reporting no source of information. Again, there is probably a reciprocal relationship. Those who have multiple sources of information may be led to use family planning; those who have used family planning are likely to seek out additional sources of information.

SUMMARY

Taiwan is a society in that stage of the demographic transition in which mortality has fallen to low levels and remained there long enough for higher survival rates to exert pressure on traditional arrangements based on high mortality. There are signs of a variety of developmental changes which may lead to lower fertility, and fertility has begun to fall in the older ages, as might be expected if many women have the children they want before the end of the child-bearing period and begin to try to limit family size. A sample survey in the city of Taichung provides evidence consistent with the hypothesis that favorable attitudes to family limitation and attempts to practice it develop in the latter half of the child-bearing period when low mortality permits the survival of the moderate number of children and sons formerly requiring a larger number of births. We do not know whether this represents a change in the desired number of children or simply a different way of reaching the same values.

The survey data show clearly that those in the more modern sectors of the population, with characteristics transcending the traditional local familial and community setting, use family-limitation methods first and most effectively; they want and have smaller families, more of the children survive, and they turn more often to methods other than abortion.

Apparently family limitation becomes so crucial to many couples that there is a fumbling experimentation with a variety of methods, including contraception, abortion, and sterilization—even if these are not considered good things to do by the population itself.

The "Growth of American Families" Studies*

Arthur A. Campbell

There have been two nationwide interview surveys of family planning in the United States. They are known as the Growth of American Families (or GAF) Studies, and were conducted in 1955 and 1960 by the Survey Research Center of the University of Michigan and the Scripps Foundation for Research in Population Problems, Miami University, Oxford, Ohio.[1]

These studies were stimulated in part by the unexpected maintenance of high birth rates in the postwar period. In 1946 and 1947 the birth rate rose rapidly to the highest level it had reached in the preceding quarter of a century. This "baby boom" was not entirely unforeseen, because a similar, though less extreme, rise occurred after World War I. What was unexpected was the length of time the birth rate remained at 24–25 per 1,000 population.

The birth rate dropped steadily during the 1920's and early 1930's from a high of 28 in 1920 to a low of 18 in 1933, and stayed in the 18–19 range during the

°*Adapted from* Welfare in Review, *1965, 3: No. 10, pp. 17–22.*

[1]The results of the 1955 study are reported in Ronald Freedman, Pascal K. Whelpton, and Arthur A. Campbell: Family Planning, Sterility, and Population Growth. McGraw-Hill, New York, 1959.

The results of the 1960 study appear in Pascal K. Whelpton, Arthur A. Campbell, and John E. Patterson: Fertility and Family Planning in the United States. Princeton University Press, Princeton, 1966.

remainder of the 1930's. Roughly parallel movements had occurred in other industrially developed countries throughout the world, and demographers had become accustomed to the generalization that as industrialization and urbanization proceed, fertility declines. A number of highly plausible explanations were offered to account for this widely observed relationship, and a body of economic thought developed to deal with the problems that presumably would be presented by stable or declining populations. The possibility that fertility might someday rise was not considered seriously.

The prevailing opinion was expressed explicitly in population projections prepared for the Census Bureau by P. K. Whelpton in 1946 and 1947. These projections were based on the assumption that the postwar spurt in the birth rate would be short-lived and that fertility would eventually decline to a level at or near the rates observed during the late 1930's. In a very short time, of course, this assumption was shown to be inaccurate. By 1950, the actual population had reached 151 million, but the highest population projected for this year was only 148 million.

This head-on collision between fact and theory had a very stimulating effect on demography and led to some exciting and useful innovations. In particular, P. K. Whelpton was the first to revise the traditional modes of fertility analysis with the development, during the early 1950's, of the cohort approach.

RECENT TRENDS IN FERTILITY

In essence, the cohort approach studies fertility as a cumulative process, making explicit use of the obvious fact that what happens early in the childbearing period affects what happens later. It follows the reproductive histories of women from the beginning to the end of the childbearing period.

First of all, cohort analysis showed that many women who were old enough to have children in the 1930's did not have them then but postponed them until the postwar period. Part of the "baby boom" represented their relatively late childbearing.

Cohort analysis also revealed that the age at which women were having children had declined considerably during the early postwar period. This resulted in the heaping of births in the younger childbearing ages, which, of course, raised the birth rate substantially. It was not clear, however, whether the women who were doing their childbearing at younger ages would go on to have more children so that on the average they would have more than the women who preceded them in childbearing, or whether they would soon curtail their fertility and have the same number. Obviously, if their completed fertility were going to be no higher, their current fertility would remain high for only a few years and then fall to previously observed low levels.

One of the principal objectives of the first GAF Study of 1955 was to find out how many children women then in the reproductive years of life expected to have. In addition, the survey was designed to obtain information on couples' ability to have children (their "fecundity") and on their control of fertility. The sample consisted of 2,713 white women 18 to 39 years old who were married and living with their husbands. They represented approximately 17 million wives throughout the United States.

The second GAF Study of 1960 was designed, in part, to see how accurately the wives interviewed in the first study had predicted the number of births that women like themselves would have. However, the same women were not interviewed in both studies. Instead, an independent sample was drawn for the 1960 study. The 1960 sample included several groups. . . . :

The 1955 study showed that the young women expected to have larger families, on the average, than earlier cohorts of women. This rise was not coming about from an increase in the proportion of couples with "large" families (say, six or more children), but from a decline in the proportion of couples with no children or only one child and an increase in the proportion with moderate-sized families of two to four children. It was clear that childlessness had lost whatever appeal it once had, but at the same time people did not want unusually large families.

What does this mean in terms of national averages? Fertility reached a low among women in the 1909 cohort (i.e., women born in 1909). By the time these women had completed their fertility, they had borne an average of 2,230 children per 1,000 women. It is not yet known which of the cohorts now reproducing will achieve the highest fertility, but it appears that the 1935 cohort will be close to the peak with about 3,350 births per 1,000 women by the end of the childbearing period, which they will reach in the 1980's. This will mean an increase of 50 percent in completed fertility between the 1909 and 1935 cohorts. Although this increase represents only one child per woman, on the average, it has already brought about a substantial rise in the rate of growth of our population.

The 1960 GAF Study fully confirmed the birth expectations collected in 1955. Over the 5 years, 1955–60, women in the reproductive ages had about as many children as wives interviewed in 1955 said they expected to have during this period.

THE USE OF CONTRACEPTION

It has been observed that women have been able to make useful predictions of the number of children they will have. How do they control their fertility? In presenting the findings on this topic, attention will be confined to white wives 18–39 years old, the group that is common to both the 1955 and 1960 studies.

First, it is important to recognize that a large majority of married couples have or expect to have some form of limitation on their fertility.

The 1960 study revealed that:

81 percent of the couples had used some form of contraception (including rhythm);

6 percent expected to use contraception;

10 percent had not used contraception and did not expect to do so, but were below normal in their physiological capacity to have children (subfecund);

1 percent were not subfecund and intended never to use contraception, but the wife reported that she regularly douched within one-half hour after intercourse, a practice that reduces the probability of conception;

2 percent had no limitation on their fertility and intended never to use contraception.

In other words, some form of fertility limitation is nearly universal in the United States. Values are consistent with practice in this area of married life, for research has shown overwhelming approval of the idea that couples should exercise some control over the number of children they have.

The proportion of couples who have used or intend to use contraception form a clear majority of every major religious and socioeconomic group, but the size of this majority varies. For example, the study showed it is 90 percent for Protestants and 80 percent for Catholics. It is 93 percent among wives with a college education and 72 percent for wives who never went beyond grade school. What causes these variations? The main factor responsible is the wide differences among socioeconomic groups in when they begin using contraception. In certain groups, it is customary for couples to delay using contraception until relatively late in the process of family growth. The longer couples put off using contraception, the more likely they are to become subfecund before they feel the need to begin using contraception.

Delay in using contraception was shown to be most common among the poorly educated. For example, among grade-school educated wives who have been pregnant three times, only 18 percent began using contraception before the first pregnancy. The comparable proportion for college wives is 55 percent. By the time they had had three pregnancies, 76 percent of the grade-school wives had begun to use contraception (or their husbands had), and most of the remaining 24 percent were subfecund and would probably never have to use contraception. By the time the college wives had three pregnancies, however, 92 percent had begun using contraception.

A similar explanation accounts for most, though not all, of the difference between the proportions of Protestants and Catholics who have used or will use contraception (90 and 80 percent for the two religious groups, respectively). The Catholics begin contraception later and more of them discover fecundity impairments before the time when they would begin use.

There is evidence that couples are beginning to use contraception earlier. For example, the proportion using contraception before the first pregnancy increased from 34 percent in 1955 to 38 percent in 1960. Also, the proportion of couples who already had used contraception by the time the wife was 18–24 years old increased from 68 to 78 percent in this 5-year period. Therefore, the younger cohorts now in the childbearing period can be expected to have higher proportions who eventually use contraception than some of the older cohorts.

The trend toward earlier use of contraception has already brought about a rise in the proportion of users in the 18–39 group as a whole. In 1955, 70 percent of white couples with wives 18–39 years old had already used contraception. By 1960, the comparable proportion was 81 percent. On the basis of the intentions expressed by the wives in the 1960 study, it is estimated that by 1965 the proportion of users will be even higher—about 85 percent.

HOW FAMILIES ARE PLANNED

As noted previously, a large majority of white couples try to exercise some control over their fertility by using contraception. However, they vary greatly in when they begin use and in how successful their efforts are. This section will describe in broad outline how couples use contraception to plan their families.

First of all, nearly two out of three newlyweds do not start using contraception before the first conception. In most cases, this is because they want to have a baby as soon as they can. Most of those who do begin contraception before the first pregnancy stop using it and conceive

only 8 or 9 months later than other couples. The first child usually arrives less than 2 years after marriage.

After the first birth, the typical couple wants to have another child fairly soon. Although most begin to use contraception before the second child comes along, they still feel no strong pressure to avoid conception. They may omit contraception occasionally or fail to use it properly.

This casual approach to family planning is fairly prevalent until the couple has the desired number of children. It helps to account for the fact that over half the couples in our sample had pregnancies that were not intended to occur when they did. After they have had the two, three, or four children they want, however, most couples become more careful. Usually this means that they use contraception more regularly.[2]

By the time the wife is between 25 and 30 years old, the majority of couples consider their families complete, but they still have an average of about 13 to 16 years of potential childbearing ahead of them. Even though they now try to use contraception regularly, some couples do have unwanted conceptions. But most manage to avoid having more children than they want.

How successful are couples in controlling their fertility? Success can be measured in a number of ways. It might be noted that 18 percent of the couples had had accidental conceptions (i.e., they occurred while contraception was being used always) or that 54 percent had had conceptions that were not intended to

[2] These are among the most important findings of the Princeton Study. See Robert G. Potter, Philip C. Sagi, and Charles F. Westoff: "Improvement of Contraception During the Course of Marriage," *Population Trends*, vol. 16, no. 2, November 1962, pp. 160–174.

occur when they did. But a more important measure of success is whether or not the couple has avoided unwanted pregnancies—that is pregnancies that were not wanted either when they occurred or later. To get at this, each wife with two or more births was asked whether she or her husband had wanted another child at any time shortly before their last conception occurred. If one or both partners did not want any more children, and if the conception was not deliberately planned by stopping contraception, then the couple was classified as having excess fertility.

Seventeen percent of the white couples in this study are classified as having excess fertility. The comparable proportion for nonwhites is 31 percent. Among whites, couples with excess fertility have 3.7 births, on the average, and expect to have 4.1 altogether. Not all of the couples with excess fertility have or expect unusually large numbers of births: 18 percent have only two births, and 33 percent have three. In terms of expectations, 14 percent expect two births and 31 percent expect three. Thus, nearly half of the excess fertility couples expect no more births than the average white couple. Only a minority of 26 percent expect five or more births.

Excess fertility is most prevalent among couples in the lower socioeconomic categories. The greatest contrast is found when couples are classified by the wife's educational attainment: 11 percent of the college group have excess fertility, compared with 32 percent of the grade school group. Differences in husband's income are also related to the prevalence of ineffective family planning: among couples with husbands earning $10,000 or more annually, the proportion with excess fertility is 15 percent; among those with husbands earning less than $3,000, it is 21 percent.

Not only do the lower income groups have relatively more couples with excess fertility, but the degree of excess fertility is most severe among them. For example, the percentage by which the number of births expected exceeds the number of children wanted is 70 percent among couples with the husband's income under $3,000, but only 27 percent if his income is $10,000 or more. This means that most of the excess fertility couples in the low income group have two or more unwanted children. The excess in the high-income group is more likely to be only one child.

Why do couples with lower socioeconomic status have so many unwanted pregnancies? Part of the reason is the fact that some do not begin to use contraception before they have more children than they want. In the grade-school group, 15 percent of the couples had unwanted pregnancies before trying to prevent conception. They account for nearly half of the excess fertility couples in this group. There were hardly any comparable couples in the college group (only 0.2 percent).

Another reason, the study shows, for the high prevalence of unwanted pregnancies among less-educated couples is that after they begin to use contraception they often fail to use it regularly.

These findings indicate that the problem of preventing unwanted pregnancies among the less educated is primarily a problem of their beginning to use contraception earlier and then to use it regularly. It is not simply a matter of making available cheap, effective, and convenient methods of contraception. It is a matter of establishing the habitual use of contraception as a normal and accepted part of married life. This has been stated many times in regard to populations in underdeveloped countries, but it is no less true for the undereducated in our own country.

SUMMARY

A large majority of wives and husbands in the United States agree that the control of fertility is desirable, and most couples who are able to have children either make some attempt to prevent pregnancy or intend to do so. Couples who have never used contraception and do not expect to begin usually have impairments of the reproductive system.

Most couples want two, three, or four children, and they want them within the first 10 years of marriage. A majority do not use contraception before the first conception. After beginning use, but before having all the children they want, some couples do not use contraception very effectively. Most of those who have had all the children they want, however, are able to prevent unwanted conceptions.

An important minority of 17 percent however, have had more children than the husband, wife, or both partners wanted. Although "excess fertility" is experienced in all socioeconomic groups, it is most common among couples with low educational attainment and low income. The 1960 study shows that the most important reasons for excess fertility in the lower socioeconomic groups are the failure of some couples to use contraception after they have all the children they want, and the tendency of other couples to use contraception irregularly.

8

SOCIALIZATION OF THE INFANT

Although young human replacements must be trained in all societies to become participating adults, just how much of the socializing and educating of the young is done by the family varies from one social context to another. The family in general and the mother in particular are the most important, if not the exclusive, sources of influence during the first few years of life. A study not reported in this volume sought to determine through interviews with mothers in six very different societies what were the bases these mothers were using to socialize their young. In all six societies the mothers varied with respect to such maternal behaviors as the use of warmth and praise and in the objectives of inducing responsibility and of controlling fighting among the children.[1]

As we pass from what mothers say to the way in which scientists conceptualize dimensions of socialization, we find Eleanor Maccoby formulating along the line of such determinants of learning observed in laboratory animals as amount of reinforcement, proportion of responses reinforced, and the ratio of rewards to punishments. But in translation to the human level the problem becomes complicated by the question: "What do we mean by reward?" Experiments can induce drive in laboratory animals by depriving them of food or water, but since most parents do not let their children "get hungry, thirsty, wet or overtired," purely physiological rewards are not as relevant with children as with animals. The more complicated nature of the problem at the human level is seen in the fact that approval, affection, and attention become rewards, and the sex of the socializer may affect the outcome of a socializing episode. Here we see Maccoby dealing with problems envisaged in chapter 1 concerning the translation of variables from concepts in measurable operations.

As science succeeds folk wisdom in contemporary society, the "child expert" displaces grandmother in knowing how to handle junior. Nathan Maccoby traces the history of the communication of child-rearing advice by the mass media and shows that the nature of this advice has changed over time and varies among different media. In an effort to show how this advice is considered by mothers, he presents the results of a study in which women were advised on proper child training procedures. His findings indicate that social scientists must undertake more than content-analyses to understand the advice-taking process.

The articles by Ferreira and Skard speak to the question, "What effects do different maternal behaviors have on infants?" Ferreira's study

[1] Leigh Minturn Triandis and William W. Lambert, "Pancultural Factor Analysis of Reported Socialization Practices," *Journal of Abnormal and Social Psychology*, 1961, 62: 631–639.

begins before babies are born; it shows that maternal attitudes measured during pregnancy covary with the subsequent behaviors of their babies. Such data are amenable to the interpretation that there is some underlying process connecting maternal prenatal attitude as cause to infants' behavior as effect. A reductionistic argument that the connecting process is biochemical[2] lends plausibility to the argument.

Aase Skard relates studies of maternal deprivation to a series of studies of mother-infant interaction among monkeys. The author also describes developmental stages of the human from birth into childhood and maternal behaviors appropriate to these stages.

The Choice of Variables in the Study of Socialization*

Eleanor E. Maccoby

Perhaps the greatest change that has occurred in the field of child development in the past 15 years has been the increasing emphasis on socialization. The change may be traced by comparing the more traditional text books with recent ones. The scholarly child psychology text by Munn [15], for example, does not bring up the topic of parent-child interaction until the 16th chapter, and here devotes only eight pages to a topic called "environmental influences and personality," a heading under which he presents all that the book has to say on "mothering," on Freudian theory of developmental stages, on ordinal position—in fact, on socialization in general. Contrast this with a book such as Watson's [22], in which more than half the book is devoted to a discussion of socialization theory and a detailed consideration of the impressive amounts

of research that have recently been done on the subject.

The same increasing emphasis on socialization may be seen in the child-development journals. And, of course, the widespread research interest in this topic has led to the development of several research instruments for the measurement of parental attitudes and behavior. There are the Fels scales [2], developed during the 40's, for the rating of parent behavior; the parent interview schedule developed by Sears and his associates at Harvard and Stanford [20], the parent attitude scales developed by Shoben at U.S.C. [21], and the widely-used Parent Attitude Research Instrument scales developed at the National Institutes of Health by Schaefer and Bell [19], to mention only a few. Each investigator, when he sat down to make a first draft of his rating scale or

[2] One way a mother may affect her unborn child is suggested by recent reports indicating that the fetus is vulnerable to drugs ingested by the mother. See "Placenta Is No Barrier: Tufts Pediatrician Reports Many Drugs Taken by Mother May Threaten Fetus," *Medical World News*, March 10, 1967, pp. 116–117. If the mother's attitude is correlated with some disposition to ingest hormonal agents, barbiturates, vitamins, or even aspirin, a causal chain can be sketched in.

*Adapted from Eleanor E. Maccoby, "The Choice of Variables in the Study of Socialization," Sociometrey, 1961, 24:357–371.

interview schedule or attitude scale items, had to ask himself the question: what shall I measure? What are the important variables in parental behavior that ought to make a difference in the development of the child? The process of selecting and defining variables is, of course, the very heart of theory-making. There are as many possible variables as there are ideas about what causes what in human development. I cannot attempt here to give any sort of roster of variables; the task would be too great and might not prove very useful. I simply want to point out some of the major classes of variables that have been used and give a little of the history of the reasons why we have chosen to measure these things and not others and perhaps point to a few ways in which we could clarify the meaning of the dimension we are using.

Let us start with the traditional child psychologist, with his interests in motor development, emotional development, intelligence, concept formation, and personality development, all grounded in traditional principles of learning and maturation. He may look upon the current work in socialization with a jaundiced eye and inquire what the excitement is all about. He may feel that he has actually been studying socialization for years without calling it by this name. He might put his question this way: If it is true that socialization is the process of transmitting culture from one generation to another, and that the child acquires the modes of behavior prescribed by his culture through the process of learning, then how is the study of socialization any different from the study of learning itself? One might reply that in socialization studies, we study not only the child as learner but the parent as teacher. But a skeptic might still wonder how much difference this actually makes. For example, laboratory studies of learning have dem-

onstrated that behavior which is followed by reward will be strengthened, and its probability of recurrence will be increased. Now, if a student of socialization does a study of dependency, and discovers that parents who reward their children for dependency have more dependent children, has he really found out anything that we didn't know already?

In my opinion, it is valuable to carry out at the human level studies which attempt to employ the standard variables that have grown out of laboratory studies on learning where most of the work has been done on sub-human species. But, in the process of applying such variables to socialization studies, the variables almost perforce undergo certain modifications and elaborations, with the result that translating traditional behavior theory variables into the socialization setting sometimes results in the addition of something new, and the possibility of getting new kinds of principles.

Let me give an example. Suppose we wanted to study the effects of a particular schedule of reward. What do we mean by reward? The traditional approach to reward has been to produce a physiological drive, such as hunger or thirst, through deprivation; and then to reinforce the desired behavior by presenting a drive-relevant reinforcing stimulus. But even in fairly young children, a rapid development of complex motivation occurs, and this changes the nature of the reinforcements to which children will be responsive. B. F. Skinner encountered this fact when he was developing his teaching machines. The early models were devised so as to emit little pieces of chocolate candy whenever a child made the correct response. But it was soon evident that a child progressed through a series of arithmetic or spelling problems just as readily without the candy; in fact, the giving of candy sometimes disrupted the learning process. Skinner, therefore, abandoned the candy rewards, and the current models of his machine rely upon no other reward than the child's interest in doing his work correctly—buttressed, no doubt, by a certain amount of pressure from the teacher and parents. This incident illustrates a major question about the definition of variables: what happens to the variable "amount of reward" when it is translated into situations of teacher-child, or parent-child, interaction? In modern societies, children's physiological drives are regularly and quite fully satisfied and are seldom used as a basis for training. That is, most parents do not let the child get hungry, thirsty, wet, or overtired, and then make the satisfaction of these needs conditional on good behavior. Rather, the rewards used are money, a trip to the zoo, being allowed to stay up for a special TV program, etc. A gift of candy for some children becomes symbolic of affection instead of vice versa. Very commonly, behavior is reinforced simply through the giving of approval, affection, or attention. So the concept "reward," when it refers to the rewards which parents use in socializing their children is not directly comparable to the concept as it was originally developed in studies of animal learning. Of course, it is not really a new idea to point out that different kinds of organisms are capable of being rewarded by different kinds of things. It is clear enough that there are as many kinds of rewards as there are distinguishable motives, and that both motives and rewards vary between species and within species. But the new idea that has been added in socialization studies is that there may be distinguishable *classes* of rewards which may have different effects. The primary distinction made in studies so far has been between material reward and praise. Material reward covers all instances of giving the child some object or privilege that he wants, conditional upon good behavior. Praise depends to some degree upon the

previous establishment of a relationship between the socializing agent and the child, such that the approval of this particular adult is something the child wants. That is, the effectiveness of praise ought to depend upon the identity of the person doing the praising and upon this person's being someone the child loves, fears, or must depend upon for the satisfaction of needs.

The same kind of differentiation of a variable has occurred with respect to punishment. Students of the socialization process have been working under the assumption that not all kinds of aversive events following a child's act will have the same effect. The distinction most commonly made is that between physical punishment and so-called love-oriented discipline, or withdrawal of love. There are other categories of punishment, too, such as withdrawal of privileges and ridicule, which are less interesting than the first two because there are fewer hypotheses about their probably effects. Let us concentrate for a moment on the distinction between physical punishment and withdrawal of love. Physical punishment is easy enough to define, although in rating its frequency and severity, the researcher is always troubled about the problem of how to weigh slaps and shakings in relation to formal spankings. More tricky by far is the matter of defining withdrawal of love. Sears and his associates [20] have defined it as any act or statement on the part of the parent that threatens the affectional bond between the parent and child. This would include the mother's turning her back on the child, refusing to speak to him or smile at him or be in the same room with him, saying she doesn't like him when he does disapproved things, etc. The system of classification of techniques of discipline presented by Beverly Allinsmith in her chapter in Miller and Swanson's book, *Inner Conflict and Defense*, [1] similarly emphasizes the distinction between "psychological" and "corporal" punishment, but defines psychological discipline somewhat differently. This classification for Allinsmith includes manipulating the child by shaming the child, appealing to his pride or guilt, and expressing disappointment over his misdeeds. But there is another dimension considered in the rating: namely, the amount of emotional control the mother displays in administering her discipline. Thus, if a mother shouts angrily at the child, "I hate you for doing that," Allinsmith would *not* classify this as psychological discipline, while Sears et al. would. But the mother who says calmly and perhaps coldly, "Now, dear, you know I don't like little boys who do that," would be classified as using psychological discipline in both systems. The difference in these two classification systems stems in part from two different views of the nature of the process which gives psychological discipline its effect. Sears et al. it as a technique which arouses the child's anxiety over whether he is loved and approved of, and thereby elicits efforts on the child's part to regain his parents' approval by conforming, apologizing, or making amends. Allinsmith, on the other hand, emphasizes two things: (1) the *modeling* function of discipline, pointing out that a mother who loses her temper at the same time she is trying to teach the child to control his, will have a child who will do as the mother *does* rather than as she *says;* and (2) the target the child chooses for the aggressive impulses aroused in him as a consequence of punishment. The reasoning here is that openly angry mother becomes a more legitimate target for the child's counter-aggression. The distinction between the two definitions of the dimension is further brought out when we consider the kinds of findings reported in the studies using them: Sears et al. found that withdrawal of love was associated with high development of conscience, physical punishment with low; Allinsmith found that psychological discipline, as she defined it, was associated with *indirect* fantasy expressions of aggression in the children they studied, corporal punishment with *direct* expression of aggression. All this illustrates the fact that fairly subtle differences in the definition of a dimension can affect the nature of child behavior that can be predicted from it. But more importantly, both these studies illustrate the fact that when we attempted to take over the variable "punishment" from the learning laboratories, we found it necessary to subdivide and differentiate the variable and gained predictive power by doing so.

I have been attempting to cite ways in which I think that socialization studies have improved upon some of the standard variables employed in laboratory studies. There are instances, alas, in which we have not taken note of the differences which exist between the laboratory and the standard socialization settings, and thus have failed to identify and make use of some potentially promising variables. For example, in laboratory studies, we can take it for granted that the experimenter is there during training sessions, administering either reinforcements or aversive stimuli in some orderly relationship to the subject's responses. In the parent-child relationship, the parent is by no means always functioning as a trainer, and parents differ greatly in the degree to which they do so. Some parents keep track quite continuously of what the child is doing, and engage in a constant flow of interaction, both verbal and nonverbal, with the child. Other parents, for a substantial portion of the time they are with their children, are bored, busy, withdrawn, intoxicated, watching television, or subject to some other state or activity which precludes their responding to the child unless he becomes very insistent. In such a household the children are, of course, in a very different learning situation than children growing up with more wholly attentive parents. I think the sheer amount of interaction may in some cases be a more important variable for predicting characteristics of the child than the nature of the interaction that does occur. Let me give you an example. In a study Dr. Lucy Rau and I are now doing at Stanford, we have selected groups of children who show discrepancies in their intellectual abilities. That is, we have one group of children who are good at verbal tasks but poor at number, another group who are good at spatial tasks but poor at verbal, etc. One of our students, Mrs. Bing, has interviewed the mothers of the children, and has also conducted some observation sessions in which the mother presents achievement tasks to the child while the observer records the kind and amount of the mother's involvement with the child's work. Mrs. Bing has found that it is the *amount*, rather than the *kind*, of mother-child interaction that best predicts what the child's pattern of intellectual skills will be. That is, the mothers of the highly verbal children use more praise, but also more criticism, than do the mothers of equally bright children whose area of special skill is non-verbal. Their total level of interaction with the child is greater, and this interaction includes the administration of what we would regard as aversive stimuli as well as reinforcements. The variable "amount of interaction" emerged in our factor analysis of the scales in the *Patterns of Child Rearing* study [20]—we titled this variable "responsible child-rearing orientation" for lack of a better name, but we never made much use of the variable because it did not fit in with the theoretical formulation of our study. But I suspect that for any future work in which we are trying to predict such things as the child's cogni-

tive maturity level or his achievement motivation, we may find that this variable is a better predictor than the less global variables (such as amount of praise) that we have been relying on up till now.

So far, I have been discussing the process of translating variables from laboratory studies of learning to the socialization setting, and have pointed out that we have been successful in employing such variables as reward and punishment, but that in the process of using these variables, we have found useful ways of subdividing them. Let us consider the theoretical meaning of the elaborations of these variables that have occurred.

When we make the distinction between material reward and praise, and the distinction between love-oriented punishment and punishment that depends for its effect upon producing direct physical pain, we are really taking note of the fact that the effect of discipline, and in fact the very nature of the discipline that is possible to use with a child, depends upon the history of the relationship that has been developed between the child and the person who is training him. And here is a new class of variables that socialization studies have added to the list of variables derived from classical studies of learning. In laboratory studies of learning, it has not been found necessary (at least until very recently) to ask whether the experimental subject loved or hated the machine that was emitting pellets of food and drops of water, or whether the characteristics of the machine or person presenting the rewards made any difference in the effectiveness of the reinforcement. Socialization studies, on the other hand, have found the identity of the socializing agent, and certain of his personality characteristics, to be important.

The emphasis on the importance of the relationship between trainer and learner came, of course, out of psychodynamic theories of personality development.

Learning theory and psychoanalytic theory differ, I think, with respect to what they believe the basic nature of the socialization process is. This is an oversimplification, but I believe it would be reasonably accurate to say that a learning theorist would regard socialization as a learning process in which certain actions of the child's are selected out by virtue of reinforcement, others tried and dropped because they are in some way punished or non-reinforced. The parents have a primary role in administering the rewards and punishments for the child's actions, although they do not necessarily do this deliberately and consciously as a teaching effort. And, of course, there are other sources of reward and punishment than the parents' reactions which will help to determine what behavior the child retains.

The psychoanalytic approach, on the other hand, would emphasize not the detailed learning of specific actions on the basis of their outcome, but the providing of conditions which will motivate the child to take on spontaneously the socialized behavior the parent wants him to have. The terms introjection, internalization, learning through role-playing, and identification have been used in this connection; they all refer to the child's tendency to copy, to take on as his own, the behavior, attitudes, and values of the significant people in his life, even when the socializing agents have not said "that's a good boy" or given him a piece of candy for performing these acts or holding these values. I will not go into the controversy concerning which so much has been written as to whether the child is more likely to identify with the person who is powerful and feared or with the person who is loved; nor will I discuss the several thoughtful efforts by personality theorists to reconcile the two points of view. The only important point for our consideration here is that the psychoanalytic view of socialization has led to an exploration of such variables as the warmth or hostility of the socializing agent toward the child.

There can be no doubt that measures of the warmth of the parent-child relationship have turned out to be enormously useful in socialization studies, in a number of ways. In some studies, warmth has been found to have a direct relationship to some dependent variable. For example, McCord and McCord [13] have found that warmth in fathers was associated with low crime rate in sons. In other studies, warmth has turned out to be a useful crosscutting variable which interacts with other variables in such a way that other variables only begin to show their effects when the sample is first sub-divided into groups differing in parental warmth. For example, in the *Patterns of Child Rearing* study, Sears et al. [20] found that withdrawal of love is associated with rapid development of conscience, but only if this technique is employed by a warm mother; also that punishment for toilet accidents disrupts the toilet training process, but that the greatest disruption occurs if punishment is administered by a cold mother.

Warmth also occupies a central role in socialization studies in its relationship to other measures of child-training variables. There have been, to my knowledge, three factor analyses carried out on sets of socialization variables. One of these was on the Fels parent behavior rating scales [17], one on the PARI [26], and one on the dimensions employed by Sears et el. in the Patterns study [20]. In the latter two, warmth emerged as a fairly clear factor. In the first, there were two factors, one called "concern for the child" and the other called "parent-child harmony," which taken together are probably close to what is meant by warmth in the other two studies. It is clear, then, that both in terms of its predictive value for the child's behavior and its central place among the other interrelated child-training variables, warmth is a variable to be taken seriously. Why is it so important? I have already pointed out why the psychodynamic theorists believe it to be so—because of its role in producing identification. But the laboratory learning theorists can acknowledge its importance for another very simple reason: before a parent can socialize a child, he must have established a relationship with the child such that the child will stay in the vicinity of the parent and orient himself toward the parent. A warm parent keeps the child responsive to his directions by providing an atmosphere in which the child has continuous expectations that good things will happen to him if he stays near his parent and responds to his parent's wishes. Fear of punishment can also make the child attentive to the parent, of course, but it establishes as well the conflicting motivation to escape out of reach of the punisher.

I'm sure I needn't belabor any further the notion that warmth is an important variable. But to say this is not enough. We still are faced with considerable difficulty in definition. It has been the experience of a number of people working with child training data that they find themselves able to make reliable distinctions between mothers they call warm and mothers they call cold, and they find it possible to train others to make similar distinctions, but find it difficult indeed to define exactly what cues they are using to make the rating.

I suspect one source of difficulty is that the behavior we look for as indicating warmth varies with the age of the child the mother is dealing with. When the child is an infant, we are likely to label a mother as warm if she gives a good deal of the contact comfort that Harlow° has described. As the child grows older, the part played by the giving of contact comfort in the total constellation of warmth undoubtedly declines. When a child is ten, a mother seldom expresses her warm feelings for him by holding him on her lap. Rather, they are more likely to be expressed by the mother showing interest in the child and what he is doing, by helping unconditionally when help is needed, by being cordial and relaxed. Now warmth as expressed this way is not the same thing as giving contact comfort, and it is not to be expected that the same individuals would necessarily be good at both. Those who have read Brody's fascinating, detailed descriptions of mothers' behavior toward their infants [4] will perhaps have noted that the mothers who gave effective contact comfort, in the sense of holding the child comfortably and close, stroking it occasionally, imparting some rocking motion, handling it skillfully and gently in the process of caring for the child—the women who could do all these things well were not necessarily the same women who expressed delight and pride in their children, who noticed their little accomplishments, or who looked upon their infants as individuals. We should therefore not be surprised if there are low correlations between a mother's warmth toward her infant and her warmth toward the same child when it is older. If a primary ingredient of warmth is being able to gratify the child's needs unconditionally, and if the child's needs change from the infantile needs for being fed and being given contact comfort to the more mature needs for various kinds of ego support,

°See H. F. Harlow, "The Nature of Love," *Amer. Psychologist*, 1958, 13, pp. 673–685—Eds.

then it is necessary for a mother to change considerably as her child changes, in order to be warm towards him at all ages. Some mothers make this change more easily than others. It is true that Schaefer and Bayley [18], in their longitudinal study of a group of mothers, did find a substantial degree of continuity in the degree of warmth displayed by a given mother toward a given child as the child grew older. There were undoubtedly individual differences in the ways warmth was manifested, and in the appropriateness of a mother's particular style of warmth-giving to the needs of her child at each developmental stage.

From the standpoint of making use of the variable in research, it appears that we should recognize that measuring the mother's current warmth at the time the child is, say, in nursery school or in the primary grades, may not be an especially good index of how warm she was to the child as an infant. Furthermore, her warmth in infancy might predict quite different characteristics of the child than her warmth in middle childhood. If there is any relation at all between nurturance to an infant and its later personality traits, infant nurturance ought to relate only to those aspects of personality that presumably have their foundation in infancy—such as Erikson's dimension of trust [6], or various aspects of orality. Achievement motivation, on the other hand, if it is related to the mother's warmth at all, ought to be related to measures of this variable taken when the child is older. A finding of Bronfenbrenner's [5] seems to support this point about the importance of warmth-giving being appropriate to the developmental level of the child. He was studying high-school-aged children and employed several variables relating to the kind and amount of affectionate interchange between these adolescents and their parents. He measured the parents' affection-giving (in the

sense of direct demonstrativeness), use of affective rewards, nurturance, and affiliative companionship. Among these variables, it was only the last one, affiliative companionship, that correlated with the child's current level of responsibility taking. We can speculate that this particular aspect of warmth is the one that fits in much better with an adolescent's needs than either giving him kisses or peanut butter sandwiches. All this means that warmth has to be defined in terms of parental responsiveness to the changing needs of the child.

I have referred to socialization variables that came originally from laboratory studies of learning, and that have been adapted for use in studying the socialization process. I have also referred to variables that originated in psychodynamic thinking. There is a set of variables that is difficult to classify in terms of these two theoretical systems; I am referring to the dimension "permissiveness vs. restrictiveness," which emerged in our factor analysis of the *Patterns* variables, and to the related dimension of "control vs. laissez-faire" which has come out of the factor analysis of the PARI scales. The theoretical status of these variables is confusing because they relate to both psychoanalytic and learning theory, but the predictions from the two theories as to the probable effects of "permissiveness" or "control" are sometimes quite different. To cite a familiar example, there is the issue of what ought to be the effects of permissive treatment of the infant's sucking responses. The question is complex, but a simplified version of the opposing positions would be this: the learning theorist would argue that if an infant is permitted extensive sucking, his sucking habit will be strengthened, and he will be more likely to suck his thumb, pencils, etc., at a later age. The psychodynamic theorist would argue that permitting extensive infantile sucking satisfies oral needs and reduces the likelihood of excessive oral behavior at a later age. The same kind of difference of opinion can be found concerning whether permissive treatment of a child's aggressive or dependent responses should increase or decrease those responses. Now, of course, the fact that different theories produce different predictions concerning the effects of a variable is no reason for abandoning the variable. On the contrary, it is cause for rejoicing, and we should by all means continue to use the variable so that we can get data which will bear upon the validity of the theories. The trouble is that when we arrive at the point of trying to get agreement on the interpretation of findings, it sometimes turns out that the two schools of thought did not mean the same thing by "permissiveness." If a study shows that the more permissive parents are toward their children's aggression the more aggressive the children become, the psychodynamic theorist may say, "Well, by permissiveness I didn't mean *license;* the child must have limits set for him but he must also be allowed to express his feelings." If, on the other hand, a study shows that children heavily punished for aggression are more aggressive on the playground, or prefer aggressive TV programs, the learning theorist may say, "Well, of course, if the parents' methods of stopping aggression are such as to provide additional instigation to aggression, than their non-permissiveness won't eliminate the behavior." We begin to see that there are some hidden meanings in such a term as "permissiveness" and that we are dealing with several dimensions. Continuing with the example of aggression, we can see that permissiveness for aggression could mean the following things:

1. The mother holds the attitude that aggression is an acceptable, even desirable, form of behavior.

2. The mother does not like aggres-

sive behavior and expects to limit it in her children, but feels that it is natural and inevitable at certain ages and so does not react strongly when her young child displays anger. A related definition of permissiveness would be placing the demands for self control placed upon the child to correspond with his developmental level.

3. The mother is not especially interested in the child or is otherwise occupied, and does not act to stop or prevent his aggression because she does not notice what he is doing unless his actions are aimed directly at her.

4. The mother does not act early in a sequence of her child's aggressive behavior, but waits till the behavior has become fairly intense.

And at the other end of the scale, the effect of *non*-permissiveness ought to depend upon how the non-permitting is done—whether by punishment, by reinforcing alternative behavior, by environmental control that removes the instigations of undesired behavior, or some other means. The basic point I wish to emphasize is that I believe "permissiveness" is not a unitary variable, and that we need to work more directly with its components.

So far I have discussed several classes of variables: the ones translated as directly as possible from laboratory studies of learning (e.g., amount and kind of reward and punishment), and variables such as warmth and permissiveness of the socializing agent, which have their origins more in psychodynamic theories. There is another class of variables which has been emerging as more and more important, namely the "social structure" variables. These variables have their origin largely in sociological thinking. I do not have time to give them more than the most cursory attention, but I do not believe they can be omitted if we are to do any sort of justice to the scope of significant variables employed in current socialization studies. One has only to list a few findings which have come out of the investigation of social structure factors to see how essential it has become to take them into account. Here is a brief sampling of such findings:

1. In adolescents, parents are most strict with children who are of the same sex as the dominant parent. [16].

2. A mother's use of strongly dominant child-rearing techniques (called "unqualified power assertion" in this study) is related to her husband's F score (authoritarian personality score), but not to her own. [10].

3. A mother's behavior toward her children is more closely related to her husband's education than her own, and her behavior is more closely related to her husband's education than is *his* behavior with his own education. Thus it appears that it is the family's social status, as indicated by the husband's education, that influences the mother's socialization practices. [5].

4. Sons are more intra-punitive if their mothers are primarily responsible for discipline than they are if their fathers are the primary disciplinarians. [9].

Aspects of social organization such as whether residence is patrilocal, matrilocal, or neolocal, and whether marriage is polygamous or monogamous, determine such aspects of culture as the length of the postpartum sex taboo, the duration of exclusive mother-child sleeping arrangements, and the amount of authority the father has over the child; these factors in turn determine such socialization practices as the age of weaning, the severity of the socialization pressures which are directed toward breaking up the child's dependency upon the mother, and the existence and nature of puberty rites at adolescence.

5. These socialization practices then in their turn determine certain aspects of personality, including certain culturally established defense systems. [23, 24, 25].

6. When offered a choice between a small piece of candy now vs. a large one later, children from father-present homes can postpone gratification more easily than children from father-absent homes. [14].

These findings all represent efforts to put socialization practices into a cultural context. In each case, socialization practices are regarded as a link in a several-step chain, and consideration is given to the factors which determine the socialization practices themselves, as well as to the effects these practices in their turn have upon the child. It is clear that the way parents treat their children will be a function of their relationship to each other (especially of the distribution of authority between them), of the place the family has in the status system of the society in which the family resides, of the society's kinship system, etc. Of course, not every student of socialization need concern himself with all the steps in the complex sequence; he may, and often does, select a set of socialization practices and relate them to the child's behavior without going back to the conditions which led to these practices. But he needs to be aware of the degree to which socialization practices are embedded in a cultural context, and even needs to be alert to the possibility that the "same" socialization practice may have different effects when it is part of different cultural settings. So far, few studies have been planned or analyzed with this possibility in mind, but it might be worth some empirical examination.

It is time to make explicit an assumption that has been implicit so far about the constancy of personality from one situation to another and from one time to another. When we select aspects of parental behavior to study, and try to relate these to measured characteristics of the child, we usually measure what we believe to be reasonably pervasive, reasonably enduring "traits" of the parent and child. Orville Brim [3] in a recent paper, has leveled a direct attack at the notion of trait constancy. He has asserted that there is no such thing as a "warm" person, nor an "aggressive" person, nor a "dependent" person, but that behavior is specific to roles. This would mean that the same individual may be aggressive with his subordinates and dependent toward his boss; that a child may be emotionally expressive with his same-sexed age mates, but not with his teachers or his parents. The question of exactly how general personality traits are, is, of course, a matter that personality theorists have struggled with for many years. But our view of this matter will have some bearing upon our selection and definition of socialization variables. For if a child's behavior is going to be entirely specific to roles, then there is no point in trying to predict any generalized traits in the child; rather, we should be looking for those aspects of the socialization situation that will determine what behavior will be adopted by the child in each different role relationship in which he will find himself. If we wanted to find what socialization practices were associated with the child's becoming dominant or submissive, for example, we would have to study how his dominant behavior had been reacted to when he was playing with same-sexed siblings, and study this separately from the socialization of the same behavior when he was playing with opposite-sexed siblings; only thus could we predict, according to Brim, how dominant he would be with other boys in the classroom, and we would have to make a separate prediction of his dominance with girls in the classroom. We have already been following Brim's advice, in essence, when we do studies in which we test how the child's behavior varies with the role characteristics of the person with whom he is interacting. A good example is Gerwitz' and Baer's study on the interaction between the sex of the experimenter and the effects of interrupted nurturance [7]. But to follow Brim's point further, we would have to investigate the ways in which the child's behavior toward specific categories of "others" was conditioned by differential socialization in these role relationships.

I do not believe that either socialization or the child's reaction tendencies are as role-specific as Brim claims; but obviously role differentiation does occur, and he is quite right in calling our attention to the fact that for some variables at least, we should be studying socialization separately within roles. Actually, role is only one aspect of situational variability; we have known ever since the days of Hartshorne and May [8] that trait behavior like "honesty" is situation-specific; they found, for example, that the child who will cheat on the playground is not necessarily the same child who will cheat in the classroom, and that cheating is a function of the specific task presented to the child. This means that in studying the effects of socialization, we either have to abandon efforts to predict characteristics like "honesty" and attempt to study only those characteristics of the child that are at least somewhat constant across situations, or we have to choose socialization variables that are themselves much more situation-specific, and make much more detailed predictions. An example of the utility of making socialization variables more specific to the situations they are intended to predict is provided in a study by Levy [12], in which it was found that a child's adjustment to a hospital experience was *not* a function of the parents having trained the child generally to meet many different kinds of stress situations; rather, the child's response to hospitalization was predicted only from the amount of training the parent gave in advance for the meeting of this *particular* stress situation.

The same sort of situation prevails with respect to trait constancy over time. In their recent article on dependency, Kagan and Moss [11] were able to present repeated measurements of dependency in the same group of individuals —measurements which began at the age of three and continued into the late twenties. The most notable feature of their findings was the absence of continuity in this trait. The children who were dependent at age three and four were not the same individuals who emerged as dependent in adulthood. There was simply no continuity at all for boys, while there was some, but not a great deal, for girls. Let us consider Kagan's finding from the standpoint of efforts to study the socialization practices that are related to dependency. The first and obvious point is that we cannot expect to find any characteristic of the parent's behavior that will correlate with dependency in the young child and also correlate with dependency when the child is an adolescent or adult. This is not to say that the only correlations we can hope for are those between socialization practices and child characteristics measured at the same point in time. It is of course most likely that we will be able to find aspects of a parent's current behavior that correlate with characteristics his child is displaying at the same time. But it is also possible that we could find aspects of the parent's current behavior whose effects will not show up until later. That is, perhaps there were things the parents of Kagan's sample of children were doing when these children were three and four that had some bearing upon how dependent the children became at the age of ten or eleven. But it is clear enough that whatever these delayed-action variables are, they could hardly be the same variables as the ones which determined how dependent the children were at age three, since it was not the same children who were displaying large amounts of dependency behavior at the two ages.

I have pointed to the way in which different theoretical systems, and different social science disciplines, have converged to define and elaborate some of the variables which have been used in studies of socialization. In some cases this convergence has produced useful new knowledge; in others it has produced confusion over the meaning of variables. More importantly, it has produced a startling range of findings which have not yet been integrated into a theory of socialization. This is a major task that remains to be done.

References

1. ALLINSMITH, BEVERLY, "The directness with which anger is expressed," in D. R. Miller and G. E. Swanson, *Inner Conflict and Defense* (New York: Holt, 1960), chapter 14.
2. BALDWIN, A. L., KALHORN, JOAN, and BREESE, FAY H., "The Appraisal of Parent Behavior," *Psychol. Monogr.*, 1949, 63.
3. BRIM, O. G., JR., "Personality development as role learning," in I. Iscoe and H. W. Stevenson, eds., *Personality Development in Children* (Austin: Univer. Texas Press, 1960).
4. BRODY, SYLVIA, *Patterns of Mothering* (New York: International Universities Press, 1957).
5. BRONFENBRENNER, U., "Some Familial Antecedents of Responsibility and Leadership in Adolescents," unpublished manuscript, Cornell University, 1959.
6. ERIKSON, E. H., *Childhood and Society* (New York: Norton, 1950).
7. GERWIRTZ, J. L. and BAER, D. M., "Does Brief Social 'Deprivation' Enhance the Effectiveness of a Social Reinforcer ('Approval')?" *Amer. Psychologist*, 1956, 11, 428–429.
8. HARTSHORNE, H. and MAY, M.A., *Studies in Deceit* (New York: Macmillan, 1928).
9. HENRY, A. F., "Family Role Structure and Self-blame," *Social Forces*, 1956, 35, 34–38.
10. HOFFMAN, M. L., "Power Assertion by Parents and Its Impact on the Child," *Child Develpm.*, 31, 1960, 129–144.

11. KAGAN, J. and MOSS, H.A., "The Stability of Passive and Dependent Behavior from Childhood through Adulthood," *Child Develpm.*, 1960, 31, 577–591.

12. LEVY, E., "Children's Behavior under Stress and Its Relation to Training by Parents to Respond to Stress Situation," *Child Develpm.*, 1959, 30, 307–324.

13. McCORD, W. and McCORD, JOAN, *The Origins of Crime* (New York: Columbia Univ. Press, 1959).

14. MISCHEL, W., "Preference for Delayed Reinforcement: An Experimental Study of a Cultural Observation," *J. Abnorm. Soc. Psychol.*, 1958, 56, 57–61.

15. MUNN, N. L., *The Evolution and Growth of Human Behavior* (Boston: Houghton Mifflin, 1955).

16. PAPANEK, MIRIAM L., "Family Structure and Child-Training Practices," unpublished doctoral dissertation, Radcliffe College, 1954.

17. ROFF, M., "A Factorial Study of the Fels Parent Behavior Scales," *Child Develpm.*, 1949, 20, 29–45.

18. SCHAEFER, E. S. and BAYLEY, NANCY, "Consistency of Maternal Behavior from Infancy to Preadolescence," *J. Abnorm. Soc. Psychol.*, 1960, 61, 1–6.

19. SCHAEFER, E. S. and BELL, R. Q., "Development of a Parental Attitude Research Instrument," *Child Develpm.*, 1958, 29, 339–361.

20. SEARS, R. R., MACCOBY, ELEANOR E., and LEVIN, H., *Patterns of Child Rearing* (Evanston: Row Peterson, 1957).

21. SHOBEN, E. J., "The Assessment of Parental Attitudes in Relation to Child Adjustment," *Genet. Psychol. Monogr.*, 1949, 39.

22. WATSON, R. I., *Psychology of the Child* (New York: Wiley, 1959).

23. WHITING, J. W. M., "Sin, Sorcery and Superego," in M. R. Jones, ed., *Nebraska Symposium on Motivation* (Lincoln: Univ. Nebraska Press, 1959), pp. 174–195.

24. WHITING, J. W. M., CHASDI, ELEANOR H., ANTONOVSKY, HELEN F., and AYRES, BARBARA C., "The Learning of Values," in C. Kluckhohn and E. Z. Vogt, eds., *The Peoples of Rimrock: A Comparative Study of Values Systems.* In press.

25. WHITING, J. W. M., KLUCKHOHN, R., and ANTHONY, A., "The Function of Male Initiation Rites at Puberty," in Eleanor E. Maccoby, T. M. Newcomb, and E. L. Hartley, eds., *Readings in Social Psychology* (New York: Holt, 1958), pp. 359–370.

26. ZUCKERMAN, M., BARRETT-RIBBACK, BEATRICE, MONASHKIN, I., and NORTON, J., "Normative Data and Factor Analysis on the Parental Attitude Research Instrument," *J. Consult. Psychol.*, 1958, 22, 165–171.

The Communication of Child-Rearing Advice to Parents[*]

Nathan Maccoby

My [purpose] . . . is to discuss the evidence on the nature and effects of various types of communications on information, attitudes, and behavior in mental health

[*]*Adapted from* The Merrill-Palmer Quarterly, *1961, 7: 199–204.*

matters. The evidence that I have to report derives mainly from a series of studies that my colleagues and I have been conducting at Stanford during the last two to three years (4, 3, 1). These studies have been concerned mainly with the role of the communications process in the acquisition of information, attitudes, and behavior changes concerning child rearing among parents. We have studied the mass media both past and present for communication content. We have interviewed parents intensively. We have obtained correlational type survey analysis data on information-seeking behavior in mothers on matters related to child rearing, and we have conducted controlled experiments on the effects of communications of various types on mothers.

Since some of our data is still in the analysis stage, . . . I shall simply report some of the more interesting results thus far obtained.

CHILD REARING ADVICE IN MEDIA

Our study of advice on child rearing in the popular magazines was modeled closely after Celia Stendler's classic study, "Sixty Years of Child Training Research" (5). We took issues of three popular women's magazines—*The Ladies Home Journal, Woman's Home Companion,* and *Good Housekeeping*—beginning in 1892, the Victorian Period. Then we took 1910, the Edwardian Pre-World War I era. Then 1925, the Post-World War I period; then 1935, the Depression years; and 1950 for Post-World War II; and finally, 1959, a more or less current year. Only the *Ladies Home Journal* was available for all these years. However, for 1910–1950 all three magazines were used. Among other things, we coded all child-rearing advice with respect to amount of copy, subject matter, specificity of advice, general method of child rearing advocated, whether the advice was couched in objective-factual terms or consisted of moralistically toned value judgements, and the source of the communication. One of our most interesting findings turned out to be the relationship between the sheer number of articles and the birth rate. During the periods of high birth rate, we found a large number of articles. The nadir for both birth rate and articles on child-rearing advice was the Depression year of 1935.

We find, as might be expected, a kind of cyclic fashion in the permissiveness-restrictiveness dimension of advice. Restrictiveness was prominent in popular articles in 1892, even more so in 1910, a little less in 1925, much less in 1935, and lowest of all in 1950. Interestingly enough, in 1959 restrictiveness shows a definite increase but has nothing like the amount of attention it enjoyed in earlier years.

It is important to note, however, that whether advice is for permissive or restrictive parental behavior seems to depend to a considerable extent on the subject matter of the article. When the subject matter consists largely of personality development or developmental stages, a la Gesell, permissiveness advice dominates. However, when physical development or socialization of infants is being discussed, the advice tends to be largely in favor of restrictiveness in child rearing. Articles dealing with the socialization of older children or with specific behavior problems tend to be intermediate along a restrictiveness-permissiveness scale.

When we now examine the kinds of content in the different years studied, we find that articles dealing with physical development and health are less prevalent in 1950 and are more prevalent earlier, as well as in 1959, when, as we recall, an upward trend in restrictiveness advice was seen. Stories dealing with personality development or with developmental stages, on the other hand, are most frequent in the permissive years and least in the restrictive years. Again, 1959 behaves like a return to restrictiveness.

Although 1959 shows this return in the direction of restrictiveness advice, it is marked also by a stiff increase in the number of articles dealing with specific behavior problems. This increase is accompanied by a decrease in global advice on child rearing. Furthermore, the nature of the behavior problems changes from such problems as getting a child to sleep, and manners, to problems of sex and modesty behavior. In 1910, bed-going was discussed as follows: "It all comes back to the matter of habit and submission to the inevitable;" in 1959, "nightmares and other fears occur at this time because the fear about injury to the genitals is too great to tolerate consciously." In general, this emphasis on a cause and effect analysis of behavior keeps increasing with the years.

In addition to the historical analysis of women's magazines, we studied a sample of the contents of current mass media. In this, we included newspapers and television, as well as magazines. Mainly, we sampled among the first six months of 1959.

Very briefly, we found some interesting differences by media in the handling of child-rearing advice. Of the three newspapers studied, the *New York Times* devoted the highest proportion of its child-rearing content to serious matters of child development and very little to humor or high adventure as compared to the *San Francisco Chronicle* and the *Palo Alto Times*. But both of the latter were exceeded by television in the proportion of "light" coverage of sports, teen-age culture, and comic material.

We coded not only explicit advice, but also the implied suggestions of fictional portrayals. It is interesting to note that the proportion of explicit parental guidance advocating the permissive handling of children is very much higher than it is in the case of fictional and other implicit advice where restrictiveness tends to be the order of the day.

A possible reason for this discrepancy between the fictional emphasis on restrictiveness and the direct literature's emphasis on permissiveness suggests itself. Parents, at a covert level, may prefer restrictive behavior or at least find themselves engaging in it more often than they would overtly prefer to do. Thus arguments for restrictive behavior are more palatable when made through fiction. The recent upward trend in restrictiveness advice in non-fiction may then indicate increased insight into this situation by parents.

Although we have no measures of the relative potency of direct versus fictional type advice, it is not unlikely that fictional may be more powerful in some respects. First, it is more likely to be attended to by larger audiences; and secondly, it can perhaps bring about changes in *emotional* responding more easily through role practice than can direct tuition. In less affective matters, one would clearly expect direct tuition to be more effective.

INFORMATION SEEKING BEHAVIOR IN CHILD REARING

Let us now turn from media content on child rearing to an examination of information-seeking behavior. We do have a fair amount of data in this area. In one series of studies, we selected women of three kinds: (a) young married women with no children; (b) women with one child, a baby in his first year; and (c) women whose youngest child was in the first or second grade. When women of these three types were offered through the mails a free copy of our booklet entitled "When to Toilet Train Your Child," (while just over a third of the childless women and of the women with older children replied) over two-thirds (71%) of the mothers of infants—our "critical-period" group—requested copies. Unsolicited and unannounced mailings were made to another sample of such women. Subsequent interviews, in which a test of the booklet contents took place, produced similar results. Just under half of the pre- and post-critical groups read the booklet, while almost nine-tenths of the critical-period mothers did so.

We were also interested in the effects of an administered communication on the information-seeking behavior of persons exposed to it. Employing Festinger's theory of cognitive dissonance (2), one could predict that those people presented with an argument at variance with their initial position would either change or stand firm. In either case, dissonance drive would increase. Among the changers, the old position would still have some attractions; and on the non-changers, the new position arguments would leave their scars. In this study, we first determined the subject's position on a nature-nurture scale and then presented a taped lecture which in some instances was consonant with the subject's initial position and in some, dissonant. More members of the two dissonant groups indicated a desire to attend a further discussion of the topic than was the case for the two consonant groups.

In other studies, we were interested in the effect of our toilet-training booklet on the information-seeking behavior of subjects. First of all, we found that some two-thirds of the women who had read the booklet did discuss its contents subsequently with someone. Furthermore, this was more likely to happen among our critical-period mothers than with other women. Although our data indicate that most people initially believe in early toilet training, most of our respondents talked to people they expected, in advance, to agree with out booklet's late training position. In fact, those changed by the booklet were much more likely to seek out and talk to people whom they ex-

pected to agree with their new position than was the case for those not so affected by our communication. On the contrary, talking with people who were expected to disagree with the message was largely confined to those people whose views remained unchanged after exposure to the booklet. Furthermore, the effect of this subsequent discussion itself was evidently to help maintain the change or non-change as the case might be. Those who changed and who did not seek out discussants were likely to backslide—to lose that change over a six-month period. However, those who did seek out discussants tended to maintain their new positions for long periods of time.

Finally, let us examine some evidence on the effects of communications on child rearing. . . . In an experiment conducted with San Francisco women, we tested the effects of a pamphlet we prepared on toilet training. We found, contrary to our expectations, that we had at least as much, if not more, immediate influence on women with no children, or with older children only, as we had on those with young infants only. These latter we labeled "critical-period" people because they were faced for the first time with the decision on when to start bowel training. We recommended delaying until the child was 24 months old or older. On a re-test of both experimentals and controls, six months later, we found that our critical-period women tended to stay changed. In our other groups, only those whose initial position was quite discrepant from the one we advocated were still influenced. Those who came close to agreeing with us initially tended to revert to their initial position, but this did not happen among the mothers of young babies. These stood firm or even, in some cases, were sleepers. That is, although they did not change immediately, they changed over time.

A year later, we attempted to find out whether our attitudinal changes would carry over to toilet-training behavior. We found that the experimental group mothers of babies did indeed start or plan to start at almost the time they had said they would. However, our control group women—those who did not read the booklet—also tended to start training almost as late. Events tended to conspire to make them delay the onset of training: Relatives visiting, illness of mother or child, moving (even people already in California show surprisingly high mobility), and other factors tended to cause mothers to start bowel training in earnest somewhat later than they had thought they should in the control group. We didn't anticipate this finding, and now wish we had obtained a measure of guilt. That is, our control mothers should feel that they have been wrong to wait, that they may have done badly by their child, while our experimental ones should feel that they started bowel training about when they should have.

Subsequent studies have been concerned with the inter-relationship of more general attitudes with specific ones. Those data are now being analyzed. I can only say that the results indicate a complex relationship between general and specific attitudes. Whether the general communication is compatible with the subject's initial position makes a difference on its effect and interacts with the order of presentation of general and specific communication.

SUMMARY

In studies analyzing the content of mass communications on child rearing, we have traced developments in popular women's magazines since 1892 where, among other things, we found a relationship between the number of articles on child rearing and the birth rate, a cyclical change in permissiveness advice with a recent mild upswing in restrictiveness. However, subject matter changes have accompanied these swings, with permissiveness advice being largely in the area of personality development and restrictiveness advice dealing with physical development and the socialization of infants.

In our analysis of the current mass media, we found that newspapers, especially the *New York Times*, were likely to concern themselves with serious advice. Television, on the other hand, contained considerable light and humorous content. Fictional advice was found to be much more in the direction of restrictiveness, and it was speculated that fictionalized content through role portrayal might turn out to be more potent than direct advice in affectively charged matters.

We next discussed findings on information seeking. We found that critical-period mothers were more likely to seek out information relevant to their needs; and, once exposed to such overt information, to attend to it. In further studies, one of the important effects of exposure to communications is the resulting seeking out of further information and discussion. This seeking tends to take the form of seeking support for either one's old position, if it is still retained after exposure to contrary information, or to seek support for the newly acquired position. These findings were interpreted in terms of Festinger's cognitive dissonance theory.

Finally, we found that although a communication, in terms of immediate effects, had no more influence on involved critical-period mothers than on women less involved, in terms of long lasting effects, it did have more influence. That is, with delayed measures, people whose initial position was distant from the one our communication advocated, tended to be changed as often in pre- and post-critical-period women as among critical-period women. However, for people whose position was initially nearer the one we advocated, only the critical-period mothers showed strong delayed effects.

References

1. ADAMS, J. S.   The reduction of cognitive dissonance by seeking consonant information. *J. abnorm. soc. Psychol.*, 1961, 62, 74–78.
2. FESTINGER, L.   *A theory of cognitive dissonance.* Evanston: Row, Peterson, 1957.
3. MACCOBY, ELEANOR E., MACCOBY, N., ROMNEY, A. K. and ADAMS, J. S. Social reinforcement in attitude change. *J. abnorm. soc. Psychol.*, 1961, 63, 109–115.
4. MACCOBY, N., ROMNEY, A. K., A-DAMS, J. S. and MACCOBY, ELEANOR E. "Critical periods" in seeking and accepting information. *Amer. Psychologist*, 1959, 14, 358.
5. STENDLER, CELIA.   Sixty years of child training practices, revolution in the nursery. *J. Pediatrics*, 1950, 36, 122–134.

The Pregnant Woman's Emotional Attitude and its Reflection on the Newborn*

Antonio J. Ferreira

Throughout the centuries, in folklore and magic, there has been a prevalent belief that some specific events, happenings, or circumstances could ominously affect the pregnant woman, alter the course of her otherwise normal physiologic processes, and ultimately print indelible marks on the offspring. However, until recently, the subject of prenatal influences aroused but little scientific interest.

In 1896 Dabney [1] described 90 cases of fetal abnormalities which he believed were associated with and caused by "maternal impressions" incurred in the course of pregnancy. But it was only in the last twenty years, mostly through the efforts of Sontag and his co-workers, that our understanding of a prenatal environment began to take shape. Sontag pointed out that "deeply disturbed maternal emotion produces a marked increase in activity of the fetus" [6], and

°*Reprinted from* The American Journal of Orthopsychiatry, *1960, 30:3: 553–561.*

unearthed some evidence of the fact that "the psychophysiological state of the (pregnant) mother exerts an influence upon the behavior pattern of the normal fetus" [7]. A similar conviction was also expressed by Ernest Jones [2], who emphasized that the mother's attitude toward the unborn child influences the course of pregnancy and labor. In recent years, Turner [8], from a survey of 100 mothers and babies, was also led to the impression that "prenatal emotional stress might . . . alter the whole pattern of postnatal behavior."

The strength of these and other studies has not sufficed, however, to establish the existence and importance of a prenatal enviroment beyond the point of plausibility. And, perhaps also because of the difficulties inherent in a systematic study of the subject, the consideration of factors in the prenatal environment has remained speculative, if not unspoken.

This paper reports on an attempt to

demonstrate the existence of a prenatal environment. Through a research study conducted at Letterman Army Hospital, San Francisco, and with the integrated participation of the Psychiatric, Obstetric and Pediatric Services, we set out to answer the question as to whether certain emotional attitudes of the pregnant mother were prenatally conveyed to the fetus and thus reflected upon the behavior of the newborn. We hoped to demonstrate experimentally the existence of a prenatal environment and, more specifically, to investigate the hypothesis that "upset" or deviant behavior in the newborn would bear a relationship with mother's prenatal "negative" attitude toward pregnancy and the baby-to-come.

THE DESIGN

The pregnant women were studied by means of a self-administered questionnaire. Utilizing the facilities of a Prenatal Clinic, every woman in her last four weeks of pregnancy (i.e., after the 36th week of pregnancy) was directed to fill out an attitude-inventory type of questionnaire. The questionnaire was based on the Parental Attitude Research Instrument (PARI) as developed by Schaefer and Bell [4]. It was composed of eight scales, seven from the PARI (constructed to measure the woman's Martyrdom, Dependency, Marital Conflict, Inconsiderateness-of-Husband, Irritability, Rejection of Homemaking Role, and Fear of Harming the Baby), and one other scale intended to measure Rejection of Pregnancy, in the same format as the other scales. Each of these scales consisted of eight items in the form of statements to which the individual was directed to respond with agreement or disagreement on a four-point scale. Weights of 3, 2, 1, 0 were assigned to the response of strong agreement, mild agreement, mild disa-

greement, and strong disagreement, respecitvely. A scale score was the sum of the weights. The scores obtained from the scales of Fear of Harming the Baby (FHB) and Rejection of Pregnancy (RP) were to be considered as the criterion scores. They resulted from answers to the following statements:

Fear of Harming the Baby

3. A mother's greatest fear is that in a forgetful moment she may let something bad happen to the baby.

11. Mothers are fearful that they may hurt their babies in handling them.

19. All young mothers are afraid of their awkwardness in handling and holding the baby.

27. Mothers never stop blaming themselves if their babies are injured in accidents.

35. You must always keep tight hold of the baby during his bath, for in a careless moment he might slip.

43. Mothers often worry that people playing with the baby might be too rough.

51. There is no excusing the mother if a baby gets hurt.

59. A good mother must always be careful so that in a sleepy or busy moment she won't neglect the baby or hurt him.

Rejection of Pregnancy

8. A wise and intelligent woman avoids becoming pregnant.

16. Pregnancy makes a woman ugly.

24. Often a woman regrets having become pregnant.

32. A woman often doubts the wisdom of being pregnant.

40. There is nothing worse for a woman than being pregnant.

48. A pregnant woman is an unhappy woman.

56. Oftentimes a pregnant woman wishes her baby never to be born.

64. For natural reasons many times a woman resents having a baby.

. . . The expectant mothers under study were wives of people in the military (all ranks) in their last four weeks of pregnancy who utilized the service of the Prenatal Clinic during the period of time covered by this project (June 11–September 18, 1958). They filled out the self-administered questionnaire in an isolated room; they were instructed "not to sign it" and upon its completion, to place it in the envelope provided and to seal the envelope. . . .

The babies were rated on the basis of the observation of their behavior during the first five days of life. The newborn's behavior was rated on five parameters: amount of crying, amount of sleep, degree of irritability, bowel movements, and feeding. Through daily interviews with the nurses who had been especially instructed to act as observers, an observational impression of each baby's behavior "for the past 24 hours" was obtained and rated in terms of each of the above-mentioned parameters. In each parameter, and for each day, the baby was described as normal (i.e., "like any average or usual newborn baby in the nurse's experience with babies"), somewhat deviant or markedly deviant (i.e., crying, sleeping, fussing, etc., "unusually more or less than the average newborn baby in the nurse's experience"). The frame of reference for such observations was carefully, repetitiously, and almost tediously emphasized by the investigator. The procedure was as follows: to the head nurse, at the end of her morning shift (about 3 P.M.), the following kind of question would be put for each baby and for each parameter. For instance, "Baby Smith . . . as a result of your observation during the morning shift . . . and the combined observations of the nurses in the two preceding shifts . . . and in terms of all of your experience with newborn babies . . . would you say that Baby Smith cried more or cried less than babies of this age usually and normally cry?"

From the ratings so obtained, a deviant day was operationally defined as any of those five days in the nursery in which the newborn baby displayed deviant behavior (scored either "somewhat" or "markedly" deviant) on any of the five parameters under consideration.

A deviant baby was then operationally defined as a baby who had two or more deviant days out of the first five days of life in the nursery. For the purpose of the study, the total baby population was thus divided into two groups operationally defined as nondeviant babies (with none or one deviant day) and deviant babies (with two or more deviant days) . . .

The hypothesis to be tested could now be formulated in its final form: that, as a group, mothers of deviant babies came from a population measurably different, in terms of the criterion variables (Fear of Harming the Baby and Rejection of Pregnancy), from mothers of nondeviant babies; and that this measurable difference was to be in the *direction* of higher criterion scores for mothers of deviant babies.

THE FINDINGS

A total of 268 mothers and 235 babies were studied. As expected, however, there were many babies "without" mothers, and mothers "without" babies. This is easily understood: Many mothers delivered outside (under the Medicare Program), others moved away before delivery, others delivered without having used and been tested at the Prenatal Clinic, a few did not fill out the questionnaire because of a language barrier, etc.

When babies and mothers were matched through code numbers, there were only 163 baby-mother pairs available for statistical treatment. Of the 163 babies involved, 28 were deviant babies (two or more deviant days out of five in the nursery) and 135 were nondeviant (none or one deviant day).

We shall now compare the two groups of mothers (mothers of deviant babies vs. mothers of nondeviant babies) in terms of the criterion variables under consideration: Fear of Harming the Baby and Rejection of Pregnancy.

Fear of Harming the Baby (FHB)

Upon the collection of the first 50 cases, the hypothesis was tested by means of a point biserial correlation. The results appeared extremely encouraging, and displayed a statistically significant difference between the two groups of mothers. However, the observation of the FHB scores versus the total scores (sum total of the scores in the other seven scales), as plotted on a scattergram, brought a curious fact into evidence: that the individual score on the FHB scale (as in the other six scales from the PARI) seemed to be a linear function of the total score of the other scales! The higher the total score, the higher the FHB score seemed to be. From this observation we concluded that the FHB scores were being influenced by a number of factors or uncontrolled variables which similarly influenced the total scores. These uncontrolled variables were probably of the same type as those that ordinarily affect and influence scores on this sort of questionnaire: educational level, response "set," the degree of acquiescence, etc. It became apparent, therefore, that the raw FHB scores did not possess the desired comparative meaningfulness, and that they would have to be "adjusted" in terms of the uncontrolled variables involved. The uncontrolled variables were reflected in the total scores. Accordingly, and since the necessary statistical conditions seemed to be met [3], the FHB scores were treat-ed by means of analysis of covariance using the total scores as a measurement of the uncontrolled variables. Thus treated, the data revealed that on the FHB scale the group of mothers of deviant babies had an adjusted mean score of $\overline{X_D} = 15.73$ versus an adjusted mean score of $\overline{X_N} = 14.07$ for mothers of nondeviant babies. These findings were statistically significant ($p < .025$, one-tailed).

It is important to mention at this point that we were also interested in investigating the construct validity of the FHB scale.[1] For this purpose, through consultation with obstetricians and other physicians, we established the soundness of a new hypothesis: that, as a group, primiparas would have a greater fear of harming the baby than multiparas. We proceeded then to test this hypothesis in terms of the criterion variable FHB for the two groups of primiparas and multiparas. Again the total score was used as a measure of the uncontrolled variables and analysis of covariance applied. The adjusted mean for the group of primiparas was $\overline{X_P} = 15.28$ and for the multiparas was $\overline{X_M} = 13.59$. This difference was statistically significant ($p < .01$, one-tailed) and thus indicated construct validity for the FHB scale.

We had anticipated that the FHB scores were to some extent a function of the educational level of the mothers. We found this to be so. When the mothers were divided into three subgroups according to the level of education attained, the obtained results were statistically significant ($p < .01$, one-tailed, analysis of variance) in terms of predicted decreased FHB scores with increased schooling. It is interesting to note that in each of

[1] Readers who are not conversant with the concept of construct validity may wish to consult Lee J. Cronbach and Paul E. Meehl, "Construct Validity in Psychological Tests," *Psychological Bulletin*, 52, 1955, 281–302—Eds.

these three subgroups, we found again that mothers of deviant babies scored appreciably higher on the FHB scale than mothers of nondeviant babies.

Rejection of Pregnancy (RP)

In terms of the scores obtained on this scale, there was no statistically significant difference between the two groups of mothers. Worth noting is that seemingly the RP scale behaved quite differently from any of the other seven scales inasmuch as there was no appreciable correlation between scores on the RP scale and the total score.

However, the examination of the RP scores brought a very curious finding to our attention. It seemed that mothers of deviant babies had responded to the RP scale in such a way as to yield scores that belonged to either of the extreme portions of the range of RP scores. In other words, mothers of deviant babies seemingly scored either very high or very low on the range of scores of the RP scale. This had not been at all predicted and it should be eyed with great caution since it was brought to light by inspection of the data *after* its collection. Nevertheless, it appeared as an interesting point worthy of further exploration. Accordingly, the range of RP scores was broken down in four portions, each with approximately the same number of cases, and the two extreme portions compared with the two in-between. A comparison of the two groups so formed proved to be statistically significant ($p < .02$, chi square), allowing us to conclude *post facto* that mothers of deviant babies tended to score on the extreme range of the RP scale.

Baby's Deviancy

As previously mentioned, a deviant baby was operationally defined as a baby

with two or more deviant days; and a deviant day was defined as any day when, on any of the five parameters, the baby was rated as deviant on the strength of the nursery nurses' observation. The nurses involved in the study were well experienced with the behavior of newborns; and throughout the study they maintained a very cooperative attitude with excellent understanding of the role they were playing as observers . . .

An attempt was made to relate deviancy in the baby with other factors in the mother of in the baby, but no relationships were found. Deviancy in the baby did not relate with any of the scores obtained on the other six scales in the mother's questionnaire and, further, there was no relationship between deviancy in the baby and any one of the following factors: (1) race, (2) mother's age, (3) mother's education, (4) primiparity or multiparity, (5) length of labor, (6) type of delivery, (7) anesthesia during delivery, (8) breast or bottle feeding, (9) birth-weight, (10) baby's weight loss (or gain) at the fifth day, (11) whether the pregnancy had been "planned" or not.

The group of deviant babies contained, however, more boys than girls, a discrepancy that when compared with the composition of the nondeviant group appeared, though unpredicted, statistically significant ($p < .05$).

DISCUSSION

We had seen that an operationally defined deviancy in the newborn's behavior was statistically associated with nothing but a "negative" maternal attitude in evidence *prior* to delivery. The mothers of deviant babies scored significantly higher on an attitudinal scale of Fear of Harming the Baby; and on a Rejection-of-Pregnancy scale, the mothers of deviant babies again responded differently insofar as they tended to score either too high or too low through the whole range of scores.

The totality of the results obtained in this study speaks well for the existence of a prenatal environment. In terms of the variable Fear of Harming the Baby, mothers of deviant babies come from a population different from mothers of nondeviant babies. We feel that this observation is not only statistically significant, but psychologically meaningful as well. Having established construct validity for the criterion scale (FHB), we may conclude then that the "average" mother of a deviant baby had, during pregnancy, a conscious fear of harming her baby greater than the "average" mother of a nondeviant baby. As implied in our choice of the FHB scale as a criterion variable, we can assume further that this consciously "greater" fear of harming the baby corresponds to a "greater" *unconscious* hostility toward the baby-to-come.

On an *ad hoc* scale of Rejection of Pregnancy, the mothers of deviant babies again behaved in a significantly different fashion. We interpret this difference to mean that mothers of deviant babies have a conscious attitude of either extreme rejection or extreme nonrejection of their state of pregnancy. To the incautious reader, we must emphasize again the *post facto* nature of this finding, though its very occurrence cannot but add weight to the hypothesis of a prenatal environment. It bears repeating that no relationship was found between deviancy in the newborn and any such factor as race, age of mother, parity, length of labor, type of anesthesia, type of delivery, type of feeding, and whether or not pregnancy had been planned.

We have established that deviant behavior in the newborn was associated solely with "negative" attitudes in the mother, as expressed by a "higher" score on a scale of Fear of Harming the Baby and by an "either extreme" score on a scale of Rejection of Pregnancy. We may not ask: Is the association between newborn's deviant behavior and mother's negative attitude the result of a prenatal influence? Or, instead, is baby's deviancy the result of a direct and immediate contact with mother *after birth* during those five days in the nursery? This is a very crucial question. To answer it we return now to a further analysis and interpretation of the available data:

1. During the baby's five days in the nursery, mother and baby were together for a maximum of 10 hours. For the first 24 hours, nursery regulations allowed no contact between the mother and her baby. In the four subsequent days, the mother was to be with her baby five times a day for a feeding period not to exceed 30 minutes. Therefore, for those five days, mother and child were together for only 10 hours, the sum total of those feeding periods. During the rest of all those five days, i.e., 110 hours approximately, the newborns stayed in the nursery and totally away from mother.

2. However, we cannot so easily discount the possible importance of those ten hours during which mother and child were in contact for the first five days of the baby's life. For those ten hours occurred at a most crucial time—the feeding time. Fortunately, by means of a new assumption, the available data lends itself to further investigation. We assumed that if the observed deviancy were the result of mother's postnatal influence upon the newborn, and that if we could further assume a cumulative effect to such influence, there would be more babies deviant on the fourth and fifth days than on the first and second. The data revealed this not to be the case. In fact, there were about just as many babies deviant on the first and second days as there were on the fourth and the fifth. Therefore, we came to the conclusion that deviancy was related *not to postnatal factors*, but to prenatal ones.

3. Among the 163 mothers in the study, only one was unwed. Prior to delivery, this unwed mother had made arrangements to have her baby adopted. No postnatal contact whatsoever was allowed between this mother and her baby. It is interesting to note, therefore, that though there was no postnatal contact, her baby belonged to the deviant group (with three deviant days), while she herself had scored obviously "high" on the scale of Fear of Harming the Baby.

4. Another finding merits reporting, and further invites us to conclude for the existence of a prenatal environment. The finding in question has to do with the behavior of babies born of women who refused to fill out the questionnaire. From 268 mothers, only 4 opposed participation in the study and outrightly refused to fill out the questionnaire. Of these 4 women, 2 gave birth to babies who rated deviant in one day, one had a baby rated deviant in two days, and the other a baby deviant in three days out of five. On the basis of the data, the probability that this might have occurred by chance alone is approximately 2 in 10,000.

. . . If we are now to put together the weight of the results of this study, we come readily to conclude that they overwhelmingly tend to confirm the hypothesis of the existence of a prenatal environment. Of course we feel that the present study is in no way a final word on the subject. The coarseness of the measurements speaks for itself. And yet—it is conceivable that the influence of prenatal maternal attitudes upon the newborn may turn out to be such a grossly obvious phenomenon that even an approach as crude and blunt as ours was, stands a chance of bringing it into the light.

We look upon the results of this study as experimental confirmation of the existence and importance of a prenatal environment and for the present we find it reasonably safe to state that the influence of the emotional environment (mother's attitude) upon behavior has its zero hour before birth.

References

1. DABNEY, W. C., "Maternal Impressions," in *Diseases of Children*, pp. 191–216 (Edinburgh: Young J. Pentland, 1896). In M. E. Rogers, A. M. Lilienfeld and B. Pasamanick, *Prenatal and Paranatal Factors in the Development of Childhood Behavior Disorders*. Acta Psychiat. Neurol., Scand., Suppl. 102, 1955.

2. JONES, E., *Psychology and Childbirth*. Lancet, 1:695–696, 1942.

3. LINDQUIST, E. F., *Design and Analysis of Esperiements in Psychology and Education*. (Cambridge, Mass.: Riverside Press, 1953).

4. SCHAEFER, E. S., and R. Q. Bell, *Parental Attitude Research Instrument (PARI): Normative Data*. Unpublished manuscript. Library, National Institutes of Health, Bethesda, Md., 1955.

5. SIEGEL, S., *Nonparametric Statistics: For the Behavioral Sciences*, pp. 145–151 (New York: McGraw-Hill, 1956).

6. SONTAG, L. W., "The Significance of Fetal Environmental Differences," *Am. J. Obst. & Gynec.*, 42:995–1003, 1941.

7. ———, "Difference in Modifiability of Fetal Behavior and Physiology," *Psychosom. Med.*, 6: 151–154, 1944.

8. TURNER, E. K., "The Syndrome in the Infant Resulting from Maternal Emotional Tension During Pregnancy," *Med. J. Australia*, 1:221–222, 1956.

Maternal Deprivation:
The Research and Its Implications *

Aase Gruda Skard

In most Utopian societies, the principle has been, in theory or in practice, to raise all children in institutions. Would such an arrangement really be "utopian" for the new generation? In some preliterate societies, children are brought up by foster parents or the children are the "common property" of the society, so that all women function as mothers for all children. Although modern society arranges for each child to be brought up by his own parents, the society has always had to care for some children, those whose parents had died or were unable or unwilling to accept responsibility for their children. A system of children's homes, organizations for adoption, and foster parents has been built up in conformity with the demands of society. This state and local control has steadily increased in scope with the growth of knowledge in this field and the extension of state responsibility to embrace such activities.

Fourteen years ago, all people concerned with children were made apprehensive by a report from the English child psychiatrist John Bowlby[1] about the damage to the child separated from his mother. The report, published by WHO, created new public demands regarding institutional care for children;

and a storm of discussion arose about children's institutions, foster homes, women in professional life, etc. The demand that a woman should stay at home appeared with new strength; and changes were strongly called for in children's institutions, hospitals, and other related arenas.

Not everybody noted that Bowlby only wrote about small children. His observations were frequently applied to much larger groups of children than he had originally envisaged. Not all realized that he thought in terms of separations of months, and many used the same arguments for absences that lasted only a few hours. But many healthy changes were implemented, e.g., in children's institutions and in the rules and regulations concerning child welfare. During the years that have passed, the meaning of Bowlby's interpretations in his first report have become clearer; and he himself has arrived at viewpoints that have more nuances as he has continued to study the problem.[2] In addition, many new investigations throw light on the mother-child relationship and what it implies. These stress the importance of understanding the way children experience their surroundings and their daily life when the mother is not there, and how they can receive what they need from the

°*Adapted from the* Journal of Marriage and the Family, *1965, 27: 333–343.*

[1] John Bowlby, *Maternal Care and Mental Health*, Geneva, Switzerland: World Health Organization Monograph Series, No. 2, 1951.

[2] John Bowlby, "The Nature of the Child's Tie to His Mother," *International Journal of Psychoanalysis*, 39 (1958), pp. 350–373.

surroundings, whether or not the mother is with them.

A great mass of recent literature in German, French, English, and other languages[3] attests that maternal deprivation is one of the problems in child psychology that has come most strongly to the forefront during the last ten to 12 years. It has been approached from many different angles, and many different methods have been used.

The early investigations on which Bowlby based his conclusions were in many ways good and served the purpose of at least directing the attention of psychologists and psychiatrists to the problem, making it possible to develop a rudimentary theory of the effects of the many and different factors in the mother-child relationship. But the first investigations were groping and included, as a rule, far too many factors that were not properly distinguished. Later research has tried to isolate the factors involved and to investigate the effects of each of them. But the more the problem has received attention, the more involved it has seemed, and the more difficult to reach definite conclusions. It is impossible to experiment with children in all the ways that a research scheme would demand. One may not arrange situations that might cause serious damage to the children.

To facilitate a more focused approach to the problem, psychologists have tried to use animals of different kinds with which they could experiment freely. Other psychologists have investigated cultural groups with the same racial background who treated their children in different ways, and where there were definite differences in the amount of time the child stayed with the mother. And at the same time, many psychologists continued to study children in different kinds of institutions—hospitals, day-nurseries, kindergartens, and so forth —where children come at different age levels and stay for varying periods. In this type of investigation, they have been studying the effects of different conditions, not only while the children were in the institution or had just left it, but over a long period.

POSSIBLE CORRELATES WITH MATERNAL DEPRIVATION EFFECT

Very important factors are age and developmental level: Are there any special developmental levels at which children or young animals are particularly sensitive to separation from their mother, to moving from one place to another, to meeting new people? Will they become more or less sensitive to such influences as time passes, or are there special stages when the effect is particularly strong?

What is the effect of the different forms of contact with the mother and the different amounts of contact on a child at different developmental levels? Can there be too much of mother at some stage? What does the child need in addition to the mother as it grows? What will happen if the mother and child are not separated enough, or not early enough?

When the time period during which a child is separated from his mother varies, how long can the period be that would be without effect on each developmental stage? And how long will the effect last after a shorter or longer period of separation?

Will some factors in the surroundings increase or decrease the effect: for exam-

[3]Cf. J. Svejcar, "Etude de l'influence de la mère sur le development psychique de l'enfant," *Courrier*, 12 (1962), pp. 469–473; and S. Lebovici, *The Concept of Maternal Deprivation: A Review of Research*, Geneva, Switzerland: World Health Organization, 1962, pp. 75–95.

ple, will a child who has been to a great extent satisfied in his need for mother contact suffer more or suffer less than one who has not received so much from the mother? What will the effect be if the milieu into which the child comes is of a different character?

What difference does it make if the mother leaves the child or the child is moved from the mother? In other words, if the child stays in the same home without the mother, or if he is moved to another home? And what influence will it have if the mother visits the child frequently or rarely in his new surroundings?

What will the effect be of the acute separation process itself? And what effect would it have on the child to stay without the mother for a long period? Does the child adjust to life without mother, and if so, how? What can the surroundings contribute to help children adjust themselves? Are there great differences here in children at different age levels, and also in individual children? Are some children tougher or more adjustable than others? Will new changes make the child more used to adapting himself to new people and relationships, or is the effect cumulative for each change of environment?

What is it that the mother gives to the child at each development stage and which the child finds so necessary? Is it breast-feeding, body warmth, an innate biological connection carried over from pregnancy or blood ties, or what? Is it right to speak about *maternal* deprivation, or is the deprivation which the child experiences something which really has nothing to do with the personal mother, such as missing the rocking or the small talk? Is it the mother love itself which others may learn and use in relationship in a child?

There are a host of questions, many more than Bowlby first thought. We have no answers to most of them. But we have some results from investigations, and these may throw some light on the problem.

THE FINDINGS OF ANIMAL PSYCHOLOGY

Everybody thinks that it is a matter of course that young mammals follow their mothers. They get their food from her and thus are able to stay alive. But it is not only because of the food that they seek the mother. Young apes cling to the fur of the mother from the time they are newly born, holding on to her belly or her back. Young kittens creep next to the mother's body, not only to suck, but also to sleep. And many other animals than mammals are strongly tied to their mothers or their parents—of course, the question can be raised if it is the young ones who stay close to the adults or vice versa. Many small birds stay in the nest, and the parents feed them until they are big enough to fly. How strong the tie is after this stage, and whether the young ones attempt to follow the parents or to follow the flock of birds, is not easy to ascertain.

Some young birds are large enough to move around as soon as they leave the egg, such as chickens, which follow the hen for a longer period while they grow. Is it to find their food, or is there something else about her that makes them follow her? Is it only the hen which has laid the egg that the chickens will follow, or the one that has been breeding them? Since it is the brood hen which becomes the mother when it comes to making the chickens follow, there can be no "blood tie." But will the chickens and others necessarily follow the brood hen?

During the last few years, birds such as hens, ducks, and geese, and mammals such as monkeys and apes have been the objects of research experiments that have provided increased insight into the mother-child relationship in these animals.

The German biologist Konrad Z. Lorenz,[4] the American Eckhard H. Hess,[5] and others have each performed a series of experiments with different kinds of birds. They have found that chickens do not necessarily follow "the mother" who has brooded them, but follow something that moves and gives certain sounds in front of them during the period when they have just left the egg. If a box is moved in front of the newly brooded chickens, they will follow the box; and if they are allowed to continue to follow it for some hours, they will only follow boxes and care nothing about the clucking mother. Lorenz, who was the first to work on this phenomenon, called the process "Prägung," or "imprinting."

Imprinting is a process whereby some impressions of early life have a lasting effect on the individual, marking the whole of his total social development. Lorenz pointed out that imprinting must happen at a critical period, at a certain developmental stage in each kind of animal, this usually lasting only for a short time. During this period, the animal is tied to a living or inanimate object which happens to be close by. The animal is thus lastingly imprinted not only by this object but also by all others of the same kind as that; only later will the animal learn to differentiate individual traits and follow a specific object.

The critical period for such imprinting which makes the chicken follow the hen, a box, or a human being, has been studied particularly by Hess.[6] He finds that in ducklings, the tendency to follow gradually increases during the first hours after the brooding, up to 13 to 16 hours, and then decreases quickly. When the ducklings are around 24 hours old, the critical period is over, and they have lost their ability to be imprinted by something and to follow a certain figure.

Certain conditions in the situation can result in a quicker and more effective imprinting in ducklings, chickens, and others. If the young ones must work hard to follow, the imprinting appears more quickly and is more effective than if they are able to follow easily. If they must walk up a hill in order to follow the box, the imprinting will be more effective and accomplished much sooner than if the road is flat and easy to walk. Difficulties that must be overcome, such as the pain of an electric shock, which the young undergo when following something, will also make imprinting quicker and more effective.

From daily life, most people have some experience of such imprinting. Puppies must live with certain human beings during the age of three-and-a-half through nine to 13 weeks if they are to become "man's best friend," and the age of seven weeks seems to be the culmination point of the critical period for social development and imprinting.[7] If no human being touches or cares for kittens from the time that their eyes are opened until they are weaned, they will stay somewhat wild and fearful of people.[8] Continuing in the biological rank order, the question arises whether there are such critical periods for imprinting in all species where there are parent-young relationships, including the human child, and whether there are times when children are particularly approachable and particularly sensitive to human ties,

[4] Konrad J. Lorenz, "Comparative Behaviourology," in *Discussions on Child Development*, ed. by I. J. Tanner and B. Inhelder, London, 1956, Vol. I, pp. 108–131.

[5] Eckhard H. Hess, "Ethology," in *New Directions in Psychology*, ed. by I. Brown *et al.*, New York, 1962, pp. 159–266.

[6] *Ibid.*

[7] J. P. Scott, "Critical Periods in the Development of Social Behavior in Puppies," *Psychosomatic Medicine*, 20 (1958), pp. 42–54.

[8] Hess, *op. cit.*

which enables them to develop love for an adult.

Animals are not only tied to a thing or a person which may be close to them. They also become scared of the unknown and show flight tendencies when faced with certain kinds of influences. Hess has observed that, as a rule, this tendency to run away needs a certain period for maturing.[9] Certain ducklings will follow anything during the first 24 hours after they have left the egg; after that period, however, they are scared of many kinds of creatures which they were earlier willing to follow but by which they were not imprinted at that time. It seems that animals must reach a certain stage of maturation before the reaction of fear appears. But this is not the whole story, because some experiments indicate that early experiences play role also. In some kinds of animals (chickens, dogs, apes), the flight tendency will only appear if the young ones have been imprinted by something at an early stage and are happily tied to somebody from the critical period. This indicates that a positive tie is a precondition for the opposite reaction, namely, flight from the unknown or the threatening. Here observations relating to human children are interesting. The well-known child psychiatrist R. A. Spitz maintains, for example, that babies who are strongly tied to their mothers or their parents will be more afraid of strange people than those children who have not had the same kind of tie to their parents.[10] Imprinting should on one hand tie young animals to something or somebody and, on the other hand, make them particularly aware of dangers from the unknown.

It seems that it is not only the need for food that makes the young animals stay by their mothers. This aspect of the problem has been studied particularly by H. F. Harlow.[11] He works with animals who are close to the human being in the developmental rank order, namely, rhesus monkeys. Many animal observers have pointed out how the newborn young monkey takes hold of the mother's fur purely as a reflex. The hands will close around anything that touches the palm, and the grasp is nearly impossible to loosen again, similar to behavior observed in a newborn baby. The young monkey will hang in the mother's fur until it gets hold of the nipples, and through the operation of the sucking reflex, it begins to get milk. Harlow thought that there must be two different characteristics in the mother that the young would seek, the fur and the milk.[12] But what was the more important? Were they tied to and did they grow to love their mother because she gave them food, or because she had fur that they could snuggle into?

Harlow started his experiments by isolating the maternal characteristics in artificial mothers, with which the young monkeys could grow up from the moment they were born.[13] He made one artificial mother out of netting and with bottles from which the monkeys could suck their milk, and another of fur and wool so that she was warm and soft but without milk. The small monkeys went to the milk-mother when they were hungry, but otherwise they kept always to the wool-mother. If they were scared or felt

[9] Ibid.

[10] R. A. Spitz and Katherine Wolf, "Anaclitic Depression," Psychoanalytic Studies of Childhood, 2 (1946), pp. 313–342.

[11] Harry F. Harlow, "The Nature of Love," American Psychologist, 13 (1958), pp. 673–685; and "The Development of Affectional Patterns in Infant Monkeys," in Determinants of Infant Behavior, ed. by B. M. Foss, London, 1961, Vol. I, pp. 75–88.

[12] Harlow, "The Development of Affectional Patterns . . . ," Ibid.

[13] Harlow, "The Nature of Love," op. cit.

unwell, they went without exception to the soft wool-mother, not to the milk-mother. This indicates that the soft and warm fur has as great value for the young monkeys as the milk. They cannot live without food, but they also need something to take hold of, something soft around them that touches their skin, and it is this that gives them the feeling of protection and security when they for one reason or another feel threatened.

Are the characteristics that the monkey mother has fur and that she has food for her young ones enough for her to fulfill her task as a mother? Newer investigations have led Harlow to answer that more is needed than fur and food.[14] He followed the development in the young monkeys that he had taken away from their living mothers and left with the two artificial mothers. They grew up as usual monkeys, were healthy and strong and apparently normal. But when they were sexually mature, it turned out that they were not normal. They showed no sexual behavior, and they refused to copulate. When Harlow placed the young female monkeys from the artificial mothers together with usual mother-educated male monkeys, these males wanted to copulate with the females, but the females steadily refused. They tried to get away from the males, and threatened and hit out at them. Copulation was accomplished with only four of these female monkeys, and then only through the "patience, persistence, knowledgeability and motor skill of the breeding males," Harlow says.

These four artificially educated females had their babies. But they did not want to care for them. The young ones would hang in their fur and snuggle up to them just like normal young mon-

keys. But the mother only shook them off herself, pushed them away, and showed no sign of maternal behavior. There must have been something wrong in these mothers' development, something that led to their not being sexually developed and maternal like other female monkeys. And the same was true for the males; they never managed to copulate properly, even with normal females who presented themselves to them. What could have been missing in the lives of these monkeys that enables usual monkeys to be normal in sexual and maternal behavior, but which evidently the artificial mothers could not give?

Harlow thinks that there are two important forms of behavior which can be observed in normal female monkeys, but that do not enter into the picture of the milk-mother and child. One is active play between mother and child. The other is the fact that the mother at a certain developmental stage begins to push the young ones away and only lets the young ones come close to her at intervals. In this way, the young monkeys have to turn to each other, to play with other young monkeys. Harlow wants to experiment with these characteristics also, but until his work is completed, other observations throw some light on the problem.

Female baboons have been closely observed by DeVore and by Jay,[15] who point out that there is a certain developmental sequence in the maternal behavior: First, the baboon mother keeps the young one tightly by her body and is only interested in this baby. During the first eight to ten days after delivery, the mother is busy licking her baby, plucking and picking him, pouting her mouth to

[14] Harry F. Harlow and Margaret K. Harlow, "The Effect of Rearing Conditions on Behavior," *Bulletin of the Menninger Clinic*, 26 (1962), pp. 213–224.

[15] Irven De Vore, "Mother-Infant Relations in Free-Ranging Baboons," in *Maternal Behavior in Mammals*, ed. by Harriet L. Rheingold, New York, 1963, pp. 305–355; and Phyllis Jay, "Mother-Infant Relations in Langurs," in *Ibid.*, pp. 282–304.

him, sniffing him, and allowing him to suck. During this first period, the young ones will hold on to the nipples almost all of the time, or will hold on to the mother's fur while she is walking around and following the group to some other place. From the age of three weeks or so, the young one will begin to sit between the mother's legs without holding on to her, but as soon as she is ready to walk somewhere, she grasps the young one and presses him to her body until he has a firm hold of her fur and can hold himself while she is walking. When the young one is about one month old, he may take one or two steps away from the mother. From now on, he begins to notice the other young monkeys in the group when the female monkeys sit together; and the young ones in this way get close to each other. Gradually mother and child fall into a kind of oscillation: the young one walks a little bit away from the mother, but returns—he will sometimes be picked up by other female monkeys and he tolerates this, but he tumbles back to his own mother afterwards, or the mother gets hold of him and draws him to her body again. Other young monkeys which are a little older now begin to try to get the younger ones to join in their games. From the age of three months, the baboon is big enough to play with other young ones for a greater length of time than he spends with his mother, but still he runs back to her regularly and cuddles into her arms. At this time, the young baboon will also become increasingly interested in the other adult monkeys, crawling over the adult male monkeys which enjoy playing with the young ones, and on the whole becoming more and more remote from the mother and seeking the company of the group. From the age of six months, the young one begins to get other food in addition to his mother's milk, but still he will sleep in his mother's arms every night.

During the nine- to ten-month period, the mother begins to push the young one away. She pushes him away from the nipples if he wants to suck, and she shakes him down from her back when he wants to ride her. At about this time, the mother begins to experience a new period of heat and seeks the company of the male monkeys. But occasionally she still takes her young one in her arms. When the young one comes to the mother, he will then experience that she sometimes takes him into her arms, sometimes pushes him away. She never takes the initiative to get the young one to come to her; it is the young one which seeks the mother, with uncertain results. She will still come to his help if other monkeys attack her young one, but if he has other kinds of difficulties and cries, she does not care any more. Some young apes get easily through this period, but others are evidently out of balance, grieve, and try hard to keep up their relationship with the mother. Instead of the relationship with the mother, the young ones now play to an increasing extent with the group of young apes of about the same age, and the relationship to this group becomes more important. When a young ape is around one-and-one-half years old, he spends so little time with his mother that it is impossible for an observer to find out which young one belongs to any particular female monkey. Only if there is a big fight in the group, the young monkeys rush each to his own mother to help her or to stay with her, or the mothers throw themselves into the fight to protect their young ones. But at the age of two years, the young ones are wholly independent of their mother, and the two have forgotten each other. The tie to the mother is replaced by the tie to the peer group.

Other kinds of monkeys show the same development: 1. Mother and child hang tightly together. 2. The young one oscillates to and from the mother and seeks steadily to return to her, and the mother always draws the young one to her. 3. The mother becomes neutral, she tolerates the fact that the young one seeks her, but she makes no effort to get hold of him. 4. The mother shakes the young one off herself and pushes him away toward life with the other young monkeys. During the different periods, different forms for play occur between the mother and the young one: hugging and plucking, pushing and playing, the mother running after the young one to get hold of him, etc.

Of course, these observations of animals can only give suggestions about what to look for in human children. The similarity in mother-child relationship between monkeys and human beings is probably greatest when the child is very small. Gradually, the particularly human characteristics come into play: more intelligent behavior and deeper, more lasting emotions than a monkey will ever have. Still, Harlow considers it important that besides getting food, other important factors exist in the monkey mother-child relationship, such as touching, protection, playing, and pushing away at the right time. Although human beings do not follow the exact pattern of monkeys, elements in the monkey mother-child relationship may be compared for the degree to which they exist in the human mother-child relationship. Where similarities exist, it may be asked at which state in human development it is natural and healthy to find these different elements and to what degree they are present.

Harlow maintains that both monkey and human mothers "have the obligation of gradually dissolving the intense physical bonds which characterize the early mother-child relationship."[16] For the monkey mother, it is easier and more

natural than for a woman, he says, because when the young one is so big that he becomes bothersome, the monkey mother pushes him away and punishes him, and the young one withdraws for a while so that she may rest; then she may be kind to him for a while when he returns. In this way, the young one becomes independent gradually. This will not happen with the wool-mother, which never gets tired of the young one, never pushes him away, never forces him over to the peer group, and in this way somehow resembles the overprotecting mothers among human beings who hold on to their children for too long and so prevent healthy ties to the peer group.

THE FINDINGS OF RESEARCH ON HUMAN MOTHER-CHILD RELATIONSHIPS

Many of the first investigations into the effect of living in a children's institution compared children from institutions with other children, but with no information about the age when they had arrived in the institution, why they had come there, what inheritance they carried with them, what they had experienced before they came, what the institution was like, or if they perhaps had been moved around from one institution to another. Newer research takes such factors into consideration.[17] The present paper compares observations of children with observations and experiments with young animals.

First of all, it is apparently extremely important at which developmental stage

16 Harlow and Harlow, *op. cit.*

17 For closer survey and analysis of available research, see L. J. Yarrow, "Maternal Deprivation: Toward an Empirical and Conceptual Re-evaluation," *Psychological Bulletin*, 58 (1961), pp. 459–490.

the child is separated from his mother,[18] and that the mother will have a different meaning to the child at different stages. On the basis of this, one may draw certain practical conclusions concerning the time when the mother and child may be separated, how often and for how long the child tolerates being without his mother, and how one may find a good substitute for the mother.

THE FIRST HALF YEAR

Apparently what may be called the "awakening of the senses" plays a great role during the first half year, perhaps most of all at the three- to six-months stage. Not all the senses are awake, and therefore not all can be used at the same time. Sight is evidently the sense that develops latest. Therefore the children cannot differentiate between different adults until they are somewhere between three and six months old. Only then will they begin to recognize mother and other people they know and differentiate them from the unknown. It is possible that they earlier have recognized the way the mother will hold them, her smell, the taste of the nipple, etc. But very little proof exists for this. Only a few children seem to suffer from being separated from their mother when they are less than three months old; and even in the age group three to six months, disturbances seem relatively slight.[19] If they suffer from being separated from their mother at this time, it may not be the mother as a person they miss, but rather something that she usually will give them and which they do not get to the same degree in a new milieu.

Now, what does a mother usually give a child at this time? Food, opportunity to suck, warmth from her body, fondling and rocking, small talk, and humming. All these things together will be called "mothering." Is there something in all this that is particularly important, more important than anything else?

The Harlow experiments with young monkeys show that they especially seek warmth and the soft skin of the mother. Other experiments with animals show that they suffer very much if they do not get any sense stimuli at all.[20] It is probable that something comparable may occur with human beings: they need sense stimuli, stimulation of the right kind. If they are moved during the first half year, it is likely that it is deprivation in general that makes them suffer rather than any special maternal deprivation.[21]

They are bored in children's institutions rather than being homesick for a personal mother. It appears that during this period one can separate mother and child if one takes care that the child gets the necessary mothering, i.e., that it gets the chance to experience body warmth from another human being; rocking and patting; and perhaps also to have something colorful to look at; to get food and something to suck; to be carried around; to have something moving around it; and to listen to voices, singing, and talking. But who stimulates the child in this manner is probably not important. The child may be said to be "care-oriented," not yet "person-oriented."[22]

[18] L. J. Yarrow, "Research in Dimensions of Early Maternal Care," *Merrill-Palmer Quarterly*, 9 (1963), pp. 101–114.

[19] *Ibid.*

[20] Donald O. Hebb, *A Textbook of Psychology*, Philadelphia, 1958.

[21] H. R. Schaffer and W. M. Callender, "Psychological Effects of Hospitalization in Infancy," *Pediatrics*, 24 (1959), p. 538 ff.

[22] H. R. Schaffer, "Some Issues for Research in the Study of Attachment Behavior," in *Determinants of Infant Behavior*, ed.

From Six Months to Three or Three-and-One-Half Years

During the second half year, the situation will be more complicated. And through the following years, much is happening to the child that makes it more difficult to move him.

The child begins to recognize the person or persons who tend to him, he begins to love and be tied to one or a few adults, and he begins to recognize things around him. From the age of five to seven months, it will be important for the child that one particular adult return again and again. The child needs real personal contact.

What happens in the mother-child relationship when the child was around seven months old is quite similar to the phenomenon of imprinting which Lorenz and others found in several animals. Observations of babies in hospitals[23] show that children under seven and over seven months old are strikingly different, and that the difference is so evident that it may seem as if there is a jump in the development from one way of reacting to a completely new reaction from this stage on. Children of less than seven months made little or no protest if they only had kind nurses who would tend to them in a pleasant way and mother them. They adjusted rather easily to the new situation in the hospital. But children over seven months old were brought totally out of balance, they cried and turned away from the adults, they did not want to eat or they reacted in other ways, showing that they were not adjusted. Other investigations indicate that the warmer the child's relationship to his mother, the harder it will be for him to be separated from her

when they have reached this new developmental stage.[24]

From around six to seven months or so, the baby evidently will become tied to the one or more adults who take care of it, and this process is a quick process, like imprinting in the animal young ones. When the children have more adults around, as for example, in the Israeli kibbutzim or in societies where all grown women care for and act as mothers for all babies, it seems as if each child has one main person to whom it is more tied than to the others. But in addition to this one, the child may also be tied to other adults without damage to his personality.[25]

When the child is becoming tied to one or more of the adults who are steadily around, he also begins to be shy and fearful of unknown people. This phenomenon may have its parallel in the flight tendency which animal young show in comparable situations. Child psychologists have already earlier noticed the so-called eight-months anxiety in the child, anxiety for new adults, but this has not been related to the process of becoming tied to a familiar figure. There is some reason to believe that this anxiety for the unknown has a close connection with the love for the familiar figure, which is just growing at this time. The tie with a few grown-ups is important for the development of basic trust which E. H. Erikson[26] regards as an extremely important process during the first year of life.

The situation for children at this age level should preferably be characterized by a few adults for a very few children. Children's institutions now rightly begin

by B. M. Foss, London, 1963, Vol. II, pp. 179–196.

[23] Schaffer and Callender, op. cit.

[24] Spitz and Wolf, op. cit.

[25] Yarrow, "Maternal Deprivation . . .," op. cit.

[26] Erik H. Erikson, "Growth Crises of the Healthy Personality," in Symposium on the Healthy Personality, New York, 1950, pp. 91–146.

to organize the environment in such a way that there are only a few children in each children's home, and frequently children of different ages are present. This enables the smallest child to have his or her own substitute mother. Children experience daily and regular impressions, both in these institutions and when a mother takes care of her own child at home, and also variations in the mood of this one person, who may at one time be in one kind of mood, sometimes in another, and who is subjective and emotional, not only objective and monotonous. This period is particularly marked by development in emotional life and in the relationship to adults. In this respect, the children need nourishment and regular, rich experiences.

If persons who are very different take care of the child in this period, this will mean a particular stress for the child because so much will be unexpected and different from what he has been used to. One adult comforts a crying child by giving it something to eat or to suck, another may pick it up and pat it, a third one will rock it, a fourth will perhaps sing or talk to the baby. In these cases, crying will not produce consistent treatment; and even if some variation may be desirable, there may be too much of a good thing.

The anatomic-physiological development in the fetus has shown that structure and organs that are in the process of rapid development are particularly vulnerable. Therefore, rubella (German measles) is particularly dangerous for the fetus if the mother contracts this illness in a definite limited time period (second or third month) of the pregnancy when certain areas of the brain and the sense organs are in rapid development. In a parallel way, psychologists are trying to formulate hypotheses about vulnerability in the mental field: that functions and processes in rapid development are particularly vulnerable. According to such

hypotheses, at the stage of development when a child is about to tie his emotions to one single or some very few adults, he would also be particularly vulnerable to separation from those to whom he was tied, and this is just the case. As pointed out by Bowlby, Spitz, and others, small children (from six to seven months upward) have great difficulties when they are separated from their mother for a long period, i.e., during several weeks continuously, especially if they have no substitute mother on whom they can fix their emotions. It may give additional security to a child to feel that he can rely upon more than one person for protection and care[27] and that he has more than one person whom he can trust.[28]

As the months and the years pass, the need for activity increases in the child. He needs freedom to move, to kick and roll around, to creep and walk, to grasp, handle things, throw, roll, wave, and hit out with things, crawl up the stairs, jump, run. But at the same time, he needs somebody to whom he may return, he needs the oscillation which was observed in the young monkeys. The mother's lap, the fathers's safe arms must be present. But the child needs also to leave the lap and the arms, to go out to play and use muscles, to be active and experiment.

Perhaps this is a period when the child needs to play with adults, as Harlow mentioned, to play peekaboo and show himself again, to pretend that the adults run hard to get hold of the child, on the whole the kind of game which creates distance and new contact.

[27] Margaret Mead, "A Cultural Anthropologist's Approach to Maternal Deprivation," in Deprivation of Maternal Care, Geneva, Switzerland: World Health Organization, 1962, pp. 45–62.

[28] Barbara Wootton, "A Social Scientist's Approach to Maternal Deprivation," in Ibid., pp. 63–73.

Not all private homes can satisfy this need for activity in children. Not all small modern apartments can give enough space for play and enough toys of the right kind. Here, gradually, other institutions must come in to supplement the home: the nursery school, the park supervisor, etc. Frequently a transitional period is necessary when the child simultaneously needs both the mother and these new surroundings. Children's homes may, if they are good, give in this respect practically equally good conditions for this type of development where the need for activity can be satisfied while the same mother figure continues to be there for the child to return to.

From Three or Three-and-One-Half Years to Seven Years

At preschool age, a relationship with a few adults seems to be important for the child. It will be less of a strain to be separated from the mother now, but it is still a strain. The child begins in this period to identify with adults, to take over the roles, attitudes, norms, and language of adults. The child learns his or her own sex role, learns what it means in his or her society to be a boy or a girl. Conscientiousness begins to develop as he acquires a feeling that it is wrong to go against the rules and the norms.

Observations of children who have grown up in large children's institutions with few adults tend to show that if the children cannot have such permanent adults with whom they can identify themselves, they begin to identify themselves with each other. One may find unusually strong coherence in groups of children and unusually deep love among them, but children are not carriers of ethical norms and values. Identification with one or more other children cannot give to each child a definite feeling of right and wrong, nor an appreciation of the value of laws and rules, of work and industry.

On the other hand, social interest and the need for social relationships with other children are increasing in this period. A good relationship to parents seems to be a good base for a good relationship to the peer group also. In addition to one or more adults, the children now need human beings of the same size as themselves. Children's homes and institutions, kibbutzim, etc., may give to the children values which a private home with only one child can provide only with difficulty, but still the ties to the few adults are more important. And the children need adults of both sexes, both "mother" and "father." In this period, both "maternal" and "paternal" deprivation" may cause them to experience stress. [29] But the memory is now so much better developed that parents may stay away from the children for a longer time, even for several months, so long as they return. And in the same way, it will take the child a shorter period of time to make up for the strain of the deprivation than it did in the earlier period.

From school age onward, and particularly during puberty and adolescence, the ties with adults will steadily loosen, and the child will gain independence and adult ability to fend for himself.

CHILDREN OF WORKING MOTHERS

The problem "children of working mothers" turns out to be difficult and complicated. It cannot be evaluated only from the child's viewpoint, or from the viewpoint of healthy development as a human being. A woman is more than just a milieu for her child or her children—

[29] Cf. R. G. Andry, "Paternal and Maternal Roles and Delinquency," in *Ibid.*, pp. 31–44.

she has her own value as a human being, and the problem must also be considered for what may serve her interests and development.

That women wish to do something different and to do more than just take care of their children is not something new that only contemporary women have begun to demand. Women in earlier times also lived for more than just their functions as mothers. They had richer and more varied work in and around their home, they baked bread, they spun and wove, they made the clothes for everybody in the family, they participated in the slaughtering of the farm animals, they had their domestic animals to care for, etc. And as a rule, many women cooperated in these functions. Today women are not so different from what they were in earlier generations, but now they live in a different situation, the work and the social milieus are different. At least in the cities, the women very often carry out their domestic work in a lonely place, where during their work they have no contact with other human beings. The field of work in the home is much reduced because so many functions have moved out of the home, and others are made easier by modern labor-saving devices. In Oslo, where the author and her colleagues have been studying certain families for some years, it has been observed that mothers were happy to stop their professional work when they expected their first baby. But when the child reached the age of three or four, many mothers felt isolated and deserted. They wanted to have a job, not so much in order to earn money as to get to a place where they could meet others, where they had work companions. But most of them wanted a job only part of the day. They wanted to be professional workers, but not only professional workers. They wanted to be mothers, but not only mothers.

For most women, it still is important that what they want might hurt their babies, and in such cases they will give up their own demands. But is it necessary to give up outside work if they like and want such work? Will it hurt the children?

It is not easy to answer these questions, because life may be arranged so differently for the children concerned: a) They may stay in the home with a grandmother, a nanny, etc.; or the father and the mother may have different times of work so that the father takes care of the child while the mother is away at work, at least part of this time. b) They may be placed under supervision in a park, day nursery, or kindergarten, this depending on the length of time the mother will spend in her work. c) They can live in a children's institution with the parents visiting them at certain times of the day, such as in the arrangement made at the Israeli kibbutzim.

On the other hand, there may be important variations in the mother's work and in her emotional experiences with regard to her job: a) She may have regular work or only occasional jobs. b) She may take on the job in order to get a larger income for the family, or she may take it on because she likes that particular work. c) She may be happy or not happy in her domestic work.

Third and not least important, it makes a great difference how old the children are, and how many of them are in the family.

And finally, it makes a great difference how the mate and the rest of the family react to the mother's work. The husband may think it is fine that the wife has a job, he may experience her as superior to him when she earns money, he may demand the same services from her around the house as from a woman working at home, the neighbors may wonder why she goes out to work. The attitudes the working mother encounters everywhere in her surroundings affect her position.

The problems concern not only employed women, but equally so women working in the home: How much do they take care of the children and to what extent do they send the children out—and to what? What is most important for the mother, the children's needs for play and activity, or order and cleanliness in the house? Does a woman working at home inhibit the children in their need to be independent? May the woman working at home inhibit the relationship between father and child, or does she make it easier for the father to spend time with the children? Is the husband happy to be the only financial supporter of the family, or is he discontented because the wife does not earn money outside the house?

Very little research has been done on all these relationships, but that which has shows that part of what people usually believe is not correct.

It is often said that "key children," the children who carry the key to the apartment on a string around their neck, easily become delinquents. In general, this is not correct. On the other hand, children of women who have occasional jobs, of women who take a job on some occasions and at other times work in the home, in many cases run into difficulties.[30] The reasons for this are varied: Perhaps nothing regular is arranged for these children since the mother is not permanently engaged in her work. Perhaps such occasional work is an expression of something moody and irregular in the mother's personality, and the same characteristics will be found also in her treatment of the children. Perhaps the mother takes a job to earn money once in

a while but is not pleased with this state of affairs, and her unhappiness spreads to the rest of the home.

Strangely enough, research indicates that employed women are frequently together with their children more than the women who remain at home, and that the working mothers strive harder to participate in activities in which the children are particularly interested.[31] The domestic women seem more content to leave the children to play alone outdoors, and then perhaps to take them on errands or to other activities that interest the mother herself. The employed women show their children more tenderness, perhaps because they love their work and on the whole have a surplus of joy to share with the children. Or perhaps because they have a bad conscience about leaving the children and try to make up for it by excessive cuddling.

Looking at the different age groups of children, it may be said that for the babies, it is good to have mother with them. But it is still more important that she return daily and regularly at specific times. For some children, it seems to be better if their mothers have always been employed, since the actual transition from having a domestic mother to a working mother is the most difficult for them.

In the preschool age, much depends on how life is organized for the children.[32] It may be difficult for active preschool children to stay at home in a small modern apartment with a mother who emphasizes cleanliness and order all the time. It may be healthy for them to have some hours daily in another milieu where life is organized in a different way. Like

[30] Sheldon Glueck and Eleanor T. Glueck, *Unraveling Juvenile Delinquency,* Boston, 1950.

[31] Marian Radke Yarrow, "Maternal Employment and Child Rearing," *Children,* 8 (1961), pp. 223–228.

[32] Eleanor E. Maccoby, "Children and Working Mothers," *Children,* 5 (1958), pp. 83–89.

the young monkeys, they need to be pushed away to play with other children. They get a richer life in this way and become less rigid. But they need at the same time a mother and a father as something permanent in life. Preschool children seem to become more anxious when mother goes to work once in a while than when she goes regularly. In kibbutzim, the children at this age will be more firmly tied to their parents than to ther substitute mother with whom they live, though they only see the parents for some hours daily. The love they encounter, and the feeling of being with persons who are "my mother" and "my father," evidently make them experience these ties.

School-age children of employed women on the whole are more independent than other children and manage better with their school subjects. But they have greater difficulties when first starting school than children from homes where the mothers do not go out to work. It is uncertain why this is so; perhaps these initial starting difficulties may have the same origin as that for mother's work, family difficulties in the home. Not enough is known about this problem so far.

Many investigations have had as their object the comparison of children of nonworking and working women. On the whole, these investigations show few or no differences. But greater differences are found if the mothers are grouped in another way, namely, in one group, those who love their outside work and those who love their domestic work,[33] and in a different group, those who are discontented with staying at home and those who are discontented in their outside work. More well-adjusted, happy children are found in the first group than in the second.

The provisional conclusion from these investigations is that for some women the best thing is to go out to work, for others it is best to stay in the home. But is seems important that the mother have a permanent arrangement. Children develop best and most harmoniously when the mother herself is happy and gay. Whether she has work outside the home or not seems rather unimportant from the child's viewpoint. But in addition to this rather general conclusion, the whole question of the motives that drive a woman to one or the other form of life must be considered. Her own experience of the situation may play a greater role than the actual situation. More important than any other single factor, however, is the developmental stage of the child and his changing needs from one age level to another.

---

[33] M. R. Yarrow, *op. cit.*

9

SOCIALIZATION OF THE CHILD

Although it is generally thought that the early experiences of the child—especially his relations with his parents—influence his personality and affect his role-performances, scholars have not yet achieved consensus as to the effects of particular parental behaviors or as to the processes by means of which parents impart such influences to their children.

Identification is a term that has been very diversely conceived, and the authors of our first two papers define it differently. David Lynn presents his theory of sex-role learning through identification as he conceives that term. He argues that male and female children have very different models from which to learn sex-typed behavior and that this difference enters into their social adjustment throughout life. Using a different definition of identification, Bandura, Ross and Ross compare three theories of identificatory learning to determine which is the best predictor of a child's role-model. By controlling the sex of the model, Bandura et al. are able to show the greatest verifiability of one theory, independent of sex-typing. The Lynn article indicates how the structure of the nuclear family may affect which behaviors are learned, while the paper by Bandura et al. illuminates certain features of the process of the learning.

Diana Baumrind shows how different patterns of parental behavior may affect the child's personality. She presents three modes of parental control—permissive, authoritarian, and authoritative. Her interpretation of the literature on parental disciplinary practices leads her to the conclusion that authoritative control is most efficient in generating behavior that is well socialized yet willful and independent.

The Process of Learning Parental and Sex-Role Identification *

David B. Lynn

The purpose of this paper is to summarize the writer's theoretical formulation concerning identification, much of which has been published piecemeal in various journals. Research relevant to new hypotheses

*Adapted from the Journal of Marriage and the Family, 1966, 28: 466–470.

is cited, and references are given to previous publications of this writer in which the reader can find evidence concerning the earlier hypotheses. Some of the previously published hypotheses are considerably revised in this paper and, it is hoped, placed in a more comprehensive and coherent framework.

THEORETICAL FORMULATION

Before developing specific hypotheses, one must briefly define identification as it is used here. *Parental identification* refers to the internalization of personality characteristics of one's own parent and to unconscious reactions similar to that parent. This is to be contrasted with *sex-role identification*, which refers to the internalization of the role typical of a given sex in a particular culture and to the unconscious reactions characteristic of that role. Thus, theoretically, an individual might be thoroughly identified with the role typical of his own sex generally and yet poorly identified with his same-sex parent specifically. This differentiation also allows for the converse circumstances wherein a person is well identified with his same-sex parent specifically and yet poorly identified with the typical same-sex role generally. In such an instance the parent with whom the individual is well identified is himself poorly identified with the typical sex role. An example might be a girl who is closely identified with her mother, who herself is more strongly identified with the masculine than with the feminine role. Therefore, such a girl, through her identification with her mother, is poorly identified with the feminine role.[1]

Formulation of Hypotheses

It is postulated that the initial parental identification of both male and female infants is with the mother. Boys, but not girls, must shift from this initial mother identification and establish masculine-role identification. Typically in this culture the girl has the same-sex parc-

[1]D. B. Lynn, "Sex-Role and Parental Identification." *Child Development*, 33:3 (1962), pp. 555–564.

ental model for identification (the mother) with her more hours per day than the boy has his same-sex model (the father) with him. Moreover, even when home, the father does not usually participate in as many intimate activities with the child as does the mother, e.g., preparation for bed, toileting. The time spent with the child and the intimacy and intensity of the contact are thought to be pertinent to the process of learning parental identification.[2] The boy is seldom if ever with the father as he engages in his daily vocational activities, although both boy and girl are often with the mother as she goes through her household activities. Consequently, the father, as a model for the boy, is analogous to a map showing the major outline but lacking most details, whereas the mother, as a model for the girl, might be thought of as a detailed map.

However, despite the shortage of male models, a somewhat stereotyped and conventional masculine role is nonetheless spelled out for the boy often by his mother and women teachers in the absence of his father and male models. Through the reinforcement of the culture's highly developed system of rewards for typical masculine-role behavior and punishment for signs of femininity, the boy's early learned identification with the mother weakens. Upon this weakened mother identification is welded the later learned identification with a culturally defined, stereotyped masculine role.

(1)[†] *Consequently, males tend to identify with a culturally defined mascu-*

[2]B. A. Goodfield, "A Preliminary Paper on the Development of the Time Intensity Compensation Hypothesis in Masculine Identification," paper read at the San Francisco State Psychological Convention, April, 1965.

[†] Specific hypotheses are numbered and in italics.

line role, whereas females tend to identify with their mothers.[3]

Although one must recognize the contribution of the father in the identification of males and the general cultural influences in the identification of females, it nevertheless seems meaningful, for simplicity in developing this formulation, to refer frequently to *masculine-role identification* in males as distinguished from *mother identification* in females.

Some evidence is accumulating suggesting that (2) *both males and females identify more closely with the mother than with the father.* Evidence is found in support of this hypothesis in a study by Lazowick[4] in which the subjects were 30 college students. These subjects and their mothers and fathers were required to rate concepts, e.g., "myself," "father," "mother," etc. The degree of semantic similarity as rated by the subjects and their parents was determined. The degree of similarity between fathers and their own children was not significantly greater than that found between fathers and children randomly matched. However, children did share a greater semantic similarity with their own mothers than they did when matched at random with other maternal figures. Mothers and daughters did not share a significantly greater semantic similarity than did mothers and sons.

Evidence is also found in support of Hypothesis 2 in a study by Adams and Sarason[5] using anxiety scales with male and female high school students and their mothers and fathers. They found that anxiety scores of both boys and girls were much more related to mothers' than to fathers' anxiety scores.

Support for this hypothesis comes from a study in which Aldous and Kell[6] interviewed 50 middle-class college students and their mothers concerning child-rearing values. They found, contrary to their expectation, that a slightly higher proportion of boys than girls shared their mothers' childrearing values.

Partial support for Hypothesis 2 is provided in a study by Gray and Klaus[7] using the Allport-Vernon-Lindzey Study of Values completed by 34 female and 28 male college students and by their parents. They found that the men were not significantly closer to their fathers than to their mothers and also that the men were not significantly closer to their fathers than were the women. However, the women were closer to their mothers than were the men and closer to their mothers than to their fathers.

Note that, in reporting research relevant to Hypothesis 2, only studies of *tested similarity,* not *perceived similarity,* were reviewed. To test this hypothesis, one must measure tested similarity, i.e., measure both the child and the parent on the same variable and compare the similarity between these two measures. This paper is not concerned with perceived similarity, i.e., testing the child on a given variable and then comparing that finding with a measure taken as to how the child thinks his parent would respond. It is this writer's opinion that

[3] D. B. Lynn, "A Note on Sex Differences in the Development of Masculine and Feminine Identification," *Psychological Review,* 66:2 (1959), pp. 126–135.

[4] L. M. Lazowick, "On the Nature of Identification," *Journal of Abnormal and Social Psychology,* 51 (1955), pp. 175–183.

[5] E. B. Adams and I. G. Sarason, "Relation Between Anxiety in Children and Their Parents," *Child Development,* 34:1 (1963), pp. 237–246.

[6] J. Aldous and L. Kell, "A Partial Test of Some Theories of Identification," *Marriage and Family Living,* 23:1 (1961), pp. 15–19.

[7] S. W. Gray and R. Klaus, "The Assessment of Parental Identification," *Genetic Psychology Monographs,* 54 (1956), pp. 87–114.

much confusion has arisen by considering perceived similarity as a measure of parental identification. It seems obvious that, especially for the male, perceived similarity between father and son would usually be closer than tested similarity, in that it is socially desirable for a man to be similar to his father, especially as contrasted to his similarity to his mother. Indeed, Gray and Klaus[8] found the males' perceived similarity with the father to be closer than tested similarity.

It is hypothesized that the closer identification of males with the mother than with the father will be revealed more clearly on some measures than on others. (3) *The closer identification of males with their mothers than with their fathers will be revealed most frequently in personality variables which are not clearly sex-typed.* In other words, males are more likely to be more similar to their mothers than to their fathers in variables in which masculine and feminine role behavior is not especially relevant in the culture.

There has been too little research on tested similarity between males and their parents to presume an adequate test of Hypothesis 3. In order to test it, one would first have to judge personality variables as to how typically masculine or feminine they seem. One could then test to determine whether a higher proportion of males are more similar to their mothers than to their fathers on those variables which are not clearly sex-typed, rather than on those which are judged clearly to be either masculine or feminine. To this writer's knowledge, this has not been done.

It is postulated that the task of achieving these separate kinds of identification (masculine role for males and mother identification for females) requires separate methods of learning for each sex. These separate methods of

[8] *Ibid.*

learning to identify seem to be problem-solving for boys and lesson-learning for girls. Woodworth and Schlosberg differentiate between the task of solving problems and that of learning lessons in the following way:

> With a problem to master the learner must explore the situation and find the goal before his task is fully presented. In the case of a lesson, the problem-solving phase is omitted or at least minimized, as we see when the human subject is instructed to memorize this poem or that list of nonsense syllables, to examine these pictures with a view to recognizing them later.[9]

Since the girl is not required to shift from the mother in learning her identification, she is expected mainly to learn the mother-identification lesson as it is presented to her, partly through imitation and through the mother's selective reinforcement of mother-similar behavior. She need not abstract principles defining the feminine role to the extent that the boy must in defining the masculine role. Any bit of behavior on the mother's part may be modeled by the girl in learning the mother-identification lesson.

However, finding the appropriate identification goal does constitute a major problem for the boy in solving the masculine-role identification problem. When the boy discovers that he does not belong in the same sex category as the mother, he must then find the proper sex-role identification goal. Masculine-role behavior is defined for him through admonishments, often negatively given, e.g., the mother's and teachers' telling him that he should not be a sissy without precisely indicating what he *should* be. Moreover, these negative admonishments are made in the early grades in the absence of male teachers to serve as mod-

[9] R. S. Woodworth and H. Schlosberg, *Experimental Psychology*, New York: Holt, 1954, p. 529.

els and with the father himself often unavailable as a model. The boy must restructure these admonishments in order to abstract principles defining the masculine role. It is this process of defining the masculine-role goal which is involved in solving the masculine-role identification problem.

One of the basic steps in this formulation can now be taken. (4) *In learning the sex-typical identification, each sex is thereby acquiring separate methods of learning which are subsequently applied to learning tasks generally.*[10]

The little girl acquires a learning method which primarily involves (a) a personal relationship and (b) imitation rather than restructuring the field and abstracting principles. On the other hand, the little boy acquires a different learning method which primarily involves (a) defining the goal (b) restructuring the field, and (c) abstracting principles. There are a number of findings which are consistent with Hypothesis 4, such as the frequently reported greater problem-solving skill of males and the greater field dependence of females.[11]

The shift of the little boy from mother identification to masculine-role identification is assumed to be frequently a crisis. It has been observed that demands for typical sex-role behavior come at an earlier age for boys than for girls. These demands are made at an age when boys are least able to understand them. As was pointed out above, demands for masculine sex-role behavior are often made by women in the absence of readily available male models to demonstrate typical sex-role behavior. Such demands are often presented in the form of punishing, *negative* admonishments, i.e., telling the boy what not to do rather than

what to do and backing up the demands with punishment. These are thought to be very different conditions from those in which the girl learns her mother-identification lesson. Such methods of demanding typical sex-role behavior of boys are very poor methods for inducing learning.

(5) *Therefore, males tend to have greater difficulty in achieving same-sex identification than females.*[12]

(6) *Furthermore, more males than females fail more or less completely in achieving same-sex identification, but they rather make an opposite-sex identification.*[13]

Negative admonishments given at an age when the child is least able to understand them and supported by punishment are thought to produce anxiety concerning sex-role behavior. In Hartley's words:

> This situation gives us practically a perfect combination for inducing anxiety—the demand that the child do something which is not clearly defined to him, based on reasons he cannot possibly appreciate, and enforced with threats, punishments and anger by those who are close to him.[14]

(7) *Consequently, males are more anxious regarding sex-role identification than females.*[15] It is postulated that punishment often leads to dislike of the ac-

[10] D. B. Lynn, "Sex-Role and Parental Identification," *op. cit.*

[11] *Ibid.*

[12] D. B. Lynn, "Divergent Feedback and Sex-Role Identification in Boys and Men," *Merrill-Palmer Quarterly*, 10:1 (1964), pp. 17–23.

[13] D. B. Lynn, "Sex Differences in Identification Development," *Sociometry*, 24:4 (1961), pp. 372–383.

[14] R. E. Hartley, "Sex-Role Pressures and the Socialization of the Male Child," *Psychological Reports*, 5 (1959), p. 458.

[15] D. B. Lynn, "Divergent Feedback and Sex-Role Identification in Boys and Men," *op. cit.*

tivity that led to punishment.[16] Since it is "girl-like" activities that provoked the punishment administered in an effort to induce sex-typical behavior in boys, then, in developing dislike for the activity which led to such punishment, boys should develop hostility toward "girl-like" activities. Also, boys should be expected to generalize and consequently develop hostility toward all females as representatives of this disliked role. There is not thought to be as much pressure on girls as on boys to avoid opposite-sex activities. It is assumed that girls are punished neither so early nor so severely for adopting masculine sex-role behavior.

(8) *Therefore, males tend to hold stronger feelings of hostility toward females than females toward males.*[17] The young boy's same-sex identification is at first not very firm because of the shift from mother to masculine identification. On the other hand, the young girl, because she need make no shift in identification, remains relatively firm in her mother identification. However, the culture, which is male-dominant in orientation, reinforces the boy's developing masculine-role identification much more thoroughly than it does the girl's developing feminine identification. He is rewarded simply for having been born masculine through countless privileges accorded males but not females. As Brown pointed out:

> The superior position and privileged status of the male permeates nearly every aspect, minor and major, of our social life. The gadgets and prizes in boxes of breakfast cereal, for example, commonly have a strong masculine rather than feminine appeal. And the most basic social institu-

tions perpetuate this pattern of masculine aggrandizement. Thus, the Judeo-Christian faiths involve worshipping God, a "Father," rather than a "Mother," and Christ, a "Son," rather than a "Daughter."[18]

(9) *Consequently, with increasing age, males become relatively more firmly identified with the masculine role.*[19]

Since psychological disturbances should, theoretically, be associated with inadequate same-sex identification and since males are postulated to be gaining in masculine identification, the following is predicted: (10) *With increasing age males develop psychological disturbances at a more slowly accelerating rate than females.*[20]

It is postulated that as girls grow older, they become increasingly disenchanted with the feminine role because of the prejudices against their sex and the privileges and prestige offered the male rather than the female. Even the women with whom they come in contact are likely to share the prejudices prevailing in this culture against their own sex.[21] Smith[22] found that with increasing age girls have a progressively better opinion of boys and a progressively poorer opinion of themselves. (11) *Consequently, a larger proportion of females*

---

[16] E. R. Hilgard, *Introduction to Psychology,* New York: Harcourt, Brace, and World, 1962.

[17] D. B. Lynn, "Divergent Feedback and Sex-Role Identification in Boys and Men," *op. cit.*

[18] D. G. Brown, "Sex-Role Development in a Changing Culture," *Psychological Bulletin,* 55 (1958), p. 235.

[19] D. B. Lynn, "A Note on Sex Differences in the Development of Masculine and Feminine Identification," *op. cit.*

[20] D. B. Lynn, "Sex Differences in Identification Development," *op. cit.*

[21] P. M. Kitay, "A Comparison of the Sexes in Their Attitudes and Beliefs About Women: A Study of Prestige Groups," *Sociometry,* 3 (1940), pp. 399–407.

[22] S. Smith, "Age and Sex Differences in Children's Opinion Concerning Sex Differences," *Journal of Genetic Psychology,* 54 (1939), pp. 17–25.

than males show preference for the role of the opposite sex.[23]

Note that in Hypothesis 11 the term "preference" rather than "identification" was used. It is *not* hypothesized that a larger proportion of females than males *identify* with the opposite sex (Hypothesis 6 predicted the reverse) but rather that they will show *preference* for the role of the opposite sex. *Sex-role preference* refers to the desire to adopt the behavior associated with one sex or the other or the perception of such behavior as preferable or more desirable. *Sex-role preference* should be contrasted with *sex-role identification*, which, as stated previously, refers to the actual incorporation of the role of a given sex and to the unconscious reactions characteristic of that role.

Punishment may suppress behavior without causing its unlearning.[24] Because of the postulated punishment administered to males for adopting opposite-sex role behavior, it is predicted that males will repress atypical sex-role behavior rather than unlearn it. One might predict, then, a discrepancy between the underlying sex-role identification and the overt sex-role behavior of males. For females, on the other hand, no comparable punishment for adopting many aspects of the opposite-sex role is postulated. (12) *Consequently, where a discrepancy exists between sex-role preference and identification, it will tend to be as follows: Males will tend to show same-sex role preference with underlying opposite-sex identification. Females will tend to show opposite-sex role preference with underlying same-sex identification.*[25] Stated in

another way, where a discrepancy occurs both males and females will tend to show masculine-role preference with underlying feminine identification.

Not only is the masculine role accorded more prestige than the feminine role, but males are more likely than females to be ridiculed or punished for adopting aspects of the opposite-sex role. For a girl to be a tomboy does not involve the censure that results when a boy is a sissy. Girls may wear masculine clothing (shirts and trousers), but boys may not wear feminine clothing (skirts and dresses). Girls may play with toys typically associated with boys (cars, trucks, erector sets, and guns), but boys are discouraged from playing with feminine toys (dolls and tea sets). (13) *Therefore, a higher proportion of females than males adopt aspects of the role of the opposite sex.*[26]

Note that Hypothesis 13 refers to *sex-role adoption* rather than *sex-role identification* or *preference*. *Sex-role adoption* refers to the overt behavior characteristic of a given sex. An example contrasting sex-role adoption with preference and identification is an individual who *adopts* behavior characteristic of his own sex because it is expedient, not because he *prefers* it nor because he is so *identified*.

SUMMARY

The purpose of this paper has been to summarize the writer's theoretical formulation and to place it in a more comprehensive and coherent framework. The following hypotheses were presented and discussed:

1. Males tend to identify with a culturally defined masculine role, whereas

[23] D. B. Lynn, "A Note on Sex Differences in the Development of Masculine and Feminine Identification," *op. cit.*

[24] Hilgard, *op. cit.*

[25] D. B. Lynn, "Divergent Feedback and Sex-Role Identification in Boys and Men," *op. cit.*

[26] D. B. Lynn, "A Note on Sex Differences in the Development of Masculine and Feminine Identification," *op. cit.*

females tend to identify with their mothers.

2. Both males and females identify more closely with the mother than with the father.

3. The closer identification of males with their mothers than with their fathers will be revealed most frequently in personality variables which are not clearly sex-typed.

4. In learning the sex-typical identification, each sex is thereby acquiring separate methods of learning which are subsequently applied to learning tasks generally.

5. Males tend to have greater difficulty in achieving same-sex identification than females.

6. More males than females fail more or less completely in achieving same-sex identification but rather make an opposite-sex identification.

7. Males are more anxious regarding sex-role identification than females.

8. Males tend to hold stronger feelings of hostility toward females than females toward males.

9. With increasing age, males become relatively more firmly identified with the masculine role.

10. With increasing age, males develop psychological disturbances at a more slowly accelerating rate than females.

11. A larger proportion of females than males show preference for the role of the opposite sex.

12. Where a discrepancy exists between sex-role preference and identification, it will tend to be as follows: Males will tend to show same-sex role preference with underlying opposite-sex identification. Females will tend to show opposite-sex role preference with underlying same-sex identification.

13. A higher proportion of females than males adopt aspects of the role of the opposite sex.

A Comparative Test of the Status Envy, Social Power, and Secondary Reinforcement Theories of Identificatory Learning*

Albert Bandura, Dorothea Ross, and Sheila A. Ross

Although it is generally assumed that social behavior is learned and modified through direct reward and punishment of instrumental responses, informal observation and laboratory study of the social learning process reveal that new responses may be rapidly acquired and existing behavioral repertoires may be considerably changed as a function of observing the behavior and attitudes exhibited by models (Bandura, 1962).

*Adapted from the Journal of Abnormal and Social Psychology, 1963, 67: 527–534.

The latter type of learning is generally labeled "imitation" in behavior theory, and "identification" in most theories of personality. These concepts, however, are treated in the present paper as synonymous since both encompass the same behavioral phenomenon, i.e., the tendency for a person to match the behavior, attitudes, or emotional reactions as exhibited by actual or symbolized models. While the defining properties of identification are essentially the same in different personality theories, a host of divergent learning conditions have been proposed as the necessary antecedent variables for matching or identificatory behavior (Bronfenbrenner, 1960; Freud, 1946; Freud, 1924, 1948; Kagan, 1958; Klein, 1949; Maccoby, 1959; Mowrer, 1950; Parsons, 1955; Sears, 1957; Whiting, 1960).

In the experiment reported in this paper predictions were derived from three of the more prominent theories of learning by identification, and tested in three-person groups representing prototypes of the nuclear family. In one condition of the experiment an adult assumed the role of controller of resources and positive reinforcers. Another adult was the consumer or recipient of these resources, while the child, a participant observer in the triad, was essentially ignored. In a second treatment condition, one adult controlled the resources; the child, however, was the recipient of the positive reinforcers and the other adult was assigned a subordinate and powerless role. An adult male and female served as models in each of the triads. For half the boys and girls in each condition the male model controlled and dispensed the rewarding resources, simulating the husband dominant family; for the remaining children, the female model mediated the positive resources as in the wife dominant home. Following the experimental social interactions the two adult models exhibited divergent patterns of behavior in the presence of the child, and a measure was obtained of the degree to which the child subsequently patterned his behavior after that of the models.

According to the *status envy theory* of identification recently proposed by Whiting (1959, 1960), where a child competes unsuccessfully with an adult for affection, attention, food, and care, the child will envy the consumer adult and consequently identify with him. Whiting's theory represents an extension of the Freudian defensive identification hypothesis that identificatory behavior is the outcome of rivalrous interaction between the child and the parent who occupies an envied consumer status. While Freud presents the child as in competition with the father primarily for the mother's sexual and affectional attention, Whiting regards any forms of reward, material and social, as valued resources around which rivalry may develop. The status envy theory thus predicts that the highest degree of imitation by the child will occur in the experimental condition in which the rivalrous adult consumes the resources desired by the child, with the consumer adult serving as the primary object of imitation.

In contrast to the envy theory, other writers (Maccoby, 1959; Mussen & Distler, 1959; Parsons, 1955) assume that the controller, rather than the consumer, of resources is the main source of imitative behavior. The *power theory* of social influence has received considerable attention in experimental social psychology, though not generally in the context of identification theories.

Social power is typically defined as the ability of a person to influence the behavior of others by controlling or mediating their positive and negative reinforcements. French and Raven (1959) have distinguished five types of power based on expertness, attractiveness, legitimacy; coerciveness, and rewarding power, each of which is believed to have somewhat differential effects on the social influence process. For example, the use of threat or coercion, in which the controller derives power from his ability to administer punishments, not only develops avoidance behavior toward the controller but also decreases his attractiveness and hence his effectiveness in altering the behavior of others beyond the immediate social influence setting (French, Morrison & Levinger, 1960; Zipf, 1960). The use of reward power, in contrast, both fosters approach responses toward the power figure and increases his attractiveness or secondary reward value through the repeated association of his attributes with positive reinforcement. Attractiveness is assumed to extend the controller's power over a wide range of behavior (French & Raven, 1959).

In the present investigation power based upon the ability to dispense rewards was manipulated experimentally. In accordance with the social power theory of identification, but contrasting with the status envy hypothesis, one would predict that children will reproduce more of the behavior of the adult who controls positive reinforcers, than that of the powerless adult model, and that power inversions on the part of the male and female models will produce cross-sex imitation.

The *secondary reinforcement theory* of identification, which has been alluded to in the discussion of social power through attractiveness, has been elaborated in greatest detail by Mowrer (1950, 1958). According to this view, as a model mediates the child's biological and social rewards, the behavioral attributes of the model are paired repeatedly with positive reinforcement and thus acquire secondary reward value. On the basis of stimulus generalization, responses which match those of the model attain reinforcing value for the child in proportion to their similarity to those made by the model. Consequently, the child can administer positively conditioned reinforcers to himself simply by reproducing as closely as possible the model's positively valenced behavior. This theory predicts that the experimental condition in which the child was the recipient of positive reinforcements will yield the highest imitation scores with the model who dispensed the rewards serving as the primary source of imitative behavior.

METHOD

Subjects

The subjects were 36 boys and 36 girls enrolled in the Stanford University Nursery School. They ranged in age from 33 to 65 months, although the variability was relatively small with most of the ages falling around the mean of 51 months.

An adult male and female served as models in the triads so as to reproduce possible power structures encountered in different types of family constellations. A female experimenter conducted the study for all 72 children.

Design and Procedure

The subjects were assigned randomly to two experimental groups and one control group of 24 subjects each. Half the subjects in each group were males, and half were females.

High rewarding power was induced experimentally through the manipulation of material and social reinforcements, and the use of verbal structuring techniques. While accompanying the child to the experimental room, for example, the experimenter informed the child that the adult who assumed the role of controller owned the nursery school "surprise room," as well as a fabulous collection of play materials. After introducing the child to the controller, the experimenter asked whether the child may play in the surprise room. The controller explained that he was on his way to his car to fetch some of his most attractive toys, but the experimenter and the child could proceed to the room where he would join them shortly. As the controller left, the experimenter commented on how lucky they were to have access to the controller's play materials.

On the way to the experimental room they met the other adult who insisted on joining them but the experimenter informed her that she would have to obtain permission from the controller since he owned the room, and it was doubtful whether sufficient play materials were available for both the adult and the child. This brief encounter with the other adult was designed primarily to create the set that rewards were available to one person only and thereby to induce rivalrous feelings over the controller's resources.

As soon as the experimenter and the child arrived in the experimental room, they sat down at a small table and played with the few Lincoln Logs and two small cars that were provided. A short time later the other adult appeared and announced that the controller also granted her permission to play in the room.

The controller then entered carrying two large toy boxes containing a variety of highly attractive masculine and feminine toys, a colorful juice dispensing fountain, and an ample supply of cookies. As soon as the controller appeared on the scene, the experimenter departed.

For children in the Adult Consumer condition, the adult who assumed the role of consumer requested permission to play with the articles and the controller replied that, since the child appeared to be occupied at his table, the consumer was free to use the play materials. This monopolistic move by the consumer adult left the child stranded at a table with two relatively uninteresting toys.

During the 20-minute play session, the controller offered the consumer, among other things, miniature pinball machines, mechanical sparkling toys, kaleidoscopes, dolls, and actively participated with the consumer in dart games and other activities. To add to the credibility of the situation, both the controller and consumer devoted most of their attention to articles, such as the pinball ma-

chine and dart game, which could be used in adult appropriate activities. Throughout the interaction the controller was most helpful, supportive, and generous in dispensing social reinforcers in the form of praise, approval, and positive attention. The consumer, in turn, commented frequently on the controller's highly attractive resources so as to further enhance the controller's rewarding status. The consumer also verbalized considerable positive affect characteristic of a person experiencing positive reinforcements.

Approximately half way through the session, the controller remarked, "Say, you look hungry. I have just the thing for you." He then brought forth the soda fountain dispenser, poured colorful fruit juices into paper cups and served them to the consumer along with a generous supply of cookies. While the consumer was enjoying his snack, the controller turned on a "TV-radio" that played a nursery melody while a revolving dial displayed a series of storybook scenes.

Toward the end of the session, the controller informed the consumer that he will be leaving on a shopping trip to San Francisco that afternoon, and asked the consumer if there was anything special she would like him to buy for her. The consumer requested a super two-wheel bicycle, a high status object among the nursery school children. The controller promised to purchase the bicycle along with any other items the consumer might think of before the controller departed for the city.

The procedure for the Child Consumer condition was identical with that described above except the child was the recipient of the material rewards and the social reinforcement. During the session the other adult sat at the opposite end of the room engrossed in a book, and was totally ignored by the controller. In discussing the prospective San Francisco shopping trip, the controller mentioned to the child that he was planning to visit some toy stores in the city that afternoon, and asked for suggestions of attractive toys he might purchase for future play sessions with children.

For half the boys and girls in each treatment condition the male model controlled and dispensed the resources, simulating the husband dominant family; for the remaining children the female model mediated the positive resources as in the wife dominant home.

At the completion of the social interaction session the controller announced that he had a surprise game in his car that the three of them could play together. The controller then asked the other adult to fetch the experimenter to assist them with the game, and as soon as the adult departed, the controller removed the toys and assembled the imitation task apparatus.

Imitation Task

The imitation task was essentially the same two-choice discrimination problem utilized in an earlier experiment (Bandura & Huston, 1961), except the response repertoires exhibited by the models were considerably extended, and the procedure used in the acquisition trials was somewhat modified.

The apparatus consisted of two small boxes with hinged lids, identical in color and size. The boxes were placed on stools approximately 4 feet apart and 8 feet from the starting point. On the lid of each box was a rubber doll.

As soon as the other adult returned with the experimenter, the controller asked both the child and the experimenter to be seated in the chairs along the side of the room, and the other adult to stand at the starting point, while the controller described the game they were

about to play. The controller then explained that the experimenter would hide a picture sticker in one of the two boxes and the object of the game was to guess which box contained the sticker. The adults would have the first set of turns, following which the child would play the guessing game.

The discrimination problem was employed simply as a cover task that occupied the children's attention while at the same time permitted observation of the models as they performed divergent patterns of behavior during the discrimination trials in the absence of any set to attend to or learn the responses exhibited by the models.

Before commencing the trials, the controller invited the other participants to join him in selecting a "thinking cap" from hat racks containing two identical sets of four sailor caps, each of which had a different colored feather. The controller selected the green feathered hat, remarked "Feather in the front" and wore the hat with the feather facing forward. The other model selected the yellow feathered hat, commented, "Feather in the back," and placed the hat on her head with the feather facing backward. The child then made his choice from the four hats in the lower rack and it was noted whether he matched the color preference, hat placement, and the verbal responses of the one or the other model.

The models then went to the starting point, the child returned to his seat, and the experimenter loaded both boxes with sticker pictures for the models' trials.

During the execution of each trial, each model exhibited a different set of relatively novel verbal and motor responses that were totally irrelevant to the discrimination problem to which the child's attention was directed. At the starting point the controller stood with his arms crossed, but at the experimenter's warning not to look, the controller placed his hands over his eyes, faced sideways, and asked, "Ready?" The other model stood with his arms on his hips, then squatted with his back turned to the boxes, and asked, "Now?"

As soon as the experimenter gave the signal for the first trial the controller remarked, "Forward march" and began marching slowly toward the designated box repeating, "March, march, march." When he reached the box he said, "Sock him," hit the doll aggressively off the box, opened the lid and yelled, "Bingo," as he reached down for the sticker. He then remarked, "Lickit-sticket," as he pressed on the picture sticker with his thumb in the upper-right quadrant of a 24 × 24 inch sheet of plain white paper that hung on the wall immediately behind the boxes. The controller terminated the trial by replacing the doll facing sideways on the container with the comment, "Look in the mirror," and made a final verbal response, "There."

The other model then took her turn and performed a different set of imitative acts but equated with the controller's responses in terms of number, types of response classes represented, structural properties, and interest value. At the starting point, for example, she remarked, "Get set, go" and walked stiffly toward the boxes repeating "Left, right, left, right," When she reached the container she said, "Down and up," as she lay the doll down on the lid and opened the box. She then exclaimed, "A sticker-oo," repeated, "Weto-smacko," and slapped on the sticker with the open hand in the lower-left quadrant of the sheet of paper. In terminating the trial, the model lay the doll on the lid of the container with the remark, "Lie down," and returned with her hands behind her back, and emitted the closing remark, "That's it."

The two sets of responses were coun-terbalanced by having the models display each pattern with half the subjects in each of the three groups.

The models performed alternately for four trials. At the conclusion of the fourth trial the controller explained that he had to check some materials in his car and while he and the other model were away the child may take his turns. Before they departed, however, the experimenter administered a picture preference test in which the models were asked to select their preferred picture from six different stickers pasted on a 5 × 8 inch card, after which the child was presented a similar card containing an indentical set of stickers and requested to indicate his preference.

In addition to the introductory block of four trials by the models, the child's 15 total test trials were interspersed with three two-trial blocks by the models. The models were always absent from the room during the child's test series. This procedure was adopted in order to remove any imagined situational restraints against, or coercion for, the child to reproduce the models' responses. Moreover, demonstrations of delayed imitation in the absence of the model provides more decisive evidence for learning by means of imitation.

The models always selected different boxes, the right-left position varying from trial to trial in a fixed irregular order, and the controller always took the first turn. Although the models received stickers on each trial, the child was nonrewarded on one third of the trials in order to maintain his interest in the cover task.

At the beginning of each of the blocks of subjects' trials, the experimenter administered the picture preference test and the selection of stickers that matched the models' choices was recorded. In addition, on the eighth trial the models removed their hats and hung them in different locations in the room. If the child removed his hat during the session and placed it along side one or the other of the model's hats, this imitative act was also scored.

At the completion of the imitation phase of the experiment, the children were interviewed by the experimenter in order to determine whom they considered to be the controller of resources, and to assess their model preferences. The latter data were used as an index of attraction to the models. In addition, for the children in the adult consumer condition, the session was concluded by providing them the same lavish treatment accorded their adult rival.

Children in the control group had no prior social interaction with the models but participated with them in the imitative learning phase of the study. The experimenter assumed complete charge of the procedures and treated the models as though they were naive subjects. This control group was included primarily to determine the models' relative effectiveness as modeling stimuli. In addition, the models alternated between subjects in the order in which they executed the trials so as to test for the possibility of a primacy or a recency of exposure effect on imitative behavior.

Imitation Scores

The imitation scores were obtained by summing the frequency of occurrence of the postural, verbal, and motor responses described in the preceding section, and the hat, color, and picture preferences that matched the selections of each of the two models.

The children's performances were scored by three raters who observed the experimental sessions through a one-way mirror from an adjoining observation room. The raters were provided with a separate check list of responses exhibited by each of the two models, and the scor-

ing procedure simply involved checking the imitative responses performed by the children on each trial. In order to provide an estimate of interscorer reliability, the performances of 30% of the children were recorded simultaneously but independently by two observers. The raters were in perfect agreement on 95% of the specific imitative responses that they scored.

RESULTS

The control group data revealed that the two models were equally effective in eliciting imitative responses, the mean values being 17.83 and 20.46 for the male and female model, respectively; nor did the children display differential imitation of same-sex ($M = 20.30$) and opposite-sex ($M = 17.92$) models. Although children in the control group tended to imitate the second model ($M = 22.21$) to a somewhat greater extent than the one who performed first ($M = 16.08$) on each trial, suggesting a recency of exposure effect, the difference was not of statistically significant magnitude ($t = 1.60$).

Table 1 presents the mean imitation scores for children in each of the two experimental triads. A $2 \times 2 \times 2 \times 2 \times 2$ mixed factorial analysis of variance was computed on these data in which the four factors in the design were sex of child, sex of the model who controlled the resources, adult versus child consumer, and the controller versus the other model as the source of imitative behavior. As shown in Table 2, the findings of this study clearly support the social power theory of imitation. In both experimental treatments, regardless of whether the rival adult or the children themselves were the recipients of the rewarding resources, the model who possessed rewarding power was imitated to a greater degree than was the rival or the ignored model ($F = 40.61$, $p < .001$). Nor did the condition combin-

TABLE 1 Mean number of imitative responses performed by subgroups of children in the experimental triads

Subjects	Objects of imitation			
	MALE *Controller*	FEMALE *Consumer*	FEMALE *Controller*	MALE *Consumer*
Girls	29.00	9.67	26.00	10.00
Boys	30.17	18.67	22.33	16.17
Total	29.59	14.17	24.17	13.09
	Controller	*Ignored*	*Controller*	*Ignored*
Girls	22.00	16.17	31.84	22.17
Boys	29.17	16.67	26.83	34.50
Total	25.59	16.42	29.34	28.34

ing resource ownership with direct reinforcement of the child yield the highest imitation of the model who controlled and dispensed the positive rewards. The latter finding is particularly surprising since an earlier experiment based on two-person groups (Bandura & Huston, 1961), demonstrated that pairing of model with positive reinforcement substantially enhanced the occurrence of imitative behavior. An examination of the remaining significant interaction effects together with the postexperimental interview data suggest a possible explanation for the discrepant results.

The differential in the controller-other model imitation was most pronounced when the male model was the controller of resources ($F = 4.76$, $p < .05$), particularly for boys. In fact, boys who were the recipients of rewarding resources mediated by the female model tended to favor the ignored male as their object of imitation. In the postexperiment interview a number of boys in this condition spontaneously expressed sympathy for the ignored male and mild criticism of the controller for not being more charitable with her bountiful resources (for example, "She doesn't share much. John played bravely even though she didn't even share. . . . She's a bit greedy.").

As a partial check on whether this factor would tend to diminish the differ-

ential imitation of the two models, six children—three boys and three girls—participated in a modified Child Consumer treatment in which, halfway through the social interaction session, the ignored adult was informed that he too may have access to the playthings. He replied that he was quite content to read his book. This modified procedure, which removed the rivalry and the exclusion of the model, yielded four times as much imitation of the controller relative to the model who was ignored by choice.

The significant triple interaction effect indicates that the differential in the controller-other model imitation was greatest when the same-sex model mediated the positive reinforcers, and this effect was more pronounced for boys than for girls.

The data presented so far demonstrate that manipulation of rewarding power had produced differential imitation of the behavior exhibited by the two models. In order to assess whether the dispensing of positive reinforcers in the prior social interaction influenced the overall level of matching responses, the imitation scores in each of the three groups were summed across models and analyzed using a Sex × Treatment design.

The mean total imitative responses for children in the Child Consumer, Adult Consumer, and the Control group

TABLE 2   Summary of the analysis of variance of the imitation scores

Source	df	MS	F
Between subjects	47	310.17	
Sex of subjects (A)	1	283.59	<1
Sex of controller model (B)	1	128.34	<1
Adult versus child consumer (C)	1	518.01	1.61
A × B	1	23.01	<1
A × C	1	1.76	<1
B × C	1	742.59	2.31
A × B × C	1	21.10	<1
Error (b)	40	321.49	
Within subjects	48	113.24	
Controller versus other model (D)	1	2,025.84	40.61***
A × D	1	297.51	5.96*
B × D	1	237.51	4.76*
C × D	1	396.09	7.94**
A × B × D	1	256.76	5.15*
A × C × D	1	19.52	<1
B × C × D	1	23.02	<1
A × B × C × D	1	184.00	3.69
Error (w)	40	49.88	

* $p < .05$.
** $p < .01$.
*** $p < .001$.

were 50.21, 40.58, and 37.88, respectively. Analysis of variance of these data reveals a significant treatment effect ($F = 3.37$, $.025 < p < .05$). Further comparisons of pairs of means by the t test, show that children in the child rewarded condition displayed significantly more imitative behavior than did children both in the Adult Consumer treatment ($t = 2.19$, $p < .05$), and those in the Control group ($t = 2.48$, $p < .02$). The Adult Consumer and Control groups, however, did not differ from each other in this respect ($t = .54$).

The model preference patterns were identical for children in the two experimental conditions and consequently, the data were combined for the statistical analysis. Of the 48 children, 32 selected the model who possessed rewarding power as the more attractive, while 16 preferred the noncontrolling adult. The greater attractiveness of the rewarding model was significant beyond the .05 level ($x^2 = 5.34$). The experimental triad in which boys were the recipients of positive reinforcers while the male model was ignored, and the female consumer-girl ignored subgroup, contributed the highest preference for the non-controlling adult.

In addition to the experimental groups discussed in the preceding section, data are available for 9 children in the Adult Consumer condition, and for 11 children in the Child Consumer treatment who revealed, in their postexperiment interviews, that they had actually attributed rewarding power to the ignored or the consumer adult despite the elaborate experimental manipulations designed to establish differential power status. A number of these children were firmly convinced that only a male can possess resources and, therefore, the female dispensing the rewards was only an intermediary for the male model (for example, "He's the man and it's all his because he's a daddy. Mommy never really

TABLE 3   Imitation as a function of attributed rewarding power to the models

TREATMENT CONDITION	Objects of imitation			
	FEMALE CONTROLLER	MALE NONCON-TROLLER	MALE CONTROLLER	FEMALE NONCON-TROLLER
Adult consumer	24.0	12.3	29.8	14.6
Child consumer	18.2	6.7	35.5	16.2

has things belong to her. . . . He's the daddy so it's his but he shares nice with the mommy. . . . He's the man and the man always really has the money and he lets ladies play too. John's good and polite and he has very good manners.") This view of resource ownership within the family constellation was often directly reinforced by the mothers (for example, "My mommy told me and Joan that the daddy really buys all the things, but the mommy looks after things."). Children who attributed the resource ownership to the consumer or ignored female model had considerable difficulty in explaining their selection (for example, "I just knowed it does. . . . I could tell, that's how."), perhaps, because the power structure they depicted is at variance with the widely accepted cultural norm.

As shown in Table 3, models who were attributed rewarding power elicited approximately twice as many matching responses than models who were perceived by the children as possessing no control over the rewarding resources. Because of the small and unequal number of cases in each cell, these data were not evaluated statistically. The differences, however, are marked and quite in accord with those produced by the experimentally manipulated variations in power status.

DISCUSSION

To the extent that the imitative behavior elicited in the present experiment may be considered an elementary prototype of identification within a nuclear family group, the data fail to support the interpretation of identificatory learning as the outcome of a rivalrous interaction between the child and the adult who occupies an envied status in respect to the consumption of highly desired resources. Children clearly identified with the source of rewarding power rather than with the competitor for these rewards. Moreover, power inversions on the part of the male and female models produced cross-sex imitation, particularly in girls. The differential readiness of boys and girls to imitate behavior exhibited by an opposite-sex model are consistent with findings reported by Brown (1956, 1958) that boys show a decided preference for the masculine role, whereas, ambivalence and masculine role preference are widespread among girls. These findings probably reflect both the differential cultural tolerance for cross-sex behavior displayed by males and females, and the privileged status and relatively greater positive reinforcement of masculine role behavior in our society.

Failure to develop sex appropriate behavior has received considerable attention in the clinical literature and has customarily been assumed to be established and maintained by psychosexual threat and anxiety reducing mechanisms. Our findings strongly suggest, however, that external social learning variables, such as the distribution of rewarding power within the family constellation, may be highly influential in the formation of inverted sex role behavior.

Theories of identificatory learning have generally assumed that within the family setting the child's initial identification is confined to his mother, and that during early childhood boys must turn from the mother as the primary model to the father as the main source of imitative behavior. However, throughout the course of development children are provided with ample opportunities to observe the behavior of both parents. The results of the present experiment reveal that when children are exposed to multiple models they may select one or more of them as the primary source of behavior, but rarely reproduce all the elements of a single model's repertoire or confine their imitation to that model. Although the children adopted many of the characteristics of the model who possessed rewarding power, they also reproduced some of the elements of behavior exhibited by the model who occupied the subordinate role. Consequently, the children were not simply junior-size replicas of one or the other model; rather, they exhibited a relatively novel pattern of behavior representing an amalgam of elements from both models. Moreover, the specific admixture of behavioral elements varied from child to child. These findings provide considerable evidence for the seemingly paradoxical conclusion that imitation can in fact produce innovation of social behavior, and that within the same family even same-sex siblings may exhibit quite different response patterns, owing to their having selected for imitation different elements of their parents' response repertoires.

The association of a model with noncontingent positive reinforcement tends to increase the incidence of imitative behavior in two person groups (Bandura & Huston, 1961), whereas the addition of a same-sex third person who is denied access to desired rewards may provoke in children negative evaluations of the rewarding model and thereby decreases his potency as a modeling stimulus. These two sets of data demonstrate how learning principles based on an individual behavior model may be subject to strict limitations, since the introduction of additional social variables into the stimulus complex can produce significant changes in the functional relationships between relevant variables.

References

BANDURA, A. Social learning through imitation. In M. R. Jones (Ed.), *Nebraska symposium on motivation: 1962.* Lincoln: Univer. Nebraska Press, 1962. Pp. 211–269.

BANDURA, A., & HUSTON, ALETHA C. Identification as a process of incidental learning, *J. abnorm. soc. Psychol.*, 1961, 63, 311–318.

BRONFENBRENNER, U. Freudian theories of identification and their derivatives. *Child Develpm.*, 1960, 31, 15–40.

BROWN, D. G. Sex-role preference in young children. *Psychol. Monogr.*, 1956, 70 (14, Whole No. 421).

BROWN, D. G. Sex-role development in a changing culture. *Psychol. Bull.*, 1958, 55, 232–242.

FRENCH, J. R. P., JR., MORRISON, H. W., & LEVINGER, G. Coercive power and forces affecting conformity. *J. abnorm. soc. Psychol.*, 1960, 61, 93–101.

FRENCH, J. R. P., JR., & RAVEN, B. The bases of social power. In D. Cartwright (Ed.), *Studies in social power.* Ann Arbor, Mich.: Institute for Social Research, 1959. Pp. 150–167.

FREUD, ANNA. *The ego and the mechanisms of defense.* New York: International Univer. Press, 1946.

FREUD, S. The passing of the Oedipus-complex. In, *Collected papers.* Vol. 2. London: Hogarth Press, 1924. Pp. 269–282.

FREUD, S. *Group psychology and the*

analysis of the ego. London: Hogarth Press, 1948.

KAGAN, J. The concept of identification. Psychol. Rev., 1958, 65, 296–305.

KLEIN, MELANIE. The psycho-analysis of children. London: Hogarth Press, 1949.

MACCOBY, ELEANOR E. Role-taking in childhood and its consequences for social learning. Child Develpm., 1959, 30, 239–252.

MOWRER, O. H. Identification: A link between learning theory and psychotherapy. In, Learning theory and personality dynamics. New York: Ronald Press, 1950. Pp. 69–94.

MOWRER, O. H. Hearing and speaking: An analysis of language learning. J. speech hear. Disord., 1958, 23, 143–152.

MUSSEN, P., & DISTLER, L. Masculinity, identification, and father-son relationships. J. abnorm. soc. Psychol., 1959, 59, 350–356.

PARSONS, T. Family structure and the socialization of the child. In T. Parsons &

R. F. Bales (Eds.), Family, socialization, and interaction process. Glencoe, Ill.: Free Press, 1955. Pp. 35–131.

SEARS, R. R. Identification as a form of behavioral development. In D. B. Harris (Ed.), The concept of development. Minneapolis: Univer. Minnesota Press, 1957, Pp. 149–161.

WHITING, J. W. M. Sorcery, sin, and the superego: A cross-cultural study of some mechanisms of social control. In M. R. Jones (Ed.), Nebraska symposium on motivation: 1959. Lincoln: Univer. Nebraska Press, 1959. Pp. 174–195.

WHITING, J. W. M. Resource mediation and learning by identification. In I. Iscoe & H. W. Stevenson (Eds.), Personality development in children. Austin: Univer. Texas Press, 1960. Pp. 112–126.

ZIPF, SHEILA G. Resistance and conformity under reward and punishment. J. abnorm. soc. Psychol., 1960, 61, 102–109.

Effects of Authoritative Parental Control on Child Behavior[*]

Diana Baumrind

An authority is a person whose expertness befits him to designate a behavioral alternative for another where the alternatives are perceived by both. This neutral definition became infused with the prejudicial connotations appropriate to the authoritarian personality syndrome following Lewin's work with authoritarian, democratic, and laissez faire social climates (Lewin, Lippitt, & White, 1939), and the publication of The Authoritarian Personality (Adorno, Frenkel-Brunswik, Levinson, & Sanford, 1950).

[*]Adapted from Child Development, 1966, 37: 888–907.

The introduction of the "authoritarian personality syndrome" into the lexicon of the psychologist, probably by Fromm (1941), provided a convenient label to apply to the controlling parent. Fromm, however, distinguished between rational and inhibiting authority. He used the term "authoritarian personality" to refer to the syndrome in which enactment of the role of inhibiting authority, not rational authority, characterizes the individual's interpersonal relations.

The practices favored by American parents to influence the actions and character of their offspring have varied from time to time, with the predominant view of the child as a refractory savage, a small adult, or an angelic bundle from heaven. These convictions have, for the most part, been based on humanistic or religious values rather than upon scientific findings. Research findings have had a salutary effect in debunking certain clinically derived notions about the obligatory neurotogenic effects of one or another common child-rearing practices, notions characterized perhaps more by creative flair and inner certitude than demonstrable validity.

The psychoanalytic view that full gratification of infantile sucking, excretory, and genital needs is essential for secure and healthful adult personalities provided a rationale for prolonged breast feeding on self-demand schedules, gradual and late weaning, and late and lenient toilet training. The ideal home or school in the late forties and fifties was organized around unlimited acceptance of the child's current needs for gratification, rather than around preparation for adult life. The child was to be granted maximum freedom of choice and self-expression in both settings. Spock's 1946 edition of *Baby and Child Care* advocated such infant-care practices and the extension into early childhood of lenient disciplinary practices. Yet the avalanche of studies on the effects of infant-care practices did not support the supposed harmful effects of such restraints on the child as scheduled feeding, early weaning, and early toilet training. Indeed, Spock's emphasis altered in the 1957 edition. Comparing the changes in child-rearing practices from 1940 to 1955, he stated that "Since then a great change in attitude has occurred and nowadays there seems to be more chance of a conscientious parent's getting into trouble

with permissiveness than strictness" (p. 2). In his recent *Redbook* columns (1964——), Spock speaks out more affirmatively for the reinstitution of parental controls and for the inculcation by the parent of ideals and standards.

The vigorous introduction into educational philosophy of permissive and child-centered attitudes began at least 40 years ago (Coriat, 1926; Naumberg, 1928) as a partial outgrowth of the psychoanalytic theory of psychosexual development. The view that the effects on the child of adult authority are inhibiting, neurotogenic, and indefensible ethically is promoted today by articulate spokesmen (Goodman, 1964; Maslow, 1954; Neill, 1964; Rogers, 1960) in the fields of education and child rearing.

While progressivism in American education claims Dewey as its founder, Dewey (1915; Dewey & Dewey, 1916) did not indorse two of the central principles of progressive education introduced by Neill: the freedom of the child to choose to go to class or to stay away, and the notion of enfranchising small children. Dewey's concern about freedom emphasized intellectual exploration and room for diverse interests and gifts in the curriculum and not the right of the individual child to determine his own conduct in the school setting. The correctives introduced by Dewey have become part of the accepted wisdom of the present age, although the child-centered approach, in the extreme form advocated by Neill, has had little permanent effect on public school education (Cremin, 1964, pp. 347–353).

Permissiveness in child rearing, like its counterpart in education, is the antithesis to the thesis that the proper way to train a child is for the parent or teacher to play the role of omniscient interpreter of an omnipotent deity and to insist forcibly, when necessary, that the child conform to absolute rules of conduct. A synthesis of the valid components of that antinomy concerning adult authority is proposed in this paper and referred to as "authoritative control."

PROTOTYPES OF ADULT CONTROL

This section consists of a presentation of three prototypes of adult control, each of which has influenced greatly the child-rearing practices of educators, parents, and child-development experts.

Permissive

The permissive parent attempts to behave in a nonpunitive, acceptant, and affirmative manner toward the child's impulses, desires, and actions. She consults with him about policy decisions and gives explanations for family rules. She makes few demands for household responsibility and orderly behavior. She presents herself to the child as a resource for him to use as he wishes, not as an ideal for him to emulate, nor as an active agent responsible for shaping or altering his ongoing or future behavior. She allows the child to regulate his own activities as much as possible, avoids the exercise of control, and does not encourage him to obey externally defined standards. She attempts to use reason and manipulation, but not overt power, to accomplish her ends.

Lawrence Frank, while affirming the positive value to the individual of adherence to cultural values, drew with some passion the "pathetic picture of individuals who in their early childhood have been unnecessarily deprived, frustrated, and coerced and so have built up a private world which is forever insecure and threatened; hence they

must react with resentment and hostility to every experience" (1940, p. 346). He expressed concern for the "young child who is striving to meet the demands made upon him, is under constant tension which is crystallized into a persistent anxiety about his own competence and functional adequacy" (1940, p. 346).

The alternative to adult control, according to Neill, is to permit the child to be self-regulated, free of restraint, and unconcerned about expression of impulse or the effects of his carelessness.

Self-regulation means the right of a baby to live freely, without outside authority in things psychic and somatic. It means that the baby feeds when it is hungry; that it becomes clean in habits only when it wants to; that it is never stormed at nor spanked; that it is always loved and protected [1964, p. 105, italics Neill's].

I believe that to impose anything by authority is wrong. The child should not do anything until he comes to the opinion—his own opinion—that it should be done [1964, p. 114, italics Neill's].

Every child has the right to wear clothes of such a kind that it does not matter a brass farthing if they get messy or not [1964, p. 115].

Furniture to a child is practically nonexistent. So at Summerhill we buy old car seats and old bus seats. And in a month or two they look like wrecks. Every now and again at mealtime, some youngster waiting for his second helping will while away the time by twisting his fork almost into knots [1964, p. 138].

Really, any man or woman who tries to give children freedom should be a millionnaire, for it is not fair that the natural carelessness of children should always be in conflict with the economic factor [1964, p. 139].

Authoritarian

The authoritarian parent attempts to shape, control, and evaluate the behavior and attitudes of the child in accordance with a set standard of conduct, usually an absolute standard, theologically motivated and formulated by a higher authority. She values obedience as a virtue and favors punitive, forceful measures to curb self-will at points where the child's actions or beliefs conflict with what she thinks is right conduct. She believes in keeping the child in his place, in restricting his autonomy, and in assigning household responsibilities in order to inculcate respect for work. She regards the preservation of order and traditional structure as a highly valued end in itself. She does not encourage verbal give and take, believing that the child should accept her word for what is right.

Authoritarian control is less consistent with the American ethos than it was in past centuries when parental discipline was directed at teaching the child to do the will of God. The authoritarian parent in a previous era generally felt that her purpose in training her child was to forward not her own desire but the Divine will. In the words of Wesley's mother:

> As self-will is the root of all sin and misery, so whatever cherishes this in children insures their after-wretchedness and irreligion; whatever checks and mortifies it promotes their future happiness and piety. This is still more evident, if we further consider, that religion is nothing else than doing the will of God, and not our own: that the one grand impediment to our temporal and eternal happiness being this self-will, no indulgences of it can be trivial, no denial unprofitable. Heaven or hell depends on this alone. So that the parent who studies to subdue it in his child, works together with God in the renewing and saving a soul. The

parent who indulges it does the devil's work, makes religion impraticable, salvation unattainable; and does all that in him lies to damn his child, soul and body forever [Susannah Wesley, quoted in Gesell, 1930, pp. 30–31].

Since the impediment to temporal and eternal happiness was thought to be self-will, the authoritarian parent was stern because she cared. Her discipline was strict, consistent, and loving. Thus Mrs. Wesley's rules:

> That whoever was charged with a fault, of which they were guilty, if they would ingenuously confess it, and promise to amend, should not be beaten. . . . That no child should ever be chid, or beat twice for the same fault; and that if they amended, they should never be upbraided with it afterwards. . . . That every signal act of obedience, especially when it crossed upon their own inclinations, should be always commended, and frequently rewarded, according to the merits of the case. . . . That if ever any child performed an act of obedience, or did anything with intention to please, though the performance was not well, yet the obedience and intention should be kindly accepted; and the child with sweetness directed how to do better for the future [Gesell, 1930, p.27].

Authoritative

The authoritative parent attempts to direct the child's activities in a rational, issue-oriented manner. She encourages verbal give and take, shares with the child the reasoning behind her policy, and solicits his objections when he refuses to conform. Both autonomous self-will and disciplined conformity are valued by the authoritative parent. Therefore, she exerts firm control at points of parent-child divergence, but does not hem the child in with restrictions. She enforces her own perspective as an adult, but recognizes the child's individual interests and special ways. The authoritative parent affirms the child's present qualities, but also sets standards for future conduct. She uses reason, power, and shaping by regime and reinforcement to achieve her objectives and does not base her decisions on group consensus or the individual child's desires.

Some quotations from Rambusch, in describing the Montessori method, illustrate the way in which authoritative control is used to resolve the antithesis between pleasure and duty, and between freedom and responsibility.

> The discipline resides in three areas in a Montessori classroom: it resides in the environment itself which is controlled; in the teacher herself who is controlled and is ready to assume an authoritarian role if it is necessary; and from the very beginning it resides in the children. It is a three-way arrangement, as opposed to certain types of American education in which all of the authority is vested in the teacher, or where, in the caricature of permissive education, all of the authority is vested in the children [1962, pp. 49–50].

> When a child has finished his work he is free to put it away, he is free to initiate new work or, in certain instances, he is free to not work. But he is not free to disturb or destroy what others are doing. If the day is arranged in such a way that at a certain time the teacher must demand of the children that they arbitrarily finish what they are doing—if it is lunch time, or recess or whatever—the child must accommodate himself to the demand of the group. It is largely a question of balance. In a Montessori class the teacher does not delude herself into believing that her manipulation of the children represents their consensus of what they would like to do. If she is manipulating them insofar as she is determining arbitrarily that this must be done at this time, she is cognizant of what

she is doing, which the child may or may not be [1962, p. 51].

> The importance of the responsibility in selecting matter for the child to learn is placed in the hands of those adults who are aware of what the culture will demand of the child and who are able to "program" learning in such a way that what is suitable for the child's age and stage of development is also learnable and pleasurable to him. Both Dewey and Montessori feel that interest and discipline are connected and not opposed. Dewey himself decried unrestrained freedom of action in speech, in manners, and lack of manners. He was, in fact, critical of all those progressive schools that carried the thing they call freedom nearly to the point of anarchy [1962, p. 63].

A CRITICAL LOOK AT EIGHT PROPOSITIONS CONCERNING THE EFFECTS ON CHILD BEHAVIOR OF DISCIPLINARY TECHNIQUES

The associations between seven dimensions of parental control and manifest behavior of nursery school and school-age children are summarized in Table 1. The effects of infant-care practices have been reviewed elsewhere (Caldwell, 1964; Orlansky, 1949; Stendler, 1950) and are not included.

A review of the literature led to the selection of 12 studies which were particularly relevant to the topic of this paper and had the following methodological characteristics: Data on parents and children were collected independently; data on the children were derived from direct repeated observations in natural or laboratory settings; and parents' scores were based on interview or direct observational data, rather than on personality test scores.

Only findings significant at the .05 level or beyond and concerned with the effects of disciplinary practices are summarized in Table 1. A more detailed

TABLE 1 Parent control and child behavior

Dimensions of Parental Control	Relevant Variables	Effects
1. *Punitive vs. nonpunitive disciplinary practices:* Parent injects threats and hostile remarks into control attempts and makes use of severe punishment, ridicule and strong disapproval to motivate the child to obey	Glueck & Glueck (1950); Physical punishment Sears, Whiting, Nowlis, & Sears (1953); Punitiveness	Higher in delinquent group Associated for boys, with dependence upon peers, and aggression; for girls, with dependency
	Bandura & Walters (1959); Nagging and scolding	For fathers, higher in aggressive than control group For fathers, higher in aggressive group
	Physical punishment Punishment for dependence Punishment for aggression towards other adults	For mothers, higher in aggressive group For both parents, higher in aggressive group
	McCord et al. (1961); Punitiveness Becker et al. (1962); Physical punishment	Higher in the most aggressive group For mothers, associated with aggression and conduct problems in boys and girls
	Kagan & Moss (1962); Restrictiveness (defined as punitive)	Associated in boys with passive dependent correlates at early ages changing to hostile, nondependent correlates by adult interview; associated in girls with passive dependent correlates at all ages
2. *Use vs. nonuse of withdrawal of love:* Child is punished by withholding or withdrawing love as a way of obtaining compliance with a parental directive	Sears et al.; Withdrawal of love	Associated with dependency, and also with high conscience when mother is warm
	Bandura et al.; Withdrawal of love	No difference between aggressive and control groups, but use of this technique correlates with resistiveness in total group
3. *Explanations offered and give and take encouraged vs. rigid maintenance of status distinctions:* Tolerates dissent, explains policy, uses reason to impel obedience, equalitarian	Baldwin (1948); Democracy	Associated with aggressiveness, fearlessness, playfulness, leadership, and cruelty
	Glueck & Glueck; Reasoning Bandura & Walters; Use of reasoning Finney (1961); Rigidity Schaefer & Bayley (1963); Equalitarianism	Higher in nondelinquent group Higher in control than aggressive group Associated with covert hostility Associated in both sexes with positive, happy, friendly behavior
	Baumrind (1967); Communication	Mature group higher than immature or alienated groups

TABLE 1 Continued Parent control and child behavior

Dimensions of Parental Control	Relevant Variables	Effects
4. *High vs. low demands for household responsibilities and orderly behavior:* Makes and enforces demands for socially desirable behavior, personal neatness, orderliness about cleaning up, and sharing in household responsibilities	Glueck & Glueck; Household duties Sears et al.; Current frustration Bandura & Walters; Demands for achievement McCord et al.; Demands for polite, responsible behavior Becker et al.; Permissiveness vs. restrictiveness (routines)	Higher in nondelinquent group No significant findings for boys or girls Higher in control than aggressive group Higher demands by parents of least hostile children No significant findings
5. *Restricts vs. permits autonomy:* Parental prohibitions and restrictions cover many areas of child's life and needs systems	Glueck & Glueck; Control (physical punishment, deprivation of privileges, threatening, etc.) Supervision Sears et al.; Current frustration: eating and sickness-danger Bandura & Walters; Parental restrictions Permissiveness for aggression toward mother McCord et al.; Supervision Control Becker et al.; Permissiveness vs. strictness with sex and aggression Schaefer & Bayley; Autonomy (correlations with positive evaluation vary with sex and age of child)	Generally higher in delinquent group Higher in nondelinquent group No significant findings for boys or girls Higher in aggressive group Higher in aggressive group Least hostile boys were supervised most Most hostile boys were either under or over-controlled No significant findings for maternal strictness; paternal strictness associated with hostile withdrawal and nervous disposition in both sexes For adolescent boys maternal ratings at 0–3 correlated positively with timidity, inhibition, courtesy, tact; for 10½–12 year boys maternal ratings at 9–14 correlated negatively with friendly, cooperative, interested behavior; for adolescent girls, ratings at 9–14 correlated negatively with defiance, hostility, unpopularity and discontent

TABLE 1 Continued Parent control and child behavior

Dimensions of Parental Control	Relevant Variables	Effects
6. Uses high- vs. low-power assertion:	Hoffman (1960); Initial unqualified power assertion	Associated in middle-class homes with resistance towards teacher
	Reactive unqualified power assertion	For both middle-class and working-class youth, associations were with assertiveness and resistance to being dominated; and in working-class youth only, associated with hostility
	Schaefer & Bayley; Wish to control	Unrelated to behavior of boys at any age; associations in adolescent girls were with discontent and turbulence
7. Firm vs. lax control: Enforces rules firmly, can resist child's demands, believes in directing child	Baldwin; Control	Negatively related to quarrelsomeness, resistance and disobedience. Higher in nondelinquent group
	Glueck & Glueck; Firm but kindly discipline Waston (1957), Strict vs. permissive parental discipline Psychologist's ratings	Permissive higher than strict group on independence and socialization
	Teacher's ratings	Strict group higher than permissive group on energetic involvement
	Bandura & Walters; Parental demands for obedience Finney; Firmness McCord et al.; Consistency of parental discipline Baumrind; Parental control	Higher in control than aggressive group Associated with conscience development Characterized parents of least hostile children Highest in mature (self-assertive and self-reliant), lowest in immature group

Note. – Prototype defined by dimensions:
Authoritarian model – low 3; high 4, 5, 6, 7, variable 1, 2.
Permissive model – low 1, 4, 5, 6, 7; high 3; variable 2.
Authoritative model – low 1, 2; high 3, 7; moderate 4, 5, 6.

review of these 12 studies is on file with the American Documentation Institute.

The subsequent discussion, while relying primarily upon the findings summarized in Table 1, also draws upon .additional studies which are relevant to the theses but do not meet the criteria set here for detailed review.

Side effects of punishment

Punitive, hostile, disaffiliated, self-righteous, and nonempathic disciplinary practices are associated clearly in the studies reviewed with cognitive and emotional disturbance in the child, including hostile withdrawal, hostile acting out, dependency, personality problems, nervousness, and reduced schoolroom efficiency. There is some evidence that paternal punitiveness, especially in working-class families, is associated with more severe disturbance in the child than maternal punitiveness, perhaps because techniques used by the father—and the working-class father in particular—are harsher.

The clearly detrimental effects of punitiveness, which can scarcely be separated from those of rejection, should not be confused with the effects on the child of particular forms of mild punishment, physical or otherwise. The possibility should be considered that mild punishment may have beneficial side effects, such as the following: (a) more rapid re-establishment of affectional involvement on both sides following emotional release, (b) high resistance to similar deviation by siblings who vicariously experience punishment, (c) emulation of the aggressive parent resulting in prosocial assertive behavior, (d) lessening of guilt reactions to transgression, and (e) increased ability of the child to endure punishment in the service of a desired end. Punishment which is severe, unjust, ill-timed, and administered by an unloving parent is probably harmful as well as ineffective. Just, mild punishment by a loved and respected parent may not have harmful side effects. It may have, like other forthright uses of power, beneficial side effects.

Effectiveness of punishment

The proposition that punishment is an extremely ineffective means of controlling human behavior may indeed be a "legend" as Solomon (1964) and Walters, Parke, and Cane (1965) suggest. Under conditions prevailing in the home setting, punishment may be quite effective in helping to accomplish particular objectives.

Punishment has been found to suppress unacceptable responses even when these responses are not eliminated, and so to require continued reinforcement. Parents frequently do not wish to eliminate a response, but wish merely to suppress its occurrence in particular places and for a limited period of time. They are willing and able to continue the process of aversive stimulation as long as is necessary to accomplish these objectives. A procedure which appears ineffective in the laboratory will then be, from the perspective of the parent, quite effective.

The use of nonreward as a substitute for punishment may be less effective than punishment as a way of altering certain behavior under actual conditions prevailing in the home setting. The very presence of the mother may be taken by the child as a tacit approval of his behavior if she merely nonrewards rather than punishes his deviant response (Crandall, 1963; Crandall, Good, & Crandall, 1964; Siegel & Kohn, 1959). Also, many of a child's disapproved acts provide their own reward. Such acts as sneaking sweets and smacking a younger sibling fall into the category of intrinsically rewarding disapproved responses which will not respond to parental nonreward. In the laboratory, the punishing agent may be avoided by the child and thus lose her power to alter the child's behavior. If the punishing agent is a loved and respected parent, such a side effect of punishment, which would render future punishment less effective, is improbable.

The child may, but need not, overgeneralize an avoidant response to a whole pattern of behavior associated by similarity or contiguity with the punished response. Sharp discrimination can result from consistent, verbally mediated social training in which an undesirable response is punished and a similar or substitute response rewarded concurrently.

Aversive stimuli may be less effective than rewarding stimuli in eliciting desired behavior in an operant conditioning laboratory. However, the conclusion does not follow that punishment, as typically used in the home, is ineffective or that its use could not be made more effective.

It is more reasonable to teach parents who wish to learn to use punishment effectively and humanely how to do so than to preserve the myth that punishment is ineffective or intrinsically harmful. For example, the timing of punishment in relation to a response is one of many controllable determinants of the long-range effectiveness of punishment as a deterrent (Aronfreed & Reber, 1965; Walters et al., 1965). Parents can also be taught to accompany punishment with an explanation in which both the changeworthy act, and where possible a more acceptable act, are specified.

2. Close Supervision, High Demands, and Other Manifestations of Parental Authority Provoke Rebelliousness in Children, Particularly at Adolescence

The findings reported here failed to support the common assumption that demands for neatness and orderliness reflect rigid obsessive qualities in the parents and should result in passive-aggressive problems in the child. In fact, Bandura and Walters (1959), Glueck and Glueck (1950), and McCord, McCord, and Howard (1961) found that higher demands were made by the parents of the *least* hostile or delinquent children. Finney (1961) found that, while rigidity was associated with covert hostility in children, firm control was associated with conscience development.

Parents who demand that their child be orderly and assume household responsibilities also seem to provide compatible surroundings conducive to the child's well-being and to involve themselves conscientiously with his welfare. Perhaps that is why such demands are viewed by the child, in most instances studied, as reasonable, and do not tend to provoke rebellion.

Findings from several additional studies suggest that parental demands provoke rebelliousness or antisocial aggression only when the parent is also repressive, hostile, and restrictive. In one study of 211 third graders' attitudes (Hoffman, Rosen, & Lippitt, 1960), the children who described their parents as coercive but also permissive of high autonomy, compared with the remainder of the sample, were higher in academic success, use of directives, successful influence of peers, group leadership, friendliness, and also conscious experience of hostility. They were striving and aggressive but not rebellious. Sears (1961) found that the antecedents at age 12 of prosocial aggression scores, in maternal interview data obtained when the child was age 5, were high permissiveness for aggression and high punishment. In the Sears study, punishment for aggression appeared to reduce antisocial but increase prosocial aggression, indicating once again that parental authority may stimulate self-assertiveness without concomitant rebellious behavior. Dubin and Dubin (1963) surveyed 25 studies on the authority inception period in socialization. They concluded, speculatively, that the apparent conflict between individuality and conformity is resolved by the imposition of parental authority in complex social relations. This teaches the child about the variable character of social demands and instructs him as to the range of acceptable choices for various situations. By authoritative acts, parents establish for the child the concept of legitimacy and provide a model for the child to emulate. Pikas (1961), in his survey of 656 Swedish adolescents, showed that significant differences occurred in their acceptance of parental authority, depending upon the reason for the directive. Authority which was based on rational concern for the child's welfare was accepted well by the child, while authority which was based on the adult's desire to dominate or exploit the child was rejected. The former, which he calls rational authority, is similar to "authoritative control," and the latter, which he calls inhibiting authority, is similar to "authoritarian control," as these terms are used in this discussion. His results are supported by Middleton and Snell (1963) who found that parental discipline regarded by the child as either very strict or very permissive was associated with lack of closeness between parent and child and with rebellion against the parent's political viewpoints.

A distinction, then, must be made between the effects on the child of unjust, restrictive, subjective authority, when compared to rational, warm, issue-oriented authority. There is considerable evidence that the former but not the latter constellation of practices is associated in the child with negative affect, disaffiliativeness, and rebelliousness.

3. Firm Parental Control Generates Passivity and Dependence

Baldwin (1948) found that high control with democracy held constant covaried negatively with prosocial as well as antisocial assertive behavior. However, contrary results have been found in other studies. It would appear that many children react to parental power by resisting the parent's pressure, rather than by being cowed. Hoffman's (1960) results indicate that parental assertiveness and submissiveness in the child are negatively correlated. Sears' (1961) findings on early socialization and later aggression suggest that high punishment for aggression, like "reactive unqualified power assertion," does not lead to submissive behavior. Baumrind's (1967, 75-1) results were that parents of the most self-reliant and approach-oriented group of children were rated highest in firm control.

There are individual differences in vigor and reactivity which may alter young children's reactions to parental power. A gentle, sensitive child might well react to high-power directives with passive, dependent responses, whereas an aggressive, vigorous child might react self-assertively or oppositionally, modeling himself after the aggressive parent.

The same parent variables which increase the probability that the child will use the parent as a model should increase the likelihood that firm control will result in assertive behavior. Thus, the controlling parent who is warm, understanding, and autonomy-granting should generate less passivity (as well as less rebelliousness) than the controlling parent who is cold and restrictive because of the kinds of behavior she will reinforce and the traits she presents as a model.

4. Parental Restrictiveness Decreases Normal Self-assertiveness and Buoyancy

The definition of restrictiveness used by different investigators varies greatly. Thus studies differ substantially in the parental correlates of this variable, particularly with hostility. Restrictiveness, when correlated positively with parental hostility (Becker, Peterson, Luria, Shoemaker, & Helmer, 1962; Kagan & Moss, 1962), tends to be associated in the child with passivity, dependence, social withdrawal, and passively expressed hostility. In studies where restrictiveness is an expression of involvement, antisocial aggression in children and parental restrictiveness seem to be correlated negatively. Bandura and Walters' (1959) findings were that parents of delinquent boys were less, rather than more, restrictive when compared to parents of nondeliquent boys. Findings of Glueck and Glueck (1950) and McCord et al. (1961) were similar. However, the studies reviewed do not suggest that moderate restrictiveness decreases self-assertiveness unless accompanied by parental hostility or overprotectiveness.

When granting autonomy is an indication of detachment rather than warmth, its opposite, restrictiveness is not associated in the child with hostility or passivity. A careful examination of the findings of Schaefer and Bayley (1963) makes the point rather well. The conceptual definition of Schaefer and Bayley's variable "autonomy" (low) is quite similar to that of Kagan and Moss's variable "restrictiveness" (high), but maternal "autonomy" does not covary positively, except for girls at ages 9–14, with maternal warmth (measured by the variable "positive evaluation"). At ages 9–14, for girls, when "autonomy" and "positive evaluation" covary positively (.40), the variable "autonomy" is associated in adolescent girls with popularity, contentment, and low hostility. At 0–3 years, when "autonomy" and "positive evaluation" are somewhat negatively related (−.28), there are no significant associations between the maternal variable "autonomy" and any of the child behavior ratings. For boys also, "autonomy" is correlated negatively (−.07 to −.33) with "positive evaluation." It is interesting, therefore, to note that "autonomy" measured at 0–3 years is associated with timid, inhibited, courteous, and tactful behavior in adolescent boys, and at 9–14 with unfriendly, uncooperative, uninterested behavior, rather than with self-reliance, buoyancy, and self-assertiveness. Maternal "autonomy," as measured by Schaefer and Bayley, seems to reflect detached uninvolvement, except for mothers of girls 9–14, when it is correlated positively with most measures of maternal warmth. The effect on the child covaries with these maternal correlates.

It would appear that no conclusions can be drawn concerning the effects on the child of variables called "autonomy" or "restrictiveness" until correlates with other parent variables, especially hostility, are known.

5. Permissiveness Frees the Child from the Presence and Authority of the Parent

When the child engages in behavior which he has reason to think is unacceptable and an adult is present and noninterfering, does the noninterference of the adult leave the child free to act as he would naturally if he did not have to fear the disapproval of the adult, or does the noninterference of the adult increase the likelihood that such socially disapproved behavior will occur in the future? The former alternative is generally assumed, but the latter appears to be more likely. The parent's nonaction signifies to the child approval of his behavior, not neutrality (Sears, Maccoby, & Levin, 1957, p. 259). In a well-controlled study, Siegel and Kohn (1959) demonstrated that the presence of a permissive adult increased the incidence of aggression shown by nursery school boys to somewhat younger boys.

"Two-thirds of the Ss in the adult-present sessions were more aggressive in the second than in the first session, and all the Ss in the adult-absent sessions were less aggressive in the second than in the first session. This finding is in confirmation of the hypothesis, which was drawn from a consideration of the nature and effects of adult permissiveness with children and of the nature of young children's controls for aggression" (Siegel & Kohn, 1959, pp. 140–141).

Their results, which indicate that the presence of a nonreacting adult affects the child in definite ways, are supported by those of Crandall et al. (1964), in which changes in children's behavior produced by adult nonreaction were greater than those produced by extinction (nonadult nonreaction).

6. Controlling Parents Are Motivated by the Authoritarian Personality Syndrome and Therefore Are Compelled, by Fear of Loss of Control, To Restrict the Child's Self-directed, Autonomous Efforts

While parents motivated by the authoritarian personality syndrome are controlling, it does not follow that the converse is true. Some subgroups of controlling parents permit high autonomy in many areas of the child's life. Lois Hoffman et al. (1960) described a subgroup of parents who were perceived by their children as both coercive and permissive of high autonomy. Martin Hoffman's (1963) findings were that the authoritarian personality syndrome, as measured by a 12-item form of the F test, was not related to use of "initial unqualified power assertion" or "reactive unqualified power assertion" for middle-class fathers or mothers or for working-class mothers, although such a relationship did exist for working-class fathers. Power need, as measured by a thematic test, was unrelated for any group to either "initial unqualified power assertion" or "reactive unqualified power assertion." Baumrind (1967) found that, whereas the parents of alienated children tended to use inhibiting control, the parents of exceptionally mature children, who exerted even firmer control, used reason to explain their directives and encouraged independent expression. This latter group of parents did not exhibit the authoritarian personality syndrome. Thus, several investigators have identified subgroups of controlling parents who are not restrictive of children's autonomy or motivated by the authoritarian personality syndrome and have shown that children react differently to firm and repressive control.

It is of interest to evaluate empirically the effects on children of various combinations of extreme scores on these two dimensions, "firm control" and "restricts child's autonomy," rather than to assume that they form a single dimension.

7. Firm Control Inhibits the Child's Creative Thrust

The parent whose orientation is nonpermissive, even when she exerts rational authority and encourages the child to make many of his own decisions, is seeking, by definition, to obtain from the child conformity with parental standards. The parent who exerts authoritative control, as that pattern of child rearing was defined earlier—even if her hope is that as the child grows older she will be able to relinquish control—does indeed exert vigorous efforts to shape the child's behavior in his early years. To the extent that her policy is effective, the child may argue and test the limits, but he is fundamentally satisfied with his relationship to his parents and does not revolt.

Intellectual endeavors which require solitary effort without concern about social approval or which demand a revolutionary rejection of the premises established by previous authorities may be initiated less frequently by children who have learned to trust and depend upon their parents' wisdom, to seek their approval, and to accept their authority. There is some indirect evidence to that effect. In one of a series of provocative studies, Bing concluded: "The findings led to the general conclusion that discrepant verbal ability is fostered by a close relationship with a demanding and somewhat intrusive mother, while discrepant nonverbal abilities are enhanced by allowing the child a considerable degree of freedom

to experiment on his own" (1963, p. 647). Along similar lines, Getzels and Jackson (1961) found that parents of children whose IQ scores were high but not their creativity scores, when compared to parents of children whose creativity scores were high but not their IQ scores (the lower score was below the top 20 per cent but not actually below the mean), were more authoritative in their discipline and more concerned about intellectual and social achievement than about inner life. Firm, intrusive parents may inhibit nonverbal achievement and enhance achievement in verbal areas.

The child-rearing procedures which generate competence, mental health, and optimism may not be the same as those which give rise to eminence. Thus Eiduson (1962), among others, found that the eminent scientists whom she studied had little contact with their fathers whom they described as rigid and aloof, and remembered their mothers as possessive and aggressive.

8. Similar Patterns of Child Rearing Affect Boys and Girls Differently

Many investigators have concluded that similar parental practices have different effects on boys and girls. Bronfenbrenner (1961, p. 269), for example, suggested that "in the absence of extreme rejection or neglect, both parental affection and authority have differential effects on the development of responsibility in sons and daughters. For boys, it is the absence of sufficient warmth or discipline which more frequently impairs dependability; for girls, it is an overdose of either variable that has deleterious effects." Bayley (1964) offered the hypothesis of genetic sex differences to explain the fact that girls' intelligence scores, unlike boys' scores, show little relation to maternal variables.

Sears (1961) suggested that sex differences in antecedents for aggression anxiety might lie in the different dynamic and genetic characteristics of aggression anxiety for boys and girls.

However, it cannot be demonstrated that sex-related differences in the relation between a particular child-rearing variable and a particular child behavior do, in fact, exist, until it can be shown that there are no mean, variance, or covariance differences for boys and girls in either the parent or child variable. Thus, indexes of warmth frequently covary differently with indexes of directiveness or restrictiveness for boys and girls, and this fact may account for many instances of differences in parent-child correlates which have been interpreted as signifying differential effects of a parental variable on the development of a particular attribute in sons and daughters. In the Schaefer and Bayley study, for example, maternal ratings of "autonomy" at 9–14 years correlated with contrasting attributes for boys and girls. Interpretation of these findings must remain ambiguous because "autonomy" covaried with other maternal variables differently for boys and girls (1963, p. 19). The same kind of question can and should be raised for what, on the face of it, are age-related differences in effects of similar parental variables on child behavior.

There is not enough known about the complex, subtle differences in child-rearing practices to indicate that we have ever succeeded in equating practices for boys and girls. We need an empirical basis for establishing equivalence of patterns of relations among parent variables and among child variables before the problem of sex-related differences in effects of child-rearing patterns can be investigated systematically.

FREEDOM AND CONTROL AS ANTINOMY OR SYNTHESIS

Behavioral scientists and philosophers still dispute vigorously the relation of control to freedom. To an articulate exponent of permissiveness in child rearing such as Neill, freedom for the child means that he has the liberty to do as he pleases without interference from adult guardians and, indeed, with their protection. Hegel, by contrast, defines freedom as the appreciation of necessity. By this he means that man frees himself of the objective world by understanding its nature and controlling his reactions to its attributes. His definition equates the concept of freedom with power to act, rather than absence of external control. To Hegel, the infant is enslaved by virtue of his ignorance, his dependence upon others for sustenance, and his lack of self-control. The experience of infantile omnipotence, if such he has, is based on ignorance and illusion. His is the freedom to be irresponsible, a freedom reserved for the very young child and the incompetent.

The ability to make an autonomous choice includes as a necessary but not sufficient condition that external agents with greater power leave the actor free to formulate, initiate, and complete his action. For a person to behave autonomously, he must accept responsibility for his own behavior, which in turn requires that he believe that the world is orderly and susceptible to rational mastery and that he has or can develop the requisite skills to manage his own affairs.

There may be good reasons for parents concerned with their children's freedom to use direct methods of influence which include cognitive appeal and power, rather than indirect methods such as nurturance withdrawal or guilt induction. In order that a child can learn to direct his energies wilfully and thus feel responsible, he needs practice in choosing a course of action under realistic conditions, conditions which include aversive as well as gratifying stimulation. In choosing an action for which he can expect punishment and for which he is then punished, he gains important information upon which to base subsequent choices. The less he is manipulated by guilt-inducing techniques of discipline or indirect threats of loss of love which condition his behavior while bypassing his conscious will, the more capable he should become of responsible (i.e., chosen) action. A conditioned reaction of guilt to a particular action limits the individual's freedom to choose that action or to choose an alternative to that action. Nurturance withdrawal by a loving parent has been shown to be a most effective means of producing guilt about wrongdoing and thus conditioned compliance (Hartup, 1958; Hill 1960; Mussen & Rutherford, 1963; Sears, 1961). The manipulation by the parent of the love relation probably poses a greater threat to the child's ability to make a conscious choice than even the use of unqualified power assertion. One may wonder about the limits which early internalization of parental standards imposes upon the development of cognitively directed responsible behavior and individuality in later life. When compliance with parental standards is achieved by use of reason, power, and external reinforcement, it may be possible to obtain obedience and self-correction without stimulating self-punitive reactions. To some extent, the parent's aggressiveness stimulates counteraggression and extrapunitive responses from the child, thus reducing

the experience of guilt or early internalization of standards whose moral bases cannot yet be grasped. When the child accepts physical punishment or deprivation of privileges as the price paid for acts of disobedience, he may derive from the interaction greater power to withstand suffering and deprivation in the service of another need or an ideal and, thus, increased freedom to choose among expanded alternatives.

Authoritarian control and permissive noncontrol may both shield the child from the opportunity to engage in vigorous interaction with people. Demands which cannot be met or no demands, suppression of conflict or sidestepping of conflict, refusal to help or too much help, unrealistically high or low standards, all may curb or understimulate the child so that he fails to achieve the knowledge and experience which could realistically reduce his dependence upon the outside world. The authoritarian and the permissive parent may both create, in different ways, a climate in which the child is not desensitized to the anxiety associated with nonconformity. Both models minimize dissent, the former by suppression and the latter by diversion or indulgence. To learn how to dissent, the child may need a strongly held position from which to diverge and then be allowed under some circumstances to pay the price for nonconformity by being punished. Spirited give and take within the home, if accompanied by respect and warmth, may teach the child how to express aggression in self-serving and prosocial causes and to accept the partially unpleasant consequences of such actions.

The body of findings on effects of disciplinary practices as reviewed and interpreted here give provisional support to the position that authoritative control can achieve responsible conformity with group standards without loss of individual autonomy or self-assertiveness. The hypotheses generated by that position must, of course, be tested empirically with a variety of subgroups. These hypotheses will need to be corrected by the data and adapted to include equivalent parental behaviors, depending upon the characteristics of the subgroup to which they are to be applied.

References

ADORNO, T. W., FRENKEL-BRUNSWIK, ELSE, LEVINSON, D. J., & SANFORD, R. N. *The authoritarian personality.* New York: Harper, 1950.

ARONFREED, J., & REBER, A. Internalized behavioral suppression and the timing of social punishment. *J. Pers. soc. Psychol.*, 1, 3–16.

BALDWIN, A. L. Socialization and the parent-child relationship. *Child Develpm.*, 1948, 19, 127–136.

BANDURA, A., & WALTERS, R. H. *Adolescent aggression.* New York: Ronald, 1959.

BAUMRIND, DIANA. Parental control and parental love. *Children*, 1965, 12, 230–234.

BAUMRIND, DIANA. Child care practices anteceding three patterns of preschool behavior. *Genet. Psychol. Monogr.*, 1967, 75–1.

BAYLEY, NANCY, & SCHAEFER, E. S. Correlations of maternal and child behaviors with the development of mental abilities: data from the Berkeley growth study. *Monogr. Soc. Res. Child Develpm.*, 1964, 29, No. 6 (Whole No. 97).

BECKER, W. C., PETERSON, D. R., LURIA, ZELLA, SHOEMAKER, D. J., & HELLMER, L. A. Relations of factors derived from parent-interview ratings to behavior problems of five-year-olds. *Child Develpm.*, 1962, 33, 509–535.

BING, ELIZABETH. Effect of childrearing practices on development of differential cognitive abilities. *Child Develpm.*, 1963, 34, 631–648.

BRONFENBRENNER, U. Some familiar antecedents of responsibility and leadership in adolescents. In L. Petrullo and B. M. Bass (Eds.), *Leadership and interpersonal behavior.* New York: Holt, Rinehart & Winston, 1961. Pp. 239–271.

CALDWELL, BETTYE M. The effects of infant care. In M. L. Hoffman and Lois W. Hoffman (Eds.), *Review of child development research.* Vol. 1. New York: Russell Sage Found., 1964. Pp. 9–87.

CORIAT, I. H. The psycho-analytic approach to education. *Progr. Educ.*, 1926, 3, 19–25.

CRANDALL, VIRGINIA C. The reinforcement effects of adult reactions and nonreactions on children's achievement expectations. *Child Develpm.*, 1963, 34, 335–354.

CRANDALL, VIRGINIA C., GOOD, SUZANNE, & CRANDALL, V. J. The reinforcement effects of adult reactions and nonreactions on children's achievement expectations: a replication. *Child Develpm.*, 1964, 35, 485–497.

CREMIN, L. A. *The transformation of the school.* New York: Vintage, 1964.

DEWEY, J. *Democracy and education.* New York: Macmillan, 1916.

DEWEY, J., & DEWEY, EVELYN. *Schools of tomorrow.* New York: Dutton, 1915.

DUBIN, ELISABETH R., & DUBIN, R. The authority inception period in socialization. *Child Develpm.*, 1963, 34, 885–898.

EIDUSON, BERNICE T. *Scientists: their psychological world.* New York: Basic Books, 1962.

FINNEY, J. C. Some maternal influences on children's personality and character. *Genet. Psychol. Monogr.*, 1961, 63, 199–278.

FRANK, L. K. Freedom for the personality. *Psychiatry*, 1940, 3, 341–349.

FROMM, E. *Escape from freedom.* New York: Farrar & Rinehart, 1941.

GESELL, A. *The guidance of mental growth in infant and child.* New York: Macmillan, 1930.

GETZELS, J. W., & JACKSON, P. W. Family environment and cognitive style: a study

316

SOCIALIZATION OF THE CHILD

of the sources of highly intelligent and of highly creative adolescents. *Amer. Sociol. Rev.*, 1961, 26, 351–359.

GLUECK, S., & GLUECK, ELEANOR. *Unraveling juvenile delinquency.* New York: Commonwealth Fund, 1950.

GOODMAN, P. *Compulsory mis-education.* New York: Horizon, 1964.

HARTUP, W. W. Nurturance and nurturance withdrawal in relation to the dependency behavior of pre-school children. *Child Develpm.*, 1958, 29, 191–201.

HILL, W. F. Learning theory and the acquisition of values. *Psychol. Rev.*, 1960, 67, 317–331.

HOFFMAN, LOIS, ROSEN, S., & LIPPITT, R. Parental coerciveness, child autonomy, and child's role at school. *Sociometry*, 1960, 23, 15–22.

HOFFMAN, M. L. Power assertion by the parent and its impact on the child. *Child Develpm.*, 1960, 31, 129–143.

HOFFMAN, M. L. Personality, family structure, and social class as antecedents of parental power assertion. *Child Develpm.*, 1963, 34, 869–884.

KAGAN, J., & MOSS, H. A. *Birth to maturity: a study in psychological development.* New York: Wiley, 1962.

LEWIN, K., LIPPITT, R., & WHITE, R. K. Patterns of aggressive behavior in experimentally created "social climates." *J. soc. Psychol.*, 1939, 10, 271–299.

McCORD, W., McCORD, JOAN, & HOWARD, A. Familial correlates of aggression in nondelinquent male children. *J. abnorm. soc. Psychol.*, 1961, 62, 79–93.

MASLOW, A. H. *Motivation and personality.* New York: Harper, 1954.

MIDDLETON, R., & SNELL, P. Political expression of adolescent rebellion. *Amer. J. Sociol.*, 1963, 68, 527–535.

MUSSEN, P., & RUTHERFORD, E. Parent-child relations and parental personality in relation to young children's sex-role preferences. *Child Develpm.*, 1963, 34, 589–607.

NAUMBURG, MARGARET. *The child and the world.* New York: Harcourt, Brace, 1928.

NEILL, A. S. *Summerhill.* New York: Hart, 1964.

ORLANSKY, H. Infant care and personality. *Psychol. Bull.*, 1949, 46, 1–48.

PIKAS, A. Children's attitudes toward rational versus inhibiting parental authority. *J. abnorm. soc. Psychol.*, 1961, 62, 315–321.

RAMBUSCH, NANCY M. *Learning how to learn: an American approach to Montessori.* Baltimore: Helicon, 1962.

ROGERS, C. R. A therapist's view of personal goals. *Pendle Hill Pamphlet 108.* Wallingford, Pa.: Pendle Hill, 1960.

SCHAEFER, E. S., & BAYLEY, NANCY. Maternal behavior, child behavior, and their intercorrelations from infancy through adolescence. *Monogr. Soc. Res. Child Develpm.*, 1963, 28, No. 3 (Whole No. 87).

SEARS, R. R. Relation of early socialization experiences to aggression in middle childhood. *J. abnorm. soc. Psychol.*, 1961, 63, 466–492.

SEARS, R. R., MACCOBY, E. E., & LEVIN, H. *Patterns of child rearing.* Evanston, Ill.: Row, Peterson, 1957.

SEARS, R. R., WHITING, J. W. M., NOWLIS, V., & SEARS, P. S. Some child rearing antecedents of aggression and dependency in young children. *Genet. Psychol. Monogr.*, 1953, 47, 135–234.

SIEGEL, ALBERTA E., & KOHN, LYNETTE G. Permissiveness, permission, and aggression: the effects of adult presence or absence on aggression in children's play. *Child Develpm.*, 1959, 30, 131–141.

SOLOMON, R. L. Punishment. *Amer. Psychologist*, 1964, 19, 239–253.

SPOCK, B. M. *The common sense book of baby and child care.* New York: Duell, Sloan, & Pearce, 1946.

SPOCK, B. M. *Baby and child care.* (2d ed.) New York: Pocket Books, 1957.

STENDLER, CELIA B. Sixty years of child training practices. *J. Pediatrics*, 1950, 36, 122–136.

WALTERS, R. H., PARKE, R. D., & CANE, VALERIE A. Timing of punishment and observation of consequences to others as determinants of response inhibition. *J. exp. child Psychol.*, 1965, 2, 10–30.

WATSON, G. Some personality differences in children related to strict or permissive parental discipline. *J. Psychol.*, 1957, 44, 227–249.

10

SOCIAL STRUCTURE AND SOCIALIZATION

The papers of this chapter consider the relation between soical structure and the sex-typing of behavior. In the first of these two papers Barry, Bacon and Child consider variation in the society—the macrostructure—and find that where physical strength is economically important, the society tends to emphasize sex differences in the process of socialization.

Orville G. Brim, Jr. is concerned with the microstructure of the family. He has reanalyzed the data of Helen Koch pertaining to same-sex compared with opposite-sex siblings in two-child families. He finds that: (1) cross-sex siblings have more traits of the opposite sex than do same-sex siblings, and (2) the effect is greater for the younger than for the older sibling.

A Cross-Cultural Survey of Some Sex Differences In Socialization *

Herbert Barry III, Margaret K. Bacon, and Irvin L. Child

In our society, certain differences may be observed between the typical personality characteristics of the two sexes. These sex differences in personality are generally believed to result in part from differences in the way boys and girls are reared. To the extent that personality differences between the sexes are thus of cultural rather than biological origin, they seem potentially susceptible to change. But how readily susceptible to change? In the differential rearing of the sexes does our society make an arbitrary imposition on an infinitely plastic biological base, or is this cultural imposition found uniformly in all societies as an adjustment to the real biological differences between the sexes? This paper reports one attempt to deal with this problem.

° Adapted from the Journal of Abnormal and Social Psychology, 1957, 55: 327–332. Most of the societies used in this article are listed in "Relation of Child Training to Subsistence Economy" by Barry, Child and Bacon, American Anthropologist, 1959, 61: 51–63.

DATA AND PROCEDURES

The data used were ethnographic reports, available in the anthropological literature, about socialization practices of various cultures. One hundred and ten cultures, mostly nonliterate, were studied. They were selected primarily in terms of the existence of adequate ethnographic reports of socialization practices and secondarily so as to obtain a wide and reasonably balanced geographical distribution. Various aspects of socialization of infants and children were rated on a 7-point scale by two judges (Mrs. Bacon and Mr. Barry). Where the ethnographic reports permitted, separate ratings were made for the socialization of boys and girls. Each rating was indicated as either confident or doubtful; with still greater uncertainty, or with complete lack of evidence, the particular rating was of course not made at all. We shall restrict the report of sex difference ratings to cases in which both judges made a confident rating. Also omitted is the one instance where the two judges reported a sex difference in opposite directions, as it demonstrates only unreliability of judgment. The number of cultures that meet these criteria is much smaller than the total of 110; for the several variables to be considered, the number varies from 31 to 84.

The aspects of socialization on which ratings were made included:

1. Several criteria of attention and indulgence toward infants.
2. Strength of socialization from age 4 or 5 years until shortly before puberty, with respect to five systems of behavior; strength of socialization was defined as the combination of positive pressure (rewards for the behavior) plus negative pressure (punishments for lack of the behavior). The variables were:

(a) Responsibility or dutifulness training. (The data were such that training in the performance of chores in the productive or domestic economy was necessarily the principal source of information here; however, training in the performance of other duties was also taken into account when information was available.)

(b) Nurturance training, i.e., training the child to be nurturant or helpful toward younger siblings and other dependent people.

(c) Obedience training.

(d) Self-reliance training.

(e) Achievement training, i.e., training the child to orient his behavior toward standards of excellence in performance, and to seek to achieve as excellent a performance as possible.

Where the term "no sex difference" is used here, it may mean any of three things: (a) the judge found separate evidence about the training of boys and girls on this particular variable, and judged it to be identical; (b) the judge found a difference between the training of boys and girls, but not great enough for the sexes to be rated a whole point apart on a 7-point scale; (c) the judge found evidence only about the training of "children" on this variable, the ethnographer not reporting separately about boys and girls.

SEX DIFFERENCES IN SOCIALIZATION

On the various aspects of attention and indulgence toward infants, the judges almost always agreed in finding no sex difference. Out of 96 cultures for which the ratings included the infancy period, 88 (92%) were rated with no sex difference by either judge for any of those variables. This result is consistent with the point sometimes made by anthropologists that "baby" generally is a single status undifferentiated by sex, even though "boy" and "girl" are distinct statuses.

On the variables of childhood socialization, on the other hand, a rating of no sex difference by both judges was much less common. This finding of no sex difference varied in frequency from 10% of the cultures for the achievement variable up to 62% of the cultures for the obedience variable, as shown in the last column of Table 1. Where a sex difference is reported, by either one or both judges, the difference tends strongly to be in a parment of an especially high order of skill. Thus training in nurturance, responsibility, and, less clearly, obedience, may contribute to preparation for this economic role. These consistencies with adult role go beyond the economic sphere, of course. Participation in warfare, as a male prerogative, calls for self-reliance and a high order of skill where survival or death is the immediate issue. The childbearing which is biologically assigned to women, and the child care which is socially assigned primarily to them, lead to nurturant behavior and often call for a more continuous responsibility than do the tasks carried out by men. Most of these distinctions in adult role are not inevitable, but the biological differences between the sexes strongly predispose the distinction of role, if made, to be in a uniform direction.[1]

The relevant biological sex differences are conspicuous in adulthood but generally not in childhood. If each generation were left entirely to its own devices, therefore, without even an older generation to copy, sex differences in role would presumably be almost absent in childhood and would have to be developed after puberty at the expense of considerable relearning on the part of one or both sexes. Hence, a pattern of child training which foreshadows adult differences can serve the useful function of minimizing what Benedict termed "discontinuities in cultural conditioning"[1].

The differences in socialization between the sexes in our society, then, are no arbitrary custom of our society, but a very widespread adaptation of

culture to the biological substratum of human life.

VARIATIONS IN DEGREE OF SEX DIFFERENTIATION

While demonstrating near-universal tendencies in direction of difference between the socialization of boys and girls, our data do not show perfect uniformity. A study of the variations in our data may allow us to see some of the conditions which are associated with, and perhaps give rise to, a greater or smaller degree of this difference. For this purpose, we classified cultures as having relatively large or small sex difference by two different methods, one more inclusive and the other more selective. In both methods the ratings were at first considered separately for each of the five variables. A sex difference rating was made only if both judges made a rating on this variable and at least one judge's rating was confident.

In the more inclusive method the ratings were dichotomized, separately for each variable, as close as possible to the median into those showing a large and those showing a small sex difference. Thus, for each society a large or a small sex difference was recorded for each of the five variables on which a sex difference rating was available. A society was given an over-all classification of large or small sex difference if it had a sex difference rating on at least three variables and if a majority of these ratings agreed in being large, or agreed in being small. This method permitted classification of a large number of cultures, but the grounds for classification were capricious in many cases, as a difference of only one point in the rating of a single variable might change the over-all

---

[1]For data and interpretations supporting various arguments of this paragraph, see Mead [2], Murdock [3], and Scheinfeld [6].

TABLE 1   Culture variables correlated with large sex difference in socialization, separately for two types of sample

	More Selective Sample		More Inclusive Sample	
Variable	N	∅	∅	N
Large animals are hunted	.48*	(34)	.28*	(72)
Grain rather than root crops are grown	.82**	(20)	.62**	(43)
Large or milking animals rather than small animals are kept	.65*	(19)	.43*	(35)
Fishing unimportant or absent	.42*	(31)	.19	(69)
Nomadic rather than sedentary residence	.61**	(34)	.15	(71)
Polygyny rather than monogamy	.51*	(28)	.38**	(64)

* $p < .05$.

** $p < .01$.

Note. — The variables have been so phrased that all correlations are positive. The phi coefficient is shown, and in parentheses, the number of cases on which the comparison was based. Significance level was determined by χ^2, or Fisher's exact test where applicable, using in all cases a two-tailed test.

classification of sex difference for a culture from large to small.

In the more selective method, we again began by dichotomizing each variable as close as possible to the median; but a society was now classified as having a large or small sex difference on the variable only if it was at least one step away from the scores immediately adjacent to the median. Thus only the more decisive ratings of sex difference were used. A culture was classified as having an over-all large or small sex difference only if it was given a sex difference rating which met this criterion on at least two variables, and only if all such ratings agreed in being large, or agreed in being small.

We then tested the relation of each of these dichotomies to 24 aspects of culture on which Murdock has categorized the customs of most of these societies[2] and which seemed of possible significance for sex differentiation. The aspects of culture covered include type of economy, residence pattern, marriage

[2] These data were supplied to us directly by Professor Murdock.

and incest rules, political integration, and social organization. For each aspect of culture, we grouped Murdock's categories to make a dichotomous contrast (sometimes omitting certain categories as irrelevant to the contrast). In the case of some aspects of culture, two or more separate contrasts were made (e.g., under form of marriage were contrasted monogamy with polygyny, and also contrasted sororal with nonsororal polygyny). For each of 40 comparisons thus formed, we prepared a 2 × 2 frequency table to determine relation to each of our sex-difference dichotomies. A significant relation was found for six of these 40 aspects of culture with the more selective dichotomization of overall sex difference. In four of these comparisons, the relation to the more inclusive dichotomization was also significant. These relationships are all given in Table 1, in the form of phi coefficients, along with the outcome of testing significance by the use of x^2 or Fisher's exact test. In trying to interpret these findings, we have also considered the nonsignificant correlations with other variables, looking for consistency and inconsistency with the general implications of the significant findings. We have arrived at the following formulation of results:

1. Large sex difference in socialization is associated with an economy that places a high premium on the superior strength, and superior development of motor skills requiring strength, which characterize the male. Four of the correlations reported in Table 2 clearly point to this generalization: the correlations of large sex difference with the hunting of large animals, with grain rather than root crops, with the keeping of large rather than small domestic animals, and with nomadic rather than sedentary residence. The correlation with the unimportance of fishing may also be consistent with this generalization, but the argument is not clear.[3] Other correlations consistent with the generalization, though not statistically significant, are with large game hunting

[3] Looking (with the more inclusive sample) into the possibility that this correlation might result from the correlation between fishing and sedentary residence, a complicated interaction between these variables was found. The correlation of sex differentiation with absence of fishing is found only in nomadic societies, where fishing is likely to involve cooperative activity of the two sexes, and its absence is likely to mean dependence upon the male for large game hunting or herding large animals (whereas in sedentary societies the alternatives to fishing do not so uniformly require special emphasis on male strength). The correlation of sex differentiation with nomadism is found only in nonfishing societies; here nomadism is likely to imply large game hunting or herding large animals, whereas in fishing societies nomadism evidently implies no such special dependence upon male strength. Maximum sex differentiation is found in nomadic nonfishing societies (15 with large difference and only 2 with small) and minimum sex differentiation in nomadic fishing societies (2 with large difference and 7 with small difference). These findings further strengthen the argument for a conspicuous influence of the economy upon sex differentiation.

rather than gathering, with the hunting of large game rather than small game, and with the general importance of all hunting and gathering.

2. Large sex difference in socialization appears to be correlated with customs that make for a large family group with high cooperative interaction. The only statistically significant correlation relevant here is that with polygyny rather than monogamy. This generalization is, however, supported by several substantial correlations that fall only a little short of being statistically significant. One of these is a correlation with sororal rather than nonsororal polygyny; Murdock and Whiting [4] have presented indirect evidence that co-wives generally show smoother cooperative interaction if they are sisters. Correlations are also found with the presence of either an extended or a polygynous family rather than the nuclear family only; with the presence of an extended family; and with the extreme contrast between maximal extension and no extension of the family. The generalization is also to some extent supported by small correlations with wide extension of incest taboos, if we may presume that an incest taboo makes for effective unthreatening cooperation within the extended family. The only possible exception to this generalization, among substantial correlations, is a near-significant correlation with an extended or polygynous family's occupying a cluster of dwellings rather than a single dwelling.[4]

[4] We think the reverse of this correlation would be more consistent with our generalization here. But perhaps it may reasonably be argued that the various nuclear families composing an extended or polygynous family are less likely to develop antagonisms which hinder cooperation if they are able to maintain some physical separation. On the other hand, this variable may be more relevant to the first generalization than to the second. Occupation of a cluster of dwellings is highly correlated with presence of herding and with herding of large rather than small animals, and these economic variables in turn are

In seeking to understand this second generalization, we feel that the degree of social isolation of the nuclear family may perhaps be the crucial underlying variable. To the extent that the nuclear family must stand alone, the man must be prepared to take the woman's role when she is absent or incapacitated, and vice versa. Thus the sex differentiation cannot afford to be too great. But to the extent that the nuclear family is steadily interdependent with other nuclear families, the female role in the household economy can be temporarily taken over by another woman, or the male role by another man, so that sharp differentiation of sex role is no handicap. . . .†

Both of these generalizations contribute to understanding the social background of the relatively small difference in socialization of boys and girls which we believe characterizes our society at the present time. Our mechanized economy is perhaps less dependent than any previous economy upon the superior average strength of the male. The nuclear family in our society is often so isolated that husband and wife must each be prepared at times to take over or help in the household tasks normally assigned to the other. It is also significant that the conditions favoring low sex differentiation appear to be more characteristic of the upper segments of our society, in socioeconomic and educational status, than of lower segments. This observation may be relevant to the tendency toward smaller sex differences in personality in higher status groups [cf. Terman and Miles, 8].

The increase in our society of conditions favoring small sex difference has led some people to advocate a virtual elimination of sex differences in socialization. This course seems likely to be dysfunctional even in our society. Parsons, Bales, et al. [5] argue that a differentiation of role similar to the universal pattern of sex difference is an important and perhaps inevitable development in any social group, such as the nuclear family. If we add to their argument the point that biological differences between the sexes make most appropriate the usual division of those roles between the sexes, we have compelling reasons to expect that the decrease in differentiation of adult sex role will not continue to the vanishing point. In our training of children, there may now be less differentiation in sex role than characterizes adult life—so little, indeed, as to provide inadequate preparation for adulthood. This state of affairs is likely to be especially true of formal education, which is more subject to conscious influence by an ideology than is informal socialization at home. With child training being more oriented toward the male than the female role in adulthood, many of the adjustment problems of women in our society today may be partly traced to conflicts growing out of inadequate childhood preparation for their adult role. This argument is nicely supported in extreme form by Spiro's analysis of sex roles in an Israeli kibbutz [7]. The

---

correlated with large sex difference in socialization. Occupation of a cluster of dwellings is also correlated with polygyny rather than monogamy and shows no correlation with sororal vs. nonsororal polygyny.

†At first glance it may appear that these findings are at variance with those of Nimkoff and Middleton, pp. 35–43 of this volume. However, this is not the case. Nimkoff and Middleton related size of family to type of economy. The present authors do not relate these two variables, but find a negative correlation between social isolation and sex-role differentiation. Type of economy is never analyzed, and the negative relations between social isolation and both size of family and sex-role differentiation buttress Nimkoff and Middleton's argument.—Eds.

ideology of the founders of the kibbutz included the objective of greatly reducing differences in sex role. But the economy of the kibbutz is a largely nonmechanized one in which the superior average strength of men is badly needed in many jobs. The result is that, despite the ideology and many attempts to implement it, women continue to be assigned primarily to traditional "women's work," and the incompatibility between upbringing or ideology and adult role is an important source of conflict for women. . . .

SUMMARY

A survey of certain aspects of socialization in 110 cultures shows that differentiation of the sexes is unimportant in infancy, but that in childhood there is, as in our society, a widespread pattern of greater pressure toward nurturance, obedience, and responsibility in girls, and toward self-reliance and achievement striving in boys. There are a few reversals of sex difference, and many instances of no detectable sex difference; these facts tend to confirm the cultural rather than directly biological nature of the differences. Cultures vary in the degree to which these differentiations are made; correlational analysis suggests some of the social conditions influencing these variations, and helps in understanding why our society has relatively small sex differentiation.

References

1. BENEDICT, RUTH, "Continuities and discontinuities in cultural conditioning," Psychiatry, 1938, 1, 161–167.
2. MEAD, MARGARET, Male and female (New York: Morrow, 1949).
3. MURDOCK, G. P., "Comparative data on the division of labor by sex," Social Forces, 1937, 15, 551–553.
4. MURDOCK, G. P., and WHITING, J. W. M., "Cultural determination of parental attitudes: The relationship between the social structure, particularly family structure and parental behavior," in M. J. E. Senn, ed., Problems of infancy and childhood: Transactions of the Fourth Conference, March 6–7, 1950. New York: Josiah Macy, Jr. Foundation, 1951. Pp. 13–34.
5. PARSONS, T., BALES, R. F., et al., Family socialization and interaction process (Glencoe, Ill.: Free Press, 1955).
6. SCHEINFELD, A., Women and men (New York: Harcourt, Brace, 1944).
7. SPIRO, M. E., Kibbutz: Venture in Utopia (Cambridge: Harvard Univ. Press, 1956).
8. TERMAN, L. M., and MILES, CATHERINE C., Sex and personality (New York: McGraw-Hill, 1936).

Family Structure and Sex Role Learning By Children:
A Further Analysis of Helen Koch's Data*

Orville G. Brim, Jr.

The structure of a social group, delineated by variables such as size, age, sex, power, and prestige differences, is held to be a primary influence upon the patterns of interaction within the group, determining in major part the degree to which any two group members interact. It is held, second, that social roles are learned through interaction with others, such interaction providing one with the opportunity to practice his own role as well as to take the role of the other. On this basis one may hypothesize that group structure, by influencing the degree of interaction between group members, would be related to the types of roles learned in the group: one would learn most completely those roles which he himself plays, as well as the roles of the others with whom he most frequently interacts. This argument is applied in this paper specifically to the relation between family structure, described in terms of age, sex and ordinality of children, and the sex role learning by the children.

ROLE LEARNING
THROUGH INTERACTION

The process of role learning through interaction, which has been described in detail by Mead [15], Cottrell [2], and others, can be sketched as follows. One learns the behavior appropriate to his position in a group through interaction with others who hold normative beliefs about what his role should be and who are able to reward and punish him for correct and incorrect actions. As part of the same learning process, one acquires expectations of how others in the group will behave. The latter knowledge is indispensable to the actor, in that he must be able to predict what others expect of him, and how they will react to him, in order to guide his own role performance successfully. Accurate or erroneous understanding and prediction are respectively rewarding and punishing to the actor, and learning proceeds systematically through the elimination of incorrect responses and the strengthening of correct ones.

It has been the distinctive contribution of sociology to demonstrate that learning the role of others occurs through the actor's taking the role of the other, i.e., trying to act as the other would act. While this role-taking of the other can be overt, as with children who actively and dramatically play the role of the parent, it is commonly covert in adults, as with the husband who anticipates what his wife will say when he returns home late, or the employee who tries to foresee his employer's reaction when he asks for a raise.

It follows that, whether taking the role of others is overt or covert, certain

*Adapted from Sociometry, 1958, 21: 1–15.

responses (belonging to the role of the other) are in fact made, run through, completed, and rewarded if successful, i.e., accurate, and that this process adds to the repertoire of possible actions of a person those actions taken by others in their own roles. Such actions, as part of one's repertoire or pool of learned responses, are available for performance by an actor, not now simply in taking the role of the other, but as resources which he can use as part of his *own* role performances.

The critical fact is that the actor not only can, but *does*, make use of responses learned in role-taking in his own role performances. There are two senses in which this happens. The first, which does not concern us in this paper, involves the direct transfer of the role of the other to a new and parallel status of one's own, where there is a straightforward adoption of the other's role. Such transfer may be appropriate and rewarded, as where the oldest child performs the role of the parent to his sibs, or simply interesting and tolerated, as where the new assistant professor plays the department chairman to the graduate students.

The second sense, which is our major concern here, involves a more complex process of convergence between one's own role and that of the other which he takes, where there is a spillover of elements belonging to another's role into one's own performance when it is not necessarily appropriate. Our basic hypothesis, set forth by Cottrell [2] and others, is that interaction between two persons leads to assimilation of roles, to the incorporation of elements of the role of the other into the actor's role. Thus, one says, husbands and wives grow more alike through time, and long-time collaborators in research begin to think alike.

ASSIMILATION OF ROLES

While not pretending to a full analysis of the process underlying assimilation, several causes can be described. First, the actor may note that the other is successful to a high degree in some of his behavior and consciously transfer to his own role such behavioral elements for trial. To the extent that they prove successful for him, in his performance, and are not eliminated through punishment from others for being inappropriate, he will adopt them. Second, faced with novel situations where his "own" behavior fails, the elements of others' roles are already learned and available for trial and hence would tend to be tried prior to the development of totally new responses; again, if successful, they tend to be assimilated to the role. Third, the actions learned by taking the role of others are ordinarily performed implicitly and under limited conditions, e.g., in interaction with the other. However, the cues which guide and elicit one's own role performance may be difficult to differentiate from cues eliciting taking the role of the other. It would appear that for the young child this is especially difficult, and data indeed show that the child has difficulty discriminating between reality and fantasy, between what his role is or even what his self is, and what belongs in the category of the "other." In this way, behavior learned through role-taking and appropriate to the other is confused with and undifferentiated from behavior learned as part of one's own role. The latter becomes tinged or diluted with characteristics belonging to someone else's role.

Among the hypotheses which are derivative of the general hypothesis of assimilation through interaction, two are pertinent here. First, the process of discrimination between what belongs to oneself and what belongs to the other is aided by the guidance of other persons. Thus, the parent helps the son differentiate between what belongs to him and what belongs to his sister; the fledgling nurse is assisted in a proper demeanor and in separating her duties from those of the physician. Rewards and punishments administered by others govern the discrimination process. Where the process of assimilation comes primarily from inability to discriminate between roles, it follows that where greater attention is paid to helping the learner discriminate, the process of assimilation is to a greater degree arrested.

Second, given two other persons with whom one interacts and who differ in power over the actor, i.e., differ in the degree to which they control rewards and punishments for the actor, one would predict that the actor would adopt more of the characteristics of the powerful, as contrasted to the less powerful, other person. This follows from the fact that it is more important to the actor to predict the behavior of the powerful figure, that he is motivated more strongly to take his role, that the rewards and punishments are more impressive and the learning consequently better. Interaction between two figures of unequal power should give a parallel result, namely, there would be a greater assimilation of the role of the other into the actor's role for the less powerful figure, for the same reasons as above. Thus the employee gravitates toward the boss more than the reverse; and the child becomes more like the parent than the other way round. However, this is not to imply that the more powerful figure need not take the role of the other,

nor that he does not assimilate (to a lesser degree) elements from the other's role. The weaker figure always has some control over rewards and punishments, requiring therefore that his reaction be considered. The displeased employee can wound his boss through expressions of dislike, and the angry child can hurt his parents in a variety of ways, from refusing to eat to threatening to leave home.

SEX-ROLE LEARNING

Turning now to a consideration of sex-role learning specifically, pertinent reviews [1, 17] of the data show that sex-role prescriptions and actual performance begin early. The accepted position is that children in a family learn their appropriate sex roles primarily from their parents. There is remarkably little data, other than clinical materials, on this topic, perhaps because of its obviousness. What systematic data there is, is not inconsistent with the role-learning propositions set forth above. Sears, Pintler, and Sears [14] have shown that in families where the father is absent the male child is slower to develop male sex-role traits than in families where the father is present, a finding predictable from the fact that there is no father whose role the child needs to take. Both Sears [13] and Payne and Mussen [12] have shown that father role-playing, identification with the father, and masculinity of attitudes are positively related to the father's being warm, affectionate, and rewarding. This strikes one as the same type of finding as the first, but at the other end of the interaction range; insofar as warm, affectionate, and rewarding fathers interact more with their sons, or are perceived as such because they interact more, it follows that the sons have more experience in taking their role.

In regard to the effects of sibling characteristics upon sex-role learning, there is again almost no information. Fauls and Smith [3] report that only children choose sex-appropriate activities more often than do children with older same-sex siblings, a finding which seems to fit none of our role-learning propositions. While one might hold that the only child has more interaction, because of sibling absence, with his same-sex parent, hence learns his sex role better, one might equally say, especially for the young boys, that it is the cross-sex parent with whom the child interacts and hence the only child should not learn his sex role well. In any case, the finding serves to stress the limitations of the data we are to report, namely, that they pertain to variations within two-child families, and that generalization to families of varying sizes is unwarranted. We return to this point later.

Even with respect to theory concerning the effects of siblings on sex-role learning, we have not noted any systematic predictions in the literature. It seems to us implicit in Parson's recent analysis [11] of sex-role learning in the nuclear family that when the child begins his differentiation between the father and mother sex roles he would be helped in making the differentiation if he had a cross-sex sibling; this is not formally stated, however, and we may be guilty of misinterpretation.

HYPOTHESES

It is against this background of comparative absence of research and theory on the effects of siblings on sex-role learning that our own report must

be viewed. The very valuable data on personality traits of children presented in recent publications by Helen Koch [4, 5, 6, 7, 8, 9, 10] provide the opportunity to apply several of the general hypotheses set forth above to the substantive area of sibling effects on sex-role learning. The specific application of these hypotheses can be summarized as follows:

First, one would predict that cross-sex, as compared with same-sex, siblings would possess more traits appropriate to the cross-sex role. When taking the role of the other in interaction, cross-sex siblings must take the role of the opposite sex, and the assimilation of roles as delineated above should take place.

Second, one would predict that this effect would be more noticeable for the younger, as compared with the older, sibling in that the latter is more powerful and is more able to differentiate his own from his sibling's role.

Third, on the assumption that siblings close in age interact more than those not close in age, one would predict that this effect would be more noticeable for the siblings who are closest together in age. This is in essence an extension of the first hypothesis to deal with variations in interaction within the cross-sex sibling groups.

PROCEDURES

Our description of procedures must of necessity be broken into two parts. The first consists of a brief description of the procedures in Helen Koch's original study; complete details are available in the publications cited previously. The second consists of our mode of further analysis of the reported data.

THE INITIAL DESIGN

In her series of papers Helen Koch has reported results from a major research project concerned with the relation between structural characteristics of the family, namely, sex of child, sex of sibling, ordinal position of child, and age difference between siblings, and the child's ratings on more than fifty personality traits. In her study, all subjects were obtained from the Chicago public schools and one large private school. The characteristics of the children used as subjects can be summarized as follows. All children were from unbroken, native-born, white, urban, two-child families. The children were five- and six-year-olds, free of any gross physical or mental defect. In most cases only one sibling in a family was a subject in the study.

The subjects numbered 384. "The experimental design included three sibspacing levels, two ordinal positions, subjects of two sexes and siblings of two sexes. There were 48 children in each of the following categories—male with a male sib older, male with a male sib younger, male with a female sib older, male with a female sib younger, female with a male sib older, female with a male sib younger, female with a female sib older, and female with a female sib younger. Each of these groups of 48 children was composed of three subgroups of 16 children, representing the following three sibling-age-difference levels: siblings differed in age by under two years, by two to four years, and four to six years, respectively. Hence our basic subgroups of 16 numbered 24" [7, p. 289]. The groups were matched, approximately, on an individual subject basis with respect to age of child and father's occupational status.

Teachers' ratings were made for each child on 58 traits. The teachers, all of whom were women, were trained in a conference or two to make the ratings. No teacher rated a child with whom contact had been less than three months, and in most cases the contact ranged from six to nine months. The 58 traits included 24 of the Fels Child Behavior Scales, and 34 items from the California Behavior Inventory for Nursery School Children. All ratings were made on line scales, converted later to 9-point scales. Ratings on each trait were subsequently normalized, prior to analysis of the data.

The relation between personality trait ratings and the structure of the family from which the children came was assessed by analysis of variance for each of the 58 traits. Helen Koch presents in her publications the findings from the variance analyses. It is this data on which we made our further study.

THE SECONDARY ANALYSIS

The procedures for the further analysis involved several steps. First, the writer, with the assistance of three professional persons as additional judges,[1] judged each of the 58 traits in terms of its pertinence to either a masculine or feminine role. Our conception of the characteristics of the two sex roles was based on recent empirical studies describing sex-role differences in small problem-solving groups [16] and in the nuclear family [18], and on the major theoretical treatment of such differences by Talcott Parsons [11]. In these studies the now-familiar distinction between the in-

[1]Dr. John Mann, Mr. David Glass, and Mr. David Lavin.

strumental or task role and the expressive or social-emotional role in a social group is shown to be related to sex-role differentiation, particularly in the family, with the male customarily taking the instrumental role and the female the expressive role. Hence in the judging process our decision as to whether a trait was masculine or feminine was essentially dependent on whether we believed the trait to belong to the instrumental or expressive role respectively.

Substantial descriptive data are available on sex-role differences in children for some of the traits which we judged. These findings, summarized by Terman and Tyler [17], were consulted after the judging was completed and strongly corroborate our assignment of traits: e.g., male children are judged higher on traits we believed instrumental, such as dominance and aggression, and lower on traits we judged to pertain to the expressive role, such as affection and absence of negativism.

In judging the traits it was recognized that many of them would be part of the role requirements for both roles.

TABLE 1   Traits assignable to male (instrumental) or female (expressive) roles

Trait name	Pertains primarily to instrumental (I) or expressive (E) role	Trait is congruent (+) or incongruent (−) characteristic of role
1. Tenacity	I	+
2. Aggressiveness	I	+
3. Curiosity	I	+
4. Ambition	I	+
5. Planfulness	I	+
6. Dawdling and procrastinating	I	−
7. Responsibleness	I	+
8. Originality	I	+
9. Competitiveness	I	+
10. Wavering in decision	I	−
11. Self-confidence	I	+
12. Anger	E	−
13. Quarrelsomeness	E	−
14. Revengefulness	E	−
15. Teasing	E	−
16. Extrapunitiveness	E	−
17. Insistence on rights	E	−
18. Exhibitionism	E	−
19. Uncooperativeness with group	E	−
20. Affectionateness	E	+
21. Obedience	E	+
22. Upset by defeat	E	−
23. Responds to sympathy and approval from adults	E	+
24. Jealousy	E	−
25. Speedy recovery from emotional disturbance	E	+
26. Cheerfulness	E	+
27. Kindness	E	+
28. Friendliness to adults	E	+
29. Friendliness to children	E	+
30. Negativism	E	−
31. Tattling	E	−

However, it was clear that there exists for each of the roles what is essentially a rank order of characteristics in terms of their importance for the role. Hence the basis for our judgments was whether the trait appeared to be higher in the rank order of requirements for the instrumental or the expressive role. Traits which seemed pertinent to neither, e.g., stammering, or for which no judgment of greater importance could be made, e.g., curiosity, were not ascribed to either role and were omitted from subsequent steps in the analysis. It was possible to assign 31 of the 58 traits to either the instrumental or expressive role. Twenty of the 31 traits pertain to the expressive role, the children evidently having been rated on a predominantly female cluster of traits.

Some of the traits were stated in a negative way which made them, while pertinent to the role, incongruent with the role conception. Thus, "uncooperativeness with group" seemed clearly to be relevant to the expressive role but as an incongruent trait. In like manner, both affectionateness and jealousy seemed most important as aspects of the expressive role, the former being congruent with the role conception, the latter incongruent. It therefore was necessary to make a second judgment regarding each trait, namely, whether it was a congruent or incongruent aspect of the role to which it pertained.

Table 1 lists the 31 traits, the role to which they seemed most pertinent, and the indication of whether the trait was a congruent or incongruent characteristic of the role.

With the judging of the traits completed, the next step was a careful reading of Helen Koch's findings. A tabulation was made of all differences on the 31 traits between the 16 basic subgroups reported by her as significant (close to or at the .05 level, based on the separate analyses of variance). Such differences involved single structural characteristics, e.g., firstborn versus second-born; single interactions of characteristics, e.g., girls with brothers versus girls with sisters; and multiple interactions, e.g., first-born boys with sisters versus first-born boys with brothers. These significant differences in traits were then entered in some preliminary forms of Tables 2 and 3. The procedure for entering differences was somewhat complicated and is described as follows:

First, with respect to a trait judged pertinent to the male or instrumental role, and considered a *congruent* aspect of that role: when any subgroup or groups were rated significantly higher than others on that trait, the number of the trait was entered in the high masculinity column for such a group; the subgroup or groups they were higher than, i.e., the low groups, had the number of the trait entered in the low masculinity column. Second, with respect to a male trait considered an *incongruent* aspect of the role: when any subgroup was rated higher than another on such a trait, the trait number was entered in the low masculinity column for such a group; for the group it was higher than, i.e., the low group, the trait number was entered in the high masculinity column. The procedure for the female or expressive traits was identical, except the female columns were used.

This procedure means that for any subgroup, entries in the high masculinity column consist of congruent male traits on which the group is high, and incongruent male traits on which it is low; entries in the low masculinity column consist of incongruent male traits on which the group is high, and congruent male traits on which it is low. Female column entries are read the same way. An example may be helpful at this point. Consider in Table 3 the subgroup "Younger Boy with Older Brother" at the four- to six-year age difference. In the high masculinity column the entry of trait number 2 means that the group was rated significantly *high* on aggressiveness; the entry of trait number 10 means that the group was rated significantly *low*

on wavering in decision. In the low masculinity column, trait number 6 indicates a *high* rating on dawdling and procrastinating, while trait number 7 indicates a *low* rating on responsibleness.

The preliminary forms of Tables 2 and 3 were complicated and two further steps toward simplification were taken before reaching the present form. The initial tables were marred by the occurrence of duplicate trait-number

TABLE 2   **Instrumental and expressive traits for five- and six-year-old girls**

SUBJECTS	SIB AGE DIFFERENCE	*Male or (Instrumental) Traits*		*Female (or Expressive) Traits*	
		HIGH MASCULINITY RATINGS	LOW MASCULINITY RATINGS	HIGH FEMININITY RATINGS	LOW FEMININITY RATINGS
Older girl with younger sister	0-2 years	2,5,7	4,6,9,10	13,14,15,16,17,18, 19,20,21,24,30	22,23,25,26, 27
	2-4 years	7	2,4,9,10,11	13,14,15,16,17,18, 19,20,21,24,30	22,23,26,27, 28
	4-6 years	7	2,4,6,9,10, 11	13,14,15,16,17,18, 19,20,21,24,30	22,23,25,26, 27,28
Older girl with younger brother	0-2 years	1,2,3,4,5, 9,10	6	13,14,15,16,19,20, 21,25,26,27,30	22,24
	2-4 years	1,2,3,4,9, 10	6	13,14,15,16,19,20, 25,26,27,30,31	22,24
	4-6 years	1,2,4,6,7, 9,10	6	13,14,15,19,20,21, 25,26,27,28,30	22,24,31
Younger girl with older sister	0-2 years	2,5,6,7,8	3,4,9,10,11	12,13,14,15,16,18, 19,20,21,22,23,30	17,25,26,27
	2-4 years		3,4,5,8,9 10,11	12,13,14,15,16,18, 19,20,21,22,23,30	17,25,26,27, 28
	4-6 years	6,7	2,3,4,9,10, 11	12,13,14,15,16,18, 19,20,21,22,23,30	17,25,26,27, 28
Younger girl with older brother	0-2 years	1,2,3,4,7, 8,9,10,11		12,13,14,15,16,18, 19,20,21,22,23,25, 26,27,28,30	
	2-4 years	1,4,6,7,10, 11		12,13,14,15,16,18, 19,20,21,22,23,25, 26,27,28,30	
	4-6 years	2,4,5,10,11		12,13,14,15,16,18, 19,20,21,22,23,25, 26,27,28,30	

Note: Trait numbers refer to listing in Table 1. Traits entered in masculinity rating column are male-congruent traits with high ratings, male-congruent traits with low ratings. The reverse is true for masculinity rating column. Female trait entries are made in the same manner.

entries in the cells, arising primarily from the multiple reporting of the original data and the multiple differences emerging between the various subgroups. Hence, where duplicate trait-entries occurred, only one entry was kept. The result is to make each entry read that that subgroup is significantly higher (or lower) than some other group *or groups* on that particular trait. Second, the tables were complicated by the fact that for all subgroups there were at least some trait numbers which appeared in *both* the high and low subdivisions of either the male or female column. This indicated, of course, that a subgroup was higher (or lower) than some other group on that trait, but also lower (or higher) than still another group; i.e., on the ranking of mean ratings on the trait, the subgroup would have differed significantly from both the top and bottom ranks. To clarify the tables, and also

TABLE 3 Instrumental and expressive traits for five- and six-year-old boys

SUBJECTS	SIB AGE DIFFERENCE	*Male (or Instrumental) Traits*		*Female (or Expressive) Traits*	
		HIGH MASCULINITY RATINGS	LOW MASCULINITY RATINGS	HIGH FEMININITY RATINGS	LOW FEMININITY RATINGS
Older boy with younger brother	0-2 years	9,10	1,2,7,11		12,13,14,15,16,19, 22,23,25,26,27,30
	2-4 years	4,9,10	1,2,5,7,11		12,13,14,15,16,19, 20,21,22,23,25,26, 27,28,30
	4-6 years	2,4,9,10	1,7,11		12,13,14,15,16,19, 20,22,23,25,26,27, 30,31
Older boy with younger sister	0-2 years	11	2,4,7,9,10	25,26,27,31	12,13,14,15,16,17, 18,19,20,21,22,23, 24,30
	2-4 years	2,3,5,11	4,7,9,10	25,26,27,28	12,13,14,15,16,17, 18,19,20,21,22,23, 24,30
	4-6 years	3	2,4,7,9,10	25,26,27,28	12,13,14,15,16,17, 18,19,20,21,22,23, 24,30
Younger boy with older brother	0-2 years	4,9,10	1,2,3,5,6, 7,8	22,23,24	13,16,18,19,21, 25,26,27,28,30
	2-4 years	4,9,10	1,3,6,7	22,23,24	13,16,18,19,20,21, 25,26,27,28,30
	4-6 years	2,4,5,8,9, 10	6,7	22,23,24,29	13,16,18,19,20,21, 25,26,27,28,30
Younger boy with older sister	0-2 years		2,4,5,6,7,8, 9,10	17,22,23,24, 25,26,27	13,19,30
	2-4 years		2,4,6,9,10	17,22,23,24, 25,26,27,28	13,16,19,20,21,30
	4-6 years		2,4,6,7,9, 10	17,22,23,24, 25,26,27,28	13,16,19,20,21,30

Note: See note to Table 2.

substantially to increase the reliability of the subgroup differences reported here, all traits on which a subgroup had both high and low entries were dropped for that subgroup. In summary, the result of this step, combined with the one above, is to make *each entry in the final tables read that that subgroup is significantly higher (or lower) than one or more groups on that trait, and is significantly lower (or higher) than none.*

RESULTS

The data presented in Tables 2 and 3 can be brought to bear upon our hypotheses by considering the distribution by subgroups of the traits indicating high or low masculinity or femininity. Our concern is with the frequency of trait entries of the four types, rather than with the descriptive content of any particular trait. Essentially we give each separate trait an equal weight, then summarize in terms of masculinity (many high rating, few low rating entries) and of femininity, associated with each subgroup.

With respect to our first hypothesis, that through interaction and taking the role of the other the cross-sex sibs would have more traits of the opposite sex than would same-sex sibs, an examination of the distribution in Table 2 shows that this is clearly the case. Controlling for ordinality, the older girl with a younger brother has more high masculinity traits and fewer low masculinity traits, than does her counterpart, the older girl with a younger sister. This distribution of traits is even more pronounced for the girls in the second ordinal position, the younger girl with older brother being substantially higher on masculinity than her counterpart with an older sister. One will note that the

acquisition of male traits does not seem to reduce the number of feminine traits of the girls with brothers. The more accurate interpretation is that acquisition of such traits adds to their behavioral repertoire, probably with a resultant dilution of their femininity in behavior, but not a displacement.

Examination of Table 3 with respect to this first hypothesis indicates that it holds for boys also. While not pronounced for the boys in the eldest child position, the boy with the sister is feminine to a greater degree than the boy with the brother. For the boys who are second-born, the difference is clear: the boy with the elder sister is substantially more feminine than his counterpart with an older brother. For the boy with the older sister the acquisition of feminine traits would seem to have displaced, rather than simply diluted, his masculinity and he thus contrasts with the girls for whom this did not occur. We can offer no explanation for this, but it may provide a lead for further study in this area.

In connection with this result, the role of the parent requires attention. While all would agree that parents actively assist cross-sex sibs in separating their sex roles, the data show they are unsuccessful in completely arresting the process of assimilation. Perhaps in earlier times, when children's sex roles were stressed more strongly, and perhaps today for some parents making an extreme effort, the effects of interaction would be reduced. However, it certainly appears that the average parent today cannot completely avoid the effects of such sib interaction. Even were more attention given by parents to cross-sex as opposed to same-sex sibs in this matter, we believe that the tremendously greater cross-sex interaction of the former would leave its mark.

With respect to our second hypothesis, that because of differences in control of rewards and punishments and in ability to discriminate between self and other roles the effects of role-taking would be more pronounced for the younger child, an examination of Tables 2 and 3 again seems to support the hypothesis. While the younger, as contrasted with the older, girl with a brother manifests only a slightly greater degree of masculinity, this difference for boys is quite striking: the younger, as contrasted with the older, boy with a sister is substantially more feminine.

With respect to our third hypothesis, that on the assumption of interaction varying inversely with age-gap and greater interaction producing greater role-taking, the effects of role-taking would be largest for the sibs closest in age, the results in both tables are negligible. One might discern some such relationship for the boy with an older sister, and the girl with an older brother, but even here it is tenuous. Because the assumption that interaction varies with sib age differences may in fact be untenable, we cannot in this instance say we have made a direct test of the hypothesis that more frequent interaction produces more role assimilation. Since the first hypothesis, which in essence states the same point, was so strongly confirmed, our inclination is to reject our assumption that interaction varies with age difference, at least to a degree sufficient to produce differences in role-taking.

DISCUSSION

There are two further aspects of Tables 2 and 3 which are quite noticeable and which need comment. We refer first to the fact that girls with brothers appear to be masculine to a greater degree than do any of the males themselves. The simplest and most likely explanation, hence the one which we favor, is that this result occurs because of certain biases in the teachers' ratings. We submit that teachers implicitly rated boys and girls on different scales, i.e., girls were implicitly rated on a girls' scale, boys on a boys' scale. The girl with an extreme masculine trait—extreme, that is, for a girl—receives a very high rating; a boy with the same absolute degree of such a trait, or even more of it, would on the boys' scale not be extreme and his rating consequently would be reduced. In the subsequent analysis of variance, where the male and female ratings are treated as if on the same absolute scale, certain girls extremely high for girls would score significantly higher than even certain boys high on the trait. To some extent we see the same effect in reverse for the younger boys with an older sister; while not being more feminine than girls, they almost tie certain girls, e.g., older girls with younger sisters. The probable use of different implicit rating scales, the implausibility of any group of girls being more masculine than all boys and the important fact that when girls and boys are assuredly rated on the same absolute scale [e.g., 3, 17] boys regularly outscore girls on masculine traits, all tend to support this interpretation.

The second additional aspect of the tables which merits discussion is that all girls seem to be more feminine than the boys are masculine; indeed, the major characteristic of the boys is to be anti-feminine, not masculine. In part this is explained by the assumed bias in the ratings mentioned above; boys are outscored on their own traits by some girls. In part also this is explained by the preponderance of feminine traits used in the ratings, so that boys could only express their masculinity, as it were, by being rated low on such traits. In part, and an intriguing part indeed, it may be explained by certain developmental processes commonly assumed in clinical theory and recently put in a role theory context by Parsons [11, pp. 95–101]. Parsons points out that both boy and girl first identify with the mother and tend to play an expressive role. In development the boy must break away and establish a new identification with the father, which is difficult and involves much new learning, in the role-taking sense. At the same time, the boy must "push far and hard to renounce dependency." Girls, continuing identification with the mother and the expressive role, face neither of these problems. It may be, then, that the girls' femininity and the boy's antifemininity and yet lack of masculinity which shows itself in Tables 2 and 3 arises in part because the children have been caught by the raters at an age where the boy is trying to shift his identification from mother to father.

To conclude, our analysis of Helen Koch's data indicates that cross-sex siblings tend to assimilate traits of the opposite sex, and that this effect is most pronounced in the younger of the two siblings. These findings support the role-learning theory presented here, and also stand as a substantive contribution to the area of sex-role learning. We wish now to stress two points mentioned earlier.

First, these findings must be subject to strict limitations to two-child families. Not only does the Fauls and Smith study demonstrate this limitation with regard to only-child families, but observation suggests that in larger families other variables come into play; e.g., in the four-child family with a three and one sex split, parents may actively help the solitary child in differentiating sex roles; or in the four-child family with a two and two split, siblings may pair off by sex and the cross-sex role-taking effect is minimized.

Second, with respect to the substantive value of these results, we would point out that even though parents must remain as the major source of sex-role learning, almost every child has a mother and father to learn from. Hence the *variations* in type and amount of sex-role learning occur on top of this base, so to speak, and in this variability the effect of a same or a cross-sex sib may play as large or larger a role than variations in parental behavior, mixed versus single-sexed schooling, sex of neighborhood playmates, and the like. Speculations on the durable and considerable effects of sex of sib on sex-role learning thus seem warranted and lead one to consider problems such as the effect of sex of sibling on one's later role in the marital relation, on career choices, and on other correlates of the adult sex role.

SUMMARY

This paper reports some relations between ordinal position, sex of sibling, and sex-role learning by children in two-child families. The findings are based on a further analysis of Helen Koch's data relating personality traits of children to their sex, sex of sibling, ordinal position, and age difference from sibling. In this analysis the personality traits were classified as pertaining either to the instrumental (masculine) role or the expressive (feminine) role. The distribution of such traits in children as a correlate of family structure was then assessed.

General propositions describing

role learning in terms of interaction with others, including taking the role of the other, leads to hypotheses that cross-sex siblings will have more traits of the opposite sex than will same-sex siblings, and that this effect will be greater for the younger, as contrasted with the older, sibling. Both hypotheses are confirmed by the data presented.

References

1. BRIM, O. G., JR., "The Parent-Child Relation as a Social System: I. Parent and Child Roles," *Child Development*, 1957, 28, 344–364.
2. COTTRELL, L. S., JR., "The Analysis of Situational Fields in Social Psychology," *American Sociological Review*, 1942, 7, 370–382.
3. FAULS, L. B., and W. D. SMITH, "Sex Role Learning of Five-Year-Olds," *Journal of Genetic Psychology*, 1956, 89, 105–117.
4. KOCH, H. L., "The Relation of 'Primary Mental Abilities' in Five- and Six-Year-Olds to Sex of Child and Characteristics of His Sibling," *Child Development*, 1954, 25, 210–223.
5. KOCH, H. L., "Some Personality Correlates of Sex, Sibling Position, and Sex of Sibling Among Five- and Six-Year-Old Children," *Genetic Psychology Monographs*, 1955, 52, 3–50.
6. KOCH, H. L., "The Relation of Certain Family Constellation Characteristics and the Attitudes of Children Toward Adults," *Child Development*, 1955, 26, 13–40.
7. KOCH, H. L., "Attitudes of Children Toward Their Peers as Related to Certain Characteristics of Their Sibling," *Psychological Monographs*, 1956, 70, No. 19 (whole No. 426).
8. KOCH, H. L., "Children's Work Attitudes and Sibling Characteristics," *Child Development*, 1956, 27, 289–310.
9. KOCH, H. L., "Sibling Influence on Children's Speech," *Journal of Speech and Hearing Disorders*, 1956, 21, 322–328.
10. KOCH, H. L., "Sissiness and Tomboyishness in Relation to Sibling Charac-

teristics," *Journal of Genetic Psychology*, 1956, 88, 231–244.
11. PARSONS, T., "Family Structure and the Socialization of the Child," in T. Parsons and R. F. Bales, *Family, Socialization and Interaction Process* (Glencoe, Illinois: Free Press, 1955).
12. PAYNE, D. E., and P. H. MUSSEN, "Parent-Child Relations and Father Identification Among Adolescent Boys," *Journal of Abnormal and Social Psychology*, 1956, 52, 359–362.
13. SEARS, P. S., "Child-Rearing Factors Related to Playing of Sex-Typed Roles," *American Psychologist*, 1953, 8, 431 (abstract).
14. SEARS, R. R., M. H. PINTLER, and P. S. SEARS, "Effect of Father Separation on Preschool Children's Doll Play Aggression," *Child Development*, 1946, 17, 219–243.
15. STRAUSS, A., *The Social Psychology of George Herbert Mead* (Chicago: Phoenix Books, University of Chicago Press, 1956).
16. STRODTBECK, F. L., and R. D. MANN, "Sex Role Differentiation in Jury Deliberations," *Sociometry*, 1956, 19, 3–11.
17. TERMAN, L. M., and L. E. TYLER, "Psychological Sex Differences," in L. Carmichael (ed.), *Manual of Child Psychology* (2d ed.) (New York: Wiley, 1954).
18. ZELDITCH, M., JR., "Role Differentiation in the Nuclear Family: A Comparative Study," in T. Parsons and R. F. Bales, *Family, Socialization and Interaction Process* (Glencoe, Illinois: Free Press, 1955).

11

SOCIAL CLASS, CULTURE, AND SOCIALIZATION

In the sense that class and ethnic memberships differentially determine socializing experiences, the theme of this chapter is a continuation of the position-conferring function of the family as pursued by Winch in Chapter 6. After showing that middle-class children stay in school longer and perform better than do lower-class children, Jackson Toby attributes such differences to the subcultures of these classes and to the family as the context through which the values are transmitted from parents to children.

Melvin Kohn provides an insight into the differences in emphasis which distinguish middle-class socialization from working-class socialization. First he finds a broad set of values that both categories of parents view as being both important and problematic of attainment. Kohn finds, however, that different priorities are given to certain values by each of the two classes. Specifically, middle-class parents are more likely than are working-class parents to value internalized standards like honesty and self-control and less likely to value more overt behaviors like obedience and cleanliness. In the present work Kohn relates this difference to the living conditions of the two classes; in subsequent articles he has also related it to class differences in occupational conditions.[1]

Fred L. Strodtbeck studies values and psychological orientations to achievement as related to style of family interaction in middle- and lower-class Jewish and Italian families. He finds a clear link between familial democracy and high valuation of achievement among adolescents. In turn, familial democracy is positively correlated with socio-economic status, but unrelated to ethnicity. By linking familial interaction with social class and ethnicity, Strodtbeck illuminates the part played by the family in the socialization of the adolescent into the role of adult.

---

[1]Melvin L. Kohn, "Social Class and Parent-Child Relationships: An Interpretation," *American Journal of Sociology*, 1963, 68: 471–480.

Orientation to Education as a Factor In the School Maladjustment Of Lower-Class Children*

Jackson Toby

Even taking an extremely crude index of school achievement, that of grade placement, *for every age level* the average grade of middle-class urban children is higher than that of lower-class children. (See Tables 1, 2, and 3.) These differences can be observed at 7 and 8 years of age as well as at 17. Apparently whatever produces the difference starts operating to differentiate lower-class from middle-class children from the early grades. Another way of looking at class selectivity of the educational process is to observe the proportion of lower-class boys in high school a generation ago (Tables 4 and 5) or in college today. [1]

Why are middle-class children more successful in their studies? Why do lower-class children drop out at younger ages and complete fewer grades? One hypothesis is that school teachers are middle-class in their values, if not in their origins, and penalize those students who do *not* exhibit the middle-class traits of cleanliness, punctuality, and neatness or who *do* exhibit the lower-class traits of uninhibited sexuality and aggression. [2] Some social scientists believe that lower-class children, even though they may have the intellectual potentialities for high levels of academic achievement, lose interest in school or never become interested because they resent the personal rejection of their teachers. Such rejection is, they say, motivated by the teachers' mistaken notion that lower-class children are deliberately defying them. Davis and Havighurst show that children are the prisoners of their experience and that lower-class children behave the way they do, not because of any initial desire to defy school authorities, but rather because of their lower-class childhood training. [3]

According to this hypothesis, teacher rejection makes the lower-class boy resentful and rebellious. His attitude is, "If you don't like me, I won't cooperate." Unfortunately for him, however, school achievement is related to later occupational advancement. Failure to cooperate with the teacher cuts off the lower-class boy from a business or professional career. . . . Professor Warner and his colleagues point out that the American public school teacher is

---

*Adapted from Social Forces, 1957, 35:259–266. Copyright, University of North Carolina Press, 1957.

[1] Helen B. Goetsch, *Parental Income and College Opportunities* (New York: Teachers College, Columbia University, Contributions to Education, No. 795, 1940).

[2] W. L. Warner, R. J. Havighurst, and M. B. Loeb, *Who Shall Be Educated?* (New York: Harper & Brothers, 1944).

[3] Allison Davis and Robert J. Havighurst, *Father of the Man* (Boston: Houghton Mifflin, 1947).

suspicious of lower-class children and unwilling to give them a chance. If they withdraw from school to escape the pressures, they must surrender their chance to realize the American dream: social mobility.

Another hypothesis attributes the inferior performance of lower-class children at school *directly* to the economic disabilities of their families. John is a poor student because he lacks the nourishing food for sustained effort or because he is compelled to work after school instead of doing his homework; or he is a truant because he is ashamed to appear at school in ragged clothes or torn shoes. Like the rejecting teacher

hypothesis, the economic disability hypothesis treats the child as essentially passive. According to both, he is victimized by a situation over which he has no control, in the one case by teachers who reject him, in the other by an economic system which does not allow him the opportunities to realize his ambitions.

But it is not at all clear that the average lower-class child has academic aspirations which are thwarted by his teachers or his economic circumstances. Studies of withdrawees from high school show that the majority leave school with no regrets; some volunteer the information that they hate school and are

TABLE 1   Median years of school completed by native white boys by monthly rental value of home and by age in cities of 250,000 inhabitants or more, 1940

AGE	Monthly Rental Value of Home						
	UNDER $10	$10-$14	$15-$19	$20-$29	$30-$49	$50-$74	$75 AND OVER
7 years	1.3	1.5	1.6	1.7	1.7	1.7	1.7
8 years	2.1	2.4	2.4	2.5	2.6	2.6	2.7
9 years	2.8	3.2	3.3	3.4	3.5	3.7	3.7
10 years	3.6	4.0	4.2	4.4	4.5	4.6	4.7
11 years	4.4	4.9	5.1	5.3	5.5	5.6	5.6
12 years	5.4	5.7	6.0	6.2	6.5	6.6	6.7
13 years	6.0	6.7	7.1	7.2	7.5	7.7	7.8
14 years	7.2	7.8	7.9	8.2	8.5	8.7	8.8
15 years	8.3	8.5	8.8	9.2	9.4	9.6	9.8
16 years	8.6	9.3	9.6	9.8	10.3	10.5	10.6
17 years	9.4	9.9	10.2	10.7	10.7	11.3	11.5

SOURCE: Bureau of the Census, *Sixteenth Census of the United States (1940), Monograph on Population Education: Educational Attainment of Children by Rental Value of Home* (Washington: Government Printing Office, 1945), p. 3.

TABLE 2   Distribution of retarded and nonretarded pupils according to occupational status of father (Sims' scale) in the New York City public schools, 1931-32

FATHER'S OCCUPATIONAL STATUS	TOTAL	SLOW PROGRESS	NORMAL PROGRESS	RAPID PROGRESS
Total	100.0	100.0	100.0	100.0
Professional	3.7	1.3	4.4	6.2
Clerical	19.8	11.2	19.4	31.9
Artisan	24.0	22.0	25.5	24.8
Skilled laborer	36.9	43.8	35.1	29.8
Unskilled laborer	15.6	21.7	15.6	7.3

TABLE 3 Percentage distribution of pupils according to father's occupational status and pupils' progress status, 1931-32

FATHER'S OCCUPATIONAL STATUS	*Pupils' Progress Status*			
	TOTAL	SLOW	NORMAL	RAPID
Professional	100.0	13.2	39.7	47.1
Clerical	100.0	21.3	32.7	46.0
Artisan	100.0	34.6	35.6	29.8
Skilled laborer	100.0	45.0	31.9	23.1
Unskilled laborer	100.0	53.0	33.6	13.4

SOURCE for Tables 2 and 3: Eugene A. Nifenecker, *Statistical Reference Data Relating to Problems of Overageness, Educational Retardation, Non-Promotion, 1900-1934* (New York: Board of Education, 1937), p. 233.

TABLE 4 High school attendance of the children of fathers following various occupations, Seattle, St. Louis, Bridgeport, and Mount Vernon, 1919-1921

Parental Occupation	*Number in High School for Every 1,000 Men 45 Years of Age or Over*
Proprietors	341
Professional service	360
Managerial service	400
Commercial service	245
Building trades	145
Machine trades	169
Printing trades	220
Miscellaneous trades	103
Transportation service	157
Public service	173
Personal service	50
Miners, lumber workers, and fishermen	58
Common labor	17

delighted to get through with it.[4] These data suggest that some lower-class children view the school as a burden, not an opportunity. Perhaps it is not only teacher prejudice and his parents' poverty that handicap the lower-class child at school. *He* brings certain attitudes and experi-

4Howard C. Seymour, The Characteristics of Pupils Who Leave School Early—A Comparative Study of Graduates with Those Who are Eliminated Before High School Graduation, unpublished Ph.D. dissertation, Harvard University, 1940; Harold J. Dillon, *Early School Leavers* (New York: National Child Labor Committee, 1949).

ences to the school situation just as his teacher does.

Whereas the middle-class child learns a socially adaptive fear of receiving poor grades in school, of being aggressive toward the teacher, of fighting, of cursing, and of having early sex relations, the slum child learns to fear quite different social acts. His gang teaches him to fear being taken in by the teacher, of being a softie with her. To study homework seriously is literally a disgrace. Instead of boasting of good marks in school, one conceals them, if he ever receives any. The lower-class individual fears not to be thought a street-fighter; it is a suspicious

TABLE 5 Percentage of students in each of two high school years from each of the occupational groups, 1919-1921

Parental Occupation	Freshman Class	Senior Class
Proprietors	17.7	22.9
Professional service	7.7	12.5
Managerial service	15.4	19.1
Commercial service	8.6	11.1
Clerical service	5.9	5.9
Agricultural service	2.3	2.3
Artisan-proprietors	4.4	3.5
Building trades	8.8	5.3
Machine trades	8.3	4.6
Printing trades	1.0	0.8
Miscellaneous trades	4.8	2.3
Transportation service	6.2	3.6
Public service	1.7	1.1
Personal service	1.4	0.9
Miners, lumber workers, and fishermen	0.5	0.3
Common labor	1.8	0.6
Unknown	3.5	3.2

SOURCE for Tables 4 and 5: George S. Counts, *The Selective Character of American Secondary Education* (Chicago: University of Chicago Press, 1922), pp. 33, 37.

and dangerous social trait. He fears not to curse. If he cannot claim early sex relations his virility is seriously questioned.[5]

Of course, not all lower-class children have a hostile orientation to the school. As a matter of fact, the dramatic contrast between the educational attainments of drafted enlisted men in the two World Wars shows that the public schools are being used more and more; and some of this increase undoubtedly represents lower-class youths who eagerly take advantage of educational opportunities.[6] Still, many lower-class children

do *not* utilize the educational path to social advancement.[7] Apparently, one reason for this is a chronic dissatisfaction with school which begins early in their academic careers. Why should middle-class children "take to" school so much better?

[7] The assumption here is that the goal of success is sufficiently widespread in the American ethos and the penalties for criminal deviance sufficiently great that the failure to utilize a legitimate channel of social mobility can usually be explained as due (1) to a failure on the part of the individual to *perceive* that channel as feasible for him and to define it as an opportunity, (2) to objective disabilities which cannot be overcome by effort, or (3) to his perception of other and better opportunities. We assume, therefore, that the lower-class subculture (uncongenial to social mobility) has its roots in a sour-grapes reaction. This does *not* mean that every lower-class boy yearns for higher socio-economic status at some time or other in his life. Some of them have been socialized into the sour grapes tradition before having the experience on which they might personally conclude that the grapes are sour.

[5] Allison Davis, *Social Class Influences on Learning* (Cambridge, Massachusetts: Harvard University Press, 1949), p. 30.

[6] 41 percent of the selectees of World War II were high school graduates or better, as contrasted with only 9 percent in World War I. Samuel A. Stouffer and others, *The American Soldier* (Princeton: Princeton University Press, 1949), I, 59. Compulsory school attendance laws may have something to do with this difference, but the average age of high school graduation is beyond the age of compulsory attendance in most states.

To begin with, it should not be taken for granted that any child, whatever his socio-economic origin, will find school a pleasant experience from the very first grade. On the contrary, there is reason to believe that starting school is an unpleasant shock. The average child cannot help but perceive school as an invasion of his freedom, an obligation imposed on him by adults. Forced to come at set times, to restrain his conversation so that the teacher may instruct the class as a group, he may not see any relationship between what she asks him to learn and what he might be interested in doing. And in terms of maximizing his pleasure at the time, he is quite right. Except for kindergarten and ultra-progressive schools, the curriculum is a discipline imposed on the pupil rather than an extension and development of his own interests. This is not to condemn the school system, but it does point up the problematic nature of school adjustment.

Middle-class parents make it quite clear that school is nothing to be trifled with. They have probably graduated at least from high school, and their child is aware that they *expect* him to do the same or better. If he has difficulty with his studies, they are eager (and competent) to help him. And not only do his *parents* expect him to apply himself to his studies, so do his *friends* and *their* parents. He is caught in a neighborhood pattern of academic achievement in much the same way some lower-class boys are caught in a neighborhood pattern of truancy and delinquency. This concern with education is insurance against the child's fall in social status. Middle-class parents convey to their children subtly or explicitly that they must make good in school if they want to go on being middle-class. This may be phrased in terms of preparation for a "suitable" occupation (an alternative

to a stigmatized occupation such as manual labor), in terms of a correlation between a "comfortable" standard of living and educational level, or in terms of the honorific value of education for its own sake.

Middle-class parents constantly reinforce the authority and prestige of the teacher, encouraging the child to respect her and compete for her approval. The teacher makes a good parent-surrogate for him because his parents accept her in this role.[8] They urge him to value the gold stars she gives out and the privilege of being her monitor. But although the middle-class child's initial motivation to cooperate with the teacher may spring from his parents, motivation functionally autonomous of parental pressure usually develops to supplement it.[9] Part of this new motivation may be the intrinsic interest of the subject matter, or at least some of it, once he has gotten well along in his course. *Learning* to read may be a disagreeable chore; but the time soon comes when interesting stories are made accessible by the development of reading skill. An even more important source of motivation favorable to school is the recognition he gets in the form of high marks. He

[8] Professor Green maintains that the middle-class boy is more closely supervised by his mother than the lower-class boy and that this "personality absorption" creates a dependence on adult authority much greater than that of the less well supervised lower-class boy. If this theory were accepted, we would thus find additional reason for the relative tractability and ·cooperativeness of the middle-class boy in school. Arnold W. Green, "The Middle Class Male Child and Neurosis," *American Sociological Review*, XI (1946), 31–41.

[9] See Gordon W. Allport, *Personality* (New York: Henry Holt and Company, 1937), pp. 191–206, for a discussion of functional autonomy.

learns that scholastic competition is somewhat analogous to the social and economic competition in which his parents participate. The object of scholastic competition is to win the approving attention of the teacher, to skip grades, and to remain always in the "bright" classes. (In grade school the "bright" and the "dull" classes take approximately the same work, but pupils and teachers have no difficulty in separating the high prestige groups. In high school, "commercial," "trade," and "general" courses have different curricula from the high prestige "college" course. Again, there is consensus among the students as well as the teachers that the non-college courses are for those who are not "college material." [10]

Of course it is not competition alone that gives the middle-class child an emotional investment in continued scholastic effort; it is the *position* he achieves in that competition. Apparently his preschool training prepares *him* much better for scholastic competition than his lower-class classmate.[11] His parents mingle with lawyers, accountants, businessmen, and others who in their day-to-day activities manipulate

[10] George S. Counts, *The Selective Character of American Secondary Education* (Chicago: University of Chicago Press, 1922), shows the middle-class orientation of the "college" course; see also R. E. Eckert and T. O. Marshall, *When Youth Leaves School* (New York: The Regents' Inquiry, McGraw-Hill, 1938), p. 67.

[11] Millie C. Almy, *Children's Experiences prior to First Grade and Success in Beginning Reading* (New York: Teachers College, Columbia University, Contributions to Education, No. 954, 1949); Dorris M. Lee, *The Importance of Reading for Achieving in Grades Four, Five, and Six* (New York: Teachers College, Columbia University, Contributions to Education, No. 556, 1933).

symbols. In the course of conversation these people use a sizeable vocabulary including many abstractions of high order. He unconsciously absorbs these concepts in an effort to understand his parents and their friends. He is stimulated in this endeavor by the rewards he receives from his parents when he shows verbal precociousness. These rewards are not necessarily material or conscious. The attention he receives as a result of a remark insightful beyond his years, the pride his mother shows in repeating a bright response of his to her friends, these are rewards enough. This home background is valuable preparation for successful competition in school. For, after all, school subjects are designed to prepare for exactly the occupational level to which his parents are already oriented. Hence he soon *achieves* in school a higher than average status. (See Tables 1, 2, and 3.) To maintain this status intact (or improve it) becomes the incentive for further effort, which involves him deeper and deeper in the reward and punishment system of the school. Thus, *his success cumulates and generates the conditions for further success.*

A similar conclusion was reached after a study of the success and failure of children in certain nonacademic activities. Dr. Anderson concluded that success and practice mutually reinforce one another, producing remarkable differentiations in performance.

> . . . a child is furnished from early life with the opportunity to hammer nails. In the course of the next ten or fifteen years, the child has 100,000 opportunities to hammer nails, whereas a second child in the same period of time has only ten or fifteen opportunities to hammer nails. At the age of twenty, we may be tremendously impressed with the ease and accuracy with which the first child hammers nails and likewise with the awk-

wardness and incapacity of the second child. We speak of the first child as an expert and the second child as a boob with respect to the nail hitting situation, and we may naïvely ascribe the ability of the first child to an inherited ability because its appearance is so inexplicable in comparison with the lack of ability of the second child.[12]

The most significant fact which comes out of these observations is the fact that if we take a particular child and record his relationship to the group, we find that in ninety-five percent of the situations with which he is presented in the play situation, he is the dominating or leading individual, whereas another child under the same conditions is found to be in the leading position only five percent of the time.

. . . the social reactions of these particular children . . . may be the product of hereditary factors, environmental factors, more rapid rate of development, or a large number of factors combined. The important fact for our discussion is that within a constant period one child is getting approximately twenty times as much specific practice in meeting social situations in a certain way as is a second child. Life is something like a game of billiards in which the better player gets more opportunity for practice and the poorer player less.[13]

For the average middle-class child, the effective forces in his life situation form a united front to urge upon him a favorable orientation to school. Of course, this may not be sufficient to produce good school adjustment. He may not have the native intelligence to perform up to the norm. Or he may have idiosyncratic experiences that alienate him from scholastic competition. But,

apparently, for the *average* middle-class child, this favorable orientation, combined with the intellectual abilities cultivated in his social milieu, results in satisfactory performance in the school situation.

The other side of the coin is the failure of some lower-class children to develop the kind of orientation which will enable them to overcome the initial frustration of school discipline.[14] To begin with, the parents of the lower-class child may not support the school as do middle-class parents. His parents probably do not have much education themselves, and, if not, they cannot very well make meaningful to him subjects that they do not themselves understand. Neither are they able to help him surmount academic stumbling blocks. Even more important, they lack the incentive to encourage him in and praise him for school accomplishment at that critical early period when he finds school new and strange and distasteful. Almost the same reasoning can be applied to the inculcation of a cooperative attitude toward school in the child as has been applied to an acceptant attitude toward toilet training. If the parents convey to the child their eagerness to have him adjust to irksome school discipline, he will probably accept it to please them and retain their love just as he learned to urinate and defecate at appropriate times and places. But toilet training and school adjustment training differ in an important particular. Parents *must* toilet train the child because permitting him to soil himself at will is a constant and immediate nuisance.

[12] John E. Anderson, "The Genesis of Social Reactions in the Young Child," *The Unconscious: A Symposium*, ed. by E. S. Dummer (New York: Alfred A. Knopf, 1928), pp. 83–84.

[13] *Ibid.*, pp. 81–82.

[14] At this point we are abstracting from such situational considerations as teacher rejection, the economic resources of the family and native capacity. We are considering only the orientations of the boy himself.

The consequences of a child's disinterest in school may also be unpleasant, both for him and for his parents, but it is not immediate. In the short run, allowing him to neglect school may be the least troublesome course for his parents to take. If they are neutral or antagonistic toward school, a result (1) of the esoteric nature of the curriculum from the point of view of skills cultivated and appreciated in the lower-class milieu and (2) of their failure to see the relevance of education to occupational advancement into a higher socio-economic class, they do not *have* to give the kind of support to the school given by middle-class parents. There is no reason to assume that the value of education is self-evident. For those lower-class people who have lost hope in social mobility, the school is a symbol of a competition in which they do not believe they can succeed. If they themselves have given up, will they necessarily encourage their children to try to be better?

Moreover, coming as he does from a social stratum where verbal skills are not highly developed, the lower-class child finds school more difficult than does his middle-class contemporary. His father, a carpenter or a factory worker, manipulates concrete objects rather than symbols in his occupational role. In so far as he learns from his father, he is more likely to learn how to "fix things" than the importance of a large vocabulary.[15] This learning does not help him with his school work, for school tends to give a competitive advantage to those with verbal facility.

This disadvantage with respect to verbal skills may account for the poorer showing of lower-class children on standard intelligence tests. . . .[16]

In other words, middle-class children have an advantage because they are more familiar with the sort of problems that occur on the tests. This does not necessarily mean that the intelligence tests are invalid. It depends upon what the investigator thinks he is measuring. If he believes he is getting at "innate" ability, abstracted from cultural milieu and idiosyncratic learning, he is naïve. An intelligence test is a valid measure of the native intellectual ability of an individual only under special circumstances, one of these being that the respondent's experience is similar to that of the group on which the test was standardized. Thus, a Navaho boy who scores 80 on the Stanford-Binet (Revised Form) may be unusually intelligent. Unitl a test is designed to tap the experiences of Navahos, there exists no reference point about which to assess superiority and inferiority.[17]

However, it is not only the *content* of the intelligence test that gives middle-class urban children a better chance at high scores. It is the *structure* of the test situation. Even if we could find items equally familiar or unfamiliar to everyone taking the test, differential interest in solving abstract problems would work against the lower-class student.

. . . finding completely unfamiliar problems is not a possible choice, because such problems (namely, those involving some relationship between esoteric geometrical figures) do not arouse

---

15 Of course this is a matter of degree. The lower-class boy acquires verbal skills but not on so high a level as the middle-class boy.

16 Walter S. Neff, "Socio-economic Status and Intelligence: a Critical Survey," *Psychological Bulletin*, XXXV (1938), 727–757.

17 Dorothy Leighton and Clyde Kluckhohn, *Children of the People* (Cambridge, Massachusetts: Harvard University Press, 1947), pp. 148–155.

as great interest or as strong a desire to achieve a solution among low socio-economic groups as among high groups. The reason is clear: such an unrealistic problem can arouse the child's desire to achieve a solution only if the child has been trained to evaluate highly any and all success in tests. No matter how un-real and purposeless the problem may seem, the average child in a high socio-economic group will work hard to solve it, if his parents, his teacher, or other school officers expect him to try hard. The average slum child, however, will usually react negatively to any school test, and especially to a test whose problems have no relation to his experience.[18]

However justified the criticisms of the intelligence test as an instrument measuring native intellectual ability, it is highly predictive of academic accomplishment. A student with a high I.Q. score does better in his studies, on the average, than one with a low I.Q. score.[19] Hence the discrepancy between the scores of lower-class students and of middle-class students is an index of the former's disadvantage in the school situation.

One possible response of the lower-class child to his disadvantages in the school situation is to increase his efforts. But his initial orientation drives him in the opposite direction. He is more likely to respond to competitive failure by going on strike psychologically, neglecting his homework, paying no attention in class, annoying the teacher. Uninterested in the curriculum, he learns as little as he can. Instead of a situation where the student and the teacher work toward a common goal, the development of the student's

understanding of certain ranges of problems, he and his teacher are oriented antagonistically to one another. The teacher tries to stuff into his head as much of the curriculum as possible; he tries to absorb as little as is consistent with his own safety, in terms of sanctions mobilized by the school and his parents.

But school subjects are cumulative. Within a few years he is retarded in basic skills, such as reading, absolutely necessary for successful performance in the higher grades. Whether he is promoted along with his agemates, "left back," or shunted into "slow" programs makes relatively little difference at this point. For whatever is done, he finds himself at the bottom of the school status hierarchy. He is considered "dumb" by the more successful students and by the teachers. This makes school still more uninteresting, if not unpleasant, and he neglects his work further. Eventually he realizes he can never catch up.

Without realizing what he was doing, he had cut himself off from the channels of social mobility. In those crucial early grades where the basis for school adjustment was being laid, he had not yet known that he wanted more out of life than his parents. Or, if he knew, he did not realize that school achievement and high occupational status are related. And he was not lucky enough to have parents who realized it for him and urged him on until he was old enough to identify with the school through choice. There is a certain ir-reversibility about school maladjust-ment. The student can hardly decide at 18 that he wants to become a lawyer if he is five years retarded in school. It is no longer possible for him to "catch up" and use school as a means to realize his ambitions. Sometimes lower-class men will rue their failure to take ad-vantage of the opportunities presented

[18] *Ibid.*, pp. 68–69.
[19] Eugene A. Nifenecker, *Statistical Reference Data Relating to Problems of Over-ageness, Educational Retardation, Non-Promotion,* 1900–1934 (New York: Board of Education, 1937), p. 111.

by the school. James T. Farrell captures the flavor of this regret in the following passage from one of his novels:

> Walking on, seeing the lights of Randolph Street before him, he wondered if they were college football players [referring to the young men walking in front of him]. That was what Studs Lonigan might have been. Even if he did admit it, he had been a damn good quarterback. If he only hadn't been such a chump, bumming from school to hang around with skunky Weary Reilley and Paulie Haggerty until he was so far behind at high school that it was no use going. It wouldn't have been so hard to have studied and done enough homework to get by, and then he could have set the high school gridiron afire, gone to Notre Dame and made himself a Notre Dame immortal, maybe, alongside of George Gipp, the Four Horsemen, Christie Flannagan and Carideo. How many times in a guy's life couldn't he kick his can around the block for having played chump.[20]

If on the other hand, the social milieu of the lower-class boy supported the school and encouraged him to bend every effort to keep up with his work, he would finish high school whether he enjoyed it or not—the way middle-class boys do. At graduation he might decide that he would like to become a plumb-

[20] James T. Farrell, *Judgment Day* (New York: Vanguard Press, 1935), p. 24.

er. That is, he might not crave middle-class status enough to suffer the discipline of continued education. But if he were not content with a lower-class status, if he wanted above all things to "be somebody," the educational route to high status would still be open. He would still have a *choice*; he would not be forced to accept a menial occupational role whether he liked it or not. As it is, the crucial decision is made before he is old enough to have a voice in it; it is made by his parents, his neighbors, and his friends.

To sum up, the middle-class child has the following advantages in school compared with the lower-class child: (1) his parents are probably better educated and are therefore more capable of helping him with his school work if this should be necessary; (2) his parents are more eager to make his school work seem meaningful to him by indicating, implicitly or explicitly, the occupational applications of long division or history; (3) the verbal skills which he acquires as part of child training on the middle-class status level prepare him for the type of training that goes on in school and give him an initial (and cumulating) advantage over the lower-class child in the classroom learning situation; and (4) the coordinated pressure of parents, friends, and neighbors reinforce his motivation for scholastic success and increase the probability of good school adjustment.

Social Class and Parental Values *

Melvin L. Kohn

We undertake this inquiry into the relationship between social class and parental values in the hope that a fuller
understanding of the ways in which
parents of different social classes differ
in their values may help us to understand why they differ in their practices. [1]
This hope, of course, rests on two assumptions: that it is reasonable to conceive of social classes as subcultures of
the larger society, each with a relatively
distinct value-orientation, and that values really affect behavior.

* Adapted from The American Journal of
Sociology, 1959, 64:4:337–351, by permission of The University of Chicago Press.

[1] There now exists a rather substantial,
if somewhat inconsistent, body of literature
on the relationship of social class to the ways
that parents raise their children. For a fine
analytic summary see Urie Bronfenbrenner,
"Socialization and Social Class through Time
and Space," in Eleanor E. Maccoby et al.,
Readings in Social Psychology (New York:
Holt; 1958). Bronfenbrenner gives references
to the major studies of class and child-rearing
practices that have been done.

For the most relevant studies on class
and values see Evelyn M. Duvall, "Concep-
tions of Parenthood," American Journal of
Sociology, LII (November, 1946), 193–203;
David F. Aberle and Kaspar D. Naegele,
"Middle Class Fathers' Occupational Role
and Attitudes toward Children," American
Journal of Orthopsychiatry, XXII (April,
1952), 366–78; Herbert H. Hyman, "The
Value Systems of Different Classes," in
Reinhard Bendix and Seymour M. Lipset
(eds.), Class, Status, and Power (Glencoe,
Ill.: Free Press, 1953), pp. 426–42.

SAMPLE AND METHOD OF DATA COLLECTION

Washington, D.C.—the locus of
this study—has a large proportion of
people employed by government, relatively little heavy industry, few recent
immigrants, a white working class drawn
heavily from rural areas, and a large
proportion of Negroes, particularly at
lower economic levels. Generalizations
based on this or any other sample of one
city during one limited period of time
are, of course, tentative.

Our intent in selecting the families
to be studied was to secure approximately two hundred representative
white working-class families, each family
having a child within a narrowly de-
limited age range. We decided on
fifth-grade children because we wanted
to direct the interviews to relationships
involving a child old enough to have a
developed capacity for verbal communication.

The sampling procedure involved
two steps: the first, selection of census
tracts. Tracts with 20 per cent or more
Negro population were excluded, as
were those in the highest quartile with
respect to median income. From among
the remaining tracts we then selected a
small number representative of each of
the three distinct types of residential
area in which the population to be
studied live: four tracts with a predominantly working-class population,
four predominantly middle-class, and

three having large proportions of each. The final selection of tracts was based on their occupational distribution and their median income, education, rent (or rented homes), and value (of owner-occupied homes). The second step in the sampling procedure involved selection of families. From records made available by the public and parochial school systems we compiled lists of all families with fifth-grade children who lived in the selected tracts. Two hundred families were then randomly selected from among those in which the father had a "white-collar" occupation and another two hundred from among those in which the father had a manual occupation.

In all four hundred families the mothers were to be interviewed. In every fourth family we scheduled interviews with the father and the fifth-grade child as well.[2] (When a broken family fell into this sub-sample, a substitute was chosen from our over-all sample, and the broken family was retained in the over-all sample of four hundred families.)

When interviews with both parents were scheduled, two members of the staff visited the home together—a male to interview the father, a female to interview the mother. The interviews were conducted independently, in separate rooms, but with essentially identical schedules. The first person to complete his interview with the parent interviewed the child.

[2] We secured the co-operation of 86 per cent of the families where the mother alone was to be interviewed and 82 per cent of the families where mother, father, and child were to be interviewed. Rates of non-response do not vary by social class, type of neighborhood, or type of school. This, of course, does not rule out other possible selective biases introduced by the non-respondents.

INDEXES OF SOCIAL CLASS AND VALUES

Social Class

Each family's social-class position has been determined by the Hollingshead Index of Social Position, assigning the father's occupational status a relative weight of 7 and his educational status a weight of 4. We are considering Hollingshead's Classes I, II, and III to be "middle class," and Classes IV and V to be "working class." The middle-class sample is composed of two relatively distinct groups: Classes I and II are almost entirely professionals, proprietors, and managers with at least some college training. Class III is made up of small shopkeepers, clerks, and salespersons but includes a small number of foremen and skilled workers of unusually high educational status. The working-class sample is composed entirely of manual workers but preponderantly those of higher skill levels. These families are of the "stable working class" rather than "lower class" in the sense that the men have steady jobs, and their education, income, and skill levels are above those of the lowest socioeconomic strata.

Values

We shall use Kluckhohn's definition: "A value is a conception, explicit or implicit, distinctive of an individual or characteristic of a group, of the desirable which influences the selection from available modes, means, and ends of action."[3]

[3] Clyde Kluckhohn, "Values and Value Orientations," in Talcott Parsons and Edward A. Shils (eds.), *Toward a General Theory of Action* (Cambridge, Mass.: Harvard University Press, 1951), p. 395.

Our inquiry was limited to the values that parents would most like to see embodied in their children's behavior. We asked the parents to choose, from among several alternative characteristics that might be seen as desirable, those few which they considered *most* important for a child of the appropriate age. Specifically, we offered each parent a card listing 17 characteristics that had been suggested by other parents, in the pretest interviews, as being highly desirable. (These appear down the left margin of Table 1. The order in which they were listed was varied from interview to interview.) Then we asked: "Which three of the things listed on this card would you say are the *most* important in a boy (or girl) of (fifth-grade child's) age?" The selection of a particular characteristic was taken as our index of value.

Later in this report we shall subject this index to intensive scrutiny.

CLASS AND VALUES

Middle- and working-class mothers share a broadly common set of values— but not an identical set of values by any means (see Table 1). There is considerable agreement among mothers of both social classes that happiness and such standards of conduct as honesty, consideration, obedience, dependability, manners, and self-control are highly desirable for both boys and girls of this age.

Popularity, being a good student (especially for boys), neatness and cleanliness (especially for girls), and curiosity are next most likely to be regarded as desirable. Relatively few

TABLE 1   Proportion of mothers who select each characteristic as one of three "most desirable" in a ten- or eleven-year-old child

CHARACTERISTICS	For Boys		For Girls		Combined	
	MIDDLE CLASS	WORKING CLASS	MIDDLE CLASS	WORKING CLASS	MIDDLE CLASS	WORKING CLASS
1. That he is honest	0.44	0.57	0.44	0.48	0.44	0.53
2. That he is happy	.44*	.27	.48	.45	.46*	.36
3. That he is considerate of others	.40	.30	.38*	.24	.39*	.27
4. That he obeys his parents well	.18*	.37	.23	.30	.20*	.33
5. That he is dependable	.27	.27	.20	.14	.24	.21
6. That he has good manners	.16	.17	.23	.32	.19	.24
7. That he has self-control	.24	.14	.20	.13	.22*	.13
8. That he is popular with other children	.13	.15	.17	.20	.15	.18
9. That he is a good student	.17	.23	.13	.11	.15	.17
10. That he is neat and clean	.07	.13	.15*	.28	.11*	.20
11. That he is curious about things	.20*	.06	.15	.07	.18*	.06
12. That he is ambitious	.09	.18	.06	.08	.07	.13
13. That he is able to defend himself	.13	.05	.06	.08	.10	.06
14. That he is affectionate	.03	.05	.07	.08	.05	.04
15. That he is liked by adults	.03	.05	.07	.04	.05	.04
16. That he is able to play by himself	.01	.02	.00	.03	.01	.02
17. That he acts in a serious way	0.00	0.01	0.00	0.00	0.00	0.01
N	90	85	84	80	174	165

* Social-class differences statistically significant, 0.05 level or better, using chi-square test.

TABLE 2 Proportion of fathers who select each characteristic as one of three "most desirable" in a ten- or eleven-year-old child

CHARACTERISTICS	For Boys		For Girls		Combined	
	MIDDLE CLASS	WORKING CLASS	MIDDLE CLASS	WORKING CLASS	MIDDLE CLASS	WORKING CLASS
1. That he is honest	0.60	0.60	0.43	0.55	0.52	0.58
2. That he is happy	.48	.24	.24	.18	.37	.22
3. That he is considerate of others	.32	.16	.38	.09	.35*	.14
4. That he obeys his parents well	.12*	.40	.14	.36	.13*	.39
5. That he is dependable	.36*	.12	.29*	.00	.33*	.08
6. That he has good manners	.24	.28	.24	.18	.24	.25
7. That he has self-control	.20	.08	.19	.00	.20*	.06
8. That he is popular with other children	.08	.16	.24	.45	.15	.25
9. That he is a good student	.04	.12	.10	.36	.07	.19
10. That he is neat and clean	.16	.20	.14	.09	.15	.17
11. That he is curious about things	.16	.12	.10	.00	.13	.08
12. That he is ambitious	.20	.12	.14	.00	.17	.08
13. That he is able to defend himself	.04	.16	.00*	.18	.02*	.17
14. That he is affectionate	.00	.04	.05	.18	.02	.08
15. That he is liked by adults	.00	.08	.00	.09	.00	.08
16. That he is able to play by himself	.00	.08	.05	.00	.02	.06
17. That he acts in a serious way	0.00	0.04	0.00	0.00	0.00	0.03
N	25	25	21	11	46	36

* Social-class differences statistically significant, 0.05 level or better, using chi-square test.

mothers choose ambition, ability to defend one's self, affectionate responsiveness, being liked by adults, ability to play by one's self, or seriousness as highly desirable for either boys or girls of this age. All of these, of course, might be more highly valued for children of other ages.

Although agreement obtains on this broad level, working-class mothers differ significantly[4] from middle-class mothers in the relative emphasis they place on particular characteristics. Significantly fewer working-class mothers regard happiness as highly desirable for *boys*. Although characteristics that define standards of conduct are valued by many mothers of both social classes, there are revealing differences of em-

phasis here too. Working-class mothers are more likely to value obedience; they would have their children be responsive to parental authority. Middle-class mothers are more likely to value both consideration and self-control; they would have their children develop inner control and sympathetic concern for other people. Furthermore, middle-class mothers are more likely to regard curiosity as a prime virtue. By contrast, working-class mothers put the emphasis on neatness and cleanliness, valuing the imaginative and exploring child relatively less than the presentable child.[5]

[5] Compare these results with Bronfenbrenner's conclusion, based on an analysis of reports of studies of social class and child-rearing methods over the last twenty-five years: "In this modern working class world there may be greater freedom of emotional expression, but there is no laxity or vagueness with respect to goals of child training.

[4] The criterion of statistical significance used throughout this paper is the 5 per cent level of probability, based, except where noted, on the chi-square test.

Middle-class mothers' conceptions of what is desirable for boys are much the same as their conceptions of what is desirable for girls. But working-class mothers make a clear distinction between the sexes: they are more likely to regard dependability, being a good student, and ambition as desirable for boys and to regard happiness, good manners, neatness, and cleanliness as desirable for girls.

What of the *fathers'* values? Judging from our subsample of 82 fathers, their values are similar to those of the mothers (see Table 2). Essentially the same rank-order of choices holds for fathers as for mothers, with one major exception: fathers are not so likely to value happiness for their daughters. Among fathers as well as mothers, consideration and self-control are more likely to be regarded as desirable by the middle class; middle-class fathers are also more likely to value another standard of conduct—dependability. Working-class fathers, like their wives, are more likely to value obedience; they are also more likely to regard it as desirable that their children be able to defend themselves. [6]

Consistently over the past twenty-five years, the parent in this group has emphasized what are usually regarded as the traditional middle-class virtues of cleanliness, conformity, and (parental) control, and although his methods are not so effective as those of his middle-class neighbors, they are perhaps more desperate" (*op. cit.*).

[6] A comparison of the values of the fathers in this sub-sample with those of the mothers in this same sub-sample yields essentially the same conclusions.

We do not find that fathers of either social class are significantly more likely to choose any characteristic for boys than they are to choose it for girls, or the reverse. But this may well be an artifact of the small number of fathers in our sample: Aberle and Naegele (*op. cit.*) have found that

We take this to indicate that middle-class parents (fathers as well as mothers) are more likely to ascribe predominant importance to the child's acting on the basis of internal standards of conduct, working-class parents to the child's compliance with parental authority.

There are important differences between middle- and working-class parents, too, in the way in which their choice of any one characteristic is related to their choice of each of the others.

We have already seen that parents of both social classes are very likely to accord *honesty* first-rank importance. But the choice of honesty is quite differently related to the choice of other characteristics in the two classes (see Table 3). Middle-class mothers[7] who choose honesty are more likely than are other middle-class mothers to regard consideration, manners, and (for boys) dependability as highly desirable; and those mothers who regard any of these as desirable are more likely to value honesty highly. Consideration, in turn, is positively related to self-control, and manners to neatness. Honesty, then, is the core of a set of standards of conduct, a set consisting primarily of honesty, consideration, manners, and dependability, together with self-control and neatness. As such, it is to be seen as one among several, albeit the central,

---

middle-class fathers are more likely to value such characteristics as responsibility, initiative, good school performance, ability to stand up for one's self, and athletic ability for boys and being "nice," "sweet," pretty, affectionate, and well-liked for girls.

[7] This analysis and those to follow will be limited to the mothers, since the sample of fathers is small. For simplicity, we shall present data separately for boys and for girls only where the relationship under discussion appears to differ for the two sexes considered separately.

TABLE 3 All cases* where mothers' choice of one characteristic as "desirable" is significantly related to their choice of any other characteristic as "desirable"

		Middle-Class Mothers		
		PROPORTION WHO CHOOSE B AMONG THOSE WHO:		
Characteristic		Choose A	Do Not Choose A	
A	**B**	(p_1)	(p_2)	p_1/p_2
Positive relationships:				
1. Honesty	Consideration	0.42	0.37	1.14
2. Honesty	Manners	.22	.16	1.38
3. Honesty	Dependability (boys)	.33	.22	1.50
4. Consideration	Honesty	.47	.42	1.12
5. Manners	Honesty	.52	.43	1.21
6. Dependability	Honesty (boys)	.54	.41	1.32
7. Consideration	Self-control	.24	.22	1.09
8. Self-control	Consideration	.41	.39	1.05
9. Manners	Neatness	.24	.08	3.00
10. Neatness	Manners	.42	.16	2.63
11. Curiosity	Happiness	.58	.43	1.35
12. Happiness	Curiosity	.23	.14	1.64
13. Happiness	Ambition (boys)	.13	.06	2.17
Negative relationships:				
1. Honesty	Popularity	.04	.24	0.17
2. Popularity	Honesty	.12	.50	0.24
3. Curiosity	Obedience	.03	.24	0.13
4. Obedience	Consideration	0.17	0.45	0.38
		Working-Class Mothers		
Positive relationships:				
1. Happiness	Honesty	0.51	0.55	0.93
2. Popularity	Honesty	.62	.51	1.22
3. Honesty	Popularity	.20	.14	1.43
4. Honesty	Defend self	.07	.05	1.40
5. Consideration	Manners (girls)	.42	.30	1.40
6. Manners	Consideration (girls)	.31	.20	1.55
7. Consideration	Curiosity	.11	.04	2.75
8. Ambition	Dependability	.29	.19	1.53
9. Happiness	Consideration (boys)	.35	.27	1.30
10. Consideration	Happiness (boys)	.32	.25	1.28
11. Happiness	Popularity (girls)	.25	.16	1.56
Negative relationships:				
1. Obedience	Popularity	.05	.24	0.21
2. Manners	Popularity	.00	.23	0.00
3. Consideration	Popularity	.02	.23	0.09
4. Popularity	Obedience	.10	.38	0.26
5. Popularity	Manners	.00	.29	0.00
6. Popularity	Consideration	.03	.32	0.09
7. Manners	Dependability (girls)	0.00	0.20	0.00

* Where it is not specified whether relationship holds for boys or for girls, it holds for both sexes. In all the relationships shown, p_1 and p_2 are each based on a minimum of 20 cases.

standards of conduct that middle-class mothers want their children to adopt.

This is not the case for working-class mothers. Those who regard honesty as predominantly important are not especially likely to think of consideration, manners, or dependability as comparable in importance; nor are those who value any of these especially likely to value honesty. Instead the mothers who are most likely to attribute importance to honesty are those who are concerned that the child be happy, popular, and able to defend himself. It is not that the child should conduct himself in a considerate, mannerly, or dependable fashion but that he should *be* happy, *be* esteemed by his peers, and, if the necessity arise, *be* able to protect himself. It suggests that honesty is treated less as a standard of conduct and more as a quality of the person; the emphasis is on being a person of inherent honesty rather than on acting in an honest way.

Note especially the relationship of popularity to honesty. For middle-class mothers these are *negatively* related. To value honesty is to forego valuing popularity; to value popularity is to forego valuing honesty. One must choose between honesty "at the risk of offending" and popularity at the sacrifice of absolute honesty. The exact opposite obtains for working-class mothers: those who accord high valuation to either are *more* likely to value the other. The very mothers who deem it most important that their children enjoy popularity are those who attribute great importance to honesty. Honesty does not interfere with popularity; on the contrary, it enhances the probability that one will enjoy the respect of one's peers.

However, working-class mothers who value obedience, manners, or consideration are distinctly unlikely to value popularity, and vice versa. They do see each of these standards of conduct as inconsistent

with popularity.[8] This further substantiates the view that working-class mothers are more likely to view honesty as a quality of the person, a desideratum of moral worth, rather than as one among several highly valued standards of conduct.

Happiness, in distinction to honesty, implies neither constraints upon action nor a moral quality; rather, it indicates a desired goal, achievable in several different ways. One way of specifying what is implied when happiness is regarded as a major value is to ascertain the other values most likely to be related to the choice of happiness.

The two choices positively related to the choice of happiness by middle-class mothers are curiosity and (for boys) ambition. Those middle-class mothers who deem it exceedingly important that their children aspire for knowledge or success are even more likely than are middle-class mothers in general to value their children's happiness highly.

Working-class mothers who value these, however, are no more likely to value happiness. Instead, curiosity is related to consideration, to the child's concern for others' well-being, and ambition to dependability, to his being the

[8] It may be that these three characteristics have more in common than that they are all standards of conduct. The fact that working-class mothers who value consideration for their *daughters* are especially likely to value manners, and the converse, suggests the possibility that consideration may be seen as a near-equivalent to manners by at least a sizable portion of working-class mothers. If so, all three values negatively related to popularity can be viewed as reflecting close conformance to directives from parents—as contrasted to directives from within. (Note, in this connection, that working-class mothers who would have their daughters be mannerly are distinctly unlikely to deem it important that they be dependable.)

type of person who can be counted on. The values that are positively related to happiness by working-class mothers are honesty, consideration (for boys), and popularity (for girls). Not aspirations for knowledge or for success, but being an honest—a worthy—person; not the desire to outdistance others, but, for boys, concern for others' well-being and for girls, enjoyment of the respect and confidence of peers: these are the conceptions of the desirable that accompany working-class mothers' wishes that their children be happy.

CLASS, SUBCULTURE, AND VALUES

In discussing the relationship of social class to values we have talked as if American society were composed of two relatively homogeneous groups, manual and white-collar workers, together with their families. Yet it is likely that there is considerable variation in values, associated with other bases of social differentiation, *within* each class. If so, it should be possible to divide the classes into subgroups in such a way as to speci-

TABLE 4   Mothers' socioeconomic status and their choice of characteristics as "most desirable" in a ten- or eleven-year-old child

	Proportion Who Select Each Characteristic Socioeconomic Stratum (on Hollingshead Index)				
CHARACTERISTIC	I	II	III	IV	V
Obedience	0.14	0.19	0.25	0.35	0.27
Neatness, cleanliness	.06	.07	.16	.18	.27
Consideration	.41	.37	.39	.25	.32
Curiosity	.37	.12	.09	.07	.03
Self-control	.24	.30	.18	.13	.14
Happiness	.61	.40	.40	.38	.30
Boys		.48	.40	.27	
Girls		.54	.40	.45	
Honesty	0.37	0.49	0.46	0.50	0.65
N	51	43	80	128	37

Still the perhaps equally important fact is that no choice, by mothers of either social class, is negatively related to the choice of happiness.

The final bit of information that these data provide concerns the conception of *obedience* entertained in the two classes. Middle-class mothers who value curiosity are unlikely to value obedience; those who value obedience are unlikely to value consideration. For middle-class mothers, but not for working-class mothers, obedience would appear to have a rather narrow connotation; it seems to approximate blind obedience.

fy more precisely the relationship of social class to values.

Consider, first, the use we have made of the concept "social class." Are the differences we have found between the values of middle- and working-class mothers a product of this dichotomy alone, or do values parallel status gradations more generally? It is possible to arrive at an approximate answer by dividing the mothers into the five socioeconomic strata delineated by the Hollingshead Index (see Table 4). An examination of the choices made by mothers in each stratum indicates that variation in values parallels socioeconomic status rather closely:

a) The higher a mother's status, the higher the probability that she will choose consideration, curiosity, self-control, and (for boys)[9] happiness as highly desirable; curiosity is particularly likely to be chosen by mothers in the highest stratum.

b) The lower her status, the higher the probability that she will select obedience, neatness, and cleanliness; it appears, too, that mothers in the lowest stratum are more likely than are those in the highest to value *honesty*.

Mothers' values also are directly related to their own occupational positions and educational attainments, independently of their families' class status. (The family's class status has been indexed on the basis of the husband's occupation and education.) It happens that a considerable proportion of the mothers we have classified as working class hold white-collar jobs.[10] Those who do are, by and large, closer to middle-class mothers in their values than are other working-class mothers (see Table 5). But those who hold manual jobs are even further from middle-class mothers in their values than are working-class mothers who do not have jobs outside the home.

So, too, for mothers' educational attainments: a middle-class mother of *relatively* low educational attainment (one who has gone no further than graduation from high school) is less likely to value curiosity and more likely to value (for girls) neatness and cleanliness (see Table 6). A working-class mother of *relatively* high educational attainment (one who has at least graduated from high school) is more likely to value self-control for boys and both consideration and curiosity for girls. The largest differences obtain between those middle-class mothers of highest educational attainments and those working-class mothers of lowest educational attainments.

Even when we restrict ourselves to considerations of social status and its various ramifications, we find that values vary appreciably within each of the two broad classes. And, as sociologists would expect, variation in values proceeds along other major lines of social demarcation as well. Religious background is particularly useful as a criterion for distinguishing subcultures within the social classes. It does *not* exert so powerful an effect that Protestant mothers differ significantly from Catholic mothers of the same social class in their values.[11] But the combination of class and religious background does enable us to isolate groups that are more

---

[9] The choice of happiness is, as we have seen, related to social class for boys only. Consequently, in each comparison we shall make in this section the choice of happiness for *girls* will prove to be an exception to the general order.

[10] No middle-class mothers have manual jobs, so the comparable situation does not exist. Those middle-class women who do work (at white-collar jobs) are less likely to value neatness and cleanliness and more likely to value obedience and curiosity.

[11] The index here is based on the question "May I ask what is your religious background?"

Even when the comparison is restricted to Catholic mothers who send their children to Catholic school versus Protestant mothers of the same social class, there are no significant differences in values.

Jewish mothers (almost all of them in this sample are middle class) are very similar to middle-class Protestant mothers in their values, with two notable exceptions. More Jewish than Protestant mothers select popularity and ability to defend one's self—two values that are not related to social class.

TABLE 5 Working-class mothers' own occupations and their choice of characteristics as "most desirable" in a ten- or eleven-year-old child

	Proportion Who Select Each Characteristic		
CHARACTERISTIC	WHITE-COLLAR JOB	NO JOB	MANUAL JOB
Obedience	.26	.35	.53
Neatness, cleanliness	.16	.18	.42
Consideration	.39	.21	.05
Curiosity	.10	.04	.00
Self-control	.13	.14	.11
Happiness	.33	.40	.26
Boys	.32	.21	
Girls	.36	.59	
N	69	77	19

TABLE 6 Mothers' education and their choice of characteristics as "most desirable" in a ten- or eleven-year-old child

	Middle-Class Mothers			
	PROPORTION WHO SELECT EACH CHARACTERISTIC			
	Male Child		Female Child	
CHARACTERISTIC	AT LEAST SOME COLLEGE	HIGH-SCHOOL GRADUATE OR LESS	AT LEAST SOME COLLEGE	HIGH-SCHOOL GRADUATE OR LESS
Obedience	0.11	0.22	0.13	0.29
Neatness-cleanliness	.03	.09	.03*	.23
Consideration	.47	.35	.41	.37
Curiosity	.31*	.13	.31*	.06
Self-control	.33	.19	.19	.21
Happiness	0.50	0.41	0.59	0.40
N	36	54	32	52

	Working-Class Mothers			
	PROPORTION WHO SELECT EACH CHARACTERISTIC			
	Male Child		Female Child	
CHARACTERISTIC	AT LEAST HIGH-SCHOOL GRADUATE	LESS THAN HIGH-SCHOOL GRADUATE	AT LEAST HIGH-SCHOOL GRADUATE	LESS THAN HIGH-SCHOOL GRADUATE
Obedience	0.29	0.43	0.28	0.32
Neatness-cleanliness	.12	.14	.21	.35
Consideration	.32	.27	.33*	.14
Curiosity	.07	.05	.12*	.00
Self-control	.22*	.07	.16	.08
Happiness	0.27	0.27	0.47	0.43
N	41	44	43	37

* Difference between mothers of differing educational status statistically significant, 0.05 level or better, using Chi-squared test.

homogeneous in their values than are the social classes *in toto*. We find that there is an ordering, consistent for all class-related values, proceeding from middle-class Protestant mothers, to middle-class Catholic, to working-class Protestant, to working-class Catholic (see Table 7). Middle-class Protestants and working-class Catholics constitute the two extremes whose values are most dissimilar.

Another relevant line of social demarcation is the distinction between urban and rural background.[12] As we did for religious background, we can arrange the mothers into four groups delineated on the basis of class and rural-urban background in an order that is reasonably consistent for all class-related values. The order is: middle-class urban, middle-class rural, working-class urban, working-class rural (see Table 8). The extremes are middle-class mothers raised in the city and working-class mothers raised on farms.

Several other variables fail to differentiate mothers of the same social class into groups having appreciably different values. These include the mother's age, the size of the family, the ordinal position of the child in the family, the length of time the family has lived in the neighborhood, whether or not the mother has been socially mobile (from the status of her childhood family), and her class identification. Nor are these results a function of the large proportion of families of government workers included in the sample: wives of government employees do not differ from other mothers of the same social class in their values.

In sum, we find that it is possible to specify the relationship between social class and values more precisely by dividing the social classes into subgroups on the basis of other lines of social demarcation—but that social class seems to provide the single most relevant line of demarcation. . . .

This study does not provide disinterested observations of the parents' behavior. Our closest approximation derives from interviews with the parents themselves—interviews in which we questioned them in considerable detail about their relevant actions. Perhaps the most crucial of these data are those bearing on their actions in situations where their children behave in *disvalued* ways. We have, for example, questioned parents in some detail about what they do when their children lose their tempers. We began by asking whether or not the child in question "ever really loses his temper." From those parents who said that the child does lose his temper, we then proceeded to find out precisely what behavior they consider to be "loss of temper"; what they "generally do when he acts this way"; whether they "ever find it necessary to do anything else"; if so, what else they do, and "under what circumstances." Our concern here is with what the parent reports he does as a matter of last resort.[13]

[12] We asked: "Have you ever lived on a farm?" and then classified all mothers who had lived on a farm for some time other than simply summer vacations, prior to age fifteen, as having had a rural background.

Ordinarily, one further line of cultural demarcation would be considered at this point—nationality background. The present sample, however, is composed predominantly of parents who are at least second-generation, United States-born, so this is not possible.

[13] This comparison and those to follow are limited to parents who say that the child does in fact behave in the disvalued way, at least on occasion. (Approximately equal proportions of middle- and working-class mothers report that their children do behave in each of these ways.)

TABLE 7 Mothers' religious background and their choice of characteristics as "most desirable" in a ten- or eleven-year-old child

| | *Proportion Who Select Each Characteristic* | | | |
CHARACTERISTIC	MIDDLE-CLASS PROTESTANT	MIDDLE-CLASS CATHOLIC	WORKING-CLASS PROTESTANT	WORKING-CLASS CATHOLIC
Obedience	0.17	0.25	0.33	0.36
Neatness, cleanliness	.08	.15	.17	.27
Consideration	.36	.38	.26	.29
Curiosity	.24	.12	.07	.05
Self-control	.28	.15	.15	.09
Happiness	.47	.42	.38	.30
Boys	.48	.32	.35	.13
Girls	0.45	0.52	0.42	0.54
N	88	52	107	56

TABLE 8 Rural versus urban background of mothers and their choice of characteristics as "most desirable" in a ten- or eleven-year-old child

| | *Proportion Who Select Each Characteristic* | | | |
CHARACTERISTIC	MIDDLE-CLASS URBAN	MIDDLE-CLASS RURAL	WORKING-CLASS URBAN	WORKING-CLASS RURAL
Obedience	0.19	0.24	0.29	0.42
Neatness, cleanliness	.11	.12	.17	.25
Consideration	.42	.27	.31	.18
Curiosity	.19	.12	.07	.04
Self-control	.20	.33	.15	.11
Happiness	.47	.42	.41	.25
Boys	.44	.47	.28	.25
Girls	0.50	0.37	0.57	0.26
N	141	33	110	55

TABLE 9 Choice of "self-control" as "most desirable" characteristic and most extreme actions that mothers report they take when their children lose their tempers

| | *Middle Class* | | *Proportion Working Class* | | *Both* | |
	CHOOSE SELF-CONTROL	DON'T CHOOSE SELF-CONTROL	CHOOSE SELF-CONTROL	DON'T CHOOSE SELF-CONTROL	CHOOSE SELF-CONTROL	DON'T CHOOSE SELF-CONTROL
Punish physically	0.26	0.20	0.44	0.26	0.32	0.23
Isolate	.20	.11	.11	.12	.17	.11
Restrict activities, other punishments	.06	.05	.17	.14	.10	.10
Threaten punishment	.06	.03	.00	.02	.04	.02
Scold, admonish, etc.	.31	.40	.17	.31	.26	.36
Ignore	0.11	0.21	0.11	0.15	0.11	0.18
	1.00	1.00	1.00	1.00	1.00	1.00
N	35	113	18	113	53	226

Mothers who regard *self-control* as an important value are more likely to report that they punish the child—be it physically, by isolation, or by restriction of activities; they are unlikely merely to scold or to ignore his loss of temper altogether (see Table 9).

To punish a child who has lost his temper may not be a particularly effective way of inducing self-control. One might even have predicted that mothers who value self-control would be less likely to punish breaches of control, more likely to explain, even ignore. They do not, however, and we must put the issue more simply: mothers who assert the value are more likely to report that they apply negative sanctions in situations where the child violates that value. This response would certainly seem to conform to their value-assertion.

A parallel series of questions deals with the mother's reactions when her child "refuses to do what she tells him to do." Mothers who assert that they regard *obedience* as important are more likely to report that they punish in one way or another when their children refuse. [14] There is also evidence that mothers who value *consideration* are more likely to respond to their children's "fighting with other children," an action that need not necessarily be seen as inconsistent with consideration, by punishing them, or at least by separating them from the others. [15]

[14] The figures are 47 versus 29 per cent for middle-class mothers; 36 versus 18 per cent for working-class mothers.

[15] The figures are 42 versus 29 per cent for middle-class mothers; 61 versus 37 per cent for working-class mothers.

There is also some indication that *working-class* mothers who value *honesty* have been more prone to insist that their children make restitution when they have "swiped" something, but the number of mothers who say that their children have ever

In all three instances, then, the reports on parental reactions to behavior that seem to violate the value in question indicate that mothers who profess high regard for the value are more likely to apply negative sanctions.

INTERPRETATION

Our first conclusion is that parents, whatever their social class, deem it very important indeed that their children be honest, happy, considerate, obedient, and dependable.

The second conclusion is that, whatever the reasons may be, parents' values are related to their social position, particularly their class position.

There still remains, however, the task of interpreting the relationship between parents' social position and their values. In particular: What underlies the differences between the values of middle- and of working-class parents?

One relevant consideration is that some parents may "take for granted" values that others hold dear. For example, middle-class parents may take "neatness and cleanliness" for granted, while working-class parents regard it as highly desirable. But what does it mean to say that middle-class parents take neatness and cleanliness for granted? In essence, the argument is that middle-class par-

swiped something is too small for this evidence to be conclusive. (The figures for working-class mothers are 63 versus 35 per cent; for middle-class mothers, 38 versus 33 per cent.)

The interviews with the children provide further evidence that parents have acted consistently with their values—for example, children whose mothers assert high valuation of dependability are more likely to tell us that the reason their parents want them to do their chores is to train them in responsibility (not to relieve the parents of work).

ents value neatness and cleanliness as greatly as do working-class parents but not so greatly as they value such things as happiness and self-control. If this be the case it can only mean that in the circumstances of middle-class life neatness and cleanliness are easily enough attained to be of less immediate concern than are these other values.

A second consideration lies in the probability that these value-concepts have differing meanings for parents of different cultural backgrounds. For example, one might argue that honesty is a central standard of conduct for middle-class parents because they see honesty as meaning truthfulness; and that it is more a quality of the person for working-class parents because they see it as meaning trustworthiness. Perhaps so; but to suggest that a difference in meaning underlies a difference in values raises the further problem of explaining this difference in meaning.

It would be reasonable for working-class parents to be more likely to see honesty as trustworthiness. The working-class situation is one of less material security and less assured protection from the dishonesty of others. For these reasons, trustworthiness is more at issue for working-class than for middle-class parents.

Both considerations lead us to view differences in the values of middle- and working-class parents in terms of their differing circumstances of life and, by implication, their conceptions of the effects that these circumstances may have on their children's future lives. We believe that parents are most likely to accord high priority to those values that seem both *problematic*, in the sense that they are difficult of achievement, and *important*, in the sense that failure to achieve them would affect the child's future adversely. From this perspective

it is reasonable that working-class parents cannot afford to take neatness and cleanliness as much for granted as can middle-class parents. It is reasonable, too, that working-class parents are more likely to see honesty as implying trustworthiness and that this connotation of honesty is seen as problematic.

These characteristics—honesty and neatness—are important to the child's future precisely because they assure him a respectable social position. Just as "poor but honest" has traditionally been an important line of social demarcation, their high valuation of these qualities may express working-class parents' concern that their children occupy a position unequivocally above that of persons who are not neat or who are not scrupulously honest. These are the qualities of respectable, worthwhile people.

So, too, is obedience. The obedient child follows his parents' dictates rather than his own standards. He acts, in his subordinate role as a child, in conformity with the prescriptions of established authority.

Even in the way they differentiate what is desirable for boys from what is desirable for girls, working-class mothers show a keen appreciation of the qualities making for respectable social position.

The characteristics that middle-class parents are more likely to value for their children are internal standards for governing one's relationships with other people and, in the final analysis, with one's self. It is not that middle-class parents are less concerned than are working-class parents about social position. The qualities of person that assure respectability may be taken for granted, but in a world where social relationships are determinative of position, these standards of conduct are both more problematic and more important.

The middle-class emphasis on internal standards is evident in their choice of the cluster of characteristics centering around honesty; in their being less likely than are working-class parents to value obedience and more likely to value self-control and consideration; and in their seeing obedience as inconsistent with both consideration and curiosity. The child is to act appropriately, not because his parents tell him to, but because he wants to. Not conformity to authority, but inner control; not because you're told to but because you take the other person into consideration—these are the middle-class ideals.

These values place responsibility directly upon the individual. He cannot rely upon authority, nor can he simply conform to what is presented to him as proper. He should be impelled to come to his own understanding of the situa-tion.[16] He is to govern himself in such a way as to be able to act consistently with his principles. The basic importance of relationship to self is explicit in the concept of self-control. It is implicit, too, in consideration—a standard that demands of the individual that he respond sympathetically to others' needs even if they be in conflict with his own; and in the high valuation of honesty as central to other standards of conduct: "to thine own self be true."

Perhaps, considering this, it should not be surprising that so many middle-class mothers attribute first-rank importance to happiness, even for boys. We cannot assume that their children's happiness is any less important to working-class mothers than it is to middle-class mothers; in fact, working-class mothers are equally likely to value happiness for *girls*. For their sons, however, happiness is second choice to honesty and obedience. Apparently, middle-class mothers can afford instead to be concerned about their son's happiness. And perhaps they are right in being concerned. We have noted that those middle-class mothers who deem it most important that their sons outdistance others are especially likely to be concerned about their sons' happiness; and even those mothers who do not are asking their children to accept considerable responsibility.

[16] Curiosity provides a particularly interesting example of how closely parents' values are related to their circumstances of life and expectations: the proportion of mothers who value curiosity rises very slowly from status level to status level until we reach the wives of professionals and the more highly educated businessmen; then it jumps suddenly (see Table 4). The value is given priority in precisely that portion of the middle class where it is most appropriate and where its importance for the child's future is most apparent.

Family Interaction, Values, and Achievement*

Fred L. Strodtbeck

. . . we [chose] those values which appeared most likely to have accounted for the differences in occupational achievement after these two groups [Jews and Southern Italians] came to the United States. This task entailed . . . a comparison of Italian-Jewish values. . . . Finally the problem narrowed to a comparison at five points, as follows:

1 Man's sense of personal responsibility in relation to the external world

. . . For the present-day achiever in the United States, rational mastery of the situation has taken the place of the "hard work" of the Calvinists, and the threat of almost continuous review of his record has been equated with anxiety over eventual salvation. There is no necessary personal deprivation which must be endured; indeed, one's accomplishment can be facilititated by "breaks." But the breaks are now of the individual's own making; it is a matter of being available with what is needed at the right place and at the right time. Just as the breaks are not doled out by a beneficent power, neither are failures. Whatever failure an individual has suffered could always have been foreseen and circumvented if the individual had been sufficiently alert. For the modern achiever there is no legitimate excuse for failure. His sense of personal respon-

sibility for controlling his destiny is enormous.

Old-culture Jewish beliefs appear to be congruent in many, if not all, respects with such a belief in a rational mastery of the world. For the Jew, there was always the expectation that everything could be understood, if perhaps not controlled. Emphasis on learning as a means of control was strong. Neither religious nor secular learning, once attained (unlike the Protestant's salvation and the achiever's status), was in continual jeopardy. For men who were learned in trades but not religious scholars, the expectations of charity to others of the community who were less fortunate was a continuing goad to keep working; but if misfortune befell a former benefactor, the community understood. The sense of personal responsibility existed along with a responsibility of the community for the individual which eased somewhat the precariousness associated with "all or none" expectations of the individual.

For the Italian, there was no real logic in striving; the best-laid plans of man might twist awry. Misfortune originated "out there," out beyond the individual. *Destino* decreed whether a particular event would or would not come to pass. A sort of passive alertness was thus inculcated. Although no one knew when he might be slated for a lucky break, at the same time there was no motivation for any rational undertaking of heroic proportions; such an undertaking might be *destined* to fail.

Adapted from David C. McClelland, Alfred L. Baldwin, Urie Bronfenbrenner and Fred L. Strodtbeck, Talent and Society, pp. 135–194. Copyright 1948, Van Nostrand Company, Inc., Princeton, New Jersey.

2 Familism versus loyalty to a larger collectivity

. . . The old Jewish pattern sanctioned separation from the family for purposes of business and education, and there was a distinct consciousness that a man's first responsibility was toward his children. That is, obligations were primarily from those who have more to those who have less—from which, practically speaking, it followed that children need not always stay to nurture parents who might be better off than they were. Although the Jews did not go so far as the present American achiever in weakening the ties to parents, the pattern contrasts sharply with that of the Southern Italians who put loyalty upward to the extended family first.

3 Perfectability of man

An aspect of Calvinism perhaps best captured for popular consumption in *Poor Richard's Almanac* by Benjamin Franklin is the insistence that at every moment of every day a man must work to improve himself. The old Jewish culture also, with its emphasis on religious scholarship and study, represented a similar belief in the responsibility for self-improvement. For the achiever in the United States, this perfectability has, in one sense, been relaxed; but insofar as it remains, it has become even more stringent. Now, we are told, the improvement should be acquired in a relaxed manner, with no apparent effort; self-improvement is something to be "enjoyed" not "endured" as earlier. But in any case, an interest in education should be (and has been) high because it is so obviously one of the ways in which man perfects himself.

For the Southern Italian there has always been considerable doubt as to whether man could perfect himself or, indeed, whether he need try. According to his interpretation of Catholicism, he must conscientiously fulfill his duties, but his "good works" do not form a rationalized system of life. Good works may be used to atone for particular sins, or, as Weber points out, stored up as a sort of insurance toward the end of one's life; but there is no need to live in every detail the ideal life, for there is always the sacrament of absolution. Furthermore, the Southern Italian sees man as living in an uneasy peace with his passions, which from time to time must be expected to break through. Man is really not perfectable—he is all too human. So he would do well not to drive himself or his mind too relentlessly in trying to reach that impossible goal, perfection.

4 Consciousness of the larger community

The Calvinist's dictum that "each man is his brother's keeper" has given way in the United States to a less moralistic rationale based upon a recognition of the interdependencies in modern society. Just as the whole Jewish community could vicariously participate in the charities of its wealthiest members, there is a sense in which the strengthening of various aspects of American society is recognized as contributing to the common good.

The Jew from the older culture, enabled by his success to assume a responsibility for the community, had little choice in the matter. The social pressures were great, and they were ordinarily responded to with pride and rewarded by prominence in the community forum. The identification went beyond the extended family. The giver was not to be rewarded in kind; his reward came from community recognition. Such community identification—as contrasted with family identification—has not been highly developed among Southern Italians. Reduced sensitivity to community goals is believed to inhibit the near altruistic orientations which in adolescence and early maturity lead individuals to make prolonged personal sacrifices to enter such professions as medicine or the law.

5 Power relations

. . . The old-culture Jew, on the other hand, did not see power in the context of some external system of pre-established impersonal relationships. He tended, like the Calvinist, to translate power questions into other terms—to the equity of a particular bargain, for example; but unlike the Calvinist, he saw these relationships always as specific, both as to persons and content, and not part of a larger system. His primary concern was to make his relationships good with others with whom he was in close contact over a particular issue. The specificity of his relations with others, including his separation of business and family matters, is also like the functional specificity of modern bureaucratic society, but again unlike it in overlooking the *system* of such functional relationships.

The old-culture Italian tended to see power entirely in immediate interpersonal terms. Power was the direct expression of who can *control* the behavior of another rather than who knows more for a job in an impersonal system. "Who's boss?" was his constant inquiry. Every relationship he turned into a "for me-against me" or "over me-under me" polarity.

THE NEW HAVEN SAMPLE

In the process of developing the sampling frame in New Haven, further data were obtained which bear upon Italian-Jewish cultural differences. A questionnaire was administered to 1151 boys between the ages of 14 and 17 (and a somewhat larger number of girls) in the New Haven public and parochial schools. Data obtained on this questionnaire were utilized primarily to identify a set of third-generation Italian and Jewish boys, who were in turn stratified by their school performance and socio-economic status. The questionnaire touched generally upon values and more particularly upon materials relating to occupational choice, parental expectations, parental control, educational aspirations, and balance of power within the family.[1]

Boys from Catholic families who reported one or more paternal and one or more maternal grandparent born in Italy were considered Italian. Boys who reported the religion of both their parents as Jewish were considered Jewish. Socio-economic status was determined from information provided by the son relating to his parents' education and his father's occupation. . . . In terms of these two criteria the following frequencies were obtained:

Socio-economic Status	Italian	Jewish	Other
High (classes 1 and 2; owners of large businesses; major and minor professionals)	8	24	52
Medium (classes 3 and 4; owners of small businesses; white-collar workers; supervisors)	80	66	213
Low (classes 5, 6, and 7; skilled workers; laborers)	182	17	455
Unclassified	15	2	59
	285	109	779

[1] A more detailed form of this questionnaire has been deposited as Document number 5501 with the ADI Auxiliary Publications

To demonstrate even more clearly the differential status distribution of the two groups, one may construct an index number using the distribution of "Others" as a base. For example, 52 out of the total 720 in column 3 (excluding the unclassified "Others") are of high socio-economic status. On a pro rata basis, 19.5 Italians of high status would be expected. Significantly fewer than this—only 8, or 41 per cent of the expected—turn up. For the Jews of high status, 310 per cent of the expected are observed. The full set of indices is as follows:

Percentage of expectation

Socio-economic Status	Italian	Jewish
High	41	310
Middle	100	209
Low	107	25

We used the boy's achievement in school as a criterion of his own performance, just as the status of the family might be used as a criterion of the father's performance. Toward this end, each boy's performance on intelligence and achievement tests was inspected, and his grade performance in terms of the norms of the particular school predicted. When the boy's school grades exceeded the expected performance, he was considered an over-achiever; when his grades fell short, he was classified as an under-achiever. The different standards and testing systems of the various schools made it necessary to adjust slightly the degree to which the boy had to depart

from expectation before he was considered an over- or under-achiever.

Being an over-achiever proved to be positively related to higher socio-economic status. This may be illustrated with the 674 "other" students for whom full information was available.

Socio-economic Status	Percentage of Over-achievers	
High	47%	(47)
Medium	35%	(201)
Low	27%	(426)

It thus becomes apparent that since socio-economic status is not an analytic element of central interest, provision must be made for controlling or removing its effect if other variables are to be understood. The standard procedure for making this correction is a factorial design. Forty-eight boys, according to our estimate, could be studied intensively, and they were selected from the larger frame of cases to be allocated as follows.[2]

Socio-economic Status	Italian Boys School Achievement		Jewish Boys School Achievement	
	"OVER"	"UNDER"	"OVER"	"UNDER"
High	4	4	4	4
Medium	4	4	4	4
Low	4	4	4	4
		Total 48		

. . . To initiate our relations with the families, each of the 48 boys was first contacted in the school during

Project, Photoduplication Service, Library of Congress, Washington 25, D.C. A copy may be secured by citing the Document number and by remitting $2.50 for photoprints, or $1.75 for 35 mm. microfilm. Advance payment is required. Make checks or money orders payable to: Chief, Photoduplication Service, Library of Congress.

[2] In making the final selection, it was necessary in scattered instances to use families with parents who were born elsewhere, but who had come to this country as very young children. The socio-economic status classification is in all cases based upon the interviewer's notes obtained in the interviews with the parents. One Italian family was obtained from a residential community adjacent to New Haven.

his study period and told that he had been selected by a random process to assist with the development of a new kind of test. The "test" consisted of a set of six 8 × 10 pictures, similar in appearance to the TAT cards, designed to elicit *n* Achievement scores.[3] These pictures were presented to the boy one at a time with instructions to make up a good story around the picture "about real people and real problems." The administration procedure adopted was comparable to what McClelland and his co-workers have described as "neutral" [1, pp. 100 ff.], and it was not assumed that the boy's achievement motivation was any more mobilized than it would ordinarily be in a school situation. The girl psychologist who administered the pictures was young and attractive; the atmosphere was casual and businesslike.

After the session, the boy's cooperation was sought in arranging a visit to his home at a time when it would be possible to talk with him and his parents. On that same day, a letter was sent from the principal explaining the investigation and stating a hope that the parents would cooperate. The experimenter then phoned the parents and completed arrangements to visit the home. The objective of the investigation was explained to the parents as an effort to illuminate ways in which parents and sons go about making occupational decisions.

The parents were almost unanimously cooperative (as soon as they were assured that we did not have anything to sell). Our only refusals came from two

families—one where there was illness and one in which the father would not participate.

THE EXPERIMENTAL PROCEDURE

In addition to the questionnaire administered to the boy at school, questionnaires were given to the father, mother, and son in the home. Some questions were asked of the son both in school and at home so that instances of shift in response might be checked against other family information.

The team visiting each home consisted of an experimenter and an assistant, who carried portable sound equipment. As soon as the answer sheets had been completed, the assistant compiled a set of items for discussion. These he selected, if the distribution of original responses made it possible, with an eye to making three coalitions of the following type:

(a) Mother and son agree, father disagrees;

(b) Father and mother agree, son disagrees;

(c) Father and son agree, mother disagrees.

While this collation of responses was being carried out by the assistant, the experimenter gave the family other forms to fill out and subsequently moved them into position around the recorder. He then presented the first item to the family with the following instructions:

> We've looked over your responses to the first set of items and, in many cases, all three of you answered the items in the very same way. In some cases, two of you agreed, but the third person picked a different alternative. What we would like to do is ask the three of you as a group to consider again some of these items on which the agreement was not complete. We would like you to talk over the item

---

[3] Briefly described, the pictures are as follows: (1) boy in classroom; (2) operation in background, boy in foreground; (3) man and boy in foreground, horses in background; (4) young man in foreground, crossroads in background; (5) two male figures in workshop; and (6) boy with broom in foreground and several teen-agers in background.

until you understand clearly why each person marked the item as he did. We want you to try to agree on one choice which would best represent the opinion of the family, if this is possible.

The experimenter then read the item in question saying, roughly:

Mr.———said———, and Mrs.——— said, and (calling the son by his first name) said———. Talk this over and see if it's possible to agree on one of the choices. When you are finished, call me.

. . . The details of the revealed-difference routine were evolved by a series of trial-and-error modifications which may be briefly described. If one contrasts conversations between husbands and wives obtained by concealed recording devices with those obtained by a recorder in full view, one finds no striking differences. Evidently (a) the importance of resolving a difference of opinion with a person with whom one had a solid relationship, and (b) the concurrent requirement of having each member act so that his behavior is consistent with the expectations developed in previous interaction, combine to give a measure which is not greatly influenced by the recording paraphernalia. At the heart of the process is the necessity for "revealing a difference," as has been most clearly demonstrated in a Cornell study by Arthur J. Vidich [7]. Vidich attempted to have married couples discover and discuss whatever differences they might have about disposing of a legacy. In this he encountered great resistance, with a tendency for couples to be most interested in explaining their respective thinking to the experimenter instead of to one another. Vidich's experience suggests that the group cohesiveness which, when a difference is revealed, creates the motivation for interaction operates to conceal and resist differences when they arise

under conditions which the group can control. . . .

To illustrate the experimental procedure concretely, we will quote from the discussion in one Italian home, along with scattered background information, Michael's father, a machinist who stopped attending school just before graduating from high school, conceived of himself as a strict disciplinarian.

I probably should be ashamed to say it, but up to a few months ago I used to beat him, I really let him have it. I still believe that sparing the rod spoils the child. I still do let him have it every so often. I wore out a strap on that boy. You can't overlook badness. It's got to be nipped in the bud.

In his discussion with the interviewers, Michael's father gave this picture of his own discussions with Michael:

Sometimes I feel he keeps quiet when I want him to put up an argument, especially when I look at things the wrong way; maybe I misunderstand the whole situation. I may be wrong, maybe I came home crabby, the kid may have an argument on his hands with me. He may be right; I may be wrong. Well, my tone of voice, my manner makes him keep quiet. Maybe he had all the right in the world in his argument, and he keeps quiet about the whole situation, and then he gets heck from me for not putting up an argument.

. . . The protocol of their discussion of the first revealed difference question is as follows:

Michael's Family

Experimenter: Two fathers were discussing their boys, one of whom was a brilliant student and the other a promising athlete. Some people believe that one father was more fortunate than the other father. Do you think that the father with the athletic son or the father with the studious son was more fortunate? Michael said that the father with the athletic son was the more fortunate and (the father and mother) said that the father with the brilliant son was more fortunate. We would like you to discuss this.

Father: Why do you say the ah, ah, father of an athlete?(8)[4]

Michael: Because if the son is an athlete he must be getting good marks in order to play sports.(5) He must be getting good marks (6) and—

Father: Not necessarily.(10) Not necessarily.(10)

Mother: While he's out playing, he doesn't get his studies.(5)

Father: No!(10) That's not it either.(10) Let's look at it this way.(6) Forget about the school part.(6) Don't attach the athletic life to the school life. (6) Don't make it—Don't make it that the boy in order to be an athlete has to have good marks. (6) We know that. (5) But take it as a kid's life; (6) as a guy's life. (6) Would you think that a guy who was a good athlete would get more out of life; (8) get ahead in life more than a kid who was smart in his studies and made every grade just like that? (5)

Michael: Well, the way you're asking the question, you're putting it a little different than the way it reads on the paper, I think. (10)

Father: No! (10) No! (10) I'm not. (10) It means the same thing. (10) It's just that I probably made it a little longer. (5)

Michael: Well, what is the last sentence on the paper exactly? (7)

Father: Look. Do you . . . (sternly) . . .? (12) I'll read the whole thing. (6)

Michael: (Attempts to protest that rereading is not necessary.) (11)

Father: Two fathers were discussing their boys; (6) one of whom was a brilliant student and the other an athlete of great promise. (6) (continues to read question given above.)

Michael: (inaudible remark) Athletic son . . . (11)

[4]The scores in parentheses are Bales' Interaction Process categories [2].

Father: Well. (6) I think if ah, ah, my son were studious and he pursued any vocation at all, (6) Michael (6), I wouldn't worry as much as I would even if I knew he were a brilliant football player. (5) What good is that? ah (8)

Michael: Well, it's like I said before. (10) If he's good in sports, he must be good in marks. (5)

Father: Yes, Michael. (3) What good is being a football player, ah, towards helping you to become something? (8) An engineer or draftsman or something? (6) Football and baseball, there's a limit to it. (5) You've got to live with it and make something out of it. (5)

Michael: I don't know. (10) What do you think, Maw? (8)

Mother: I'd still say the studious type. (5)

Father: Try to make your son understand, Mother, that even if he were a great football or basketball player, after he's 35 or 40 he can't play any more. (4)

Mother: Play any more. (3) That's right, Michael. (5)

Father: What are you going to do then? (8) Live on your laurels? (12)

Michael: No! (3) No! (3) You'd have to quit by then (3) but I mean, I mean you'd have to have good marks before. (10)

Mother: Yes, but—(10)

Father: In other words you agree. (5) You agree you have to be studious first? (8)

All protocols were scored directly from the recordings and were not transcribed. The subsequent processing of the data may be illustrated with Michael's family's protocol. In Table 1 the number of acts by each family member is shown for each decision in each of the three coalition patterns. Previous research [4] leads one to expect that persons who talk most should have most power in the sense of winning the most decisions; and that an isolate role, necessitating an explanation of one's position to two others, should also increase participation.

In Michael's family, the differentia-

TABLE 1 Acts by person by decision for Michael's family

TYPE OF DECISION	Originator			
	FATHER	MOTHER	SON	TOTAL
	47	16	28	91
Fa vs. Mo-So	65	19	37	121
	76	23	41	140
	188	58	106	352
	39	16	17	72
Mo vs. Fa-So	31	16	10	57
	52	39	43	134
	122	71	70	263
	52	6	17	75
So vs. Fa-Mo	23	4	21	48
	47	2	26	75
	122	12	64	198
Total	432	141	240	813

tion in participation is marked, with the father accounting for more than half of the total acts originated. Even in instances where others are the isolates, he continues to dominate. To anticipate the statistical analysis, the acts originated are converted to percentage values, then transformed to angular readings in this way:

	Father	Mother	Son
Original acts	432	141	240
Percentage	53%	17%	30%
Arc sine	47	24	33

Throughout the statistical analysis and in subsequent tables, arc sine values are used to stabilize the variance.

To form a power score based upon decisions won, it is convenient to assign arbitrary scores, so that winning, or holding one's position when in the minority, is weighted more heavily when one is an isolate than when one is a member of the larger coalition. The conventions are as follows:

Nature of Decision	Coalition Members		Minority Member
Coalition Wins	1	1	0
Minority Wins	0	0	2
No Decision	.5	.5	1

In Michael's family, the resultant measure of power is markedly differentiated:

	Father	Mother	Son
Original Score	9.5	5.0	3.5
Percentage	53%	28%	19%
Arc Sine	47	32	26

and it may be noted that Michael's father, who participated most heavily, also demonstrated the highest power. Michael had the second highest participation, but ranked third in power. . . .

THE V-SCALE AND OTHER ATTITUDINAL DIFFERENCES

Fifteen items were included in the original screening questionnaire. These items, adapted from research of the Harvard Seminar in Social Mobility,[5] dealt very generally with the types of value differences which have been previously described as characterizing older Italian-Jewish differences. Not all points in the value analysis were covered in the questionnaire. The analysis was completed late in the study, and the questionnaire had been the original device for selecting subjects for the study by the revealed difference technique.

In the first stage of the analysis, we were looking for items which would discriminate at the .05 level between overachieving and under-achieving students

V-score	Percentage Above Average	Number
0	0	2
1	0	6
2	17	46
3	20	82
4	23	146
5	26	207
6	30	226
7	42	220
8	51	76

(both Italians and Jews being excluded from this comparison). The original set of 15 items was reduced to 8 (see Table 2). Although in this process items of uneven coverage resulted, it was nonetheless apparent that these scores could be combined (1 for achievement-related responses, 0 for the alternate responses) to provide a moderately efficient discrimination of students receiving above average grades.

Since neither the Italians nor the Jews had been involved in the original computations, Italian-Jewish differences provide an independent check on the dis-

tribution of one type of "achievement potential" in the two populations. From inferences made on the basis of status mobility, it was predicted that Jews would have higher achievement-related responses than Italians. Table 2 shows that this prediction was significantly confirmed for six of the eight items, with no differences observed in the other two cases. . . .

As to the validity of the scale so developed, three bits of evidence are relevant.

(1) The first is based upon the way the fathers responded to the V-items on the questionnaires administered in the home. One assumes that second-generation fathers of higher status have by their own work personally accounted for some appreciable part of their mobility. In terms of such an assumption, one might preeict that fathers of higher status would have higher V-scores than those of lower status. These data, presented in Table 3, may be analyzed so that each effect associated with the factorial design (including status) is isolated. The form of the analysis is as follows:

Source of Variation	Degrees of Freedom
Corrected sum of squares	47
between groups	11
1. Linear SES	1
2. Quadratic SES	1
3. Italian (I) v Jews (J)	1
4. (O) v (U) Achievers	1
5. I v J × O v U	1
6. I v J × Linear SES	1
7. I v J × Quadratic SES	1
8. O v U × Linear SES	1
9. O v U × Quadratic SES	1
10. I v J × O v U × Linear SES	1
11. I v J × O v U × Quadratic SES	1
Residual	36

[5] The assistance of Florence Kluckhohn, Talcott Parsons, and Samuel A. Stouffer, joint directors of this seminar, is gratefully acknowledged.

It will be our practice throughout the analysis to examine the variance associated with each degree of freedom.

TABLE 2 V-scale items, factor loadings and Italian-Jewish response levels

Factor Loading			Percentage Who Disagree	
FACTOR I "MASTERY"	FACTOR II "INDEPEN- DENCE OF FAMILY"	ITEMS	JEWS	ITALIANS
.64	.00	(1) Planning only makes a person unhappy since your plans hardly ever work out anyhow.	90	62
.49	.28	(2) When a man is born, the success he's going to have is already in the cards, so he might as well accept it and not fight against it.	98	85
.58	.15	(3) Nowadays, with world conditions the way they are, the wise person lives for today and lets tomorrow take care of itself.	(80)*	(79)
.04	.60	(4) Even when teen-agers get married, their main loyalty still belongs to their fathers and mothers.	64	46
.21	.60	(5) When the time comes for a boy to take a job, he should stay near his parents, even if it means giving up a good job opportunity.	91	82
.29	.68	(6) Nothing in life is worth the sacrifice of moving away from your parents.	82	59
−.02	.28	(7) The best kind of job to have is one where you are part of an organization all working together even if you don't get individual credit.	54	28
−.05	.00	(8) It's silly for a teen-ager to put money into a car when the money could be used to get started in business or for an education.**	(65)	(63)

* The difference is not significant at the .05 level for pairs of values in parentheses; for the remaining values the differences are significant at the .05 level or greater.

** Percent "Agree" reported for this item.

In this instance three significant effects are observed:

Primary Sources of Variation for Father's V-scores

Line 1. Higher SES groups have higher values	$F = 10.85$ $p \leq 0.01$
Line 4. Fathers of over-achievers are higher than fathers of under-achievers	$F = 4.74$ $p \leq 0.05$
Line 6. There is a greater linear SES trend for Jews than Italians	$F = 4.16$ $p \leq 0.05$

Of primary interest is the relation between the father's class position and the V-score. This effect is significant and in keeping with the hypothesis that persons who have achieved higher status have higher V-scores. We must not, of course, lean too heavily upon this finding, because we have not demonstrated that the higher V-scores preceded the attainment of higher status; the opposite might well be the case. But if there had been no relationship, or a reversed relationship, then there would have been less ground for believing that a high V-score in high school would necessarily be associated with status mobility. The observed finding leaves open the possibility that the higher V-scores of the higher-status fathers may have been continuously operative and contributed to the status attained.

From line 6 one learns that there is a greater difference between the V-score of high-status and low-status Jewish fathers than there is between high- and low-status Italian fathers. This finding, which in itself appears to be of little consequence, serves merely to draw our attention to the fact that, save for this exception, there were *no* Italian-Jewish differences. That is, the two items—stratification by class and educational achievement of son—remove the Italian-Jewish differences found originally in the school population.

(2). From line 4 one obtains a second, slightly different, validation of the significance of the V-score: fathers of over-achievers have higher V-scores than fathers of under-achievers.

Would the same effects be present for mothers, or is the pattern of their relationship different? To conserve space, the table of actual values for mothers'

TABLE 3 Fathers' V-score by SES, ethnicity, over- and under-achievement

SOCIO-ECONOMIC STATUS SES	Italians		Jews	
	OVER-ACHIEVERS	UNDER-ACHIEVERS	OVER-ACHIEVERS	UNDER-ACHIEVERS
High	6	6	8	7
	6	6	8	6
	8	5	8	7
	6	7	8	7
Medium	5	6	6	8
	7	2	7	6
	8	6	8	8
	7	5	7	6
Low	5	5	5	6
	6	8	6	3
	4	5	6	4
	7	6	6	6

V-score is omitted, and the results of an analysis of variance examined directly.

Primary Sources of Variation for Mothers' V-scores

Line 3.	Jewish mothers are higher than Italian mothers	$F = 4.46$ $p \leq 0.05$

In this case, mothers of higher socio-economic status are not differentiated from those of lower socio-economic status. As an after-the-fact speculation, one might say that the status of a family is primarily established by the husband's occupation; therefore there is less reason to believe that higher-status wives personally contributed by extra-familial efforts to the mobility. Hence the lack of SES effects would not controvert the finding in the case of the fathers. Equally interesting is the fact that the mothers of over-achieving boys do not show disproportionately higher V-scores. Again the mother's contribution to a highly achieving son might involve something other than parallel attitudes about the universe, family ties, work relations, and the like. The ethnic difference in the case of the mothers is not removed by the stratification; the expected cultural relationship persists; Jewish women have higher V-scores than Italian women. These data are provocative. Yet the one instance of V-score variation which goes toward validation—that is, the ethnic difference—is counterbalanced by the absence of higher V-scores for mothers of over-achievers.

(3) There remains, of course, the matter of particular interest—the sons' V-scores:

Primary Sources of Variation for Sons' V-scores

Line 4.	Over-achievers have higher V-scores than under-achievers	$F = 5.17$ $p \leq 0.05$

For sons, as for fathers, there are, after stratification, no ethnic differences, but over-achieving boys are significantly higher than under-achieving boys. In so far as both Italian and Jewish boys were excluded from the sample at the time the eight items were selected, this finding constitutes, on an independent sub-population, a third instance of validation of the V-scale as a measure of values which are associated with actual achievement. When both parents are in agreement on the positive alternative of the V-score item—or other attitudinal points, for that matter—then the son may be prevented from playing the parents against each other. It is notable that instances of joint V-score agreement in the positive direction are significantly more frequent among Jewish parents than Italian parents.

Primary Sources of Variation for Joint Parental "Achievement Positive" Responses to V-items

Line 1.	Parents from higher SES groups agree more	$F = 9.78$ $p \leq 0.01$
Line 3.	Jewish parents agree more than Italians	$F = 13.43$ $p \leq 0.01$

Choice of occupation for the son is another point at which the value structure of the family members is obviously apparent. Data on this point were obtained from the questionnaire. All the boys in our high-school sample, as well as the parents of the 48 boys in the intensive sample, were asked whether they would be pleased or disappointed if the sons chose the following occupations (listed by status rank):

1. Doctor, advertising executive
2. Druggist, jewelry store owner
3. Bank teller, bookkeeper
4. Carpenter, auto mechanic
5. Mail carrier, bus driver
6. Night watchman, furniture mover

The results have been reported in full elsewhere [6]. What is relevant here is that in the total sample, the slope of self-reported pleasure in the occupations by Jewish boys was significantly steeper ($p < .01$) than for Italian boys, meaning that the Jewish boys rejected the occupations of lower status more decidedly. The same result was obtained for the parents; Jewish parents rejected lower-status occupations for their sons more decidedly ($p < .05$) than Italian parents. Finally, there was more agreement among parents and sons ($p < .05$) in the Jewish than in the Italian families.

The difference in emphasis upon education also stands out. For example, the percentage of the respondents in the large sample who "want to" and "expect to" go to college is sharply differentiated between Italians and Jews; but, interestingly enough, Italians are not differentiated from "others."

SES	Italians	Jews	Other
High	(75%)*	83%	77%
Middle	45%	83%	51%
Low	38%	(71%)*	31%

* Values in parentheses are based on low frequencies. See p. 366 *supra*.

Some of the same factors differentiate over- and under-achievers. In cases where boys differed from their parents, the over-achieving boys preferred the higher status occupations significantly more frequently than under-achieving boys ($p < .01$). Also there was more initial consensus among the three family members over all the "revealed differences" in the families of over-achievers. In short, these data support strongly the conclusion based on V-scale results: Jews have values more likely to promote high achievement than Italians do, and there is greater agreement among family members. The additional findings agree with the V-scale also in that they show higher

occupational aspiration and greater family consensus among over-achievers than among under-achievers.

ACHIEVEMENT SCORES

A point of articulation between the V-score and prior research arises in connection with the n Achievement scores. The scores for each boy in the sample, based on the presence or absence of achievement imagery in the stories written about the pictures shown him, have been analyzed in the manner illustrated with the V-scores.

Primary Sources of Variation for Sons' n Achievement Scores

Line 4. Over-achievers have higher n Achievement than under-achievers	$F = 4.79$ $p \leq .05$

In view of previously reported differences between Italians and Jews as to "age of mastery," the absence of an Italian-Jewish difference is surprising, notwithstanding the stratification. The small difference present, an average of 3.2 stories with n Achievement imagery for Italians to 3.7 for Jews, is in the expected direction but *not* significant. The difference between over-achievers (3.9) and underachievers (3.0) is significant at the 0.05 level and constitutes an additional confirmation of the relationship of n Achievement to high-school grades [3].

FAMILY INTERACTION AND POWER

Examination of the family patterns of interaction in terms of Bales interaction process categories showed no significant relationships to socio-economic status, to ethnicity, to over- and under-achievement, to V-scores, or to n Achievement. Only two significant effects emerged for the supportiveness index. The first was a greater supportiveness toward their sons by Italian than by Jewish fathers. The interpretation seems to be that there was a tendency for the Italian father to look upon his son as a less mature person; hence it suggests a denial of near-adult status. Second, mothers were more supportive to fathers as the status of the fathers improved.

The point to be emphasized is the very great similarity of Italian and Jewish interaction patterns. If there has been differential achievement—and according to our data this is indeed the case—then one must conclude that ethnic differences in family interaction are not of great relevance in explaining it. . . .

[With respect to power] the significant trends within the family are as follows:

Primary Source of Variation in Family Power Sources

Fathers:

Line 1. Fathers from higher SES groups have higher power scores. $F = 11.82$ $p \leq 0.01$

Line 8. There is a greater linear SES trends for fathers of over-achievers than for fathers of under-achievers $F = 5.09$ $p \leq 0.05$

Mothers:

Line 3. Jewish mothers have higher power scores than Italian mothers $F = 4.19$ $p \leq 0.05$

Sons:

Line 1. Sons from higher SES groups have lower power scores $F = 6.47$ $F \leq 0.05$

The higher the status of the families, the less the power of the sons and the greater the power of the fathers (just as the sons had reported). The mothers' power scores do not seem to be influenced by status, but Jewish mothers have more power than Italian mothers. One significant interaction is found; namely, the trend over status is steeper for fathers of over-achievers than for fathers of under-achievers. There were no ethnic differences in fathers' and sons' power scores and no differences in the sons' power scores related to school achievement.

To test the assertions that there were more departures from equality among Italians than Jews, a coefficient was formed by squaring the mean deviations of the power scores within each family. Analysis of this measure by the standard techniques reveals:

Primary Sources of Variation for Coefficient of Dispersion of Family Power (Transformed to Rankits)

Line 3. Power dispersion is greater in Italian than Jewish families $F = 3.15$ $p \leq 0.05$

In short, our data show less equality among the family members in Italian than in Jewish families. This fact agrees with the ratings of power in Jewish-Italian families in the Greater Boston area reported earlier, as well as with the distribution of parental power as reported by Jewish and Italian boys in our own larger sample.

Although participation scores, like the other Bales categories, are not related to any of the variables in this study, they were significantly associated with power scores, as in the author's previous study of husband-wife interaction [5]. The residual correlations (after effects of classificatory variables are removed) are for the father .57 ($p < .001$), for the mother .48 ($p < .01$), for the son .56 ($p < .001$). In short, he who talks most wins most.

SUMMARY

. . . There is . . . evidence . . . that the following three values contained in the V-scale are important for achievement in the United States.

1. *A belief that the world is orderly and amenable to rational mastery; that, therefore, a person can and should make plans which will control his destiny (three items in the V-scale)*. The contrary notion, that man is subjugated to a destiny beyond his control, probably impeded Southern Italians in their early adjustment to the United States, just as in this study it impeded boys in school of less successful fathers in their choice of occupations. Unfortunately, we cannot say with any assurance in which direction the curse worked—whether the poor performance of the Italians and of the less successful fathers or sons was the result of their belief in fate, or whether the belief in fate was the result of their poor performances. But since we do know, in the case of the Italians, that the belief was part of their earlier culture and therefore antedated their performance, we may feel justified in concluding that the belief came first so far as the adjustment of Southern Italians to the United States is concerned.

2. *A willingness to leave home to make one's way in life*. Again, the South Italian stress on "familism," for which we found evidence in the V-scale, may well have interfered with upward mobility and contributed to the lower occupational achievement of Italians as compared with Jews. Family balance of power also affects willingness to leave home, as we shall see in a moment—a fact which demonstrates that one's position in life can produce a value disposition as well as the reverse. But whether the willingness to break up the family comes from an "old culture," from the power balance in the family, or from the father's or son's relative lack of success in job and school, it is certainly a value of importance in the achievement complex.

3. *A preference for individual rather than collective credit for work done*. Because our evidence is based upon only one item of the V-scale, it must be interpreted with caution. We have earlier argued

that for achievement to arise from a heightened desire for individual credit, a certain basic competence and discipline within a larger relationship system (i.e., a profession or modern bureaucracy) is required. Familistic organization with emphasis upon collateral rewards has not historically fitted the requirements for achievement of intermediate status in the United States—particularly not as well as more individualistic orientations. Our finding that Jews are more inclined toward individual credit than Italians has positive implications for achievement, but this ethnic difference is less important to our argument than the more general emphasis that individual credit must be sought within a framework of norms which, like the Calvinist's, are pointed toward the betterment both of society and the particular actor.

Beyond the V-scale results, which are impressive because they reflect differential achievement of cultures (Jews versus Italians), of fathers (high versus low SES) and of sons (over- versus under-achievement in school), there are two facts from the larger questionnaire study which relate to a fourth expected value difference between Italians and Jews—namely, the value placed on the *perfectability of man*. The Jews definitely had higher educational and occupational expectations for their sons. Practically speaking, this would mean they believed that man could improve himself by education and that no one should readily submit to fate and accept a lower station in life, the way the Italians were prepared to do.

The fifth and final expected Italian-Jewish value difference had to do with power relationships. From ethnographic reports and other studies, we had been led to believe that Italians would be more concerned than Jews with establishing dominance in face-to-face relationships. Such indeed turned out to be the case. Both in the boys' reports of who was dominant at home and in the actual decision-winning in the homes we studied intensively, the Italians showed greater variations from equality of power than the Jews. While this finding is probably of less importance than those presented above, it nonetheless sharpens our curiosity about the effects of power balance on the son's achievement. Is it perhaps true that when relatively equalitarian relations exist in the home, the son can move to new loyalties for larger systems of relationship, such as those provided by college or a job, without an outright rupture of family controls? Is such an adjustment to new institutions outside the home harder the more the home has tended to be dominated by one parent or the other? Furthermore, what would be the cost to the son of such a rupture—both in performance and in motivation to continue on his own? One wonders, of course, whether the conflict would not be less, the frustration less, when the break came—and consequently the emotional and intellectual adjustment more efficient—if the son had come from a home where controls were already diffuse and equalitarian as they are in many situations in life? The present research involved only a single visit with the families; in subsequent research it is to be hoped that more contact can be arranged as the child is growing up. Thus one could follow the effects of a balance of power on the child's adjustment inside the family and subsequently to life outside it.

So we come back to one of the most persistent and important themes of this study: what have power and the adjustment to power to do with achievement? Let us review the steps of the argument briefly. We held that, to achieve on the American scene, one must adjust to a more or less impersonal, bureaucratic system where power lies not with the individual but with the system, and is used to reward and punish according to the way individuals live up to impersonal specialized standards of performance. In addition, we argued that the family is also a "power system" and that the son's adjustment to it should generalize to his life outside. Of course, the reverse should generalize (at least for the fathers) to performance inside the family. Our data confirm this expectation. Fathers who have adjusted successfully to the American scene (and therefore have high SES in our terms) are significantly more powerful in their homes too. Interestingly enough, the same is not true of sons: those who have done well outside (the over-achievers) do not necessarily have more power at home. This is because the family consists of two adults whose largely complementary roles tend to create a strong coalition working on and for the child; the latter could wield influence only if both the other members were very weak or disunited. The father's occupational success is something else again. He is a key member of the parental coalition; if he fails in his function of "bringing home the bacon"—of adapting successfully outside—his power is reduced at home, too.

But to return to our main concern here—the generalization of the boy's experience with power at home to his possible future achievement—our data on this point are especially striking. They point most clearly to a link between family "democracy" (that is, a relatively powerful mother) and the V-scale. Now, since we have just shown that the V-scale contains values (belief in control of one's destiny, willingness to leave home) related to three types of achievement, we can feel justified in assuming that power balance in the family is of importance in giving a child ideas which will bear on his later success or failure. And oddly enough, it is the power balance that is correlated with the ideas and not whether those same ideas are held by the parents or not. A clear case of the children believing what the parents do and not what they say! For example, a father may have a high V-score and believe that one can control his destiny, as perhaps he himself has done in achieving a high-status occupation. But is his son likely to accept this belief if his father pushes him around all the time? Apparently not, to judge by our data. The son is more likely, at least in this stage of his life, to resign himself to the notion that there are forces beyond his control—in this instance, father.

This analysis immediately suggests the popular notion that there is alternation of generations in the production of great men in a family, or Franz Alexander's analysis of "chronic" achievers as persons who experience guilt for having usurped their father's role.[6] At least it provides a fairly solid ground for such theories to build on: father's power is *inversely* related to V-scale values. It also adds one further item to the growing

[6]Franz Alexander, in the *Age of Unreason (1)*, explains ultra-aggressive, ruthless, and belligerently self-centered personality

body of evidence that power relations in the family are an important determinant of personality development. Finally, it provides an interesting example of how the theoretical analysis of family structure, so ably made by Parsons and Bales [2], can be tested by empirical studies of the sort reported here.

---

types produced by impoverished immigrant families in terms of the failure of the parental coalition: "A common solution is that the son usurps the father's place in the mother's affection as well as in economic importance and acquires an inordinate ambition. He wants to justify all his mother's hopes and sacrifices and thus appease his guilty conscience about his father. He can do this only by becoming successful at whatever cost. Success becomes the supreme value and failure the greatest sin because it fails to justify the sacrifice of the father. In consequence of this all other defects such as insincerity in human relationships, unfairness in competition, disloyalty, disregard of others, appear comparatively slight, and the result is a ruthless careerist, obsessed by the one idea of self-promotion, a caricature of the self-made man, and a threat to Western civilization, the principle of which he has reduced to absurdity."

References

1. MCCLELLAND, D. C., ATKINSON, J. W., CLARK, R. A., and LOWELL, E. L., *The Achievement Motive* (New York: Appleton-Century-Crofts, 1953).

2. PARSONS, T., and BALES, R. F., *Family, Socialization and Interaction Process* (Glencoe, Illinois: Free Press, 1955).

3. RICCIUTI, H. N., and SADACCA, R., "The Prediction of Academic Grades with a Projective Test of Achievement Motivation: II. Cross-Validation at the High School Level," Princeton, N. J.: Education Testing Service, 1955.

4. SHANNON, J., "Early Detachment and Independence in a Study of Creativity," unpublished manuscript, Univ. of Chicago, 1957.

5. STRODTBECK, F. L., "Husband-Wife Interaction over Revealed Differences," *Amer. Soc. Rev.*, 1951, 16, 468–473.

6. STRODTBECK, F. L., MCDONALD, M. R., and ROSEN, B. C., "Evaluation of Occupations: A Reflection of Jewish-Italian Mobility Differences," *Amer. Soc. Rev.*, 1957, 22, 546–553.

7. VIDICH, A. J., "Methodological Problems in the Observations of Husband-Wife Interaction," unpublished manuscript, Cornell Univ., 1957.

12

THE WORLD OF THE ADOLESCENT:
PARENTS, PEERS, AND CULTURE

As children grow up they become increasingly involved in extra-familial activities. This involvement becomes an important source of conflict in many families because it is often incompatible with roles and role expectations which have evolved during the socialization process. Thus the adolescent may find himself feeling the strains and pressures of a tug-of-war between familial and extra-familial roles.

The chapter is introduced by August B. Hollingshead's definition of "adolescence." By noting the ambiguity of role and status which is characteristic of adolescence, Hollingshead clarifies both its structural importance for society and its personal meaning for the adolescent.

Talcott Parsons analyzes the position of the adolescent in American society and points to the sources of increased pressure. Parsons attributes this increased strain to (1) "the increased differentiation of the nuclear family from other structures in which it was formerly embedded," and (2) "the enhanced level of expectation in functioning outside the family for both adults and children." Parsons then uses this analysis to describe the reaction of adolescents to these social pressures. He calls their response a "Youth Culture."

Adolescence: A Sociological Definition *

August B. Hollingshead

In the past half-century physiologists, psychologists, educators, clergymen, social workers, and moralists have turned their attention to the physical and psychological phenomena connected with adolescence, and . . . of the millions of words written on the subject most have had a worried tone. This interest in the adolescent, with its emphasis on the "problems" of adolescence, can be traced to the monumental work of G. Stanley Hall.[1] Hall blended evolutionary theory, the facts of physical growth (as they were then known), instinct psychology, and a liberal sprinkling of ethnographic facts taken out of their cultural context with a set of strong moral judgments. He assumed that the individual in the course

*Adapted from August B. Hollingshead, Elmtown's Youth, New York: John Wiley & Sons, Inc., 1949, pp. 5–7.

[1] G. Stanley Hall, Adolescence, Its Psychology and Its Relations to Physiology, Anthropology, Sociology, Sex, Crime Religion, and Education, New York, D. Appleton and Company, 1904, two volumes.

of his life recapitulates the evolutionary development of the human species.[2]

Hall conceived of adolescence as the period in the life cycle of the individual from age 14 to 24, when the inexorably unfolding nature of the organism produces a "rebirth of the soul" which brings the child inevitably into a conflict with society. This was believed to be a period of "storm and stress," of "revolution," in the individual. In the "new birth" the "social instincts undergo sudden unfoldment."[3] Hall also asserted that "the adolescent stage of life" is marked by a struggle between the needs of the organism and the desires of society, which is "biologically antagonistic to genesis."[4] "All this is hard on youth . . .'[5] This psychology of adolescence included in its scope physiology, anthropology, sociology, sex, crime, religion, and education. Needless to say, this is a broad area which only a system maker who ignored facts as they exist in society could cover in a single sweep.

Hall's prestige as a psychologist, educator, and university president was so great and his influence over students so dominant that his theories were accepted widely by psychologists and educators. Gradually, however, the weight of empirical information indicated that these views were largely doctrinal. But, even now, the idea that adolescence is a period of "storm and stress," of conflict between individual and society, is held by many people, in spite of the fact that this has never been demonstrated to be true. On the contrary, common-sense observation will cast grave doubts upon its validity. Nevertheless, a recent summary of the field of adolescent psychology insisted upon the "casual" connection between the physical manifestations of adolescence and social behavior.[6]

Eventually, the conclusion was reached that, from the viewpoint of the sociologist, adolescence is distinctly different from psychologists', physiologists', and educators' concepts of it. *Sociologically, adolescence is the period in the life of a person when the society in which he functions ceases to regard him* (male or female) *as a child and does not accord to him full adult status, roles, and functions.* In terms of behavior, it is defined by the roles the person is expected to play, is allowed to play, is forced to play, or prohibited from playing by virtue of his status in society. It is not marked by a specific point in time such as puberty, since its form, content, duration, and period in the life cycle are differently determined by various cultures and societies. Sociologically, the important thing about the adolescent years is the way people regard the maturing individual. The menarche, development of the breasts, and other secondary manifestations of physical adolescence in the female, and the less obvious physical changes in the male connected with sex maturation, such as rapid growth, voice changes, the appearance of labial, axial, and pubic hair, derive their significance for the sociologist from the way they are regarded by the society in which the adolescent lives.

---

[2]*Ibid.*, vol. I, p. viii.
[3]*Ibid.*, p. xv.
[4]*Ibid.*, p. xvi.
[5]*Ibid.*, p. xviii.

[6]Wayne Dennis, "The Adolescent," in *Manual of Child Psychology*, edited by Leonard Carmichael, John Wiley and Sons, Inc., New York, 1946, pp. 633–666. We would agree with Dennis if he or any other psychologist demonstrated any "causal" connection between the physical phenomenon of puberty and the social behavior of young people during the adolescent period, irrespective of cultural milieu.

Youth in the Context of American Society*

Talcott Parsons

THE POSITION OF AMERICAN YOUTH

. . . It is in [the] broad picture of the American social structure and its development that I should like to consider the position of American youth. Contrary to prevalent views that mainly stress the rising standard of living and the allegedly indulgent and easy life, I think it is legitimate to infer that the general trend of development of the society has been and will continue to be one which, by and large puts greater rather than diminished demands on its average individual citizen—with some conspicuous exceptions. He must operate in more complex situations than before. He attempts to do many things his predecessors never attempted, that indeed were beyond their capacities. To succeed in what he attempts, he has to exercise progressively higher levels of competence and responsibility. These inferences seem to me inescapable when full account of the nature of the society and its main trends of development is taken.

If capacities and relevant opportunities developed as rapidly as do demands, it would follow that life on the average would be neither more nor less difficult. There seems reason to believe that if anything demands have tended somewhat to outrun the development of capacities—especially those for orient-

°Adapted and reprinted from Youth: Change and Challenge, edited by Erik H. Erickson, ©1961 by the American Academy of Arts and Sciences, ©1963 by Basic Books, Inc., Publishers, New York.

ing to normatively complex situations—and in some respects even opportunities, and that this is a major source of the current unrest and malaise. My broad contention, taking due account of the process of change just outlined, is that this society, however, is one that is relatively well organized and integrated with reference to its major values and its major trends of development. If those values are intact and are by and large shared by the younger generation (there seems to be every indication that they are), then it ought to be a society in which they can look forward to a good life. In so far as their mood is one of bewilderment, frustration, or whatever, one should look for relatively specific sources of difficulty rather than to a generalized mal-integration of the society as a whole.

It may be well to set the tone of the following analysis by an example of the ways in which current common sense can often misinterpret phenomena that raise distressing problems. American society, of course, is known for its high divorce rate. Until the peak following World War II, moreover, the trend was upward throughout the century, though since then it has appreciably declined. This divorce rate has widely been interpreted as an index of the "disintegration of the family" and, more importantly, of the levels of moral responsibility of married persons.

That it results in increased numbers

of broken families is of course true, though the seriousness of this is mitigated by the fact that most divorces occur between childless couples and that most divorced persons remarry, a large proportion stably. In any case, the proportion of the population of marriageable age that is married and living with their spouses is now the highest it has been in the history of the census.

The main point, however, is that this point of view fails to take into account the increased strain put on the marriage relationship in the modern situation. In effect, it says, since an increased proportion fail in a difficult task relative to those who previously failed in an easier task, this increased rate of failures is an index of a declining level of responsibility; seen in this light, this interpretation is palpably absurd, but if the underlying situation is not analyzed, it is plausible.

The increased difficulty of the task has two main aspects. One is the increased differentiation of the nuclear family from other structures in which it was formerly embedded, notably the farm and other household or family enterprises from which economic support was derived. This differentiation deprives the family and the marriage relationship within it of certain bases of structural support. This is clearly related to the component of freedom mentioned above; the freedom of choice of marriage partners is clearly related to the spread of the view that really serious incompatibility may justify breaking the marriage tie.

The other factor is the enhanced level of expectation in functioning outside the family for both adults and children. For adults, particularly men, the central obligation concerns the levels of responsibility and competence required by their jobs; for children, these requirements of growing up in a more complex and competitive world, going farther in education, and undertaking substantially more autonomous responsibility along the way impose greater demands than before. It is my impression that the cases in which marriage was undertaken irresponsibly are no more numerous than in any other time, and that divorce is not often lightly resorted to but is a confession of failure in an undertaking in which both parties have usually tried very hard to succeed.[1]

I cite this example because it is a conspicuous special case of the more general considerations I wish to discuss. The first keynote here is the rising general level of expectations. The primary reference point, of course, is that of adult roles at their peak of responsibility in middle age. The most prominent example is that of the higher levels of masculine occupational roles, in which (in those with technical emphasis) the requisite levels of training and technical competence are continually rising. With respect to managerial roles, the size and complexity of organizations is increasing, and hence the requirements necessary for their successful management also. Similar things, however, are true in various other fields. Thus the whole range of associational affairs requires membership support for leadership as well as responsible leadership itself, both of which involve complicated responsibilities. These range from the many private associations and "good causes" through participation on boards and staffs (including university departments and faculties) to participation through voting and other forms of exercising public responsibility.

The family in this context is a further case. The feminine role is typically anchored in the first instance in the family. Family duties may not be more onerous in such senses as drudgery and hard work than they were, but they involve a higher level of competence and responsibility, particularly, though not exclusively, in the field of the psychological management of both children and husbands, as well as of selves—the latter because wives are now far more autonomous on the average than they were. What we may call the independence training of children is more delicate and difficult than was the older type of training in strict obedience—that is, if autonomy for the young is to be accompanied by high levels of self-discipline and responsibility. But in addition, the typical married woman participates far more extensively outside the home than she formerly did, and in particular she forms a rapidly increasing proportion in the labor force.

Perhaps the central repercussion of this general upgrading of expectations (and hence of the norms with which conformity is expected) on the situation of youth is in the field of formal education. Here, of course, there has been a steady process of lengthening the average period of schooling, with the minimum satisfactory norm for all approaching the completion of high school, while nearly forty percent of the total age cohort now enter college, and a steadily increasing percentage complete college. Finally, by far the most rapidly growing sector has been that of post-graduate professional education. Uneven as standards are, and unsatisfactory as they are at many points, there is no solid evidence of a general tendency to deterioration and much evidence of their improvement, especially in the best schools at all levels.[2]

It seems fair, then, to conclude that in getting a formal education the average young American is undertaking a more difficult, and certainly a longer, job than his father or mother did, and that it is very likely that he is working harder at it. A growing proportion is prolonging formal education into the early adult years, thus raising important problems about marriage, financial independence, and various other considerations.

Furthermore, he is doing this in a context in which, both within and outside the school, he must assume more autonomous responsibility than did his predecessors. In the school itself—and in college—the slow though gradual trend has been in the direction of a mildly "progressive" type of education, with a diminution of the amount of drill and learning by rote. In certain respects, parents have grown distinctly more permissive within the family and with regard to their children's activities outside. This throws an important stress on the child's relations to his age peers, one that becomes particularly important in adolescence. This is the area least under adult control, in which deviant tendencies can most readily be mutually reinforced, without being immediately checked by adult intervention. This is to say that in general the education process puts increased demands on the younger group.

Three other factors seem involved in this situation of strain from the combination of enhanced expectations and autonomy. They concern one aspect of the psychological preparation for the tasks of maturing, one aspect of the choices that are open, and one aspect of the situation with reference to normative regulation.

First, with respect to psychological preparation, there seems to have been a trend within the family to *increase* the dependency of the young pre-oedipal child, particularly on the mother, of course. This trend is the consequence of the structural isolation of the nuclear family. There is less likelihood of there being close relatives either directly in the home or having very intensive and continual contact with the family. For middle-class families, the virtual disappearance of the domestic servant has also left less room for a division of responsibility for child care. Further, the proportion of very large families with five or more children has been sharply decreasing, while those with three and four children have been increasing. All these factors contribute to a concentration of relationships within the family and of the parents' (especially the mother's) sanctioning powers—both disciplinary and rewarding.

Psychological theory, however, indicates that under the proper circumstances this enhanced dependency contributes to developing motivations for high levels of achievement. These circumstances include high levels of aspiration for the child on the part of the parents and the use of the proper types of discipline. The essential point is that high dependency provides a very strong motivation to please the parent. This in turn can be used to incite him to learn what the parent sets him, if he is suitably rewarded by parental approval. The general findings of studies on the types of discipline used in middle-class families—the use of the withdrawal of love and approval as the predominant type of negative sanction—seem to fit in this picture.

The dependency components of motivation, however, are seldom if ever fully extinguished. The balance is so delicate in their relation to the autonomous components that it is easily upset, and in many cases this is a source of considerable strain. Attempting to maintain this balance, for example, may very well contribute to the great increase in the practice of "going steady" and its relation to the trend to early marriages. Emerging in adolescence, the dyadic heterosexual relation is the main component of the relational system of youth that articulates most directly with the earlier dependency complex—though some of it may also be expressed in same-sex peer groups, and indeed in "crushes" on the teacher. It is striking that the main trend seems to be toward intensive, and not merely erotic but diffuse, dyadic relations, rather than to sexual libertinism. This is in turn reflected in the emotional intensity of the marriage relationship and hence in the elements of potential strain underlying the problem of divorce.

This brings me to the second of the factors mentioned above, the range of choices open. A progressive increase in this range is a consequence of the general process of social change sketched above, namely, differentiation in the structure of the society. As this process goes on, types of interest, motivation, and evaluation that were embedded in a less differentiated complex come to be separated out, to become more autonomous and more visible in that they are freed from more ascriptive types of control. Ties to class and family, to local community and region become more flexible and hence often "expendable" as more choices become available.

One of the most conspicuous cases in relation to the present interest is the erotic component of sex relations. In an earlier phase of our society, it was rather rigidly controlled even within marriage, indeed, not infrequently it was partially suppressed. The process by which it has become differentiated, allowing much greater freedom in this area, is closely related to the differentiation of function and the structural isolation of the nuclear family.[3] In a society in which autonomous freedom is so widespread, there is much greater freedom in this field as in many others, not only in practice but also in portrayals on the stage, in the movies and television, and in the press, magazines, and books.

In this connection, since much of the newer freedom is illegitimate in relation to the older standards (normative upgrading and value generalization take time), it is very difficult to draw lines between the areas of new freedom in process of being legitimated and the types which are sufficiently dysfunctional, even in the new state of society, so that the probability is they will be controlled or even suppressed. The adolescent in our society is faced with difficult problems of choice and evaluation in areas such as this, because an adequate codification of the norms governing many of these newly emancipated areas has not yet been developed.

The third factor, that of normative regulations, is essentially a generalization of the second factor. We have maintained (though of course without documentation) that, contrary to various current opinions, the basic pattern of American values has not changed. Value patterns, however, are only part of the normative culture of the society. At the lower levels, both at the more specific levels of values and of what we technically call norms, it is in the nature of the type of process of change we have been discussing that there should be a continual reorganization of the normative system. Unfortunately, this does not occur as an instantaneous adjustment to the major innovations, but is a slow, uneven, and often painful process. In its course, at any one time (as we have noted), there are important elements of indeterminancy in the structure of expectations—not simply in the sense that there are areas of freedom in which autonomous decision is expected, but also in the sense that, where people feel there ought to be guidance, it is either lacking altogether, or the individual is subject to conflicting expectations that are impossible to fulfill all at once. This is the condition that some sociologists, following Durkheim, call *anomie*.

There seems to be an important reason why this source of strain and disturbance bears rather more heavily on the younger generation than on others. This is owing to the fact that the major agents for initiating processes of change lie in other sectors of the society above all, in large-scale organization, in the developments of science and technology, in the higher political processes, and in the higher ranges of culture. Their impact tends to spread, and there is a time lag in change between the locations of primary change and the other parts of the social structure.

Though there is of course much unevenness, it seems correct to say that, with one major exception, the social structures bearing most directly on youth are likely to be rather far down the line in the propagation of the effects of change. These are the family and the school, and they are anchored in the local residential community. The major exception is the college, and still more, the university which is one of the major loci of innovation and which can involve its students in the process more directly.

By and large, it seems fair to suggest that adults are on the average probably more conservative in their parental roles than when their children are not involved, and that this is typical of most of their roles outside the family. Similarly, schools, especially elementary and secondary schools, are on the whole probably more conservative in most respects than are the organizations that employ the fathers of their children. In the present phase of social development, another important institution of the residential community, the parish church or synagogue, is probably distinctly on the conservative side as a rule.

This would suggest that, partly as a matter of generation lag, partly for more complex reasons of the sort indicated, the adult agencies on which the youth most depends tend to some extent to be "out of tune" with what he senses to be the most advanced developments of the time. He senses that he is put in an unfair dilemma by having to be so subject to their control.

If we are right in thinking that special pressures operate on the younger generation relative to the general pressures generated by social change, on the other side of the relationship there are factors which make for special sensitivities on their part. The residua of early dependency, as pointed out above, constitute one such factor. In addition, the impact on youth of the general process of social differentiation makes for greater differences between their position and that of children, on the one hand, and that of adults, on the other, than is true in less differentiated societies. Compared to our own past or to most other societies, there is a more pronounced, and above all (as noted) an increasingly long segregation of the younger groups, centered above all on the system of formal education. It may be argued especially that the impact of this process is particularly pronounced at the upper fringe of the youth period, for the rapidly increasing proportion of the age cohort engaged in higher education—in college, and, very importantly, in postgraduate work. These are people who are adults in all respects except for the element of dependency, since they have not yet attained full occupational independence.

THE YOUTH CULTURE

The question may now be raised as to how young people react to this type of situation. Obviously, it is a highly variegated one and therefore occasions much diversity of behavior, but there are certain broad patterns which can be distinguished. These may be summed up under the conception, now familiar to social scientists, of a relatively differentiated "youth culture." Perhaps S. N. Eisenstadt is its most comprehensive student, certainly in its comparative perspective.[4]

It is Eisenstadt's contention that a distinctive pattern of values, relationships, and behavior for youth tends to appear and become more or less institutionalized in societies that develop a highly universalistic pattern of organization at the levels of adult role involvements. Since all lives start in the family, which is a highly particularistic type of structure, there is not only the difficulty of rising to higher levels within the same type of relationship system, but also of learning to adjust to a very different type. What has been discussed above as the enhancement of dependency in early childhood is a special case of this general proposition. Totalitarian societies attempt to bring this period under stringent centralized control through officially organized, adult-directed youth organizations such as the Soviet *Komsomols*, or earlier, the *Hitlerjugend*. In democratic societies, however, it tends to be relatively free, though in our own it is rather closely articulated with the system of formal education through a ramifying network of extracurricular activities.

As a consequence of youth's being exposed to such strains, it might be expected that youth culture would manifest signs of internal conflict and that it would incorporate elements of conformity as well as of alienation and revolt. In nonrational, psychological terms, rather than in terms of rational aims, youth culture attempts to balance its need for conforming to the expectations of the adult agencies most directly involved (parents and the local residential community) with some kind of outlet for tension and revolt and with some sensitivity to the winds of change above and beyond its local situation.

For two reasons, one would expect to find the fullest expression of these trends at the level of the peer group. For one thing, this group is the area of greatest immunity to adult control; indeed, the range of its freedom in this respect is particularly conspicuous in the American case. The other reason is that this is the area to which it is easiest to displace the elements of dependency generated in early experience in the family—on the one hand, because the strong stress on autonomy precludes maintaining too great an overt dependence on parents or other adult agencies, and, on the other, because the competitive discipline of school achievement enforces autonomous responsibility in this area. The peer group then gradually differentiates into two components, one focusing on the cross-sex relationship and one focusing on "activities," some of which occur within the one-sex group, others, relatively nonerotic, in mixed groups.

In general, the most conspicuous feature of the youth peer group is a duality of orientation. On the one hand, there tends to be a compulsive independence in relation to certain adult expectations, a touchy sensitivity to control, which in certain cases is expressed in overt defiance. On the other hand, within the group, there tends to be a fiercely compulsive conformity, a sharp loyalty to the group, an insistence on the literal observance of its norms, and punishment of deviance. Along with this goes a strong romantic streak. This has been most conspicuous in the romantic love theme in the cross-sex relationship, but it is also more generalized, extending to youth-culture heroes such as athletes and group leaders of various sorts, and sometimes to objects of interest outside the youth situation.

It is my impression (not easy to document) that important shifts of emphasis in American youth culture have occurred in the last generation. For the main trend, notably the increasingly broad band we think of as middle class, there has been a considerable relaxation of tension in both the two essential reference directions, toward parents and toward school expectations—though this relaxation is distinctly uneven. In the case of the school, there is a markedly greater acceptance of the evaluation of good school work and its importance for the future. This, of course, is associated with the general process of educational upgrading, particularly with the competition to enter good colleges and, at the next level, especially for students at the better colleges, to be admitted to graduate schools. The essential point, however, is that this increased pressure has been largely met with a positive response rather than with rebellion or passive withdrawal. The main exception is in the lowest sector, where the pattern of delinquency is most prominent and truancy a major feature. This is partly understandable as a direct consequence of the upgrading of educational expectations, because it puts an increased pressure on those who are disadvantaged by a combination of low ability, a nonsupportive family or ethnic background.

As to youth's relation to the family, it seems probable that the institutionalizing of increased permissiveness for and understanding of youth-culture activities is a major factor. The newer generation of parents is more firmly committed to a policy of training serious independence. It tolerates more freedom, and it expects higher levels of performance and responsibility. Further, it is probably true that the development of the pattern of "going steady" has drained off some tension into semi-institutionalized channels—tension formerly expressed in wilder patterns of sexual behavior. To be sure, this creates a good many problems, not only as to how far the partners will go in their own erotic relations, but also possibly premature commitments affecting future marriage. It may be that the pendulum has swung too far and that adjustments are to be expected.

Within this broad framework, the question of the content of peer-group interests is important. What I have called the romantic trend can be broadly expressed in two directions; the tentative terms "regressive" and "progressive" are appropriate, if not taken too literally. Both components are normally involved in such a situation, but their proportions and content may vary. They derive specifically from the general paradigm of social change outlined above, the former, at social levels, tending to resist change, the latter to anticipate and promote it.

One of the most striking interests of American youth culture has been in masculine physical prowess, expressed in particular in athletics. It seems quite clear that there has been a declining curve in this respect, most conspicuous in the more elite schools and colleges, but on the whole it is a very general one, except for the cult of violence in the delinquent sector. The cult of physical prowess has clearly been a reflex of the pressure to occupational achievement in a society in which brains rather than brawn come increasingly to count. From this point of view, it is a regressive phenomenon.

The indication is that the lessened concentration on this cult is an index of greater acceptance of the general developmental trend. Alcohol and sex are both in a somewhat different category. For the individual, they are fields of emancipation from the restrictions of childhood, but they are definitely and primarily regressive in their significance for the adult personality. However, as noted above, the emancipation of youth in this respect has been connected with a general emancipation which is part of the process of differentiation in the adult society, which permits greater expressiveness in these areas. I have the impression that a significant change has occurred from the somewhat frenetic atmosphere of the "flaming youth" of the 1920's and to some extent of the 1930's. There is less rebellion in both respects, more moderation in the use of alcohol, and more "seriousness" in the field of sexual relations. Youth has become better integrated in the general culture.

On the other side, the progressive one, the most important phenomena are most conspicuous at the upper end of the range, both in terms of the sociocultural level and of the stage of the life cycle. This is the enormous development of serious cultural interests among students in the more elite colleges. The most important field of these interests seem to be that of the arts, including highbrow music, literature, drama, and painting.

The first essential point here is that this constitutes a very definite upgrading of cultural standards, compared with the philistinism of the most nearly corresponding circles in an earlier generation. Second, however, it is at least variant and selective (though not, I think, deviant) with respect to the main trends of the society, since the main developments in the latter are on the "instrumental" rather than the "expressive" side. As to the special involvement of elite youth in the arts, it may be said that youth has tended to become a kind of "loyal opposition" to the main trends of the culture, making a bid for leadership in a sphere important to a balanced society yet somewhat neglected by the principal innovating agencies.

The question of youth's relation to the political situation is of rather special interest and considerable complexity. The susceptibility of youth groups to radical political ideologies, both left and right, has often been remarked. It appears, however, that this is a widely variant phenomenon. It seems to be most conspicuous, on the one hand, in societies just entering a more "developed" state, in which intellectuals play a special role and in which students, as potential intellectuals, are specially placed. In a second type of case, major political transitions and instabilities are prominent, as in several European countries during this century, notably Germany.

Seen in this context, American youth has seemed to be apathetic politically. During the 1930's and 1940's, there was a certain amount of leftist activity, including a small Communist contingent, but the main trend has certainly been one of limited involvement. Recently, there seems to have been a kind of resurgence of political interest and activity. It has not, however, taken the form of any explicit, generalized, ideological commitment. Rather, it has tended to focus on specific issues in which moral problems are sharply defined, notably in race relations and the problems of nuclear war. It does not seem too much to say that the main trend has been in accord with the general political characteristics of the society, which has been a relatively stable system with a strong pluralistic character. The concomitant skepticism as to generalized ideological formulae is usually thought deplorable by the moralists among our intellectuals. In this broad respect, however, the main

orientation of youth seems to be in tune with the society in which they are learning to take their places.

The elements in youth culture that express strain because of deviations from the main standards of the adult society are by no means absent. One such deviation is what we have called the "romantic," the devotion to expectations unrealistically simplified and idealized with respect to actual situations. A particularly clear example has been the romantic love complex. It is interesting, therefore, that a comparable pattern seems to have appeared recently in the political field, one that is connected with a pervasive theme of concern: the "meaningfulness" of current and future roles in modern industrial society.

. . . in the field of politics, one not very explicit interpretation of a meaningful role for youth in general is to exert a major personal influence on determining the "big" political decisions of our time. The realistic problem, of course, is the organization of large-scale societies on bases that are not rigidly fixed in tradition, not authoritarian, and not unduly unstable. In this respect, public opinion (though in the long run extremely important) is necessarily diffuse and, with few exceptions, unable to dictate particular decisions. The main policy-making function is of necessity confined to relatively few and is the special responsibility of elected representatives who, in large-scale societies, become professionalized to a considerable degree. The average adult citizen, even if high in competence and responsibility, is excluded from these few. Yet this is not to say that in his role as citizen his responsibilities are meaningless or that his life in general can become meaningful only if his principal concerns (e.g., his nonpolitical job) are sacrificed to the attempt to become a top "influential" in national politics. If this were true, representative democracy as we know it would itself be meaningless. The alternative, however (if large-scale society is to exist at all), is not populistic direct democracy but dictatorship.

This particular syndrome, of course, is a part of a larger one: the general difficulty of accepting the constraints inherent in large-scale organizations—in particular, the "instrumental" aspect of roles other than those at the highest levels. We have already pointed out some of the features of our developing social system that make this a focus of strain. Equally, through the development of institutionalized individualism, there is a whole series of factors making for an increasing rather than a diminishing autonomy. The question, however, concerns the spheres in which the autonomy of various categories of individuals can operate. Differentiation inevitably entails mutual dependence: the more differentiation, the more dependence. In a system characterized by high levels of differentiation, it is to be expected that organizational policy making will also become differentiated. Hence, only a few will become very intimately concerned with it. The problem of what mechanism can control these few is indeed a complex one which cannot be analyzed here. The political role, however, seems to provide particularly striking evidence of a romantic element in current youth ideology.

Perhaps the most significant fact about current youth culture is its concern with meaningfulness. This preoccupation definitely lies on the serious and progressive side of the division I have outlined. Furthermore, it represents a rise in the level of concern from the earlier preoccupation with social justice —even though the problem of race relations is understandably a prominent one. Another prominent example is the much discussed concern with problems of "identity." This is wholly natural and to be expected in the light of *anomie*. In a society that is changing as rapidly as ours and in which there is so much mobility of status, it is only natural that the older generation cannot provide direct guidance and role models that would present the young person with a neatly structured definition of the situation. Rather, he must find his own way, because he is pushed out of the nest and expected to fly. Even the nature of the medium in which he is to fly is continually changing, so that, when he enters college, there are many uncertainties about the nature of opportunities in his chosen field on completing graduate school. His elders simply do not have the knowledge to guide him in detail.

It is highly significant that the primary concern has been shifting since early in the century from the field of social justice to that of meaningfulness, as exemplified by the problem of identity—except for the status of special groups such as the Negro. In terms of the social structure, this enhances the problem of integration, and focuses concern more on problems of meaning than on those of situation and opportunity in the simpler sense. It is a consequence of the process of social change we have outlined.

It is also understandable and significant that the components of anxiety that inevitably characterize this type of strained situation should find appropriate fields of displacement in the very serious, real dangers of the modern world, particularly those of war. It may also be suggested that the elite youth's resonance to the diagnosis of the current social situation in terms of conformity and mass culture should be expected.[5] Essentially, this diagnosis is an easy disparagement of the society, which youth can consider to be the source of difficulty and (so it seems to them) partially unmanageable problems.

CONCLUSION

The above analysis suggests in the main that contemporary American society is of a type in which one would expect the situation of youth to involve (certainly, by the standards of the society from which it is emerging) rather special conditions of strain. As part of the more general process of differentiation to which we have alluded, youth groups themselves are coming to occupy an increasingly differentiated position, most conspicuously, in the field of formal education. Though an expanding educational system is vital in preparing for future function, it has the effect of segregating (more sharply and extensively than ever before) an increasing proportion of the younger age groups. The extension of education to increasingly older age levels is a striking example.

The other main focus of strain is the impact on youth of the pace and nature of the general process of social change. This is especially observable in the problem of *anomie*. In view of this change, youth's expectations cannot be defined either very early or very precisely, and this results in considerable insecurity. Indeed, the situation is such that a marked degree of legitimate grievance is inevitable. Every young person is entitled in some respects to complain that he has been brought into "a world I never made."

To assess the situation of American youth within the present frame of reference presents an especially difficult problem of balance. This is an era that lays great stress, both internally and externally, on the urgencies of the times, precisely in the more sensitive and responsible quarters. Such a temper highlights what is felt to be wrong and emphasizes the need for change through active intervention. With reference to the actual state of society, therefore, the tendency is to lean toward a negative evaluation of the status quo, because both the concrete deficiencies and the obstacles to improvement are so great.

That this tendency should be particularly prominent in the younger age groups is natural. It is both to be expected and to be welcomed. The main feature of the youth situation is perhaps the combination of current dependence with the expectation of an early assumption of responsibility. I think that evidence has been presented above that this conflict is accentuated under present conditions. The current youthful indictments of the present state of our society may be interpreted as a kind of campaign position, which prepares the way for the definition of their role when they take over the primary responsibilities, as they inevitably will.

It seems highly probable that the more immediate situation is strongly influenced by the present phase of the society with respect to a certain cyclical pattern that is especially conspicuous in the political sphere. This is the cycle between periods of "activism" in developing and implementing a sense of the urgency of collective goals, and of "consolidation" in the sense of withdrawing from too active commitments and on the whole giving security and "soundness" the primary emphasis. There is little doubt that in this meaning, the most recent phase (the "Eisenhower era") has been one of consolidation, and that we are now involved in the transition to a more activistic phase.

Broadly speaking, youth in a developing society of the American type, in its deepest values and commitments, is likely to be favorable to the activistic side. It is inculcated with the major values of the society, and strongly impressed with the importance of its future responsibilities. At the same time, however, it is frustrated by being deprived of power and influence in the current situation, though it recognizes that such a deprivation is in certain respects essential, if its segregation for purposes of training is to be effective—a segregation which increases with each step in the process of differentiation. A certain impatience, however, is to be expected, and with it a certain discontent with the present situation. Since it is relatively difficult to challenge the basic structure of the youth situation in such respects (e.g., as that one should not be permitted to start the full practice of medicine before graduating from college), this impatience tends to be displaced on the total society as a system, rather than on the younger generation in its specific situation. From this point of view, a generous measure of youthful dissatisfaction with the state of American society may be a sign of the healthy commitment of youth to the activist component of the value system. However good the current society may be from various points of view, *it is not good enough to meet their standards.* It goes almost without saying that a fallibility of empirical judgment in detail is to be expected.

The task of the social scientist, as a scientific observer of society, is to develop the closest possible approach to an objective account of the character and processes of the society. To him, therefore, this problem must appear in a slightly different light: he must try to see it in as broad a historical and comparative perspective as he can, and he must test his judgments as far as possible in terms of available empirical facts and logically precise and coherent theoretical analyses.

Viewed in this way (subject, of course, to the inevitable fallibilities of all cognitive undertakings), American society in a sense appears to be running a scheduled course. We find no cogent evidence of a major change in the essential pattern of its governing values. Nor do we find that—considering the expected strains and complications of such processes as rapid industrialization, the assimilation of many millions of immigrants, and a new order of change in the power structure, the social characteristics, and the balances of its relation to the outside world—American society is not doing resonably well (as distinguished from outstandingly) in implementing these values. Our society on the whole seems to remain committed to its essential mandate.

The broad features of the situation of American youth seem to accord with this pattern. There are many elements of strain, but on the whole they may be considered normal for this type of society. Furthermore, the patterns of reaction on the part of American youth also seem well within normal limits. Given the American value system we have outlined, it seems fair to conclude that youth cannot help giving a *relative* sanction to the general outline of society as it has come to be institutionalized. On the other hand, it is impossible for youth to be satisfied with the status quo, which must be treated only as a point of departure for the far higher attainments that are not only desirable but also obligatory.

Clearly, American youth is in a ferment. On the whole, this ferment seems to accord relatively well with the sociologist's expectations. It expresses many dissatisfactions with the current state of society, some of which are fully justified, others are of a more dubious validity. Yet the general orientation appears to be, not a basic alienation, but an eagerness to learn, to accept higher orders of responsibility, and to "fit," not in the sense of passive conformity, but in the sense of their readiness to work within the system, rather than in basic opposition to it. The future of American society and the future place of that society in the larger world appear to present in the main a *challenge* to American youth. To cope with that challenge, an intensive psychological preparation is now taking place.

References

1. See Talcott Parsons and Robert F. Bales, *Family, Socialization and Interaction Process* (Chicago: The Free Press of Glencoe, Illinois, 1955), especially ch. 1.
2. For example, I am quite certain that the general level of academic achievement on the part of students of Harvard College and the Harvard Graduate School has substantially risen during my personal contact with them (more than thirty years).
3. The emancipation of components that were previously rigidly controlled by ascription is of course a major feature of the general process of differentiation, which could not be detailed here for reasons of space.
4. S. N. Eisenstadt, *From Generation to Generation*. Chicago: The Free Press of Glencoe, Illinois, 1956. See also his paper in this issue of *Daedalus*.
5. For an analysis of this complex in the society, see Winston R. White, *Beyond Conformity*. New York: The Free Press of Glencoe, 1961.

13

ADULTS AND THEIR PARENTS

Let us think of young adults as being around twenty-five years old and their parents as approximately fifty. The first article in this chapter looks at the relationships between these generations. Dorrian Sweetser integrates many studies of intergenerational relationships, and documents the effect of industrialization on the increasing importance of the wife's kin. She finds cross-cultural support for the hypothesis that intergenerational solidarity will be greater between the nuclear family of the young couple and the husband's parents where the young man inherits the farm from his father or goes into business with him. Where there is no such succession, Sweetser finds greater solidarity with the wife's parents.

For the balance of this chapter the parents comprise society's senior generation; their children have advanced into middle age. Irving Rosow presents seven factors which determine the welfare of a society's aged and then ranks the United States on each criterion. The importance of family relationships for the support of the aged is apparent in Rosow's review of mechanisms which can serve to integrate an older person into society.

The importance of the family and a bleak prospectus for the elderly is echoed by Elaine Cumming in her theory of disengagement. This theory is a system of hypotheses which attempts to account for the range and limits of the aging process. In her essay, Dr. Cumming describes the personal, familial, and societal processes which cause the elderly to become disengaged from one social role after another. Of particular interest is the special primacy of the family for the aged. Cumming asserts that the ascriptive basis of family membership allows people to continue functioning as family members long after they have relinquished the achievement-based ties to other areas of social participation.

Although urban in location, Bethnal Green has more the atmosphere of a working-class village, for established residents claim to "know everyone." Both in social integration and in housing it differs from Woodford, a suburb of middle- and working-class people. Willmott and Young show how these differences are related to the lives of old people.

Thompson and Streib describe family interaction during the last forty years of marriage. They show that disengagement proceeds in stages by virtue of the fact that the elderly are really two distinct age groups: those aged 65 to 74 who are generally integrated with society, and those above 75 who are relatively disengaged.

The Effect of Industrialization
On Intergenerational Solidarity [*][1]

Dorrian Apple Sweetser

The characteristic form of the family in modern urban-industrial societies is the independent nuclear family with bilateral kindred. Ties of affection and helpfulness do exist between relatives, particularly between parental families and the families of their children, as has been pointed out by a number of writers,[2] but there are no normatively sanctioned obligations for the nuclear family to live nearby, help, or otherwise unite itself with any adult kin. The family *may* do so, but it is not *obliged* to.

Given the existence of this type of family, with its bilateral kindred, the evidence now at hand of generally closer ties in urban-industrial societies between the nuclear family and the wife's parents than with the husband's parents requires explanation. This offers a general hypothesis to account for this matrilateral asymmetry in intergenerational ties. In brief, the general hypothesis states that, where there is succession in male instrumental roles, solidarity will be greater between the nuclear family and the lineal relatives of males, and, where there is no succession, solidarity will be greater with the wife's family. Since succession in male instrumental roles, as this term will be defined, means that the family is an economic unit of production, and since the process of industrialization weakens or does away with this function of the family, the general hypothesis states a change in the focus of intergenerational family solidarity which is a consequence of industrialization.

The correctness of this general hypothesis will be scrutinized by examining three bodies of data: first, some illustrative material from pre-industrial societies or subsocieties on the relationship between succession in male instrumental roles and intergenerational solidarity; second, evidence of change in the focus of intergenerational solidarity in industrializing societies or subsocieties; finally, data on the predominance of female ties between generations in industrial societies.

°*Adapted from* Rural Sociology, *1966, 31: 156–170.*

[1]Revision and abridgement of a paper read at the 1965 meeting of the Rural Sociological Society entitled "Rural-Urban Differentiation in Intergenerational Solidarity." This work is part of a project, "Family Interaction and Ecology," supported by the National Science Foundation.

[2]Eugene Litwak, "Occupational Mobility and Extended Family Cohesion," *American Sociological Review*, 25 (February, 1960), pp. 9–21, and "Geographic Mobility and Extended Family Cohesion," *American Sociological Review*, 25 (June, 1960), pp. 385–394; Marvin B. Sussman and Lee Burchinal, "Kin Family Network: Unheralded Structure in Current Conceptualizations of Family Functioning," *Marriage and Family Living*, 24 (August, 1962), pp. 231–240.

MALE SUCCESSION AND FAMILY SOLIDARITY

Succession here means actual collaboration and continuity of related males in a particular instrumental role, not what might be termed mere occupational coincidence, in which the younger man follows the same line of work as the older. The term implies stem or extended families, since such instrumental succession requires that adjacent generations live together. The term also implies that the family is a unit of production and therefore that occupational placement of men is largely a direct result of their family position, rather than of broader societal processes such as the operation of a labor market or the channels of formal education. "Corporate family group" is a convenient term to apply to such families. In such a corporate family group, we would expect to find, and we do find, that solidarity (meaning helpfulness, loyalty, and obligations) focuses on the group, rather than on the mother's relatives in patrilocal societies, or the father's relatives in matrilocal societies. The economic advantage to men of this arrangement no doubt contributes to intergenerational solidarity. The excerpts to follow illustrate the type.

Sheldon's study of a farming village in Finnish Karelia illustrates family organization with male succession and the focusing of solidarity on the patrilocal corporate family group.

> In the old days the individual was closely identified with his family. What he earned by his own efforts belonged to the family as a whole. . . . The Karelian type family . . . consisted of a man, his wife, his unmarried children, and his married sons with their wives and children. The old man was the head of the family. . . . Any member of the family was free to leave if he wanted to, except that wives were not free to leave their husbands, but if he stayed he was expected to act under the authority of the master and mistress; and in practice this custom seems to have been strictly followed. . . . The person in authority ordered, and the others agreed. If they could not or would not agree, they could not remain members of the group, and they split off to live elsewhere. If the members of a family could not get along and finally split, the fact of their inability to get along was the subject of derision by the other villagers.[3]

Dore gives a detailed analysis of the original Japanese family system, or rather "a description of how most people think most people *used* to behave and everyone used to expect people to behave."[4] It consisted of a stem family, in LePlay's use of the term, surrounded by a cluster of branch families of younger sons, which would be single-family households for the first generation and then would develop into stem families. The *doozoku*, or larger family group consisting of one main and a cluster of branch families, rested on a complex economic base supported by legal and moral rules.

> Neither occupation, property, house tradition nor ancestors belong to the individual, but to the family as a whole. . . . Honour, too, pertains not simply to the individual but to the family. A man's acts bring praise and blame not only on himself but on his family, his parents and brothers, his ancestors and descendants.[5]

Ishwaran's study of Dutch families included a description of the stem farm family, found mostly in the "sandy soil"

[3] Richard C. Sheldon, "Socio-economic Development in a Karelian Village," Unpublished Ph.D. dissertation, Cambridge: Harvard University, 1952, pp. 118–122.

[4] Ronald P. Dore, *City Life in Japan*, Berkeley: University of California Press, 1963, p. 96.

[5] *Ibid.*, pp. 99–100.

areas of the Netherlands.[6] Farming was a way of life, not a business. Marriage united not only man and wife but also farm with farm and cows with cows.

> The farm family was a productive as well as a consumptive unit; it cared for old as well as young, performed educational, religious, protective, and other similar activities. The importance of the family as a productive as well as a consumptive unit was to be observed in the functional roles of individuals, especially in the interdependence of parents and children.[7] Old parents gradually relinquish activity and control in the home and on the farm in favour of the son, usually the eldest. The farmer's son receives the possession of the land from his father in return for "rental charges" and continues to live under the same roof, but with an independent hearth of his own.[8]

The traditional stem farm family is still quite common in the "sandy soil" areas, as indicated by a survey made in 1956 by Kooy.[9] In the Achterhoek area, 46.5 percent of farm households were of the traditional type, consisting of a nuclear family plus one or more close kin. In two-thirds of the cases, these were husband's kin. The same ancient form of social security, by transmission of farms to sons on a contractual basis, is found in Finland and Sweden today.[10]

Patrilineal kin groups in a Lebanese village, described by Fuller, rested on a similar basis of economic cooperation and mutual protection.[11]

In the family type just illustrated, the coexistence of male succession with the focusing of family solidarity on the line of descent to which the men belong is true by virtue of the definition of the type. The common residence of nuclear families in a corporate family group requires at least some degree of allegiance of individuals to the group. However, though the definition of the type is not by itself evidence of a causal link between male succession and the direction of family solidarity, the definition furnishes a needed starting point for evaluating the hypothesis that such a causal link exists. Evidence of the causal linkage will consist of (1) studies of change in the focus of intergenerational solidarity when male succession disappears, and (2) studies of intergenerational solidarity in societies in which the family is not a unit of production.

Evidence is lacking on the focus of intergenerational solidarity in an important third type of society. These are societies in which the family is a unit of production but is organized as independent nuclear families rather than as stem or extended families. The independent nuclear family is common among hunters, gatherers, and fishers[12] and is likewise found in many predominantly agricultural societies, including much of

[6] K. Ishwaran, *Family Life in the Netherlands*, The Hague: Uitgeverij van Keulen, 1959.

[7] *Ibid.*, pp. 40–41.

[8] *Ibid.*, p. 55.

[9] Gerrit A. Kooy, "The Traditional Household in a Modernized Rural Society," in *Recherches sur la Famille*, vol. III, Göttingen: Vandenhoeck and Ruprecht, 1958, pp. 188–192.

[10] Dorrian Apple Sweetser, "Urbanization and the Patrilineal Transmission of Farms in Finland," *Acta Sociologica*, 7 (1964), pp. 215–224.

[11] Anne H. Fuller, "The World of Kin in Lebanon," in W. J. Goode (Ed.) *Readings on the Family and Society*, Englewood Cliffs, New Jersey: Prentice-Hall, 1964, pp. 176–180.

[12] M. F. Nimkoff and R. Middleton, "Types of Family and Types of Economy," *American Journal of Sociology*, 66 (1960), pp. 215–225.

pre-industrial Europe.[13] Data on the focus of intergenerational solidarity in such instances would be an important addition to the body of evidence and the theoretical framework of this paper, but none is available.

THE IMPACT OF INDUSTRIALIZATION ON INTERGENERATIONAL SOLIDARITY

Two studies, one of the Japanese family and one of farm families in Finland and Sweden, contain evidence of change, related to industrialization, toward greater solidarity with the wife's relatives.[14]

In Japan, the extended family is losing ground to the independent nuclear family. Shared households, once the rule because of the custom requiring the eldest son to succeed to the family headship and live with his aged parents, are declining in frequency. However, the dissolution of the extended family, though it would include a decrease in the prevalence of shared households, would not automatically change their composition. Nevertheless, a change toward sharing households with wife's parents can be inferred from the number that exist.

Dore reports from his study of Shitayama-cho, a neighborhood of about 300 households near the center of Tokyo, that

there are good reasons for thinking that daughters are in future likely to play a bigger part than sons in looking after parents . . . it is, in fact becoming a widespread custom. Of these forty-three families in Shitayama-cho in which parents are living with married children, thirty-four . . . do conform to the patterns of the "family system." That is to say, the married child is either a son (in twenty-seven cases) or, in the other seven, an inheriting daughter who has taken an adopted husband—a husband who takes his wife's surname and succeeds his father-in-law (rather than his own father) as head of his wife's family. The remaining fifth of these families, however, do not conform to these patterns at all. Although in form the daughter has married out of her family into her husband's, the young couple live with her, and not with her husband's, parents.

There are . . . reasons for expecting this to become gradually more common nowadays when the chief reasons for parents to live with their married children is to solve the young couple's housing problem or to make some provision for the parents' old age, rather than simply because "it is the proper thing to do."[15]

Dore summarizes data from his Tokyo study as follows:

. . . the bias toward patrilineal ties in the old family depended primarily on the practice of patrilocal marriage. . . . If anything, there is, perhaps, a tendency for the new family to have relations of greatest solidarity with the wife's parental family and with her siblings. . . .[16]

Dore discusses as contributing factors to the change toward independent nuclear family life, with more stress on the husband-wife bond than on the patrilineal ties of men, the following

---

[13] John Mogey, "Family and Community in Urban-Industrial Societies," in H. T. Christensen (Ed.), *Handbook of Marriage and the Family*, Chicago: Rand McNally, 1964, p. 509.

[14] Just as the corporate family group is not found in all pre-industrial societies, neither is industrialization the only process of social change which can weaken or do away with the corporate family. It is, however, the process involved in the studies presented here.

[15] Dore, *op. cit.*, pp. 132–133. See also Takashi Nakano, "Recent Studies of Change in the Japanese Family," *International Social Science Journal*, 14 (1962), pp. 527–538.

[16] *Ibid.*, p. 154.

aspects and correlates of industrialization: (1) demographic change, especially falling mortality and a resulting increase in the number of sons who survive and consequently of branch families, (2) weakening of the *doozoku* group by the move of younger sons from the country to the cities to enter different occupations from those traditional in their families, by the different occupations available to younger sons of urban families, and by the increasing importance of education as the doorway to work, at the expense of traditional family occupations, (3) the increase in the number and variety of jobs, so that the "ideal of following in father's footsteps is replaced with the ideal of doing better than father," (4) the change from family production to wage employment, and from family ownership to individual ownership of property, (5) an increase in participation in nonkinship groupings, such as schools, factories, or military service, and (6) opportunity for women to work, with a resultant broadening of their knowledge of the world.[17] Many of these factors conduce to the weakening of male succession, including a weakening of the corporate family group and of patrilineal solidarity.

In the writer's investigation of Finnish and Swedish family relations, signs of a change in the patrilocal stem farm family were noted.[18] A statistically significant rank correlation (*tau* = .54) was found between the degree of urbanization of areas in Finland and the proportion of shared farm households which included an older parent or parents and a daughter and her husband, rather than a son and his wife. Urbanization was measured by the proportion of people in an area who lived in relatively densely populated settlements. The more

urbanized an area was, the greater was the tendency for shared farm households to include the daughter rather than the son. For Sweden, evidence of a change in the patrilocal stem farm family was also noted. Married daughters predominated among younger couples living in a shared farm household, while married sons predominated, as in the old days, in older shared farm households. The matrilineal emphasis typical of industrial societies appears to be spreading to farm families also.

The precise causes of this change are not known. One factor, differential migration of the sexes before marriage, was investigated in Finland by using the sex ratio in rural communes as an indicator of such differential migration rates. In general, regions in which there were more farm households shared by sons were regions with an excess of males; where there were more farm households shared by sons-in-law, there was an excess of females. It can be conjectured that in more urbanized areas there are more occupational alternatives available to sons, who therefore move away from the farms and are reluctant to return, leaving openings for upwardly mobile rural boys to marry the farmer's daughter.

MOTHER-DAUGHTER TIES IN URBAN SAMPLES IN INDUSTRIAL SOCIETIES

This section will review evidence from five industrial societies, the U. S., Britain, the Netherlands, Finland, and Sweden, on the differing closeness of a couple to the husband's or the wife's parents in one or more of the following areas: household sharing, residential proximity, interaction and ties of sentiment, and help of various kinds.

[17] *Ibid.*, pp. 111–116.
[18] Sweetser, *op. cit.*

Household Sharing

Data from 14 samples in five countries show a moderate, but strikingly consistent, tendency for parents of wives to be found more often than parents of husbands in households shared by parents and married couples.[19] Table 1 summarizes these studies.

Residential Proximity

Residential proximity, as well as household sharing, also displays a bias toward the wife's family. In Bethnal Green, a working class area in London, married daughters were likely to settle closer to the parental home than were married sons.[20] The same phenomenon was reported in a study of a working class area in Oxford.[21] On the other

[19] Wives tend to be younger than their husbands, and hence their parents are presumably younger on the average and more likely to be living. The effect of this age difference on the predominance of wives' parents in shared households was tested in my study cited in Table 1 and found to be negligible. Another alternative explanation might be that girls, before marriage, do not move as far away from home as boys, and hence married daughters tend to settle closer to home than married sons. This would make it easier for married daughters and their husbands to move in with wife's parents, or for the wife's parents to move in with the daughter. The effect on intergenerational solidarity of differential migration of the sexes before marriage is under investigation in the project entitled "Family Interaction and Ecology."

[20] Peter Townsend, The Family Life of Old People, London: Routledge and Kegan Paul, 1957, p. 33. Michael Young and Peter Willmott, Family and Kinship in East London, London: Routledge and Kegan Paul, 1957, ch. 2.

[21] John M. Mogey, Family and Neighborhood, Oxford: Oxford University Press, 1956, p. 54.

hand, there was no tendency in Oxford for more of the husband's or the wife's kin to be known.[22]

Similar evidence of greater residential proximity to the wife's kin is available from two American samples. Rogers and Leichter, in a study of New York families of Eastern European Jewish origin, report that there were many more wife's kin than husband's kin living in the same building or within walking distance.[23] Aldous and Hill obtained from a series of area probability samples in the Minneapolis-St. Paul area a sample consisting of 88 white, three-generation lineages, each composed of an independently residing nuclear family linked vertically to two other nuclear families, and all residing within 100 miles of the two cities.[24] Of the three-generation lineages, 36 percent were composed of the families of grandmother, mother, and daughter, and 17 percent were composed of the families of grandfather, father, and son. The remaining were divided almost equally between grandfather-father-daughter lineages and grandmother-mother-son lineages.

Interaction and Sentiment

Visiting, communication, and ties of sentiment show the same matrilineal bias in intergenerational ties. Mogey summarized a number of community studies in Britain by saying that

[22] Ibid., p. 80.

[23] Candace L. Rogers and Hope J. Leichter, "Laterality and Conflict in Kinship Ties." Paper delivered at the National Conference on Social Welfare, New York City, 1962, p. 7.

[24] Joan Aldous and Reuben Hill, "Family Continuities through Socialization over Three Generations." Paper presented at the American Sociological Association annual meeting, August 28, 1963.

TABLE 1 Summary of studios reporting household sharing by married couples and parents in urban-industrial societies

Author	Location and sample	Date of data collection	Percent of such shared households containing wife's parents
U. S. Census Bureau[a]	U. S. probability	1946	55 (parents living in child's household)
U. S. Census Bureau[a]	U. S. probability	1946	60 (young couples living in parents' household)
U. S. Census Bureau[b]	U. S. probability	1950	60 (young couples living in parents' household)
Smith, Britton, and Britton[c]	all 3-generation families in a Penn. town	1952	64 (estimate)
Smith, Britton, and Britton[c]	all 3-generation families in a Penn. rural community	1952	77 (estimate)
Koller[d]	Ohio and Va. community samples; some probabilistic, some purposive	1954(?)	"most 3-generation households were created by the mother of the wife moving in"
Young and Willmott[e]	working class area of London; probability sample	1953–1955	67
Willmott and Young[f]	London suburb; probability sample	mid-1950's	71
Rogers and Leichter[g]	clients of East European Jewish origin in a random sample of N.Y.C. social agency clients	late 1950's	of "wife's kin," 54% share present household and 93% shared past household; latter were "most often young couples in the home of the wife's parents"
Thompson and Finlayson[h]	Aberdeen; 5-year follow-up of probability sample of women at first confinement	1955–1958	"usually the wife's mother"
Bellin[i]	wid., sep., div. older people in a probability sample in Syracuse, N.Y.	1959	79

[a] U. S. Bureau of the Census, "Characteristics of Secondary Families in the United States: February, 1916." Series P.S. No. 15, Table 2, Washington, D. C.: Bureau of the Census, 1947.

[b] U. S. Bureau of the Census, *U.S. Census of Population: 1950,* Vol. IV, *Special Reports,* Washington, D. C.: Govt. Printing Office, 1953, Part 2, Ch. D. Table 1.

[c] W. M. Smith, Jr., J. H. Britton, and Jean O. Britton, "Relationships within Three-Generation Families," University Park: Pennsylvania State University College of Home Economics, Res. Pub. No. 155, 1958.

[d] M. R. Koller, "Studies of Three-Generation Households," *Marriage and Family Living,* 16 (1954), pp. 205–206.

[e] Michael Young and Peter Willmott, *Family and Kinship in East London,* London: Routledge and Kegan Paul, 1957, Table 5.

[f] Peter Willmott and Michael Young, *Family and Class in a London Suburb,* London: Routledge and Kegan Paul, 1960.

[g] Candace L. Rogers and Hope J. Leichter, "Laterality and Conflict in Kinship Ties." Paper presented at the National Conference on Social Welfare, New York City, 1962.

[h] Barbara Thompson and Angela Finlayson, "Married Women Who Work in Early Motherhood," *British Journal of Sociology,* 14 (June, 1963), pp. 150–168.

[i] Seymour S. Bellin, "Relations among Kindred in Later Years of Life: Parents, Their Siblings, and Adult Children." Dittoed, 1961.

TABLE 1   (Continued)

Author	Location and sample	Date of data collection	Percent of such shared households containing wife's parents
Sweetser[j]	secondary analysis; data from probability sample by Helsinki City Statistical Office.	1955	58
Sweetser[j]	secondary analysis; non-farm shared households in a national probability sample in Sweden studied by Central Bureau of Statistics	1958	76
Sweetser[j]	secondary analysis; non-farm shared households in a probability sample in rural areas studied by the Bureau of Social Research of the Finnish Ministry of Social Affairs	1959–1960	87

[j] Dorrian Apple Sweetser, "Mother-Daughter Ties between Generations in Industrial Societies," *Family Process,* 3 (September, 1964), pp. 332–343. Predominance of wife's parents persisted when household headship (older parent versus son or son-in-law) was held constant. Conclusions from Swedish and Finnish rural nonfarm samples considered to be "tentative" because of small numbers of cases.

In older wage-earning districts the extended family, combining grandparents, parents, and children, is common; not all of joint residence is due to the housing shortage, for close relations within the kindred are very important to these people. The "community" of such districts has been found to be characterized by kinship ties rather more than by neighborhood ties. . . . In central town areas, women, as mothers and grandmothers, run the social, domestic, and child-rearing sides of life; men, as husbands and wage earners, stand a little aside from this intensive interaction and are more involved in neighborhood affairs. The tie which carries most *affect* in this social system is that between a mother and her daughters; but "mum" is an immensely important figure to all her children, and to their children. With her death this kinship pattern usually breaks up and reforms with each daughter occupying the status position "mum" to her own daughters. This pattern of social relations has been described for Scotland, Manchester, Liverpool, Oxford, East London, and Wolverhampton. [25]

Rogers and Leichter report of their New York Jewish sample that the wife's relatives are more likely to drop in unannounced or to have a key. Husbands, however, maintained more telephone contact with their own relatives. [26] In a study of area probability samples in two Pennsylvania cities, Smith reports that although the same percentage (about 40 percent) of couples lived with or near the husband's parents as lived with or near the wife's parents, there was more frequent letter-writing to wife's parents than to husband's parents. [27] In a study

[25] John Mogey, "Social Aspects of English Housing," in *Recherches sur la Famille,* vol. III, p. 230.

[26] Rogers and Leichter, *op. cit.,* pp. 7–8.

[27] W. M. Smith, Jr., "Family Living Plans for Later Years," *Marriage and Family Living,* 16 (February, 1954), p. 40.

of farm migrants, urban migrants, and native families in Des Moines, Bauder and Burchinal indicate that the number of husband's relatives in Des Moines was about the same as the number of wife's relatives in each group, but that the yearly frequency of large family gatherings (location unspecified) was greater with wife's relatives.[28]

From the Netherlands, Ishwaran reported of the urban middle class family that

> It is not surprising, in view of the great influence of the mother, that young people have proportionately more contact with relatives on the distaff side than on the spear. Association was greatest with uncles, aunts, and cousins on the mother's side, whom the mother also visited.[29]

HELP AND THE FAMILY CYCLE

In this section, additional and some previously cited studies will be summarized so as to indicate precisely what tasks and activites, apart from visiting and letter-writing, family get-togethers and other forms of sociability and sentiment, are involved in intergenerational relationships at different stages of the urban-industrial family cycle. The direction and nature of this help vary with the stage in the life cycle of the family; the side of the family from which it comes differs according to whether the activity has to do with woman's work or man's work; but help and interaction involving the wife's side predominate because of the characteristic urban-industrial separation between the principal male role (occupational) and the family.

Young couples just starting out, or in the early stages of child-rearing, got direct financial aid such as loans more often from the husband's family, in both a blue-collar and a white-collar American sample.[30] Indirect financial aid, in the form of substantial, non-reciprocated gifts, came more from the wife's family, in both samples. Services to the young couple, such as care in sickness, childbirth, baby sitting, sewing or yard work, came more from the wife's family in the blue-collar sample and about equally from either side in the white-collar sample.

Young couples solve a housing shortage or cope with parents' indigence by living with the wife's parents to an increasing extent in Tokyo.[31] Presumably the same problems led young couples to live with parents, predominantly wife's parents, in the samples studied by the Census Bureau in 1946 and 1950, and in the nonfarm samples studied by the writer in Finland and Sweden.[32] In many urban communities in Britain, the wife's mother finds for the young couple a place to live near her.[33]

Maternal grandmothers, or other relatives of the wife, are more common as baby sitters and child tenders in New York[34] and Aberdeen.[35] A broad spectrum of mutual assistance with these and other housewifely tasks unites

[28] Ward W. Bauder and Lee G. Burchinal, "Farm Migrants to the City," Ames: Iowa State University, Agr. and Home Econ. Exp. Sta. Research Bulletin 534, 1965, Table 17.

[29] Ishwaran, op. cit., p. 171.

[30] Bert N. Adams, "Structural Factors Affecting Parental Aid to Married Children," Journal of Marriage and the Family, 26 (August, 1964), pp. 327–331.

[31] Dore, op. cit., pp. 132–133.

[32] See Table 1.

[33] John Mogey, "Family and Community in Urban-Industrial Societies," loc. cit., p. 520.

[34] Rogers and Leichter, op. cit., p. 7.

[35] Thompson and Finlayson (cited in Table 1), p. 160.

"Mum" and her daughters in British urban communities.[36]

Help to the husband in getting a job is reported to come from the husband's father in Britain

> when the father can vouch for his son as responsible in unskilled occupations like dockers in London, porters in the major London markets, or college servants in Oxford. Even among the skilled trades, like printing composition, where entry to an occupation is strictly controlled by union locals or branches dominated by a few family lines, the right of entry to an occupation may in this fashion become almost a family inheritance.[37]

In Rogers and Leichter's New York sample, if the husband was in business with kin, it was with his own kin.[38]

Coming to the later stages of the life cycle, assistance to the elderly with finances, care, and housework, usually came more from the daughter than from the son, in Smith's Pennsylvania samples,[39] Townsend's Bethnal Green sample,[40] and other British urban samples.[41] Dore noted in Tokyo a tendency for more of such help to come from daughters, as the extended family weakens.[42] A national probability sample of persons aged 65 and over in the U. S., reported by Shanas, more often said they would turn to a daughter rather than a son if they needed convalescent care.[43] The

tendency for older parents to live with married daughters and their husbands, rather than married sons and their wives, noted in the Census Bureau data of 1946, in a number of smaller U. S. samples, and in nonfarm families in Finland and Sweden, is further evidence of the predominance of a matrilineal link between generations.[44]

THE DAUGHTER-IN-LAW PROBLEM

Although positive factors, discussed in the next section, contribute to matrilateral solidarity in the urban-industrial family, an important negative factor is the conflict between mother and daughter-in-law.

It appears as a general rule, in the broad range of family types that we have been discussing, that the most common and most troublesome in-law conflict is that between mother and daughter-in-law. Sheldon says of the Karelian farm family that

> all kinds of stories are told about the unhappiness of daughters-in-law who had stern mothers-in-law and who in turn were strict with their own daughters-in-law. When I was investigating reasons for the splitting-up of families, one of the commonest explanations I received was that the daughters-in-law could not get along with their mothers-in-law or with each other.[45]

Dore says that in Japan the "'mother-in-law-daughter-in-law' problem' is a common phrase although it was until recently simply considered a part of the natural order like earthquakes, not as a 'problem' in the sense of something to be dealt with and solved."[46]

[36] John Mogey, "Social Aspects of English Family Housing," *loc. cit.*, p. 230.

[37] John Mogey, "Family and Community in Urban-Industrial Societies," · *loc. cit.*, p. 516.

[38] Rogers and Leichter, *op. cit.*, p. 8.

[39] Smith, *op. cit.*, p. 40.

[40] Townsend, *op. cit.*, pp. 84–87, 110.

[41] John Mogey, "Social Aspects of English Family Housing," *loc. cit.*, p. 230.

[42] Dore, *op. cit.*, p. 132–134.

[43] Ethel Shanas, *Family Relationships of Older People*, New York: Health Information Research Series, No. 20, 1961.

[44] Studies cited in Table 1.

[45] Sheldon, *op. cit.*, p. 119.

[46] Dore, *op. cit.*, p. 126.

In discussing the "traditional" household in the sandy soils area of the Netherlands, Kooy surveyed 15 polemic articles or books on such households written by family life experts, and all mentioned the daughter-in-law, frequently as a problem. Kooy observed that

> they form a much larger group than the sons-in-law (3:1) and . . . their life situation, much more than that of the latter, conditions the possibility of a conflict with the other members of the household. The son-in-law's opinion on the farm management may differ from that of the father-in-law, but the daughter-in-law has the risk to become involved in a struggle about home management and education as well as about farm operation, at least if the "old woman" is still alive.[47]

The other mother-in-law problem, that arising between the husband and his mother-in-law, is of course less likely to arise in patrilocal societies such as the Karelian, Japanese, and Dutch farm families represent. Probably also conflict between persons of the same sex is more likely than between persons of different sex and different age. Even in neolocal societies, however, although we find the husband's mother-in-law problem rising to notice, as in English music hall jokes and the Amos and Andy show, the wife-mother-in-law problem is the more severe. Both Wallin[48] and Duvall[49] report that the mother-in-law problem was the most severe of all in-law problems and that

the wife's mother-in-law was the more prominent in such conflicts, and Rogers and Leichter agree on the predominance of the husband's kin in marital discord.[50]

DISCUSSION

The various evidence just reviewed of predominantly matrilateral ties between generations in industrial societies can be summarized as meaning that, in matters pertaining to the wife's role, such as child care, homemaking, the maintenance of expressive relationships, and succorance, the mother-daughter link is stronger than the mother-daughter-in-law link, and that where the matter pertains to the husband's role, such as money or work, the father-son link is stronger than the father-son-in-law link; and that since the husband's occupational and financial role is largely divorced from family connections, ties between the couple and the wife's immediate family predominate. Contributing factors to this matrilateral asymmetry are mother-daughter-in-law conflict and (possibly) differential migration and the greater dependency of girls on their family than boys.

It should be emphasized that intergenerational kin relations exhibit behavioral regularities, not normatively enforced regularities. The whole situation of intergenerational kin relations is extremely flexible and open to a thousand influences, such as differences in interpersonal relationships between families, and the occurrence of families with children of only one sex. Considering the fluidity and lack of norms governing intergenerational relations, the consistency of even modest differences in closeness between the nuclear family and one set of relatives rather than another is the

[47] Kooy, op. cit., p. 193. See also Ishwaran, op. cit., p. 55.

[48] Paul Wallin, "Sex Differences in Attitudes to In-laws: A Test of a Theory," American Journal of Sociology, 59 (March, 1954), pp. 466–469.

[49] Evelyn M. Duvall, In-laws, Pro and Con, New York: Association Press, 1954, p. 184.

[50] Rogers and Leichter, op. cit., p. 11.

more striking. It is suggested here that the moderate prevalence of matrilateral links in intergenerational relationships is only the top of the iceberg, so to speak. If we suppose that in 40 percent of cases circumstances dictate that aid and interaction must involve a son, and that in another 40 percent it must involve a daughter, while in only 20 percent is there the possibility of choice, and that the choice almost always goes toward a daughter, we would have a result such as that which we observed: a moderate, though strikingly consistent, prevalence of ties with the daughter.

Intergenerational solidarity follows the line of male succession in instrumental tasks; when the latter disappears, matrilateral solidarity between generations becomes the rule. We have a society in which kin can rarely be of use to men in their daily business, while kin can be of considerable use to women in their daily business. While the father in the modern family is still the breadwinner and the mother the homemaker, as in the old days, the father's sphere of operation is the office or factory, not the home. This means that the line of succession from father to son in the masculine role of making a living has for the most part been broken. The son does not inherit a farm from his father or go into business with him. True, the son may go into the same kind of work as his father, but this is occupational coincidence, not succession, and usually means only that the father sees that his son obtains the necessary formal education, or is hired at the shop or factory. There need not be any work relations between father and son which bind them together and which consequently would foster residential proximity and solidarity between the son's household and that of his parents.

This absence of a necessity for father and son to collaborate or work together in their breadwinner roles enhances the influence of the women on intergenerational solidarity. Besides, as noted, women have the responsibility for the daily running of the household. Consequently, the question of whether ties between parental generations and daughters' families tend to be more or less close than ties between parental generations and sons' families reduces to the question of whether the mother-daughter relationship or the mother-daughter-in-law relationship is likely to be closer. Both positive and negative factors favor the former.

In summary, for instrumental reasons the important intergenerational link in non-industrial settings is the tie between men. Again for instrumental reasons, namely the detachment of men's work from the family, in urban-industrial societies the important intergenerational link is the tie between women.

·

And Then We Were Old[*]

Irving Rosow

The old are with us, but not of us.

More than 17,000,000 persons over sixty-five live in America today, making up almost nine percent of the population; but this is not why they are a problem. They increase ever more rapidly—one million every three years; nor is this why they are a problem.

They trouble us precisely because we are such an affluent society. They have become a standing embarrassment, a mute reproach to social conscience. Our productivity makes the sheer cost of meeting such social problems of secondary importance; we can view them against larger national goals and the kind of society we want to become. The price of social change is not a critical economic issue—it is basically a moral concern and a value choice.

The old lack money and they lack medical care. But even if these needs were met, their problem would still not be solved. We must not confuse provision for material needs with a general solution. Although many specific needs are involved, the old in America suffer primarily from lack of function and status. . . .

How do other cultures handle their aged? What conditions support the social position of old people—their prestige, status, or power? What fosters their social integration?

°*Originally published in* Trans-Action Magazine, *Community Leadership Project, Washington University, St. Louis, Missouri, 1965, 2: 21–26.*

Leo Simmons has studied this problem among almost a hundred primitive societies represented in the Yale cross-cultural files. Others, such as Conrad Arensberg and Solon Kimball, provide supplemental data on more recent nonindustrial cultures as well. Taken together, they cover all stages of pre-industrial development, from the simplest food-gathering groups to advanced agricultural economies with complex systems of private property.

These studies show that the welfare of the aged varies according to seven factors which involve the resources that old people command, the functions they perform, and the state of social organization. Their position in their society is relatively stronger if:

1. They own or control property on which younger people are dependent. In this way they maintain their own independence while simultaneously governing the opportunities of the young. In rural Ireland, for instance, a son may not succeed to his inheritance before his fifties, and he may be deferential to his parents almost into their senility.

2. Their experience gives them a vital command or monopoly of strategic knowledge of the culture, including the full range of occupational skills and techniques, as well as healing, religion, ritual, warfare, lore, and the arts. As the principal bearers and interpreters of cultures in which there is little change and no science, the old have a strategic func-

tion in transmitting this knowledge to younger people.

3. They are links to the past and to the gods in tradition-oriented societies. In classical China, for example, old age was honorific and revered on religious as well as other grounds; and when the old died they were worshiped as ancestors.

4. The extended family is central to the social structure. A clan can and will act much more effectively to meet crises and dependency of its members than a small family. Mutual obligations between blood relatives—specifically including the aged—are institutionalized as formal rights, not generous benefactions.

5. The population clusters in relatively small, stable communities in which the governing values are sacred rather than secular; community structure is fairly clear cut, with formal age-grading and definite roles linked to different ages; almost all contacts between group members are face-to-face and personal; and an individual relates to the same group of people in many different contexts instead of many diverse groups— one at home, a second at work, and a third in church, for example.

The final two factors are rather surprising. They show that the relative welfare of the old person in his group improves to the extent that:

6. The productivity of the economy is low and approaches the ragged edge of starvation. The greater the poverty and the struggle to survive, the *relatively* better off old people are by the standards of their group. With low marginal productivity and a primitive division of labor, labor may be cheap, but the contribution of each additional pair of hands to the small gross product is valued.

To be sure, in such primitive economies extremely dependent old people are not sentimentally cared for indefi-

nitely. Their fates are determined by the balance between what they put in and take out of the system. But, so long as an old person's productivity exceeds his consumption, including the time and effort required for his care, the culture retains and makes a place for him. However, when the balance shifts and his dependency threatens the group, then he tends to be expelled. Although the particular form of this fate may vary, swift death is common. The Masai of Africa unceremoniously throw the old dependent outside the village *bwoma* and forget about him, while the Polar Eskimos rather sorrowfully "put him out on the ice"— in both cases to die. But when his needs impose a severe strain on the group's resources, his *social* death precedes the physical.

7. Finally, there is high mutual dependence within a group. The great interdependence among members promotes mutual aid in meeting survival problems. Here the aged are benefactors as well as beneficiaries of reciprocity.

A range of studies indicate that even in America, old people are relatively better off and accepted when they own family farm land, live in small communities, are members of racial or ethnic minorities with extended kinship obligations, or belong to unskilled, working class groups where interdependence and mutual aid are standard conditions of survival. These findings argue well for the generality of the seven principles.

However, social change is systematically weakening these principles, regardless of local variations.

Property ownership

This has spread broadly through the population during the past generation. But it has been attended by an important separation between capital ownership and management in which control is *not* particularly centered in the hands of older people. Further, the growth of the economy has created many new jobs, but mainly for younger people. At the same time, changes in higher education have opened the gates of the universities to many more of them.

These developments have increased young people's opportunities and reduced their dependence. While an old property owner may be financially independent, he no longer has significant control over the life chances of the young; and they have less need to defer to him.

Strategic knowledge

Old people's skills, experience, and knowledge are no longer critical factors in our culture and seldom make them authorities. The speed and pervasiveness of social change now transform the world within a generation, so that the experience of the old becomes largely irrelevant to the young. The lifetime of a seventy-five-year-old person spans man's leap from the horse and buggy to the hydrogen bomb and space travel. Occupational and other skills are now taught through formal education rather than informally. The young and middle-aged learn attitudes and life styles largely from age mates and the mass media. Nor have the old solved the problems of the world successfully enough to inspire respect and confidence. Therefore, they are considered neither strategic agents of instruction nor founts of wisdom.

Religious links

Our society has never venerated the aged as peculiarly sacred links to ancestors, gods, or the past. The old are not protected by religious tradition.

Kinship and extended family

Kinship and family ties have been weakened in this century by occupational demands and frequent moving. Shifting job markets require flexibility of movement at the same time that urban homes have shrunk in size. The smaller isolated family has become the norm, and responsibility to one's spouse and children now takes clear priority over obligations to parents. Although children still do help aged parents, especially in the working classes, the major responsibility for old people has shifted to the government and other organizations.

Community life

Urbanization and residential mobility have also seriously weakened local community ties. Changing neighborhoods, turnover of residents, and urban impersonality have undermined those stable neighborhood structures which used to accommodate older people.

Productivity

Clearly, by any conceivable index, our productivity is tremendously high and growing. Because of automation, there is widespread displacement and no general labor scarcity outside of selected occupations. Since old people do not appreciably command skills in those occupations where labor is short, they are in little demand on the labor market. Except under special conditions, such as boom or war, they are not important to the work force.

Mutual dependence

Our economic growth and the drastic rise in living standards have undermined our mutual dependence. Greater income and opportunity have extended the range of personal choice and the freedom of action. Many goals can now be achieved with comparatively little reliance on other individuals, but this independence has been bought at the expense of solidarity and reciprocity. Except for the civil rights movement, it is a far cry indeed from the collective action of industrial unionization in the thirties.

Therefore, those factors which reinforce the position of old people in less advanced societies undermine the aged in America. We are too wealthy as a nation and too prosperous as individuals to *need* the old person. He can do little for us that we cannot do ourselves . . .

THE HIGH COST OF AGING

Some features of American life are positively *inimical* to old people. We are youth-oriented, so that children and the young persons have a prior claim on our resources. We view this as an investment in the future rather than in the past, and it reflects pragmatism if not equity.

Also, though it has traditionally been difficult for men over forty to get employment, occupational obsolescence is occurring at steadily younger ages. Moreover, technological development affects not only the manual and less skilled workers, but is now reaching relentlessly into higher professional and managerial ranks and into the most advanced complex levels of science.

In many fields, the fund of human knowledge doubles in about ten years, and as new ideas and techniques are introduced, experience counts for less and less. Consequently, the electronics engineer will eventually step aside for the solid-state physicist. Because of reluctance and the decline in learning ability as people grow older, we cannot expect easy retraining in new skills during middle age or later. Actually,

advances in knowledge will result in a shorter work life and a younger retirement age in the future. By the end of the century the twenty-five hour week and retirement at fifty may well be commonplace—and these are conservative estimates.

While older workers can still make some contribution, their productive capacity and quality are generally lower at sixty-five than at thirty or forty. They may be kept productive if they are placed in carefully selected jobs, but it is another question whether they can be kept working at competitive costs. Beyond sheer obsolescence lie two *other* obstacles to their continued employment:

1. Less productive older workers involve higher direct and indirect costs. Therefore, employers are asked to subsidize the aged either by absorbing higher expenses or by lowering profit margins. In either case, we expect them to assume the costs, and in our economy, their lack of enthusiasm for this is scarcely surprising.

2. The second obstacle to continued employment is the "efficiency" norm of large scale enterprises. Routine personnel procedures in recruitment, hiring, and job placement aim to eliminate inefficient individual processing. But the optimum assignment of old workers requires custom job-tailoring and personal attention. In other words, sheer bureaucratic pride in "running a taut ship" itself militates against individual treatment.

Thus changes in technology, the occupational system, urbanization, residential mobility, and the family have all been harmful to old people. The aged have been shorn of their major functions and supports; they have lower social status and no incentive to accept old age as rewarding. Consequently, to avert the stigma of age, they systematically deny that they are declining or getting old. To admit to being old is the final surrender.

How can they preserve the illusion of youth, of keeping age at bay? In general only by maintaining those factors that integrate an old person into society. But can their middle age patterns be continued into old age?

Property and power

We have seen earlier that old people cannot easily retain the bases of power, and that property may give them independence, but little control over or deference from others.

Group memberships

People are integrated into society not only by the resources they command and the functions they perform, but also through their social networks. Here the picture for the old is equally clear. Data on their associations show that participation in clubs and organizations declines steadily with age as low income, widowhood, and illness increase. Their informal relationships similarly diminish as neighborhoods change, families separate when children marry and pursue jobs, relatives and friends move away or die. More of their time is spent at funerals than ever before. In other words, old people progressively lose their group supports as networks of relatives, friends, and neighbors wither away through time.

What possible substitutes exist for these deteriorating social ties? One is the formation of new friendships with younger people nearby. However, younger age groups tend to be indifferent to or reject the old. This is trenchantly expressed in Joyce Cary's novel, *To Be a Pilgrim:*

> Love is a delusion to the old, for who can love an old man? He is a nuisance; he

has no place in the world. The old are surrounded by treachery, for no one tells them truth. Either it is thought necessary to deceive them, for their own good, or nobody can take the trouble to give explanation or understanding to those who will carry both so soon into a grave. They must not complain of what is inevitable; they must not think evil. It is unjust to blame the rock for its hardness, the stream for its inconstancy and its flight, the young for the strength and the jewel brightness of their passage. An old man's loneliness is nobody's fault. He is like an old fashioned hat which seems absurd and incomprehensible to the young, who never admired and wore such a hat.

It is consistent with this that research shows small chance of success for the development of friendships between old and young. Younger people have negative stereotypes about the old; and their attitudes do *not* change as a result of contact, exposure to, or experience with them. For example, my own studies of local friendship patterns show that in a large apartment building with old and young residents, less than four percent of friendships in the building were between the age groups. There is an effective social barrier between older and younger people which proximity does not destroy. The aged, incidentally, are the only group for which this is true. Contact and exposure do break down invidious stereotypes about other groups; but not about old people. This is not only because age is devalued, but also because different age groups seldom are peers sharing a common role, similar life experiences, and a common fate.

Major social roles

People are also defined and located in society according to their major role attributes, such as marital status, work, income, and health. To the extent that an older person can maintain his middle-age characteristics in this respect, his later years pose few serious problems. But if these change, old age becomes strained, problematic, and demoralized. Older people are relatively well off and socially integrated if they are: (a) married and living with spouse; (b) still at work; (c) have no major loss of income; and (d) are in good health. But they are apt to be in serious difficulty if they are widowed, retired, have suffered a large drop in income, and are in poor health.

What chances have they of showing up favorably on these four factors?

Marital status

As expected, the aged show more marital disruption than any other age group. Of those over sixty-five, only about 45 percent are still married and living with spouses. One-fourth of the men and more than one-half of the women are widowed.

But even these overall figures conceal the sharp rise in marital dissolution with increasing age. Each ten-year period after sixty-five finds an additional 20 percent widowed. For example, 15 percent of the men 65–69 are widowed compared to 58 percent of those over 85. For women, widowhood increases from 41 percent of those 65–69 to 83 percent of those 85 or older. Widowhood affects more women than men and probably has a harder impact on them. This will probably continue because women are generally younger than their husbands, they have lower mortality rates at every age, and their life expectancy rises even faster. For example, in 1920, there were about equal numbers of men and women over sixty-five; in 1940, there were almost eleven women for every ten men; by 1950, there were fully twelve women for every ten men. The surplus of older women will presumably in-crease—and so will the strains of widowhood.

Work

The proportion of people over sixty-five in the labor force has declined steadily for the past sixty years. Two-thirds of the men were working in 1900 compared to scarcely one-third today, only about half of them full-time.

More important, of those men still working, almost one-half are *self-employed*, but precisely in those sectors of the economy where the independent operator is steadily giving way. The family farmer and small businessman are losing out to corporations; and pro-fessionals are increasingly entering business or government as salaried em-ployees. Thus, the economy itself is steadily undermining the possibilities for self-employment.

What about the remaining older workers, those on wages? Except for a minority protected by effective seniority and flexible retirement provisions, they are very vulnerable. On the free labor market, older workers are in the traditionally marginal position of Ne-groes—the last hired and first fired. Apart from illness and a few atypical industries, one overriding factor governs whether older people work: when labor is scarce, old people have jobs; when labor is abundant, they do not. It is as stark as that. And in an era of automation, labor shortages promise to be ephemeral and localized.

Income

So long as older people continue to work, their income holds up reasonably well. Indeed, if their health is good, they may even be better off than earlier because their homes are usually paid off, their children independent, and their own needs more modest. But for the two-thirds who are retired, income is chopped to approximately *half* of their former earnings. Furthermore, despite steady increases in social security benefits from the early 'fifties, retirees have not received a *pro rata* share of our growing productivity. Between 1940 and 1960, all workers' *real* income after taxes rose by 51 percent while real social security benefits increased by only 17 percent, or one-third as much.

For the aged as a whole, income figures are appalling, and one cannot conceive how many of them manage to keep body and soul together at today's prices. It is perhaps a tribute to human resilience and adaptability. According to the Social Security Administration, among persons over sixty-five in 1960, about one-fourth of the women had no income at all, almost three-fourths had less than $1,000 per year, and fewer than one in ten had as much as $2,000 annually. The situation of men was not quite so bad, but it was bad enough. More than one-fourth had less than $1,000, one-third between $1,000 and $1,999, and about 40 percent had $2,000 or more per year. Fewer than one person in four had an income approaching $40 per week. Try to imagine an old couple or even a single person subsisting on less than this at recent price levels!

Health

Modern medicine has reduced infectious diseases so that the aged suffer mostly from chronic illness. Older people generally expect more aches, pains, and creaks in their daily lives, and they accept this as normal so long as they are still able to get around and function independently. For the most part, they do manage. Only about 15 percent have serious loss of mobility or capacity to function.

The foregoing losses do not affect persons over sixty-five uniformly. A major dividing line occurs at seventy-five. Significantly more people over seventy-five are widowed, retired, have low incomes, and are in very poor health. . . .

BEYOND SECURITY

There are no simple answers to the question, "What is the solution to the problems of the aged?" for the question itself has different levels; it can refer to symptoms or to causes. Some limited, practical measures are possible—even though they only ameliorate symptoms. After all, if we try to make terminal cancer patients as comfortable as possible, we can do at least as much for the aged.

We might consider two alternatives. First, we can provide adequately for old people's material welfare and security. This means assuring them of all the medical care they need without quibbling about their eligibility or whether it will cost two billion or three billion dollars and without burying the patient, the doctor, or the hospital in paperwork. This is possible. It also means assuring all older people of a genuinely adequate income and decent standard of living, again without quibble or cavil. This would require major revision of the entire social security program and its income provisions. But this too is possible. . . .

Second, we must consider how best to insulate old people from the social insults of age; specifically how to ease their loss of status and the indifference of younger people. Isolation and other problems grow as the aged lose their roles and their contacts, but these demoralizing pressures might slacken if the aged had ready access to other old people of similar background. Similarity of life experience and a common fate are a firm basis of communication, mutual understanding, and group formation. We are not advocating the formal segregation of the aged; but insofar as potential friends are found in the immediate environment, this might insulate them from the rebuffs of society, increase the prospect of new social ties, and partially revitalize their lives. Environments which integrate old people into local groups warrant careful study, and some research on this is being completed.

But we must not concentrate only on symptoms—particularly if we are successful in treating them. There is little doubt that some important concessions will be made, whether willingly or grudgingly, to the material needs of the aged, especially medical care and income. These must not be neglected; but we may still be barely scratching the surface of the problem.

More fundamental answers must be sought to the status issue. Basic solutions will be almost impossible unless our material values shift and our institutions change. We will have to place a higher value on our human resources, on social rights, on truth and beauty, not because they are practical but for their own sake. This is necessary before a life of genuine dignity and respect will be possible for older people—or for the young.

Actually, the crucial people are *not* the aged, but the *younger* groups. It is *we* who determine the status and position of the old. The problem is that of alienation—not only the alienation of old from young, but of the young from each other, and of man from man. No real way out of this dilemma exists without a basic reworking of our national aspirations and values. Anything less than this will see us treating only symptoms, nibbling at the tattered edges of our social problems without penetrating to their heart.

*Further Thoughts on the Theory of Disengagement**

Elaine Cumming

The usefulness of a theory depends upon its ability to explain the present and predict the future. In this essay, I shall amplify and elaborate the 'disengagement' theory of ageing that W. E. Henry and I developed with our colleagues between 1957 and 1960.[1] I hope

in this way to make that theory better able to describe and predict both the range and the limits of the ageing process. In its original form, the theory was too simple; it had only enough detail to account for the main outlines of the process of growing old. By adding new elements and elaborating the basic propositions in more detail, I hope to be

°*Reprinted from* International Social Science Journal, *1963, 15: 377–393.*

[1] The theory was first suggested in 'Disengagement, a tentative theory of aging,' by Elaine Cumming, Lois R. Dean, and David S. Newell, *Sociometry*, vol. 23, no. 1, March 1960, and developed in greater detail in *Growing Old*, by Elaine Cumming and William E. Henry, New York, Basic Books, 1961.

THE GENERAL THEORY OF DISENGAGEMENT

The disengagement theory was developed during a five-year study of a sample of ageing people in an American city. The sample consisted of 275 individuals between the ages of 50 and 90 years; they were in good health and had the minimum of money needed for independence.[2] Briefly, the theory proposes that under these conditions normal ageing is a mutual withdrawal or 'disengagement' between the ageing person and others in the social system to which he belongs—a withdrawal initiated by the individual himself, or by others in the system. When disengagement is complete, the equilibrium that existed in middle life between the individual and society has given way to a new equilibrium characterized by greater distance, and a changed basis for solidarity.

Engagement is essentially the interpenetration of the person and the society to which he belongs. The fully-engaged person acts in a large number and a wide variety of roles in a system of divided labour, and feels an obligation to meet the expectations of his role partners. There are variations, however, in the type of engagement. It is possible to be broadly engaged in a number of social systems that exert little influence over the remainder of society, and it is possible to be deeply engaged in the sense of having roles whose function is to make policies that affect others in large numbers. It is possible to be symbolically engaged by epitomizing some valued attribute—by being a famous scientist, poet or patriot. A few men have roles that combine all three types of engagement and carry with them the extreme constraints that must accompany such a number and variety of obligations; presidents and prime ministers are among them. Roughly, the depth and breadth of a man's engagement can be measured by the degree of potential disruption that would follow his sudden death.[3] The death of someone who has an important symbolic engagement with his society, however, can result in both loss and gain because the survivors can rally around the symbols he embodied and thus reaffirm their value. For many Americans, Dag Hammarskjöld's death brought into sharp focus the need for world order.

In its original form, the disengagement theory concerned itself with the modal case which, in America, is first, departure of children from families, and then, retirement for men or widowhood for women. It did not take account of such non-modal cases as widowhood before the marriage of the last child or of work protracted past the modal age of retirement. Most importantly, it did not, and still does not, concern itself with the effects of the great scourges of old age, poverty and illness.[4] This essay will modify and elaborate the theory somewhat and suggest some character-

[2] This means that they were able to live on their incomes from whatever source without seeking public assistance.

[3] Obviously this is an over-simplification. There are many structural safeguards in any society to keep this kind of disruption to a minimum; included among them is the rational-legal system of authority.

[4] The population of study was a representative sample of the Greater Kansas City metropolitan area with the lowest and the highest socio-economic groups and all who could not fill their major roles on account of illness removed.

istics of ageing people that might make an important difference to their patterns of disengagement. Like the original statement, this modification has the status of a system of hypotheses. Some of the elements are close to being operational as they stand; others are still too general for testing.

Before proceeding further, an asymmetry in the earlier discussions of the theory must be dealt with. Disengagement has been conceived as a mutual withdrawal between individual and society, and therefore the process should vary according to the characteristics of both. In earlier statements, consideration was given to the different ways in which the environment retreats—retirement, loss of kin or spouse, departure of children, and so on—but the only individual difference to be considered in any detail was that between the sexes. Eventually, if the process is to be described adequately, we must have typologies of withdrawal and retreat. I suggest that deeply-rooted differences in character are a good starting point because it is reasonable to suppose that they colour all of life, including the disengagement process.

TEMPERAMENT AND DISENGAGEMENT

In its original form the disengagement theory did no more than suggest an ultimate biological basis for a reduction of interest or involvement in the environment. Variations in the process were attributed to social pressures, especially as they are differently experienced by men and women. A vital difference in style, however, can be expected between people of dissimilar temperaments, no matter what their sex. Combining biological and social variables within the framework of the disengagement theory, it might be possible to suggest a wider variety of styles of interaction in old age than would otherwise be possible.

A proposed temperamental variable, basically biological, is the style of adaptation to the environment. It seems well established that humans must maintain a minimum of exchange with the environment, or a clear anticipation of renewing exchange with it, in order to keep a firm knowledge both of it and of themselves.[5] There appear to be different modes of maintaining this relationship, which can perhaps be called the 'impinging' mode and the 'selecting' mode.[6] The impinger appears to try out his concept of himself in interaction with others in the environment and to use their appropriate responses to confirm the correctness of his inferences about himself, the environment, and his relationship to it. If the feedback from others suggests that he is incorrect, he will try to bring others' responses into line with his own sense of the appropriate relationship. Only if he fails repeatedly will he modify his concept of himself. In contrast, the selector tends to wait for others to affirm his assumptions about himself. From the ongoing flow of stimulation he selects these cues that confirm his relationship to the world. If they fail to come, he waits, and only reluctantly brings his own concepts into line with the feedback he receives. The selector may be able to use symbolic residues of old interactions to maintain his sense of self more effi-

[5] Philip Solomon, et. al., Sensory Deprivation. Cambridge, Mass., Harvard University Press, 1961.

[6] For a discussion of the implications of this typology of temperament for psychopathology, see, John Cumming and Elaine Cumming, Ego and Milieu, New York, Atherton Press, 1962.

ciently than the impinger, and thus be able to wait longer for suitable cues.

We assume that temperament is a multi-determined, biologically-based characteristic, and therefore that the temperamental types are normally distribute in the population with few people at the extremes. We also assume that the modal person can both impinge and select as the occasion demands, although perhaps favouring one style rather than the other. A normal person will shift to the alternate pattern when it becomes necessary either for appropriate role behaviour or for the prevention of 'diffusion feelings.'[7] If there are no complicating ego problems, a pronounced selector will probably be known as 'reserved,' or 'self-sufficient' or 'stubborn,' and a pronounced impinger as 'temperamental,' 'lively,' or 'brash.' We would expect the impinger, as he grows older, to experience more anxiety about loss of interaction, because he needs it to maintain orientation.[8] The selector, being able to make more use of symbols, may have less difficulty with the early stages of disengagement.[9]

[7] I use this phrase in the way that Erikson does in *Childhood and Society,* New York, W. W. Norton, 1950. Roughly, it refers to the anxiety that attends the doubt that others will confirm in the future either the relationship presently established or the identity currently implied by the interaction.

[8] It is fairly obvious that these proposed temperaments are related to the psychological dimension, introversion-extroversion.

[9] This raises a problem of the difference between the *appearance* of engagement and the *experience* of it. This problem is enhanced by a tendency to contrast disengagement with activity (see, Robert Havighurst, 'Successful aging,' *Gerontologist*, vol. 1, p. 8–13, 1961). In fact, activity and engagement are not in the same dimension. A disengaged person often maintains a high level of activity in a small number and narrow variety of roles, although it is doubtful if it

The disengaging impinger can be expected to be more active and apparently more youthful than his peers. His judgment may not be as good as it was, but he will provoke the comment that he is an unusual person for his age. Ultimately, as he becomes less able to control the situations he provokes, he may suffer anxiety and panic through failure both to arouse and to interpret appropriate reactions. His problem in old age will be to avoid confusion.

is possible to be at once firmly engaged and inactive. In any event, the opposite of disengagement is engagement, a concept different from, though related to, the concept of activity. The result of confusing these two variables is that *active* people are judged to be *engaged*. They may, however, be *relatively disengaged impingers*. They may also, depending upon the type of activity, be exceptionally healthy or restless. There is no real way to judge because the issue has not been put to the test. Unfortunately, many of the populations used for gerontological studies are volunteers and thus can be expected to include a disproportionately large number of impingers. For example Marc Zborowski (in: 'Aging and recreation,' *Journal of Gerontology*, vol. 17, no. 3, July 1962) reports that a group of volunteers reported little change over time of their recreational activities and preferences. The author concludes from this that the subjects are not disengaging, using the concept in Havighurst's sense as the opposite of active. His finding is only unexpected inasmuch as the disengagement theory would predict a *rise* in recreational activities after retirement among a population that might include numerous disengaging impingers. In contrast to this report is a careful study of a *general population* of older people in New Zealand (see, 'Older People of Dunedin City: A Survey,' J. R. McCreary, and H. C. A. Somerset, Wellington: Dept. of Health, 1955) among whom only 10 per cent belonged to, or wanted to belong to, recreational groups, and only 9 per cent of those not working would seek work if the restrictions on their pensions would allow them.

The selector, in contrast to the impinger, interacts in a more measured way. When he is young he may be thought too withdrawn, but as he grows older his style becomes more age-appropriate. In old age, because of his reluctance to generate interaction, he may, like a neglected infant, develop a kind of marasmus. His foe will be apathy rather than confusion.

These are not, of course, ordinary aging processes; the extreme impinger and the extreme selector are almost certain to get into trouble at some crisis point because they cannot move over to the opposite mode of interacting when it is adaptive to do so. In general in an achievement-oriented society, the impinger may be more innately suited to middle age, the selector perhaps to childhood and old age.

To sum up, some biologically-based differences among people may be expected to impose a pattern upon their manner of growing old. I shall now return to the theory, with this variable in mind, and at the same time suggest other concepts that it might profitably include.

AT THE OUTSET
OF DISENGAGEMENT

Disengagement probably begins sometime during middle life when certain changes of perception occur, of which the most important is probably an urgent new perception of the inevitability of death. It is certain that children do not perceive the meaning of death and it is said that 'no young man believes that he will ever die.' It is quite possible that a vivid apprehension of mortality—perhaps when the end of life seems closer than its start—is the beginning of the process of growing old. Paradoxically, a sense of the shortness of time may come at the height of engagement; that is, competition for time may

draw attention to both its scarcity and its value. There may be a critical point beyond which further involvement with others automatically brings a sense of 'there is no time for all that I must do' which, in turn, leads to evaluations of what has been done compared to what was hoped for, and then to allocations and priorities for the future. If this process is common to many people, those who have never been very firmly engaged should feel less sense of urgency than those who are tightly enmeshed with society—all other things, including temperament, being equal.

Accompanying the need to select and allocate is a shift away from achievement. Achievement, as Parsons says, [10] demands a future; when confidence in the existence of a future is lost, achievement cannot be pursued without regard to the question, 'Shall it be achievement of this rather than of that?' Such a question is the beginning of an exploration of the meaning and value of the alternatives. [11] In American life, where achievement is perhaps the highest value, its abandonment has always been tinged with failure. We would, therefore, expect the relinquishment of achievement to be a crisis, and, indeed, general knowledge and some research tell us that in middle life competent men with a record of achievement feel sudden painful doubts about the value of what they have done. [12] Once any part of achieve-

[10] Talcott Parsons, 'Toward a healthy maturity,' *Journal of Health and Human Behavior*, vol. 1, no. 3, 1960.

[11] Of course, at all times in the life span, priorities must be set up because it is impossible to do more than one thing in one space of time. But as long as there is the possibility of postponement until a later date, the problem of allocation has little poignancy.

[12] William E. Henry, 'Conflict, age, and the executive,' *Business Topics*, Michigan State University, no date.

ment is given up, some binding obligations are gone, and even if they are replaced with less demanding ties, a measure of disengagement has occurred.

Disengagement may begin in a different way, somewhat as follows: the middle-aged person who has not undergone an inner period of questioning reaches a point where losses, both personal and public, begin to outrun his ability to replace them. A friend dies, a business closes, his children move far away. For the healthy, ageing impinger these losses may be replaced; for the selector they may not, and an awareness of their permanence may be a turning point. With each loss, the ageing person must surrender certain potential feelings and actions and replace them with their symbolic residues in memory.[13] In a sense, this substitution of symbol for social action changes the quality of the self. Even if the role partners themselves are replaced, they cannot often substitute for the lost relationship because sentiments built up over the years cannot be copied.

The most crucial step in the disengagement process may lie in finding a new set of rewards. The esteem that achievement brings can be replaced by the affection generated in socio-emotional activity. The approval that comes from meeting contracted obligations can be replaced by the spontaneous responses of others to expressive acts. The inner rewards of weaving the past into a satisfactory moral fabric can partly replace

the public rewards of achievement. Nevertheless, in America today there is a net loss because achievement is more highly valued than meaning or expression and because its symbols are more easily calibrated. To be rich is to be recognized a success; wisdom is often its own reward.

Finally, and perhaps most importantly, freedom from obligation replaces the constraint of being needed in an interlocking system of divided tasks. The fully engaged man is, in essence, bound; the disengaged man is free—if he has resources and health enough to allow him to exercise that freedom. The ability to enjoy old age may be the ability and the opportunity to use freedom.[14]

No matter how important the effects of the perception of time and the shift in rewards, the essential characteristic of disengagement is that once started it tends to be self-perpetuating. If the search for meaning becomes urgent, and the impulse toward seeking out others becomes less rewarding, there will be a tendency not to replace ties broken by loss.

Once withdrawal has begun, it may become more difficult to make new contacts. Not knowing quite how to behave under strange circumstances inhibits exploration, and this difficulty, in turn, can reinforce the disengaging process—many elderly people refuse to fly in aircraft, not because they are afraid but because they do not know airport etiquette! A sense of strangeness cannot, of course, in itself lead to withdrawal; any middle-aged adult feels discomfort if he finds himself in an unknown situation without a role. Prisoners of war must be helped to re-engage after long periods of isolation from their culture. For the ageing, such diffusion feelings enhance a

[13] No concept of 'economy of libido' is implied here. The inference is quite simply that a person with a store of memories is less likely to give full attention to the world around him than the person who has fewer symbolic residues to capture his attention. Of course, there are obvious limits on preoccupation with the past including some minimum level of interaction that seems almost mandatory for life itself.

[14] See Emile Durkheim, *Suicide*, Glencoe, Ill., Free Press, 1951, p. 157-9.

process that is already under way—a process made inevitable by man's mortality.

Thus, empirically, we see ageing people interacting less and in fewer roles. Modally, ties to kindred become more salient, while more distant, impersonal, and more recent ties become less important and finally disappear. This process of reduction and simplification leaves the individual freer from the control that accompanies involvement in a larger number and greater variety of roles. Concretely, this means that the broadly engaged person receives fewer of the positive and negative sanctions that accompany and guide all interactions and control the style of everyday behaviour, and, therefore, idiosyncratic personal behaviour becomes possible. At the same time, ideas, removed from the scenes in which they can be tested out, become more stereotyped and general.[15]

It seems possible that those who have been deeply engaged in roles that influence considerable areas of society or those who have rare and valuable skills will remain engaged longer than those less deeply involved with the affairs of their generation. This is because the values that inform major decisions are slower to change than everyday norms, and those who have been consciously enmeshed with them may, in old age, symbolize their continuity for those who have not. Those who have been successful mathematicians, politicians, and poets can count on society remaining closer to them than those who have not influenced or represented their fellow men.

[15] When the Kansas City respondents were asked the question, 'What do you think of the younger generation?' the middle-aged people gave concrete examples of youthful behaviour that they found compelling or unattractive while the older people answered in large generalizations, usually negative.

As the number of groups to which an ageing person belongs is reduced, his membership in those remaining becomes more important because he must maintain a minimum of stimulation. The memberships of old age—kinship, friendship, and perhaps church—are all marked by a high level of agreement among members and many explicit common values. In such groups, it is very difficult to deviate far from the common viewpoint. Thus, the more the elderly person disengages from a variety of roles, the less likely is he to take on new ideas. The conservatism of old age is partly a security measure, related to the need to maintain harmony among the remaining companions.

As withdrawal of normative control is an essential aspect of the disengagement theory, it must be asked why old people should enter a spiral of decreasing conformity when middle-aged people, except in extreme cases, are able to endure prolonged interpersonal disruptions and quickly reconstitute contact with the norms. Moving from one city to another is an interpersonal crisis, but it does not often set in motion a process that leads to a new orientation to life. The difference seems to be that for the ageing a combination of reduced biological energy, the reduction of freedom, preoccupation with the accumulated symbols of the past, and licence for a new kind of self-centredness cannot be resisted. Furthermore, all this is expected of the older person, and so the circle is further reinforced.

In contrast, if the middle-aged person feels that he is in a situation of reduced social control, he has both the energy and the opportunity to seek new constraints, and if he retreats too far from conformity he is sanctioned. In some ways, an ageing person is like an adolescent; he is allowed more freedom and expressiveness than a middle-aged adult. Later, when he is very old, he is permitted the dependency and individuation of the small child.

In this view, socialization is the encouragement of children to abandon their parochialism and individuation and to accept conformity to the demands of the major institutions of society, while disengagement is a permission to return again to individuation. In all, for the old person, the circular process of disengagement results in the social tasks getting harder and the alternatives more rewarding, while for the young person, the social tasks remain rewarding and the alternatives are felt as alienation. Were it not for the value placed on achievement, the chains that the adult so willingly allows to bind him might be put off at least as readily as they are taken on.

SOCIETY'S WITHDRAWAL

The disengagement theory postulates that society withdraws from the ageing person to the same extent as that person withdraws from society. This is, of course, just another way of saying that the process is normatively governed and in a sense agreed upon by all concerned. Everyone knows how much freedom from constraint is allowable and where the line between the oddness of old age and the symptoms of deviance lies. There seem to be deeply-rooted reasons, in both the culture and the social structure, for this withdrawal process.

In the first place the organization of modern society requires that competition for powerful roles be based on achievement. Such competition favours the young because their knowledge is newer. Furthermore, the pressure of the young on to the highest roles cannot be met in a bureaucracy by an indefinite expansion of the powerful roles. Therefore, the older members must be discarded to make way for the younger. In America, a disproportionately large number of young adults will soon be competing for jobs that are becoming relatively fewer as industry moves toward complete automation.[16] If Americans are to remain engaged in any serious way past the seventh decade, as many observers insist they must, roles must be found for them that young people *cannot* fill.[17] Only an elaboration of available roles can accomplish this because it is impossible for a society organized around standards of achievement and efficiency to assign its crucial roles to a group whose death rate is excessively high. When a middle-aged, fully-engaged person dies, he leaves many broken ties, and disrupted situations. Disengagement thus frees the old to die without disrupting vital affairs.

Finally, at the end of life when one has outlived one's peers, social withdrawal consists in failure to approach. In this sense, the young withdraw from the old because the past has little reality for them. They cannot conceive of an old person in any but a peripheral role. Thus,

[16] The whole problem of retraining for automation is complex. On the surface, retraining an older person seems wasteful, but if the rate of technical change remains the same, retraining may be necessary so frequently that older workers may economically be included in the programme. Retraining may not be necessary if Parsons is right in suggesting that as American society becomes more sophisticated there will be more variety of roles for old people just as there are more available to women past the child-bearing age. If this is true, there should be demonstrable differences in the attitude toward older people between groups with different levels of sophistication and between countries with different kinds of cultural elaborations.

[17] For a full discussion of this possibility, see Parsons, *op. cit.*

they approach him with condescension, or do not approach at all because of embarrassment. This gulf between generations is a by-product of a future-oriented society; when it changes, America will have changed. In the meantime, it seems clear that the older person may find it more rewarding to contemplate a moment of past glory than to try to make new relationships, especially with the young. In the intimate circle, no such effort is needed; the only real social problem for the very old, given health and enough money, may be lack of such a circle.[18]

DISENGAGEMENT FROM ROLES

Whether disengagement is initiated by society or by the ageing person, in the end he plays fewer roles and his relationships have changed their quality.

Socialization ensures that everyone learns to play the two basic kinds of roles that are known as instrumental and socio-emotional. In this essay, the instrumental roles in any given social system are those primarily concerned with active adaptation to the world outside the system during the pursuit of system goals. Socio-emotional roles are concerned with the inner integration of the system and the maintenance of the value patterns that inform its goals.[19]

[18] It is interesting that American ideology holds that it is not good for an old person to live in his adult child's household. Nevertheless a very large number do so, and apparently successfully. In these cases there seems to be a tendency to define the situation as in some way extraordinary so as to keep honouring the shibboleth in the breach. See, Seymour Bellin, 'Family and kinship in later years,' doctoral dissertation, Columbia University.

[19] In this general statement, the word 'system' means any social system. In any particular case the system must be specified

Men, for reasons at once too obvious and too complex to consider here, must perform instrumental roles on behalf of their families, and this, for most men, means working at an occupation. Although men play socio-emotional roles, in business and elsewhere, they tend to assign the integrative tasks to women when they are present. In patriarchal societies, a man conceivably can live his whole adult life without playing a socio-emotional role, if, in both his family and in his work, others are willing to integrate social systems around him. A married woman, on the other hand, in addition to the socio-emotional role she plays in her family as a whole, must be instrumental in relationship to small children. Very few women, and those only perhaps among the wealthiest, can totally avoid instrumentality. Thus, women are in the habit of bringing either kind of role into salience with more ease than men.

Whether there is any inherent quality that makes it easier to play one role than another is obscure, although the impinging temperament may predispose toward socio-emotionality. Empirically, we see a spectrum that includes goal-directed men, all of whose roles are instrumental (officers in the regular Army whose wives tremble when they shout); men who play socio-emotional roles in some circumstances (comforting the baby when he falls), men who seek out socio-emotional roles (in America, perhaps the personnel man); women who play instrumental roles whenever the situation allows it (club presidents),

because the same acts can be part of an instrumental role viewed from one system and a socio-emotional role viewed from another. The clergyman plays an integrative role in society in general, but an instrumental role vis-à-vis his family—and all his professional acts can thus be categorized differently according to the system of reference.

women who shift from instrumental work roles to socio-emotional family roles, and women who play socio-emotional roles almost all the time (the helpful maiden aunt living in a relative's household).

Most married couples with children, no matter what secondary roles they may hold, have a basic division of labour in which the husband plays a core instrumental role *vis-à-vis* his family by working, and the wife a core socio-emotional one by maintaining their home and caring for their children. By the time the children have left home and the husband has retired, the original division of labour has lost much of its basis.

A man has no clear-cut role upon retirement. He may still play an instrumental role relative to his wife, but it loses its public label; there is no special place to go to perform it, and there is no paycheck that is the obvious consequence of his daily round. He must bring his capacities for integrative activity into salience much of the time and perhaps even share the instrumental roles that remain available with other retired men. For these reasons, the disengagement theory proposes that it is more difficult for a man to shift to socio-emotional roles and integrative activities than it is for him to assume new instrumentalities, both because it is a less familiar mode for him and because he is in danger of competing directly with his wife and possibly with his grandchildren for roles within kinship or friendship circles. Therefore, the theory predicts that retirement will bring a period of maladjustment to many American men.

A man's response to retirement may be coloured by the type of work role from which he withdraws. If his role has been part of a 'true' division of labour, such that he can see the contribution that he is making to the functioning of society, he is likely to have considerable ego involvement in his work—it is to him as children are to a woman, a persistent palpable achievement. If, on the other hand, the division of labour is such that the outcome of his contribution is invisible to him, he will tend to be alienated from the meaning of his work and will find his rewards in his personal relationships with his fellow workers. In the first case, his instrumental role has three facts: he can see his contribution to the larger society, to his immediate working group, and to his family; in the second case, he can see a contribution only to the primary groups, work and family. Men in these two situations may react quite differently to retirement. The first might be expected to suffer more sense of loss immediately upon retirement—as women do when children first depart—but eventually to take much satisfaction from recalling his contribution to social goals and perhaps seeing others build upon it. The second may be relieved at leaving a meaningless work role but eventually suffer from lack of the symbolic connexion with his own past, especially if he is a selector and accustomed to depending upon symbols for his orientation and sense of self.

Disengagement from central life roles is basically different for women than for men. This seems to be because women's roles are essentially unchanged from girlhood to death. In the course of their lives women are asked to give up only pieces of their core socio-emotional roles or to change their details. Their transitions are therefore easier[20]—

[20] This point is strikingly made by Peter Townsend who has described (*The Family Life of Old People*, Glencoe, Ill.: Free Press, 1957) how working-class women in London pass smoothly through the roles of daughter, mother, and grandmother. The pattern in America may be somewhat less straightforward, but the disjunction for women still seems far less acute than for men.

the wife of a retired man can use her integrative skills to incorporate him in new groupings. She must, if she is tactful, become even more integrative through abandoning to him the more adaptive of her domestic tasks. Similarly, the problems raised by widowhood are more easily resolved than the problems raised by retirement. Moreover, the loss of status anchorage that women suffer at the time of a husband's death is less severe than the loss of status suffered at retirement because widowhood, unlike retirement, has no tinge of failure in it.[21] It is the blameless termination of a valued role. Furthermore, the differential death rate that leaves about 20 per cent of American women living without a conjugal bond by the age of 60, provides a membership group for them.[22] Men in contrast, have difficulty finding memberships to compensate for work associations.

In general we might say that a woman's lifelong training to a role that is primarily socio-emotional but nevertheless includes adaptive skills leaves her more diffusely adaptable than a man's working career leaves him, because he does not automatically need integrative skills. Integrative skills are, in a sense, the *lingua franca* wherever

people interact with one another. Adaptive skills, in contrast, tend to be more functionally specific and less easily transferred. The disposition toward the instrumental role can remain after retirement, but the specific skills lose relevance. Only rarely does a woman find herself with no membership group that can use her integrative contribution.

Finally, a retired man loses suitable role models—that is, role partners with whom he can try out patterns of adaptation and hence learn alternatives. He must seek out other retired men—who are themselves tinged with failure in his eyes—or learn from women. Women, again because of the differential death rate, have more models, and these are more familiar. For both men and women, however, the roles of old age must be learned from others who are themselves relatively free of constraints —unlike children who are taught the roles they anticipate filling by adults who are as fully engaged and constrained as they will ever be.

Among married couples, a crucial event after retirement may be a shifting of the representative role from the man to the woman. While he works, a husband endows his family with its position in society, but after he enters the socio-emotional world of women and leisure, his wife tends to represent their conjugal society at kinship gatherings and social affairs—even in church activities. In this regard, also, men are more freed by retirement than women are by widowhood.

If these differences between men and women are important, there should be a visible contrast in their ability to cope with the discontinuities of the disengagement process. Two obvious examples are available, that appear related, on the one hand, to women's abilities in finding roles in social systems

[21] When the data from which the disengagement theory was induced were gathered, the responsibility of women to feed their husbands in such a way as to avoid coronary heart disease had not appeared in the mass media. There may be a tendency since then for widowhood under some circumstances to be construed as role failure.

[22] This does not mean that women go out and 'join' a group of widows. My impression is that they re-establish old bonds, or move closer to other women who have lost their husbands or never married. They probably tighten their ties to their children at this time also.

and, on the other, to the sudden freedom from constraint of retirement. In Table 1 we see the relative proportions of men and women in a study sample who, when seeking help from a public relief agency, were found to be homeless as well as in need of money. At no age are men who are in economic distress as able as women to maintain membership in a domestic unit. Indeed, there is no female counterpart in America to the 'homeless man.' In Table 2, we see that among a cohort of men and women over 60 years of age entering a mental hospital for the first time, one-third of the non-married men had been living in shelters and old people's homes, whereas less than one-tenth of the non-married women had come from such institutions. Women without husbands appear able to accommodate themselves to both the households of others and the hospital environment more readily than men without wives.[23] The differences in both tables are statistically significant at better than the 1 per cent level of confidence.

In Fig. 1, we see the rates of suicide, by age, for men and women. At the age that disengagement is postulated to occur, 65–75, the rate of suicide among women drops and continues to drop, while among men it rises persistently.[24]

[23] In the area of study, a shelter, which is really a 'poorhouse,' and even an old people's home is considered much less desirable than a nursing home or hospital.

[24] This may be an exaggerated phenomenon in America. In England, for example, the rates for men and women are more nearly parallel.

TABLE I Proportion of homeless[1] men and women in a time sample of applicants to two relief agencies

Age and sex	Total	Percentage homeless
Men	227	27.7
Under 60 years	185	27.6
Age 60 and over	42	28.6
Women	144	6.3
Under 60 years	100	6.0
Age 60 and over	44	6.8

[1] Excluding migrant workers, and those temporarily stranded away from home. These data are from a study of the division of labour among the integrative agents of society financed in part by NIMH (National Institute of Mental Health) Grant M4735, Principal Investigator Elaine Cumming.

TABLE 2 Living arrangements of 100 consecutive first admissions, aged 60 and over, to a mental hospital[1]

		Percentage who had been living in		
SEX AND MARITAL STATUS	NUMBER	DOMESTIC UNIT	HOSPITAL OR NURSING HOME	SHELTER OR HOME FOR AGED
Men	43			
Married	16	81.3	12.5	6.2
Non-married	27	44.4	18.5	37.1
Women	57			
Married	16	87.5	12.5	0.0
Non-married	41	63.4	26.8	9.8

[1] I am grateful to Mary Lou Parlagreco and John Cumming for permission to use these data from an unpublished study.

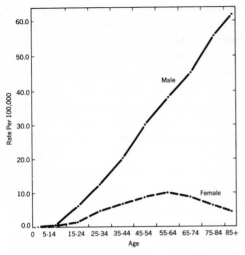

FIG. 1. Rates of suicide per 100,000 population for all white residents of continental United States, 1957. (Adapted from Table CO, *Summary of Mortality Statistics: United States, 1957,* Washington, D.C. National Office of Vital Statistics.)

The figure leads to the speculation that women go from a little too much constraint to just the right amount of freedom while men go from too much of the one to too much of the other. In spite of this dramatic difference, it is unlikely that men who survive the transition crisis of retirement are as disadvantaged as these data make them seem; they are more likely to resemble Charles Lamb, who says of his sudden and unexpected retirement: 'For the first day or two I felt stunned—overwhelmed. I could only apprehend my felicity; I was too confused to taste it sincerely. I wandered about, thinking I was happy, and knowing that I was not. I was in the condition of a prisoner in the old Bastille, suddenly let loose after a forty years' confinement. I could scarce trust myself with myself. It was like passing out of Time into Eternity—for it is a sort of Eternity for a man to have all his Time to himself. It seemed to me that I had more time on my hands than I could ever manage.

From a poor man, poor in Time, I was suddenly lifted up into a vast revenue; I could see no end of my possessions; I wanted some steward, or judicious bailiff, to manage my estates in Time for me. And here let me caution persons growing old in active business, not lightly, nor without weighing their own resources, to forego their customary employment all at once, for there may be danger in it. I feel it by myself, but I know that my resources are sufficient; and now that those first giddy raptures have subsided, I have a quiet home-feeling of the blessedness of my condition.'[25]

CHANGES IN SOLIDARITY

I have discussed disengagement as it affects temperamental types, as an inner experience, as a social imperative, and as a response to changing roles. Perhaps the most economical way of describing it is in terms of shifting solidarities that may have roots in middle life. In general, ageing brings change from solidarity bonds based on differences of function and hence on mutual dependency to bonds based on similarities and common sentiments. The post-retirement part of a man's life can be considered, therefore, in terms of a two-stage shift in the nature of his relationships with his wife, his kinsmen, and the rest of the world that starts with departure of children and retirement. On the one hand, the 'organic solidarity' of a divided labour that marked his conjugal life is weakened because after retirement he no longer has a clearly marked, publicly recognized, instrumental role; therefore, the 'mechanical solidarity' of

25 Charles Lamb, 'The superannuated man,' in *Aging in Today's Society,* eds. Clark Tibbitts and Wilma Donahue, New York: Prentice-Hall, 1960, p. 99–100.

common belief and sentiments that must precede and accompany the division of labour becomes more salient.[26] On the other hand, the man and his wife, as a unit, are no longer functioning as a factory for making adults from children and hence are now related to other segments of society through common characteristics. Thus, both men and women abandon the mutual obligations and power problems of a divided labour among themselves as well as between themselves and society. They move into a more equalitarian relationship with each other and with the world—a relationship in which solidarity is based almost entirely upon a consensus of values and a commonality of interest. Most importantly, the new segmental solidarity is marked by an essential redundancy of the parts.[27] Loss of a member from a system of divided labour disrupts the system. Loss of a member from a group of peers diminishes the society but does not disrupt it.

The second stage of old age comes when the old person is no longer able to carry out the minimum adaptive behaviour necessary to maintain health, or cleanliness or propriety. At that point, someone else must enter the conjugal society to perform adaptive functions for both man and wife, and thus they return

[26] It is, of course, impossible to imagine a division of labour between people who are not bound by any common sentiments.

[27] This is not so for the conjugal society toward the end of life. Immediately after retirement, husbands seem redundant to many women who have developed lives of their own since the termination of child raising. However, extremely old people, with no division of labour at all, become dependent upon one another to such an extent that if one dies the other is likely to follow quickly. This special case of a very binding mechanical solidarity is probably the result of these extremely old people being almost merged into one identity like twin infants.

to the asymmetrical social condition of infants—their contribution to the solidarity lies not in what they do but what they are—members by birthright of a family. A very old person with no family ties has the pathos of an orphaned child and society deals with him accordingly. This terminal dependency excludes all other social relations. Indeed, among the extremely aged, 'collective monologues' such as Piaget describes among children may replace conversation, for as Durkheim says—'society has retreated from the old person, or what amounts to the same thing, he has retreated from it.'

Summarizing the shift in solidarity in more concrete terms, we may say that men at work are tied together by sentiments about the work itself and women by sentiments about children, schools[28] and domestic matters. After work ceases, the bonds between a man and those he worked with must literally be reforged if they are to survive, because they must have new substance. After children leave home, while much must be rewrought between women, it is less than for men because they still have in common the roles of spouse and mother—although the latter may be somewhat attentuated.

Among kindred there are values and sentiments arising from many common experiences, and, therefore, it is easy for solidarity to persist after disengagement. In other words, it is the diffusely-bonded solidarities that survive and the specifically-bonded ties that wither. If a specific bond involves some divided labour, the attachment is stronger, but once the conditions of mutual dependency are removed, it is weakened. In diffusely-bonded relationships, of which kinship is the prototype,

[28] American society strongly encourages women to belong to school-related organizations and thus to meet the mothers of other children.

common sentiments, values and traditions inevitably form around many activities and events. For this reason, such stable solidarities persist through role changes and become the salient relationships of old age. The energy to force such strong links as exist between siblings or very old friends because of common history, common experience, and interlocking membership, may be lost as soon as biological energy begins to fade.

It should be noted that there are certain 'atemporal' roles available to men that do not become outmoded and can be the basis of a divided labour until extreme old age. The clergyman's role, for example, is concerned with persistent values; it resists obsolescence because it ties society to its timeless values. The clergyman is the instrumental leader in his family but with the larger society as the social system of reference, he performs an integrative function in an important socio-emotional role. Such roles seem to perform for the whole society the function that women perform for the

family—they maintain the pattern of values that inform the goals and they reduce the tension generated by the effort of adaptation. Their content is the *lingua franca* of the general culture.

IMPLICATIONS

In this discursive account of the disengagement theory, I have raised more problems than I have begun to solve. The additions to the theory are untidily grafted on to the orginal formulation without regard to whether or not they contradict it or shift its focus. The next task is to formalize the propositions and whereever possible cast them in terms that can be tested—but this is another undertaking for another time. Given the choice, I have taken what is for me the pleasanter alternative ot thinking widely rather than rigorously, and in doing so I have drawn attention to the theory's need for greater rigour.

*Family, Class, and Generation in London**

Peter Willmott and Michael Young

In one important way, Woodford has turned out to be much as we expected. Kinship ties there are much looser than in Bethnal Green. When a couple marry

Woodford is a middle- and working-class suburb of London. Bethnal Green is a working-class "village in the middle of London." There follows an excerpt from the conclusions of a study comparing the family in these two settings—Eds.

*Adapted from Family and Class in a London Suburb. London: Routledge & Kegan Paul Ltd., 1960, pp. 123-127, Chapter II.

they set up a genuinely independent household; relatives' homes are more often connected by occasional missions, not by the continuous back and forth which make two homes into one in Bethnal Green. Kinship matters less—friendship more. That is no surprise. But we also asked other questions, whose answers were not as we expected. This applies particularly to four important points— old age, the feminine core to the kinship system, the friendliness of the suburb and the difference between the working classes of the two districts.

1. OLD AGE

Money apart, Bethnal Green could almost have been designed expressly for aged parents, so well is it suited to their needs, providing them with company, care, and, at least if they are mothers, a place of eminence in the family. How could Woodford reach such a standard? Was it not inevitable that more independence for the young would mean less security for the old? It sounds plausible, but it is not true, not wholly so at any rate . . . the generations do come together, but not so much on marriage as on bereavement. Bethnal Green daughters give up adolescent freedoms and return to their mother's hearth when they marry; Woodford parents come to their children's door when one of them is left widowed or when both are too old or too infirm to take care of themselves any longer. From a purely physical point of view, Woodford seems to look after its old as well as Bethnal Green.

This is not to say there is nothing to worry about. Physical care is only one of the needs of old age. Others are not so well satisfied in Woodford—the need for respect, the need to give as well as receive, the independence which is necessary to a sense of identity. To some extent this is inevitable. Woodford belongs more fully to a modern technological world than does Bethnal Green, and is therefore less in awe of tradition. Woodford wives do not pay great heed to their mothers' opinions about baby-care, as they do in Bethnal Green; they are more likely to consult the clinic, their doctor or each other. The wisdom of age is not valued in the same way. The generations have been apart for many years and, this being so, they are almost bound to have grown apart too. It may be a shock to both sides when they re-unite, and find each other so prickly.

But if the friction of which we saw evidence is partly unavoidable, it is not wholly so. A good deal of the trouble arises because the generations so often have to live under the same roof. Here Woodford is at a disadvantage compared with Bethnal Green. The latter has more variety of accommodation, one- and two-room flats and floors, tiny houses as well as large, and Mums can use their influence with rent-collectors to get suitable quarters for each segment of their family. The old can live in their own little place across the road from their daughter. But things change as one goes towards the periphery of the city—at the centre there are more small dwellings in large buildings, flats and old houses, and in the suburbs more large dwellings in small houses. In Woodford the housing is as nearly uniform as the most hidebound municipal estate—it has almost nothing but three- or four-bedroom houses, for families with children, ill-designed for the elderly. The generations move in together because they have no alternative—there is no suitable accommodation nearby.

In the long run more small houses will presumably be built, mixed up with the larger, so that whole families can more often live *near* to each other. There is scope for a private counterpart to the Council dwellings which are becoming increasingly popular with the old. Meanwhile, most people will have to make do as best they can in houses not designed with the needs of three generations in mind. It seemed to us that wherever a semblance of a separate dwelling for the old had been carved out inside the house, a cooking-stove and a wash-basin installed, or best of all a separate bathroom and kitchen, the aged were more content because they enjoyed more independence and suffered less wound to their pride. The younger people benefited through being on their own too, for at least some of the time. What can be done depends upon the size and lay-out of the house, and how many people have to fit into it. But some sort of physical conversion should often be possible and worthwhile. It is now obligatory, under the House Purchase and Housing Act of 1959, for local authorities to make grants for conversions and improvements. This could be a most useful measure for old people. But perhaps Councils could, in co-operation with voluntary bodies, do something more—not just to publicize the existence of this new Act (which is probably unknown to almost all the citizens of Woodford, as of everywhere else), but to provide a source of architectural advice. The husbands of Woodford, as we noticed in Chapter II, are many of them formidable handyman already. But this does not mean they would be averse to suggestions made on the spot by a knowledgeable person about ways of reorganizing rooms, plumbing and heating to suit the needs of old people without impairing the eventual value of the house. This new architectural service would naturally draw together what is already known—and it is considerable—about the special housing needs of old people. Where a local authority was already building bungalows for them it would be particularly easy to add on the additional function of advising private owners and landlords about conversions and adaptations.

There is another service which would be especially helpful to the young. One of our informants was an aged woman who had recently spent six weeks in the nearby Langthorne Hospital so that her children could have an urgently needed break. She was exceptional. Far more help of this sort is needed. Langthorne Hospital has been a pioneer in providing for temporary admissions of aged patients in order to relieve their relatives.[1] Sheldon[2] suggested short-stay hostels to help meet the same objective; other measures include the fuller use of day hospitals and home helps. Relief of this sort not only helps hard-pressed relatives; by assisting old people to stay well, it also eases the pressure of demand for beds in chronic wards.

The social services generally can do much to relieve the financial pressure on old people. They can usually manage at the moment, without being an intolerable burden on the younger generation, because they have some support from their pension. This is not to say it is adequate. . . . we saw how much the income of manual workers falls upon retirement, and how much scope there is for an improved pension which would do a little more to maintain their standard of living in old age. There is another vital job for the social services, State and voluntary, and that is to care for the large minority of people who have no families to aid them. . . . we would say that the task of supporting them adequately has only been started. The kind of old people who were isolated in Woodford needed more frequent visits from somebody—a few of them saw practically nobody. They also needed more help with housing, small old people's homes with a family atmosphere about them, "foster children" and, generally, the sense that society had not deserted them.

2. MOTHERS AND DAUGHTERS.

In the light of our research in Bethnal Green, and that in other working-class districts of Britain, we ventured to expect "the stressing of the mother-

[1] DeLargy, J., "Six Weeks In: Six Weeks Out."

[2] Sheldon, J. H., *The Social Medicine of Old Age*, pp. 197–8.

daughter tie to be a widespread, perhaps universal, phenomenon in the urban areas of all industrial countries." But we went on to qualify this statement by saying "at any rate in the families of manual workers."[3] Manual workers seemed to have more need for the extended family as the "woman's trade union." Working class mothers suffered more from insecurity. They received uncertain and ungenerous housekeeping allowances even when their husbands were not out of a job. Death rates were high, and if husbands were not killed in war or in peace, they were always liable to desert. Woman's only protection, we argued, was herself. The wife clung to the family into which she was born, and particularly to her mother.

Since middle-class wives were not beset by such insecurity we did not expect them to be so dependent on their own families of origin. We imagined that the closeness of husband and wife . . . might

[3]*Family and Kinship in East London,* p. 163.

exclude any special bond between a wife and her mother. We were not completely wrong—the mother-daughter tie is not so tight as in Bethnal Green. But it is there all the same; the feminine relationship is still stressed; it is very often still the axis of such extended family relationships as there are . . . occupational mobility did not seem to set up barriers between mothers and daughters as it did between fathers and sons. Insecurity or not, married women have a common interest in children and housekeeping, in their common occupation, which is stronger than the interest shared by fathers and sons engaged in quite different occupations.† We would now remove the qualification from the above statement.

†Michael Young and Hildred Geertz suggested that the same tie between mothers and daughters could be observed in a San Francisco suburb. See Michael Young and Hildred Geertz, "Old Age in London and San Francisco: Some Families Compared," *British Journal of Sociology,* 1961, 12: 124–141. —Eds.

Meaningful Activity in a Family Context*

Wayne E. Thompson and Gordon F. Streib

VARIATIONS IN FAMILY STRUCTURE

. . . The primary purpose of this article is to describe the family of the mature years and to suggest its relevance to the

Reprinted from Aging and Leisure: A Research Perspective into the Meaningful Use of Time, *edited by Robert W. Kleemeier. New York: Oxford University Press, 1961, pp. 177–211.* ©1961 by Oxford University Press, Inc.

question of how people use their leisure time. This seems to imply discussion of a relatively constant social factor in the lives of mature individuals. In point of fact, however, the family cannot usefully be so conceptualized. Within any given family, the patterns of relationships vary considerably through time, following what has been called the life cycle of the family. . . .

In the paragraphs which follow we will consider in turn the settings which are characteristic of the family of "late maturity" which typically still includes dependent children; the family of pre-retirement which typically involves the husband and wife living alone but with the husband still gainfully employed; the family of early retirement which typically differs from the previous type principally in the fact that the husband has retired; and the family of later retirement in which widowhood becomes the typical case.

THE LIFE CYCLE OF THE FAMILY THROUGH THE LATER YEARS

The Family of Late Maturity

Family Composition

In the age group 45 to 54, almost 90 per cent of both males and females live in households which include one or more relatives—what the Bureau of the Census has defined as a primary family.[1] The overwhelming majority of these people are married and living with their

[1]It should be noted in passing that the figures on which our presentation is based are dated by now, for they are reports of the 1950 Census. With reference to the chronological cutting points which are used in our discussion of the life cycle of the family, needless to say, there is no magic in their selection. As a matter of fact, the usual obstinacy of the population is manifested here: there are always many exceptions to the generalizations which are advanced. At the same time, the categories are not simply arbitrarily selected. They are convenient because they are used by the Bureau of the Census in its tabulations; they are useful and important because they differ significantly in the properties of the modal family at each stage.

spouses in their own households, and in these husband-wife families, somewhat more than half have children under 18 still living in the household (Glick, 1957, Table 44, p. 73). In other words, while many have by this age completed their role as parents of dependent children, most adults of the modal family of early maturity are just at the end of this role.

Family relationships

At this stage of the family cycle, many of the patterns of activities within the family context may represent an extension of whatever patterns were prevalent earlier. At this point, however, the relationship between parents and children is undergoing a significant transition as the child reaches the end of his period of dependency; the patterns of activities associated with this relationship are undergoing transition as well.[2] A wide variety of leisure time pursuits, both formal and informal, which were associated with the parent-dependent-child relationship lose their meaning at this point, and for the parents the stage is set for working out a *modus vivendi* for two. To be sure, sloughing off the patterns of an earlier period may not come easily: this is the period in which parents are hurt and bewildered when their child protests at such a simple thing as the parents' wishing to go along to a ball game. Yet, wishes to the contrary notwithstanding, the process of "de-socialization" does proceed and new patterns are established for the next stages of the family cycle. In fact, if one were to choose a label for this stage

[2]Cf. Anderson (1953) who shows differences both in participation in formal and informal organizations to be associated with the stages of parent-child relationships. Cf. also Rohrer and Schmidt (1954).

of the family cycle, it might well be *transitional stage*.

In an important sense, the patterns of family relationships which are established in this period are crucial for all subsequent stages of the family cycle. Here parents and children establish the beginnings of their relationships as adults; and, closely related to this, here the two-generation family group is being dismembered and the parent-child relationships are being reformulated as an aspect of what has been called a network of social relationships (Bott, 1957, p. 58). Success in establishing satisfactory relationships in this sense clearly relates to the probable realization of a wide range of meaningful activities associated with contacts with the nuclear families formed by children's marriages, including the very important contact with grandchildren. At the same time, the aging parents suddenly face the necessity to become reacquainted and to develop activities which take into account the new composition of the family group, namely, only the two of them again after many years in which the family group not only included but also centered on the youngsters.

As this reorganization takes place, leisure time activities which are not aspects of family duties become increasingly significant, for release from the obligations of parental responsibility provides an impressive amount of free time. This is especially true in the case of the wife, for whom "retirement" from the role of mother provides the opportunity for increased leisure time activities. Clearly, "retirement" from the role of father also requires considerable readjustment. In the case of the husband, however, excessive free time is not so much at issue, and for this reason it may be that the wife plays the dominant role in choosing the patterns of

meaningful activity to be pursued through the later years. [3]

Socialization for the later years

Learning the new patterns specific to the changing family relationships of this stage of the family cycle certainly involves the process of socialization. But the changing relationships among parents and children in this transitional period may give rise also to a more pervasive socialization and anticipatory socialization process. That is to say, the conception of self bound up with the role of parent to dependent children becomes outmoded at this point, and it may be that this fact is associated with the beginning of the self-conception of "middle-age." The effects of such a re-definition of self upon selection and pursuit of meaningful activity are, of course, manifold. Among other things, it may be that this represents the crest of future orientation, the point at which "onward and upward" is replaced by "onward and downward." To the extent that this involves radical differences in what is perceived as meaningful and appropriate activity, this point of re-orientation may mark the point at which it makes practical sense to start encouraging consideration of the needs of later maturity. [4]

It may also be, however, that such a redefinition of self involves ill-advised

[3] The increasing number of mothers in the labor force is an important qualification of this point, of course.

[4] As a matter of conjecture, one might also consider the effects upon future orientation of too much preparation for later maturity presented too early. It might prove very interesting indeed to compare the careers of students who ask placement officers about opportunities for advancement with the careers of students who ask about provisions of retirement plans.

sloughing off of interests and activities which would help to enrich the years of later maturity, but which are considered to be appropriate only to the "young." The extent to which this occurs may be an index of the degree to which later maturity is prejudged beyond all hope of a satisfactory and rich adjustment.

Factors other than changing relationships among parents and children are also relevant to this changing definition of self. Chronological labels are important: "life begins at forty," suggesting, of course, the beginning of the end. Also, this period is the most probable time of the climacteric with its inevitable psychological repercussions; and the manner in which these problems are handled has a most important bearing upon subsequent marital adjustments of the spouses, both sexually and in the more general patterns of companionship and compatibility. Thus, not only definition of the self, but also redefinition of the marital relationship may be affected, and precisely at that point at which the family is being reorganized into the two-person group. . . .

The Family of Pre-retirement

Family composition

In the age range, 55 to 64, the differences in family composition between older males and females are beginning to be greater (Figures 1A and 1B). That is to say, differences already evident in the earlier period take on the characteristics of trends. The most striking of these is the greater incidence of widows: there are more than four times as many widows as widowers. This trend, which continues through the later years, reflects both the differences in mortality of females as compared with males and the fact that in our society, husbands tend to be older than their wives. Thus, mortality of males in any given age bracket is par-

tially reflected in the number of widows in the subsequent age category.

Over-all, however, just as in late maturity, the majority of both males and females in the 55 to 64 age range are still living with their spouses in their own households. But these husband-wife families differ in an important way from the modal family of late maturity, namely, the percentage of dependents under 18 years of age has by this time declined from over half to less than a quarter (Glick, 1957, Table 44). In other words, at this stage of the family cycle, the fledglings typically have left the nest.

Family relationships

We have spoken earlier of "retirement" from the parental role. Yet, in a sense it would be more accurate to speak of a change in the earlier role, for in the pre-retirement period, parents very frequently play an important part in helping their children to establish their own households. A fairly common practice is assistance by the mother at the time of birth of grandchildren; also, in certain class levels of society, financial assistance is frequent. In other words, it might be held that generally the parental role in this stage of the family cycle does involve significant contact, but that the emphasis has changed from *responsibility* to *assistance*.

The parent-child relationship at this point includes all the vicarious joys and woes involved in watching the children get established on their own. Furthermore, more often than not, it involves the pleasures of grandparenthood. As we have suggested, however, an important difference between the parental role of this period and of earlier periods is the degree to which parental responsibility is involved. Despite ties of affection, despite vicarious attachment, despite contact and usefulness in helping the

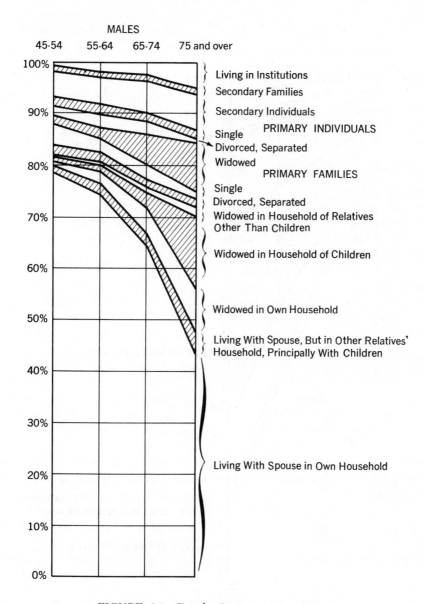

FIGURE 1A Family Living Arrangements of the Population According to Sex Within Designated Age Ranges (Males). (Adapted from Bureau of Census tabulations, U.S. Bureau of the Census, U.S. Census of Population 1950. Vol. IV. Special Reports, Chap. D, Marital Status, Table 1, pp. 2D–20, 21, 22.)

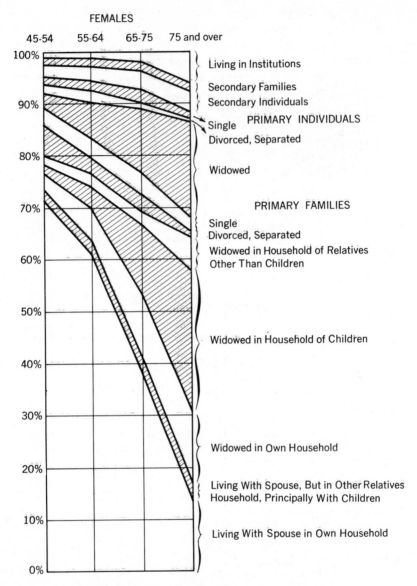

FIGURE 1B Family Living Arrangements
of the Population According to Sex Within
Designated Age Ranges (Females).

children, both parents and children by this time come to subscribe to the norm of independence for children. Although parents who have in fact maintained relationships with their children express little need to substitute new activities for extended family activities, they claim to be pleased to have more freedom to do what they desire (Sussman, 1955). And objectively they *are* more free to pursue activities of their own choice. Moreover, not only are they unencumbered by restrictive responsibilities toward children, but also typically they have not yet encountered the impediments of poor health and economic deprivation, which become more frequent in the later years.

Continued contact varies with factors other than the stage of the family cycle, of course. For example, Sussman found that proximity to children and closeness of family ties are associated with activity patterns of those whose children have left home (*ibid.*). That is, when young adults who have withdrawn from the parental home live near their parents (within a radius of 50 miles) and maintain harmonious relationships, the older generation experiences no basic change in its activity patterns.[5]

Socialization for retirement

At this stage, retirement from the occupational role begins to come into focus. In fact, it may be that the freedom from family responsibilities serves logically and practically as the point at which systematic preparation for retirement should begin. In other words, in this

[5] The importance of congenial relationships for continued activity as revealed by these research findings underscores the point made in the earlier section of this chapter that the relationships established in the transitional period are crucial to the later stages of the family cycle.

period the family relationships of the couple are the prototype of the pattern of relationships which will obtain in retirement; and the patterns of meaningful activity evolved here can therefore be expected to serve in later maturity, at least as long as both the spouses survive in reasonably good health.

The latter qualification is important, however. The person who would plan systematically for his retirement must take into account the fact that his children will become increasingly preoccupied with the responsibilities of their own nuclear family and the fact that one spouse almost always survives the other. Herein lies a problem. It is probably always difficult to plan for a situation radically different from the situation in which one finds one's self; and planning for the eventualities of the later years is particularly difficult, inasmuch as both dis-attachment from children and death of spouse are unpleasant to contemplate. As one older worker described it:

> I know they are trying to help me when they come around and talk about my retirement, but as far as I am concerned it just reminds me that I am getting up in years and can expect to start having the ailments that old people have. Worst of all, you start realizing that you've all got to go sometime.

Thus, while most people can look forward to a portion of retirement in which family patterns are essentially the same as in the pre-retirement period, a longer range perspective must take into account other contingencies. The problem is to reconcile the probability of a period in which the older couple will be living alone after retirement and the fact that this situation will not last forever. Townsend's concept of "desolates" we would take to include those persons whose meaningful activity was predicated on the assumption that the significant other person in the relationship would always be there and able to share the relationship. The facts of illness and death belie such an assumption. . . . .

The Family of Early Retirement

In the age category 65 to 74, there is a pronounced variation in the family living arrangements of males as compared with females, a further development of the trends we have discussed previously (Fig. 1). As before, the single most frequent living arrangement for both sexes is living with the spouse in their own household. However, this category constitutes less than 40 per cent among the females, of whom nearly half are widowed as compared with less than one-fifth of the men. In considering the family structure of people in early retirement, therefore, it might be useful to consider separately the family context of men and women.

Men in early retirement

About 65 per cent of the men in this age bracket live with their spouse in their own household, more often than not with no other relatives present. Inasmuch as this is the period in which retirement becomes frequent, one might contend that the problems of meaningful activity here devolve upon the relationship between the husband and wife in their own home. The circumstances of retirement may markedly alter the range of possible activities for such older couples; but to the extent that situational resources allow, the activities of the couples of this age probably represent an expression of interests which were developed earlier.

We have called this stage of the family cycle "early retirement," for it might be argued that the years from 65 to 74 differ significantly from the later period (cf. Confrey and Goldstein, 1960).

While the incidence of family patterns of this period shows important changes from the previous two decades, for most men of this age the pattern of family relationships is essentially a continuation of earlier periods. Putting it another way, while a reordering of family composition is going on continuously throughout the later years, the incidence of changes for men is greatest after the age of 75. Moreover, not only are the family relationships of early retirement a continuation of previous relationships, but also in this period the health of the older person is less often a barrier to the enjoyment of the time freed by retirement.

Again, we emphasize that there are important exceptions to every generalization. For some people retirement certainly involves a time in which the older couple may be free to "do what we have always wanted to do." But for others, it may represent a more equivocal opportunity. Instead of being able to enjoy free time with the spouse, the older person may find the retirement years to be a long, drawn out hassle. On the face of it, this would not seem to be a particularly attractive way of life, although it might be well for those of us who would study meaningful activity not to prejudge what can and cannot be meaningful.[6]

Also, just as in the case of short-sighted pre-retirement planning, the activities of this period of early retirement may set the older couple upon a pattern of mutual dependency which is completely desolating when death finally

[6]The authors are reminded of a retiree who insisted in interviews that retirement was grand because it afforded him an opportunity to spend much time with his wife. He then called the wife to meet the interviewer and the next half-hour was spent in a vicious, back-biting interchange between the two of them—from which both were obviously getting a good deal of pleasure.

does overtake one of the partners. . . . we would take the position that the extent to which family relationships are conducive to wholesome meaningful activity is related to the extent to which those relationships are seen as a part of a whole program of life patterns. Typically the individual is so inexorably tied to other members of his family that the process of self-assessment and adjustment always in part involves assessment of family activities and relationships. This process of assessment, however, must necessarily include the inevitability that some of the family relationships will cease to exist.

With regard to contact with children and grandchildren in the period of early retirement, following Sussman (1955), we would expect that, given proximity of some of their children and congeniality of the relationship, frequency of contact would not appreciably decline. This hypothesis is further supported by our research at Cornell, for we find that 71 per cent of a group of nearly 1,800 70-year-old respondents see some of their children occasionally, and only 6 per cent hardly ever or never see their children.[7]

But although frequency of contact may remain more or less constant, by this stage of the family cycle the *content* of parent-child relationships normally has been significantly changed. Insofar as there is contact between parents and children, it is more akin to that of close friends than to a set of institutionalized obligations, and the way is paved for relationships which may be regarded as meaningful activities in themselves. Similarly, this period usually involves a continuation of rather free enjoyment of grandchildren.

[7]These data are from the Cornell Study of Occupational Retirement, which is described by Streib, Thompson, and Suchman, 1958.

To be sure, relationships with children and grandchildren have their trials and tribulations also. The classic instance of difficulties arises when the parents forget that their children are grown up and established and, in forgetting, revert to patterns of earlier periods. The interfering parent of this age is the person who has never quite given up the parental role of assistance or, albeit more rarely, the role of parent to dependent children. Also the rate of change in child-rearing practices is such that grandparents could not hope to keep up with the shifts. In the interest of giving the older person an important opportunity for meaningful activity and from the perspective of all three generations, there is much to be said for letting grandparents "spoil" their grandchildren rather than having the grandchildren ruined by a confusion of discipline as practiced simultaneously by parents and grandparents. The problems involved in the relationships of the three generations probably are aggravated in those instances in which all live in the same household, for in such a setting confusion of responsibilities, obligations, and privileges may run rampant.

Among the men in early retirement, one nonmodal category stands out as being of particular significance: the widowers who are living alone. For these older men, this stage of the family cycle very frequently has initiated not only retirement and its attendant problems, but also the lonely and unfamiliar tasks of keeping house. Because of the multiple adjustments which must be made, it may well be that of all the categories of older persons, this one is beset with the greatest problems. Of course, the fact of being a widower living alone certainly does not preclude the possibility of contact with children, and it would not be fair to overstate the seriousness of the widower's plight. At the same time, the combination of role changes and alteration of the marital relationship for this category of older men clearly creates unique problems of adjustment.[8]

Women in early retirement

Among women in the age bracket 65 to 74, exceptional family living arrangements become the rule. Although the most frequent single living arrangement is living with spouse in their own home, the most frequent marital status is widowed (Fig. 1). As noted previously, the higher incidence of widows reflects the mortality difference between men and women and the tendency for wives to be younger than their husbands in our society.

For women in the upper ages of this category, the fact of being younger than their husband may be of considerable significance even when the spouse is still living. At this age, the incidence of women caring for an incapacitated husband undoubtedly shows a sharp increase. Also, whether incapacitating illness be involved or not, women at this

[8] It might be appropriate in this context to introduce what Nelson Foote has called a "neglected member of the family," namely, the family dog (1956). In general, the role of pets as an object of interest and as a source of companionship for the older person has been neglected as a focus for research. Yet, in connection with problems of meaningful activity in the mature years, it should be acknowledged that for some people this relationship may be of paramount importance. There is a story, writ large in every instance, of a cat or dog who falls heir to the fortune of his reclusive master; and for every one who leaves such a fortune there are hundreds who spend a good deal of time worrying about what will happen to their animals when they die.

age face a considerably increased probability of widowhood. Again, it may be hard to reconcile "rational planning" for widowhood with maintenance of established and satisfying relationshps at a given time.

For those women in this age bracket who are already widowed, the most frequent living arrangement is that of the primary individual, which usually means living alone. As in the case of the widower, this may involve a lonely existence. But for the widow, unlike the widower, the housewifely tasks usually do not represent a marked change of pattern and problem of adjustment. In fact, for a great many widows living alone, the day-to-day tasks involved in keeping house constitute a very important variety of meaningful activity; and ability to maintain certain standards of good housekeeping often represents a challenge and a test of the degree to which the older woman is avoiding "getting old."

The widow who lives alone may have frequent contacts with her children and grandchildren, of course, and in many instances may be able to live a full meaningful life within a pattern that includes very little more than her house and these contacts. Among other things, the role of grandmother in our culture probably includes a wider range of meaningful activities than the role of grandfather and on this account may be a more important factor in the adjustment of the elderly widow. Moreover, insofar as women set the pattern of relationships with children, these patterns may differ very little from those which would obtain were the spouse still alive.

The second most frequent living arrangement among widows in this age grouping is residence in the household of children, usually the homes of daughters. Very often at this age these widowed mothers are alert and in perfectly good health. Thus the possibility of overt interference in the affairs of their children and of conflict in the household centering on parent-child relationships is maximal here. The image which comes to mind is, of course, the stereotypical mother-in-law (cf. Duvall, 1954). But it would be very interesting indeed to determine through research just how formidable mothers-in-law really are.

Socialization for old age

We have already mentioned that the age differences between spouses often provide firsthand experience for women with the problems of "infirmities of old age." In general, this period of life cycle marks increased awareness of such problems on the part of both men and women, for among persons of this age there is an increased frequency of incapacitating illness and death. From the perspective of the aging individual the implications of these facts are enormous. Most people seem to be able to accept the inevitability of death in a rather matter-of-fact way; but very few are able to accept the possibility of incapacitating illness and increased dependence on their children.[9] Yet, the subsequent stage of the family cycle is a period in which very considerable numbers of

[9] People who have contact with the aged frequently are struck by the fact that obituary columns are avidly "followed" by the older person. Far from repressing the inevitability of death, many seem preoccupied with the phenomenon. It has been suggested that old people in fact are no different from anyone else: it is within the obituary notices that they read about their peers. For the younger reader this footnote may seem to be a morbid aside, reflecting the fact that few younger people are successfully able to identify with the aged or to see life and death from their perspective.

older people do in fact become dependent, either directly in the sense of taking up residence with the child or indirectly in the sense of having to depend on the child for financial assistance and for the major part of their close, personal relationships. In a sense, therefore, the emphasis on independence in the parent-child relationship serves as a barrier to effective socialization for the contingencies of later retirement.

The Family of Later Retirement

Family composition

The age category of 75 and over contains a widespread diversity of family living arrangements, both among males and females. In fact, it could be argued that the plotting of statistical information about this portion of the population most clearly reflects the sociological, psychological, and physiological aspects of old age (Fig. 1). For example, although still a very small proportion of the total number, inmates of institutions cease to be a statistical rarity at this time. Also, both among men and women, the incidence of widowhood increases sharply. Among the women for the first time the modal family living arrangement is no longer that of the couple in their own household. Rather, it is that of a widow living in the household of her children. Moreover, the number of widowed primary individuals among the women over 75 also is greater than the number living with their husband in their own house.

In the case of the elderly men, as before, the single most frequent living arrangement involves living with the wife in their own house. But for the first time during the mature years, this living arrangement accounts for less than a majority of the population. As among the women, this proportionate decline reflects the sharp increase in those who are within the several categories of the widowed.

Family relationships

What can be said of the family patterns in this oldest age group? Most probably the safest generalization which might be advanced is that, just as in the case of the wide variation in living arrangements, this category shows the greatest variation in the patterns which structure family relationships.

In those instances in which both spouses are still living, the old couple may continue in much the same patterns they have been following for the previous decade or so. Especially for the couple who have matched their activities to the probability of a gradual slowing down, this period may constitute a thoroughly happy and well integrated time of life, albeit largely lacking in the excitements of the earlier years. In those instances in which congenial relationships with children have been established in the earlier years, it would be expected that such relationships would persist. In fact, as the children themselves begin to reach later maturity and as *their* children reach the age of independence, the old parents and children may become closer friends and approach a relationship akin to that of peers. Close relationships with children in this sense are not limited to the elderly couple, of course. Although as a whole widows and widowers are relatively more often discontented, many live their later years with considerable satisfaction; and continued close relationships with children and grandchildren provide a major share of such satisfaction.

To be sure, while family contacts may be a major factor in satisfaction in old age, such contacts by no means ex-haust the inventory of meaningful activities open to the old person. It would be a mistake to assume that everybody in advanced years is a potential Grandma Moses; but it also would be a mistake to suppose that persons of advanced years are necessarily passive and incapable of a considerable range of meaningful activity actively pursued. In fact, in the extreme case family obligations are perceived as an obstacle to the pursuit of preferred leisure time activities.

In some instances, however, other meaningful activity is lacking and contact with children and grandchildren does become crucial. These relationships with the younger generations may take many forms. For some, the contact represents the harvest of a lifetime of good family relationships. Here the children and grandchildren interact with their aging relative largely because they want to; and for the elderly person these contacts are a pleasant social relationship happily awaited and remembered. In such a relationship, benefits are reciprocal: the old person gives to the relationship as well as receives from it.

In other instances the benefits accrue largely to the old person and not to the "youngster." That is to say, the old person's dependence on the child for interpersonal relationships may follow a pattern in which emotional sustenance is provided almost exclusively by the visits of the children or grandchildren. For some, this will take the form of continuing vicarious experiences for, quite understandably, at this age vicarious pleasures provide one alternative to despair. Putting it another way, at this age, except for those who hold a strong religious conviction of an afterlife, there really is very little more to look forward to as individuals. Dependence on children and grandchildren in this sense does not necessarily require frequent visits or affection on the part of the children. All that is needed is minimal contact enabling the old person to garner to himself material for the vicarious life.

But for some, this is not enough. Although emotional dependence is also present in these cases, it is a demanding sort of thing and from the perspective of the old person there is neglect. This reflects the fact that as family contact comes to constitute almost the entire content of meaningful activity, the same frequency of interaction comes to hold disproportionate importance. To the extent that there actually is nothing else in the life of the old person, infrequent contact with children does constitute a pathetic or tragic phenomenon; and it clearly is important for the old person to avoid insofar as possible the vulnerability which comes of having nothing else.

Feelings of neglect probably are experienced with a greater incidence among the very old than in any other age category, and, on the whole, such feelings probably increase at a rate much greater than the actual changes in patterns of family relationships. All of this tends to assume, however, that the old person enjoys and wants contact with his children. This is by no means a safe assumption. Following the findings of the Kansas City studies, one might hypothesize that the process of disengagement from the norms of society would affect family relationships as well as other institutional commitments (Williams, 1960, pp. 291 ff.). That is to say, with increasing age the individual tends to return to a more or less egocentric outlook. At this advanced age the old person tends to stress individual satisfaction as the most important value rather than more normatively structured activities such as family relationships. At this age

interest in the feelings of others declines to a considerable degree and the old person becomes increasingly direct— even blunt and impolite—in his interpersonal relationships.

To the extent that disengagement occurs in this extreme sense, it might be hypothesized that if such old people are physically and economically capable, they should be left alone and free to pursue whatever they choose to regard as meaningful activity. As it happens, however, disengagement as a correlate of aging is found much more frequently in the very advanced age levels—a time at which physical and mental decline also is more probable. Thus such egocentric old people very often may be found living with their children. This creates a dilemma not only for the children torn between generational loyalties but also for the old person himself.

As we have suggested, for the egocentric old person, complete dependence of this sort may provide the opportunity to behave as a martinet; and such a person may derive considerable "meaning" from pushing the role to its hilt. Such circumstances usually bode ill for the children and grandchildren of the household. For many old people, however, dependence in this sense is a personal disaster which precludes a satisfactory old age. In fact, for those of clear mind this most probably constitutes the modal reaction to complete dependency. For many, life in an institution is a much preferable alternative to a life of dependency; and, the considerable increase in the numbers of inmates in institutions in this age group probably arises in part from these circumstances or from anticipation of such circumstances. In fact, in some instances in which institutional living is not a possible alternative, the old person quite literally would rather die.

The Family Cycle and the Meaningful Use of Leisure Time

In the preceding sections we have discussed some of the major family structures at various stages of the later years. The emphasis has been primarily on a description of the settings within which patterns of use of leisure time are established and carried out, and on the ways in which these settings change through time.

Thus, focusing on the modal family at each stage of the family cycle, we note that in the family of late maturity much of the use of leisure time centers around the obligations of parenthood. This includes not only the duties specific to the parental role but also a wide range of activities which reflect patterns of conjoined family activity as the children are growing up. At this stage of the family cycle, it might be hypothesized that there is roughly a balance of activity distributed among family obligations, those which are extra-familial, centering on occupation and community activities, and those which are concerned with satisfaction for the self.

This period of late maturity, which few people other than the very young would consider a part of "old age," is a transitional period. It is at this time and at the next stage of the cycle that the major socialization for the later years might best occur. Here, for example, patterns of relationships with adult children are becoming established. Insofar as these relationships are important to meaningful use of leisure time in the later years, success in this endeavor is vital.

In the family of pre-retirement, in considerable measure, the locus of meaningful activity shifts to the older couple living alone. Here patterns of parental

duties normally have changed to patterns of voluntary assistance, and the balance among meaningful activities may well involve a lessening importance of those activities associated with family obligations. Insofar as there is a gradual tapering off of parental duties, further adjustment to the later years may be facilitated. In the process, however, the older person must be wary lest the relationship with children retain too much importance, thereby rendering life meaningless at a later stage of maturity when the parental role can no longer be maintained. For people of early retirement patterns of meaningful activity established in the preceding decade— either in fact or in anticipation—may serve as useful guidelines for behavior. To be sure, the relationship between the spouses may seriously be affected by their reaction to retirement. Yet, insofar as retirement is an established fact, the older persons must learn to live with one another. One of the programmatic implications of this fact might be to include employees' wives in pre-retirement counseling programs which are designed to facilitate adjustment.

In the early retirement years, more often than not the elderly retired couple tends still to be living in their own household with considerable time on their hands. In this period, family obligations involving children most probably have further declined. The older persons in this age category typically no longer have either parental responsibility or binding obligations of assistance. Instead, family relationships may be marked by considerable freedom and spontaneity. In fact, as we have implied, to the extent that health and economic status permit, on almost every count this stage of the family cycle is one of free choice for the use of leisure time. Moreover, with retirement the meaningful activities associated with the job are largely terminated. This period, then, both provides the opportunity for wider self-expression and for involvement in various activities outside the home and the challenge to make the most of these opportunities. At the same time, the freedom of early retirement may create a serious problem of adjustment, and the older person faces here the pitfalls of an undue retreat to family centeredness or a premature withdrawal into the self.

The period of late retirement, age 75 and above, marks the culmination of trends in changing family patterns which can be noticed much earlier. Stereotypes of the aged to the contrary notwithstanding, there probably is less social structural and cultural standardization of individual and family behavior patterns in this last stage of the family cycle than in any other period. The keynote is diversity: diverse patterns of contact with children and grandchildren; diverse conditions of health and ability to care for one's self; and even, in some, diverse orientation toward life itself. Unlike every other stage of the family cycle, activities planned on the basis of long-term prospects have little meaning at this point, and this fact may be reflected in the phenomenon of disengagement. Insofar as any general statement can be made, it could be argued that at this time the greatest impoverishment of meaningful activity occurs. Self-centeredness for these old persons may take priority over both family-related and extra-familial activities. . . .

References

ANDERSON, W.A. *Rural Social Participation and the Family Life Cycle*. Part I. Formal participation, Memoir 314; Part II. Informal participation, Memoir 318. Ithaca: Cornell University, Agricultural Experiment Station, 1953.

BLUMBERG, L. and R. R. BELL. Urban migration and kinship ties. *Social Problems*, 1959, 6, p. 328–33.

BOTT, E. *Family and Social Network*. London: Tavistock Publications, 1957.

BURGESS, E. W. and H. J. LOCKE. *The Family: From Institution to Companionship*, 2nd ed. New York: American Book, 1953.

CAVAN, RUTH S. Family life and family substitutes in old age. *Amer. Sociol. Rev.*, 1949, 14, p. 71–82.

CONFREY, E. A. and M. S. GOLDSTEIN. The health status of aging people, Chapter 7. In C. Tibbitts (ed.), *Handbook of Social Gerontology: Societal Aspects of Aging*. Chicago: U. of Chicago Press, 1960.

CONNOR, R., T. B. JOHANNIS, JR., and J. WALTERS. Family recreation in relation to role conceptions of family members. *Marriage and Family Living*, 1955, 17, p. 306–9.

DUVALL, E. M. *In-laws—Pro and Con: An Original Study of Interpersonal Relations*. New York: Association Press, 1954.

DYER, W. G. and D. URBAN. The institutionalization of equalitarian family norms. *Marriage and Family Living*, 1958, 20, p. 53–8.

FOOTE, N. N. A neglected member of the family. *Marriage and Family Living*, 1956, 18, p. 213–8.

GLICK, P. C. *American Families; Census Monograph Series*. New York: Wiley, 1957.

GRAVATT, A. F. Family relations in middle and old age: a review. *J. of Gerontol.*, 1953, 8, p. 197–201.

HAVIGHURST, R. J. and K. FEIGENBAUM. Leisure and life-style. *Amer. J. of Sociol.*, 1959, 64, p. 396–404.

HAWKINS, H. and J. WALTERS. Family recreation activities. *J. of Home Economics*, 1952, 44, p. 623–6.

LANSING, J. B. and L. KISH. Family life cycle as an independent variable. *Amer. Sociol. Rev.*, 1957, 22, p. 512–9.

ROHRER, W. G. and J. F. SCHMIDT. *Family Type and Social Participation*. Misc. Publication No. 196. College Park, Maryland: Agricultural Experimental Station, U. of Maryland, 1954.

STREIB, G. F. and W. E. THOMPSON. The older person in a family context, Chapter 13. In C. Tibbitts (ed.), *Handbook of Social Gerontology: Societal Aspects of Aging*. Chicago: U. of Chicago Press, 1960.

STREIB, G. F., W. E. THOMPSON and E. A. SUCHMAN. The Cornell study of occupational retirement. *J. of Social Issues*, 1958, 14, p. 3–17.

SUSSMAN, M. B. Activity patterns of postparental couples and their relationship to family continuity. *Marriage and Family Living*, 1955, 17, p. 338–41.

SUSSMAN, M. B. The isolated nuclear family. *Social Problems*, 1959, 6, p. 333–40.

TOWNSEND, P. *The Family Life of Old People*. London: Routledge & Kegan Paul, 1957.

WILLIAMS, R. H. Changing status, roles and relationships, Chapter 9. In C. Tibbitts (ed.), *Handbook of Social Gerontology: Societal Aspects of Aging*. Chicago: U. of Chicago Press, 1960.

PART THREE

The Husband-Wife Relationship

14

MATE-SELECTION:
PRINCIPLES THAT SPECIFY
THE FIELD OF ELIGIBLES

Embedded in each culture is an approved way of deciding who shall marry whom. In some societies it is believed that this is and should be an individual matter, that each can best select his own spouse. Other societies regard mate-selection as too important to be left to the ill-considered judgment of naive and passionate youngsters.

The selections by Sugimoto and by Vogel describe the drift of Japanese mate-selection in the twentieth century. Sugimoto's two vignettes from traditional Japan show a wedding of two strangers and a father's reaction to a son who selects his own woman. Vogel shows that in Mamachi, a middle-class suburb of Tokyo, the mate-selective practice is a compromise between the arranged marriage of traditional Japan and the voluntary selection of the United States.

In considering marriage with and without love, Freeman views ethnocentrism and the avoidance of incest as two considerations defining the field of eligibles. He sets up a classification of mate-selective procedures on the basis of the width of the field of eligibles and the arrangement versus voluntary selection of mates.

Goode notes that marriage is a link between kin lines and that it affects the ownership of property and the exercise of influence. He then asserts that mate-selection and love are have been considered "too important to be left to the children" in virtually every society. He distinguishes several methods of "love control," such as child marriage and segregation of the sexes. Since the upper strata of society have much more at stake in the maintenance of the social structure, they will exercise stricter control over love and courtship and keep mate-selection within a specified field of eligibles. Hence there will be less free choice of mates among upper strata than in the lower strata.

Old Love and New[*]

Etsu Inagaki Sugimoto

THE HONOURABLE ALL ORDAINS

This family council was the largest that had been held since Father's death. Two gray-haired uncles were there with the aunts, besides two other aunts, and a young uncle who had come all the way from Tokyo on purpose for this meeting. They had been in the room for a long time, and I was busy writing at my desk when I heard a soft "Allow me to speak!" behind me, and there was Toshi at the door, looking rather excited.

"Little mistress," she said with an unusually deep bow, "your honourable mother asks you to go to the room where the guests are."

I entered the big room. Brother was sitting by the *tokonoma*, and next to him were two gray-haired uncles and the young uncle from Tokyo. Opposite sat Honourable Grandmother, the four aunts, and Mother. Tea had been served and all had cups before them in their hands. As I pushed back the door they looked up and gazed at me as if they had never seen me before. I was a little startled, but of course I made a low, ceremonious bow. Mother motioned to me, and I slipped over beside her on the mat.

"Etsu-ko," Mother said very gently, "the gods have been kind to you, and your destiny as a bride has been de-

°*Adapted from* A Daughter of the Samurai, *by E. I. Sugimoto. Copyright 1925 by Doubleday & Company, Inc., pp. 55-58, 88-89.*

cided. Your honourable brother and your venerable kindred have given much thought to your future. It is proper that you should express your gratitude to the Honourable All."

I made a long, low bow, touching my forehead to the floor. Then I went out and returned to my desk and my writing. I had no thought of asking, "who is it?" I did not think of my engagement as a personal matter at all. It was a family affair. Like every Japanese girl, I had known from babyhood that sometime, as a matter of course, I should marry, but that was a faraway necessity to be considered when the time came. I did not look forward to it. I did not dread it. I did not think of it at all. The fact that I was not quite thirteen had nothing to do with it. That was the attitude of all girls. . . .

THE HONOURABLE ALL DEFIED

I must have been very young when my brother went away, for though I could distinctly recall the day he left, all memory of what went before or came immediately after was dim. I remember a sunny morning when our house was decorated with wondrous beauty and the servants all wore ceremonial dress with the Inagaki crest. It was the day of my brother's marriage. . . .

Ishi and I wandered from room to

room, she explaining that the bride for the young master would soon be there. . . .

. . . The "seven-and-a-half-times" messenger in his stiff-sleeved garment . . . had returned from his seventh trip to see if the bridal procession was coming, and though the day was bright with sunshine, was lighting his big lantern for his last trip to meet it halfway—thus showing our eagerness to welcome the coming bride. . . .

Then suddenly something was wrong. Ishi caught my shoulder and pulled me back, and Brother came hurriedly out of Father's room. He passed us with long, swinging strides, never looking at me at all, and stepping into his shoes on the garden step, he walked rapidly toward the side entrance. I have never seen him after that day.

The maiden my brother was to have married did not return to her former home. Having left it to become a bride, she was legally no longer a member of her father's family. This unusual problem Mother solved by inviting her to remain in our home as a daughter; which she did until finally Mother arranged a good marriage for her.

In a childish way I wondered about all the strangeness, but years had passed before I connected it with the sudden going away at this time of a graceful little maid named Tama, who used to arrange flowers and perform light duties. . . . Tama was not a servant. In those days it was the custom for daughters of wealthy tradesmen to be sent to live for a short time in a house of rank, that the maiden might learn the strict etiquette of *samurai* home life. The position was far from menial. . . .

The morning after my brother went away I was going, as usual, to pay my morning greetings to my father when I met Tama coming from his door, looking pale and startled. She bowed good morning to me and then passed quietly on. That afternoon I missed her and Ishi told me that she had gone home.

Whatever may have been between my brother and Tama I never knew; but I cannot but feel that, guilt or innocence, there was somewhere a trace of courage. . . . In that day there could be only a hopeless ending to such an affair, for no marriage was legal without the consent of parents, and my father, with heart wounded and pride shamed, had declared that he had no son.

It was not until several years later that I heard again of my brother. One afternoon Father was showing me some twisting tricks with a string. . . . A maid came to the door to say that Major Sato, a Tokyo gentleman whom my father knew very well, had called. . . . I shall never forget that scene. Major Sato, speaking with great earnestness, told how my brother had gone to Tokyo and entered the Army College. With only his own efforts he had completed the course with honour and was now a lieutenant. There Major Sato paused.

My father sat very still with his head held high and absolutely no expression on his stern face. For a full minute the room was so silent that I could hear myself breathe. Then my father, still without moving, asked quietly, "Is your message delivered, Major Sato?"

"It is finished," was the reply.

"Your interest is appreciated, Major Sato. This is my answer: I have daughters, but no son."

Modern Japanese Marriage*

Ezra F. Vogel

Formerly the *ie* [extended family] had considerable power in arranging marriages and jobs for the young. Since marriage was viewed as a change of *ie* for a girl or an adopted son-in-law, it was considered appropriate that the decision be made both by the *ie* receiving the member and the *ie* giving up the member. This attitude has not entirely disappeared, and wedding negotiations, arrangements, gift exchanges, and even the formal ceremonies still distinguish between the *ageru hoo* (the family which is "giving up" a person) and the *morau hoo* (the family which is "receiving" a person).

The investigations and negotiations leading to marriage, generally were carried out by a go-between (sometimes one for each side), who performed his services at the request of the *ie*. The view and temperament of the young man and young lady were considered, but it was expected that their wishes should be subordinated to the *ie*. This was not without some reason, for in the case of the first son, the young bride, after all, was coming to live with her husband's family, and might spend more time with her mother-in-law than with her husband. Even in the marriage of a second son, over which the family exercised less supervision, the family had to bear the responsibility for marital difficulties. Hence, the parents felt that their children (who until the time

of marriage had virtually no opportunity for meeting with members of the opposite sex) required their help in selecting a spouse.

The young people of Mamachi now regard such marriage arrangements as remnants of antiquated feudalistic society whereby the *ie* imposes its will on the young people who must sacrifice themselves for the good of the *ie*. While the Mamachi young people no longer are expected to conform to the wishes of their *ie* as such, their parents still retain influence in deciding whom the children should marry. The residents of Mamachi differentiate between two kinds of marriage: the *miai* (arranged marriage) and the *renai* (love marriage). In the *miai*, typically the parents, and sometimes relatives and family friends, have more influence, and in *renai* the young people themselves have more say.[1] While only about half of the recent marriages are officially arranged, in the overwhelming majority parents take an active role, checking on details of the other family. Some families will engage friends or private detectives to investigate the other family. Families frequently argue about the degree of independence that young people should have in selecting a spouse, but the range of freedom subject

*Adapted from Ezra F. Vogel, Japan's New Middle Class. Berkeley, Calif.: University of California Press, 1963, pp. 175–178.

[1] Regarding these two forms of marriage, see Ezra F. Vogel, "The Go-Between in a Developing Society," *Human Organization*, 1961, 20:112–120. The distinction between these two types of marriage will be explored more fully in a forthcoming work by Professor Robert Blood.

to dispute is relatively narrow if one considers the overwhelming power of the family in the Japan of an earlier era or the much broader freedom given most young people in the United States.

Yet, compared to the previous age, siblings and friends increasingly are replacing parents as sources of introductions, and coeducational schools and places of work provide limited opportunities which did not exist a few decades ago for respectable middle-class children to meet on their own. Nevertheless, there are few acceptable ways for young people to meet without some kind of introduction. Too much freedom is still suspect. A girl who has had dates with more than two or three men before marriage is still considered a bit free and worldly, and some will wonder whether she will make a good wife. What is emerging to some extent is a combination of *miai* and *renai*—a combination considered desirable by most parents. Under this combination, an appropriate person whom the family already has investigated thoroughly and found acceptable is introduced to the young person. The young people are permitted a few meetings (preferably not too many) to fall in love and make a decision. Under such arrangements they feel they have the best of two worlds: responsible arrangements and romantic love. If a child were given freedom to make his own decision, few discussions with his parents would be necessary, but in Mamachi where the decision is typically shared between the child and his parents, the selection of a spouse may dominate family discussions for years. Certainly both parents and the older children will be included, and sometimes knowledgeable or thoughtful friends. These discussions (or arguments) turn on such questions as what kind of person is desirable, who can help locate a promising

candidate, what are the relative assets and weak points of various candidates, how can they get a desirable candidate to agree, what kind of arrangements can be worked out for the marriage and living arrangements afterward. Particularly if the child is a daughter, these items are discussed, rediscussed, investigated, and reinvestigated. A family tries to arrive at a consensus on each minor step along the way. Indeed, they must arrive at a consensus if arrangements are to proceed smoothly. These discussions give the parents, and especially the mother, a purpose and function which they do not enjoy in many Western countries.

Considering how vehemently some adolescents insist on the freedom to find their own spouses, a surprisingly large number later acquiesce to arrangements or suggestions made by their parents. Many young people, especially the overprotected, the bashful, the cautious, those with high standards, those with a proud family history, the undesirable *urenokori* (leftovers) who did not find a spouse on their own, find the *miai* their best opportunity to get married and accept this pattern even if opposed to it ideologically. The willingness of children to let parents take an active part in the decision is undoubtedly related also to the close mother-child relationship and the fact that mothers have sacrificed so much for the children.[2]

[2] Evidence for this, based on projective test material given to Japanese, is presented in George DeVos, "The Relation of Guilt to Achievement and Arranged Marriage among the Japanese," *Psychiatry*, 1960, 23:287–301. Judging from De Vos's work, even in rural Japan the willingness to follow the mother's wishes has less to do with the concept of duty to *ie* than with the emotional bond between mother and child.

Furthermore, because children have had little opportunity to meet contemporaries of the opposite sex, they have little confidence in their own ability to make a proper decision. The modern parent of Mamachi does not object in principle to a child's selecting his own spouse; nor does a parent insist that the child follow his parents' choice out of duty to them and their *ie*, but by questioning the wisdom of the child's choice or questioning what the child would do if something went wrong, they can instill sufficient doubt so that he is willing to accede to the parents' advice.

A daughter is especially responsive to her parents' feelings because she would have to turn to them for help in case of marital difficulty. A generation ago divorce was not simply a separation of man and wife, but the husband's *ie* returning her to her parents' *ie*. It was necessary for the divorced woman to have the support of her *ie* if she were to have a source of livelihood and a reasonable chance of finding another spouse. Even today, because a widow or a divorcee has few chances for earning a living or finding a new spouse, the wife generally is reluctant to get a divorce. The rate of divorce among residents of Mamachi is still very low.[3] Even today a wife with marital difficulty, in effect, puts her case before her family and secures their approval before she decides to divorce, no matter how serious the trouble. . . .

Marriage Without Love: Mate-Selection in Non-Western Societies*

Linton C. Freeman

Virtually all societies consider married life the most desirable type of existence for adults. The details may vary from one society to another, but all societies encourage marriage; all advocate a relatively stable union between two or more persons. And in most cases the marital union involves such activities as living together, working together, having children, and rearing them. This is marriage; it is the rule in every known human group, past or present, "primitive" or modern.

If marriage is the rule in every society it is also the practice. Most people marry. In America Bill Brown marries

*Adapted from Robert F. Winch, Mate-Selection. New York: Harper & Row, Publishers, 1958, pp. 20–39.

Alice Jones because he loves her. But a couple of centuries ago in feudal Japan it was different. There, Ito Satake took Haru Taira as his wife, although he had never met her, because she was selected by his family, and he by hers. Among the Yaruro Indians of Venezuela, José Miguel was wed to Anita because she was his mother's brother's daughter. But in Southwest Africa, Gogab Garub, a Hottentot man, could not marry Hoaras Garis even though he wanted to because she was his seventh cousin, a very distant relative indeed! People marry every-

[3] Though I do not have adequate survey data, my impression is that it would be somewhat lower than the national average, which is about 10 percent.

where, but the person whom they select to marry and their reasons for selecting that person show wide variation. It is some of this variation which we shall explore in the present chapter.

Nowhere is mate-selection a random activity. It is always guided by two principles which underlie the process of selection. These are (1) *preferential mating*, which serves to define and delimit a field of eligible mates—sometimes narrow, sometimes wide—into which a person is encouraged to marry, and (2) *marriage arrangement*, which refers to the degree to which persons other than those marrying participate in the process of selection. These principles will be discussed in turn below.[1]

PREFERENTIAL MATING

All societies have rules prohibiting certain classes of persons from marrying one another. One part of these rules results from the prohibition of incest, or the tendency of all peoples to prohibit sexual activities—and hence marriage—among people who are close kinsmen. In mate-selection incest prohibition is expressed as the universal tendency to prohibit marriage between mother and son, father and daughter, or brother and sister. And many societies extend these prohibitions. Sometimes they include all known blood relatives and even persons with whom kinship ties are very distant. Some Australians, for example, prohibit marriage between persons of similarly named clans living a hundred miles away, and most probably entirely unrelated.[2] From this point of view,

then, the ideal mate for any person would be a stranger, an outsider, an individual not related to him in any real or imagined way.

In every society there is also a principle of mate-selection which runs counter to the incest prohibition, namely, the force of ethnocentrism, or group-conceit, which is common to all human groups. More or less universally the outsider is suspect; people tend to distrust and to dislike persons of different races, creeds, or cultural backgrounds. On the other hand, members of one's immediate family and community are accepted; they share the same traditional cultural values. In mate-selection ethnocentrism is expressed through prohibiting marriage with outsiders. Almost all societies, for example, oppose marriages between persons of markedly different racial or cultural backgrounds. Very often marriage with individuals outside the village or tribe is prohibited, and those from other social classes are considered unacceptable. From this point of view, the ideal mate for a man would be his mother or sister or some other member of his immediate family, since it is with these persons that he shares the most social relationships, that he feels the most cohesion. But as we have seen in the preceding paragraph, selection of a close relative as a mate, which would be a case of extreme ethnocentrism, is prohibited by the incest taboo.

From this discussion we can observe two conflicting tendencies which govern preferential mate-selection. They may be viewed as forces operating in opposite directions to locate a field of eligible mates. The location of the field of eligibles in any society will be determined by the relative strength of these two principles in that particular situation.

[1] This discussion is based in part upon G. P. Murdock's "Social Laws of Sexual Choice," as outlined in his *Social Structure*, New York, Macmillan, 1949. The present scheme represents a modification and simplification of Murdock's analysis.

[2] Robert H. Lowie, *An Introduction to Cultural Anthropology*, New York, Farrar & Rinehart, 2nd ed., 1940, p. 233.

For some groups ethnocentrism may be particularly forceful, and the result will be a high proportion of marriages among persons who are closely related to each other. Such was the case among the rulers of ancient Hawaii, Egypt, and the Incas, where brother-sister marriage was common. In our own country the intermarriage of cousins has been remarked in two very different settings: among the highlanders of the southeastern states and among the "proper Bostonians."[3] Other groups, however, have stressed incest prohibitions. Traditionally, among the Chinese, for example, one could not marry a person with the same family name as oneself, no matter how distant the relationship, and in a nation of China's size such a relationship might be distant indeed! In certain African tribes persons with a common ancestor cannot marry even though they may be quite remotely related. Just so, certain societies have prohibited marriage between persons of the same village or even of the same tribe.

In most cases neither of these forces is expressed in the extremes described above. Rather, the forces of ethnocentrism and of incest prohibition are both applied to isolate a field of eligibles within which mate-selection is expected to occur. The field of eligible or approved mates may be large or it may be small, its limits may be vague or they may be well defined, but in any case all societies have rules which tend to establish such a field. Even in modern American society we are expected to marry a person from our own race, religion, class, and age group, but one who is not too closely related to us by blood ties. In other societies the rules of preferential mating

may take different forms, but some rules will always be present.

MARRIAGE ARRANGEMENT

The second principle guiding mate-selection refers to the process of choosing a person within the field of eligibles. The field is established according to the rules for preferential mating, but very often a choice must be made among several eligibles within the field; this is where the principle of marriage arrangement comes into play. This principle is a reflection of the fact that almost every society has rules according to which persons other than those marrying participate in the process of mate-selection to a greater or lesser degree. As we shall see, some societies specify extreme intervention; they encourage the practice of fully arranged marriages. Others, such as our own, allow very little outside intervention and permit the person marrying to make his or her own choice. But in any case, the principle of marriage arrangement constitutes a real dimension of marriage choice once the field of eligibles has been established through the principle of preferential mating.

•

THE FAMILY AND MATE-SELECTION[4]

Variations in the bases upon which mates are selected can perhaps best be understood through examining the setting in which marriage occurs in various societies. Marriage takes place in every

[3] J. S. Brown, "The Conjugal Family and the Extended Family," *American Sociological Review* (1952), 17:297–306; Cleveland Amory, *The Proper Bostonians*, New York, Dutton, 1947, chap. 1.

[4] This discussion of the contemporary American family is, for the most part, based upon the following sources: John Sirjamaki, *The American Family in the Twentieth Century*, Cambridge, Harvard University Press, 1955, and Robert F. Winch, *The Modern Family*, New York, Holt, 1952.

society, and in each case it results in the formation of a marriage group or nuclear family. Such families consist of mates and their offspring.

Some societies, such as our own, consider this nuclear family as *the* family. To us, the family includes a married couple and their unmarried children. They usually live in a separate residence, often far from other relatives. Although a relationship with others, say grandparents, uncles, aunts, and cousins, is recognized, these relatives are almost outsiders; they are not included in the intimate family interaction. The family, then, is small and independent of other ties, but even this small unit is somewhat loosely organized and is seldom the center of the activities of its members. This is especially true of the father, who spends the larger part of his waking hours away from home and family at his place of work. Then too, after infancy the children are busy outside of the home most of the time, either in school or in recreational activities. The mother is more likely to be involved with home and family. Mothers with young children are by necessity more home-bound and family-oriented than others in our society, but today, with the working wives and the clubwomen, even more mothers show progressive emancipation from family ties.

Interaction and intimacy are certainly not absent in the small family group, but contacts outside that core tend to be made with age-group friends rather than with relatives. Such contacts may even preclude activities within the small family—the poker party or bowling night removing the father, the bridge club taking the mother, and the soda bar or other neighborhood hangout demanding the presence of the youngster.

Such is the typical family life of the contemporary American middle class. It is a small family and a loosely integrated one. It is a family which reflects the individualistic stress of our way of life. Individuals are taken as such; a person is known—is understood—by his job, his income, his education, his personal achievements, and, above all, his individual personality. Questions concerning his race, his religion, and his neighborhood, may be important in classifying him, but his background, his grandfather's occupation, and so on, are relatively unimportant. He may move to a position of greater or lesser prestige in the society; in fact, he is encouraged to succeed." He is an individual, and his successes and failures are his own. They reflect little upon his antecedents or his descendants—they tend to be his and his alone. It is true that his family, his wife and children, will be affected by a man's success or failure in the economic world. But a working wife may mediate this position considerably, and then the children are encouraged to go out on their own to succeed or fail for themselves.

This same individualism is reflected in American patterns of mate-selection. Bill Brown, it was said above, marries Alice Jones because he loves her. This is the ideal American middle-class pattern. They meet, "love strikes," and they marry. The basis for their feeling is undetermined—unquestioned; love is enough. However, it is likely that she will be selected from a field of eligibles which is determined according to the principle of preferential mating. The incest prohibitions will force him to choose a mate among those outside of his immediate family group. Ethnocentrism, on the other hand, dictates that he marry within his own race, his own social class, his own general age group, and usually from his own neighborhood or at least his own town. This provides him with a field of eligibles, people who are pretty much like him, sharing the same values, attitudes, and interests. Geographical migration may have led him away from his family spatially, and his own success or failures may have led him away in terms of attitudes and interests. But he will probably have more in common with the women in his field of eligibles than with his more distant relatives. Thus, though the range of acceptable mates is wide, it serves to provide him with a potential wife with whom he has much in common, and still someone who is outside of his own family group.

Ideally, within this field of eligible mates, American society gives the person marrying great leeway in selecting a spouse. Parental opposition may provide a minor setback, but since the parents have no direct personal interest in the union other than their children's happiness, their recalcitrance can usually be overcome or ignored. After all, the children have already been largely independent of their parents for some years. They have run with their own peers, made their own decisions, and somewhat governed their own lives. So selecting their own mates is merely another instance of their independence. Parents do not feel that they should interfere in the selection process, and probably they frequently doubt that they could intervene effectively if they wished to. Sometimes parents are not even consulted, for love is a personal affair between the two who experience it. Marriage, too, is their affair. When young people marry they usually leave their parents both spatially and emotionally; they go off by themselves and start their own family in their own home. Marriage usually destroys the last vestiges of dependence upon their parents. They are free—their new family is an independent unit in an individualistic world.

Most societies, however, are organized along very different lines. Imagine a society without specialists in various occupations, without schools or teachers, without churches or clergymen, without jails or police, without courts or judges. This is a society in which there are no governmental bureaucrats, no physicians or nurses, no farmers or merchants, one in which the only division of labor is made along age and sex lines. In such a society everyone would be pretty much like everyone else. Within age and sex groups all would do the same things and have the same rights and the same duties. But how would such a society be organized? Without teachers, who would educate the children? Without clergymen, who would guide the religious life of the community? Without police, who would apprehend criminals, and without judges, who would determine their guilt or innocence? Who would run the society, cure the ill, grow the food, sell the basic necessities? The same answer may be given for all of these questions: the family.

Instead of the individual, the family is the key unit of social organization. An individual's position comes not from his occupation or income, or even from his accomplishments, but rather from his family. An individual has identity only in his family setting. Aginsky provides some notion of the importance of the family in his report of a statement of an old Pomo Indian:

> A man must be with his family to amount to anything with us. If he had nobody else to help him, the first trouble he got into he would be killed by his enemies because there would be no relatives to help him fight the poison of the other group. No woman would marry him because her family would not let her marry a man with no family. He would be poorer than a newborn child; he would be poorer than a worm, and the family would not consider him worth anything. He would not bring renown or glory with him. He would not bring support of other relatives either. The family is important.

If a man has a large family and a profession and upbringing by a family that is known to produce good children, then he is somebody and every family is willing to have him marry a woman of their group. It is the family that is important. In the white ways of doing things the family is not so important. The police and soldiers take care of protecting you, the courts give you justice, the post office carries messages for you, the school teaches you. Everything is taken care of, even your children, if you die; but with us the family must do all of that.[5]

Thus, people living in such societies view the family very differently from the way we do. The family to them is a larger kinship group consisting of the nuclear marriage group and various other relatives including grandparents, uncles, aunts, cousins, grandchildren, and so on. In these societies the larger kinship group or extended family often shares a common residence and is a self-supporting cooperative unit. It is the center of activities for the individuals comprising it, and the various marriage groups within it are submerged into the larger system.

THE YARUROS OF VENEZUELA[6]

Earlier we said that among the Yaruros of Venezuela José Miguel married Anita because she was his mother's brother's daughter. Let us explore the background for such a marriage in order to determine its basis. The Yaruros

are a tribe of river nomads who inhabit a vast plain southeast of the Andes in inland Venezuela. Throughout most of the year the climate is hot and dry, the temperature climbing well above 100 degrees each day. This suffocating heat is made bearable only by the trade winds, which blow incessantly with a gale force over the level sands.

During the dry season the land is a veritable desert—miles of flat sand with very little animal or plant life. But during the rainy season the land is overrun with flora and fauna, food is plentiful, and life is relatively easy. Easy, that is, except for the insects. Insects are more than plentiful; they are omnipresent, and only the constant winds save the people from these pests.

The Yaruros are a short, dark small-boned people who have a definite Mongoloid appearance. They consider themselves to be one people but divide their lands according to recognized territorial limits. Each band has a large area along a river over which its members roam in quest of food.

The life of the Yaruros is simple to the extreme. Their economy is based upon fishing, hunting, and gathering, and although they travel far and wide in search of food, they never venture far from the river. They migrate in canoes and their only possessions can be carried in this fashion. Aside from a few baskets and pots, and some hunting equipment, they own nothing. They move on whenever food becomes scarce and settle again, but only temporarily, in any likely-looking spot.

Men do all the hunting and fishing, using bows and arrows and fishhooks. Women gather plants and herbs and roots, which they carry in baskets slung from their heads. The diet is variable, but young crocodiles are the basic staple. Crocodile eggs, turtles, turtle eggs, and various plants and roots are also com-

[5] B. W. Aginsky, "An Indian's Soliloquy," *American Journal of Sociology* (1940), 46:43–44.

[6] This description is based upon Vincenzo Petrullo, "The Yaruros of the Canpanaparo River, Venezuela," *Smithsonian Institution, Bureau of American Ethnology, Bulletin 123,* Anthropological Papers, No. 11, 1938, pp. 161–290.

mon. And honey and tobacco are continually sought. Except for dogs, the Yaruros have no domesticated animals.

The clothing worn by men consists only of a loincloth, while the women wear more elaborate girdles fashioned from foliage. Due to their sparse clothing and their constant exposure to the bright sun these people are tanned a rich brown most of the time.

The Yaruros are a peaceful people, given to religious musings. They travel in small hunting groups, and shamans or religious leaders are common. A typical camp might consist of an old man and his wife, their unmarried sons and daughters, their married daughters and husbands, their grandchildren, and sometimes their unmarried brothers and sisters. This family travels and hunts and camps as a group.

Campsites may be found anywhere along the river. The only shelters are temporary windbreaks fashioned out of branches, but these must not be too elaborate or effective or they will allow insects to gather. People find shelter from the sun and wind by sitting behind them, but they keep warm at night by burying themselves in the sand.

Yaruro society is divided into two moieties or halves on the basis of kinship. Each person belongs to one or the other moiety. Descent is traced in the female line; one inherits his moiety from his mother. And one must marry into the opposite moiety.

For the Yaruro, this means that a man must marry one of his cross-cousins, that is, one of his mother's brother's daughters or one of his father's sister's daughters. Each hunting group is made up of a single family, and other hunting groups nearby are usually closely related to it. Contacts with other more distant groups are very infrequent, It would seem, therefore, that a Yaruro man might marry only among his close relatives. However, it is considered incest to marry his sisters, his mother, and his mother's sisters, whom he calls mother also. Likewise, his mother's sister's daughters are called sister, and marriage with them is prohibited. And his father's brother's daughters belong to his own moiety. So this seems to leave only his mother's brother's daughters and his father's sister's daughters, that is, his cross-cousins. But since cross-cousin marriage probably took place in the parental generation also, his mother's brother's daughters *are* his father's sister's daughters. And it is among these cross-cousins that a Yaruros man is expected to marry.

When a young man among the Yaruros reaches marriageable age he talks with his father. The father takes him to the shaman—the religious leader—who instructs him in the obligations of marriage. Then the shaman goes to one of the boy's uncles, who selects one of his daughters, and the boy simply moves into his uncle's household. Thereafter he is obligated to work and hunt with his uncle. In effect, he takes the place of the uncle's sons who go off to live in the camps of their own wives.

Yaruro marriage practices, therefore, typify a procedure which serves to delimit an extremely narrow field of eligibles. Taken together, the incest taboos and the attitudes of ethnocentrism restrict the field of eligibles for the typical Yaruro man to one of his cross-cousins. Such an arrangement solves the problems raised by poor communication and sparse population. It affords access to a potential mate in the immediate vicinity but requires that the mate be obtained from another camp. This promotes interaction between camps and tends to maintain interfamilial solidarity.

While the dictates of preferential

mating tend to limit a person's freedom to select a mate in Yaruro society, marriage arrangement carries this restriction farther still. Preferential mating requires that a person marry his cross-cousin; marriage arrangement allows his uncle to select which particular cross-cousin it shall be. Such a pattern differs from the American one in the two important respects which we are considering here. First, one must select a mate from a small field of eligibles, i.e., from among one's cross-cousins. Persons other than cross-cousins are not defined as suitable marriage partners. Second, the choice of spouse from the field of eligibles is made not by the person to be married but by another—the uncle of the boy, who is also father of the girl.

FEUDAL JAPAN[7]

Some societies are permissive in both preferential mating and marriage arrangement, like the Americans; and

[7] This description is based principally upon the following sources: Lafcadio Hearn, *Japan, an Attempt at Interpretation*, New York, Macmillan, 1904; Kenneth S. Latourette, *The Development of Japan*, New York, Macmillan, 1920; George Bailey Sansom, *Japan: A Short Cultural History*, New York, Appleton-Century, 2nd ed., 1943; Etsu Sugimoto, *Daughter of the Samurai*, New York Doubleday, Page, 1925.

The following sources were also consulted: Alice Mabel Bacon, *Japanese Girls and Women*, Boston, Houghton Mifflin, 1902; Ruth Benedict, *The Chrysanthemum and the Sword*, Boston, Houghton Mifflin, 1946; Frank Brinkely, *A History of the Japanese People from the Earliest Times to the End of the Meiji Era*, New York, Encyclopedia Britannica, Inc., 1915; John Embree, *The Japanese Nation*, New York, Farrar & Rinehart, 1945; Douglas G. Haring, "Japan and the Japanese," in Ralph Linton (ed.), *Most of the World*, New York, Columbia University

some, like the Yaruros, are restrictive in both. Others, however, permit selection from a wide field of eligibles but restrict the persons marrying from participating in the choice. To illustrate this, we must remember that in feudal Japan Ito Satake married Haru Taira because she was selected by his family and he by hers. Let us examine the setting in which this marriage took place and try to uncover some of the factors involved in this type of marriage choice.

Arranged marriage was found in its purest form among the aristocracy of Japan during the feudal era. Let us say, therefore, that our couple were aristocrats and that they lived during the early 1700's, the height of Japanese feudalism.

Japan is a group of about three thousand islands lying off the east coast of continental Asia. The four main islands are Hokkaido, Honshu, Shikoku, and Kyushu. These form a long chain running for 1500 miles from northwest to southeast. The terrain consists chiefly of mountainous areas covered with vast forests, and only 15 percent of it is arable.[8] The climate shows great variation from region to region, and no single description will hold for all of Japan; northern Japan is subject to long and bitter winters while the south is typically subtropical.

The people of Japan are also varied. They are predominantly Mongoloid, but much Malayan and some Caucasian Ainu ancestry is evident. They are short-legged people with straight black hair

Press, 1949; Arthur M. Knapp, *Feudal and Modern Japan*, Boston, J. Knight Co., 1897, 2 vols.; Inazo Ota Nitobe, *The Japanese Nation*, New York, Putnam, 1912; George Bailey Sansom, *The Western World and Japan*, New York, Knopf, 1950.

[8] H. A. Meyerhoff, "Natural Resources in Most of the World," in Ralph Linton, *op. cit.*, p. 63.

and dark eyes. Skin color ranges from an almost Nordic pink and white to the light brown of the Pacific Islanders. Since they are a heterogeneous group, few generalizations could be made which would accurately describe the physical characteristics of the people of Japan.

During the feudal era Japan was divided into small duchies, each ruled by a local lord backed by armed knights. A hereditary military leader governed the entire nation and relegated the Emperor to comparative insignificance. Social classes were defined rigidly, and one's class was reflected in his dwelling, his style of dress, his food, etc. Both commoners and knights owed allegiance to the local lord.

However, more important even than his responsibility to his lord was a person's responsibility to his family. His thoughts, his feelings, his behavior were so completely bound up in family life that understanding him is unthinkable without first examining his family.

Family life in feudal Japan was organized around the patriarch. A typical household might include the patriarch, his wife, all his sons and their wives and children, his unmarried daughters, servants, and younger brothers of the patriarch and their wives and children. Such a family was a relatively large-scale coöperative unit under the direction of the patriarch. He was the director of the household. He handled all household business except for the purchase of supplies, and even there he might intervene and make the final decision. He was the priest in family worship and the manager of family properties. In short, the patriarch was the almost absolute ruler of all members of the Japanese family.

The power of the patriarch, however, was not unlimited. Important decisions were usually made by the family council, which included most of the mature males and the old women in the family. This group met to decide such things as adoption of a child or marriage of a family member, but day-to-day decisions were made by the family patriarch.

Children were reared into a pattern of male dominance and rigid conformity. Infants were fondled and petted, but after the first few years permissive treatment gradually gave way to a demand for conformity. This gradual increase in restriction was manifest in a range of techniques. The emphasis, however, was never upon forcing the child to express himself within the vague framework of abstractions like "good" or "bad." Rather, self-expression was denied; children learned to conform to a rigid pattern of expectations which demanded almost ritual performance of even the simplest tasks. In the Japanese desire to create and maintain "face," etiquette played a major role. Children were taught polite customs by their mothers, who actually manipulated the child's body into the desired positions. This way a child learned to bow, and to sit on the floor attentively, for hours if necessary, while studying. And young girls were taught to sleep flat on their back, legs straight together and arms straight and at their sides.

Children were forced to succumb to these rigid demands through the continual threat of humiliation or withdrawal of family affection. Regular teaching and emphasis upon "family honor" tended to center the child's attention upon the family. The threat of denial of the satisfactions of the family was, therefore, a real and effective mechanism in insuring conforming behavior.

The relative social positions of men and women were learned quite early, as was the position of each family in the social hierarchy. Most important, the child learned the intricate system of duties and obligations which characterized Japanese culture. He learned to think and act, not as an individual, but as a family member. His position in the family and the position of his family in the larger society determined his fate. He grew to accept that fate—to behave always in terms of his proper station in life.

Ideally, by the time they reached adulthood the Japanese had learned to view each other, not as individuals at all, but almost completely as stereotypes. If two people were members of the same family they treated each other in terms of their relationship. They met neither as personalities nor as persons, but only as representatives of particular relationships. All fathers treated, and were treated by, their sons in much the same way. Their interaction was based upon their kinship, not upon personal feelings.

Relationships with persons outside the family were governed by the importance of the families involved. Even here, personalities were relatively unimportant; people met as representatives of their families, not as individuals. It was more important to know that a person was a member of the Nakamura family than to know that he was Kiyoshi Nakamura. As a person he did not count; as a representative of a certain family he became important. In short, in traditional Japanese society individuality was almost completely submerged in the family system.

In studying traditional Japan we see a society in which the family was central to all activities. Everything an individual did—each of his interpersonal relationships—was organized around his position in the family. Marriage, then, like any other interpersonal relationship was an affair of the entire family. People married, not to start a new family, but rather to perpetuate the already existing one. In a sense, a marriage was not a union between two persons but a technique for

adding another person in order to keep the family going. Selecting the right person was important to everyone in the family since he or she might either contribute to the general welfare or be an active source of disorganization. Moreover, marriage established a long-term bond between two families. When considering marriage they looked for an eligible person from a family whose position might enhance their prestige and security.

Thus marriage among the traditional Japanese aristocracy was too important for all members of both families for them to allow the choice to be made by two young, inexperienced people. It was too big even for the patriarch to handle alone. So marriages were arranged by the family council.

When the family of a young man considered their son at an appropriate age for marriage they engaged the services of a family friend to act as go-between. This was necessary in order to save "face." For if they themselves started negotiations with the family of some prospective bride and were rejected, their loss of face or public esteem would be irreparable. It would be a personal affront to them—one from which recovery would be impossible. So some trusted family friend was elected, who might suggest several young ladies of suitable social standing and after discussion proceed to contact the family of one of these. After preliminary negotiations the girl's family usually appointed their own go-between, and thereafter followed a long period of careful investigation and negotiation. Considerations of social class, and honor and health among each family turned out to be healthy, honorable, and socially acceptable, agreement was reached and the betrothed was informed of the decision. The prospective bride and groom had little or no voice in the proceedings and often did not meet until the wedding ceremony.

The wedding ceremony was held at the groom's home. At the start of the ceremony the bride was often dressed in white (to signify her sorrow at losing her family), but during the proceedings she changed to a colorful kimono. Sake was drunk by the bride and groom, and the wedding ceremony was complete.

Marriage in traditional Japan thus presented a picture of almost complete subjugation of individual initiative in the familial group. The field of eligibles was relatively wide, but the marrying individuals were not even consulted in preparing for their marriage, the family council making all decisions. This pattern is understandable in light of the importance of family ties for the Japanese individual. It affords an illustration of the degree to which persons other than the ones being married may dominate the process of mate-selection.

Some societies have gone further still. Among villagers in India, the medieval English, and the inhabitants of the island of Buka in Melanesia child betrothal was quite common. The parents of young children would get together and contract a marriage for their immature offspring. Such a contract was binding even though the union could not be consummated for several years. This practice was common also among the Kazaks of central Asia. In some cases two Kazak fathers might agree to unite their as yet unborn children. Such a practice represents an extreme of parental intervention in the mate-selection of their offspring.

THE HOTTENTOTS[9]

A fourth form of mate-selection is typified by the pattern among the Hot-

[9]This description is based upon the following sources: S. S. Dornan, *Pygmies and*

tentots of Southwest Africa. Here, you will recall, Gogab Garub, a Hottentot man, could not marry Hoaras Garis because she was his seventh cousin. Although the Hottentots allow the persons marrying a more or less free choice of a mate, the mate must be chosen from within a relatively small field of eligibles. Thus, for these people the rules of preferential mating are restrictive, but marital arrangement plays only a minor part in the selection process.

The Hottentots are a group of nomadic herders who live in a great grassy plateau in the southwestern corner of Africa. The climate is cool and dry; it provides little in the way of vegetation except for grass, but animal life is abundant. Animals of all sizes and kinds—from the elephant to the tiniest insect—literally cover the plain, but a few roots, berries, bulbs, and melons are the only edible vegetation.

Today the Hottentots number about twenty thousand. Once they were far more numerous, but warfare and disease have steadily diminished their number ever since European contact. They are extremely small people—men average about five feet three inches; women, four feet eleven. Their skin is light brown in color, and it is often very wrinkled. Their bodies are relatively hairless, and the hair on their heads is usually short, black, and quite kinky.

Hottentot economy is based upon hunting and herding. The people hunt game, large and small, and gather roots and berries. They raise large herds of cattle and sheep, but these are seldom

Bushmen of the Kalahari, London, Seeley Service, 1925; George P. Murdock, *Our Primitive Contemporaries*, New York, Macmillan, 1934; I. Schapera, *The Khoisan Peoples of South Africa*, London, Routledge, 1930; I. Schapera and B. Farrington (eds.), *The Early Cape Hottentots*, Cape Town, The Van Rebeeck Society, 1933.

slaughtered. Instead, they milk the cows and ewes, and use oxen as beasts of burden. Thus, meat and milk constitute the basic part of the Hottentot diet.

Women do most of the work, and the men are characterized as lazy. The women milk the animals, gather the edible plants, carry water and firewood, cook, maintain the houses, and make clothing and pottery. The herds are tended by young boys or captive servants, while the men spend their days hunting. Sometimes men prepare skins, or work with wood or metal, but for the most part they confine their activities to the hunt.

The Hottentots are divided into twelve tribes. Although each tribe is associated with a general territorial location, the members of a tribe do not live together in a single community. Instead, each tribe is broken down into a number of clans—groups of persons united by a common ancestor. In general, the members of a clan form a single community, or sometimes, if a clan is large, it may split up into several extended families, each of which goes off to live by itself.

The Hottentots are a seminomadic people. A typical community consists of a number of light portable dome-shaped huts. They are made of sticks and covered with rush mats and are constructed in such a manner that when the water supply runs low, or hunting or grazing becomes difficult, they may be torn down, loaded on oxen, and transported to a new location where water, grass, or game is more plentiful. A single hut is occupied by a nuclear family—a man, his wife, and their unmarried children.

In any encampment the huts are arranged according to age seniority. The Hottentots place great value upon age, and the eldest male member of any clan is the chief. But political and judicial authority are vested in the chief only with reservation. A clan is governed by a council consisting of the older men of the clan. This council directs the activities of clan members, settles quarrels within the clan, and punishes minor offenders. On the tribal level these activities are performed by the tribal council composed of the chiefs of all the clans in the tribes.

Marriage for the Hottentots is usually monogamous. However, some of the wealthier men take more than one wife. Each wife lives in a separate hut along with her children. Later or secondary wives give precedence to the first wife, whose children enjoy preferred rights of inheritance. Women own their huts and their own herds of animals. They also control the distribution of household provisions. A husband must respect his wife's rights in these matters, and if he violates them he is obliged to pay a penalty of sheep or cattle.

Neither boys nor girls are considered marriageable until they have passed through a series of rites at puberty. Each boy must also demonstrate his proficiency as a hunter by killing some big-game animal. Once these rites have been completed, however, the young people are allowed considerable sexual freedom. There is also marked freedom in the choice of mate, the principal limitation on which is the prohibition against marrying a person of their own clan or a person bearing their clan name even though from another tribe. On the other hand, they are discouraged from marrying a person too alien; they are—like the Yaruros—required to marry a cross-cousin, that is, a daughter of either the mother's brother or the father's sister. Thus among the Hottentots the range of potential mates is severely restricted from the start.

From this description we can see that the field of eligibles for the Hottentots is established on the basis of kinship. Incest prohibitions are strong-they are extended to include every member of a person's clan—everyone in his local encampment. The Hottentots camp in clan groups like the Yaruros, and most interpersonal contacts are with kinsmen. And like the Yaruros, isolation and ethnocentrism force them to seek a spouse from a neighboring encampment. In both cases the person sought is a cross-cousin. But here the resemblance ends. For while Yaruro custom dictates that the choice among cross-cousins be made by the uncle, the Hottentots allow the persons marrying to make their own choice.

Thus within the field of eligibles —his cross-cousins—a young man is free to choose his own mate. When he finds a desirable prospect, a young Hottentot man speaks to his parents. They, in turn, send emissaries to the parents of the girl to ask her hand. Tradition dictates that they refuse. But the young man is undaunted by this seeming opposition. He attempts to enlist the support of the girl. He watches her house at night until he determines the location where she sleeps. Then, when everyone has retired, he goes in and lies down next to her. Usually she gets up and moves to another part of the hut but he remains in her place until morning. The next night he returns to her hut. If he finds her in the same spot he knows that his suit is favored. She may leave again, but sooner or later she will stay and the marriage is consummated.

The marriage feast is conducted the same day. He provides a cow for slaughter and goes off to hunt game for a feast. He presents gifts of cattle to her family but receives an equal number in return. The couple resides in the camp of the bride for about a year or until their first child is born. Thereafter they move to the camp of the groom's parents and establish their permanent residence in their own hut.

For the Hottentots, then, the process of actually selecting a mate is one of great freedom and individual initiative. Both bride and groom have a voice, and there is usually little or no outside interference. They are in this respect like the modern Americans, but for them, unlike the Americans, the range of potential mates from which the choice is made is relatively small.

We have defined two principles which govern the process of mate-selection: (1) preferential mating and (2) marriage arrangement. And we have indicated that each of these principles may vary from society to society. Some societies may delimit a narrow field of eligibles and some a wide one. Some may allow extreme intervention—by parents, for example—in the choice of a mate while others allow no intervention whatsoever. In order to illustrate their operation we have described four extreme types.

The first type is familiar to all of us who live in American society. Here we are allowed to choose a mate within a relatively wide field of eligibles, and outside intervention in our choice by parents or others is minimal.

The opposite of the American form in both respects was typified by the Yaruros of Venezuela. Here the field of eligibles is extremely narrow, and choice within that field is made by persons other than the ones being married.

A third extreme form is exemplified by the Japanese of feudal times. In this case the field of eligibles was wide, but the person marrying had little voice in the proceedings.

The fourth and final extreme may be illustrated by the Hottentots of Southwest Africa. This society prohibits marriage except within a relatively narrow field of eligibles, but within that field the persons marrying make their own choice.

We may summarize these points as follows:

	Preferential Mating	
DEGREE OF ARRANGEMENT OF THE MARRIAGE	HIGHLY SPECIFIED PREFERENCES LEADING TO NARROW FIELD OF ELIGIBLES	LITTLE SPECIFICATION OF PREFERRED MATE LEADING TO WIDE FIELD OF ELIGIBLES
High: Parents or others select one's spouse	Yaruros	Feudal Japan
Low: Principal selects own spouse	Hottentots	Middle-class U.S.A.

The Theoretical Importance of Love*

William J. Goode

Because love often determines the intensity of an attraction[1] toward or away from an intimate relationship with another person, it can become one element in a decision or action.[2] Nevertheless, serious sociological attention has only infrequently been given to love. Moreover, analyses of love generally have been confined to mate choice in the Western World, while the structural importance of love has been for the most part ignored. The present paper views love in a broad perspective, focusing on the structural patterns by which societies keep in check the potentially disruptive effect of love relationships on mate choice and stratification systems.

TYPES OF LITERATURE ON LOVE

For obvious reasons, the printed material on love is immense. For our present purposes, it may be classified as follows:

1. Poetic, humanistic, literary, erotic, pornographic: By far the largest body of all literature on love views it as a sweeping experience. The poet arouses our sympathy and empathy. The essayist enjoys, and asks the reader to enjoy, the interplay of people in love. The storyteller—Bocaccio, Chaucer, Dante—pulls back the curtain of human souls and lets the reader watch the intimate lives of others caught in an emotion we all know. Others—Vatsyayana, Ovid, William IX

*Adapted from the American Sociological Review, 1959, 24: 38–47.

[1]On the psychological level, the motivational power of both love and sex is intensified by this curious fact: (which I have not seen remarked on elsewhere) Love is the most projective of emotions, as sex is the most projective of drives; only with great difficulty can the attracted person believe that the object of his love or passion does not and will not reciprocate the feeling at all. Thus, the person may carry his action quite far, before accepting a rejection as genuine.

[2]I have treated decision analysis extensively in an unpublished paper by that title.

Count of Poitiers and Duke of Aquitaine, Marie de France, Andreas Capellanus—have written how-to-do-it books, that is, how to conduct oneself in love relations, to persuade others to succumb to one's love wishes, or to excite and satisfy one's sex partner.[3]

2. Marital counseling: Many modern sociologists have commented on the importance of romantic love in America and its lesser importance in other societies, and have disparaged it as a poor basis for marriage, or as immaturity. Perhaps the best known of these arguments are those of Ernest R. Mowrer, Ernest W. Burgess, Mabel A. Elliott, Andrew G. Truxal, Francis E. Merrill, and Ernest R. Groves.[4] The antithesis of romantic love, in such analyses, is "conjugal" love; the love between a settled, domestic couple.

A few sociologists, remaining within this same evaluative context, have in-

stead claimed that love also has salutory effects in our society. Thus, for example, William L. Kolb[5] has tried to demonstrate that the marital counselors who attack romantic love are really attacking some fundamental values of our larger society, such as individualism, freedom, and personality growth. Beigel[6] has argued that if the female is sexually repressed, only the psychotherapist or love can help her overcome her inhibitions. He claims further that one influence of love in our society is that it extenuates illicit sexual relations; he goes on to assert: "Seen in proper perspective, [love] has not only done no harm as a prerequisite to marriage, but it has mitigated the impact that a too-fast-moving and unorganized conversion to new socioeconomic constellations has had upon our whole culture and it has saved monogamous marriage from complete disorganization."

In addition, there is widespread comment among marriage analysts, that in a rootless society, with few common bases for companionship, romantic love holds a couple together long enough to allow them to begin marriage. That is, it functions to attract people powerfully together, and to hold them through the difficult first months of the marriage, when their different backgrounds would otherwise make an adjustment troublesome.

3. Although the writers cited above concede the structural importance of love implicitly, since they are arguing that it is either harmful or helpful to various values and goals of our society, a third group has given explicit if unsystematic attention to its structural importance. Here, most of the available propositions

[3]Vatsyayana, The Kama Sutra, Delhi: Rajkamal, 1948; Ovid, "The Loves," and "Remedies of Love," in The Art of Love, Cambridge, Mass.: Harvard University Press, 1939; Andreas Capellanus, The Art of Courtly Love, translated by John J. Parry, New York: Columbia University Press, 1941; Paul Tuffrau, editor, Marie de France: Les Lais de Marie de France, Paris L'edition d'art, 1925; see also Julian Harris, Marie de France, New York: Institute of French Studies, 1930, esp. Chapter 3. All authors but the first also had the goal of writing literature.

[4]Ernest R. Mowrer, Family Disorganization, Chicago: The University of Chicago Press, 1927, pp. 158–165; Ernest W. Burgess and Harvey J. Locke, The Family, New York: American Book, 1953, pp. 436–437; Mabel A. Elliott and Francis E. Merrill, Social Disorganization, New York: Harper, 1950, pp. 366–384; Andrew G. Truxal and Francis E. Merrill, The Family in American Culture, New York: Prentice-Hall, 1947, pp. 120–124, 507–509; Ernest R. Groves and Gladys Hoagland Groves, The Contemporary American Family, New York: Lippincott, 1947, pp. 321–324.

[5]William L. Kolb, "Sociologically Established Norms and Democratic Values," Social Forces, 26 (May, 1948), pp. 451–456.

[6]Hugo G. Beigel, "Romantic Love," American Sociological Review, 16 (June, 1951), pp. 326–334.

point to the functions of love, but a few deal with the conditions under which love relationships occur. They include:

(1) An implicit or assumed descriptive proposition is that love as a common prelude to and basis of marriage is rare, perhaps to be found as a pattern only in the United States.

(2) Most explanations of the conditions which create love are psychological, stemming from Freud's notion that love is "aim-inhibited sex."[7] This idea is expressed, for example, by Waller who says that love is an idealized passion which develops from the frustration of sex.[8] This proposition, although rather crudely stated and incorrect as a general explanation, is widely accepted.

(3) Of course, a predisposition to love is created by the socialization experience. Thus some textbooks on the family devote extended discussion to the ways in which our society socializes for love. The child, for example, is told that he or she will grow up to fall in love with some one, and early attempts are made to pair the child with children of the opposite sex. There is much joshing of children about falling in love; myths and stories about love and courtship are heard by children; and so on.

(4) A further proposition (the source of which I have not been able to locate) is that, in a society in which a very close attachment between parent and child prevails, a love complex is necessary in order to motivate the child to free him from his attachment to his parents.

(5) Love is also described as one final or crystallizing element in the decision to marry, which is otherwise structured by factors such as class, ethnic origin, religion, education, and residence.

(6) Parsons has suggested three factors which "underlie the prominence of the romantic context in our culture": (a) the youth culture frees the individual from family attachments, thus permitting

him to fall in love; (b) love is a substitute for the interlocking of kinship roles found in other societies, and thus motivates the individual to conform to proper marital role behavior; and (c) the structural isolation of the family so frees the married partners' affective inclinations that they are able to love one another.[9]

(7) Robert F. Winch has developed a theory of "complementary needs" which essentially states that the underlying dynamic in the process of falling in love is an interaction between (a) the perceived psychological attributes of one individual and (b) the complementary psychological attributes of the person falling in love, such that the needs of the latter are felt to be met by the perceived attributes of the former and *vice versa*. These needs are derived from Murray's list of personality characteristics. Winch thus does not attempt to solve the problem of why our society has a love complex, but how it is that specific individuals fall in love with each other rather than with someone else.[10]

(8) Winch and others have also analyzed the effect of love upon various institutions or social patterns: Love themes are prominently displayed in the media of entertainment and communication, in consumption patterns, and so on.[11]

4. Finally, there is the cross-cultural work of anthropologists, who in the main have ignored love as a factor of importance in kinship patterns. The implicit understanding seems to be that love as a pattern is found only in the United States, although of course individual cases of love are sometimes recorded. The term "love" is practically never found in indexes of anthropological monographs on specific societies or in general anthropology textbooks. It is perhaps not an

[7] Sigmund Freud, *Group Psychology and the Analysis of the Ego*, London: Hogarth, 1922, p. 72.

[8] Willard Waller, *The Family*, New York: Dryden, 1938, pp. 189–192.

[9] Talcott Parsons, *Essays in Sociological Theory*, Glencoe, Ill.: Free Press, 1949, pp. 187–189.

[10] Robert F. Winch, *Mate-Selection*, New York: Harper, 1958.

[11] See e.g., Robert F. Winch, *The Modern Family*, New York: Holt, 1952, Chapter 14.

exaggeration to say that Lowie's comment of a generation ago would still be accepted by a substantial number of anthropologists:

> But of love among savages? . . . Passion, of course, is taken for granted; affection, which many travelers vouch for, might be conceded; but Love? Well, the romantic sentiment occurs in simpler conditions, as with us—in fiction. . . . So Love exists for the savage as it does for ourselves—in adolescence, in fiction, among the poetically minded. [12]

A still more skeptical opinion is Linton's scathing sneer:

> All societies recognize that there are occasional violent, emotional attachments between persons of opposite sex, but our present American culture is practically the only one which has attempted to capitalize these, and make them the basis for marriage. . . . The hero of the modern American movie is always a romantic lover, just as the hero of the old Arab epic is always an epileptic. A cynic may suspect that in any ordinary population the percentage of individuals with a capacity for romantic love of the Hollywood type was about as large as that of persons able to throw genuine epileptic fits. [13]

In Murdock's book on kinship and marriage, there is almost no mention, if any, of love. [14] Should we therefore conclude that, cross-culturally, love is not important, and thus cannot be of great importance structurally? If there is only one significant case, perhaps it is safe to view love as generally unimportant in social structure and to concentrate rather on the nature and functions of romantic

love within the Western societies in which love is obviously prevalent. As brought out below, however, many anthropologists have in fact described love *patterns*. And one of them, Max Gluckman, [15] has recently subsumed a wide range of observations under the broad principle that love relationships between husband and wife estrange the couple from their kin, who therefore try in various ways to undermine that love. This principle is applicable to many more societies (for example, China and India) than Gluckman himself discusses.

THE PROBLEM AND ITS CONCEPTUAL CLARIFICATION

The preceding propositions (except those denying that love is distributed widely) can be grouped under two main questions: What are the consequences of romantic love in the United States? How is the emotion of love aroused or created in our society? The present paper deals with the first question. For theoretical purposes both questions must be reformulated, however, since they implicitly refer only to our peculiar system of romantic love. Thus: (1) In what ways do various love patterns fit into the social structure, especially into the systems of mate choice and stratification? (2) What are the structural conditions under which a range of love patterns occurs in various societies? These are overlapping questions, but their starting point and assumptions are different. The first assumes that love relationships are a universal psychosocial possibility, and that different social systems make different adjustments to their potential disruptiveness. The second does not take love for granted, and supposes rather that such

[12] Robert H. Lowie, "Sex and Marriage," in John F. McDermott, editor, *The Sex Problem in Modern Society*, New York: Modern Library, 1931, p. 146.

[13] Ralph Linton, *The Study of Man*, New York: Appleton-Century, 1936, p. 175.

[14] George Peter Murdock, *Social Structure*, New York: Macmillan, 1949.

[15] Max Gluckman, *Custom and Conflict in Africa*, Oxford: Basil Blackwell, 1955, Chapter 3.

relationships will be rare unless certain structural factors are present. Since in both cases the analysis need not depend upon the correctness of the assumption, the problem may be chosen arbitrarily. Let us begin with the first. [16]

We face at once the problem of defining "love." Here, love is defined as a strong emotional attachment, a cathexis, between adolescents or adults of opposite sexes, with at least the components of sex desire and tenderness. Verbal definitions of this emotional relationship are notoriously open to attack; this one is no more likely to satisfy critics than others. Agreement is made difficult by value judgments: one critic would exclude anything but "true" love, another casts out "infatuation," another objects to "puppy love," while others would separate sex desire from love because sex presumably is degrading. Nevertheless, most of us have had the experience of love, just as we have been greedy, or melancholy, or moved by hate (defining "true" hate seems not to be a problem). The experience can be referred to without great ambiguity, and a refined measure of various degrees of intensity or purity of love is unnecessary for the aims of the present analysis.

Since love may be related in diverse ways to the social structure, it is necessary to forego the dichotomy of "romantic love—no romantic love" in favor of a continuum or range between polar types. At one pole, a strong love attraction is socially viewed as a laughable or tragic aberration; at the other, it is mildly shameful to marry without being in love with one's intended spouse. This is a gradation from negative sanction to positive approval, ranging at the same time from low or almost nonexistent institutionalization of love to high institutionalization.

The urban middle classes of contemporary Western society, especially in the United States, are found toward the latter pole. Japan and China, in spite of the important movement toward European patterns, fall toward the pole of low institutionalization. Village and urban India is farther toward the center, for there the ideal relationship has been one which at least generated love after marriage, and sometimes after betrothal, in contrast with the mere respect owed between Japanese and Chinese spouses. [17] Greece after Alexander, Rome of the Empire, and perhaps the later period of the Roman Republic as well, are near the center, but somewhat toward the pole of institutionalization, for love matches appear to have increased in frequency—a trend denounced by moralists. [18]

This conceptual continuum helps to clarify our problem and to interpret the propositions reviewed above. Thus it may be noted, first, that individual love relationships may occur even in societies in which love is viewed as irrelevant to mate choice and excluded from the decision to marry. As Linton conceded, some violent love attachments may be found in any so-

[16] I hope to deal with the second problem in another paper.

[17] Tribal India, of course, is too heterogeneous to place in any one position on such a continuum. The question would have to be answered for each tribe. Obviously it is of less importance here whether China and Japan, in recent decades have moved "two points over" toward the opposite pole of high approval of love relationships as a basis for marriage than that both systems as classically described viewed love as generally a tragedy; and love was supposed to be irrelevant to marriage, i.e., noninstitutionalized. The continuum permits us to place a system at some position, once we have the descriptive data.

[18] See Ludwig Friedländer, *Roman Life and Manners under the Early Empire* (Seventh Edition), translated by A. Magnus, New York: Dutton, 1908, Vol. 1, Chapter 5, "The Position of Women."

ciety. In our own, the Song of Solomon, Jacob's love of Rachel, and Michal's love for David are classic tales. The Mahabharata, the great Indian epic, includes love themes. Romantic love appears early in Japanese literature, and the use of Mt. Fuji as a locale for the suicide of star crossed lovers is not a myth invented by editors of tabloids. There is the familiar tragic Chinese story to be found on the traditional "willow-plate," with it lovers transformed into doves. And so it goes—individual love relationships seem to occur everywhere. But this fact does not change the position of a society on the continuum.

Second, reading both Linton's and Lowie's comments in this new conceptual context reduces their theoretical importance, for they are both merely saying that people do not *live by* the romantic complex, here or anywhere else. Some few couples in love will brave social pressures, physical dangers, or the gods themselves, but nowhere is this usual. Violent, self-sufficient love is not common anywhere. In this respect, of course, the U.S. is not set apart from other systems.

Third, we can separate a *love pattern* from the romantic love *complex*. Under the former, love is a permissible, expected prelude to marriage, and a usual element of courtship—thus, at about the center of the continuum, but toward the pole of institutionalization. The romantic love complex (one pole of the continuum) includes, in addition, an ideological prescription that falling in love is a highly desirable basis of courtship and marriage; love is strongly institutionalized.[19] In contemporary United States, many individuals would even claim that entering marriage without being in love requires some such rationalization as asserting that

[19] For a discussion of the relation between behavior patterns and the process of institutionalization, see my *After Divorce*, Glencoe, Ill.: Free Press, 1956, Chapter 15.

one is too old for such romances or that one must "think of practical matters like money." To be sure, both anthropologists and sociologists often exaggerate the American commitment to romance;[20] nevertheless, a behavioral and value complex of this type is found here.

But this complex is rare. Perhaps only the following cultures possess the romantic love value complex: modern urban United States, Northwestern Europe, Polynesia, and the European nobility of the eleventh and twelfth centuries.[21] Certainly, it is to be found in no other major civilization. On the other hand, the *love pattern*, which views love as a basis for the final decision to marry, may be relatively common.

WHY LOVE MUST BE CONTROLLED

Since strong love attachments apparently can occur in any society and

[20] See Ernest W. Burgess and Paul W. Wallin, *Engagement and Marriage*, New York: Lippincott, 1953, Chapter 7 for the extent to which even the engaged are not blind to the defects of their beloveds. No one has ascertained the degree to which various age and sex groups in our society actually believe in some form of the ideology.

Similarly, Margaret Mead in *Coming of Age in Samoa*, New York: Modern Library, 1953, rates Manu'an love as shallow, and though these Samoans give much attention to love-making, she asserts that they laughed with incredulous contempt at Romeo and Juliet (pp. 155–156). Though the individual sufferer showed jealousy and anger, the Manu'ans believed that a new love would quickly cure a betrayed lover (pp. 105–108). It is possible that Mead failed to understand the shallowness of love in our own society: Romantic love is, "in our civilization, inextricably bound up with ideas of monogamy, exclusiveness, jealousy, and undeviating fidelity" (p. 105). But these are *ideas* and ideology; *behavior* is rather different.

[21] I am preparing an analysis of this case. The relation of "courtly love" to social structure is complicated.

since (as we shall show) love is frequently a basis for and prelude to marriage, it must be controlled or channeled in some way. More specifically, the stratification and lineage patterns would be weakened greatly if love's potentially disruptive effects were not kept in check. The importance of this situation may be seen most clearly by considering one of the major functions of the family, status placement, which in every society links the structures of stratification, kinship lines, and mate choice. (To show how the very similar comments which have been made about sex are not quite correct would take us too far afield; in any event, to the extent that they are correct, the succeeding analysis applies equally to the control of sex.)

Both the child's placement in the social structure and choice of mates are socially important because both placement and choice link two kinship lines together. Courtship or mate choice, therefore, cannot be ignored by either family or society. To permit random mating would mean radical change in the existing social structure. If the family as a unit of society is important, then mate choice is too.

Kinfolk or immediate family can disregard the question of who marries whom, only if a marriage is not seen as a link between kin lines, only if no property, power, lineage honor, totemic relationships, and the like are believed to flow from the kin lines through the spouses to their offspring. Universally, however, these are believed to follow kin lines. Mate choice thus has consequences for the social structure. But love may affect mate choice. Both mate choice and love, therefore, are too important to be left to children.

THE CONTROL OF LOVE

Since considerable energy and resources may be required to push young-

sters who are in love into proper role behavior, love must be controlled *before* it appears. Love relationships must either be kept to a small number or they must be so directed that they do not run counter to the approved kinship linkages. There are only a few institutional patterns by which this control is achieved.

1. Certainly the simplest, and perhaps the most widely used, structural pattern for coping with this problem is child marriage. If the child is betrothed, married, or both before he has had any opportunity to interact intimately as an adolescent with other children, then he has no resources with which to oppose the marriage. He cannot earn a living, he is physically weak, and is socially dominated by his elders. Moreover, strong love attachments occur only rarely before puberty. An example of this pattern was to be found in India, where the young bride went to live with her husband in a marriage which was not physically consummated until much later, within his father's household.[22]

2. Often, child marriage is linked with a second structural pattern, in which the kinship rules define rather closely a class of eligible future spouses. The marriage is determined by birth within narrow limits. Here, the major decision, which is made by elders, *is when* the marriage is to occur. Thus, among the Murngin, *galle*, the father's sister's child, is scheduled to marry *due*, the mother's brother's child.[23] In the case of the

[22] Frieda M. Das, *Purdah*, New York: Vanguard, 1932; Kingsley Davis, *The Population of India and Pakistan*, Princeton: Princeton University Press, 1951, p. 112. There was a widespread custom of taking one's bride from a village other than one's own.

[23] W. Lloyd Warner, *Black Civilization*, New York: Harper, 1937, pp. 82–84. They may also become "sweethearts" at puberty; see pp. 86–89.

"four-class" double-descent system, each individual is a member of *both* a matri-moiety and a patri-moiety and must marry someone who belongs to neither; the four-classes are (1) ego's own class, (2) those whose matri-moiety is the same as ego's but whose patri-moiety is different, (3) those who are in ego's patri-moiety but not in his matri-moiety, and (4) those who are in neither of ego's moieties, that is, who are in the cell diagonally from his own.[24] Problems arise at times under these systems if the appropriate kinship cell—for example, parallel cousin or cross-cousin—is empty.[25] But nowhere, apparently, is the definition so rigid as to exclude some choice and, therefore, some dickering, wrangling, and haggling between the elders of the two families.

3. A society can prevent widespread development of adolescent love relationships by socially isolating young people from potential mates, whether eligible or ineligible as spouses. Under such a pattern, elders can arrange the marriages of either children or adolescents with little likelihood that their plans will be disrupted by love attachments. Obviously, this arrangement cannot operate effec-

tively in most primitive societies, where youngsters see one another rather frequently.[26]

Not only is this pattern more common in civilizations than in primitive societies, but is found more frequently in the upper social strata. *Social* segregation is difficult unless it is supported by physical segregation—the harem of Islam, the zenana of India[27]—or by a large household system with individuals whose duty it is to supervise nubile girls. Social segregation is thus expensive. Perhaps the best known example of simple social segregation was found in China, where youthful marriages took place between young people who have not previously met because they lived in different villages; they could not marry fellow-villagers since ideally almost all inhabitants belonged to the same *tsu*.[28]

24 See Murdock, *op. cit.*, pp. 53 ff. *et passim* for discussions of double-descent.

25 One adjustment in Australia was for the individuals to leave the tribe for a while, usually eloping, and then to return "reborn" under a different and now appropriate kinship designation. In any event, these marital prescriptions did not prevent love entirely. As Malinowski shows in his early summary of the Australian family systems, although every one of the tribes used the technique of infant betrothal (and close prescription of mate), no tribe was free of elopements, between either the unmarried or the married, and the "motive of sexual love" was always to be found in marriages by elopement. B. Malinowski, *The Family Among the Australian Aborigines*, London: University of London Press, 1913, p. 83.

26 This pattern was apparently achieved in Manus, where on first menstruation the girl was removed from her playmates and kept at "home"—on stilts over a lagoon—under the close supervision of elders. The Manus were prudish, and love occurred rarely or never. Margaret Mead, *Growing Up in New Guinea*, in *From the South Seas*, New York: Morrow, 1939, pp. 163–166, 208.

27 See Das, *op. cit.*

28 For the activities of the *tsu*, see Hsien Chin Hu, *The Common Descent Group in China and Its Functions*. New York: Viking Fund Studies in Antrhopology, 10 (1948). For the marriage process, see Marion J. Levy, *The Family Revolution in Modern China*, Cambridge: Harvard University Press, 1949, pp. 87–107. See also Olga Lang, *Chinese Family and Society*, New Haven: Yale University Press, 1946, for comparisons between the old and new systems. In one-half of 62 villages in Ting Hsien Experimental District in Hopei, the largest clan included 50 per cent of the families; in 25 per cent of the villages, the two largest clans held over 90 per cent of the families; I am indebted to Robert M. Marsh who has been carrying out a study of Ching mobility partly under my direction for this reference: F. C. H. Lee,

It should be emphasized that the primary function of physical or social isolation in these cases is to minimize informal or intimate social interaction. Limited social contacts of a highly ritualized or formal type in the presence of elders, as in Japan, have a similar, if less extreme, result.[29]

4. A fourth type of pattern seems to exist, although it is not clear cut; and special cases shade off toward types three and five. Here, there is close supervision by duennas or close relatives, but not actual social segregation. A high value is placed on female chastity (which perhaps is the case in every major civilization until its "decadence") viewed either as the product of self-restraint, as among the 17th Century Puritans, or as a marketable commodity. Thus love as play is not developed; marriage is supposed to be considered by the young as a duty and a possible family alliance. This pattern falls between types three and five because love is permitted before marriage, but only between eligibles. Ideally, it occurs only between a betrothed couple, and, except as marital love, there is no encouragement for it to appear at all. Family elders largely make the specific choice of mate, whether or not intermediaries carry out the arrangements. In the preliminary stages youngsters engage in courtship under supervision, with the understanding that this will permit the development of affection prior to marriage.

I do not believe that the empirical data show where this pattern is prevalent, outside of Western Civilization. The West is a special case, because of its peculiar relationship to Christianity, in which from its earliest days in Rome there has been a complex tension between asceticism and love. This type of limited love marked French, English, and Italian upper class family life from the 11th to the 14th Centuries, as well as 17th Century Puritanism in England and New England.[30]

5. The fifth type of pattern permits or actually encourages love relationships, and love is a commonly expected element in mate choice. Choice in this system is *formally* free. In their 'teens youngsters begin their love play, with or without consummating sexual intercourse, within a group of peers. They may at times choose love partners whom they and others do not consider suitable spouses. Gradually, however, their range of choice is narrowed and eventually their affections center on one individual. This person is likely to be more eligible as a mate according to general social norms, and as

---

[29] For Japan, see Shidzué Ishimoto, *Facing Two Ways*, New York: Farrar and Rinehart, 1935, Chapters 6, 8; John F. Embree, *Suye Mura*, Chicago: University of Chicago Press, 1950, Chapter 3,6.

Ting Hsien. *She-hui K'ai-K'uang t'iao-ch'a*, Peiping: Chung-hua p'ing-min Chiao-yu ts'u-chin hui, 1932, p. 54. See also Sidney Gamble, *Ting Hsien: A North China Rural Community*, New York: International Secretariat of the Institute of Pacific Relations, 1954.

[30] I do not mean, of course, to restrict this pattern to these times and places, but I am more certain of these. For the Puritans, see Edmund S. Morgan, *The Puritan Family*, Boston: Public Library, 1944. For the somewhat different practices in New York, see Charles E. Ironside, *The Family in Colonial New York*, New York: Columbia University Press, 1942. See also: A. Abram, *English Life and Manners in the Later Middle Ages*, New York: Dutton, 1913, Chapters 4, 10; Emily J. Putnam, *The Lady*, New York: Sturgis and Walton, 1910, Chapter 4; James Gairdner, editor, *The Paston Letters, 1422–1509*, 4 vols., London: Arber, 1872–1875; Eileen Power, "The Position of Women," in C. G. Crump and E. F. Jacobs, editors, *The Legacy of the Middle Ages*, Oxford: Clarendon, 1926, pp. 414–416.

judged by peers and parents, than the average individual with whom the youngster formerely indulged in love play.

For reasons that are not yet clear, this pattern is nearly always associated with a strong development of an adolescent peer group system, although the latter may occur without the love pattern. One source of social control, then, is the individual's own 'teen age companions, who persistently rate the present and probable future accomplishments of each individual.[31]

Another source of control lies with the parents of both boy and girl. In our society, parents threaten, cajole, wheedle, bribe, and persuade their children to "go with the right people," during both the early love play and later courtship phases.[32] Primarily, they seek to control love relationships by influencing the informal social contacts of their children: moving to appropriate neighborhoods and schools, giving parties and helping to make out invitation lists, by making their children aware that certain individuals have ineligibility traits (race, religion, manners, tastes, clothing, and so on). Since youngsters fall in love with those with whom they associate, control over informal relationships also controls substantially the focus of affection. The results of such control are well known and are documented in the more than one hundred studies of homogamy in this country: most marriages take place between couples in the same class, religious, racial, and educational levels.

As Robert Wikman has shown in a generally unfamiliar (in the United States) but superb investigation, this pattern was found among 18th Century Swedish farmer adolescents, was widely distributed in other Germanic areas, and extends in time from the 19th Century back to almost certainly the late Middle Ages.[33] In these cases, sexual intercourse was taken for granted, social contact was closely supervised by the peer group, and final consent to marriage was withheld or granted by the parents who owned the land.

Such cases are not confined to Western society. Polynesia exhibits a similar pattern, with some variation from society to society, the best known examples of which are perhaps Mead's Manu'ans and Firth's Tikopia.[34] Probably the most familiar Melanesian cases are the Trobriands and Dobu,[35] where the systems resemble those of the Kiwai Papuans of the Trans-Fly and the Siuai Papuans of the

---

31 For those who believe that the young in the United States are totally deluded by love, or believe that love outranks every other consideration, see: Ernest W. Burgess and Paul W. Wallin, *Engagement and Marriage,* New York: Lippincott, 1953, pp. 217–238. Note Karl Robert V. Wikman, *Die Einleitung Der Ehe. Acta Academiae Aboensis (Humaniora),* 11 (1937), pp. 127 ff. Not only are reputations known because of close association among peers, but songs and poetry are sometimes composed about the girl or boy. Cf., for the Tikopia, Raymond Firth, *We, the Tikopia,* New York: American Book, 1936, pp. 468 ff.; for the Siuai, Douglas L. Oliver, *Solomon Island Society,* Cambridge: Harvard University Press, 1955, pp. 146 ff. The Manu'ans made love in groups of three or four couples; cf. Mead, *Coming of Age in Samoa, op. cit.,* pg. 92.

32 Marvin B. Sussman, "Parental Participation in Mate Selection and Its Effect upon Family Continuity," *Social Forces,* 32 (October, 1953), pp. 76–81.

33 Wikman, *op. cit.*

34 Mead, *Coming of Age in Samoa, op. cit.,* pp. 97–108; and Firth, *op. cit.,* pp. 520 ff.

35 Thus Malinowski notes in his "Introduction" to Reo F. Fortune's *The Sorcerers of Dobu,* London: Routledge, 1932, p. xxiii, that the Dobu have similar patterns, the same type of courtship by trial and error, with a gradually tightening union.

Solomon Islands.[36] Linton found this pattern among the Tanala.[37] Although Radcliffe-Brown holds that the pattern is not common in Africa, it is clearly found among the Nuer, the Kgatla (Tswana-speaking), and the Bavenda (here, without sanctional sexual intercourse).[38]

A more complete classification, making use of the distinctions suggested in this paper, would show, I believe, that a large minority of known societies exhibit this pattern. I would suggest, moreover, that such a study would reveal that the degree to which love is a usual, expected prelude to marriage is correlated with (1) the degree of free choice of mate permitted in the society and (2) the degree to which husband-wife solidarity is the strategic solidarity of the kinship structure.[39]

[36] Gunnar Landtman, *Kiwai Papuans of the Trans-Fly*, London: Macmillan, 1927, pp. 243 ff.; Oliver, *op. cit.*, pp. 153 ff.

[37] The pattern apparently existed among the Marquesans as well, but since Linton never published a complete description of this Polynesian society, I omit it here. His fullest analysis, cluttered with secondary interpretations, is in Abram Kardiner, *Psychological Frontiers of Society*, New York: Columbia University Press, 1945. For the Tanala, see Ralph Linton, *The Tanala*, Chicago: Field Museum, 1933, pp. 300–303.

[38] Thus, Radcliffe-Brown: "The African does not think of marriage as a union based on romantic love, although beauty as well as character and health are sought in the choice of a wife," in his "Introduction" to A. R. Radcliffe-Brown and W. C. Daryll Forde, editors, *African Systems of Kinship and Marriage*, London: Oxford University Press, 1950, p. 46. For the Nuer, see E. E. Evans-Pritchard, *Kinship and Marriage Among the Nuer*, Oxford: Clarendon, 1951, pp. 49–58. For the Kgatla, see I. Schapera, *Married Life in an African Tribe*, New York: Sheridan, 1941, pp. 55 ff. For the Bavanda, although the report seems incomplete, see Hugh A. Stayt, *The Bavenda*, London: Oxford University Press, 1931, pp. 111 ff., 145 ff., 154.

[39] The second correlation is developed

LOVE CONTROL AND CLASS

These sociostructural explanations of how love is controlled lead to a subsidiary but important hypothesis: From one society to another, and from one *class* to another within the same society, the sociostructural importance of maintaining kinship lines according to rule will be rated differently by the families within them. Consequently, the degree to which control over mate choice, and therefore over the prevalence of a love pattern among adolescents, will also vary. Since, within any stratified society, this concern with the maintenance of intact and acceptable kin lines will be greater in the upper strata, it follows that noble or upper strata will maintain stricter control over love and courtship behavior than lower strata. The two correlations suggested in the preceding paragraph also apply: husband-wife solidarity is less strategic relative to clan solidarity in the upper than in the lower strata, and there is less free choice of mate.

Thus it is that, although in Polynesia generally most youngsters indulged in considerable love play, princesses were supervised strictly.[40] Similarly, in China lower class youngsters often met their spouses before marriage.[41] In our own society, the "upper upper" class maintains much greater control than the lower strata over the informal social contacts of their nubile young. Even among the Dobu, where there are few controls and little stratification, differences in control

from Marion J. Levy, *The Family Revolution in China*, Cambridge, Harvard University Press, 1949, p. 179: Levy's formulation ties "romantic love" to that solidarity, and is of little use because there is only one case, the Western culture complex. As he states it, it is almost so by definition.

[40] E.g., Mead, *Coming of Age in Samoa, op. cit.*, pp. 79, 92, 97–109. Cf. also Firth, *op. cit.*, pp. 520 ff.

[41] Although one must be cautious about China, this inference seems to be allowable

exist at the extremes: a child betrothal may be arranged between outstanding gardening families, who try to prevent their youngsters from being entangled with wastrel families.[42] In answer to my query about this pattern among the Nuer, Evans-Pritchard writes:

> You are probably right that a wealthy man has more control over his son's affairs than a poor man. A man with several wives has a more authoritarian position in his home. Also, a man with many cattle is in a position to permit or refuse a son to marry, whereas a lad whose father is poor may have to depend on the support of kinsmen. In general, I would say that a Nuer father is not interested in the personal side of things. His son is free to marry any girl he likes and the father does not consider the selection to be his affair until the point is reached when cattle have to be discussed.[43]

from such comments as the following: "But the old men of China did not succeed in eliminating love from the life of the young women. . . . Poor and middle-class families could not afford to keep men and women in separate quarters, and Chinese also met their cousins. . . . Girls . . . sometimes even served customers in their parents' shops." Olga Lang, op. cit., p. 33. According to Fried, farm girls would work in the fields, and farm girls of ten years and older were sent to the market to sell produce. They were also sent to towns and cities as servants. The peasant or pauper woman was not confined to the home and its immediate environs. Morton H. Fried, Fabric of Chinese Society, New York: Praeger, 1953, pp. 59–60. Also, Levy (op. cit., p. 111): "Among peasant girls and among servant girls in gentry households some premarital experience was not uncommon, though certainly frowned upon. The methods of preventing such contact were isolation and chaperonage, both of which, in the 'traditional' picture, were more likely to break down in the two cases named than elsewhere."

[42] Fortune, op. cit., p. 30.

[43] Personal letter, dated January 9, 1958. However, the Nuer father can still refuse if

The upper strata have much more at stake in the maintenance of the social structure and thus are more strongly motivated to control the courtship and marriage decisions of their young. Correspondingly, their young have much more to lose than lower strata youth, so that upper strata elders *can* wield more power.

CONCLUSION

In this analysis I have attempted to show the integration of love with various types of social structures. As against considerable contemporary opinion among both sociologists and anthropologists, I suggest that love is a universal psychological potential, which is controlled by a range of five structural patterns, all of which are attempts to see to it that youngsters do not make entirely free choices of their future spouses. Only if kin lines are unimportant, and this condition is found in no society as a whole, will entirely free choice be permitted. Some structural arrangements seek to prevent entirely the outbreak of love, while others harness it. Since the kin lines of the upper strata are of greater social importance to them than those of lower strata are to the lower strata members, the former exercise a more effective control over this choice. Even where there is almost a formally free choice of mate—and I have suggested that this pattern is wide-spread, to be found among a substantial segment of the earth's societies—this choice is guided by peer group and parents toward a mate who will be acceptable to the kin and friend groupings. The theoretical importance of love is thus to be seen in the sociostructural patterns which are developed to keep it from disrupting existing social arrangements.

he believes the demands of the girl's people are unreasonable. In turn, the girl can cajole her parents to demand less.

15

SPECIFYING THE FIELD OF ELIGIBLES IN AMERICAN MATE-SELECTION: PROPINQUITY AND HOMOGAMY

Chapter 13 treated the specification of the *size* of the field of eligible mates. The present chapter will discuss the specification of the *social characteristics* of the field of eligibles in American mate-selection. Six characteristics will be discussed: race, religion, age, ethnic origin, social class, and residential propinquity. The principle which seems to define the field of eligibles is "homogamy" or "like attracts like."

Americans are most homogamous with respect to race. The very low percentage of interracial marriages reported by David Heer attests to this. Heer further comments on how racial homogamy perpetuates social inequality.

The influences of age, religion, ethnic origin, and social class on mate selection are demonstrated in August B. Hollingshead's study of New Haven. Although the sample is drawn from only one city, the results are generally consistent with those of other American studies.

Our concluding characteristic is residential propinquity. Katz and Hill integrate the literature and construct a theory which attempts to explain why spouses tend to live near each other before marriage. Their theory combines normative and time-cost explanations of the positive correlation between residential propinquity and marital selection. In addition to this they explain the relations between residential propinquity and variables like social class, occupational status, income status, ethnicity, and educational attainment.

Negro-White Marriage in the United States [*]

David M. Heer

. . . restrictions on racial intermarriage may well be closely linked to economic discrimination. The well-known American sociologist, Kingsley Davis, has listed the main social functions of the family as the reproduction maintenance, place-

ment, and socialisation of the young. Let us focus our attention on the placement function of the family in the contemporary United States—i.e., on the consequences which birth into a given family has for the youngster's future social position.

First, the transfer of wealth in the

[*] *Adapted from* New Society, *August, 26, 1965, 6: 7–9.*

United States is largely accomplished by bequeathal from one family member to another. Secondly, it must be recognized that although objectively recognized merit may be the predominant criterion for the matching of job applicants to job vacancies, pull and family connections are also quite important. For example, in the building trades, jobs cannot be obtained without admittance to the union's apprenticeship programme and in many instances it is almost impossible to obtain admittance unless one is a son or other close relative of a union member. Thirdly, research has established that entry to elite positions in modern industrial societies is most easily obtained by those who grow up from birth in a family with relatively high status. Birth in a high status family provides the financial means for obtaining advanced education. In addition it is invaluable for giving one a sense of familiarity with the activities and functioning of high status society. This familiarity not only reduces the fear of interpersonal contacts in such a society but also increases the motivation to become a full participant.

How may the consequences of birth affect the relative status of Negroes and whites in the United States? Consider first the pattern of familial inheritance. On a per capita basis, white persons hold a far higher share of the nation's wealth than do negroes. The formal and informal prohibitions on intermarriage serve to perpetuate this pattern of inequality since they make it unlikely that a Negro will inherit wealth from any white person. Secondly, Negroes are by and large excluded from those jobs to which entrance is strongly determined by pull and connections. This occurs simply because the existing jobs are usually held only by whites. Thirdly, the lack of close relatives among whites prevents many Negroes from having an easy familiarity

on the terrain of the social world of white persons and hence makes them afraid to apply for jobs demanding such familiarity, even when their technical qualifications are completely satisfactory.

A relaxation of the norms militating against miscegenation might have a significant and crucial effect on the socio-economic position of negroes in American society. Unfortunately, current data on this subject are very incomplete. At the present time, there are 31 states in which marriage between whites and Negroes is legal.† However, in only three states is there any officially published record of such intermarriages. These states are Hawaii, Michigan and Nebraska. For selected years before 1960 the state of California made public a cross-tabulation of marriages by race of bride and race of groom. However, in 1960 this practice was discontinued because in that year new legislation went into effect to prohibit a record of the race of bride and groom on marriage licences. For the period from 1950 to 1962, the only data on Negro-white marriages tabulated by state offices of vital statistics are as follows: California, for 1955, 1957, 1958 and 1959; Hawaii, from 1956 to 1962; Michigan, for each year from 1953 to 1962; Nebraska for 1961 and 1962.

Some readers may question the quality of the official data on Negro-white marriage. On the one hand, it might be argued that social sanctions against such marriages are so severe that the reported number of such marriages would be less than the actual number. On the other hand, it might be argued that because the true number of negro-white marriages is very small, the reported number exceeds the actual number due to misreporting of race for one partner

---

† In June 1967 the United States Supreme Court ruled unconstitutional a state law prohibiting interracial marriages.—Eds.

on the marriage certificate. Some caution in the interpretation of the reported data is therefore necessary.

ANALYSIS OF STATE DATA

In the table we show four sets of reported data: (1) the proportion of white grooms who marry Negro brides, (2) the proportion of white brides with Negro grooms, (3) the proportion of Negro grooms with white brides, and (4) the proportion of Negro brides with white grooms. Data are presented for the states and years mentioned previously, and for comparison, also for New York State (excluding New York City) for the years 1921 to 1924. All data are tabulated by area in which the marriage license was issued rather than by area of residence of bride or groom.

Of the four states with recent data, the reported incidence of Negro-white intermarriage is highest in Hawaii. The rank of the remaining states, in descending order of Negro-white intermarriage, is California, Michigan and Nebraska (where there were no inter-racial marriages in either 1961 or 1962). This rank order holds true regardless of which of the four columns of data is examined. Thus, there is considerable variation between these states in the reported proportion of interracial marriage. Hawaii has long been well known as an interracial melting pot. However, one should also note the contrast between Michigan and California, both large industrial states with similar proportions of negro population. In 1959, the latest year in which data are available for both states, the proportion of Negro-white marriages in California was more than double that in Michigan according to each of the four indices shown in the table.

The table also reveals a differential incidence of Negro-white marriage by sex. For each of the three states having Negro-white marriages, marriages between Negro men and white women are much more common than between white men and Negro women. This may possibly be because the initiative in proposing marriage in the United States rests largely with the male. Moreover, because it enhances their self-esteem, Negro males have a much stronger motivation to marry white women than white males have to marry Negro women.

COMPARISON OF RECENT DATA

The question whether the trend in interracial marriages is one of increase or of decrease is always interesting. Unfortunately, for the four states for which we have recent statistics, we have no data of more ancient vintage. For the areas, mostly cities, for which we have earlier statistics, the recent data are not readily available. The best we can do is to compare the recent data in the four states of California, Hawaii, Michigan and Nebraska with the available data from previous generations. It is apparent from the table that the rate of Negro-white marriage for Negroes in New York State (excluding New York City) in the early 1920s was higher than the contemporary rate for either Michigan or California. On the other hand, the intermarriage rate for whites is higher in California and Michigan in the recent period than in New York State 40 years ago. The Negro-white intermarriage rate for Negroes in Hawaii during 1960 was higher than any previously recorded rate for members of that race in any part of the United States during any time period. The closest competitor to Hawaii in this respect is the city of Boston in the period 1900–1904. For Boston during this period the proportion of Negro grooms marrying white brides was 13.7 per cent as compared with 14.7 per cent in Hawaii in 1960, and the

Negro-White Intermarriage Percentages

STATE AND YEAR	WHITE GROOMS MARRYING NEGRO BRIDES	WHITE BRIDES MARRYING NEGRO GROOMS	NEGRO GROOMS MARRYING WHITE BRIDES	NEGRO BRIDES MARRYING WHITE GROOMS
California				
1955	0.06	0.21	3.36	1.02
1957	0.06	0.28	3.47	0.78
1958	0.08	0.26	3.35	1.02
1959	0.09	0.33	3.96	1.16
Hawaii				
1956	0.00	0.31	0.09	0.00
1957	0.00	0.47	13.33	0.00
1958	0.06	0.16	4.08	5.00
1959	0.11	0.36	9.80	8.33
1960	0.16	0.34	14.71	12.50
1961	0.11	0.52	16.00	8.00
1962	0.05	0.46	17.78	4.17
Michigan				
1953	0.04	0.10	1.09	0.40
1954	0.04	0.09	1.10	0.46
1955	0.05	0.11	1.12	0.48
1956	0.04	0.13	1.32	0.46
1957	0.01	0.14	1.37	0.14
1958	0.05	0.13	1.37	0.50
1959	0.04	0.16	1.62	0.40
1960	0.06	0.14	1.39	0.63
1961	0.05	0.18	1.76	0.48
1962	0.05	0.19	1.90	0.49
Nebraska				
1961	0.00	0.00	0.00	0.00
1962	0.00	0.00	0.00	0.00
New York (excluding New York City)				
1921	0.01	0.06	5.63	0.66
1922	0.02	0.05	3.60	1.40
1923	0.03	0.06	2.87	1.46
1924	0.03	0.10	4.09	1.13

proportion of Negro brides marrying white grooms was 1.1 per cent as compared with 12.5 per cent in Hawaii in 1960.

We are on somewhat surer ground when we try to investigate the trend of interracial marriage in the United States within the last few years. The available data shown in the table for the three states of California, Hawaii and Michigan are certainly not conclusive, but they give a strong indication of an upward trend during recent years. Because we have not only a ten year time series for Michigan, but also a large base population, the most valid measurement of increase in interracial marriage can be made for that state. For Michigan all four indices show an increase of the interracial marriage rate with time. However, there is considerable variation in the consistency of this increase. For the indices involving white women and negro men, the trend in interracial marriage has been one of very steady rise. On the other hand, the trends for marriages involving white men and Negro women show only a weak and inconsistent increase over the ten year interval.

The recent data pointing to an upward trend in Negro-white marriage are of enhanced interest because statistics for previous periods in the United States indicated a decreasing trend in such marriages. For example, data are available concerning interracial marriage rates for both whites and Negroes in the city of Boston for the period from 1900 to 1938. These indicate an almost continuous decline in the intermarriage rate for both white and Negroes. The most drastic decline occurred between 1900-1904 and 1914–1918. The sociologists Wirth and Goldhamer have attributed this decline in the city of Boston to the fact that in the 19th century the city was the centre of the abolitionist movement and was "unusually and almost sentimentally receptive to Negroes." As the pro-Negro sentiments fostered during and after the Civil War declined in their intensity, the willingness of whites to marry Negroes declined correspondingly.

It is also interesting to note that the sharp decline in Negro-white intermarriage occurring in Boston after the turn of the century was almost entirely due to a decline in marriages involving Negro grooms and white brides. These data taken in combination with the more recent Michigan data suggest that the volatile element in Negro-white intermarriage may be the marriage between the Negro male and the white female, and that the interracial marriage rate between white males and Negro females remains relatively constant.

I have argued that racial discrimination against Negroes in American society will not be completely eliminated until Negroes and whites become racially amalgamated. However, racial intermarriage in the United States does appear to be increasing. Is it then possible to project the time necessary for interracial marriage to accomplish racial amalgamation in the United States?

NEARLY "NEVER"

This problem intrigued me. I therefore decided to spell out certain sets of assumptions concerning future trends in negro-white marriage and then calculate on a high-speed computer the length of time which according to each set of assumptions would be necessary to achieve interracial amalgamation. Altogether I made twelve sets of assumptions ranging from the most conservative to the most liberal which I thought imaginable. According to my most conservative assumption, complete amalgamation would not be attained even after 1,000 generations, or approximately 27,000 years. This is almost equivalent to the "Never" emblazoned on the buttons worn by the Alabama and Mississippi segregationists. On the other hand, according to the most liberal of the twelve sets of assumptions, complete amalgamation could be achieved in 13 generations, or approximately 351 years.

All twelve projections possessed one uniformity. This was that none of them showed substantial progress toward racial amalgamation to occur within the next 100 years. Thus, unless the most liberal set of assumptions is unnecessarily conservative, we can safely say that racial intermarriage will have little effect on the racial composition of the United States within the next four generations. If racial amalgamation is indeed necessary to achieve full equality for the Negro, one may conclude that this equality will not be soon forthcoming. If American Negroes continue to insist on full equality (and there is no reason to believe that they will not), one may also conclude that an early resolution of the current tension between the races will not be possible.

Cultural Factors in the Selection of Marriage Mates [*]

August B. Hollingshead

The question of who marries whom is of perennial interest, but only during the last half-century has it become the subject of scientific research. Throughout American history there has always been a romantic theory of mate selection, supported by poets, dramatists, and the public at large. Social scientists, however —a group of jaundiced realists, by and large—have little faith in this pleasant myth as an explanation for the selection of marriage mates.[1] Their theories can be divided between (1) the homogamous and (2) the heterogamous.[2] The theory of homogamy postulates that "like attracts like;" the theory of heterogamy holds that "opposites attract each other."

Certain aspects of each theory have been investigated by psychologists and sociologists. The psychologists have confined their attention almost exclusively to individual physical[3] and psychologi-

cal[4] characteristics. Sociologists have focused, in the main, upon factors external to the individual. As a consequence, sociological research has stressed such things as ethnic origin,[5] residential

The studies reviewed primarily dealt with physical characteristics: deafness, health, longevity, age, stature, cephalic index, hair and eye color.

[4] Harold E. Jones, "Homogamy in Intellectual Abilities," American Journal of Sociology, 35 (1929), 369–382; E. L. Kelly, "Psychological Factors in Assortive Mating," Psychological Bulletin, 37 (1940), 493 and 576; Helen M. Richardson, "Studies of Mental Resemblance Between Husbands and Wives and Between Friends," Psychological Bulletin, 36 (1939), 104–120.

[5] Bessie B. Wessel, "Comparative Rates of Intermarriage Among Different Nationalities in the United States," Eugenical News, 15 (1930), 105–107; Bessie B. Wessel, An Ethnic Survey of Woonsocket, R.I., Chicago, University of Chicago Press, 1931; James H. S. Bossard, "Nationality and Nativity as Factors in Marriage," American Sociological Review, 4 (December, 1939), 792–798; Ruby Jo Reeves, Marriages in New Haven since 1870 Statistically Analyzed and Culturally Interpreted, doctoral dissertation Yale University (unpublished), 1938; Ruby Jo Reeves Kennedy, "Single or Triple Melting-Pot? Intermarriage Trends in New Haven, 1870–1940," American Journal of Sociology, 39 (January, 1944), 331–339; Milton L. Barron, Intermarriage in a New England Industrial Community, Syracuse, Syracuse University Press, 1946. Barron has a good bibliography of studies in this area, pp. 355–366.

[*] Adapted from the American Sociological Review, 1950, 15: 619–627.

[1] For a discussion of this theory and some facts to refute it see A. B. Hollingshead, "Class and Kinship in a Middle Western Community," American Sociological Review, 14 (August, 1949), 469–475.

[2] E. W. Burgess and Paul Wallin, "Homogamy in Social Characteristics," American Journal of Sociology, 49, (September, 1943), 109–124.

[3] J. A. Harris, "Assortive Mating in Man," Popular Science Monthly, 80 (1912), 476–492. This is the earliest review in the literature that tries to give a scientific explanation of the question of who marries whom.

propinquity,[6] race,[7] religion,[8] socio-economic status,[9] and social characteristics in general.[10] While all of these re-

[6] James H. S. Bossard, "Residential Propinquity as a Factor in Marriage Selection," *American Journal of Sociology*, 38 (1932), 219–224; Maurice R. Davie and Ruby Jo Reeves, "Propinquity in Residence Before Marriage," *American Journal of Sociology*, 44 (1939), 510–517; Ruby Jo Reeves Kennedy, "Pre-Marital Residential Propinquity and Ethnic Endogamy," *American Journal of Sociology*, 48 (March, 1943), 580–584; John S. Ellsworth, Jr., "The Relationship of Population Density to Residential Propinquity as a Factor in Marriage Selection," *American Sociological Review*, 13 (August, 1948), 444–448.

[7] Romanzo Adams, *Interracial Marriage in Hawaii*, New York, The Macmillan Co., 1937; Otto Klineberg, *Characteristics of the American Negro*, New York, Harper, 1944, especially Part V where Negro-white intermarriage and the restrictions on it imposed by law are discussed; U. G. Weatherly, "Race and Marriage," *American Journal of Sociology*, 15 (1910), 433–453; Robert K. Merton, "Intermarriage and the Social Structure," *Psychiatry*, 4 (August, 1941), 371–374; Constantine Panunzio, "Intermarriage in Los Angeles, 1924–1933," *American Journal of Sociology*, 47 (March, 1942), 399–401.

[8] Reuben R. Resnick, "Some Sociological Aspects of Intermarriage of Jew and Non-Jew," *Social Forces*, 12 (October, 1933), 94–102; J. S. Slotkin, "Jewish-Gentile Intermarriage in Chicago," *American Sociological Review*, 7 (February, 1942), 34–39; Ruby Jo Reeves Kennedy, "Single or Triple Melting-Pot?" *op. cit.*

[9] Richard Centers, "Marital Selection and Occupational Strata," *American Journal of Sociology*, 54 (May 1949), 530–535; Donald M. Marvin, "Occupational Propinquity as a Factor in Marriage Selection," *Publications of the American Statistical Association*, 16 (September, 1918), 131–156; Meyer F. Nimkoff, "Occupational Factors and Marriage," *American Journal of Sociology*, 49 (November 1943), 248–254.

[10] Walter C. McKain, Jr., and C. Arnold

searches have used empirical data, only a few of them have attempted to measure the significant cultural factors that impinge upon mate selection against the background of the theories of homogamy and heterogamy. We shall attempt to do this in this paper.

My attack upon this problem will be to state the theoretical limits within which mate selection may take place, then turn to a body of data to determine how, and to what extent, specific factors influence the selection of marital partners.[11]

Viewed in the broadest theoretical perspective of democratic theory, the choice of marriage mates in our society might be conceived of as a process in which each unattached biologically mature adult has an equal opportunity to marry every other unattached biologically mature adult of the opposite sex. Viewed from the narrowest perspective of cultural determinism, biologically mature, single males or females have only limited opportunity to select a marital partner. The first proposition assumes complete freedom of individual choice to select a mate; the second assumes that mates are selected for individuals by controls imposed on them by their culture. If the first assumption is valid we should find no association between cultural factors and who marries whom; if the second is descriptive of the mate selection process we should expect to find a strong association between one or several cultural fac-

Anderson, "Assortive Mating in Prosperity and Depression," *Sociology and Social Research*, 21 (May-June, 1937), 411–418; E. W. Burgess and Paul Wallin, "Homogamy in Social Characteristics," *American Journal of Sociology*, 49 (September, 1943), 109–124.

[11] For purposes of this paper we shall rely upon tests of significance and measures of association to tell us what cultural factors are of greater or lesser importance in the determination of who marries whom.

tors and who marries whom. The second proposition, however, allows for individual choice within limits of cultural determinism; for example a Jew is expected to marry a Jew by the rules of his religion; moreover, he is more or less coerced by his culture to marry a Jewess of the same or a similar social status, but he has a choice as to the exact individual.

In the remainder of this paper I shall test five factors—race, age, religion, ethnic origin, and class—within the limits of the theories of homogamy and heterogamy and the abstract model I have outlined. The data utilized to measure the influence of these factors on the selection of marriage mates were assembled in New Haven, Connecticut, by a research team during the last year through the cooperation of the Departments of Vital Statistics of the State of Connecticut and the City of New Haven. All marriage license data on marriages in New Haven during 1948 were copied. Then parents, relatives, in some cases neighbors, were asked in February, 1949, to supply the addresses of each newly married couple. Addresses were obtained for 1,980 couples out of a total of 2,063 couples married in the city in 1948. Nine hundred and three couples, 45.8 per cent, had moved from the city, and 1,077, 54.4 per cent, were living in it in February, 1949. A 50 per cent random sample, drawn by Census Tracts from the 1,077 couples resident in New Haven, was interviewed with a schedule. The interview, which lasted from about an hour and a quarter to three hours, took place in the home of the couple, usually with both the husband and wife present, and occurred most generally in the evening or late afternoon.[12]

In addition, twenty-eight census-like items such as age, occupation, birthplace, residence, and marital status, were available on all of the 1,980 couples.

The 523 interviewed couples were compared with the 1,457 non-interviewed couples, census item by census item, to determine if the interviewed group differed significantly from the non-interviewed group. No significance of difference was found at the 5 per cent level for any item, except where the husband and wife were both over 50 years of age.[13] Having satisfied ourselves that the interviewed group was representative of the total group, we proceeded with a measure of confidence to the analysis of our data.

RACE

Our data show that the racial mores place the strongest, most explicit, and most precise limits on an individual as to whom he may or may not marry. Although interracial marriages are legal in Connecticut, they are extremely rare; none occurred in New Haven in 1948. Kennedy's analysis of New Haven marriages from 1870 through 1940 substantiates the rule that Negroes and whites marry very infrequently. Thus, we may conclude that a man's or woman's marital choice is effectively limited to his or her own race by the moral values ascribed to race in this culture. Race, thus, divides the community into two parts so far as marriage is concerned. Because there were no interracial marriages in 1948, and

reliability from one month to four months after the original interview.

[13]The principal reasons for this deviation were (1) twice as many older couples refused to be interviewed as those below fifty years of age, and (2) the age gap between interviewers and potential interviewees influenced the situation.

[12]Eighty-seven per cent of the interviewing was done by senior undergraduates and graduate students, 5 per cent by an assistant, and 8 per cent by the writer. Six per cent of the interviews were checked for

TABLE 1 Age of husband and wife by five-year intervals for New Haven marriages, 1948

AGE OF HUS-BAND	Age of Wife								TOTAL
	15-19	20-24	25-29	30-34	35-39	40-44	45-49	50 & UP	
15-19	42	10	3						55
20-24	153	504	51	10	1				719
25-29	52	271	184	22	7	2			538
30-34	5	52	87	69	13	5			231
35-39	1	12	27	29	21	2	3		105
40-44		1	9	18	17	8	2	1	56
45-49	1		3	6	16	16	7	1	49
50 & up			1	4	11	15	21	43	95
Total	254	850	365	168	86	47	33	45	1848

$\chi^2 = 2574.8905$ $P < .01$ $C = .76$ $\bar{C} = .80.$

C = The coefficient of contingency.

$\bar{C}$ = The corrected coefficient of contingency corrected for broad grouping by the formula given in Thomas C. McCormick, *Elementary Social Statistics*, McGraw-Hill, 1941, p. 207.

because of the small percentage of Negroes in New Haven, we will confine the rest of our discussion to whites.

AGE

Age, like race, is a socio-biological factor that has a definite influence on marital choice. The effects of cultural usages and values on the selection of a marriage partner may be seen by a study of Table 1. While there is a very strong association between the age of the husband and the age of the wife at all age levels, it is strongest when both partners are under 20 years of age. Men above 20 years of age tend to select wives who are in the same 5 year age group as they are, or a younger one. After age 20 the percentage of men who marry women younger than themselves increases until age 50. After 50 the marital partners tend to be nearer one another in age. Table 1 indicates further that controls relative to age rather effectively limit a man's choice to women of his age or younger, but that the woman cannot be too much younger or counter controls begin to operate. Evidence accumulated in the interviews

shows it is widely believed that a young woman should not marry "an old man." The effects of this belief and practice are reflected in the lower left hand section of Table 1. There we see that only 4 men above 45 years of age, out of a total of 144, married women under 30 years of age. The age-sanctions that impinge on a woman with reference to the age of a potential husband narrow her marital opportunities to men her age, or to slightly older men. This usage is reflected in the upper right corner of Table 1, where marriages between older women and younger men are conspicuous by their absence. In short, differences in the customs relative to age and marital partners place greater restrictions on a woman's marital opportunities than a man's. Nevertheless, it is clear that the values ascribed to age restrict an individual's marital opportunities within narrow limits; and a woman's more than a man's.

RELIGION

The effects of religious rules on an individual's marital choices were very

TABLE 2   Religious affiliation in the parental and present generations

A. Wife's Father and Mother*

Wife's Father	WIFE'S MOTHER		
	Catholic	Protestant	Jewish
Catholic	274	11	0
Protestant	9	75	0
Jewish	2	1	65
Total	285	87	65

$$\chi^2 = 522.4592 \quad P < .01 \quad C = .74$$

B. Husband's Father and Mother

Husband's Father	HUSBAND'S MOTHER		
	Catholic	Protestant	Jewish
Catholic	273	12	0
Protestant	14	70	0
Jewish	0	0	68
Total	287	82	68

$$\chi^2 = 494.4359 \quad P < .01 \quad C = .73$$

C. Husband and Wife

Husband	WIFE		
	Catholic	Protestant	Jewish
Catholic	271	20	0
Protestant	17	61	0
Jewish	1	1	66
Total	289	82	66

$$\chi^2 = 636.0297 \quad P < .01 \quad C = .77$$

* The religious affiliation claimed by the interviewees is used here.

clear.[14] Next to race, religion is the most decisive factor in the segregation of males and females into categories that are approved or disapproved with respect to nuptiality. Ninety-one per cent of the marriages in this study involved partners from the same religious group. In the case of Jews, this percentage was 97.1, among Catholics it was 93.8 per cent; it fell to 74.4 per cent for Protestants. The differences in percentage, we believe, are a reflection of the relative intensity of in-group sanctions on the individual in the three religious groups. A striking point that emerged from our data is that the effect of religion on marital choice has not changed between the parental and present generation.[15] Table 2 shows that the number of Catholics who

[14] R. J. R. Kennedy, "Single or Triple Melting-Pot? Intermarriage Trends in New Haven, 1870–1940," *op. cit.*

[15] Our discussion on this and subsequent points includes only white marriages where the religion of the couple and of their four parents was known. Moreover, the tabular materials include only white cases where the specific data called for by the table were complete. "Unknown" cases were eliminated in particular instances.

married Catholics, and Jews who married Jews, was almost the same in both generations. The number of Protestants who married Protestants dropped in the present generation, but not significantly in terms of the numbers involved.[16] The influence of religious affiliation on the selection of a marriage mate is obviously strongest in the Jewish group and weakest in the Protestant. This is reflected in the number of mixed marriages. On this point, we would remark that there is no consistent bias between sex and mixed Catholic-Protestant marriages; either partner is likely to be a Catholic or a Protestant. On the other hand, in Jewish-Gentile marriages it has been a Jewish male who has married a Gentile female.

I shall point out, in passing, that the very high association we found between religion and marriage is not unique. Burgess and Wallin reported a coefficient of contingency of .75 for the 1,000 engaged couples they studied in Chicago;[17] our data revealed a coefficient of contingency of .77 in the present generation. This is not essentially different from theirs. Because religion is so effective a control in the selection of marriage mates I shall hold it constant and analyze other factors in terms of it.

ETHNIC ORIGIN

New Haven remained almost wholly Protestant religiously, and British ethnically, from its settlement in 1638 until the late 1830's. Between 1830 and 1880 Irish arrived by the hundred; Germans and Scandinavians by the score. The Irish

[16] The religious affiliation of marital partners in the present and parental generations was tested for significance; none was found; $x^2 = 6.7015$ with 8 degrees of freedom.

[17] E. W. Burgess and Paul Wallin, op. cit., p. 115.

and a minority of the Germans were Catholic and they soon established themselves in this burgeoning railroad and manufacturing center. An expanding economy, coupled with political and economic unrest in Southern and Eastern Europe, resulted in the influx of thousands of Polish and Russian Jews, and tens of thousands of Italians between 1890 and 1914. After 1914, the stream of immigration became a trickle that has never again been allowed to run freely. Thus, today, New Haven is composed mainly of three large religious groups and seven European-derived ethnic stocks: British, Irish, German, Scandinavian, Italian, Polish, and Polish Jewish.[18]

We cannot discuss how ethnicity is related to the selection of a marriage mate apart from religion, because religion and ethnic origin are so closely related. Observation of . . . Tables 3 through 6 . . . will show that ethnicity within a religious group has been a very potent factor in influencing the mate selection process in both the parental and the present generations, but it was stronger a generation ago than it is now. Although ethnic lines are crossed within the Catholic and the Protestant faith more frequently in the present than in the parental generation, this is not true for the Jews. Furthermore, ethnic lines in both generations were crossed, for the most part, within religious groups. This means that the Catholics are becoming a mixture of Irish, Polish, and Italian as a result of intermarriage between these groups, but there is still a large block of unmixed Italian stock in New Haven and smaller blocks of Irish and Polish. The Protestants, on the other hand, select marriage partners mainly from the British segment of the city's population; a mi-

[18] We are excluding Negroes from our discussion.

TABLE 3.† Per cent of Interethnic and Intra-ethnic Marriages in the Present and Parental Generations among Catholics°

	Couples	Parents
Intra-ethnic	56	84
Interethnic	44	16
	100	100
	(N = 271)	(N = 542)

TABLE 4.† Per cent of Interethnic and Intra-ethnic Marriages in the Present and Parental Generations among Protestants°

	Couples	Parents
Intra-ethnic	34	68
Interethnic	66	32
	100	100
	(N = 61)	(N = 122)

TABLE 5.† Per cent of Interethnic and Intra-ethnic Marriages in the Present and Parental Generations among Jewish°

	Couples	Parents
Intra-ethnic	100	100
Interethnic	0	0
	100	100
	(N = 66)	(N = 132)

TABLE 6.† Per cent of Interethnic and Intra-ethnic Marriages in the Present and Parental Generations among Mixed Religions°

	Couples	Parents
Intra-ethnic	18	86
Interethnic	82	14
	100	100
	(N = 39)	(N = 78)

° The religious affiliation claimed by the interviewees is used here.
† Adopted from table 3 in original—*Eds.*

nority chose a partner from a Northwestern European group, and in some cases both partners will be of German or Scandinavian descent. Kennedy discovered this process in her study of New Haven marriage records from 1870 to 1940, and developed her theory of the triple melting-pot in terms of it. [19]

. . . Table 6 . . . indicates that, in most cases, marriages across religious lines involve the mixing of ethnic stocks. This is true whether Catholics and Protestants marry, or Jews and Gentiles, because the members of each religious group came from such different parts of Europe. From the viewpoint of assimilation, marriages across religious lines are crucial if the triple melting-pot is to become a single melting-pot. But as Kennedy's and our data show, we are going to have three pots boiling merrily side by side with little fusion between them for an indefinite period. Furthermore, if the rules relative to mixed marriages in the Roman Catholic and Jewish churches were followed strictly there would be no mixing of the contents of one pot with those of another. To be sure, ethnic intermixture would occur, but within each respective religious group.

CLASS

Our discussion of the relationship between social class and marriage will be based on cases where the husband, the wife, and both parental families were *de*

[19] For a discussion of this theory see Ruby Jo Reeves Kennedy, "Single or Triple Melting-Pot? Intermarriage Trends in New Haven, 1870–1940," *op. cit.*

TABLE 7   Residential class of husband and wife for residents of New Haven

CLASS OF HUSBAND	Class of Wife						
	I	II	III	IV	V	VI	TOTAL
I	13	7	1	0	3	1	25
II	8	56	8	12	13	8	105
III	1	4	15	5	7	7	39
IV	0	8	4	55	35	38	140
V	0	12	8	30	252	87	389
VI	0	5	9	40	60	196	310
Total	22	92	45	142	370	337	1008

$$\chi^2 = 1045.0605 \quad P < .01 \quad C = .71 \quad \bar{C} = .77$$

facto residents of New Haven.[20] The analysis of 1,008 marriages where the husband, the wife, and their families were residents of New Haven revealed that the class of residential area in which a man's or a woman's family home is located has a very marked influence on his or her marital opportunities. In 587 of these 1,008 marriages, or 58.2 per cent (see Table 7), both partners came from the same class of residential area. When those that involved a partner from an adjacent class area were added to the first group the figure was raised to 82.8 per cent of all marriages.

Careful study of the data presented in Table 7 will reveal that the residential class in which a family has its home has a different effect on a woman's marital opportunities in comparison with a man's. While the modal, as well as the majority, of marriages at all levels united class equals, when class lines were crossed the

[20] The index of class position used here was developed by Maurice R. Davie on the basis of the ecological analysis he had made of the city of New Haven. Davie has ranked the 22 natural ecological areas that are primarily residential into six classes. Class I is the best and class VI the worst type of residential area. For a discussion of the project on which these ratings are made, see Maurice R. Davie, "The Patterns of Urban Growth," *Studies in the Science of Society*, G. P. Murdock, *ed.*, New Haven, 1937, pp. 133–161.

man selected a woman from a lower class far more frequently than was true for women. For instance, if you look at Table 7 you will see that 12 men from class I married women from lower ranking areas, and four of the twelve married girls from class V and class VI areas. On the other hand, 9 women from class I areas married men from lower ranking areas, but 8 of the 9 came from a class II area and 1 from a class III area. No man from class IV, V, or VI areas married a woman from a class I area. If you follow down the successive class levels on Table 7 you will see that this tendency is repeated all the way to class VI. It is clearest, however, in classes IV and V. In class IV, only 12 women from classes II and III combined married men from class IV. On the other hand, class IV men married 35 class V and 38 class VI women, for a total of 73. Fifty class V men married women from classes II, III, and IV, but 87 married class VI women. These figures reveal that the man has a wider range of choice than a woman, but he tends, when he goes outside of his own class, to marry a woman in a lower class. From whatever way we view Table 7, it is evident that the class position of a family is a factor that exerts a very important influence on the marriage choice of its children.

Now that we have seen the larger picture, we will look at it from the special perspective of a combination of religion

TABLE 8 Residential class of husband and wife by religious groups

A. Catholic

RESIDENTIAL CLASS OF HUSBAND	RESIDENTIAL CLASS OF WIFE	
	I-III	IV-VI
I-III	16	7
IV-VI	12	161
Total	28	168

$$\chi^2 = 74.8413 \quad P < .01$$

B. Protestant

RESIDENTIAL CLASS OF HUSBAND	RESIDENTIAL CLASS OF WIFE	
	I-III	IV-VI
I-III	12	4
IV-VI	1	18
Total	13	22

$$\chi^2 = 18.0923 \quad P < .01$$

C. Jewish

RESIDENTIAL CLASS OF HUSBAND	RESIDENTIAL CLASS OF WIFE	
	I-III	IV-VI
I-III	24	2
IV-VI	3	15
Total	27	17

$$\chi^2 = 26.6687 \quad P < .01$$

and residential class. Because the number of cases where we knew both religion and class level was small in some residential areas, we have combined classes I through III, and classes IV through VI in Table 8. Table 8 indicates very clearly that the class factor operates independently of religion, and with about equal force in each religious group. What is especially significant is that the effects of class position on who marries whom are so strong in each religious group.

Education operates in the same way as residence to sort potential marriage mates into horizontal status groups within the confines of religion. Within each religious group men with a particular amount of education married women with a comparable amount of education in very significant numbers. This tendency was strongest in the Jewish and weakest in the Catholic group. The strong association between the educational level of the husband and the wife, so evident in Table 9, is not a new development. We compared the education of husbands and wives in the parental generation by religious groups and found that for both the husband's parents and the wife's parents the association held. Moreover, the coefficients of contingency for each set of parents by religion were almost the same, as the following tabulation shows:

Religion	Husband's Parents'	Wife's Parents'
Catholic	.57	.58
Protestant	.58	.59
Jewish	.59	.59

TABLE 9   Years of school completed by husband and wife by religion

A. Catholic

YEARS OF SCHOOL HUSBAND	YEARS OF SCHOOL WIFE		
	9 & LESS	10-12	13 & MORE
9 & less	35	19	1
10-12	33	128	27
13 & more	5	15	19
Total	73	162	47

$$\chi^2 = 80.9784 \quad P < .01$$

B. Protestant

YEARS OF SCHOOL HUSBAND	YEARS OF SCHOOL WIFE		
	9 & LESS	10-12	13 & MORE
9 & less	11	3	0
10-12	10	26	7
13 & more	3	6	16
Total	24	35	23

$$\chi^2 = 38.9932 \quad P < .01$$

C. Jewish

HUSBAND YEARS OF SCHOOL	YEARS OF SCHOOL WIFE		
	9 & LESS	10-12	13 & MORE
9 & less	0	0	0*
10-12	0	22	11
13 & more	0	8	26
Total	0	30	37

$$\chi^2 - 12.6033 \quad P < .01$$

* The zero cells were not included in the χ^2.

These coefficients indicate that education, along with religion, has influenced the mate selection process for at least two generations.

In summary, this paper has attempted to throw light on three questions: *first*, does a biologically mature unattached adult have an equal opportunity to marry an unattached mature adult of the opposite sex? *Second*, what restrictions are placed on his choice by society, and *third*, how effective are certain selected restrictions in limiting his choice? These questions become meaningful only when we relate them to the two propositions outlined in the introduction. There I set up a model with theoretical limits of absolute freedom of individual choice in the selection of a marital partner at one pole, and no choice at the other.

The data presented demonstrate that American culture, as it is reflected in the behavior of newly married couples in New Haven, places very definite restrictions on whom an individual may or may not marry. The racial mores were found to be the most explicit on this point. They divided the community into two pools of marriage mates and an individual fished for a mate only in his own racial pool. Religion divided the white race into three smaller pools. Persons in the Jewish pool in 97.1 per cent of the cases married within their own group; the percentage was 93.8 for Catholics and 74.4 for Protestants. Age further subdivided the potential pool of marriage mates into rather definite age grades, but the limits here were not so precise in the case of a man as of a woman. The ethnic origin of a person's family placed further restrictions on his marital choice. In addition, class position and education stratified the three religious pools into areas where an individual was most likely to find a mate. When all of these factors are combined they place narrow limits on an individual's choice of a marital partner. At the moment we cannot go beyond this point and assign a proportionate probable weight to each one.

In conclusion, I think the data we have presented strongly support the proposition that one's subculture, and one's race, age, and class positions in the society effectively determine the kind of a person one will marry, but not the exact individual. In a highly significant number of cases the person one marries is very similar culturally to one's self. Our data clearly support the theory of homogamy, rather than that of heterogamy, *but* a generalized theory of the precise influence of cultural and individual factors on the selection of marriage mates remains to be formulated. This is an objective for sociologists to work toward.

Residential Propinquity and Marital Selection: A Review of Theory, Method, and Fact*

Alvin M. Katz and Reuben Hill

BOSSARD'S GENERALIZATION

. . . The focal generation of the residential propinquity (or r.p.) sequence of studies was given by Bossard (2). He wrote that the proportion of marriages of an r.p. sample "decreases steadily and markedly as the distance between contracting parties increases." This verbal generalization can best be interpreted as a statement which describes, in summary fashion, the usual propinquity distribution. . . . [Bossard's generalization is based on] . . . the assumption that one way in which r.p. distance is related to marital choice is through an intervening factor, namely the probability of meeting. . . .

Of all the r.p. studies, Koller (9) has

been the only researcher to attempt to test the propinquity null hypothesis, that a random formation of couples, outside of r.p. considerations, would lead to a propinquity distribution similar, in proportions, to that found among naturally chosen couples. He rejected the null hypothesis having found that chance couples formed randomly from his r.p. sample were "markedly" less propinquitous than natural couples.

Koller (9) has also controlled for what might be called national socioeconomic milieu, essentially depression and war, and has judged that Bossard's Generalization holds during *normal* as well as *emergency* national periods [italics ours].

*Adapted from the Journal of Marriage and the Family, 1958, 20: 27–35.

THEORY

Wishing to explain their various propinquity distributions, several r.p. researchers have categorized sample couples according to certain characteristics and then attempted to show that these sub-samples have understandable propinquity distributions. The rationale underlying these explanatory attempts may be called the *norm-segregation* theory.

The assumptions of this theory are:

1. *The marriage decision is normative.* That is, the right to free choice is limited by cultural considerations. Every individual selector, according to the particular cultural group with which he identifies, has a *field of eligibles*[1] of the opposite sex from among whom he selects his marital partner. He, in turn, belongs to a complementary field of eligibles.

2. *Cultural groups that form fields of eligibles tend to be residentially segregated.*

It follows then that through the mechanism of segregation normative marriages would tend to cluster at low r.p. distances.

While it was Bossard (2) who introduced residential segregation as an explanatory variable, Davie and Reeves (4) were the first to present the full norm-segregation theory and to subject it to empirical test. Davie and Reeves found that 73.6 per cent of all within city selectors in New Haven chose mates residing in the same type of natural area, and that only 3.9 per cent of the sample chose mates from other areas "far removed in social, economic and cultural traits." But Davie and Reeves were not

completely satisfied since even with culture held constant "the largest group selected mates from near at hand . . . rather than from similar areas farther removed."

The conclusion that even within fields of eligibles Bossard's Generalization still holds as a first approximation was found to be correct by Kennedy (nee Reeves) (7).

To this point we have proceeded on the assumption that norms govern behavior without residue. But this assumption is contrary to one of the basic postulates of sociology, that *norms govern behavior as probabilities*.[2] Hollingshead[3] found, for example, that one of the most decisive norms governing marital choice, religion, was broken in 9 per cent of the New Haven marriages in 1948. For the understanding of propinquity distributions then it is essential to explain the r.p. distances of normative deviants.

If fields of eligibles are residentially segregated, the number of potential non-normative mates close by should be low. Thus, under these conditions we would expect normative deviants to have relatively higher r.p. distances between marital selectors. Kennedy found this inference to be correct for each ethnic group in New Haven except the Irish. With r.p. distances over twenty blocks, the relative proportions of deviant marriages were greater than those of comparable normative marriages.

The non-conformity of the Irish sub-sample can be attributed, with the

[1] See Robert F. Winch, "The Theory of Complementary Needs in Mate-Selection: A Test of One Kind of Complementariness," *American Sociological Review*, 20 (February, 1955), p. 52.

[2] See Emile Durkheim, *The Rules of Sociological Method.* Translated by A. Solovay and J. H. Mueller. Chicago: University of Chicago Press, 1938, pp. 67 ff.

[3] August B. Hollingshead, "Cultural Factors in the Selection of Marriage Mates," *American Sociological Review*, 15 (Ocotber, 1950), pp. 619–627.

theory at hand, either to the lack of an ethnic marriage norm or to relatively less residential segregation for that group. The latter possibility indicates the effect on the propinquity distribution of a sub-sample as the degree of residential segregation is varied; the less the segregation, the greater the r.p. distances for normative choices and the less the r.p. distances for deviant choices.

There are marriage norms, specifically those related to age grades and previous marital status, which tend not to be bases for residential segregation. The finding of Davie and Reeves (4) that deviant choices with regard to age grades and previous marital status are relatively more propinquitous (that is, their r.p. distances are relatively low compared to conforming choices) would then be theoretically expected. For if these choices are otherwise in conformity to ethnic and/or socio-economic class marriage norms, then the low distances could be explained as due to segregation. But if they are also deviant in these respects, we can postulate either residential segregation on the basis of anomie—the famous rooming house area—or, as suggested above, that the normative group is simply not segregated and so there is greater chance that deviant selectors will live closer together.

We can now see that the two explanatory factors, norms and residential segregation, under appropriate conditions may lead to higher as well as lower r.p. distances.

Kennedy's (7) retest of the theory exemplifies this view. Since her results were similar to Davie and Reeves (4), she extended the analysis to a study of sixty-three marriages where the partners came from "dissimilar ecological areas" and found that more than half of these choices were ethnically endogamous or, as we would say, normative.

The discussion of the norm-segregation theory to this point can be sum-marized by Chart 1. In this chart segregation, by amount and type, and norm, by degree of conformity, are the conditional or independent variables. Within the boxes we predict, according to the theory, the relative propinquity situation for the meting of the two variable conditions as indicated in stub and caption.

As already indicated, the norm-segregation theory should be equally valid in explaining propinquity differences among socio-economic groups. Research into this factor however has given little attention to segregation. Considering occupation as a social class index, the data of several studies indicate that lower prestige groups have the lower r.p. distances (3, 6, 9, 14).

Assuming a socio-economic norm governing marital choice,[4] and assuming general conformity to this norm, the norm-segregation theory would predict a greater degree of segregation among semi- and unskilled workers, than among other occupational groups—a reasonable prediction.

The inference that income levels would be similarly related to r.p. distance is indicated by Kerckhoff's Nashville data (8).

When we turn to the factor of educational attainment we find that r.p. distance of marital selectors appears to be random—that is, not predicted by categories of educational level (3, 8).

Given the norm-segregation theory, we are first led to suspect that the educational factor is not normatively involved in marital selection. But Hollingshead's[5] finding of a strong association between the educational level of husband and wife for all religious groups undermines this inference. We are thus led to the conclusion that there is little or no segregation of groups according to educational attainment and thus all educa-

[4] Hollingshead, *op. cit.*
[5] *Ibid.*

CHART 1 Norm-segregation theoretical predictor

	Segregation by Groups Holding Norm	Segregation by Groups Deviating from Norm	No Segregation
Conformity to Norm	Lower r.p. Distance	Higher r.p. Distance	Higher r.p. Distance
Deviant from Norm	Higher r.p. Distance	Lower r.p. Distance	Lower r.p. Distance

tional levels would tend to have similar r.p. distances. Possibly those levels in Kerckhoff's data with lower distances are more deviant regarding the norm.

A further normative element investigated by the r.p. researchers was age at marriage. With some within-table exceptions, the empirical generalization arising from the data is that r.p. distance is a curvilinear function of the age of the male; the youngest and oldest age groups being more propinquitous, the central age groups being less so (6, 8, 9). Clarke's (3) finding is a major exception. His age groups follow a linear function, men over thirty years old being least propinquitous and the group eighteen to twenty-two years old being most propinquitous. In general we would identify those in their middle twenties, twenty-four to twenty-seven years old, as the least propinquitous class.

Since segregation by age is unlikely, probably the simplest explanation we can give using the norm-segregative theory is that the youngest and oldest male age groups are more likely to deviate from the norm governing age of marital partners and thus tend to have lower r.p. distances than the more conforming central age group of males.

Though the norm-segregative theory, as we have seen, does have some explanatory power, a second scheme which focuses more on the behavioral than the normative factors has been developed by r.p. researchers. This second approach may be characterized as the *interaction-time-cost theory*.

The basic assumptions of this theory are:

1. *The marriage decision follows upon a period of courtship interaction. The greater the potential amount of courtship interaction, the higher will be the probability of marital choice.*

2. *The amount of potential interaction is inversely related to a time-cost function; the greater the cost, the less the potential interaction.*

3. *The time-cost function is directly related to distance.*

Since the amount of potential courtship interaction is inversely related to r.p. distance through the intervening time-cost function, it follows, through the first assumption above, that the propinquity distribution is explained.

Harris (6) was the first to advance the interaction-time-cost theory in the r.p. sequence of studies. And while his research was not directly designed to test this theory, his findings lend themselves to interpretation by this theory. Harris found that the lower the prestige of occupation, the lower the r.p. distance separating marital selectors. We had explained this finding in terms of segregation, but an alternate, or possibly supplementary, explanation is now available.

Assuming that prestige is directly related to income, the higher group could conceivably perceive the time-cost function differently than the lower. The higher groups might require, for example, a greater increase in cost to change the subjective utility of any given potential interaction. That is, for the same utility they would be willing to travel farther and at greater cost than lower groups. The propinquity differences of occupational groups then can be ascribed to differential perception of the time-cost function. The higher the prestige group the larger would be the segment of time-cost that would constitute a just noticeable difference.

In general we can say that the relationship of the individual utility functions to the time-cost functions of a propinquity sample is a determinant of the propinquity distribution of that sample.[6]

This rationalistic proposition does not necessarily contradict the cultural theory advanced earlier. Its predictive strength may well reach its maximum *within* normative fields of eligibles. The Davie-Reeves couples who formed normative marriages at greater distances might be best explained by the utility postulate.

Starting with the interaction factor we are led to still another postulate. It would seem that at *any given distance* the amount of potential interaction is dependent upon the number of potential interactants at that distance. In other words, the more potential interactants at a given distance, the greater is the potential interaction.

Mitchell (12) appears to be the first r.p. researcher to have suggested the population factor. He had found no statistical differences when he compared the propinquity distributions of two rural counties in Minnesota but when either Minnesota county was compared to the propinquity distribution of a rural Michigan county studied by McClusky and Zander (11) statistically significant differences were found in five of eight comparisons. Mitchell hypothesized that the differences could possibly be accounted for by the fact that the Minne-

sota counties were close to a large metropolitan area while the nearest metropolitan area was more than fifty miles away for the Michigan county.

Ellsworth (5) followed this start by focusing on the town of Simsbury, Connecticut, for the years 1930 to 1939. As seen in Table I, the Bossard Generalization was found not to hold.

However when population was held constant, the propinquity distribution transformed to the more acceptable pattern as seen in Table II.

The inference that as the population available at the point of origin of a selector increases, the probable r.p. distance of marital pairs decreases is suggested in Kerckhoff's data (8). We might also hypothesize that as the population of the sample city increases, the proportion of in-out marriages decreases.

With the addition of the population postulate we can see that Bossard's original generalization can be expanded into a population over distance statement, where proportion marrying varies inversely with r.p. distance and directly with number of potential mates at that distance.

The revised generalization can be seen to fall into the class of formulas developed in studies of migration phenomena.[7] The most important of these, conceptually, is Stouffer's formula for it in-

---

[6]The structure of this explanatory scheme is similar to those of decision making theories in economics and psychology. See, for example, Ward Edwards, "The Theory of Decision Making," *Psychological Bulletin*, 51 (July, 1954), pp. 380–417.

[7]See, for example, Fred L. Strodtbeck, "Population/Distance and Migration from Kentucky," *Sociometry*, 13 (May, 1950), pp. 123–130; Joseph A. Cavanaugh, "Formulation Analysis and Testing of the Interactance Hypothesis," *American Sociological Review*, 15 (December, 1950), pp. 763–766; and Theodore R. Anderson, "Intermetropolitan Migration: A Comparison of the Hypotheses of Zipf and Stouffer," *American Sociological Review*, 20 (June, 1955), pp. 287–291. S. A. Stouffer "Intervening Opportunities: A Theory Relating Mobility and Distance," *American Sociological Review*, 5 (December, 1940), pp. 845–867.

TABLE I   Numerical distribution of couples by r.p. distance. Simsbury, 1930 to 1939. Source: Ellisworth (5)

r.p. Distance in Miles	Number of Couples
Simsbury: in-in couples	86
5– 6 miles	26
7– 8	12
9–10	4
11–12	12
13–14	7
15–16	49
17–18	18
19–20	7

TABLE II   Distribution of couples per one thousand population by r.p. distance. Simsbury, 1930 to 1939. Source: Ellisworth (5)

r.p. Distance in Miles	Couples per 1,000 Population
Simsbury: in-in couples	22.71
5– 6 miles	7.51
7– 8	2.46
9–10	1.56
11–12	.34
13–14	.46
15–16	.26
17–18	.19
19–20	.06

troduces the idea of *intervening opportunities*. Stouffer's verbal statement of his hypothesis is "that the number of persons going a given distance is directly proportional to the number of opportunities at that distance and inversely proportional to the number of intervening opportunities." Since in r.p. studies opportunities could be defined as members of the appropriate complimentary field of eligibles, it would seem a more incisive concept than population in general. Also the concept of intervening opportunities allows us to generalize the residential segregation factor, for is segregation not a geographic clustering of opportunities?

At this point we can synthesize theories and understand propinquity distri-

butions more generally with a *norm-interaction* theory. The basic assumptions are:

1. That *marriage is normative*.

2. That, *within normative fields of eligibles, the probability of marriage varies directly with the probability of interaction*.

3. That *the probability of interaction is proportional to the ratio of opportunities at a given distance over intervening opportunities*.

As Strodtbeck's work[8] indicates, with the simplifying use of equal opportunity intervals, we find that Stouffer's ratio curve is theoretically *invariant* over all fields of eligibles. That is, the basic mechanism leading to the choice of a mate for any *mass* sample whose members share the same marriage norms is the same for all groups, whether of high or low socio-economic status, of whatever ethnic group, or of whatever age class. The differences in propinquity of these groups are due to differences in their prior geographic distribution of opportunities. If this hypothesis is correct, then the propinquity tables that we work with are seen to be the complex summing up of these various distribution differences.

At the probability level it is not necessary to specify which particular individual within a field of eligibles will have the higher r.p. distance, but if such explanation is called for subjective utility or some other value or psychological theory may be used.[9]

[8] Fred L. Strodtbeck, "Equal Opportunity Intervals: A Contribution to the Method of Intervening Opportunity Analysis," *American Sociological Review*, 14 (August 1949), pp. 490–497.

[9] In addition to the decision making approach cited earlier, R. F. Winch, *op. cit.*, and A. Strauss, "The Influence of Parent Images upon Marital Choice," *American Sociological Review*, 11 (October, 1946), pp. 554–59, represent an empirical sociological approach to this particular area.

POSSIBLE EMPIRICAL COMPLICATIONS

The hypothesis that Stouffer's ratio curve is invariant must be modified, of course, by the term "under certain conditions." We might here suggest a few of the complicating variables that seem to define these "certain conditions."

Actually, no matter what the distance between residences, it is safe to assume that marital selectors do minimize distance during courtship interaction. We will call the places in geographic space where these meetings occur *organizational points*. Kerckhoff's (8) concept of the degree of neighborhood self-sufficiency, defined as the presence of shopping areas, schools, churches, recreation centers, and places of work, we would define as the geographic concentration of organizational points. Let us call the distance between a selector's residence and an organizational point the organizational propinquity distance or o.p. distance.

Clarke (3) has offered data in this area. His report indicates that the lower the r.p. distance, the lower the o.p. distance for both selectors. Further Clarke found differences in r.p. distance according to the social agency of introduction as well as according to type of organizational point of meeting.

It appears to be well founded that the spatial distribution of organizational points has some effect upon the consequent propinquity distribution. We might speculate that the attraction of any given organizational point for the surrounding population is given by an inverse distance formula or possibly even by Stouffer's formula, where the population is determined by normative considerations. We would thus guess that Stouffer's ratio for marital selection is invariant only under the condition that organiza-

tional points are random in space relative to population as distributed in space. Any spatial concentration of organizational points would effect the propinquity distribution in a manner similar to residential segregation. Kerckhoff's (8) theorizing leads to a similar conclusion . . .

Two other possibly disturbing factors are variations in time-cost by direction and the difficulty of determining the potential opportunities of deviant selectors. In the first case, such things as subway and bus lines can be seen as factors that tend to distort, perceptually, the spatial distribution of opportunities. Where present it might be controlled by consideration of direction as well as distance in the analysis. Stouffer's invariance will be most likely found where such variations in time-cost by direction are minimal. In the second case, we have seen that unless an anomic field of eligibles can be identified, the best prediction of deviants' r.p. distances is given by the spatial situation of the norm-conforming group. Possibly the deviant couples should be set aside for separate analysis. It would seem that Stouffer's ratio will reach its maximum predicting power when deviation from norms is minimized or adjusted for in some fashion . . .

Bibliography

1. ABRAMS, RAY H. "Residential Propinquity as a Factor in Marriage Selection: Fifty Year Trends in Philadelphia," *American Sociological Review*, 8 (June, 1943), pp. 288–294.
2. BOSSARD, JAMES H. S. "Residential Propinquity as a Factor in Marriage Selection," *American Journal of Sociology*, 38 (September, 1932), pp. 219–224.
3. CLARKE, ALFRED C. "An Examination of the Operation of Residential Propinquity as a Factor in Mate Selection," *American Sociological Review*, 17 (February, 1952), pp. 17–22.

4. DAVIE, M. R. and REEVES, R. J. "Propinquity of Residence before Marriage," *American Journal of Sociology*, 44 (January, 1939), pp. 510–517.

5. ELLSWORTH, JOHN S., JR. "The Relationship of Population Density to Residential Propinquity as a Factor in Marriage Selection," *American Sociological Review*, 13 (August, 1948), pp. 444–448.

6. HARRIS, DANIEL. "Age and Occupational Factors in the Residential Propinquity of Marriage Partners," *Journal of Social Psychology*, 6 (May, 1935), pp. 257–261.

7. KENNEDY, RUBY JO REEVES. "Premarital Residential Propinquity and Ethnic Endogamy," *American Journal of Sociology*, 48 (March, 1943), pp. 580–584.

8. KERCKHOFF, ALAN C. "Notes and Comments on the Meaning of Residential Propinquity as a Factor in Mate Selection," *Social Forces*, 34 (March, 1956), pp. 207–213.

9. KOLLER, MARVIN R. "Residential Propinquity of White Mates at Marriage in Relation to Age and Occupation of Males. Columbus, Ohio, 1938 and 1946," *American Sociological Review*, 13 (October, 1948), pp. 613–616.

10. MARCHES, J. R. and TURBEVILLE, GUS. "The Effect of Residential Propinquity on Marriage Selection," *American Journal of Sociology*, 58 (May, 1953), pp. 592–595.

11. McCLUSKY, H. Y. and ZANDER, ALVIN. "Residential Propinquity and Marriage in Branch County, Michigan." *Social Forces*, 19 (October, 1940), pp. 79–81.

12. MITCHELL, DONALD. "Residential Propinquity and Marriage in Carver and Scott Counties, Minnesota, as Compared with Branch County, Michigan," *Social Forces*, 20 (December, 1941), pp. 256–259.

13. SCHNEPP, G. J. and ROBERTS, LOUIS A. "Residential Propinquity and Mate Selection on a Parish Basis," *American Journal of Sociology*, 58 (July, 1952), pp. 45–50.

14. SUNDAL, A. P. and McCORMICK, T. C. "Age at Marriage and Mate Selection: Madison, Wisconsin, 1937–1943," *American Sociological Review*, 16 (February, 1951), pp. 37–48.

16

DATING:
LOVE AS A CRITERION IN MATE-SELECTION

Where marriages are agreed upon by the persons directly involved rather than by their families, the society must make some provision for premarital association and for mate-selection. In its context the American practice of dating makes good sense. Winch's analysis of dating in middle-class America comes to the conclusion that this practice serves not only the objective of mate-selection but also of recreation, status-grading, and socialization for sex-roles and, to a degree at least, for marital roles.

Hollingshead describes the social context in a midwestern town in which adolescents learn to date. He surveyed the youth of Elmtown in 1941–1942. It is interesting to note the marked similarities and slight differences between the dating pattern he observed and that of contemporary America.

Describing the American college campus with the air of an ethnologist investigating an exotic tribe on a remote sun-drenched island, John Finley Scott finds that middle-class America has its mate-selective procedures nearly as well institutionalized as do many primitive societies. Focussing on the college sorority, he concludes that its alumnae select the "right kind" of girls to associate with their daughters and that the sorority is organized so that the daughters marry the "right kind" of boys. The editors might add that there are numerous other social contexts that serve as marriage markets, for example, the formal debut, computerized matching, the lonely hearts club, and the anxious mother.

There are two studies not included in this volume that illuminate dating as a mate-selective process. Walster et al. report that, compared with intelligence and personality, physical attractiveness is most salient in the early stages of the process.[1] Heiss found that at early stages men and women behaved toward each other with considerable emphasis on culturally defined sex-roles (for example, the man behaving dominantly) but that as they became better acquainted, their behavior came to reflect more of their psychic idiosyncrasies.[2]

Winch and Ktsanes and Ktsanes have attempted to operationalize the concept of love. In the present volume the latter two authors summarize the theory of complementary needs in mate-selection and describe a case that illustrates the theory. According to this theory, the homogamy in

[1]Elaine Walster, Vera Aronson, Darcy Abrahams, and Leon Rottmann, "Importance of Physical Attractiveness in Dating Behavior," *Journal of Personality and Social Psychology*, 1966, 4: 508–516.

[2]Jerold S. Heiss, "Degree of Intimacy and Male-Female Interaction," *Sociometry*, 1962, 25: 197–208.

social characteristics, which was observed in chapter 15, creates for each individual a field of eligible spouse-candidates; within the field of eligibles it is believed that mate-selection proceeds on the basis of complementary needs. This means that rather than select a mate psychically similar to oneself, a person tends to select a mate whose pattern of needs is complementary to one's own.

In the final selection Winch reviews his own test of the theory, comments on subsequent studies, and on the basis of relevant investigations and critiques, seeks to indicate how the theory might be improved.

The Functions of Dating in Middle-Class America*

Robert F. Winch

Morton Hunt speaks of dating as an American social invention of the 1920s and as

> "the most significant new mechanism of mate selection in many centuries. In place of the church meeting, the application to father, and the chaperoned evenings in the family parlor, modern youth met at parties, made dates on the telephone and went off alone in cars to spend their evenings at movies, juke joints, and on back roads."[1]

Insofar as it is related to marriage, dating is the "window-shopping" period —it carries no commitment to buy the merchandise on display. Dating in American culture has a number of functions, some of which are only remotely related to marriage. In the first place, dating is a popular form of recreation, and thereby an end in itself. In the current setting, at least where the urban ethos prevails, a date carries no future obligation on the part of either party except, perhaps, for some reciprocation in entertainment.

A second function, especially in the school situation concerns the status-grading and status-achieving function. As Mead expresses it, "the boy . . . longs for a date [but not] . . . for a girl. He is longing to be in a situation, mainly public, where he will be seen by others to have a girl, and the right kind of girl, who dresses well and pays attention."[2] In his famous article on "The Rating and Dating Complex"[3] Waller made the point that in campus dating there was exploitation in two senses: (a) each party tried to make the other fall in love "harder" and earlier, and (b) each was interested in the other for status considerations. So far as fraternity men and women are concerned, the latter point has been corroborated on the campus of one midwestern university by Ray, who asserts that dating is "one of the ways of gaining, maintaining or losing prestige for the house."[4] He found this to be considerably more true of women's than of men's

[2]Margaret Mead, *Male and Female*, New York, Morrow, 1949, pp. 286–287.

[3]Willard Waller, *American Sociological Review*, 2, 1937, 727–737.

[4]J. D. Ray, *Dating Behavior as Related to Organizational Prestige*, Department of Sociology, Indiana University, 1942, p. 42 (unpublished master's thesis).

°*Adapted from* The Modern Family. *New York: Holt, Rinehart and Winston, Inc.,* 1963.

[1]Morton M. Hunt, *The Natural History of Love*, New York, Alfred Knopf, 1959, p. 356.

organizations and pointed out that while dating was one of the principal ways in which a sorority accumulated and maintained prestige, a fraternity had other avenues to prestige, such as athletics. Both in sororities and fraternities dating was found to be quite homogamous with respect to social status, but the men's dates tended to diverge more from their own statuses than did those of the women.

In such a setting as the coeducational campus considerable pressure to date is exerted upon those who would prefer not to. It is consistent with the directness and cruelty of adolescence that such pressure is often expressed as group ridicule. The social conditions of college life, then, stimulate one (a) to date, and (b) to date the type of person approved by one's social group. It follows that a date does not always signify a man's spontaneous and voluntary affectional interest in a girl. It should not be thought, however, that fraternities and peer groups generally represent the only source of such pressure. Families are frequently interested in the courtship progress of their young people, and are traditionally disposed to encourage the mating interest of their spinster daughters, irrespective of whether the age of spinsterhood be defined as beginning at eighteen or twenty, as in Colonial times, or a decade or so later, as in the college-trained groups of today.

A third function of the phenomenon of dating is that of socialization. It provides males and females with an opportunity to associate with each other, and thus to learn proper deportment and the social graces. It serves to eliminate some of the mystery which grows up about the opposite sex—a mystery which is fostered by the small-family system in which many children have no siblings of the opposite sex near their own age.

There is a fourth function, which is a corollary of the third. The opportunity to associate with persons of the opposite sex gives a person the chance to try out his own personality and to discover things about the personalities of others. In our discussion of the adolescent we noted that the social situation caused persons of both sexes to be somewhat uncertain as to how successfully they would work through their various tasks of self-validation, especially that of achieving the appropriate sex-type. The dating process is a testing ground—both in the sense of providing repeated opportunities for the adolescent to ascertain his stimulus value to persons of the opposite sex, and of providing learning situations so that he can improve his techniques of interaction. Dating allows him an opportunity to discover that potential love-objects are also insecure; thus the adolescent can universalize his insecurity and thereby reduce his own feelings of inadequacy. In the process of learning about the personalities of the opposite sex, the male, for example, ceases to react to all females as "woman" and discovers that there are "women," i.e., that females too are individuals and have idiosyncrasies. Another way of speaking of this function is to interpret it as a means of defining the dater's identity:

> "To a considerable extent adolescent love is an attempt to arrive at a definition of one's identity by projecting one's diffuse ego images on one another and by seeing them thus reflected and gradually clarified. This is why many a youth would rather converse, and settle matters of mutual identification, than embrace."[5]

The third and fourth functions of dating facilitate the fifth—mate-selection. Dating enables young men and women to test out a succession of relationships

[5] Erik H. Erikson, *Childhood and Society*, New York, Norton, 1950, p. 228. Hunt quotes D. H. Lawrence as making roughly the same point. Cf. Morton H. Hunt, *op. cit.*, p. 355.

with persons of the opposite sex. One finds that one "gets along nicely" with some, not so well with others, that some relationships are thrilling—at least for a time—that others are satisfying, and still others are painful and laden with conflict. Through dating one can learn to interpret the behavior and thereby to diagnose the personalities of persons of the opposite sex.

By noting with what kind of person one's interaction is most gratifying one can learn something about the personality and values one would find desirable in a spouse. Armed with this experience one is in a vastly improved position to set about the task of selecting a mate. In the urban setting there is an emphasis on the need-meeting aspect of the marital relationship (in terms of affection, security, etc.) and because of the heterogeneity of the population there is considerable variation in values, life styles, etc. Accordingly, because of the complexity of the checks to be made, two or three dates barely allow the testing function to get under way.

A sixth function of dating is that of intensifying the anticipatory socialization of the dating individual into marital and other adult familial roles. Such a process is begun of course in the person's family of orientation for he learns a version of the content of the roles of husband and of wife, of father and of mother in his parental home. It is to be expected, however, that in a dynamic, non-traditional society like ours each generation will believe that there are ways to improve upon their parents' conceptions of familial roles, and in the dating relationship there is opportunity for discussion of other versions. The quest for more satisfactory definitions of familial roles can be illuminated by the explorations of the dating couple into each other's values, opinions, life style and life plans, desire as to number of children, location and kind of community to live in, devoutness of religious orientation, occupational goals, and standard of living.

When viewing dating as a procedure for selecting a mate and for beginning the adjustment to marriage, it is important to recall the ways in which the dating relationship is *not* a rehearsal for marriage. Dating provides an opportunity to explore the personality and values of another human being in a situation of erotically tinged, fun-oriented recreation. Much of the content of marital and parental roles, on the other hand, involves the task-oriented activities of making and financing purchases, keeping a house clean, orderly, and stocked, and of tending children. For this reason the efficiency of dating as a procedure for mate-selection and particularly as a context for anticipatory socialization into marital roles and adjustment to marriage can be only partial.

Dating in Elmtown *

August B. Hollingshead

Local folkways define picnics, dances, parties, and hayrides as date affairs at

*Adapted from August B. Hollingshead, Elmtown's Youth. New York: John Wiley & Sons, Inc., 1949, pp. 223–227.

which a boy is expected to pair with a girl. The testimony of many students demonstrates that the vast majority have their first formal date on these occasions. Individuals recalled vividly whom the first date was with, where they went, who was there, and other details which marked this important step in the transition from childhood to adolescent life. The first date is often a cooperative enterprise which involves the members of two cliques of the opposite sex. Two illustrations will be given to illuminate the process; both were taken from autobiographies of seniors. The first was written by a class III girl.†

> I began to date in the eighth grade with boys I had played with all my life. I ran with a group of girls, and there was also a group of fellows we liked. At all social functions where boys and girls mixed, these two groups came together. We started running around in the fifth grade at Central School, but we did not date yet. We were always together at all school parties, and by the eighth grade we were having our own private parties to which these two groups and no one else was invited. We held these parties at the homes of the girls fairly frequently, usually on a Friday or Saturday night, sometimes on Sunday, but not often. We still did not have any regular dates until the end of the eighth grade.
>
> [Then] Marion Stowe's mother had a party for us. She invited all the kids in both our groups. The fellows got together and decided they would have dates. Tom Biggers asked me to go to the party with him. I was so thrilled and scared I told him to wait until I talked it over with Mother. Mother thought I was too young to start having dates. I argued with her for two days. Dad couldn't see anything wrong with me going to the party with

† Hollingshead divides Elmtown families into five social classes. Class I carries the most prestige, and class V, the least. Class III families, then, tend to cluster around the midpoint of Elmtown's prestige spectrum, while the generally "poor but honest" families of class IV are presented as distinctly lower in prestige than those of class III. For a description of the sub-cultural characteristics of Elmtown's five classes, see A. B. Hollingshead, *op. cit.*, chap. 5—*Eds.*

Tom; so Mother let me say "Yes." Tom's dad came by for us in their car and took us to the party, but we walked home. My next date was with Joe Peters during the summer before I started to high school.

Eddie Parker, a class IV junior, believed that his interest in dating went back to the seventh grade, when he and his friends began "to feel shy in the presence of girls," whereas they had been indifferent, aloof, or hostile to them before. His clique talked "a lot" about dates, girls they would like to date, and "women" in general, but no one was bold enough to make a date. This went on until the spring "we were in the eighth grade when all of us [his clique] decided one Saturday we would make dates with the girls in our class who lived in the neighborhood. We went around to their houses and asked them if they would go to the show with us. We made dates with five of them, and that night we all went to the show together." In this case, it would appear that the boys, and probably the girls as well, derived support from one another. If we accept student reports, common characteristics of these first dates are shyness, fear of doing the wrong thing, of making statements the other person will resent, and overcautiousness in the physical approaches of one partner to another. Both persons have been filled with so much advice by parents, usually the mothers, about how to act and what to expect from the date that both play their roles clumsily. They are told precisely what to say and do, when to come home, what they should not do, and what the consequences will be if they violate their instructions. As one class III girl said:

> I was so scared by what Mother told me Jim might do I did not like the experience at all. He did not even try to hold my arm. I knew I was supposed to "freeze up" if he did and I was so ready to "freeze up" we walked all the way home without

saying much. I knew he was afraid of me so we just walked along. I was so disappointed in that first date I did not have another for a year. I had several crushes on boys, but I couldn't bring myself to say "Yes" when they asked me for a date. In the latter part of my sophomore year, I had a crush on Larry Jacobs, and when he asked me for a date I said "Yes." We went together a few times when Frank Stone asked me for a date. I went to the Junior Play with him. After the play we went to Burke's [a popular restaurant] with the rest of the kids and then home. Oh, we had fun! Since then, I have had a lot of dates, and now I really enjoy them.

The more adventurous youngsters begin to date when they are 12 years of age—at picnics and family group get-togethers—and the parents are usually present. A definite dating pattern becomes clear during the fourteenth year; 20 per cent of the girls and 15 per cent of the boys report that they had their first dates when they were 13. A much larger number begins to date in the fifteenth year, and by the end of it approximately 93 per cent of both sexes are dating with some regularity. Among the sixteen-year-olds, dating is the accepted procedure, and the boy or girl who does not date is left out of mixed social affairs. Our data make it clear that between the beginning of the fourteenth and the end of the sixteenth years the associational pattern of these adolescents changes from almost exclusive interaction with members of their own sex to a mixed associational pattern similar to that found in adult life. In this period, certain activities, such as girls' "hag parties" and hunting and baseball among the boys, are organized on a single sex basis; and others, such as dances and parties, are almost exclusively mixed.

Forty-three per cent of the boys and 58 per cent of the girls report that they experienced the thrill of their "first date" before they entered high school.

Dating before entry into high school is not related significantly to age, town or country residence, or class. On the contrary, it is associated with clique membership. Some cliques have a much higher ratio of dates than others, but we did not search for an explanation of this fact either within the cliques which dated or those which did not. The discrepancy between boys and girls with dating experience prior to entry into high school continues throughout the freshman year. This differential disappears in the sophomore year, and by the time the junior year is reached more boys than girls report dates. At this level only 1 boy out of 13 and 1 girl out of 10 claim they have never had a date. All senior boys report they have had dates, but 3 girls are still looking forward to this event.

About 51 per cent of 553 dates the students reported during April, 1942, were with other students who belonged to the same school class; that is, freshman with freshman, and so on.[1] When the dating partners belong to different school classes, the pattern is significantly different between the boys and the girls. One-third of the boys' dates are with girls who belong to a class *below* them in school, whereas 31 per cent of the girls' dates are

[1] All statistical data on the dating pattern unless otherwise indicated, such as the figures on dates and no dates before high school, are derived from the analysis of the dates the students reported they had during April, 1942. April was selected as our sample month because by that time we knew the students personally and had asked them so many questions that we assumed, and correctly, that they would give us information about their dating behavior. A second reason for choosing April was the belief that by this late in the year the dating pattern of the student group would be well established. We also believed that it was better to attempt a complete study of dating behavior for a single month than to trust student memories over a longer period.

with boys *above* them in school. This gives the freshman girl a wider opportunity for dates than the freshman boy, for she can be dated by a freshman or a boy from the sophomore, junior, or senior classes. Freshmen and sophomore boys are reluctant to ask a girl who belongs to a class above them in school for a date. Many girls do not like to date younger boys unless they possess specific prestige factors, such as athletic prowess, "family background," or "good looks." Only 15 per cent of the boys' dates are with girls from a higher school class than theirs. Almost two-thirds of these mixed dates (62 per cent) are between senior girls and junior boys; the remainder are between sophomore boys and junior and senior girls.

These figures bring out the effects of two customs on the dating relations of these young people. In the first place, the folkways of courtship encourage a boy to date a girl younger than himself. The complement of this is that the girl expects to date a boy older than herself. The operation of this rule results in boys dating girls either the same age as themselves or younger. With the school classes graded principally along age lines, this means that the boys date girls from their own class or a lower class in school. Thus, the freshman, sophomore, and junior girls have more opportunities for dates than the senior girls. In the sec-

ond place, the senior girls' dating chances are limited still further by an administrative rule which restricts to high school students any high school party at which there is dancing. This rule severely restricts the senior girls' dating field, and to a less extent the juniors', particularly in class IV, because boys at this level drop out of school sooner than girls. Thus, a shortage of senior boys, combined with the school rule that only students may attend high school dances, forces the senior girls to ask junior boys for dates or let it be known that they would like to go with a junior boy or not date at school affairs. Another effect of this aspect of the dating system is the limited opportunity open to the freshman boy to date girls. Within the high school, the only girls he can date readily are freshmen, and here he competes with sophomore and junior boys who have more prestige in the eyes of the girls than he does. Then, too, the older boys are more sophisticated, more experienced in the arts of love, usually have more money, and give the girls more status in their own eyes than a "green kid" whom they have known through years of close contact in elementary school. The net effect of these factors on dating is a significantly lower ratio of dates among freshman boys in comparison with freshman girls, and of more junior and senior girls dating younger boys or boys outside the student group.

Sororities and the Husband Game*

John Finley Scott

Marriages, like births, deaths, or initiations at puberty, are rearrangements of structure that are constantly recurring in any society; they are moments of the continuing social process regulated by custom; there are institutionalized ways of dealing with such events.   A. R. Radcliffe-Brown, *African Systems of Kinship and Marriage*

In many simple societies, the "institutionalized ways" of controlling marriage run to diverse schemes and devices. Often they include special living quarters designed to make it easy for marriageable girls to attract a husband: the Bontok people of the Philippines keep their girls in a special house, called the *olga*, where lovers call, sex play is free, and marriage is supposed to result. The Ekoi of Nigeria, who like their women fat, send them away to be specially fattened for marriage. Other peoples, such as the Yao of central Africa and the aborigines of the Canary Islands, send their daughters away to "convents" where old women teach them the special skills and mysteries that a young wife needs to know.

Accounts of such practices have long been a standard topic of anthropology lectures in universities, for their exotic appeal keeps the students, large numbers of whom are sorority girls, interested and

°*Originally published in* Trans-action Magazine, *Community Leadership Project, Washington University, St. Louis, Missouri, 1965, 2: 10–14.*

alert. The control of marriage in simple societies strikes these girls as quite different from the freedom that they believe prevails in America. This is ironic, for the American college sorority is a pretty good counterpart in complex societies of the fatting houses and convents of the primitives.

Whatever system they use, parents in all societies have more in mind than just getting their daughters married; they want them married to the *right* man. The criteria for defining the right man vary tremendously, but virtually all parents view some potential mates with approval, some with disapproval, and some with downright horror. Many ethnic groups, including many in America, are *endogamous*, that is, they desire marriage of their young only to those within the group. In *shtetl* society, the Jewish villages of eastern Europe, marriages were arranged by a *shatchen*, a matchmaker, who paired off the girls and boys with due regard to the status, family connections, wealth, and personal attractions of the participants. But this society was strictly endogamous—only marriage within the group was allowed. Another rule of endogamy relates to social rank or class, for most parents are anxious that their children marry at least at the same level as themselves. Often they hope the children, and especially the daughters, will marry at a higher level. Parents of the *shtetl*, for example, valued *hypergamy*— the marriage of daughters to a man of higher status—and a father who could afford it would offer substantial sums to acquire a scholarly husband (the most highly prized kind) for his daughter.

The marriage problem, from the point of view of parents and of various ethnic groups and social classes, is always one of making sure that girls are available for marriage with the right man while at the same time guarding against marriage with the wrong man.

THE UNIVERSITY CONVENT

The American middle class has a particular place where it sends its daughters so they will be easily accessible to the boys—the college campus. Even for the families who worry about the bad habits a nice girl can pick up at college, it has become so much a symbol of middle-class status that the risk must be taken, the girl must be sent. American middle-class society has created an institution on the campus that, like the fatting house, makes the girls more attractive; like the Canary Island convent, teaches skills that middle-class wives need to know; like the *shtetl*, provides matchmakers; and without going so far as to buy husbands of high rank, manages to dissuade the girls from making alliances with lower-class boys. That institution is the college sorority.

A sorority is a private association which provides separate dormitory facilities with a distinctive Greek letter name for selected female college students. Membership is by invitation only, and requires recommendation by former members. Sororities are not simply the feminine counterpart of the college fraternity. They differ from fraternities because marriage is a more important determinant of social position for women than for men in American society, and because standards of conduct associated with marriage correspondingly bear stronger sanctions for women than for men. Sororities have

much more "alumnae" involvement than fraternities, and fraternities adapt to local conditions and different living arrangements better than sororities. The college-age sorority "actives" decide only the minor details involved in recruitment, membership, and activities; parent-age alumnae control the important choices. The prototypical sorority is not the servant of youthful interests; on the contrary, it is an organized agency for controlling those interests. Through the sorority, the elders of family, class, ethnic, and religious communities can continue to exert remote control over the marital arrangements of their young girls.

The need for remote control arises from the nature of the educational system in an industrial society. In simple societies, where children are taught the culture at home, the family controls the socialization of children almost completely. In more complex societies, education becomes the province of special agents and competes with the family. The conflict between the family and outside agencies increases as children move through the educational system and is sharpest when the children reach college age. College curricula are even more challenging to family value systems than high school courses, and children frequently go away to college, out of reach of direct family influence. Sometimes a family can find a college that does not challenge family values in any way: devout Catholic parents can send their daughters to Catholic colleges; parents who want to be sure that daughter meets only "Ivy League" men can send her to one of the "Seven Sisters"—the women's equivalent of the Ivy League, made up of Radcliffe, Barnard, Smith, Vassar, Wellesly, Mt. Holyoke, and Bryn Mawr— if she can get in.

The solution of controlled admissions is applicable only to a small proportion of college-age girls, however. There are nowhere near the number of separate, sectarian colleges in the country that would be needed to segregate all the college-age girls safely, each with her own kind. Private colleges catering mostly to a specific class can still preserve a girl from meeting her social or economic inferiors; but the fees at such places are steep. It costs more to maintain a girl in the Vassar dormitories than to pay her sorority bills at a land-grant school. And even if her family is willing to pay the fees, the academic pace at the elite schools is much too fast for most girls. Most college girls attend large, tax-supported universities where the tuition is relatively low and where admissions policies let in students from many strata and diverse ethnic backgrounds. It is on the campuses of the free, open, and competitive state universities of the country that the sorority system flourishes.

When a family lets its daughter loose on a large campus with a heterogenous population, there are opportunities to be met and dangers to guard against. The great opportunity is to meet a good man to marry, at the age when the girls are most attractive and the men most amenable. For the girls, the pressure of time is urgent; though they are often told otherwise, their attractions are in fact primarily physical, and they fade with time. One need only compare the relative handicaps in the marital sweepstakes of a 38-year old single male lawyer and a single, female teacher of the same age to realize the urgency of the quest.

The great danger of the public campus is that young girls, however properly reared, are likely to fall in love, and—in our middle-class society at least—love leads to marriage. Love is a potentially random factor, with no regard for class boundaries. There seems to be no good way of preventing young girls from falling

in love. The only practical way to control love is to control the type of men the girl is likely to encounter; she cannot fall dangerously in love with a man she has never met. Since kinship groups are unable to keep "undesirable" boys off the public campus entirely, they have to settle for control of counter-institutions within the university. An effective counter-institution will protect a girl from the corroding influences of the university environment.

There are roughly three basic functions which a sorority can perform in the interest of kinship groups:

1. It can ward off the wrong kind of men.

2. It can facilitate moving-up for middle-status girls.

3. It can solve the "Brahmin problem"—the difficulty of proper marriage that afflicts high-status girls.

Kinship groups define the "wrong kind of man" in a variety of ways. Those who use an ethnic definition support sororities that draw an ethnic membership line; the best examples are the Jewish sororities, because among all the ethnic groups with endogamous standards (in America at any rate), only the Jews so far have sent large numbers of daughters away to college. But endogamy along class lines is even more pervasive. It is the most basic mission of the sorority to prevent a girl from marrying out of her group (exogamy) or beneath her class (hypogamy). As one of the founders of a national sorority artlessly put it in an essay titled "The Mission of the Sorority":

> There is a danger, and a very grave danger, that four years' residence in a dormitory will tend to destroy right ideals of home life and substitute in their stead a belief in the freedom that comes from community living . . . culture, broad, liberalizing, humanizing culture, we cannot get too

much of, unless while acquiring it we are weaned from home and friends, from ties of blood and kindred.

A sorority discourages this dangerous weaning process by introducing the sisters only to selected boys; each sorority, for example, has dating relations with one or more fraternities, matched rather nicely to the sorority on the basis of ethnicity and/or class. (A particular sorority, for example, will have dating arrangements not with all the fraternities on campus, but only with those whose brothers are a class-match for their sisters.) The sorority's frantically busy schedule of parties, teas, meetings, skits, and exchanges keeps the sisters so occupied that they have neither time nor opportunity to meet men outside the channels the sorority provides.

MARRYING UP

The second sorority function, that of facilitating hypergamy, is probably even more of an attraction to parents than the simpler preservation of endogamy. American society is not so much oriented to the preservation of the *status quo* as to the pursuit of upward mobility.

In industrial societies, children are taught that if they study hard they can get the kind of job that entitles them to a place in the higher ranks. This incentive actually is appropriate only for boys, but the emphasis on using the most efficient available means to enter the higher levels will not be lost on the girls. And the most efficient means for a girl—marriage—is particularly attractive because it requires so much less effort than the mobility through hard work that is open to boys. To the extent that we do socialize the sexes in different ways, we are more likely to train daughters in the ways of attracting men than to motivate them to

do hard, competitive work. The difference in motivation holds even if the girls have the intelligence and talent required for status climbing on their own. For lower-class girls on the make, membership in a sorority can greatly improve the chances of meeting (and subsequently marrying) higher-status boys.

Now we come to the third function of the sorority—solving the Brahmin problem. The fact that hypergamy is encouraged in our society creates difficulties for girls whose parents are already in the upper strata. In a hypergamous system, high status *men* have a strong advantage; they can offer their status to a prospective bride as part of the marriage bargain, and the advantages of high status are often sufficient to offset many personal drawbacks. But a *woman's* high status has very little exchange value because she does not confer it on her husband.

This difficulty of high status women in a hypergamous society we may call the Brahmin problem. Girls of Brahmin caste in India and Southern white women of good family have the problem in common. In order to avoid the horrors of hypogamy, high status women must compete for high status men against women from all classes. Furthermore, high status women are handicapped in their battle by a certain type of vanity engendered by their class. They expect their wooers to court them in the style to which their fathers have accustomed them; this usually involves more formal dating, gift-giving, escorting, taxiing, etc., than many college swains can afford. If upperstratum men are allowed to find out that the favors of lower class women are available for a much smaller investment of time, money, and emotion, they may well refuse to court upper-status girls.

In theory, there are all kinds of ways

for upper-stratum families to deal with surplus daughters. They can strangle them at birth (female infanticide); they can marry several to each available male (polygyny); they can offer money to any suitable male willing to take one off their hands (dowries, groom-service fees). All these solutions have in fact been used in one society or another, but for various reasons none is acceptable in our society. Spinsterhood still works, but marriage is so popular and so well rewarded that everybody hopes to avoid staying single.

The industrial solution of the Brahmin problem is to corner the market, or more specifically to shunt the eligible bachelors into a special marriage market where the upper stratum women are in complete control of the bride-supply. The best place to set up this protected marriage-market is where many suitable men can be found at the age when they are most willing to marry—in short, the college campus. The kind of male collegians who can be shunted more readily into the specialized marriage-market that sororities run, are those who are somewhat uncertain of their own status and who aspire to move into higher strata. These boys are anxious to bolster a shaky self-image by dating obviously high-class sorority girls. The fraternities are full of them.

How does a sorority go about fulfilling its three functions? The first item of business is making sure that the girls join. This is not as simple as it seems, because the values that sororities maintain are more important to the older generation than to college-age girls. Although the sorority image is one of membership denied to the "wrong kind" of girls, it is also true that sororities have quite a problem of recruiting the "right kind." Some are pressured into pledging by their parents. Many are recruited straight out of high school, before they know much about what really goes on at college. High

school recruiters present sorority life to potential rushees as one of unending gaiety; life outside the sorority is painted as bleak and dateless.

A membership composed of the "right kind" of girls is produced by the requirement that each pledge must have the recommendation of, in most cases, two or more alumnae of the sorority. Membership is often passed on from mother to daughter—this is the "legacy," whom sorority actives have to invite whether they like her or not. The sort of headstrong, innovative, or "sassy" girl who is likely to organize a campaign inside the sorority against prevailing standards is unlikely to receive alumnae recommendations. This/is why sorority girls are so complacent about alumnae dominance, and why professors find them so bland and uninteresting as students. Alumnae dominance extends beyond recruitment, into the daily life of the house. Rules, regulations, and policy explanations come to the house from the national association. National headquarters is given to explaining unpopular policy by any available strategem; a favorite device (not limited to the sorority) is to interpret all nonconformity as sexual, so that the girl who rebels against wearing girdle, high heels, and stockings to dinner two or three times a week stands implicitly accused of promiscuity. This sort of argument, based on the shrewdness of many generations, shames into conformity many a girl who otherwise might rebel against the code imposed by her elders. The actives in positions of control (house manager, pledge trainer or captain) are themselves closely supervised by alumnae. Once the right girls are initiated, the organization has mechanisms that make it very difficult for a girl to withdraw. Withdrawal can mean difficulty in finding alternative living quarters, loss of prepaid room and board fees, and stigmatization.

Sororities keep their members, and particularly their flighty pledges, in line primarily by filling up all their time with house activities. Pledges are required to study at the house, and they build the big papier-mache floats (in collaboration with selected fraternity boys) that are a traditional display of "Greek Row" for the homecoming game. Time is encompassed completely; activities are planned long in advance, and there is almost no energy or time available for meeting inappropriate men.

The girls are taught—if they do not already know—the behavior appropriate to the upper strata. They learn how to dress with expensive restraint, how to make appropriate conversation, how to drink like a lady. There is some variety here among sororities of different rank; members of sororities at the bottom of the social ladder prove their gentility by rigid conformity in dress and manner to the stereotype of the sorority girl, while members of top houses feel socially secure even when casually dressed. If you are born rich you can afford to wear Levi's and sweatshirts.

PRELIMINARY EVENTS

The sorority facilitates dating mainly by exchanging parties, picnics, and other frolics with the fraternities in its set. But to augment this the "fixer-uppers" (the American counterpart of the *shatchen*) arrange dates with selected boys; their efforts raise the sorority dating rate above the independent level by removing most of the inconvenience and anxiety from the contracting of dates.

Dating, in itself, is not sufficient to accomplish the sorority's purposes. Dating must lead to pinning, pinning to engagement, engagement to marriage. In sorority culture, all dating is viewed as a movement toward marriage. Casual, spontaneous dating is frowned upon; formal courtship is still encouraged. Sorority ritual reinforces the progression from dating to marriage. At the vital point in the process, where dating must be turned into engagement, the sorority shores up the structure by the pinning ritual, performed after dinner in the presence of all the sorority sisters (who are required to stay for the ceremony) and attended, in its classic form, by a choir of fraternity boys singing outside. The commitment is so public that it is difficult for either partner to withdraw. Since engagement is already heavily reinforced outside the sorority, pinning ceremonies are more elaborate than engagements.

The social columns of college newspapers faithfully record the successes of the sorority system as it stands today. Sorority girls get engaged faster than "independents," and they appear to be marrying more highly ranked men. . . .

The Theory of Complementary Needs in Mate-Selection*

Thomas Ktsanes and Virginia Ktsanes

WHO MARRIES WHOM?

The question of "who marries whom" is one which has aroused "common sense" as well as scientific interest. The common sense answer is paradoxical, for while everyone knows that "like marries like" and that "birds of a feather flock together," it is also equally clear that "opposites attract." As is frequently the case in folk wisdom, both assertions are probably true depending upon the characteristics considered. If by "like" one means similarity in regard to a variety of social characteristics such as ethnic origin, religion, occupation, residential location, and social status, then indeed the view that mates tend to be similar seems correct. If, on the other hand, "like" is used to denote similarity in a variety of psychological attitudes, traits, tendencies, or needs, then the situation is by no means clear. This being the case, it is in order to take a brief look at some studies which have attempted to answer the question of the degree to which homogamy or heterogamy prevails in marital choice. The tendency of persons to select mates who have certain characteristics similar to their own is called homogamy or assortative mating. Conversely, heterogamy refers to the selection of mates who are opposites or are merely different. We shall begin with a brief review of the research literature on homogamy. Later we shall present the theory of complementary needs as a special type of heterogamy.

Homogamy in Social Characteristics

Interest in the problem of assortative mating is probably an analogical extension out of the field of biology where for lower animals there seems to be a trend toward similarity in size and vitality. On the human level also there is some slight evidence for homogamy in physical characteristics.[1] With human beings, however, physical similarity has not been the principal concern. Most work on assortative mating has concerned a variety of social characteristics. We shall now briefly examine some of this evidence.

In an early study by Marvin[2] it was noted that there was a greater than chance tendency for marriages to occur between persons with similar occupations.

*Original manuscript. The theory of complementary needs was first set forth by Robert F. Winch. For a more detailed exposition of the theory see his book Mate-Selection. New York: Harper & Row, Publishers, 1958.

[1] In Mary Schooley, "Personality Resemblance Among Married Couples," *Journal of Abnormal and Social Psychology*, 31 (1936), 340–47, some low positive correlations were found to exist between mates on height, weight, visual acuity, and appearance.

[2] Donald Marvin, "Occupational Propinquity as a Factor in Marriage Selection," *Journal of the American Statistical Association*, 16 (1918–19), 131–50.

More recently Centers[3] has pointed out that there tend to be no wide differences in the occupational statuses of spouses. Burgess and Wallin[4] have shown that there is homogamy in educational level. Further, basing their conclusions on the ratings by the couple of the social status of their parents and on their report of the present income of their fathers, Burgess and Wallin state ". . . it is clear that there is a considerable excess over chance for young people to fall in love and become engaged to those in the same social and economic class."[5] Kennedy[6] has indicated that there is a strong trend toward homogamy in regard to religious affiliation and a tendency, though less marked, toward homogamy in ethnic origin.

Bossard,[7] in a study repeated by subsequent researchers, showed that people usually select their mates from those who live nearby. In Bossard's classic study more than half of the marriages in his sample were between persons living within twenty blocks of each other. However, the effect of this factor of mere spatial propinquity must not be overemphasized for it overlaps with the factors discussed before. The various ecological areas of the city are characterized by heavy concentrations of certain socioeconomic classes, ethnic and religious groups; and these groups as noted above tend to be endogamous.[8]

In summary, the studies reviewed indicate that persons who marry tend to be similar in regard to a variety of characteristics such as social class, ethnic background, educational level, religion, occupation, and area of residence. However, these findings actually bear little direct relationship to our problem. They are of some interest in that they give us a notion of the limits within which another principle of selection may operate. As we interpret them, these factors tend to define a field of eligibles from which a mate may be selected on psychological grounds.

Homogany in Psychological Characteristics

Psychological characteristics which have been studied with respect to homogamy include a long and varied list. Characteristics investigated by means of "paper-and-pencil" personality inventories include neuroticism, dominance, self-sufficiency, etc. One early study[9] found moderately high correlations between mates on neurotic tendency and dominance. Burgess and Wallin[10] in their more recent study of 1000 engaged couples found homogamy in regard to a few traits. Their correlations, however, were of a rather low order and are therefore not too convincing. In regard to various "content" attitudes, e.g., religious and political attitudes, there is some

[3] Richard Centers, "Marital Selection and Occupational Strata," *American Journal of Sociology*, 54 (1949), 530–35.

[4] E. W. Burgess and Paul Wallin, "Homogamy in Social Characteristics," *American Journal of Sociology*, 49 (1943), 109–24.

[5] *Ibid.*, p. 114.

[6] R. J. R. Kennedy, "Single or Triple Melting-Pot? Intermarriage Trends in New Haven, 1870–1950," *American Journal of Sociology*, 58 (1952), 56–59.

[7] J. H. S. Bossard, "Residential Propinquity as a Factor in Marriage Selection," *American Journal of Sociology*, 38 (1932), 219–24.

[8] Endogamy refers to marriage within the group.

[9] E. L. Hoffeditz, "Personality Resemblances Among Married Couples," *Journal of Abnormal and Social Psychology*, 5 (1934), 214–27.

[10] E. W. Burgess and Paul Wallin, "Homogamy in Personality Characteristics," *Journal of Abnormal and Social Psychology*, 39 (1944), 475–81.

evidence for similarity.[11] These similarities, however, may have developed after marriage. The results in this area are thus considerably short of being definitive. Stagner in reviewing the studies on homogamy in psychological characteristics has pointed out that correlations indicating similarity are higher with respect to intellectual, interest, and attitude scores, but that measures of temperament do not show this tendency as clearly.[12] The measures of temperament referred to by Stagner are those estimates of various traits such as dominance, self-sufficiency, etc., which are arrived at by means of paper-and-pencil tests. Confidence in paper-and-pencil tests is vitiated by the fact that subjects can "fake" their responses and thereby create what they regard as favorable impressions.[13] When we try to get behind the picture of personality which the subject wants us to accept, and more particularly, when we want to understand a subject's motivational patterns of which he may be only partially aware, we find no systematic research on the question of homogamous vs. heterogamous mate-selection.[14] In the absence of experimental evidence various writers have been theorizing on this problem.

[11] T. M. Newcomb, and G. Svehla, "Intra-family Relationships in Attitude," Sociometry, 1 (1937), 180–205.

[12] Ross Stagner, Psychology of Personality, New York, McGraw-Hill, 1948, p. 387.

[13] Cf. Albert Ellis, "The Validity of Marriage Prediction Tests," American Sociological Review, 13 (1948), 710–718.

[14] A few individual cases have been reported at this "deep" level of analysis, but they have been neurotic patients and the authors' reports have lacked experimental control. Cf., e.g., C. P. Oberndorf, "Psychoanalysis of Married Couples," Psychoanalytic Review, 25 (1938), 453–57.

Toward a More Adequate Theory

Ideas about types of harmonic intermeshing of needs have been suggested by various theorists and researchers. Many of these owe a debt to Freud, who made a distinction between "anaclitic" and "narcissistic" love.[15] By the anaclitic type Freud meant a love which was expressed in attitudes of self-derogation and reverential admiration toward the love-object. In this type of love one is dependent on the loved one toward whom he can express his need to revere and admire. Narcissistic love is essentially self-love but the narcissist has a great need to be admired by others as well as himself. Thus in his formulation of the narcissistic-anaclitic typology, Freud posited a type of complementary relationship, i.e., the dependent person who has the need to revere and admire is attracted to the narcissistic person who has a great need to be admired and receive adulation.

Following the suggestion that persons with complementary psychic make-ups are attracted to each other, several psychoanalysts have proposed that matching occurs between those who are complementarily neurotic.[16] According to this hypothesis, for example, a dependent male with unresolved emotional ties to his mother would be attracted to an aggressive and dominant woman burdened with conflicts over her sex role. As

[15] Sigmund Freud, "On Narcissim: An Introduction," in Collected Papers, vol. 4, London, Hogarth, 1925, pp. 30–59.

[16] Cf., e.g., C. P. Oberndorf, op. cit.; Edmund Bergler, Unhappy Marriage and Divorce, New York, International Universities Press, 1946; and Bela Mittleman, "Complementary Neurotic Reactions in Intimate Relationships," Psychoanalytic Quarterly, 13 (1944), 479–91.

a general theory of mate-selection, however, this literature is inadequate because the writers have explained attraction only in terms of the highly individualized neurotic patterns of their patients. What we are seeking is a theory which will be generally applicable, not merely to Freud's anaclitic and narcissistic types of persons, not merely to dependent people who marry nurturant people, not merely to neurotics, but to all kinds of personalities.

Gray[17] has used a broader approach to this problem. He hypothesized that mate-selection would be complementary with respect to the types of personality formulated by Jung (extrovert-introvert, etc.). His empirical findings, however, were not convincing.[18]

Other theorists have tried to identify various motivation-linked aspects of interaction. Bernard, for example, suggests various dimensions of love.[19] She notes the usual dimension of dominance and also dwells upon the desire for response or acceptance and on the differential ability of persons to "give" as she calls it. As we shall see later, these are similar to some of the "needs" in our conceptual scheme. Bernard did not systematically state that attraction occurred between persons who were complementary in regard to these dimensions. Others, however, have come very close to this notion. Ohmann[20] stated this idea by saying that we are attracted to those who complete us psychologically. We seek in a mate those qualities which we do not possess.

Taking leads from all of the foregoing, Winch attempted to pull them together. He began by defining love in terms of needs:

> Love is the positive emotion experienced by one person (the person loving, or the lover) in an interpersonal relationship in which the second person (the person loved, or love-object) either (a) meets certain important needs of the first, or (b) manifests or appears (to the first) to manifest personal attributes (*e.g.*, beauty, skills, or status) highly prized by the first, or both[21]

Then he hypothesized that mate-selection would take place according to what he called the theory of complementary needs:

> In mate-selection each individual seeks within his or her field of eligibles for that person who gives the greatest promise of providing him or her with maximum need gratification.[22]

Perhaps this can be phrased more simply by hypothesizing that the personality needs of marriage partners tend to be complementary rather than similar. Two points require further clarification: (a) What are personality needs and which needs are germane to our problem? and (b) What exactly is meant by the term "complementary?"

---

[17] Cf., *e.g.*, H. Gray, "Psychological Types in Married People," *Journal of Social Psychology*, 29 (1949), 189–200; and "Jung's Psychological Types in Men and Women," *Stanford Medical Bulletin*, 6 (1948), 29–36.

[18] Winch applied tests of significance to some of Gray's data. These tests showed that the selection of mates in terms of Jung's types was not significantly greater than might have been expected by chance.

[19] Jessie Bernard, *American Family Behavior*, New York, Harper and Brothers, 1942, pp. 435–56.

[20] Oliver Ohmann, "The Psychology of Attraction," in Helen Jordan (*ed.*), *You and Marriage*, New York, Wiley, 1942, chap. 2.

[21] Robert F. Winch, *The Modern Family*, New York, Holt, 1952, p. 333.

[22] *Ibid.*, p. 406. In the phrase "field of eligibles" Winch takes account of the previously noted homogamy with respect to such social characteristics as race, religion, and social class.

Needs

One can think of the term "need" as meaning a goal-oriented drive. Goal in this sense refers not only to such things as material objects and status in the social structure but more particularly to such things as the quality and kind of response desired in interpersonal situations. Examples of the latter are the desire to give help or adulation to others, the desire to take care of others, the desire to control, etc. When these goals are attained, the need is gratified. However, gratification is a dynamic process, and a need once gratified does not cease to function. Patterns of behavior which are tension-reducing tend rather to be reinforced. In a marriage, for example, a woman who finds in her interaction with her spouse gratification for a need to control will continue to want to control him. One further characteristic of needs should be noted. Needs function at both the conscious and unconscious levels. A person may be conscious, partly conscious, or not at all conscious of the goals he desires.

Henry A. Murray has defined "need" in a more formal way:

> A need is a construct . . . which stands for a force . . . which organizes perception, apperception, intellection, conation, and action in such a way as to transform in a certain direction an existing, unsatisfying situation.[23]

Further, he has elaborated an extensive list of emotional needs. However, because Murray's list is so detailed, we found it necessary to depart from it in a number of ways. The following list of needs[24] is nevertheless based upon Murray's scheme.

[23] H. A. Murray, et al., Explorations in Personality, New York, Oxford University Press, pp. 123–24.

[24] R. F. Winch, op. cit., pp 408–409.

Needs

n Abasement[25]	To accept or invite blame, criticism or punishment. To blame or harm the self.
n Achievement	To work diligently to create something and/or to emulate others.
n Approach	To draw near and enjoy interaction with another person or persons.
n Autonomy	To get rid of the constraint of other persons. To avoid or escape from domination. To be unattached and independent.
n Deference	To admire and praise a person.
n Dominance	To influence and control the behavior of others.
n Hostility	To fight, injure, or kill others.
n Nurturance	To give sympathy and aid to a weak, helpless, ill, or dejected person or animal.
n Recognition	To excite the admiration and approval of others.
n Sex	To develop an erotic relationship and engage in sexual relations.
n Status Aspiration	To desire a socioeconomic status considerably higher than one has. (A special case of achievement.)
n Status Striving	To work diligently to alter one's socio-economic status. (A special case of achievement.)

[25] The notation "n" before the name of a variable is used as a shorthand form for the term "need," and where it is found on following pages, that is what it represents.

n Succorance	To be helped by a sympathetic person. To be nursed, loved, protected, indulged.
	General Traits
Anxiety	Fear, conscious or unconscious, of harm or misfortune arising from the hostility of others and/or social reaction to one's own behavior.
Emotionality	The show of affect in behavior.
Vicariousness	The gratification of a need derived from the perception that another person is deriving gratification.

A study to test this theory has been undertaken with a group of middle-class subjects. Because striving for upward mobility (or higher socioeconomic status) is so central to the middle-class value system, it was decided to include two variables pertaining to status.

Complementariness

To explain this theory let us imagine two persons, A and B, interacting with each other. Let us assume that both are deriving gratification from this interaction. Then the interactional sequence will be in accordance with the theory of complementary needs if:

I. the same need is gratified in both A and B but at very *different* levels of *intensity;* or

II. *different needs* are gratified in A and B.

An example of I is the interaction between a person who wants others to do his bidding (high n Dominance) and one lacking the ability to handle his environment who is looking for someone to tell him what to do (low n Dominance). An example of II is found in the case of a person desirous of attention and recognition (n Recognition) who finds gratification in relationship with a person who tends to bestow admiration on the former (n Deference). These are referred to as Type I and Type II complementariness respectively and constitute two forms of heterogamy.

ILLUSTRATION OF THE THEORY

To illustrate the theory of complementary needs we have chosen a case from a sample of middle-class married couples and have attempted to show how these two partners complement each other need-wise. It will be noted that in this case the male shows some dependent trends. We do not feel that this case is atypical of our middle-class sample. Dependent needs in the personality of the middle-class male are probably more frequent than is popularly supposed.[26] It is to be emphasized that the man and wife discussed here are a normally functioning couple.

The Case of Anne and Frank Hamilton[27]

Before we can understand how individual needs function for mutual gratification in a marital relationship, it is

[26] For further elaboration on this point, *cf.*, for example, Arnold Green, "The Middle Class Male Child and Neurosis," *American Sociological Review*, 11 (1946), 31–41; and Talcott Parsons, *The Social System*, Glencoe, Ill., The Free Press, 1951, esp. pp. 262–69.

[27] The material upon which the case analysis was done consists of a case-history type interview, Thematic Apperception Test protocols, and a second type of interview designed to get at the more behavioral aspects of personality. The full case analysis was made by the research staff of this project which consists of Dr. Robert F. Winch, Mrs. Sandra K. Oreck, Dr. Oliver J. B. Kerner,

first necessary to present the personalities involved. We shall consider first the wife and then the husband before we attempt to understand their relationship to each other.

Anne Hamilton is best described in build as "hefty." Her outstanding features facially are her large mouth and rather prominent teeth. That her mouth is so noticeable the interviewer attributes to the fact that "it never seems to be still." She talks loud and fast. She punctuates her words by dramatic use of her hands and facial expressions. Even when she is listening, her face does not relax. She smiles broadly or raises her eyebrows or in some other way responds aggressively to what is said.

Anne's energy is also evident in her capacity to work. To finish college in three years, she carried extra courses each term and still sailed through her undergraduate work. She earned most of the money to pay her college expenses even though her family was able and willing to pay them. But she just liked to keep busy, so not only did she work and keep up her grade average, but she also held responsible positions in numerous extra-curricular affairs. She was so efficient in getting ads for the school yearbook that for the first time that publication had a financial surplus.

Going along with this terrific need to achieve, there is a high need to dominate others, which Anne describes as "a

and the authors of this article. The present report is a synopsis of their findings, which cannot be presented in their entirety because the analysis runs to about two hundred pages of manuscript. Much of the documentation for generalizations must be omitted. All names and identifying characteristics have been changed in order to preserve the anonymity of the couple without impairing the crucial facts of the case. It is our desire to present the case as simply as possible for the purpose of illustrating the theory.

certain element of bossiness in me." She feels that her way of doing things is best and she wants people to do things "in the manner I so designate."[28]

She does not like to be "stepped on" nor does she admire people who can be pushed around. Such people she cannot respect. "People that I cannot look up to, I have a tendency to shove out of my way or to trample on, just shove, push." Thus we see in Anne little need to feel sympathy for other persons (n Nurturance) but rather a hostile attitude towards them.

She tends to be critical of other people and apparently because of this she has encountered some difficulty in forming close friendships. She says that people usually like her if they can overcome their first impression which frequently is one of antagonism. She says on this point, "I'm very quick spoken and rarely stop to think that I may be hurting somebody's feelings or that they are not going to take it just the way I meant it." But she needs people and she wants them to like her.

The competitiveness and the need to manipulate people undoubtedly indicate compensatory behavior for feelings of insecurity at some level. There is some evidence to indicate that these feelings stem from her doubts about her being a feminine person. She tends to be jealous of pretty women. She is contemptuous towards them when their attractiveness and "poise" win them positions of prestige which they are not equipped to handle because of a lack of the "executive ability" that she possesses. All her life she states that she wanted to be like her mother who is pretty and sweet and "gives a lot, perhaps too much." She feels, however, that she has not

[28] Shortly we shall note that this domination of others occurred very early in her life in her relationship to her parents and other members of the household.

succeeded in becoming this sort of woman. She regards herself as a person who is "quick, uneven-tempered and impatient, ambitious . . . ready to tell others how to do things." Evidence that she rejects this "masculine" component in her personality is her view that she would not want a daughter to be like herself, but "more like Mother."

The postulation of such a conflict helps to explain why Anne did not continue with her career plans. She took a master's degree in advertising the year following her undergraduate work. She then set out to make a career in this field, but there were no jobs immediately available. Employers did not want college graduates who had their own bright ideas about the business, and, according to her account, they were unwilling to employ her for menial jobs which she was willing to take because they felt she was too intelligent and soon would become disinterested.

At this point Anne's career drive began to fluctuate. She took a job in an office. While there and while formally engaged to another man, she met Frank. She and Frank were married six months after their meeting, and they moved to a city where she had obtained a good job and where he enrolled in college. At the end of a year she became pregnant and stopped working for awhile. By the third month of her pregnancy, however, she became bored with "sitting around home" and took a job as a waitress, much against the doctor's orders. She lost the child three months later. She stated that she wanted the child very badly and that she was broken up over her loss. This wish would be consistent with the feminine desire to be a "mother." In addition to the conscious desire to be feminine, it seems probable that she had an unconscious wish to abort and to deny willingness to play a feminine (maternal) role.

Perhaps if we look into Anne's background for a moment we can see more clearly the circumstances which led to development of her pattern of aggressive behavior and the confusion over appropriate sex-role behavior.

Anne was the only child in a family of four adults. Her father was a self-made man, one who built up a trucking business to the point where it netted him an income of around $700 monthly even during the depression years. She describes him as being a short man, one who was hot-tempered and stubborn. He was 30 when Anne was born and her mother was only 18. The mother is described as being even-tempered, calm and dependent. The third adult was Anne's maternal grandmother who came to live with the family shortly after Anne was born. She managed the house and Anne's mother and apparently Anne's father as well. Anne says her grandmother often warned the father against his outbreaks of wrath in front of the child. The grandmother brought with her one of her sons who was about the age of Anne's father and who was similar to Anne's mother in temperament. He was very good to Anne and gave her everything she wanted. He married for the first time and left the household when he was 50 years old.

Anne was the center of attention for these four persons. What she could not get from one, she could get from another. This pattern of relationships was conducive to her manipulation of persons and the need for recognition from them which we have noted earlier.

Grounds for the competitiveness may also be found in this network of relationships. Anne's mother was very young and still dependent upon her mother who looked upon Anne as "her youngest child." Thus the relationship between mother and daughter resembled sibling rivalry, not only for the "mutual mother's" love but for the husband-father's love as well. Here were two bases for Anne to dislike her mother, but her mother was such a sweet young thing that she never gave Anne any rationalization for hating her. This left Anne with an unexpressed hostility which apparently has been partially sublimated into an achievement drive and partially displaced onto "feminine" women like her mother. Her mother was better looking than she, so Anne could not compete with her on these grounds but had to seek other means of achieving superiority.

To strive in an aggressive manner was satisfactory in another way too because the father, who wanted a son, approved of such behavior in his little tomboy. Further, grandmother was a model of aggressive behavior. Anne's gratifying relationship with her fostered an identification. The aggressive pattern was fairly well set by the time Anne reached adolescence as is evident in her report that, in junior high school, teachers commented on it. One teacher advised her to change her ways or she would never get a husband. Father also changed his mind about what he wanted and began to look upon her as "feminine" and wanted her to become dependent on him while she was in college. These undoubtedly are the sources of some of the ambivalence we note in her picture, especially concerning career and motherhood.

Although she had doubts about her "feminine appeal," Anne apparently had little trouble in finding dating relationships. Though she confesses she was not the most popular girl on campus and that her weekend calendar was not always filled, she dated from the time she first entered high school. She had only one serious relationship before meeting Frank. This was an engagement to a man described as "suave and smooth . . . and with nice manners." It apparently was a

stormy affair, off and on several times. The engagement was broken finally over the issue of whether or not there should be a formal wedding. Anne wanted one, but her fiance's family did not.

Frank is unlike Anne in many ways. Whereas she gets much gratification from work and positions of responsibility, he much prefers just loafing and being with people. He is now in college, at Anne's request, and very much looks forward to the time when he will be through. College is just a means to an end for him; the less work he has to do to get through, the happier he will be. He wants the degree, however, because it will facilitate his getting a good job. He looks to the job to bring him status and prestige and to provide a large income so that he can buy sports cars and a big house. Nevertheless, he does not like to work for such a position and is just as content if someone gets it for him.

Frank likes people and he gets along with them very well. It is important to him that they like him and give him attention. He loves to talk and to joke, and generally he is successful in winning friends. "I'm an easy person to get along with . . . I do a fair job of amusing people although I feel that people don't regard me as entirely full of nonsense." His physical appearance contributes to his acceptability for he is a good-looking man, tall and slightly heavy. His build is somewhat athletic but his muscles seem to lack the firmness and tonus of a well-developed athlete. He is light-hearted, pleasure-oriented, and loves to eat. [29]

[29] In terms of the Freudian stages of development, this aspect of his personality would place him at the "oral" stage, the stage at which the infant, for example, does little more than *receive* love, care, and attention from the mother. The passive-dependent trends which we note in Frank's personality are considered the psychological

To achieve acceptance Frank relates to people in a deferent manner. He consciously admires and accepts his allies almost uncritically. He shows no tendency to control them nor to compel them to do what he wants; in other words, he reveals no need to dominate. Though he likes very much to have the spotlight himself, he is willing to share it with others and even to concede it without resentment to people who are better attention-getters than he. He tends to establish friendships with such persons and to identify with them. Thus he receives vicarious gratification for his own need for recognition. This is illustrated in the fact that he joined the fraternity to which most of the "big wheels" on campus belonged though he himself was not a big wheel. Merely through association he felt he was able to share in their glory.

It is interesting to note that Frank does not limit his struggle for recognition to a few fields or a select group of persons as mature adults generally do. He is almost child-like in his willingness to perform. Once when drunk, he paid the singer in a night club twenty-five dollars to let him sing with her in front of the microphone. He still wears the badge that he received when he was deputized a sheriff for a week in his hometown. The importance of this incident was shown when Frank flipped his lapel so the interviewer could see the badge.

In addition to recognition, Frank seems to want love and affection. He tells that he was the "mascot" of a sorority at the first college he attended, and he was chosen "king of the prom" one season. If he feels blue, which he says is rare, he can be cheered by having women, peers

or the mothers of peers, tell him how handsome he is.

Apparently since high school Frank always got along well with women because he always had a girl. He tended to date one girl at a time and to go with her pretty "seriously." He expected the same of her, and as a result most of these relationships broke up by his becoming jealous when the girl would date another fellow. He became jealous he says because he wanted "all her attention." The girls he dated were all short and very attractive. The conformed to his "ideal" of "one other fellows thought highly of, a popular girl in other words." Apparently a girl of this type brought vicarious recognition to Frank in the same manner as did the "big wheels" in the fraternity.

Now let us consider Frank's background. Frank was the third son in a family of four boys, all of whom were born during a period of eight years. His father, who was 57 when Frank was born, was a successful salesman until the depression. After losing everything in the depression, the father stopped working. The major burden of supporting the family then fell upon his mother who was about 28 years younger than the father. In time this responsibility was shared by the oldest son. The mother was a petite and good-looking woman.[30] She was a very hard-working, efficient sort of person who, besides working at a full-time job, kept her house, herself, and her sons immaculately neat and also found time to participate in a few club activities. She had considerably more education than her husband in that she had a B.A. degree whereas he completed only the eighth grade. Frank remembers her as being undemonstrative in her affections and as a reasonably impartial judge in the children's quarrels but with a tendency to side with the un-

---

counterparts of this stage of development. We shall note, however, that this characteristic is by no means the whole picture and that he is considerably more active than is implied for this stage.

[30] It will be recalled that the girls he dated were of similar stature.

derdog. Frank had little to say about his father's personality. Though the man had died only two years before the interview, Frank gave the impression that his father had participated little in family affairs. Frank's few descriptive comments portrayed an opinionated man, harsh in his judgments.

Among the seemingly more important aspects of this family is the absence of daughters. Having two sons already, both parents had desired that the next children be girls. Indeed Frank can remember the time when his mother gave him a girl's haircut. It would appear therefore that this attitude on the part of his parents, and especially his mother, laid the groundwork for the passive-dependent trends we have noted in his personality. It seems logical that Frank wanted the love and attention that is given to the baby. At the age of two years, however, he could not longer be gratified in these desires because of the arrival of the fourth and final brother. It appears that Frank resented this brother greatly. In one two-hour interview he mentioned both of the older brothers but not this one. Undoubtedly as a consequence of this situation Frank has developed a fear of rejection to which he has responded by always doing what is expected of him and by endeavoring to please people in order not to be rejected by them. Frank did not react to his feeling of rejection by rebellion. Perhaps this was because the mother never actually rejected him; she just did not give him all the affection he desired. To avoid losing what he did receive and to try to get more he reacted by being a "good boy."

But Frank was not a sissy in the common use of the term. He was interested in athletics and became captain of his high school football team. He liked mechanics and cars. Currently he is studying mechanical engineering and hopes someday to become a salesman for some large engineering firm.[31]

These masuline interests are very important for understanding Frank's personality. We have shown the tendency towards dependency in his personality which culturally is considered "feminine." Generally, males in our culture who tend to be passive experience some conflict if they are not able to live up to the cultural imperatives that they be assertive and "masculine." Frank shows little anxiety on this score, however, and appears to be very well adjusted. His not having developed a conflict on this score may be due to his having achieved such successful identifications with male authority figures that he consciously never questions his "maleness."

Undoubtedly, the oldest brother is a significant figure in understanding these identifications with males. Very early this brother became a counsellor to the mother. Frank felt ambivalent towards him. He was jealous because this brother played such an important role with the mother. On the other hand, if he hated his brother, then the mother would reject him completely; but if he were like his brother, he would get his mother's attention and at the same time establish a good relationship with the brother, who was moderately successful in his own business and popular with people. Thus, the brother became an ego-model for him and at the same time was a person who could meet some of Frank's dependent needs.

Thus, we now see Frank as an amiable, non-anxious person who does not have a great deal of ambition but who has the knack of relating himself to people who can do things for him.

Up to this point we have attempted to describe both Anne and Frank with very little reference to each other. Now

[31] It is not surprising that Frank wants to become a salesman because he enjoys so much talking with people and feels certain that he is able to get along with them well.

we shall discuss their case with relation to complementary need theory.

Frank says that he was attracted to Anne because "she's probably the smartest woman I've run into, and I admired her a great deal I think before I truly loved her." On the other hand, Anne admired his easy-going manner and his ability to get along with people. Knowing what we do about each of them individually, we can see in these two remarks alone some ground for their complementary matching. First of all, we have pointed out that Anne has had some difficulty in getting along with people and that she would like to be able to do so more easily. Frank's ability to attract friends and to keep them facilitates Anne's social relationships in that he attracts their mutual friends. For Frank, Anne's initiative and her ability to attain the financial and other goals she sets for herself complements his lack of drive. The question is open, however, whether or not this particular pattern of interaction which is now mutually gratifying will continue to be so if Frank becomes a successful salesman.

In their interaction with each other we note that Anne has the authority. She handles their finances, and she decided that he should go back to school. As we have seen, this is the way she likes to do things and we have also noted that Frank shows little need to dominate and he accedes quite willingly to her plans.

Anne tends to be a very emotional person who is easily aroused and upset. At such times Frank's calm and easy-going manner is consoling to her. He has a good shoulder to cry on and he is willing to listen to her problems. She feels that he is helping to calm her down.

About the only thing that disturbs Anne about Frank's personality is that he does not have as much ambition as she would like to see. Indeed she has been somewhat bothered by his rather lethargic attitude towards school work. She would prefer to see him as excited about it as she has always been, but she feels that she is learning to accept his attitude that graduation is the important thing and that the level of one's performance in school is soon forgotten.

Occasionally Frank is a little perturbed by Anne for sometimes he is embarrassed when she pushes ahead in a crowd and drags him along with her, but he goes along and says nothing about it. Undoubtedly he is ambivalent about her aggressiveness. On the one hand, her behavior and her drive facilitate the realization of such desires as the new car which they recently bought. On the other hand, Frank fears that the same aspects of Anne's personality may put him in a position of stepping on other people which might result in their rejecting him. However, this aggressiveness does not constitute one of the things he would change about her if he could push a button to change anything. He would want to modify only her quick temper and her heaviness.

Anne is very different from the girls that Frank dated. The other girls were like his mother in physical characteristics in that they were all short and attractive. Anne has none of these physical characteristics, but does resemble Frank's mother in her efficiency. Although very different from Anne's father, Frank tends to be more like Anne's uncle and Anne's mother who are calm, easy-going, and dependent.

Both Anne and Frank desire considerable recognition from other people. Frank is attentive to Anne and considerate of her. She undoubtedly regards his submissiveness to her as admiration. Anne does not pay as much attention to Frank as he would like. It would seem that although Frank would like more in the way of demonstrated "hero-worship," he does not feel too deprived because she facilitates his getting the symbols (*e.g.*, the new sports car) which enable him to attract attention from other persons.

There is one other thing about Frank which Anne finds gratifying and which is worthy of mention here. Frank's attractive appearance and engaging manner enable Anne to compete successfully on a feminine basis with other women. Although this appeal on his part is gratifying to her in one sense, in another sense it threatens her. She mentioned that she is jealous if he pays too much attention to other women at parties. He also becomes jealous when she has occasion to lunch with another man. This mutual jealousy is understandable in terms of the marked

need for recognition which each of them exhibits. On Frank's part, it undoubtedly is a manifestation of his fear of rejection; and from Anne's point of view, the insecurity stems from doubts about her feminine ability "to hold a man."

The complementariness that is described in this couple can be summarized generally as a case of a passive-dependent male finding gratification in relationship with a striving aggressive woman (and vice versa). Indeed, they are not complementary on all counts, *e.g.*, neither is willing to surrender his own desire for recognition in favor of the other. However, it would seem that the mutual choice that has been made satisfies the major, predominating trends within the personalities of each.

Another Look at the Theory of Complementary Needs in Mate-Selection *

Robert F. Winch

The previous paper was written in 1952–53 to present the theory of complementary needs in the first edition of this book. What has happened to the theory since then? We shall consider its subsequent course under the following headings: the original test of the theory, subsequent efforts by others, criticisms, developments, and some thoughts on a reformulation of the theory.

THE ORIGINAL TEST OF THE THEORY

In 1950 twenty-five young married couples served as test subjects for the

theory. At the time of testing one or both members of each couple were undergraduate students. In 1950 a considerable number of veterans of World War II were still completing their education, and a considerable number of the husbands in this study were veterans. An effort was made to obtain couples as soon after marriage as possible.[1] No couple had been married more than two years; the median couple had been married for one. At the

°*Adapted from the* Journal of Marriage and the Family Living, *1967, 29:* pp. 756–762.

[1] It was reasoned that to select them before marriage was to run the risk that they might not marry, whereas the theory is about mate-selection, and to select them later in their marriages was to risk that their need-patterns might have undergone substantial change.

time of being interviewed no couple had children.

The data-gathering procedure employed two interviews and a projective test. The main interview (called a "need interview") was based on nearly fifty open-ended questions. Each question was designed to elicit information on the intensity of one of the needs or traits, i.e., to give an indication as to the strength of the need in the person being interviewed and the manner in which that person went about obtaining gratification for the need or expressing the trait. For example, to elicit information about the subject's hostile need (n Hos), he was asked the following: Let us suppose that you have entered a crowded restaurant, have stepped in line, have waited your turn, and presently someone enters and steps in front of you in line. What would you do? Has this ever happened to you? When was the last time this happened? Tell me about it.

A second interview sought to uncover the subject's perceptions concerning the salient relationships in his life and how he saw these as being related to his psychic and social development. In particular, he was asked to recount from his earliest memories the history of his relationships with his parents and siblings, as well as those in school and peer group. The third procedure was an abridged (ten-card) version of the Thematic Apperception Test, wherein a person is presented with a somewhat ambiguous picture concerning which he is asked to tell a story.

From each of these three sets of information a separate set of ratings was developed. For each instrument at least two raters were employed.

The theory was interpreted as predicting two types of complementariness:

Type I: The same need is gratified in both person *A* and person *B* but at very different levels of intensity. A negative interspousal correlation is hypothesized. For example, it is hypothesized that if one spouse is highly dominant, the other will be very low on that need.

Type II: Different needs are gratified in *A* and *B*. The interspousal correlation may be hypothesized to be either positive or negative, contingent upon the pair of needs involved. For example, it is hypothesized that if one spouse is highly nurturant, the other will be found to be high on the succorant (or dependent) need.

Statistical analysis of the results came out in the hypothesized direction, and the data were interpreted as providing adequate, though not overwhelming, support for the theory of complementary needs in mate-selection.[2]

[2] The theory and the immediately relevant data were presented in a series of three articles in the *American Sociological Review*: Robert F. Winch, Thomas Ktsanes and Virginia Ktsanes, "The Theory of Complementary Needs in Mate-Selection: An Analytic and Descriptive Study," 1954, 19, 241–249; Robert F. Winch, "The Theory of Complementary Needs in Mate-Selection: A Test of One Kind of Complementariness," 1955, 20, 52–56; and Robert F. Winch, "The Theory of Complementary Needs in Mate-Selection: Final Results on the Test of the General Hypothesis," 1955, 20, 552–555. Further consideration of the data by means of multivariate analysis appears in two articles: Thomas Ktsanes, "Mate Selection on the Basis of Personality Type: A Study Utilizing an Empirical Typology of Personality," *American Sociological Review*, 1955, 20, 547–551; and Robert F. Winch, Thomas Ktsanes and Virginia Ktsanes, "Empirical Elaboration of the Theory of Complementary Needs in Mate-Selection," *Journal of Abnormal and Social Psychology*, 1955, 51, 508–513. In addition there were two articles on methodological features of the study: Robert F. Winch and Douglas M. More, "Quantitative Analysis of Qualitative Data in the Assessment of Motivation: Reliability, Congruence, and Validity," *American Journal of*

Qualitative analysis of the same fifty persons suggested that there were two principal psychological dimensions underlying the various needs: (1) nurturance-receptivity, or a disposition to give versus a disposition to receive, and (2) dominance-submissiveness. On the basis of these dimensions the following types of complementariness were induced:

DOMINANT-SUBMISSIVE DIMENSION	Nurturant-Receptive Dimension	
	HUSBAND NURTURANT WIFE RECEPTIVE	HUSBAND RECEPTIVE WIFE NURTURANT
Husband Dominant Wife Submissive	Ibsenian* Ibsenian*	Master-Servant Girl
Husband Submissive Wife Dominant	Thurberian**	Mother-Son

* After *A Doll's House.*
** After James Thurber's conception of the relation (battle?) between the sexes.

SUBSEQUENT EFFORTS BY OTHERS TO TEST THE THEORY

why They didn't work

Unfortunately no one has ever replicated the original study. For a time the literature bristled with articles purporting to be tests of the theory, and it seemed that the more categorical the claims of the authors in this regard, the less directly their results actually bore on the theory.

Sociology, 1956, 61, 445–452; and Robert F. Winch and Douglas M. More, "Does TAT Add Information to Interviews? Statistical Analysis of the Increment," *Journal of Clinical Psychology,* 1956, 12, 316–321. The most general treatment of the theory appears in: Robert F. Winch, *Mate-Selection: A Study of Complementary Needs,* New York, Harper, 1958.

There is one probably very significant difference between the original study and all subsequent studies of complementary needs in mate-selection of which the author is aware. In the original study each test subject was interviewed about his need-pattern and then his answers were assessed by two or more trained analysts, whereas all subsequent studies of which the author is aware used some paper-and-pencil test in which the subject assessed himself. Some critics of the original study have made the seemingly absurd observation that the analysts on the mate-selection study were probably more subjective in their ratings (and hence less valid) than would have been the subjects themselves. How can it be reasoned that the analysts would be more concerned whether Subject 17, whom they did not know, was rated high or low on need dominance, say, than Subject 17 himself? It is this author's view that the frequently observed disposition of test subjects (like human beings generally) to portray themselves in a favorable light biases their responses.

In 1954 Allen Edwards published the Personal Preference Schedule (PPS), a paper-and-pencil test designed to measure fifteen of the needs that had been postulated and nominally defined by Murray. By name ten of the fifteen needs in the PPS were similar with or cognate to those used in the Winch study. Presumably this fact encouraged a considerable number of social scientists to think that an easy way to duplicate the Winch study was to use the PPS. The fact is that no evidence was presented to show that the Edwards test was valid either by means of a behavioral or a peer-rating criterion. Undaunted by this fact, a very considerable number of studies have purported to have tested the theory of complementary needs by means of the PPS.

Other ways in which subsequent studies have failed to be true replications include: extraneous variables (when all of the variables of the PPS are used, more than half of the resulting matrix of correlations involves variables not even proposed by name in the original study), incomplete concept of complementariness (a good many studies have ignored what is designated above as type II complementariness), and inappropriate subjects (instead of a sample of newly married couples selected in order to have complementariness at its presumed maximum, various studies used dating couples, couples married ten to thirty years, couples belonging to one unspecified church, and couples selected in such a way that they could be called only a "grab" sample).

Perhaps one should expect that if the theory were a really good one, then even with poor samples and even with a very questionable instrument the results should support the theory. In the original study, the support was visible though not overwhelmingly strong. In the subsequent studies, the general result was to show no correlation between members of couples and such correlation as did appear was more often in the direction of similarity than of complementarity.

CRITICISMS OF THE THEORY

Several thoughtful critiques of the theory have been published. Irving Rosow is the author of the first of these to come to this writer's attention.[3] Beginning with the observation that the theory had applicability to other social groups as well as to marital dyads,[4] Rosow went

[3] Irving Rosow, "Issues in the Concept of Need-Complementarity," *Sociometry*, 1957, 20, 216–233.

[4] An example of such an application is: Rudolf H. Moos and Joseph C. Speisman,

on to point out that Winch's statement of the theory did not make clear at what level the needs were hypothesized to be functioning, i.e., whether at the overt or behavioral level or at some covert or perhaps even unconscious level. The locus of gratification he saw as another problem; by this is meant the question of what happens to the expression of a need within the marriage if the person is obtaining gratification of that need outside the marriage, or if the gratification of that need is being frustrated outside the marriage.[5] Perhaps Rosow's most important

"Group Compatibility and Productivity," *Journal of Abnormal and Social Psychology*, 1962, 65, 190–196.

[5] Actually Winch had anticipated these problems and had developed a simple methodology to deal with them:

"Although Freudian psychology specifically denotes three kinds or levels of consciousness . . . , Freud and others have remarked that this three-fold classification is a heuristic device and that they really think of consciousness as a continuum with an unlimited number of levels of awareness from the most deeply repressed unconsciousness to completely verbalizable consciousness. Avenues of expression are proliferated, moreover, through the numerous mechanisms of defense. In an effort to keep our conceptual (and hence operational) schema as simple as possible, we posited only two levels—overt and covert. We accepted the overt-covert dichotomy as the most workable compromise with the Freudian view of psychic complexity.

"Similarly, the recognition that to a considerable degree behavior is situation-specific can lead to the postulation of a classification containing an unlimited number of situations. Our prime concern is with marital situations. Accordingly, we chose the simplest classification: (a) within the marriage, and (b) all other situations."

From p. 243 of first article cited in n. 2 above. It is of course possible that the proce-

criticism of the theory is that it does not provide criteria for determining which needs are complementary; a further difficulty he says, is that in many cases similarity of need may be as compatible and as functional as complementarity.

Levinger has proposed some remedies for the difficulties posed by Rosow. The former writer has suggested an operation that he believes removes the conceptual ambiguity between complementarity and similarity of needs. He advocates having the testing procedure concentrate on gratification derived from within the marital relationship in order to remove the problem about the locus of gratification, and he sees the formulation of needs by Schutz as clarifying the idea of complementarity by offering the more limited idea of compatibility.[6] Another proposal, about which more will be said below, is that of Tharp, who advocates substituting the sociological concept of role for the psychological concept of need.[7]

DEVELOPMENTS BEARING ON A REFORMULATION OF THE THEORY

Two studies have contributed to the development and refinement of the theory of complementary needs. Kerckhoff and Davis have studied a sample of un-

dergraduates who were "engaged, pinned or 'seriously attached' " and concluded that there was a sequence of filtering factors such that first individuals sort out each other by characteristics of social background (social class, religion, etc.), later by consensus on familial values (place in the community, having healthy and happy children, etc.), and still later by need complementarity.[8] It is perhaps worth noting that this is the first time the theory of complementary needs received support from a study using a paper-and-pencil test; that test was not the Edwards PPS but Schutz's FIRO– B, each scale of which deals with the desire of the respondent to act toward others with respect to inclusion, control, and affection and also to have the others act towards him with respect to the same three variables.

A very interesting development comes from an application of the theory of complementary needs in a context other than that of mate-selection. Bermann has been studying the stability of

dures used with respect to the resulting double-dichotomy of each variable (overt-covert and within-without) was not sufficiently sensitive and sophisticated to overcome Rosow's objection.

[6] George Levinger, "Note on Need Complementarity in Marriage," *Psychological Bulletin*, 1964, 61, 153–157. Cf. also William C. Schutz, *FIRO: A Three-Dimensional Theory of Interpersonal Behavior*, New York, Rinehart, 1958.

[7] Roland G. Tharp, "Reply to Levinger's Note," *Psychological Bulletin*, 1964, 61, 158–160.

[8] Alan Kerckhoff and Keith E. Davis, "Value Consensus and Need Complementarity in Mate Selection," *American Sociological Review*, 1962, 27, 295–303. The idea of a sequence of selective procedures is present in the earlier formulations of the field of eligibles and of homogamy with respect to interests and attitudes. Kerckhoff and Davis have provided empirical support for the proposition that such a sequence exists and have proposed the useful term "filtering" to denote the process. A re-analysis of these data has produced some findings that may be interpreted as consistent with certain features of Winch's "Pygmalion" hypothesis, viz., that Pygmalionizing individuals are attracted to potential mates who differ greatly from the former and present the former with a challenge to make the latter over into the formers' likeness. Cf. Alan C. Kerckhoff and Frank D. Bean, "Role-Related Factors in Person Perception Among Engaged Couples," *Sociometry*, 1967, 30, 176–186, esp. pp. 184–186.

dyadic relationships among female students at the University of Michigan.[9] He dealt with three categories of undergraduate women: student nurses, women residents of a co-operative house, and residents of a sorority house. He determined that membership in each category involved a set of norms distinctive from each of the others. That is, his investigation revealed that a nursing student is expected to be friendly, gregarious, affiliative, abasing, to suppress concern about any bodily ailments she might experience, and to be low on dependent needs as well as needs for recognition. This set of norms may be regarded as defining part of the role of the student nurse. Normative traits contributing to a definition of the role of the resident of the co-operative house were that she should be politically progressive and active, rebellious, sorority shunning, avoid the constraints of conventional dormitories, and be a member of religious or ethnic minority, of urban residence, highly intellectual, achieving, autonomous, non-deferent, aggressive, nonabasing, and individualistic. The only norm Bermann lists as pertaining to the role of the sorority girl is that of emitting highly dominant behavior.

Bermann reports on a study of 44 pairs of roommates in a dormitory for nursing students. Of these 22 pairs were rated by themselves and by peers as highly stable pairs whereas the other 22 were rated as being of low stability. As in Winch's study, interviews provided the basis for assessing the needs of the subjects; the questions designed to elicit data about needs were open-ended. The protocols of the interviews were coded for nine needs: dominance, deference, ex-

hibition, aggression, abasement, nurturance, succorance, achievement, and affiliation.

Bermann sought to predict the stability of pairs of roommates on the basis of the relationship between the pattern of needs of one girl in each pair to the pattern of her roommate. To do this, he used role theory and the theory of complementary needs to generate competing hypotheses. Using role theory, he reasoned that if both roommates were close to the ideal specified by the appropriate set of norms —in the case of student nurses, if both were friendly, abasing, etc.—each would serve the other as an object of identification with a resulting solidarity that would bind the two roommates into a stable relationship. From this reasoning he inferred, e.g., that if both should be low on the need to dominate, the pair should be stable (since low dominance was found to be an element in the definition of the role of student nurse). Using the theory of complementary needs, however, Bermann reasoned, as was done in Winch's study of mate-selection, that a more solidary relationship should exist where one was high and the other low on dominance (type I complementariness). [10] More formally, Bermann hypothesized (1) compatibility with respect to role is predictive of stability, (2) that complementariness of needs is predictive of stability, and (3) that both of these predictors considered together predict stability better than either does when taken separately. Generally, Bermann's data supported all of these propositions. Need complementarity predicted stability, but role compatibility predicted it better. Bermann's index of total compatibility, which is a combination of need complementarity and role

---

[9] Eric A. Bermann, "Compatibility and Stability in the Dyad," paper presented before the American Psychological Association, New York, September 1966.

[10] It may be recalled that Rosow had made the point that the theory of complementary needs might be generalizable beyond the marital dyad, a point made also by Winch in *Mate-Selection*, pp. 305–309.

compatibility, was the most effective predictor of stability.

SOME THOUGHTS ON A REFORMULATION OF THE THEORY

The theory of complementary needs is a psychological theory in that it refers to the actor's personality, conceived as the organization of a set of needs and traits. Role theory is a sociological theory in that its referent is a role, which is the product of the consensus of some collectivity. What Bermann has done is to show that the psychological *plus* the sociological theory is better than either of these standing alone.[11]

Before attempting to integrate the significance of these findings and formulations, it may be useful to distinguish a bit more explicitly between role and personality. Very simply, the distinction is seen as follows. Role directs our attention to behaviors and attitudes that are appropriate to a situation, irrespective of the actor, whereas personality directs our attention to behaviors and attitudes that are characteristic of the actor, irrespective of the situation. As Bermann has shown, both role and personality may be stated in terms of needs.

How can Bermann's results, obtained from studying pairs of girls rooming together, bear on the marital dyad? In the general statement of the theory of complementary needs the sex of the actor is not significant; the gender of the actor became significant in Winch's study because he placed the test of the theory in the context of mate-selection.

This writer would argue that the theoretically significant feature is not whether the members of the dyad are of the same or different sexes but whether their roles are or are not differentiated. The student nurses were enacting identical roles; there is always some difference between the familial roles of men and women because of the fact that women bear and nurse children. The degree to which roles of the sexes are differentiated beyond this inescapable consideration varies from one societal and cultural context to another. Elsewhere the present writer has argued that the degree of differentiation of sex roles varies inversely with the use of non-human power.[12]

At the beginning of a relationship it appears that physical attractiveness is salient,[13] and that the behavior of each party conforms closely to traditional sex roles (e.g., with the male emitting dominant behavior). At this time there may be a good deal of posing to the extent that such is necessary to bring one's behavior into conformity with the traditional sex role. In this way the difference in behavior between the sexes tends to be emphasized.[14] As the man and woman become

---

[11] Students of social thought may note that this outcome seems pragmatically to give the lie to the stricture of Durkheim to the effect that the explanation of a "social fact" must be another social fact, or in our language, that it is intellectually illegitimate and logically indefensible to combine the two levels of explanation (psychological and sociological) in a single problem. Cf. Emile Durkheim, *The Rules of Sociological Method*, (transl. by Sarah Solovay and John H. Mueller) Chicago, University of Chicago Press, 1938.

[12] *The Modern Family*, New York, Holt, Rinehart & Winston, 1963 (rev. ed.), pp. 399–401. The findings of Barry, Bacon and Child, pp. 318–324 above, support this proposition.

[13] Elain Walster, Vera Aronson, Darcy Abrahams and Leon Rottman, "Importance of Physical Attractiveness in Dating Behavior," *Journal of Personality and Social Psychology*, 1966, 4, 508–516.

[14] The qualifying phrase "tends to" seems warranted by the fad of self-presenta-

better acquainted, however, there is a decline in traditional behavior and hence of posing.[15] Part of the process of becoming acquainted is a filtering process in which the members of the couple explore each other's behavior and values to determine the degree to which they participate in the same sub-culture. In general, a finding of similarity results in acceptance and liking. After that, according to Kerckhoff and Davis, selection occurs on the basis of complementarity.[16] But is this complementarity of personality or of role or of both?

Before trying to answer the foregoing question, the writer must pause for a slight detour. It has been noted above that the study of complementary needs concluded with the proposal that there were two underlying dimensions of complementariness: nurturance-receptivity and dominance-submissiveness. Subsequent reflection leads the writer to the view that those same data revealed a third dimension that was not quite as well determined as the other two but seems, nevertheless, to be conceptually distinct from them. This dimension may be called "achievement-vicariousness." In the theory of complementary needs, it will be recalled, it makes no difference which spouse is high on needs pertaining to which end of any of these three dimensions—if one spouse is high on one, e.g., nurturance, the other spouse is predicted to be low on that need and to be high on its complement, in this case receptivity.[17]

As we try to incorporate role theory into the above formulation, the first question is whether or not any of these variables enters into the specification of the role of husband or of wife. If so, what bearing would this have? It seems justified to assert that the traditional public image of the husband-father in the American middle class represents him as the dominant member of the family and as being strongly oriented to achievement. The wife-mother is traditionally portrayed as nurturant but as having the children as the objects of her nurturance; also she is traditionally seen as deriving vicarious gratification from the achievements of her husband.

If these statements of role-specification are correct (or to the extent that they are correct), it does follow that the variables of Winch's study of mate-selection can be related to roles that are familial, including marital. At this point it is useful to recall that roles, through what

---

tion during the latter 1960's in a manner that seems to minimize such differences.

[15] Jerold S. Heiss, "Degree of Intimacy and Male-Female Interaction," *Sociometry*, 1962, 25, 197–208.

[16] The sequence outlined above pertains to a single relationship. A parallel development seems to occur in the individual as he moves through a series of relationships in his dating experience. At the outset, one is likely to seek a potential mate that conforms to the cultural ideal, but frustrations and lack of gratifications experienced in relationships with those who conform to cultural standards may cause one to modify one's ideal mate in the direction of an idiosyncratically conceived psychic ideal. Cf. *The Modern Family*, pp. 641–648.

[17] Actually, the name used to designate the need is "succorance." In Table 7 of *Mate-Selection* (p. 125) evidence of type I and type II complementarity for these dimensions may be noted for the following pairs of variables: nurturance and succorance (the nurturance-receptivity dimension); dominance and abasement (the dominance-submissiveness dimension); and achievement and vicariousness (the achievement-vicariousness dimension). Of the 12 cells (3 dimensions × 2 variables in each dimension × 2 spouses) referred to in that table there is one cell that fails to support the theory: with respect to the interspousal correlation on the trait of vicariousness the data show no relationship instead of the predicted negative correlation.

Gross et al.[18] call the "norm-senders," put a strain on personality to conform to the specifications of the roles. To the extent that one sees that one's need-pattern (personality) is consistent with present and prospective roles, one can feel comfortable and adjusted. But where personality is inconsistent with role(s)—e.g., the succorant or submissive or non-achievement-oriented husband—there is room for regarding oneself a misfit and for developing intrapsychic conflict. Placed in the present context, the Bermann study suggests a hypothesis:

> A pair of spouses who are attracted to each other on the basis of complementary needs will be a less stable pair if the complementarity is counter to role-specification than if it is consistent with role-specification.

The point here is that where personality and role are mutually consistent, this state of affairs should not generate intrapsychic conflict, while the pair of actors should find that their relationship is given normative support. On the other hand, where personality is in conflict with role, each actor is put in a situation to suffer intrapsychic conflict (unless each accepts a self-definition as a deviant) and the marital relationship is open to criticism on normative grounds.

Perhaps an example is in order. Let us assume there are two persons, A and B, in a dyadic relationship. A is high on dominance and low on submissiveness; B has the opposite need-pattern. At this point we do not specify which is male, which is female. With respect to needs they are complementary on this dimension. Accordingly, the theory of complementary needs predicts they are more likely to select each other as mates than a pair in which both are dominant or both

are submissive. (And of course the theory of complementary needs purports to predict only mate-selection, not marital happiness nor marital stability.) With respect to role what is the situation? If we are given the information that they are members of a society wherein the male role is defined as dominant and the female role submissive, then we are part way home. If, in addition, we learn that A is the male and B the female, we conclude that their need-complementariness on the dominance-submissiveness dimension is consistent with their role-specifications. Then, on the basis of the hypothesis derived from the Bermann study, we might predict that this relationship would be a relatively stable one. Of course if we were told that B was the man and A the woman, the prediction about their being attracted to each other would still stand but the prediction about the stability of their marriage would be reversed.[19] This case has been over simplified for heuristic purposes; one would not be justified in predicting either mate-selection or marital stability on only this narrow view of the two parties.

---

[18] Neal Gross, Ward S. Mason, and Alexander W. McEachern, *Explorations in Role Analysis*, New York, Wiley, 1958.

[19] In practice, such a prediction would have to be made contingent on the pair having an opportunity to get well acquainted. As suggested above, it appears that initially men and women tend to create images of their ideal mates in terms of normative definitions. At this stage they are disposed to reject as spouse-candidates those who complement their need-patterns if, at the same time, they deviate from the normative standards (i.e., from role-specifications). Later some discard normatively defined ideals after experience convinces them that a better fit results from one who complements their idiosyncratic need-patterns. Case materials supporting this point can be seen in the previous paper, in chapters 7–13 of *Mate-Selection*, and in *The Modern Family*. See also the discussion of the cultural ideal and the psychic ideal in *The Modern Family*.

The next step in the prediction of mate-selection and marital stability would seem to be the further analysis of marital and other familial roles. It is not clear whether or not it is desirable to continue working with the needs and traits used by Winch and by Bermann. The latter has shown that, to a limited extent at least, such variables may be used as elements of both personality and of role and thus can be used to integrate the two kinds of theory. It is in contemplating further, even exhaustive, analysis of marital and other familial roles where there arises some uncertainty as to just how adequately such an analysis can be made in terms of, or translated into, needs and traits. Some idea of the task can be seen from the following examples taken from a list of components of marital roles derived from a middle-class sample by Hurvitz:[20] performer of domestic chores; companion of spouse; friend, teacher, and guide of offspring; sexual partner; and model for offspring. The present author has previously published the following list of conceptually derived components or subroles:[21]

progenitor or progenitrix
father or mother (nurturer, disciplinarian, socializer, model)
position conferrer (provider of position in society for self, spouse, offspring)
emotional gratifier
sexual partner

The list of five subroles shown just above is intended to be universal, or culture-free, although precisely how they are defined is of course specified in each culture. For the specific setting of the American middle class the following might be added:

host or hostess
home manager
companion in leisure

Presumably the task of translating such subroles into needs is to analyze (a) how the spouses complement each other with respect to these subroles, and (b) the needs involved in such complementariness.

There are two further ideas to be taken into account in suggesting a possible direction for the analysis of marital roles. First, there will be variation from one society to another and from one segment to another within even moderately differentiated societies as to the number and nature of the subroles relating to each other. In general, the more functional the nuclear family is, the greater will be the number of such subroles. Second, the importance of complementary needs as a mate-selective criterion appears to vary inversely with the functionality of the extended family.[22] It may be surmised that the relevance of complementary needs to marital stability is also inversely related to the functionality of both the nuclear and extended family forms. In other words, in societal contexts where the family—extended and/or nuclear—is highly functional, the resulting subroles are important; it should follow that the more important such subroles are, the less importance the culture will give to the idiosyncratic needs of the individual. In middle-class America, where the extended family appears to be relatively non-functional and where the functions of the nuclear family also tend toward the low end, love can exist as a criterion for mate-selection and its absence as a criterion for marital dissolution. Hence it is reasoned that complementariness of needs, as a basis for such love, tends to assume importance with respect to both

[20] Nathan Hurvitz, "The Components of Marital Roles," *Sociology and Social Research*, 1961, 45, 301–309.

[21] This set appears in *The Modern Family*, p. 664.

[22] *The Modern Family*, pp. 41–43 and 318–320.

mate-selection and marital stability in family systems of low functionality, whereas role compatibility tends to assume importance for both the selection and retention of mates in more functional family systems.

One final consideration not to be lost sight of is that with the passage of time very significant changes take place in roles and in gratifications and frustrations, and quite possibly in need-patterns. As we follow a couple from their period of engagement into early marriage with its concomitants of occupational demands for the man and domestic demands for the wife-mother into middle and later years when their offspring have been launched and the breadwinner retires, it is obvious that the roles are modified and energy-levels changed and aspirations modified.

SUMMARY

Twenty-five recently married young couples were examined by means of two lengthy interviews and a projective technique in order to provide a test of the theory of complementary needs in mate-selection. The data were interpreted as providing some support of the theory. Originally two dimensions of complementariness were induced from the data: nurturance-receptiveness and dominance-submissiveness. Subsequently a third has been proposed: achievement-vicariousness. A spate of non-replicative tests based on the PPS has provided no support for the theory; however, Kerckhoff and Davis' study based on Schutz's FIRO–B has shown a culturally homogenizing filtering process followed by mate-selection on the basis of complementary needs. Whether or not replication of the study of mate-selection would provide additional support of the theory remains an unanswered question.

In a study of roommates in a dormitory of nursing students Bermann has strongly suggested the advisability of adding the concept of role compatibility to that of need complementarity; he showed that the stability of pairs of roommates could be predicted better by using both concepts together than by using either singly.

17

THE MARITAL DYAD

There has been speculation that the husband and the wife fulfill totally distinct roles within the marital dyad. George Levinger points out that this is only half the story. He finds that task-related roles are indeed specialized but that within the marital dyad, social-emotional behavior requires mutuality rather than specialization. He concludes that there must be a minimum of three persons involved before there will be specialization in social-emotional roles.

In a paper not included in this book Donald Wolfe has presented a method for studying power and authority in the family. He found that wives who reported their husbands as dominant tended also to report high annual income and high social status. The highest levels of marital satisfaction were expressed by wives in marriages categorized as husband-dominant or as shared authority (syncratic). Wolfe also finds that wives become more dominant as their marriages persist. Levinger's article depicts the mutuality of socio-emotional relationships, Wolfe's essentially describes specialization in task behavior.[1]

Robert Blood addresses two time-honored questions of the sociology of the family: Do the structure and functions of the family differ in urban and rural settings? Has the urbanized family adapted successfully to the loss of its traditional functions? Blood's replies are respectively, "no, not now" and, "yes." Pointing to the great difficulty in studying the rural family of the past, Blood reveals that housewives in both the rural and urban settings of southern Michigan gave little emphasis to the functions of protection, economic production, and childbearing and relatively more to marital affection and companionship and to childrearing.

[1]Donald M. Wolfe, "Power and Authority in the Family," in Dorwin Cartwright ed., *Studies in Social Power*, Ann Arbor, Mich.: The Institute for Social Research, Univ. of Michigan, 1959, pp. 99–117.

Task and Social Behavior in Marriage*

George Levinger

The welfare of any human group depends on the fulfillment of two kinds of functions: the performance of tasks for coping with the objective environment and the maintenance of social relationships among the members.[1] From research on five-man problem solving groups, Bales and Slater[2] have concluded that these two kinds of functions tend to interfere with each other. The two functions seemed best carried on by different individuals in the group, referred to as the task and the social-emotional specialist.

Parsons[3] has drawn on that conclusion in writing about family interaction. He proposed that generally the "husband-father" role is that of task specialist, while the "wife-mother" role is that of social-emotional specialist. Zelditch[4] has tried to substantiate Parsons' generalization. In a review of anthropological essays and field reports, he noted that in the large majority of cultures husbands and wives adhere to a division of roles, in which husband copes mainly with the external environment and wife maintains the home.

This view of marital roles is supported by folk wisdom. For example, in Korea the husband is sometimes referred to as "outside master" and the wife as "inside master,"[5] a seeming acknowledgment of task versus social-emotional specialization. In our own culture, the poet Ogden Nash has noted with his typical irreverence that a husband and wife are incompatible, if ". . . he has no income and she isn't patible."

Nevertheless, Parsons' and Zelditch's broad generalization must be qualified. It appears largely correct for describing the roles of father and mother in the childbearing nuclear family, a multiperson group. Yet it does not apply as readily to the roles of husband and wife, considered purely in the context of the marriage relationship.

Consider the definitions of task and of social-emotional behavior. *Task behavior* refers to activity that involves ". . . the manipulation of the object-world . . . for the achievement of goals defined within the system."[6] Such behavior is not necessarily satisfying in itself, but is a means toward attaining a group goal. In principle, task behavior

---

*Adapted from Sociometry, 1964, 27: 433–448.

[1] John W. Thibaut and Harold H. Kelley, *The Social Psychology of Groups*, New York: Wiley, 1959, p. 274.

[2] Robert F. Bales and Philip E. Slater, "Role Differentiation in Small Decision-Making Groups," in Talcott Parsons and Robert F. Bales, editors, *Family, Socialization, and Interaction Process*, Glencoe, Ill.: Free Press, 1955.

[3] Talcott Parsons, "The American Family," in Parsons and Bales, *op. cit.*

[4] Morris Zelditch, Jr., "Role Differentiation in the Nuclear Family," in Parsons and Bales, *op. cit.*

[5] Cornelius Osgood, *The Koreans and Their Culture*, New York: Ronald, 1959, p. 48.

[6] Zelditch, *op. cit.*, p. 310.

can be performed by any subpart of the group, and even *can be delegated* to persons who are not formal members.

Social-emotional behavior, in contrast, is activity that maintains the relations between the members. Zelditch terms it ". . . the expression of affection . . . and a symbolization of common membership through supportive, accepting behavior."[7] The expression of negative feeling would also, of course, be considered social-emotional behavior with repercussions for group maintenance. Social-emotional behavior is ultimately reciprocal and therefore it *cannot be delegated* to persons outside the group. Thus, while task activity refers to a subject-object relation, social activity represents instead a subject-subject relation.

According to these definitions, task and social behavior differ in their potentiality for delegation. A group's task orientation encourages specialization in its division of labor,[8] particularly when there are many different tasks to be performed and when the members' relations are cooperative.[9] However, social-emotional behavior cannot be delegated in this way, except to the extent that two members' relations to a third party are nominally equivalent. If A's and B's bonds to C are equivalent, then B's maintenance of the social-emotional relation with C serves to strengthen A's and C's relation. In that sense, social-emotional

specialization does occur in groups of *three or more* persons such as in the child rearing family;[10] the wife's care of children would be considered a social-emotional function.

From the standpoint of the marriage group, however, child care and other aspects of a wife's "inside mastery" must be considered tasks. The two members of a pair may differ in their propensity for *initiating* overt social-emotional interaction, but over the long run the maintenance of a given level of interaction depends on the degree of reciprocation by the less demonstrative partner. Back to Ogden Nash: the importance of the wife's "patibility" derives from the assumption that the husband wants to pat. A marriage where only one partner engages in social-emotional actions breaks down in its *inter*action. The lower its reciprocity, the lower should be the total level of social-emotional behavior.

It is proposed, therefore, that in the marriage group *per se* both spouses are task specialists and neither spouse is a social-emotional specialist. Furthermore, it would seem that an American middle class husband need not differ substantially from his wife in his marital aspirations. The satisfactoriness of such marriages may depend as much on the husband's as on the wife's performance in the social-emotional realm.

METHOD

The sample consisted of sixty middle class couples, all of whom had children, had been married between four

---

[7] *Ibid.*, p. 311.

[8] This view is consistent with that of Durkheim. See Emile Durkheim, *The Division of Labor in Society,* translated edition, Glencoe, Ill.: Free Press, 1947.

[9] Deutsch has explained how a group's cooperative goal orientation enhances members' ability to take on specialized, nonoverlapping tasks. See Morton Deutsch, "A Theory of Cooperation and Competition," *Human Relations,* 2 (May, 1949), pp. 129–152.

[10] Even this more limited interpretation of the tendency toward social-emotional specialization has been criticized by Slater in his conceptual discussion of Parsons' approach to parental role differentiation. See Philip E. Slater, "Parental Role Differentiation," *American Journal of Sociology,* 67 (November, 1961), pp. 296–308.

and twenty-two years, and lived in the area of Greater Cleveland. The average couple was in the late thirties, had been married 13.6 years, had three children, and came from the upper part of Class III on Hollingshead's occupational-educational index.[11] Thirty-six couples were parents of children in an elementary school; the other 24 couples were clients at a family service agency, who were comparable in the above-mentioned social characteristics. This selection of the sample ensured a relatively broad variation in marital satisfaction and also enabled use of the agency counselors for providing independent validating judgments.

Each couple participated in a two- to three-hour long interview and performance session, in which husband and wife were seen first separately and later jointly. The respondents each gave information on the following matters. Each partner ranked the importance of certain marital goals, and described both spouses' real and ideal performance in the task and social-emotional areas of marriage. Questions about task performance covered ten representative duties such as doing dishes or repairs. Questions about social-emotional matters asked about each partner's supportiveness, the couple's frequency of communication, and the sexual relationship.

Indices of marital satisfaction were derived from questions about general happiness, from those about specific satisfaction areas, and from the discrepancies between statements about real versus ideal behavior.

A laboratory performance part of the session consisted of joint performance on four tests, of which a parallel form had previously been administered individually. The first two group tests required

subjects to discuss and rank the importance of two sets of goals; the third was a joint vocabulary test; and the fourth was the Color-Symbol Test, our own special group adaptation of the Wechsler-Bellevue Digit-Symbol Test.[12] The joint session was observed and tape recorded. Three observation indices of behavior were obtained, on which two judges arrived at agreement that exceeded 80 per cent. These indices described a couple's *activity level, acceptance* of the other's contributions, and *rejection* of his contributions.

Fifteen months after the first interview, 49 of the 60 couples completed an additional set of instruments, consisting primarily of personality tests.

RESULTS

Findings will be presented under two general headings: (1) specialization versus mutuality in husbands' and wives' task and social behavior; and (2) difference versus similarity in their marital goals, their needs, and their sources of marital satisfaction.

Specialization Versus Mutuality

It is accepted that husbands and wives differ in the kinds of family tasks that they generally perform. Thus Herbst[13] and Blood and Wolfe[14] have published findings on Australian and American samples, showing that husbands and wives each have special areas

11 August B. Hollingshead, "Two Factor Index of Social Position," New Haven, Conn., 1957 (dittoed).

12 David Wechsler, *The Measurement of Adult Intelligence*, third edition, Baltimore: Williams and Wilkins, 1944.

13 P. G. Herbst, "The Measurement of Family Relationships," *Human Relations*, 5 (February, 1952), pp. 3–35.

14 Robert O. Blood, Jr., and Donald M. Wolfe, *Husbands and Wives*, Glencoe, Ill.: Free Press, 1960.

TABLE 1 Equality and inequality between husbands' and wives' reported performance of task and social-emotional items (60 couples)

Items	Husbands' Reports		Wives' Reports	
	$H \neq W_a$	$H = W$	$H \neq W$	$H = W$
TASK PERFORMANCE: Who [how frequently do you]				
repairs things around the house?	59*	1	55*	5
does the evening dishes?	53*	7	56*	4
pays the monthly bills?	53*	7	54*	6
keeps in touch with relatives?	51*	9	51*	9
does the grocery shopping?	50*	10	51*	9
puts out the trash?	48*	12	49*	11
gets information about insurance, talks to insurance agents?	39**	21	49*	11
makes complaints . . . to salesmen, workmen, landlord?	41*	19	45*	15
gets information before you buy big items . . . ?	30	30	35	25
gets ideas and information about . . . vacation?	32	28	27	33
SOCIAL-EMOTIONAL PERFORMANCE: [How often] do you [does spouse] . . .				
talk about feelings with [other] when . . . bothered or upset?	36	24	40**	20
when there is a difference of opinion, make a great effort to see [other's] point of view?	34	26	36	24
ask [other] about what [other] has done during the day?	33	27	32	28
tell [other] about the things [done] during the day?	29	31	33	27
praise [other] when [other] has done something [you like]?	32	28	27	33
kiss [other] when [you, husband] leave for or return from work?	12	48*	6	54*

$_a$ H $\neq$ W columns indicate number of reports that spouses perform a given activity to a different degree; H = W columns show number of reports that the activity is performed equally often by both partners.

* P < .01, by binominal test for N = 60.

** P < .05.

of both performance and decision-making. For example, the husband is generally more likely to do and decide about house repairs, while the wife is more prone to care for and decide about child care and family health. Furthermore, Blood and Wolfe reported that on eight representative 'inside' and 'outside' household tasks, there is only a small percentage of equality in performance. Their sample of 731 Detroit households showed a high degree of "role specialization" on these tasks, with either husband or wife taking greater responsibility on any single task.

Our own findings are similar. Table 1 shows that on eight of the ten family tasks covered in our interview schedule there was significant specialization. On all of the tasks, except getting information about "buying big items" or about "what to do on vacation," it was reported that one spouse took predominant responsibility. The two exceptions, which covered topics not dealt with in previous studies, do not deal with routinized household matters.

On the other hand, in the social-emotional realm, Table 1 shows considerably less contrast between the husband's and wife's activity. There is significantly more inequality on only one of the six items—i.e., "talking about one's feelings with [spouse] when one is bothered or upset;" here the wife was usually seen as the more vocal partner. On the remaining five items, there was as much or more mutuality in the spouses' reported behavior as there was specialization.

Table 1 showed the comparison of $H = W$ with $H \neq W$ frequencies within each of the sixteen relevant items. A different analysis would compare the percentages of task and social-emotional $H = W$ items for each single respondent.[15] Would such a procedure yield a similar result?

The results clearly support the present thesis. Forty-nine of the sixty husbands showed a larger percentage of $H = W$ items on the social than on the task set; similarly, 53 of 60 wives reported greater equality on the social-emotional items. By sign test, these results show a task-social difference significant at far beyond the .001 level.

The most convincing evidence in support of the present thesis is drawn from an item-by-item correlational analysis. This analysis is based on the assumption that specialization would be indicated by *negative* correlations between husband's and wife's performance, while mutuality would be shown by *positive* correlations. Table 2 shows that, indeed, all task items had negative correlations[16] and all social-emotional items had positive correlations.

15 This procedure was suggested by an anonymous reviewer.

16 In the original study, the form of the task questions precluded the present correlational analysis. Respondents had given only one response to describe both husband's and wife's task activity. For that reason, it became necessary to readminister the questionnaire about task performance, using the same

While all correlations in Table 2 were in the predicted direction, some were very high and others were near zero. To begin with, the correlations between two independent ratings ($H_w \times W_b$) were almost uniformly lower than those between ratings by the same judge. Obviously, two spouses' ratings within any pair often differed. The independent ratings constitute the most valid test of the hypothesis, but one should not disregard the strong support from the non-independent ratings in the last two columns of Table 2. The latter correlations indicate that the research participants perceived that tasks tend to be specialized while social maintenance is a mutual matter.

It seems meaningful that some items, such as making repairs or getting insurance information, produced very high negative correlations; one partner's activity on such items almost precludes the other's activity. Other items, such as doing the dishes or making complaints, do not represent mutually exclusive behavior; it is feasible either to do dishes jointly or to delegate the function almost entirely, and it is possible that neither or both partners may voice their complaints to outside agencies. In the social-emotional realm, "asking the spouse about his daily activities" showed the lowest positive correlation, while kissing behavior showed the highest one, once again a reflection of common sense.

Two other sources of data are pertinent. The spouses' interaction, as observed in the laboratory session, also showed a positive correlation between husband's and wife's social-emotional behavior: (a) acceptance of each other's

question-answer format as employed on the social-emotional items—with husband's and wife's activity described separately. Of the original 60 couples, 37 pairs completed the new form.

TABLE 2 Correlations between husband's and wife's reported performance on task and social-emotional items

Items	Correlations		
	$H_w \times W_b$[a]	$H_h \times H_w$[b]	$W_w \times W_h$[c]
Task Performance.[d] [How often] do you [does spouse]...			
repair things around the house?	−.46	−.91	−.71
do the evening dishes?	−.02	−.30	−.10
pay the monthly bills?	−.92	−.98	−.98
keep in touch with relatives?	−.45	−.56	−.66
do the grocery shopping?	−.73	−.87	−.74
put out the trash?	−.30	−.50	−.61
get information about insurance, talk to insurance agents?	−.69	−.80	−.90
make complaints . . . to salesmen, workmen, landlord?	−.19	−.46	−.65
get information before you buy big items . . . ?	−.29	−.29	−.33
get ideas and information about . . . vacation?	−.32	−.56	−.47
Social-Emotional Performance.[e] [How often] do you [does spouse] . . .			
talk about feelings with [other] when . . . bothered or upset?	.24	.30	.35
when there is a difference of opinion, make a great effort to see [other's] point of view?	.21	.28	.37
ask [other] about what [other] has done during the day?	.01	.53	.37
tell [other] about the things [done] during the day?	.19	.40	.27
praise [other] when [other] has done something [you like]?	.25	.31	.68
kiss [other] when [you, husband] leave for or return from work?	.48	.86	.91

[a] $H_w \times W_h$ refers to husband's rating of wife's performance as correlated with the wife's rating of husband's performance. This is the only correlation between independent ratings.
[b] $H_h \times H_w$: Husband's rating of own performance related to his rating of wife's performance.
[c] $W_w \times W_h$: Wife's rating of own performance related to her rating of husband's performance.
[d] N = 37. In order to compute correlations for the task items, the sample of respondents had be recontacted. All task items were reworded to correspond to the format of social-emotional items.
[e] N = 60.

contributions, r = .12, p = n.s.; (b) rejection of each other's contributions, r = .31, p < .02. Incidentally, the reported social-emotional behavior from the interview correlated .15 with spouses' observed acceptance of each other and −.24 with their observed rejection during the laboratory session.

Additional validating evidence in favor of the social-emotional index came from the Agency caseworkers' ratings. Considering their sub-sample of 24 couples, the caseworkers' ratings of supportiveness correlated positively with the interview index: for husbands, r = .33, for wives, r = .42.[17]

These findings, then, confirm the proposition that while task-oriented behavior in marriage tends to be specialized, social-supportive activity en-

[17] Ratings by Agency caseworkers also showed a strong positive correlation between their perceptions of husband's and wife's social supportiveness in the 24 Agency couples: r = .59, p < .01. This finding supports the present interpretation, but has limited validity due to the non-independence of the ratings.

courages reciprocation. In the latter area, two spouses within the same marriage tend to be more similar than husbands or wives across different marriages.

Difference Versus Similarity

Husbands and wives in this study do not differ as widely in the social-emotional contribution to marriage as one might have believed. In part, this conclusion derives from our limited definition of social-emotional behavior. It leads one to ask, though, whether husbands and wives *necessarily* differ in other aspects of their social-emotional relationship. How different or similar are they in their marital goals, their needs, or their satisfactions?

SIMILARITY IN MARRIAGE GOALS

Some experts in marriage research[18] claim that American marriage has become predominantly concerned with companionship. If that claim is correct, it would suggest that men and women are equally concerned with primarily social-emotional goals. On the other hand, a study by Farber[19] has reported that wives attached significantly higher importance than did husbands to social-emotional as opposed to task-oriented goals.

In our own study, each respondent ranked a set of nine general marital goals adapted from Farber's set, ordering them according to their importance for achieving a good marriage. The nine goals are shown in Table 3. Two are pri-

marily social-emotional—Affection and Companionship—and four are mainly task-oriented—Economic Security, an Attractive Home, Wise Financial Planning, and a respected Place in the Community.

Table 3 indicates that there was no difference between husbands' and wives' ranking of Affection and Companionship. These two goals were ranked at the top, the other four goals near the bottom of the order. Nor was there any difference between the husband and wife groups in their mean ratio of ranks for social versus task goals (t = .43, n.s.). On rankings of single goals, the only significant differences occurred on Economic Security (H > W, p < .01) and Religion (H < W, p < .05).

Why are these results unlike Farber's? One explanation might be that the two lists of marital goals are somewhat different; another, that the present definition of "social-emotional" goals is more restricted than Farber's. Both these variations seem of minor import.

A more convincing explanation is that social class differences account for the discrepancy. Despite the relatively high social class homogeneity of the present sample, the class index and the ratio of social-emotional versus task-oriented preferences correlated negatively for the husbands (r = −.23) and positively for the wives (r = .27). Thus husbands and wives at the upper end of the class continuum showed the smallest difference between their ranks. And it turns out that Farber's sample, in which husband-wife rankings differed more, was drawn on the average from a social class stratum somewhat lower than the present sample.[20]

[18] Ernest W. Burgess and Harvey J. Locke, *The Family: From Institution to Companionship*, New York: American Book Co., 1953.

[19] Bernard Farber, "An Index of Marital Integration," *Sociometry*, 20 (June, 1957), pp. 117–134.

[20] This inference is based on Farber's description of his sample in another paper, from which it appears that his respondents were significantly lower than ours in both education and income. Bernard Farber, *Ef-*

TABLE 3   Relative importance of nine marriage goals as ranked by sixty couples

Goals in Marriage [a]	Mean Ranks [b]		
	COUPLES	HUSBANDS [c]	WIVES
Affection. Having family members satisfied with the amount of love they give to each other.	1	3	1
Companionship. Having family members enjoy doing things together and feel comfortable with each other.	2	1	3
Happy children. Helping the children to become well-adjusted and to enjoy their lives.	3	2	2
Personal development. Giving each family member the opportunity to develop as an individual.	4	4	4
Religion. Living according to religious principles and teaching.	5	6	5
Economic security. Keeping up or improving the family's standard of living.	6	5	8
Attractive home. Having a place which is comfortable and attractive to live in.	7	7	6
Wise financial planning. Making sound decisions in budgeting for present and future purchases, and making intelligent use of money.	8	8	7
A *place in the community.* Giving family members a respected place in the community.	9	9	9

[a] The goals, which were presented in a different order to the subjects, were introduced somewhat as follows: ". . . . Indicate which of these goals is most important to you, . . . second, . . . third, . . . and so on . . ."

[b] The numerals show the mean rank for each goal for each group. On the average, therefore, Affection was seen as first in importance by both the couples and the wives, and third by the husbands.

[c] Rho between husbands' and wives' mean ranks was .83.

* $P < .05$ (sign test), wives' ranks were higher than husbands'.

** $P < .01$ (sign test), husbands' ranks were higher than wives'.

It appears therefore that companionship marriage is more a reflection of middle or upper-middle than of lower class position. Evidence from Blood and Wolfe sustains that interpretation: they found that "mean intensity of companionship" was highest for high-status white collar husbands and lowest for low-status blue collar husbands.[21] The more a couple is assured of economic security and occupational stability, the more likely it is that the husband will share the wife's concern with social-emotional matters.

---

fects of a Severely Mentally Retarded Child on Family Integration, Lafayette, Ind.: Society for Research in Child Development, 1959.

[21] Blood and Wolfe, *op. cit.,* p. 168, Table 79.

SOCIAL-EMOTIONAL NEEDS

Another set of findings pertains to the partners' descriptions of their manifest personal "needs." During a follow-up visit 15 months after the first study, 49 of the initial 60 couples completed questionnaires concerning the relative strength of various needs. Data were collected on two forms: a 144–item condensation of the Edwards Personal Preference Schedule,[22] measuring the strength of twelve general needs; and a parallel form of this Schedule, in which Edwards' items for most needs were rewritten to refer specifically to the

[22] Allen L. Edwards, *Manual for the Edwards Personal Preference Schedule,* New York: Psychological Corporation, 1954.

TABLE 4 Differences between husbands' and wives' social-emotional needs in general and in marital environment (49 couples)

Need Name	General Test Form			Marital Test Form		
	HUSBANDS' MEAN	WIVES' MEAN	t[b]H-w	HUSBANDS' MEAN	WIVES' MEAN	t[b]H-w
nAutonomy	11.67	9.87	2.19**	6.77	6.34	.56
nNurturance	10.32	12.24	2.57***	14.67	14.06	.72
nSuccorance	6.30	8.87	2.73****	13.59	14.91	1.50
nAffiliation	13.38	14.75	1.85*	—	—	—
nInterdependence [a]	—	—	—	16.97	16.85	.17

[a] Edwards' original items for nAffiliation had to be entirely rewritten for the Marital Form, since completely parallel construction was inappropriate. The resulting items were labeled Need for Interdependence.

[b] Two-tailed t-test with 96 df, comparing husbands' and wives' mean scores.

* $P < .07$.   ** $P < .04$ *** $P < .02$.   **** $P < .01$.

marital partner as the reference object.[23]

Four of Edwards' needs pertain to the social-emotional area: the needs for Autonomy, for Affiliation, for Nurturance, and for Succorance. Table 4 shows that on all four of these needs there were significant differences between the mean scores of husbands and wives on the *general* form of the schedule. Husbands scored higher than wives on their preference for Autonomy, and lower on their needs for Affiliation, Nurturance, and Succorance. On the *marital* schedule, however, these differences disappeared. In describing their need preferences in marriage, both partners showed markedly lower desire for autonomy, and acknowledged a far higher desire for interdependence, for giving nurturance to, and for receiving succor from the spouse. It appears that these latter needs are conventionally suppressed in the general environment, particularly by men; in marriage, though, these needs are given preference by *both* partners over other more achievement-oriented desires.

[23] These revisions of the EPPS were made by Barbara Allan in connection with research on her doctoral dissertation. The findings were obtained as part of the larger research program.

Would other samples of married partners show the same tendency? Until that is known, these findings support the assumption that marriage legitimizes the expression and gratification of needs that are inhibited in the general environment.

MARITAL SATISFACTION

The findings on marital goals and needs suggest that these husbands and wives would place a considerably higher value on social-emotional than on task satisfactions in their marriage, and also that husbands and wives would be relatively similar in their profiles.

This study emphasized the collection of diverse indices of marital satisfaction. Measures ranged from two indices of global happiness, to ratings of single areas of the marriage, to differences between a partner's reported real and ideal behavior. On the basis of fifteen such indices of satisfaction, two separate factor analyses were conducted for the husband and wife samples.

The present discussion will consider only the first factor extracted from the correlation matrix, which accounted for much more variance than other factors

TABLE 5 Principal factors in husbands' and wives' marital satisfaction (60 couples)

INDICES OF MARITAL SATISFACTION	Husband Factors						Wife Factors					
	I	II	III	IV	V	h²	I	II	III	IV	V	h²
Task satisfaction												
1. Couple's division of labor	-02	-02	54	-12	-09	32	21	12	-14	-13	38	24
2. Couple's decision-making balance	20	04	25	14	-57	44	-02	-42	-27	04	13	27
3. Husband's work	29	12	-01	39	13	27	20	11	43	-07	-04	24
4. Wife's work	49	06	59	26	-05	66	41	07	59	18	16	58
Social-emotional satisfaction												
5. Use of leisure	55	25	10	47	-18	63	34	13	18	35	44	47
6. Affection	55	58	32	-06	11	75	66	30	10	06	16	57
7. Communication frequency	42	03	-10	-17	-37	36	64	08	14	15	57	56
8. Husband's social-emotional role	53	23	08	-28	-04	42	56	76	03	03	24	62
9. Wife's social-emotional role	63	44	-11	-19	-39	77	40	58	03	02	-04	63
Sexual satisfaction												
10. General sexual relationship	27	80	13	14	04	76	07	-04	-07	63	11	40
11. Husband's desired frequency	10	72	-28	-03	-19	65	-11	07	05	38	-17	20
12. Wife's desired frequency	-06	03	47	09	13	25	12	-02	-53	19	-03	33
General satisfaction												
13. Achievement of nine marital goals	72	14	24	09	-17	63	48	13	33	43	21	58
14. Estimate of spouse's happiness	90	15	13	10	-03	87	91	14	08	07	04	86
15. Global happiness	89	18	-04	04	-06	83	93	14	-02	-09	-14	92
Percentage of variance	28	13	8	5	4	—	24	8	7	7	6	—

Decimal points are omitted for factor loadings and communalities. All values are rounded to two significant digits. Principal axes solution with varimax rotation. The program was provided by Dr. James Lingoes of the University of Michigan.

(see Table 5). For both husbands and wives, Factor I represented general marital satisfaction. Factor I showed high similarity between husband and wife samples; Kaiser's coefficient of factor similarity was .96.[24] For both spouses, Factor I was loaded more highly with social-emotional than with task adjustment variables. Satisfaction with either the husband's work or with the couple's division of tasks and decisions was related very little to either spouse's general happiness. In contrast, feelings about affection, use of leisure time, and each other's social supportiveness were rather highly related with general happiness. For husbands, sexual satisfaction was more related to general satisfaction, while for wives, marital communication was of greater importance.

Many of the correlations used in the factor analysis are highly reliable, but the reliability of the factor structure is more suggestive than definitive. One would therefore turn to other studies for corroboration of these factors. Tharp's[25] recent factor-analytic study of marriage roles, based on Kelly's[26] extensive survey of married couples, provides perhaps the best comparative information. Tharp found that for both husbands and wives the factor of Intimacy accounted for the largest amount of variance in describing both the *expected* and the *enacted* marriage roles. This factor comes closest to what has here been defined as social-emotional behavior, although under that rubric Tharp found additional factors which he labeled Socio-Emotional Integration and Understanding. Incidentally, Tharp's men and women differed as regards sexual and communicative relations in a way that parallels our subjects; for his husbands, the Intimacy factor was more highly loaded with sexual pleasure than for the wives, who associated Intimacy relatively more with adequacy of understanding.

DIFFERENCES BETWEEN HIGH AND LOW SATISFIED COUPLES

One other set of findings shows that marital satisfaction was related far more to social than to task performance. A comparison was made between two groups of fifteen couples, selected from the high and low extremes of the satisfaction continuum.[27] This comparison showed almost no significant differences in task performance, but many differences in social-emotional relations. The *high* satisfied couples reported significantly more socially supportive activity[28] and, in the laboratory, showed less rejecting behavior than the *lows*.[29] The *highs* also reported a higher frequency of marital communication;[30] specifically, *highs*

[24] Appreciation is acknowledged to Dr. James Lingoes of the University of Michigan for providing the appropriate computer program. The program was based on a dittoed paper by Henry F. Kaiser, "Relating Factors between Studies Based upon Different Individuals," Bureau of Educational Research, University of Illinois, July, 1960.

[25] Roland G. Tharp, "Dimensions of Marriage Roles," *Marriage and Family Living*, 25 (November, 1963), pp. 389–404.

[26] E. Lowell Kelly, "Consistency of the Adult Personality," *American Psychologist*, 10 (November, 1955), pp. 659–681.

[27] The High group consisted of the fifteen couples from the School sample who had the highest factor score on Factor I of Marital Satisfaction; the Low group were those fifteen Agency couples with the lowest marital satisfaction factor scores.

[28] Both spouses in the High group reported significantly greater positive social-emotional performance by the other partner than did spouses in the Low group: husbands, $t = 2.97$, $p < .01$; wives, $t = 4.07$, $p < .001$.

[29] $t = 2.43$, $p < .03$.

[30] $t = 2.47$, $p < .02$.

talked with each other more on nine of eleven standard topics, the only exceptions being the discussion of unpleasant feelings and of money matters.

In the task area, though, the only significant difference between the *high* and *low* satisfied couples concerned the husbands' reports of their own decision influence. *Low* husbands reported their influence to be lower than did the *high* husbands, but the *high* and *low* wives' reports did not corroborate this.[31] Also, there was no clear difference between the *high* and *low* groups in the dominance pattern they displayed during the laboratory session.

Consider one last finding, which occurred during the laboratory session. Contrary to the writer's original hypothesis, the *high* and *low* satisfied groups showed no difference in their joint performance on the two specially designed objective tests: the Vocabulary and the Color-Symbol test. In terms of a ratio of the couple's joint score to the previous average individual score, the *highs* worked together no better than did the *lows*. However, the *highs* tended to exceed the *lows* in their *expected* joint performance when they were asked to predict the couple's score before the first joint trial on the Color-Symbol Test.[32] This laboratory finding is quite important: it shows that test performance did not, in fact, co-vary with the subjects' mutual feelings. The result adds support to the belief that these couples' marital satisfaction was associated less with their objective task performance than with their subjective evaluation of their relationship.[33]

DISCUSSION

What does one conclude from these diverse findings? They suggest that social-emotional performance is the essence of the marital relationship as seen by both spouses in these American middle class marriages, and further that it is a mutual rather than a specialized matter. This interpretation does not conflict with the probability that the average wife *indicates* more than half of the socially supportive interaction. In fact, other findings from our research program suggest that the wife's perceived social-emotional role may be a more important indicator of marital cohesiveness than is the husband's.[34] Yet it is clear that a simple dichotomy of task versus social-emotional specialization in marriage receives neither logical nor empirical verification.

Several matters deserve further comment. These include a caution about limitations and some conclusions about task and social roles in groups of varying size.

With respect to limitations, the study was confined to sixty married couples, selected from the general population through their willingness to participate together in research on family life. The sample consisted predominantly of urban, white, American, middle class spouses, in the second decade of their marriage, and with young children in the home. It is possible that such couples would show greater value- and need-

---

[31] For husbands' reports, $t = 1.92$, $p < .06$; for wives', $t = .04$, n.s.

[32] $t = 1.72$, $p < .10$.

[33] These results are limited, of course, to the particular tests used in our present setting. One should note O'Rourke's recent conclu-

sion that the nature of the interaction situation—both in field and in laboratory—has a determinate effect on interaction patterns. John F. O'Rourke, "Field and Laboratory: The Decision-Making Behavior of Family Groups in Two Experimental Situations," *Sociometry*, 26 (December, 1963), pp. 422–435.

[34] George Levinger, "Instrumental and Expressive Functions in Marriage," Working Paper #1, January, 1963 (mimeographed).

similarity than that found in the average pair. The peculiarities of our present sample can only be estimated through future parallel research. However, our findings do not depart radically from those of other studies cited earlier. [35]

The findings that show the mutuality of social-emotional behavior have implications for the understanding both of family groups and of other kinds of groups. Concerning marriage, doubt is cast on the stereotype that the wife is principally interested in social-emotional relations while the husband forages merely for the material things in life. If the husband is indeed emotionally absent, the wife's ability to sustain social-emotional relations in the marriage is clearly limited. As mother, she can play a social role regardless of the husband's actions; as wife, she cannot. [36]

This research also leads one to reconsider task and social behavior in non-family groups. Assuming that Bales' hypothesis of task versus social role specialization in problem solving groups is correct, it would need to be qualified by the effects of group size. According to our present reasoning, social-emotional specialization approaches zero when group size is reduced to two persons. In a group of two partners, unilateral social-emotional behavior has little function for group maintenance—although it may be important for the initiator himself. Thus, either expressing one's feelings or telling a joke has a social maintenance function only when the other party reciprocates in some way.

The act of quiet listening to the initiator is one such form of reciprocation. However, listening behavior is difficult to observe and to operationalize, and it has not been included in existing systems of social observation. Furthermore, Bales' own observation system defines "social-emotional" to include actions which are task-oriented agreement or disagreement. [37] For these two reasons, Bales and Borgatta's interaction profiles [38] comparing two-person and larger groups do not offer an adequate test of our present assertion. The proposition that social-emotional specialization is absent in two-person groups requires new data for its general verification. [39]

[35] Blood and Wolfe, op. cit.; Farber, op. cit.; Tharp, op. cit.

[36] A similar observation has recently been made by Leik. He noted that in the male-female dyad ". . . the standard role differentiation is more a consequence of interaction outside the dyad" than within the pairwise interaction. Robert K. Leik, "Instrumentality and Emotionality in Family Interaction," Sociometry, 26 (June, 1963), pp. 131–145 (p. 132, italics are Leik's).

[37] Robert F. Bales, Interaction Process Analysis, Cambridge, Mass.: Addison-Wesley, 1950.

[38] Robert F. Bales and Edgar F. Borgatta, "Size of Group as a Factor in the Interaction Profile," in A. Paul Hare, Edgar Borgatta, and Robert F. Bales, editors, Small Groups, New York: Knopf, 1955.

[39] A recent review of studies on group size does not indicate any other empirical research on this issue. See Edwin J. Thomas and Clinton F. Fink, "Effects of Group Size," Psychological Bulletin, 60 (July, 1963), pp. 371–384.

Impact of Urbanization on American Family Structure and Functioning*

Robert O. Blood, Jr.

In the "good old days," most American families lived on farms, remote and isolated. Pioneer family members clung together with a desperation born of economic necessity. They depended on one another for most essential services. Survival required the cooperation of the entire household. The rudimentary nature of other social institutions imposed religious, political, and educational responsibilities on the family. Divorce was unthinkable, since neither man nor woman could afford to lose the services of the other. Childlessness or even limited childbearing was a hardship to be endured with regret.

The compulsory nature of family life on the frontier is indisputable. The controversial question is whether such family life was not only compulsory but "golden." To many Americans the past has a lustre which the present lacks. Pioneer families seem in retrospect to have found unique satisfaction in working and playing together. Family life then was rewarding and satisfying, vital, and meaningful. By contrast, modern family life seems brittle, tenuous, and often meaningless.

Is this picture true? Unfortunately it is impossible for the methods of social science to be used to measure the family life of the past. However, it is possible to examine contemporary rural and urban

families to see whether the "golden past" still survives on the modern farm and whether urban family life is obsolescent. If contemporary rural and urban families do not differ greatly from one another and if urban families have a stable structure and perform vital functions for their members, then the past may not have been so golden, and the present not so tarnished.

URBANIZATION OF THE AMERICAN FARM FAMILY

A total of 178 farm wives were interviewed in southeastern Michigan (a random sample of three counties extending west of Detroit). The information they provided is fundamentally similar to that derived from the Detroit Area Study. For instance, the city and farm families are equally democratic in their patterns of making family decisions. When the urban families are arbitrarily divided into husband and wife dominated segments of equal size, the farm families have an equally large proportion of equalitarian cases.

The chief way in which these farm and city couples differ is in their division of labor. As tradition suggests, farm wives are more involved than city wives in practical tasks. Farm women engage in such outside tasks as raising poultry and vegetables. They also get less help in the home from their busy husbands. Since city wives are geographi-

*Adapted from Sociology and Social Research, 1964, 49: 5–16.

cally separated from the husband's place of work, they can't assist him directly. Similarly, the fact that the commuter leaves his work behind when he comes home makes him more available to help with household tasks.[1]

Does this greater service of farm wives mean that rural families are better than city families? That depends on the criterion for what is better. If the criterion is divorce rates, farm families score somewhat better. But if it is the wife's satisfaction with her marriage partner, the rural advantage largely disappears. In these samples, farm wives are slightly more satisfied ˴with their standard of living and the husband's understanding, less satisfied with the love and affection received and equally satisfied with the companionship. Since in the American scheme of values, companionship is the crucial test of marriage, the overall evaluation of family life by rural and urban wives is essentially the same.

This brief comparison of contemporary city and farm families suggests that in most respects their family patterns are similar. It gives no conclusive answer to the question whether farm family living in the past was more "golden" than in the present. But it does suggest that city and farm families shine with essentially the same hue today.

Contemporary farm families have become urbanized, at least in Southern Michigan. They read the same newspapers, listen to the same radio broadcasts, and watch the same telecasts as their urban counterparts. Their children attend consolidated schools in urban centers. Their cars and all-weather roads give them access to the city where they participate in community activities. Modern farming has become a business which happens to be located in the country and differs little from urban family businesses in its effect on family life. Viewed in the large, city families and farm families have more common characteristics than differences, for today the metropolitan community and its hinterland are a single social unit.

VITALITY OF THE MODERN AMERICAN FAMILY

If farm families resemble city families, perhaps that only proves that they, too, are decadent. Perhaps all American families and not just urban ones have disintegrated. It is not enough to compare city and farm families relative to one another. Some assessment of the actual level of functioning of contemporary families must be made. For the sake of simplicity, this assessment will focus on urban families, but in almost every case, the same findings characterize the farm families studied.

The vitality of family life can be looked at from two points of view. First, how sound is the structure of American family life? Secondly, how effectively do these families carry out their functions?[2]

STABILITY OF MODERN FAMILY STRUCTURE

The structure of a family consists of the configuration of positions which

___

[1] See Robert O. Blood, Jr., "The Division of Labor in City and Farm Families," *Marriage and Family Living*, 20 (May, 1958), 170–74.

[2] For a complete report and analysis of the Detroit Area Study data on marriage, see Robert O. Blood, Jr., and Donald M. Wolfe, *Husbands and Wives: The Dynamics of Family Living* (New York: The Free Press of Glencoe, 1960.)

the family members occupy. This paper is concerned with the positions which the husband and wife occupy in relation to one another. These positions (or statuses) and the roles attached to them may be analyzed in terms of the power structure and the division of labor in the family.

For present purposes, it is not enough to describe these structural characteristics since no evidence is available that one structure is inherently more stable than another. Rather, the question must be raised as to the basis for contemporary structural forms. Are they based on outmoded conventions undermined by changing times? Or, do they vary randomly with no rhyme nor reason, reflecting chaotic or meaningless social conditions? If, by contrast, family structures are determined by factors which produce efficient results, it may be assumed that they will be stable over a period of time. Efficient social structures create their own rewards, leading the participants to be satisfied with them rather than to wish for change.

An efficient power structure may be defined as one which produces "right" decisions. In the past, husbands were considered the best qualified to make decisions by virtue of being men. However, the improved status of American women has increased their contribution to the decision-making process. Some alarmists suggest that the American wife has already seized domestic power, not necessarily by wresting it from her husband but at least through his abdication of authority.

The Detroit data fail to disclose an American matriarchate. Rather, the general mode of decision-making is equalitarian. Around this mode, however, there are significant variations. In some marriages the wife is more dominant while in others the husband dominates.

What is the basis for these variations? Concrete factors which affect the power structure can be summarized under the heading of "competence." Whichever partner has the greater ability to make a decision usually does so. Sometimes competence results from the individual's experience in a certain activity. For example, husbands generally choose their own job and purchase cars whereas wives make decisions about food purchases. However, the crucial question is not the competences husbands generally share but rather the variations which occur between couples.

Table 1 provides one example of a source of competence affecting marital power structure. In this case, the resource is the time the husband and wife work outside the home. Taken by itself this might not suggest individual competence so much as an economic interpretation of marriage. However, other data show that unpaid participation in the community has a similar relationship to family power structure. For example, whichever partner attends church more often and whichever partner belongs to more organizations tends to make more of the family decisions. Taken together this suggests that participation in activities outside the home provides social experience and knowledge which carry over into marital decision-making. Even more directly reflecting personal competence is the evidence that whichever partner has more education makes more decisions.

If family decisions are made by the best qualified partner, family power structures are geared to the most efficient accomplishment of their objective. Apparently, therefore, these power structures are basically stable and unlikely to be a source of complaint or unrest.

An efficient division of labor gets tasks done with the least effort. This is

TABLE I Husband's power by comparative work participation of husband and wife

	Wife not Employed			Wife Employed		
	HUSBAND OVERTIME	HUSBAND FULLTIME	HUSBAND NONE	HUSBAND OVERTIME	HUSBAND FULLTIME	HUSBAND NONE
Husband's mean power score	5.62	5.28	4.88	4.50	4.46	2.67
Number of families*	195	218	25	44	57	3

* White families only

precisely the pattern which Detroit families follow. In general, the division follows traditional sex lines, with women doing most of the housework and men concentrating on technical repairs and outside work. The fact that these are traditional sex roles does not mean that they are inefficient. Women's tasks are naturally associated with childbearing and child-rearing and men's with muscular strength and mechanical aptitude.

In Detroit, the division of labor at home is drastically affected by the out-of-the-home work schedules of both husband and wife. Housework is primarily the province of the wife, but when she works outside the home, the time left for housework is severely limited. Under these circumstances, the husband tends to come to her rescue, unless he is preoccupied with responsibilities of his own.

It has already been suggested that farm wives do more housework and get correspondingly less help from their husbands because the latter's chores are readily accessible at all hours of the day and every day of the week. Since farmers are seldom far from exterior tasks needing their efforts, they tend to be perennially busy and unable to help around the house.

Although household tasks are generally done by whichever partner has the most time, tasks requiring special skill are less easily interchanged. In Detroit, a task closely linked to personal competence is keeping track of the money

and bills. In some families, the wife "has the head for figures," while in others the husband is the better bookkeeper. In general, whichever partner has more education handles this responsibility, but in the higher income brackets this task is increasingly performed by the husband. Presumably as income exceeds the subsistence level, it is less limited to the wife's usual provinces of consumption and increasingly available for saving, investment, and tax options familiar to the husband from his business experience.

In general, then, the division of labor, like the power structure, is so organized as to accomplish the family's objectives. Hence the modern family's structure is usually stable, no matter what its form.

QUALITY OF MODERN FAMILY SERVICES

What about the functions performed by the urban family? They have changed drastically. Old functions have dwindled with the rise of specialized institutions. Protective functions are shared with the police and the army, religious functions with church and Sunday School, educational functions with the school, and recreational functions with the cinema. The once crucial function of home production has shriveled to vestigial proportions in Detroit. Food growing and processing are minority experiences in the metropolitan area, the former because of the unavailability of garden space, the latter because of the ready availability of processed foods at the corner store. Dressmaking has been taken over by the factory, and even the baking company is superseding the housewife in her kitchen. One sixth of our Detroit housewives report that they purchase all their bread and most of their cakes, cookies, and pies, while an additional 7 per cent confess that they never bake at all.

At the same time that economic production has nearly vanished from the urban home, the production of children has dwindled, too. To some extent this results from the children's transformation from useful "hands" into dregs on the family labor market. Partly, however, the decreased number of children born has been offset by the increasing proportion who survive to maturity. Under pioneer conditions, the average family lost at least one child through sickness. Today childhood fatalities are so rare that childbearing can be reduced accordingly.

The emphasis with respect to children has shifted from childbearing to child-rearing, from the quantity of children produced to the quality of children raised. While the emphasis on quality began in the middle class, it is spreading to the masses. As a result of the growing homogenization of parental aspirations for children and of the filtering down of family planning practices to the working class, families at all levels of society are beginning to gear their birthrate to their "ability to pay." For the first time in American history, couples predict that those with greater resources will have more children. (see Table II)

People in other countries often wonder what the American wife does with the leisure time provided by her labor-saving devices. One of the important answers is that she spends more time on her children's social development. Whereas she used to be preoccupied with subsistence tasks, today she can focus on her children's personality problems and achievements.

This shift has occurred with respect to parents, too. Whereas the economic and biological functions of the family once monopolized the attention of the parents, today there is time left over for each other's subtler needs. As a result, new functions emerge.

When our Detroit wives were asked to rank several new functions in comparison with the traditional economic and child bearing ones, the shifting pattern of functions appeared. Asked which of five functions they considered "the most valuable part of marriage," they most often chose "companionship in doing things together with the husband" (47 per cent). "The chance to have children" was a poor second at 26 per cent, leaving 13 per cent who chose "the husband's understanding of the wife's problems and feelings," 10 per cent for "the husband's expression of love and affection," and only 3 per cent for "the standard of living" provided by the husband's income. Exactly how many functions the family performs depends on one's analytic framework but in the light of these statistics there can be no question of the emerging significance of several new ones.

Whereas traditional family functions were directed toward the welfare of the children or of the family as a whole, the new functions focus on the husband-wife relationship. Perhaps for the first time in history, the marriage bond has become important in its own right, even after children arrive. This reflects the emergence of a whole new stage in family living after the departure of the last child from the home.[3] Whereas a

[3]See Paul C. Glick, "The Life Cycle of

TABLE II   Expected number of children by wife's education for wives under age 45

	Years of Education		
	GRADE SCHOOL	HIGH SCHOOL	COLLEGE
Expected number	2.51	2.64	2.86
Number of families*	50	318	40

* White families only

few decades ago the typical wife was widowed before her last child married, today's wives experience more than a decade of living alone with their husbands. Under these circumstances, the marital relationship increases in importance.

These new functions are oriented toward the personal needs of the marriage partners. The affectional function meets the need for acceptance and appreciation, the mental hygiene function the need for release from emotional tension, and the companionship function offsets the anonymity and loneliness of urban life.

Two empirical questions can be raised with respect to these functions. (1) How actively do the Detroit couples try to meet these needs? (2) How well do they succeed?

Companionship involves doing things for pure enjoyment through joint use of leisure time. While no overall measure of companionship is available from the Detroit Area Study, several specific facets were measured. A majority of Detroit husbands tell their wives every day or almost every day about things that happened at work. This "informative companionship" reduces the urban gap between the workplace and the home though it does not match the even higher communication level of farm husbands and wives about the business on which they depend for their livelihood.

Other types of companionship re-

quire more effort than just talking over the day's events, and therefore cannot be expected to occur so often. Nevertheless the median Detroit couple get together with relatives at least once a week, and with other friends several times a month. This joint sociability results in shared friendships, for most of the Detroit wives know at least half their husband's friends quite well.

In addition, the typical Detroit male goes to church once or twice a month, almost always with his wife, providing a significant amount of religious companionship. Joint participation in secular organizations, however, is rare beyond a small circle of high status couples.

In general, Detroit married couples engage in a considerable amount and variety of joint activity both inside and outside the home. As a result, 30 per cent of the wives are enthusiastic about the companionship they have with their husbands while most of the rest express considerable satisfaction. Should such expressions of satisfaction be discounted as mere rationalizations? Certainly they are subjective evaluations of the marital situation. But they testify to the effectiveness of the marital relationship in meeting the wife's need for companionship.

While no measures of the frequency of expressing affection are available, the wives' enthusiasm about this marital function is even greater. Affection is the one aspect of marriage where urban satisfaction markedly exceeds the rural. Apparently urban husbands particularly

the Family," *Marriage and Family Living,* 17 (February, 1955), 3–9.

excel in giving love. Perhaps they also perform better in the closely related sexual function. In any case, the average Detroit couple is bound together by mutual affection. This interpretation is reinforced by the fact that the majority of urban wives feel that their families are more closely knit than "most other families" they know.

Perhaps the newest family function dealt with is the mental hygiene function. At least this aspect of marriage has seldom been studied. Assuming that peace of mind is a basic human need, what contribution do marriage partners make to it? Particularly after a crisis has disturbed the individual's emotional equilibrium, how does the partner respond?

To be able to respond one must know about the difficulty. The typical Detroit wife tells her husband her troubles about half the time. The rest of the time, she deals with her tensions by herself or turns elsewhere for help. The problems she shares with her husband depend on his availability, his own frame of mind, and the seriousness of the problem. The typical wife relies on her husband for therapeutic assistance whenever she especially needs it and he is capable of giving it.

A majority of Detroit husbands respond with sympathy, advice, or help and the wives feel much relieved as a result. Only a small minority of husbands react so negatively that the wife feels worse or learns that it is better not to tell him at all. Apparently, the mental hygiene function operates effectively when it is really needed.

This brief exploration of three non-traditional functions of marriage reveals sources of strength in modern urban marriages which probably were less effective in the past under more arduous living conditions. In any case, they are rewarding aspects of contemporary fam-

ily life which reinforce the stability inherent in the modern family's social structure.

VARIATION IN MODERN FAMILY PATTERNS

While it is possible to generalize about "the urban family," there are significant differences between various segments of the population. Detroit's religious and ethnic groups differ little in most aspects of their family life. But educational, occupational, and income groups which involve differential social status produce varying patterns of family structure and functioning.

The Landecker-Lenski Index of Social Status provides a convenient combination of education, occupation, income, and the reported social esteem of ethnic background.[4] Table III shows the direct relationship which exists in Detroit between the husband's social status and the amount of power he wields in the family.

Although the difference between high and low status families in power structure is substantial, there is a regular progression over the social status continuum. Therefore, this is better described as a difference in degree rather than kind. Nevertheless, the difference is great enough at the extremes to become almost qualitative in nature.

Detailed analysis of the Detroit data suggests that high status contributes to the husband's power through increasing his knowledge and skill relevant to decision-making. His wife usually defers to him, recognizing his special competence, rather than being forced to submit to his arbitrary exercise of power. The low status wife frequently finds that

[4] Gerhard E. Lenski, "Status Crystallization: A Non-Vertical Dimension of Social Status," *American Sociological Review,* 19 (August, 1954), 405–13.

TABLE III Husband's power by social status

	Percentile Ranking on Social Status				Index
	0-19	20-39	40-59	60-79	80-99
Husband's mean power	4.39	4.79	5.00	5.33	5.56
Number of families*	41	147	204	177	86

* Entire urban sample (both white and Negro).

TABLE IV Husband's power by occupation and race

	Occupation			
Husband's mean	BLUE COLLAR		WHITE COLLAR	
power by race	Low	High	Low	High
White	5.07	4.98	5.36	5.52
	(162)	(161)	(78)	(151)
Negro	4.31	4.60		5.00
	(78)	(20)		(5)

Numbers in parentheses represent the number of families on which means are computed.

TABLE V Frequency wife tells husband her troubles after a bad day, by husband's occupation

	Husband's Occupation			
Frequency Wife	BLUE COLLAR		WHITE COLLAR	
Tells Her Troubles	LOW	HIGH	LOW	HIGH
Always	25%	23%	19%	17%
Usually	23	20	34	24
Half the time	23	26	30	32
Seldom	16	21	10	21
Never	13	10	7	6
Total	100%	100%	100%	100%
Mean	2.32	2.24	2.49	2.26
Number of families*	173	173	88	157

* White families only

she must take over the reins of the family as a result of her husband's incompetence, negligence, or indifference. Insofar as there are matriarchs in America, they are found at the bottom of the social scale. However, they rule by default rather than conquest.

Everything which applies to low status families generally applies in greater degree to Negro families. Table IV shows how much lower Negro husbands' power is than white husbands'

within the same occupational category. Extra economic and social disadvantages undermine the Negro husband's morale with the result that he plays a marginal role in family decision-making. This difference in power structure between Negro and white families is correlated with the high incidence of divorce and desertion in low status families generally and Negro families in particular.

In general, high social status is associated with marital satisfaction, though the husband's community responsibilities sometimes conflict with his marital relationship. Especially when the husband is preoccupied with vocational success, companionship with the wife suffers. However, such preoccupation hardly mars the general positive correlation between social status and marital satisfaction.

High social status couples usually do more things together. On all the types of companionship measured in the Detroit Area Study, high status families report more sharing. However, in the mental hygiene area, high status wives are more selective about telling their troubles to the husband.

Table 5 shows that wives of high status men typically "bother" their husbands half the time whereas wives of low status men are more apt to tell them always or not at all. Perhaps low status extremism reflects greater impulsivity. If the wife is the impulsive partner, she unburdens herself every time. On the other hand, if the husband is the impulsive one, the wife learns it isn't safe to approach him with her troubles. Wives of professional and managerial husbands, by contrast, balance their own needs against the husband's in determining how often to approach him.

CONCLUSION

Variations between social strata (and the other changes which occur over the family life cycle) are important but fail to alter the basic generalizations about urban families as a whole. In general, data from the Detroit Metropolitan Area suggest that modern urban families possess structural characteristics which enable them to function effectively. The range of functions performed by the family has shifted with the rise of the metropolis, but the reduction of old functions has released time and energy for new ones.

Urbanization, then, has enabled the family to undertake new functions and to make structural alterations appropriate to a new division of labor between the family and other social institutions and to the growing equalization of external participation by the husband and wife. These urban influences extend beyond the metropolis to adjacent farm families with the result that contemporary rural and urban families closely resemble each other in most essential features.

18

MARITAL DISSOLUTION

It is a universal cultural ideal that life should be orderly and that families, like clocks, should run smoothly, quietly lending continuity to life. However, reflection brings the realization that ideals are not often reality, that disorder is generally as familiar as order, disease as natural as health, and that marital dissolution is not confined to television soap operas.

Marital dissolution is not merely a euphemism for "divorce." It is a generic term that includes all forms of termination of marriage, including separation, divorce, and death. It will become evident from the readings that both the causes and personal significance of the various forms of marital stability are complex and varied.

The first article, by Hugh Carter and Alexander Plateris, describes trends in divorce and family disruption in the United States from 1920 to 1960. Their analysis indicates how separated and divorced persons are distributed with respect to age, length of marriage, number of children, place of residence, and remarriages. The second article, by J. Richard Udry, continues the analysis of social characteristics by relating race, sex, education, occupation, and income to marital instability.

George Levinger constructs a conceptual framework for the analysis of marital dissolution. He extends existing studies to a higher level of abstraction by examining marriage as an example of group cohesiveness. Levinger suggests that the strength of the marital relationship is a direct function of social and psychological attraction and barrier forces within the relationship. The utility of the schema may be judged by its application to a review of studies.

Operating on a level less abstract than that of Levinger, John Scanzoni discusses the cultural and structural determinants of family disorganization. He bases a review of the literature on Charles Ackerman's finding that the incidence of divorce is low when spouses maintain predominantly common affiliations, and high when separate affiliations are maintained.[1] Scanzoni then identifies four aspects of networks of family-friend affiliation which affect marital disorganization, and suggests that they be used in an extension of Ackerman's analysis. He also notes that while divorce may be dysfunctional for a "companionship family," it can be functional for the personal welfare of the individuals involved.

[1] Charles Ackerman, "Affiliations: Structural Determinants of Differential Divorce Rates," *The American Journal of Sociology*, 1963, 69: 13–20.

Trends in Divorce and Family Disruption*

Hugh Carter and Alexander Plateris

The great majority of adults in the United States are married, but each year a substantial number of marriages end in divorce. The more than 390,000 divorces in 1960 vitally affected the lives of 780,000 adults and their 460,000 children —in many instances permanently.

While these figures are disconcerting, the current level of divorces is more than a third below the peak level of 1946. Moreover, the oft-quoted figure of "one marriage in four" ending in divorce is misleading in that it relates current divorces to current marriages whereas current divorces occur to marriages that took place at any time to still-living persons. A more adequate or sensitive measure is the divorce rate per 1,000 married females aged 15 years and over, which has been under 10 (or one percent) each year since 1953. In terms of married couples, only one in every 109 obtained a divorce in 1960.

After indicating the proportions of persons by marital status and the . . . legal grounds for divorce, this paper concentrates on the numbers and characteristics of the marital partners involved in separation, divorce, and remarriage.

MARITAL STATUS
OF THE POPULATION

Two-thirds of all persons 14 years of age and over in the United States are mar-

°*Adapted from* Health, Education, and Welfare Indicators, *National Vital Statistics Division, Public Health Service, September, 1963.*

ried (Table 1). In 1962, one woman in five and one man in four had never been married; one woman in eight and one man in 29 were widowed. The greater number of widowed women than men is associated with lower mortality and the earlier age at marriage among women and the greater remarriage rate of older men. The divorced population included one of every 37 women and one of every 48 men. Of the "ever married" population, about one person in seven had been married more than once.

LEGAL GROUNDS FOR DIVORCE

The legal grounds for divorce are not necessarily the real reasons for obtaining a final decree. They reflect only in part the marital difficulties which preceded the divorce; they also depend upon statutory provisions in each State, and, perhaps even more important, on judicial interpretations and precedents. Some evidence points to the conclusion that a majority of divorces are obtained on grounds least unpleasant to advance under existing State law and easiest to establish in a legal proceeding. For the entire group of 16 States reporting divorces by legal grounds in 1959, *cruelty* was the legal ground in slightly over half the cases, and *desertion* in almost one-fourth. Indignities and incompatibility were included among a variety of other grounds given.

DIVORCE TREND, 1920-1960

The trend in divorce during the past four decades illustrates the impact of war

TABLE 1 Marital status of the civilian population March 1962 (in thousands)

MARITAL STATUS	Males AGED 14 AND OVER	PERCENT	Females AGED 14 AND OVER	PERCENT
Total	62,129	100.0	67,166	100.0
Single	15,708	25.3	13,134	19.6
Married	43,019	69.2	43,846	65.3
Widowed	2,128	3.4	8,399	12.5
Divorced	1,274	2.1	1,787	2.7
Ever Married	46,421	74.7	54,032	80.4
Married once	39,541	63.6	46,191	68.8
Married more than once	6,880	11.1	7,841	11.7

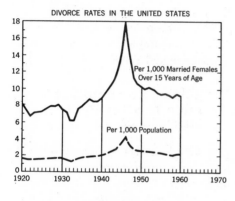

CHART 1

and economic conditions upon the legal dissolution of marriage (Chart 1). This may be seen in both the crude rate per 1,000 population and especially the more sensitive rate per 1,000 females aged 15 years and over (Table 2). The latter reached a peak in 1929. In the fall of that year a stock market crash indicated that the Great Depression was approaching. The rate was low in 1932 and 1933 in the trough of the depression but moved upward with only minor interruptions until in the first post-war year of 1946, with a total of 610,000 divorces, the rate reached the all-time high of 17.9 per 1,000 married females 15 years of age and over. Many marital difficulties of the war years did not reach the courts until after the close of hostilities, thus greatly

increasing the total number of divorces for 1946 and affecting one married couple in every 56. Thereafter the rate dropped steeply as the Nation returned to more normal living conditions. During the 1950–1960 decade, the rate showed considerable stability with a slight decline, particularly in the recession years of 1954 and 1958; the annual number of divorces during this decade ranged between 368,000 and 395,000, and the rate was less than one for every 100 married couples.

DIVORCED AND SEPARATED POPULATION

The distribution of the divorced and separated population shows marked *differences by age*. In 1962, as in 1950, the greatest proportion *divorced* was found among persons 45 through 54 years of age. (Table 3 shows the numbers and the percentages of separated and divorced in the total population of each age group.) Most persons are divorced at an early age, but the 45–54 age group contains the greatest proportion of persons who were divorced and had not remarried at the time of enumeration.

Less concentrated by age is the distribution of *separated* persons—those who are living apart from their spouses

TABLE 2 Divorces

YEAR	NUMBER (000's)	Rate per 1,000 POPU-LATION	MARRIED FEMALE AGED 15+
1920	171	1.6	8.0
1921	160	1.5	7.2
1922	149	1.4	6.6
1923	165	1.5	7.1
1924	171	1.5	7.2
1925	175	1.5	7.2
1926	185	1.6	7.5
1927	196	1.6	7.8
1928	200	1.7	7.8
1929	206	1.7	8.0
1930	196	1.6	7.5
1931	188	1.5	7.1
1932	164	1.3	6.1
1933	165	1.3	6.1
1934	204	1.6	7.5
1935	218	1.7	7.8
1936	236	1.8	8.3
1937	249	1.9	8.7
1938	244	1.9	8.4
1939	251	1.9	8.5
1940	264	2.0	8.8
1941	293	2.2	9.4
1942	321	2.4	10.1
1943	359	2.6	11.0
1944	400	2.9	12.0
1945	485	3.5	14.4
1946	610	4.3	17.9
1947	483	3.4	13.6
1948	408	2.8	11.2
1949	397	2.7	10.6
1950	385	2.6	10.3
1951	381	2.5	9.9
1952	392	2.5	10.1
1953	390	2.5	9.9
1954	379	2.4	9.5
1955	377	2.3	9.3
1956	382	2.3	9.4
1957	381	2.2	9.2
1958	368	2.1	8.9
1959	395	2.2	9.3
1960	393	2.2	9.2

because of marital discord. For men the highest proportion of separated was in the age group 45 through 54 years; for women, in the group 25 through 44 years of age.

However, for both separated and divorced, whether men or women, between 40 and 50 percent were found in ages 35 through 54 years. At both younger and older ages the numbers dropped off.

Between 1950 and 1962 the most marked increase (one-eighth) was in the proportion of women who were divorced. Of all females 14 years of age and over, 2.7 percent were reported as divorced in 1962 as compared with 2.4 percent in 1950. Comparable figures for men were 2.1 percent and 2.0 percent.

DURATION OF MARRIAGE PRIOR TO SEPARATION AND DIVORCE

Some marriages end in divorce in less than one year; others continue for more than 40 years (Chart 2). *Most divorces occur within a few years after marriage*—in 1960 more than 30 percent of the divorces occurred in less than four years and over one-half occurred in less than eight years after marriage. In most cases the husband and wife are separated for a time prior to the final decree. There is evidence that previous marital experience of husband and wife is related to the duration of marriage prior to separation, as well as prior to divorce. In a District of Columbia court, the longest median duration from marriage to separation (4.9 years) and to divorce (10.5 years) occurred when neither husband nor wife had been married previously. The briefest duration to separation (1.7 years) and to divorce (5.1 years) occurred when husband and wife had both been previously married. Duration figures were intermediate if only one spouse had been married previously (Chart 3).

TABLE 3 Separated and divorced persons by sex and age (in thousands)

Sex and age	Separated				Divorced			
	1950		1962		1950		1962	
	Number	Per-cent	Number	Per-cent	Number	Per-cent	Number	Per-cent
Males								
14 and over	852	1.6	1,004	1.6	1,071	2.0	1,274	·2.1
14–19	10	0.2	6	0.1	6	0.1	8	0.1
20–24	66	1.2	78	1.5	51	0.9	34	0.7
25–29	94	1.6	101	2.0	103	1.7	86	1.7
30–34	92	1.7	92	1.6	116	2.1	144	2.6
35–44	198	1.9	239	2.0	264	2.5	255	2.2
45–54	174	2.1	231	2.2	251	3.0	375	3.6
55–64	123	1.9	155	2.0	173	2.6	238	3.1
65–74	72	1.8	69	1.3	84	2.1	103	2.0
75 and over	23	1.3	33	1.3	22	1.3	31	1.2
Females								
14 and over	1,169	2.0	1,433	2.1	1,373	2.4	1,787	2.7
14–19	40	0.6	42	0.5	17	0.3	14	0.2
20–24	133	2.3	139	2.4	97	1.7	99	1.7
25–29	160	2.5	175	3.2	159	2.5	167	3.0
30–34	149	2.5	190	3.2	176	3.0	214	3.6
35–44	290	2.7	382	3.1	388	3.6	459	3.7
45–54	210	2.4	279	2.6	302	3.5	438	4.1
55–64	121	1.8	127	1.5	161	2.4	278	3.4
65–74	54	1.2	80	1.3	60	1.4	95	1.6
75 and over	11	0.5	19	0.6	13	0.6	23	0.7

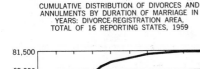

CUMULATIVE DISTRIBUTION OF DIVORCES AND ANNULMENTS BY DURATION OF MARRIAGE IN YEARS: DIVORCE-REGISTRATION AREA, TOTAL OF 16 REPORTING STATES, 1959

CHART 2

Age at divorce

Evidence from one-fifth of the States indicates that divorce usually takes place at an *early age*. For 10 States, in 1959, the median age at divorce following a first marriage was about 31 years for men and 28 years for women; but for the much smaller group of persons married more than once, the median ages were about 41 years for men and 37 years for women. In 1960 about 47 percent of divorcing women were under 30 years of age; and 52 percent of divorcing men were under 35 years of age (Table 4).

CHILDREN OF DIVORCED COUPLES

The number of children under 18 years of age of divorcing couples has risen in recent years; in 1960 more than 460,000 children were involved. The number has been increasing despite the relative stability of the number of divorces because both the proportion of couples with children and the average

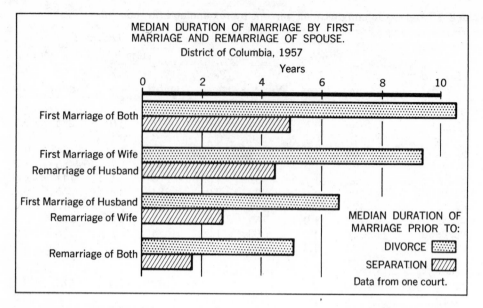

MEDIAN DURATION OF MARRIAGE BY FIRST
MARRIAGE AND REMARRIAGE OF SPOUSE.
District of Columbia, 1957

CHART 3

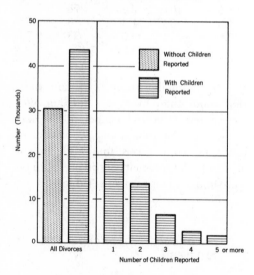

DIVORCES AND ANNULMENTS BY NUMBER OF
CHILDREN REPORTED: DIVORCE-REGISTRATION AREA,
TOTAL OF 16 REPORTING STATES, 1959

CHART 4

TABLE 4   Percentage distribution of divorces by age of spouse at time decree was granted in 1960[1]

Age	Husband	Wife
Total[2]	100.0	100.0
Under 20	1.7	7.7
20–24	15.9	22.2
25–29	18.4	16.8
30–34	16.4	15.2
35–39	13.4	13.8
40–44	12.1	10.5
45–49	8.9	6.1
50–54	6.8	3.8
55–59	2.9	2.2
60–64	1.6	0.9
65 and over	1.7	0.8

[1] Includes data for 11 States.
[2] For persons stating age.

number of children per divorce has been rising.

In recent years, in reporting States, about one-half of the divorced couples had no children under 18 years of age, while the other half had a varying number of children, up to eight or more. In 1959, 15 percent of the divorcing couples had 3 or more children (Chart 4). For the United States, in 1960, 57 percent of the divorcing couples had children under 18 years of age . . .

TABLE 5 Percent separated and divorced in the population by residence and color, 1960[1]

RESIDENCE AND COLOR	Males			Females		
	TOTAL, MARRIAGE DISRUPTED	SEPARATED	DIVORCED	TOTAL, MARRIAGE DISRUPTED	SEPARATED	DIVORCED
Total	3.6	1.5	2.1	4.8	2.0	2.8
White	3.1	1.0	2.1	4.0	1.3	2.7
Nonwhite	8.0	5.6	2.4	11.9	8.3	3.6
Urban	3.9	1.6	2.3	5.6	2.3	3.3
White	3.4	1.1	2.3	4.6	1.4	3.2
Nonwhite	9.0	6.2	2.8	13.7	9.4	4.3
Rural	2.8	1.1	1.7	2.7	1.2	1.5
White	2.7	0.9	1.8	2.3	0.8	1.5
Nonwhite	5.5	4.0	1.5	6.4	5.0	1.4

[1] Computed on the basis of the population 14 years old and over, in the respective sex-color-residence groups.

DIFFERENTIAL IMPACT OF DIVORCE ON THE POPULATION

The probability of divorce varies markedly for various segments of the population—between regions, between city and country, between white and nonwhite. It seems to be related to age at marriage and to the occupation of the principal breadwinner. However, the evidence of these differences sometimes is incomplete and fragmentary.

Divorce Rate by Region

In 1960 the divorce rate per 1,000 population was 2.2. Since two persons are involved in a divorce action, 4.4 persons in every thousand of the population, or about one in every 227 persons was divorced. However, the rate varied widely among the four regions. The lowest rate was in the Northeast Region (0.9), followed by the North Central Region (2.1), South (2.8), and West (3.4). The rate was almost four times as high in the West as in the Northeast. These rates are affected by the age distribution of the population, since most of the persons obtaining di-

vorces are young or middle aged adults. The rates are also affected to some extent by migratory divorces, for some persons move temporarily from one State to another to obtain a divorce under less stringent divorce laws. However, the regional differences are believed to be greater than could be accounted for by these factors . . .

Place of Residence (Urban and Rural, White and Nonwhite)

The 1960 Census provides considerable information about the basic demographic characteristics of persons who reported themselves as separated or divorced. The place of residence of divorced persons indicates a greater concentration in urban than in rural areas (Table 5).

In *urban areas*, reported percentages of women who were divorced and separated at the time of enumeration were substantially higher than those for men; the number of women in these marital statuses exceeded the total for men by about one-third.

TABLE 6   Percentage distribution of spouses married and of husbands and wives divorced by age at marriage, 1960

	Males		*Females*	
AGE	GROOMS	DIVORCED HUSBANDS	BRIDES	DIVORCED WIVES
Total	100.0	100.0	100.0	100.0
Under 20	13.4	16.0	37.4	44.9
20–24	41.8	40.3	32.1	27.7
25–29	17.1	18.0	10.1	10.9
30–34	8.2	9.9	5.4	6.4
35–39	5.3	5.9	4.5	3.8
40 and over	14.2	9.9	10.5	6.3

In general, the *nonwhite* population had substantially higher percentages of divorced persons, but it was in the proportion of the separated that the differences were most marked between white and nonwhite persons. The percentage of nonwhite separated males was more than five times, and of females more than six times, that of the corresponding white population. However, for the divorced population in rural areas the percentage of nonwhite residents was lower than for white residents.

It should be emphasized that these figures refer only to place of residence at the time of the Census enumeration. Since there is a great deal of movement of population from rural to urban areas, the figures can not be interpreted as giving the relative frequency of divorce or separation in rural and urban areas. A rural resident may be divorced and subsequently move to an urban area to seek employment or for other reasons.

Age at Marriage and Divorce

Age at marriage appears to have an important effect on the likelihood of divorce. The very young marriages, in which the husband or wife was under 20 years of age, seem to be overrepresented in the divorced population. In the 1960

divorces, 16 percent of the males and about 45 percent of the females had been married before reaching 20 years of age (Table 6). By contrast, the proportion of all 1960 marriages contracted before age 20 was about 13 percent for males and about 37 percent for females. In data for 1950, Glick found that divorce rates were highest in the youngest ages and decreased steadily with age. There were 12.6 divorces per 1,000 married females 15 through 19 years of age, but only 2.2 per 1,000 married females 45 through 54 years of age. There is no reason to believe that this general relation has changed since 1950.

Remarriages of Divorced and Widowed Persons

The picture of divorce and family disruption in the United States would not be complete without reviewing some of the facts concerning remarriage.

In recent years over three-fourths of a million persons have been divorced annually. A substantial majority were young: the women under 35 years of age at divorce and the men under 40. Many of these persons remarried. There were also a large number of marriages ended by death of spouse: in 1960 the total was 790,000. Most widows and widow-

TABLE 7 Remarriages by marital status of bride and groom, 1959[1] (In thousands)

Sex and age	Remarriages Number	Previous Marital Status			
		WIDOWED		DIVORCED	
		Number	Percent	Number	Percent
Brides					
All ages[2]	150.8	41.1	27.3	109.7	72.7
Under 25	27.2	1.7	6.1	25.6	93.9
25–34	45.9	5.3	11.5	40.7	88.5
35–44	36.9	9.6	26.0	27.3	74.0
45–54	23.3	11.4	49.1	11.9	50.9
55 and over	17.0	12.9	75.9	4.1	24.1
Grooms					
All ages[2]	144.3	35.9	24.9	108.3	75.1
Under 25	11.4	0.3	3.0	11.1	97.0
25–34	41.5	2.3	5.6	39.2	94.4
35–44	35.9	4.9	13.7	30.9	86.3
45–54	25.8	8.1	31.4	17.7	68.6
55 and over	29.3	20.1	68.5	9.2	31.5

[1] For 28 States.

[2] Includes age not stated.

ers are in the older age groups, and a relatively small percentage of them remarry.

In 1959 close to 300,000 persons were remarried in 28 reporting States. (Table 7 shows the numbers of remarried brides and grooms, and the percentages of all remarried who previously were widowed or divorced). About three-fourths of them were divorced at the time of remarriage and one-fourth were widowed. A slightly higher percentage of the men remarrying were divorced, and correspondingly, a higher proportion of women were widowed. Men and women under 55 years of age at remarriage were generally in the divorced group; the divorced outnumbered the widowed almost five to one. But for persons 55 years of age and over, the widowed outnumbered the divorced by five to two.

Of the 1,523,000 marriages in the United States in 1960, about 78 percent were first marriages and 22 percent, remarriages. About three out of four remarriages involved a divorced bride, or a divorced groom; one out of four involved a widow or widower. In that year, about 17 percent of all brides were divorced and 6 percent widowed; for grooms 16 percent were divorced and 5 percent were widowed. In 1959 similar proportions held for the reporting States.

Divorce and Family Disruption: Past and Future

War and economic conditions have had an impact on family disruption as well as on family formation. The peak number of divorces in one year in the United States—610,000 in 1946—reflected both a failure of spouses to readjust after wartime separation and a backlog of court cases. In the decade from 1950 to 1960 the annual number of divorces remained under 400,000, declining slightly during the years of economic recession.

Children born in the early postwar years are now entering the marriageable ages. Since a high rate of divorce has been associated with early marriage, if there is a continuance of a low age at marriage, there may be a relatively high number of divorces. A rising proportion of young married adults may tend to raise the divorce rates for the general population and for married females aged 15 and over.

With childbearing occurring in the early years of marriage, more children may be involved in divorce actions in the years ahead.

Divorce varies for the major regions of the Country and is related to broad occupational groups. There is no reason to expect that these differences will disappear in the near future.

Marital Instability by Race, Sex, Education, Occupation, and Income Using 1960 Census Data[*][1]

J. Richard Udry

Until about twenty-five years ago, it seems to have been generally believed that divorce was more prevalent in the well-to-do groups. In 1938 Terman wrote: "it is well known that more divorces occur in the higher classes."[2] The lower-status groups, it was believed, tended either to separate informally or suffer together. As Goode indicates, this may well have been true at some previous period when the general standard of living and level of development was lower.[3] After 1940, as better data became available, sociological studies in the United States showed the inadequacy of this generalization.[4] These

studies, based usually on small populations, consistently have demonstrated that the higher the socioeconomic status of a group, the lower their divorce and separation rates.

With the 1950 Census came the first opportunity to measure the relationship between status-related variables and certain aspects of marital stability, using the entire population. Glick, using 1950 Census data to calculate separation and divorce rates by race and education, found a curvilinear relationship of divorce to educational level for each race, with divorce rates highest in the middle levels of education. His data show a consistent inverse relationship between separation rates and educational level for each race.[5]

°Adapted from The American Journal of Sociology, 1966, 72: 203–209, and (1967), pp. 673–674, by permission of The University of Chicago Press.

[1] The writer is indebetd to the Bureau of the Census for providing for this analysis unpublished data from the 1960 Census of Population.

[2] Lewis M. Terman, Psychological Factors in Marital Happiness (New York: McGraw-Hill Book Co., 1938), p. 167.

[3] William J. Goode, World Revolution and Family Patterns (New York: Free Press of Glencoe, 1963).

[4] H. Ashley Weeks, "Differential Divorce Rates by Occupation," Social Forces, XXI (1943), 334–37; August B. Hollings-

head, "Class Differences in Family Stability," Annals of the American Academy of Political and Social Science, CLXXII (1950), 39–46; Willaim A. Kephart, "Occupational Level and Marital Disruption," American Sociological Review, XX (1955), 456–65; William J. Goode, After Divorce (Glencoe, Ill.: Free Press, 1956).

[5] Paul C. Glick, American Families (New York: John Wiley & Sons, 1957), p. 154, Table 102. Glick's rates are calculated as rate of divorce or separation among those "subject to" divorce or separation. "Subject to"

Hillman used 1950 Census data to calculate separation and divorce rates by sex for each race by status-related variables.[6] The breakdown of the data by sex showed the relationships between various status indexes to be quite complex. According to her method of calculation, the inverse relationship between marital instability (divorce and separation) and status held only for white males, with varying patterns occurring for non-white males and for females of both races. Figure 1 is prepared from her data, based on 1950 Census tabulations for race, sex, and educational level. Other tables in her original article present similar data for occupational and income groups by race and sex.

These conclusions fly in the face of conclusions from small studies, and also contain patterns which are difficult to reconcile. For example, Hillman's tables show an inverse relationship between education and marital instability for white men, but a direct relationship for white women. In a population in which educational homogamy is the rule the result is improbable.[7] The problem is in

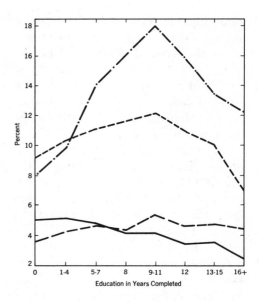

FIG. 1. Percentage of those ever married who were divorced and separated at the 1950 Census. *Solid line*, white males; *long-dash line*, white females; *short-dash line*, non-white males; *dash-dot line*, non-white females. (Source: Hillman, *op. cit.*)

---

divorce is defined as married plus one half of those divorced at the time of the census who divorced in the two years previous to the census. His rates are adjusted for age.

[6] Karen G. Hillman, "Marital Instability and Its Relation to Education, Income, and Occupation: An Analysis Based on Census Data," in Robert F. Winch, Robert McGinnis, and Herbert R. Barringer (eds.), *Selected Studies in Marriage and the Family* (rev. ed.; New York: Holt, Rinehart & Winston, 1962), pp. 602–8.

[7] In 1960 the probability of a married college-graduate female being married to a no-college male was about 0.25, while the probability of a no-college male being married to a female college graduate was about 0.07 (calculated from *U.S. Census of Population, 1960: Families*. PC (2) 4A, Tables 25 and 26).

the method of calculation of instability rates used by Glick and Hillman, necessitated by the limitations of their data. They had available only figures from which to calculate the proportion of those ever married who were *at the time of the Census* either divorced or separated. It is possible that differences in the rate of remarriage and time lag in remarriage explain the differences in rates shown in their analyses, or at least the discrepancies between the Census data and previous studies. For example, if two groups have the same over-all percentage of couples who divorce each year, but one group has a remarriage rate of 90 per cent in five years and the second has a remarriage rate of 45 per cent in five years, then at any one time many more people in the second group will be in a divorced status. Likewise, if the remarriage rate for the first group is 50 per cent in two years, and in the second is 50 per cent in four years, then at any one time the second group will have many more persons in a divorced status, even though the ultimate divorce and even remarriage rates for the two groups are identical.[8]

The data presented below are calculated from unpublished tables from the 1960 Census, based on a 5 per cent sample of the U.S. population, and provided the author by the Bureau of the Census. For most of the categories calculated by Hillman for 1950, the 1960 data offer the same relationships. For some categories data are not available for one census or the other. The 1960 analysis contains no rates by income. The 1950 data provide no rates for females by occupational status of the woman. Differences in educational categories between 1950 and 1960 should also be noted.

In order to take into account the fact that most persons who divorce remarry, disruption rates were calculated in the present analysis by adding together the number divorced, the number separated, and the number married more than once, and dividing by the number ever married.[9] In the total population, of course, this calculation is contaminated by the

number of widowed persons who have remarried, which might conceivably vary by socioeconomic status. Death rates also vary by race, marital status, and socioeconomic status, and serve as another contaminant, removing from enumeration more Negroes, low-status persons, and divorced persons than their proportion in the population. Therefore all calculations were also made on the age groups 25–34. In this group most persons who will ever marry are married,[10] most have been married long enough to have a chance for disruption,[11] and few have had time to be widowed and remarried.[12] However, the data for the age group 25–34 so calculated show relationships identical to those calculated on all persons over 14 years old (see Figs. 2 and 3) . . .

---

[8] Exactly the same problems are inherent in Glick's analysis of marital disruption using the 1960 Census data (Paul C. Glick, "Marriage Instability: Variations by Size of Place and Region," Milbank Memorial Fund Quarterly, XLI [January, 1963], 43–55). Neither Glick nor Hillman had available the category "persons married more than once" to add to the numerators of their ratios, and hence they were unable to discuss the extent of marital instability at all but were required to limit themselves to marriages currently disrupted.

[9] This calculation cannot catch the instability which takes the form of separation and reunion with the same spouse, since there is no category "ever separated."

[10] Of all females who eventaully marry, about nine in ten do so before age 25, and of all males who eventually marry, about nine in ten do so before age 30 (calculated from Paul H. Jacobson, American Marriage and Divorce [New York: Holt, Rinehart & Winston, 1959], pp. 78, 80).

[11] For all couples who divorce, the median number of years of marriage before divorce in 1957 was 6.7 years (National Office of Vital Statistics, Special Reports, L, No. 18 [1959], lviii). But most of these were separated earlier. Kephart reported that in Philadelphia more than half of those divorcing were separated by the fifth year of marriage (William M. Kephart, "The Duration of Marriage," American Sociological Review, XIX [June, 1954], 287–95). The modal length of marriage at separation in Kephart's figures was less than one year, and Jacobson (op. cit., p. 94) reported that post-World War II marriages which end in divorce had a modal length of less than two years.

[12] Of course using a young age group introduces other biases. Negroes, low-status persons, and females marry earlier and are therefore exposed to the risk of disruption more years by a given age than whites, high-status persons, and males, respectively.

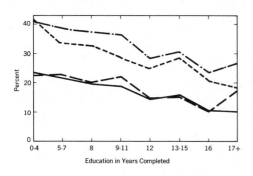

FIG. 2. Percentage of those ever married who were divorced, separated, or had been married more than once at the 1960 Census, by education (age 14 and over). Legend same as in Fig. 1. (Source: Unpublished data furnished by the Bureau of the Census.)

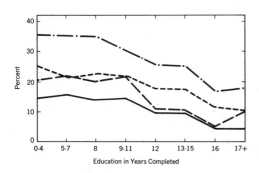

FIG. 3. Percentage of those ever married who were divorced, separated, or had been married more than once at the 1960 Census, by education (ages 25–34). Legend same as in Fig. 1. (Source: Unpublished data furnished by the Bureau of the Census.)

EDUCATION AND MARITAL STABILITY

When looking at total disruption rates, it is obvious that there is a clear inverse relationship between disruption rate and educational status for both sexes and both races. The elevated rate for women with graduate training compared

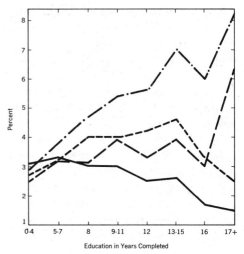

FIG. 4. Percentage of those ever married who were divorced but not remarried at the 1960 Census, by education (age 14 and over). Legend same as in Fig. 1. (Source: Unpublished data furnished by the Bureau of the Census.)

with the low rate for men with graduate training (most of whom are married to women without graduate training) is an interesting but minor exception (see Figs. 2 and 3). When we compare non-whites and whites of the same sex, non-white rates of disruption are from one and a half to more than two times the rates for whites of the same educational level. The higher the educational level, the more different are white and non-white rates of divorced status at the time of the 1960 Census (Fig. 4), but a comparison with Figure 3 suggests that this is largely due to differences in rates and lags in remarriage, since it does not hold when the "married more than once" group is added to the numerator. The ratio between white and non-white disruption rates in 1960 is fairly constant over different educational levels (Fig. 3). These observations do not give unqualified support to the frequent suggestion that increasing non-white status will obliterate racial differences in marital patterns, although they indicate that it should reduce these differences.

Being separated is still a characteristic reported primarily by the uneducated and the non-white (Fig. 5). Since these data only show those separated at one point in time, the pattern of Figure 5 cannot be taken to represent the relative frequency of the occurrence of separation in each category. In this sense it has the weakness inherent in the data Hillman and Glick worked with.

The percentage divorced may be viewed as a way of estimating differentials in the rate and time lag in remarriage among divorced groups. Comparison among the figures presented invites (but does not establish) the following interpretations as hypotheses for futher exploration. Among whites without college, the men remarry more rapidly than the women, while among whites with college, the women remarry more rapidly than the men. Younger white females with graduate education remarry more rapidly than older white women with similar education. The divorced per cent for these educated women age 25–34 is only 0.5 per cent, while among all white women with graduate education it is 6.3 per cent. There is virtually no difference for white men of this educational level between percentage divorced among the young and percentage divorced among all ages. Among non-whites, more-educated women remarry more slowly than less-educated women, while the relationship for men is curvilinear. There are, of course, other interpretations of these differences in rates. Many of the differences are no doubt due to differential accuracy of reporting in different groups, and to other limitations in the data discussed above.

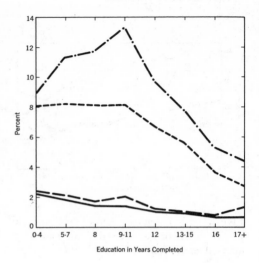

FIG. 5. Percentage of those ever married who were separated at the 1960 Census, by education (age 14 and over). Legend same as in Fig. 1. (Source: Unpublished data furnished by the Bureau of the Census.)

OCCUPATION AND MARITAL STABILITY

Occupational status and its relationship to marital stability must be considered a different phenomenon for each sex (Fig. 6), since marital disruption may lead some women into certain occupational categories, while it is more difficult to conceive of men being led into certain occupations as a result of marital disruption. Generally speaking, there is lowest marital stability in the lowest-status occupation for men, and highest stability in the high-status occupations, with highest instability in men in personal service and domestic service. Occupational status has the same relationship to marital stability in non-white and white males, except that non-white rates are more than double the white rates. The relationship between occupational status and marital

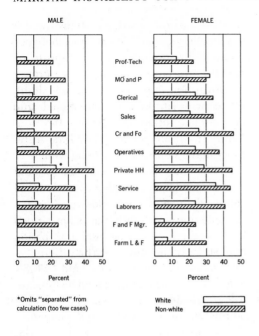

MALE FEMALE

Prof-Tech
MO and P
Clerical
Sales
Cr and Fo
Operatives
Private HH
Service
Laborers
F and F Mgr.
Farm L & F

Percent Percent

*Omits "separated" from
calculation (too few cases)

White
Non-white

FIG. 6. Percentage of those ever married who were divorced, separated, or had been married more than once at the 1960 Census, by occupation (ages 25–34). (Source: Unpublished data furnished by the Bureau of the Census.)

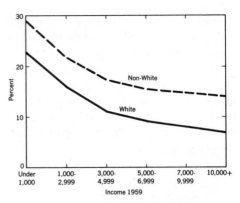

FIG. 7. Percent of ever-married males 25–34 years of age who were separated, divorced, or had been married more than once at the time of the 1960 Census, by income and race. (Based on a 5% sample). (*Source:* U.S. Bureau of the Census, U.S. Census of Population: 1960. Subject Reports: Marital Status. Final Report PC(2)-4E. Washington: U.S. Government Printing Office, 1966. Table 6.)

TABLE 1   Ratio of nonwhite to white marital instability by income for males ages 25-34 (From Figure 1)

Under 1,000	1.24
1,000–2,999	1.38
3,000–4,999	1.59
5,000–6,999	1.74
7,000–9,999	1.81
10,000+	1.95

stability for men is direct and unequivocal.

Peculiar disruption rates are associated with each occupational category among women who are employed, and these rates cannot be said to be associated with the status level of the occupational group. Since occupational status of employed women cannot be said to be a primary socioeconomic status attribute of women, and since less than half of women are included, this finding does not vitiate the fundamental inverse relationship between socioeconomic status and marital disruption. The female rates by occupation are unexplained, and the pattern invites research into the functional relationship between marriage and various occupations for women . . .

INCOME AND MARITAL STABILITY

Figure 7 below presents marital instability by personal income by race for males ages 25–34 in the same form as the data in Figure 1 above. The female data are confusing, and I am not presenting them here. It is too easy to see how marital status of women can influence their personal income to try to explain from these data how women's income might affect their marital status. This problem seems much less important in the case of men. In Figure 7, the inverse relationship of income to marital instability is quite unmistakeable. It is also quite clear that the ratio of nonwhite to white marital instability grows consistently with increasing income (See Table 1). These income data serve only to reinforce the arguments given above that the white-nonwhite difference in marital instability cannot be explained solely by differences in present socioeconomic status.[13]

SUMMARY AND DISCUSSION

Analysis of 1960 Census data shows the relationship between status and marital disruption to be inverse for both sexes and for both whites and non-whites, when status is measured by educational level. When measured by occupational status [and by income level] the relationship of status to marital disruption is still inverse and clear for men. The far greater instability of non-white marriages is shown not to be attributable solely to the general low [income] educational and occupational status of this group, but a characteristic of non-white groups of all educational and occupational levels. By

[income and] occupational status there is practically no overlap in rates between white and non-whites of any status level, and the overlap between the two groups on disruption rates by education is slight. Of course [income,] occupational and educational differences within the non-white group are related to marital instability in the same way as among whites.

The analysis presented here does not explain white–non-white differences but simply delineates them more clearly. Socioeconomic status differences not tapped by [income,] education and occupation may still explain much of the difference. For example, non-whites and whites matched on occupation or education are still grossly unequal in income, which may be related to divorce rates independently of occupational status. Perhaps the "caste" position of Negroes has a relationship to marital instability. Perhaps a historical-cultural explanation, tracing the Negro family pattern to roots in the slavery system, is made more tenable in the light of the above data.[14] Census data cannot lead to a definitive choice among the possible explanations.

[13] For further analysis of 1960 Census data on this topic the reader is referred to an article by Jessie Bernard, and comments thereon by others *Journal of Marriage and Family*, November, 1966.

[14] E. Franklin Frazier, *The Negro in the United States* (New York: Macmillan Co., 1957) and *The Negro Family in the United States* (Chicago: University of Chicago Press, 1939).

Marital Cohesiveness and Dissolution: An Integrative Review[*]

George Levinger

What makes a marriage "stick"? And what breaks it apart? Such questions have answers, but the answers do not yet rest on an explicit theoretical base. There is an abundance of descriptive findings and of empirical generalizations, but as yet a scarcity of conceptual construction.[1]

Consider the following instance. In a review of "willed departures" in marriage, Goode[2] has summarized a number of variables related to divorce proneness "which seem to be based on good evidence": urban background, marriage at very young ages, short acquaintanceship before marriage, short or no engagement, marital unhappiness of parents, nonattendance at church, mixed religious faith, disapproval by kin and friends of the marriage, dissimilarity of background, and different definitions by spouses of their mutual roles. Goode also notes that husband's occupation and income are inversely related to divorce proneness.[3] Other writers have shown associations between divorce proneness and childless-

ness,[4] low conventionality,[5] disjunctive affiliation networks,[6] and a series of other factors.[7]

It seems reasonable to seek a common conceptual base that will assist in explaining those findings. This paper presents such a conceptual frame, in which marriage is conceived as a special case of all two-person relationships. Marital cohesiveness becomes a special case of group cohesiveness in general. The findings from some major studies of divorce and of marital adjustment are interpreted according to this framework.

COHESIVENESS IN MARRIAGE

The marriage pair is a two-person group. It follows, then, that marital cohesiveness is analogous to group cohe-

[*] Adapted from the Journal of Marriage and the Family, 1965, 27: 19-28.

[1] This state of affairs has not been uncommon in other areas of sociological investigation. See Hans L. Zetterberg, On Theory and Verification in Sociology, Totowa, N.J.: Bedminster, 1963.

[2] William J. Goode, "Family Disorganization," in Contemporary Social Problems, ed. by Robert K. Merton and Robert A. Nisbet, New York: Harcourt, Brace, 1961, p. 425.

[3] Ibid., pp. 417-418.

[4] Paul H. Jacobson, "Differentials in Divorce by Duration of Marriage and Size of Family," American Sociological Review, 15 (April 1950), pp. 235-244.

[5] Harvey J. Locke, Predicting Adjustment in Marriage, New York: Holt, 1951, pp. 236-243.

[6] Charles Ackerman, "Affiliations: Structural Determinants of Differential Divorce Rates," American Journal of Sociology, 69 (July 1963), pp. 13-20.

[7] See also William J. Goode, After Divorce, Glencoe, Ill.: Free Press, 1956; Paul C. Glick, American Families, New York: John Wiley, 1957; Hugh Carter and Alexander Plateris, "Trends in Divorce and Family Disruption," HEW Indicators (September 1963), pp. v-xiv.

siveness and can be defined accordingly. Group cohesiveness is "the total field of forces which act on members to remain in the group."[8] Inducements to remain in any group include the attractiveness of the group itself and the strength of the restraints against leaving it; inducements to leave a group include the attractiveness of alternative relationships and the restraints against breaking up such existing relationships. Thus the strength of the marital relationship would be a direct function of the attractions within and barriers around the marriage, and an inverse function of such attractions and barriers from other relationships.

In marriage, a spouse is attracted to his mate because of her intrinsic worth, her love, her charm, her ability to please his wants, or perhaps because she gains him external prestige or will further extrinsic goals. Barriers against a breakup emanate from other sources: the emotional, religious, and moral commitments that a partner feels toward his marriage or toward his children; the external pressures of kin and community, of the law, the church, and other associational memberships.

Thus marital strength is a function of bars as well as bonds. Yet the strength of barriers matters little if the partners' attraction is high enough. In many marriages, the barriers have trivial importance. The spouses' close attachment precludes that either one would seriously consider breaking the relationship.

In other marriages, though, barriers have crucial importance. In the absence of positive feelings, they maintain outward signs of marital togetherness. Goode has called the latter case an "empty shell" marriage:

. . . The atmosphere is without laughter or fun, and a sullen gloom pervades the household. Members do not discuss their problems or experiences with each other, and communication is kept to a minimum. . . . Their rationalization for avoiding a divorce is, on the part of one or both, "sacrifice for the children," "neighborhood respectability," and a religious conviction that divorce is morally wrong. . . . The hostility in such a home is great, but arguments focus on the small issues, not the large ones. Facing the latter would, of course, lead directly to separation or divorce, but the couple has decided that staying together overrides other values, including each other's happiness and the psychological health of their children.[9]

This illustration of an "empty shell" family evokes contrasting images of "full shell" and "no shell" families. To carry Goode's metaphor farther, a "full shell" marriage would be one in which not only the boundaries but also the attractions are strong for both partners; a marriage in which there is warm emotional interchange. In contrast, the "no shell" couple is in a state of dissolution; it consists of two disconnected individuals, living separate lives. In this latter instance, boundaries as well as attractions have been eroded by the events over time, until eventually alternatives to the marital state are preferred. Goode's metaphor is appropriate. It implicitly refers to two underlying continua: fullness-emptiness of attraction, and strength-weakness of boundaries.

Finally, consider the attractions and barriers outside the marriage. These are forces that pertain to relations with parents, children, lovers, friends, enemies, employers, employees, or any of a host of alternate persons. Husband or wife may be more or less attracted to any of these relationships, and he or she will have a

[8] Leon Festinger, Stanley Schachter, and Kurt Back, *Social Pressures in Informal Groups*, New York: Harper, 1950, p. 164.

[9] Goode, "Family Disorganization," *op. cit.*, pp. 441–442.

varying sense of obligation to maintain them. Such alternate relationships can be fully compatible with the existence of a strong and stable marriage. The maintenance of relations with in-laws or employers, for example, does not necessarily conflict with the primary marital bond. However, an extreme commitment to such a relationship would interfere with the marriage; as would also, of course, a commitment to a third party that fully excludes the spouse.

COHESIVENESS AND DIVORCE

In studying marriage, high cohesiveness is far harder to detect than low cohesiveness. The privacy of the marital relationship prevents outsiders from judging how "truly happy" a particular union might be; even insiders, the spouses themselves, cannot be fully aware of all the attractions and restraints that they feel.

On the other hand, the extremes of low cohesiveness eventuate in the dissolution of the relationship. If divorce is the result, it is a public index that can be studied. For this reason, it is useful to give particular consideration to research on divorce to illustrate how the present framework can be applied.

Yet consideration of such research must note the distinction between divorce and separation. In certain groups of our society, de jure separation (divorce) is a less likely occurrence than de facto separation. Undoubtedly, the less socially visible a couple is, the more likely it is to resort to informal procedures of separation. The less clear a family's ties to stable norms of kin and community, the less necessary it is to make a break formal. Thus desertion has been a far more common phenomenon in the lowest socioeconomic stratum than in the higher

strata. This point must be remembered in interpreting findings on divorce rates.[10]

Possible Differences in the Forces Affecting the Two Partners

The term cohesiveness is drawn from a physical analogy. The cohesiveness of a physical bond between two nuclei in a molecule may be indicated by the amount of energy required to break it. The physical model, though, assumes homogeneity in the forces among the nuclei. A social group model of bond strength cannot assume such homogeneity. Feelings of attraction and restraint can and do vary among the members of a group.

In marriage, too, the two partners' feelings are not identical. One spouse may consider separation, while the other remains fully bound to the relationship. Nevertheless, by definition, both partners must value another alternative over that of the present marriage before both will agree to a separation. Usually, the wife is plaintiff in divorce proceedings. Nationally, the figure is about 70 per cent.[11] The preponderance of wife-initiated divorce suits results in part from cultural prescription, yet some of the author's unpublished evidence indicates that the balance of the wife's feelings is more important than the husband's as an indicator of divorce proneness.[12]

[10]Glick, op. cit., p. 156.

[11]Paul H. Jacobson, American Marriage and Divorce, New York: Rinehart, 1959, p. 119.

[12]Goode, After Divorce, op. cit., has pointed out that in many divorce cases, the husband has precipitated the break by providing reasons for the wife's complaint. Nevertheless, the wife's tolerance for the husband's normative deviation is a crucial determinant of the decision to seek a divorce.

TABLE 1 Factors found to differentiate between high and low cohesive marriages

Sources of Attraction	Sources of Barrier Strength	Sources of Alternate Attraction
Affectional rewards	Feelings of obligation	Affectional rewards
esteem for spouse[11,14,17,24]*	to dependent children[11,15,27]	preferred alternate sex partner[11,14,18,34]
desire for companionship[4,20]	to marital bond[25]	disjunctive social relations[1,24]
sexual enjoyment[18,24,32]	Moral proscriptions	opposing religious affiliations[21]
Socio-economic rewards	proscriptive religion[8,21,30]	Economic rewards
husband's income[(2),5,12,24,31,(32),34]	joint church attendance[9,11,24,31]	wife's opportunity for independent income[12,16,28]
home ownership[5,24,31]	External pressures	
husband's education[10,28,35,36]	primary group affiliations[1]	
husband's occupation[11,19,28,33,38]	community stigma: rural-urban[3,5,7,31,37]	
Similarity in social status	legal and economic bars[13]	
religion[4,6,8,21,29,30,33]		
education[4,13,20,39]		
age[4,5,24]		

* Numerals pertain to positive findings in the corresponding references listed below. Numerals in parentheses indicate which studies reported an absence of a difference between High and Low cohesive couples.

1 Charles Ackerman, "Affiliations: Structural Determinants of Differential Divorce Rates," *American Journal of Sociology*, 69 (July 1963), pp. 12–20.
2 Jessie Bernard, "Factors in the Distribution of Success in Marriage," *American Journal of Sociology*, 40 (July 1934), pp. 49–60.
3 Robert O. Blood, Jr., *Marriage*, Glencoe, Ill.: Free Press, 1962.
4 Robert O. Blood, Jr. and Donald M. Wolfe, *Husbands and Wives*, Glencoe, Ill.: Free Press, 1960.
5 Ernest W. Burgess and Leonard S. Cottrell, Jr., *Predicting Success or Failure in Marriage*, Englewood Cliffs, N. J.: Prentice-Hall, 1939.
6 Ernest H. Burgess and Paul Wallin, *Engagement and Marriage*, Philadelphia: Lippincott, 1953.
7 Hugh Carter and Alexander Plateris, "Trends in Divorce and Family Disruption," *HEW Indicators* (September 1963), pp. v–xiv.
8 Loren E. Chancellor and Thomas Monahan, "Religious Preference and Interreligious Mixtures in Marriages and Divorces in Iowa," *American Journal of Sociology*, 61 (November 1955), pp. 233–239.
9 Eustace Chesser, *The Sexual, Marital, and Family Relationships of the English Woman*, New York: Roy, 1957.
10 Paul C. Click, *American Families*, New York: John Wiley, 1957.
11 William J. Goode, *After Divorce*, Glencoe, Ill.: Free Press, 1956.
12 William J. Goode, "Marital Satisfaction and Instability: A Cross-Cultural Analysis of Divorce Rates," *International Social Science Journal*, 14:3 (1962), pp. 507–526.
13 Gilbert V. Hamilton, *A Research in Marriage*, New York: Boni, 1929.
14 Harry C. Harmsworth and Mhyra S. Minnis, "Nonstatutory Causes of Divorce: The Lawyer's Point of View," *Marriage and Family Living*, 17 (November 1955), pp. 316–321.
15 Paul H. Jacobson, "Differentials in Divorce by Duration of Marriage and Size of Family," *American Sociological Review*, 15 (April 1950), pp. 235–244.
16 Paul H. Jacobson, *American Marriage and Divorce*, New York: Rinehart, 1959.

17 E. Lowell Kelly, "Marital Compatibility as Related to Personality Traits of Husbands and Wives as Rated by Self and Spouse," *Journal of Social Psychology,* 13 (February 1941), pp. 193–198.

18 William M. Kephart, "Some Variable in Cases of Reported Sexual Maladjustment," *Marriage and Family Living,* 16 (August 1954), pp. 241–243.

19 William M. Kephart, "Occupational Level in Marital Disruption," *American Sociological Review,* 20 (August 1955), pp. 456–465.

20 Clifford Kirkpatrick, "Community of Interest and the Measurement of Adjustment in Marriage," *The Family,* 18 (June 1937), pp. 133–137.

21 Judson T. Landis, "Marriages of Mixed and Non-Mixed Religious Faith," *American Sociological Review,* 14 (June 1949), pp. 401–406.

22 Richard O. Lang, *A Study of the Degree of Happiness or Unhappiness in Marriages as Rated by Acquaintances of the Married Couples,* M.A. thesis, University of Chicago, 1932; cited in Goode (11), p. 57.

23 J. P. Lichtenberger, *Divorce,* New York: McGraw-Hill, 1931.

24 Harvey J. Locke, *Predicting Adjustment in Marriage: A Comparison of Divorced and a Happily Married Group,* New York: Holt, 1951.

25 Thomas P. Monahan, "How Stable Are Remarriages?" *American Journal of Sociology,* 58 (November 1952), pp. 280–288.

26 Thomas P. Monahan, "Divorce by Occupational Level," *Marriage and Family Living,* 17 (November 1955), pp. 322–324.

27 Thomas P. Monahan, "Is Childlessness Related to Family Stability?" *American Sociological Review,* 20 (August 1955), pp. 446–456.

28 Thomas P. Monahan, "Educational Achievement and Family Stability," *Journal of Social Psychology,* 55 (December 1961), pp. 253–263.

29 Thomas P. Monahan and Loren E. Chancellor, "Statistical Aspects of Marriage and Divorce by Religious Denomination in Iowa," *Eugenics Quarterly,* 2 (September 1955), pp. 162–173.

30 Thomas P. Monahan and William M. Kephart, "Divorce and Desertion by Religious and Mixed-Religious Groups," *American Journal of Sociology,* 59 (March 1954), pp. 454–465.

31 Clarence W. Schroeder, *Divorce in a City of 100,000 Population,* Peoria, Ill.: Bradley Polytechnic Institute Library, 1939.

32 Lewis M. Terman, *Psychological Factors in Marital Happiness,* New York: McGraw-Hill, 1938.

33 U. S. Bureau of Census, *Marriage and Divorce: 1887–1906,* Bulletin 96, Washington, D.C.: Government Printing Office, 1908, pp. 25–27.

34 U. S. Bureau of Census, *U. S. Census of Population: 1950.* Vol. IV, *Special Reports,* Part 2, Chapter D, Marital Status, Washington, D.C.: Government Printing Office, 1953, Table 6, pp. 47–48.

35 U. S. Bureau of Census, *U. S. Census of Population: 1950.* Vol. IV, *Special Report,* Part 5, Chapter B, Education, Washington, D.C.: Government Printing Office, 1953, Table 8, pp. 63–64.

36 U. S. Department of Health, Education and Welfare, *Vital Statistics–Special Reports,* 45:12 (September 9, 1957), p. 301.

37 U. S. Bureau of Census, *Current Population Reports,* Series 20, No. 87 (November 14, 1958), pp. 11–12.

38 H. Ashley Weeks, "Differential Divorce Rates by Occupations," *Social Forces,* 21 (March 1943), pp. 334–337.

39 Edith W. Williams, "Factors Associated with Adjustment in Rural Marriage," Ph.D. Dissertation, Cornell University, 1938, p. 98; cited in Goode (11), p. 99.

REVIEW OF FACTORS
ASSOCIATED WITH DIVORCE

How do findings from actual studies illustrate the framework? Attractions that act to secure a marriage derive from love and money. The rewards that spouses receive are linked to their affection for each other, to their financial income and social position, and also to the degree that husband and wife share similar characteristics. Barriers against a breakup can be coordinated to the partners' feelings of obligation to their family, to their moral values, and to external pressures exerted on them from various sources—these are the sorts of pressures that serve to maintain the boundaries of their marriage. Finally, one can consider alternate sources of affectional and financial reward; these serve as a contrast to the internal attractions and have a potentially disruptive effect.

Table 1, together with its accompanying discussion, organizes published findings that pertain to marital cohesiveness under the three headings of attraction, barrier, and alternate attraction.

Attractions in Marriage

Esteem for spouse

It appears obvious that marital cohesiveness is positively associated with the spouses' mutual esteem and affection. Yet in what areas is esteem most apparent, and in what forms is it present or absent? Locke (24)[13] has found that spouses in happy marriages described their partners' traits in a far more positive way than did divorced persons; the former were far more likely to report the mate's traits as superior or at least equal to their own. Kelly (17) also has reported that this ten-

[13] Numerals in parentheses in this review section pertain to the references in the footnote to Table 1.

dency is positively related to marital happiness. Regarding negative esteem, Goode (11), Harmsworth and Minnis (14), and Locke (24) have reported a far higher incidence of complaints about the partner among divorcees or divorce applicants than among normally adjusted spouses.

Desire for companionship

In some cultures, such as the Japanese, marriage does not promote companionship with the spouse. However, two studies of American marriages by Blood and Wolfe (4) and Kirkpatrick (20) found that desire for companionship is strongly related to marital adjustment.

Sexual enjoyment

Locke (24) has reported that happy and divorced spouses differed significantly, both in their enjoyment of actual intercourse and in their desire for it. Terman (32) found that the most adjusted couples had the highest ratio of actual/preferred frequency of sexual relations. To qualify this finding, one should note Kephart's report (18) that concern with sexual incompatibility was found primarily among divorce applicants from the higher social strata. (The present author, in an unpublished study, has obtained a similar finding.) Sexual gratification is one vital source of marital attraction, but its lack apparently is less keenly felt among spouses who have not achieved a satisfactory material standard of living.

Husband's income

In Western nations, as Goode (12) has recently pointed out, divorce rates were greater for high-income than for low-income marriages until the advent of industrialization. However, since some unspecifiable transition point during the early part of this century, divorce rates have been negatively associated with husband's income (12). It would appear that the attractions within the marriage are lowest for the poor, and that attractions outside the marriage are relatively greater. With the reduction of legal obstacles and of economic costs of divorce, there has occurred a large increase in divorce among low-income couples.

These reasons, then, explain the inverse relation between income and divorce found in modern studies. One of the first studies to suggest this was Schroeder's (31) analysis of divorce rates in Peoria; by an ecological tehcnique, he found a correlation of −.32 between divorce rates and average income in different districts of that city. Locke (24), in his comparison between happily married and divorced spouses, found that an income "adequate for the needs of the family" lessened the likelihood of divorce. Burgess and Cottrell (5) also found a moderate positive relationship. In contrast, neither Bernard (2) nor Terman (32) found such an association; however, their samples were probably too restricted in the range of financial income. When wide ranges of income and marital satisfaction are considered, as in studies of the entire U.S. population by the Census (34), there is a clear inverse correlation between income and divorced status, and even more between income and separated status. [14]

[14] A forthcoming paper by the author will report that income is also closely related to the outcome of *applications for divorce*, once such applications have actually been filed. This study avoids a criticism by Day, pertaining to some published studies of divorce. He points out that Census enumerations of persons currently occupying the status "divorced" have sometimes been erroneously taken to represent the *rate* of divorce itself. He suggests that ". . . socioeconomic differences in rates of remarriage or in the interval between divorce and remarriage could seriously affect the relative sizes of these ratios." See Lincoln H. Day,

Home ownership

The proportion of couples who obtain a divorce is lower for owners than for nonowners of a home. This finding is reported by Schroeder (31), by Burgess and Cottrell (5), and by Locke (24). Much of the association may be a function of family income and of length of marriage. However, even if the influence of those two variables is controlled, home ownership itself probably contributes to the stability of family life. [15] It would seem that home ownership is not only a source of attraction, but also helps to stabilize the boundaries that hold the marriage together. All else being equal, the mere fact of owning a home probably increases a couple's reluctance to dissolve their relationship.

Husband's amount of education

The amount of the husband's education is higher for durable than for dissolved marriages. This is indicated by data reported by Glick (10), by Monahan (28), and by U.S. Census reports (35, 36). One would speculate, *ceteris paribus*, that a wife's attraction varies with her spouse's educational status. These findings, of course, are linked to variations in other variables, such as husband's income or prestige. His years of education undoubtedly are correlated positively with prestige, with the husband's relative superiority over his wife, and with his ability to maintain a masculine role. If the husband's education is lower than his wife's, there is more likely to be a rever-

"Patterns of Divorce in Australia and the United States," *American Sociological Review*, 29 (August 1964), p. 509. Day's reminder, published after this paper was written, is well to bear in mind in assessing findings reviewed here.

[15] Unpublished data from the author's research indicate that homeowners are also more likely to dismiss an already filed divorce suit than are nonowners.

sal in the male-female power balance with an ensuing loss of the husband's attractiveness as her marital partner.

Husband's occupation

Numerous studies have shown that divorce proneness is also inversely related to husband's occupational rank. Thus, Goode (11), Kephart (19), Monahan (26), and Weeks (38) have each shown that couples in which the husband's occupation ranks high have less divorce proneness than those where it ranks low. Part of this result may be attributed to the contribution of income, another part to the higher prestige of the professions and managerial occupations.

A third reason for the difference in divorce proneness among occupational groups relates to the stability of the husband's home life, as associated with his occupation. Thus Monahan (26) reported that physicians have a higher divorce rate than dentists, taxicab drivers a higher rate than truck drivers. One would hypothesize that the divorce rate of general practitioners or internists, whose home life is constantly disrupted, would be higher than that of doctors with regular working hours (e.g., pathologists, radiologists, or X-ray specialists); that it would be higher for long-haul truckers than for intra-city truck drivers. High degrees of instability would tend to reduce the attractiveness of the relationship and also to erode the boundaries that contain it.

Occupational differences may also be linked to differences in susceptibility to alternate attractions. Members of certain occupations (e.g., internists, taxicab drivers, or masseurs) have a greater than average probability for extended intimate contacts with members of the opposite sex. Thus they will have a greater opportunity to explore alternate attractions that would compete with their current marital relationship. In contrast, members of other occupations (e.g., clergymen or politicians) are particularly vulnerable to externally imposed norms about boundary maintenance, which would restrain any proclivity toward divorce.[16]

Such additional considerations are important in weighing the impact of occupational factors in affecting marital stability. Future empirical studies may be able to distinguish among the separate influences of each of these components.

Similarity in social status

Many studies have linked marital adjustment to similarity of religious preference—particularly Chancellor and Monahan (8), Landis (21), Monahan and Chancellor (29), Monahan and Kephart (30), and Weeks (38). Burgess and Wallin (6) noted that frequency of broken engagements was lower for same-faith couples. Hamilton (13), Kirkpatrick (20), and Williams (39) have indicated that

[16] There are few good data to substantiate these predictions, because published divorce statistics do not generally reveal detailed occupational information. Possibly the best single source is a 1908 U.S. Census Bulletin (33), which relates occupation to divorce. Although its national returns were qualified as "incomplete and hardly acceptable," its New Jersey data for 1887–1906 covered 81.1 per cent of all husbands divorced. New Jersey husbands occupied in agricultural, mechanical, and manufacturing pursuits showed lower than average divorce rates; those in professional or personal service or in trade and transportation had a higher rate. Particularly low were farmers, agricultural laborers, blacksmiths, carpenters, clergymen, engineers, and manufacturing officials. Clearly on the high side were actors, commercial travelers, musicians, bartenders, physicians and surgeons, sailors, and barbers and hairdressers, in that order. Husbands in the high-rate occupations seem to have been highly exposed to alternate attractions.

marital attraction is positively related to similarity in education. Burgess and Cottrell (5) and Locke (24) found that it is significantly associated with age similarity, particularly when the husband is older. Blood and Wolfe (4) have found that all three kinds of similarity relate positively to marital satisfaction. Undoubtedly, these are all different aspects of status similarity. Communication between the spouses would tend to be enhanced by relative likeness on these characteristics.

Sources of Barrier Strength

Sources of barrier forces exist both inside and outside the individual. The following examples of restraints against marital dissolution include some cases where the restraints are primarily internal, others where they are mainly external, and still others where their source is difficult to locate.

Obligation to dependent children

It is widely held that as long as there are no children involved, divorce is the couple's own affair. For that reason, one might expect that husbands and wives with children would feel a greater restraint than those without children—particularly minor children.

Early writings on divorce gave the impression that childless couples have indeed a vastly higher divorce rate,[17] but those studies neglected to adjust divorce rate by *duration* of marriage. More sophisticated analyses by Jacobson (15) and by Monahan (27) have shown that if length of marriage is controlled, the difference in separation rate between

[17] E.g., Alfred Cahen, *Statistical Analysis of American Divorce*, New York: Columbia U. Press, 1932; Walter F. Willcox, *Studies in American Demography*, Ithaca, N.Y.: Cornell U. Press, 1940.

childless and child-rearing couples is much smaller, but still noticeable. According to Jacobson (15), between 1928 and 1948 this disparity decreased to a ratio of less than 2:1. Even the most skeptical analysis of this difference by Monahan (27) showed some excess of divorce frequency in the childless groups.

The real question is, perhaps, what obligations do the parents *feel* toward their children? To what extent do they feel that divorce of an unattractive marriage would either damage or promote their children's well-being? If parents believe the former, then the existence of children will create barrier forces; if they believe the latter, then they would be likely to be attracted to an alternative other than the present marriage. Goode (11), for example, has taken the position that, in an inevitably conflicted home, children may actually benefit from the divorce.

So far, there is no published evidence which differentiates between parents' feelings of obligation to children as *barriers* that prevent a breakup and such obligations as sources of *negative attraction* to the marriage. Until such evidence is obtained, the issue will remain unresolved.

Obligations to the marital bond

In a large proportion of marriages, both partners are firmly committed to respect the marital contract, and divorce is not considered as a possibility. Each partner has certain qualms against even thinking of such a thing. On the other hand, if one or both have previously experienced a divorce proceeding, then either partner would be more likely to consider divorce. Thus, the barriers against the dissolution of the present marriage would be weaker. A study by Monahan (25) has indeed shown that first marriages are more resistant to dissolution than are second or later marriages. His data were confined to population statistics and did not pertain longitudinally to particular individuals. Nevertheless, it would be hypothesized that marriages of divorcees tend to have weaker boundaries than those of first-married spouses; further evidence is needed, however, to arrive at any sound generalization.

Proscriptive religion

It is popularly believed that Catholics are less likely to break their marriages than persons of other religious persuasions. This is only partly true. A more correct statement is that like-faith marriages in which both members are either Catholics, Jews, or reasonably strict Protestants have the lowest probability of divorce. This has been pointed out by studies of Chancellor and Monahan (8), Landis (21), and Monahan and Kephart (30). Such studies have also shown that persons of unconventional religious convictions are most prone to use divorce as a solution to their marital problems.

Joint church attendance

Various studies have shown that divorce proneness is inversely related to joint church attendance. Joint membership and regular attendance at church places a couple in a network of connected affiliations and exposes them to conventional values. One would assume that membership in such a net is a source of powerful external pressures. If necessary, such pressures would come into play to prevent the marriage from breaking up.

Reports by Chesser (9), Locke (24), and Schroeder (31) each indicate that, in their samples of couples, marital dissolution was less frequent among regular church attenders than among nonattenders. In his study of divorcees, Goode (11) found that (in his group of Catholics) regularity of church attendance was positively associated with duration of marriage before separation.

Primary group affiliation

Affiliation with a church or with other sorts of organizations is one source of barrier forces; affiliation with kinfolk is another vital source. In a recent paper, Ackerman (1) has proposed that divorce rates vary across different cultures to the extent that the culture encourages "conjunctive" as opposed to "disjunctive" affiliations with kin. Ackerman defines the former case as one where husband and wife share a common network of kinfolk and friends; in the latter, their loyalties go in different directions. One would suppose that a conjunctive net of affiliations acts to restrain marital dissolution more than a disjunctive net. Ackerman's analysis of cross-cultural data shows empirical support for this supposition.

Community stigma

Another source of barriers against divorce is community disapproval. Such disapproval seems more characteristic of rural than of urban communities, which leads to the expectation that rural divorce rates are lower than urban ones. This expectation is borne out by 1955 Census data (37) and by 1960 Census data cited by Carter and Plateris (7). Also, studies by Schroeder (31) and by Burgess and Cottrell (5) have reported that divorced persons are less likely to be born and reared in a rural setting. [18]

Blood (3) has drawn attention to the importance of the visibility of the marriage relationship in the community where the couple lives. When both partners are known, when their behavior is

[18] William J. Goode (personal communication) has suggested that rural divorce rates in the United States may be low only for farmers, but higher for nonowners of farms.

observed, there are greater restraints against social transgressions such as extramarital affairs. Life in the country would seem more restrictive than that in the city; relations in the suburb more constraining than in the urban center.

In describing life in the modern suburb, Whyte has noted that it exerts a "beneficient effect on relations between husband and wife. The group is a foster family." Whyte quotes a minister as follows: "The kind of social situation you find here discourages divorce. Few people, as a rule, get divorces until they break with their groups. I think the fact that it is so hard to break with a group here has had a lot to do with keeping some marriages from going on the rocks." [19]

Legal and economic bars

It goes almost without saying that legal and financial considerations exert restraints against a breakup. The wide differences in divorce rates among different states can, in part, be accounted for by differences in divorce laws—as Jacobson (16) has pointed out. And, when considering differences between high- and low-income husbands, one notes that a high-income husband is likely to pay more, both absolutely and proportionately, to support his ex-wife after separation. Thus both legal and financial factors provide important restraints against going through with a divorce.

Sources of Alternate Attraction

Popularly, it might seem that alternate attractions are the chief or the only reason for broken marriages. This impression is sustained by legal fiat, which emphasizes adultery as a reason for divorce. In one state, New York, adultery

[19] William H. Whyte, Jr., *The Organization Man*, New York: Simon and Schuster, 1956, pp. 392–393.

is the only legal grounds for dissolving a marriage contract.

It is logically necessary that the alternative environment be more attractive than the marital relationship, if the partners are to be willing to undergo the costs of divorce. However, it is not necessary that the attraction be "another woman" or "another man." The marital relationship itself may be so unattractive that any alternative condition—with or without another partner—is preferred.

Opposing religious affiliations

What are the effects of obligations toward alternative competing relationships? Little direct study of this question has been made. However, one bit of evidence indicates the direction in which the answer may lie.

Landis' (21) study of divorce rates in Catholic-Protestant marriages showed clearly that mixed-faith unions were less durable than same-faith marriages of Catholics or Protestants. However, Catholic-Prostestant marriages were three times more likely to break up when the wife was Protestant than when the husband was Protestant.

This result is explainable by the framework as follows. Assume that both partners are attracted to their own religious group, but that the wife's feelings are stronger. Assume, also, that the children in each of these marriages are to be raised as Catholics, as in the usual agreement in Catholic-Protestant marriages. Finally, assume that the wife takes prime responsibility for child-rearing. It follows, then, that the Protestant mother is exposed to more conflict—negative attraction toward spouse's religion and disruptive pressures from own religion—than is the Protestant father. The strength of this conflict would depend on the strength of her religious identification—probably weakest in the lowest strata and strongest in the middle or higher strata. This line of reasoning has clearcut empirical derivations and may well be testable in Landis's existing data. Additional studies of this question are desirable.

Wife's opportunity for independent income

One other important source of alternate attraction or repulsion lies in the possibility of the wife's separate financial maintenance. The more readily she can support herself outside the marital relationship or can be assured of such support from other means (including her ex-husband's), the more ready he would be to break the marriage.

Preferred other sex partner

Aside from reports on official complaints lodged with the Court, which frequently are colored to sustain the legal fiction, relatively few studies contain data about spouses' alternate attractions outside the marriage. It is difficult to inquire about this without asking the parties to a divorce action to compromise their personal and legal position vis-à-vis their spouse. Nevertheless, several published studies have reported that preference for an outside sexual partner does play a part in a significant proportion of divorce actions. The proportion may vary anywhere from 15 to 35 per cent of all cases —e.g., Goode (11), Harmsworth and Minnis (14), Kephart (18), and Locke (24). Complaints about external sexual attachments are more frequently reported by wives; but when the husband reports them in a divorce suit, they may be even more serious. [20]

[20] In an unpublished study by the author, a comparison was made of two groups of divorce applicants, one set of whom later dismissed the action. It was found that husband's complaints of "infidelity" were more frequent in the divorcing group, while wives' complaints of the husband's "infidelity"

Disjunctive kin affiliations

Another source of outside attraction forces would be the loyalty toward one's kin or friends. If these ties conflict with those of the spouse, they will at the least lead to strain in the marriage. As mentioned earlier, Ackerman (1) has suggested that competing primary group affiliations are associated with divorce proneness. Locke (24) found that his "happy" couples freuqently reported "a little" conflict with their own parents, i.e., (alternate) attractions to parents were at less than maximal strength. This source of marital disruption is worthy of fuller exploration in future studies of divorce.

In cases of disjunctive affiliation, one would hypothesize that the marital bond would be strengthened if the couple increases its physical and psychological distance from *both* sets of alternate affiliation groups, reducing thereby the disruptive forces. For example, partners in a heterogamous marriage that involves antagonistic in-laws would strengthen their relationship by moving away from the community where either set of parents resides. No systematic evidence to support this hypothesis can be cited, but it does coincide with informal observation.[21]

In most cases where the husband's income is extremely low, and where the wife's earnings are a substantial proportion of family income, these conditions would seem to be met. In the upper economic strata, however, income differentials between wife and husband are large, and the wife has more reason to

were more frequent in the group of couples who dismissed their action and rejoined their marriage.

[21] E. Lowell Kelly (personal communication) has reported anecdotal evidence from his own marriage research that substantiates this notion concerning mixed-religious marriages.

maintain the marriage (see Goode, 12, p. 516). In other words, wives in the lower strata appear to have less to lose and more to gain from a divorce. Economic sources of alternate attraction for the wife require further attention in research on divorce. Today, when certain forms of relief payment are contingent upon proof of the husband's nonsupport, it is particularly likely that economic factors exercise an influence on divorce proneness.[22]

Considering the wife's attraction to alternate relationships, one may also note interesting differences in divorce rates between the Eastern and Western states. Both Jacobson (16) and Lichtenberger (23) have reported that the Mountain, Southwestern, and Pacific states have had high rates, while the Middle Atlantic and New England states have had low rates. Traditionally, there has been a scarcity of women in the Western states, leading to greater opportunity for remarriage and also to greater female power.

CONCLUSION

This paper introduces an elementary framework for integrating the determinants of marital durability and di-

[22] In an article based on assumptions similar to Goode's and the present author's, Heer has recently dealt with propositions about the wife's relative power in marriage. David M. Heer, "The Measurement and Bases of Family Power: An Overview," *Marriage and Family Living*, 25 (May 1963), pp. 133–139. Heer writes: ". . . the greater the difference between the value to the wife of the resources contributed by her husband and the value to the wife of the resources which she might earn outside the existing marriage, the greater the power of her husband, and vice-versa" (p. 138). We would propose that in cases of *low* difference, if the husband does not readily yield power within the marriage itself, the wife is inclined instead to dissolve the marriage.

vorce. The framework is based on merely two components—attractions toward or repulsions from a relationship, and barriers against its dissolution. The former correspond to Lewin's concept of "driving forces," which are said to drive a person either toward a positively valent object or away from a negatively valent one.[23] The latter correspond to Lewin's concept of "restraining forces," which act to restrain a person from leaving any particular relationship or situation.[24] These components can be used to subsume a large diversity of published findings. For example, findings about the effects of both income differentials and kinship affiliation could logically be fitted within the same scheme. Marital cohesiveness was thus interpreted as a special case of group cohesiveness.

Both the limitations and the advantages of the present analysis should be noted.

Limitations

First, the scheme is based on a hypothetical conception of the attractions and barriers that affect the partners in a marriage. These influences can rarely be inferred directly from changes in overt indices. This is one reason why this paper has not attempted to examine the complex interaction effects between different sets of such influences.

Second, the concept of group cohesiveness, from which this scheme is drawn, is itself the subject of critique and reformulation.[25] Theoretically, it is difficult to define cohesiveness so that it des-

[23] Kurt Lewin, *Field Theory in Social Science*, New York: Harper, 1951, p. 259.

[24] *Ibid.*, p. 259.

[25] For detailed discussions of conceptual and operational issues in research on group cohesiveness, see *Group Dynamics*, ed. by Dorwin Cartwright and Alvin Zander, Evanston, Ill.: Row Peterson, 1960, Chapter

cribes under the same rubric the forces that act on both the group and the separate individuals who compose the groups.

Third, the present review of earlier studies has been illustrative rather than comprehensive. Some pertinent studies were omitted. The discussion was often limited to single findings of available studies that were occasionally taken out of their wider context.

Advantages

At this time, it is *not* intended to offer either a general theory or to present an entirely complete review. It *is* intended to understand existing studies at a more general level of abstraction. It is suggested that marriage research can fruitfully be linked to small group research, that simple general hypotheses can be derived in the beginning stages of such a linkage, and that existing evidence about marital dissolution is suitable for documenting such hypotheses.

The present approach draws on the insights of Goode and other writers on marriage and divorce. Yet it aims to go farther in several ways. First, it points to the development of a general framework, congruent with theories about all social groups. It avoids *ad hoc* theories about "marriage" or "family," but aims to integrate the subject with knowledge of social relationships in general.

Second, the scheme intends to deal not only with actuarial rates of divorce nor only with a particular cultural milieu. Its social-psychological concepts are, in principle, applicable to any given marriage in any society. Although marriages and societies differ in the constellation of forces that determine cohesiveness, it is

assumed that these determinants ultimately will be measured and precisely described.

Third, and most important, the components of the present scheme are derived from one basic assumption about the existence of psychological and social forces. Such "forces" are hypothetical. They are not easily accessible to measurement. Yet the present statement aims to prepare for eventual measurement.

Previous attempts to explain divorce have sometimes precluded a clear operational assessment. For example, Goode recently accounted for differences in divorce rates in terms of *both* "social pressures from kinfolk and friends" and a culture-based "equialitarian ethos."[26] Yet his two concepts, kin pressures and cultural ethos, are on quite different levels of conceptualization; the former is vaguely contained in the latter. In contrast, the presently proposed framework offers an opportunity for describing the relations among such concepts. To obtain a precise estimate of the various factors which influence divorce, one would need eventually to establish some common measuring unit that would indicate the magnitude of each force. . . .

To summarize, a conceptual framework has been outlined for integrating research on marital cohesiveness and dissolution. The concepts are the same as those employed for understanding the cohesiveness of other social groups. The strength of the marital relationship is proposed to be a direct function of hypothetical attraction and barrier forces inside the marriage, and an inverse function of such influences from alternate relationships. The scheme was then applied to a review of some major findings about divorce, and its implications were discussed.

3; Annie Van Bergen and J. Kockebakker, "Group Cohesiveness in Laboratory Experiments," *Acta Psychologica*, 16 (1959), pp. 81–98; Neal Gross and William Martin, "On Group Cohesiveness," *American Journal of Sociology*, 57 (May 1952), pp. 546–554.

[26] Goode, "Family Disorganization," *op. cit.*, pp. 413–414.

A Reinquiry into Marital Disorganization *

John Scanzoni

Although scientific interest in other forms of disorganization (e.g., personal, criminal) has been maintained in recent years, it seems that relatively little thought and research have been expended on marital disorganization. Aside from one or two major contributions, *fresh* attention to this once popular area appears to have been steadily decreasing. This is perhaps a reaction to the moralistic fervor which was sometimes attached to the early studies of divorce and desertion.

One recent exception to the lack of fresh thinking about divorce comes from Farber. In contrast to the Burgess theme which has dominated family sociology, i.e., that divorce is dysfunctional given the ideal of the "companionship family," Farber argues that divorce is functional, given his ideal type of "universal permanent availability." [1] What he means by this is that individuals are free to select a mate from any segment of society they wish, for the chief purpose of personal welfare. If "personal welfare" is not achieved, then divorce serves as a way to escape this incompatibility. The divorced person is free to "shop around" until he finds someone else with whom he may attempt to be "compatible." Thus, divorce becomes a useful mechanism for the attainment of what is now purported to be the major goal of contemporary marriage, viz., personal welfare.

Whatever the merits or weaknesses of Farber's arguments, it seems clear that he is suggesting that family disorganization is best explained in terms of personality variables. While these kinds of factors are no doubt important in this connection, it must not be forgotten that even the nuclear family is, after all, a *group*. Therefore, it is legitimate to posit that certain cultural and structural variables may also play a part in family disorganization. Nevertheless, in so doing we are not overlooking "marital organization," or those marriages in which dissolution does not occur. If one attempts to deal with disorganization, it becomes theoretically difficult to fail to deal also with marital organization. Consequently, the framework which is presented should aid us in understanding why some marriages remain organized, as well as why some become disorganized. Actually, there appear to be few theoretical explanations and even fewer pieces of evidence as to why either situation should take place. Present plans call for the following schema to be soon tested empirically and thus modified where necessary.

THE DEPENDENT VARIABLE

To approach the issue of family disorganization, we shall use as our dependent variable, "conflict resolution." We shall avoid a bias which Coser has

°Adapted from the Journal of Marriage and the Family, 1965, 27: 483–491.

[1] Bernard Farber, *Family: Organization and Interaction*, San Francisco: Chandler Publishing Co., 1964, pp. 104–134.

observed exists in family research, viz., that conflict is, *ipso facto*, considered dysfunctional for the family.[2] Instead, we shall assume neither that it is functional or dysfunctional, but that it is simply endemic to or inherent in any social system including the nuclear family. In other words, it is "there," and the question becomes, "How is it resolved?" Before we can answer this question, however, we must define what we mean by conflict. By "conflict" we refer to dissensus between marital partners over values, beliefs, goals, norms, and behaviors which make up the structure of the nuclear unit. The conflict may center on any or all conceivable areas of marital interaction, such as economic activities (both production and consumption of income), leisure pursuits, child-rearing, decision-making (use of power), performance of household tasks, religious and/or community activities, sex relations, in-laws, and so on.

Further, when discussing marital conflict, it is vital to make a distinction which has long been made in other areas of sociology, viz., the distinction between conflict over basic principles or those goals and beliefs which hold a group together, and conflict over norms or the specific means by which agreed-upon goals are achieved.[3] In the first type of conflict, the existence of a group or system is threatened because the bonds of consensus which maintain the collectivity are being called into question, i.e., basic ground rules become challenged and perhaps blurred. When conflict is merely over the *means* to attain commonly held values or goals, the bonds of consensus are not threatened but instead reaffirmed, i.e., the particular means or norms which are finally utilized

are those which presumably best achieve common ends. In conflict over norms, appeals are constantly made to more abstract values to legitimate varied avenues of action. Conflict takes place within the group, but generally the group remains intact.[4]

With this background in mind, we may now address ourvelves to the question of the ways in which marital conflict is resolved. There are three possible categories: *dissolution* of the marriage (divorce, desertion, and so on); *change* of orientations on the part of one or both partners so that dissensus is removed; or *institutionalization*, i.e., the conflict becomes an accepted part of the system, or, in common parlance, partners "agree to disagree." Conflict over basic values or goals is most likely to be resolved by dissolution, next by institutionalization, least by change. Conflict over norms within a context of value consensus is most likely to be resolved by change or institutionalization, less likely to be resolved by dissolution. For example, if both partners believe that their standard of living should be "affluent," there may still be conflict over means to attain this goal, i.e., "Should we buy a yacht or an extra sports car?" However, the basic value consensus over affluence tends to reduce the possibility of conflict resolution by means of dissolution. But if one partner holds to affluence, and the other believes only in an "adequate" living standard, there exists a basic clash in values. As a result, one partner holds norms which will achieve his values ("buy a sports car"), the other holds norms derived from his goals ("buy a small compact"). The conflict of basic values gives rise to normative conflict which cannot be resolved within a framework of value consensus. Since there is no common ground of agreement or consensus, conflicts of

[2] Lewis A. Coser, *The Functions of Solid Conflict*, Glencoe, Ill.: Free Press, 1956, p. 73.

[3] *Ibid.*, p. 77 ff.

[4] *Ibid.*

these sorts tend to increase the probability that dissolution becomes a viable means of resolution. Institutionalization contains a weaker degree of probability, and change of orientations becomes less probable still.

THE INDEPENDENT VARIABLES

It will be noted from the above discussion that the use of "conflict resolution" as our dependent variable gives us an entering wedge toward the understanding of why some marriages remain organized and why others become disorganized. The question is taken out of the realm of value judgments as to what is or is not functional for the family, and the theoretical issue becomes, "How is inherent conflict resolved within the nuclear unit?" To expand our reinquiry further, we must now suggest certain independent variables which might help to account for particular categories of the dependent variable. Perhaps a fruitful way to isolate significant independent variables is, first of all, to consider certain historical factors surrounding the American family prior to widespread industrialization.[5] In doing so, we observe two general kinds of notions which are by no means startling, but which may be connected in some way.

THE EXTENDED FAMILY

First, we note that the extended family maintained much more dominance over the nuclear family than is the case today. As Goode indicates," A qualitative change . . . has taken place . . . relatives are now assimilated to the status of ascriptive friends . . . one has an obligation to be friendly to them, but they, in turn, have an obligation to reciprocate, and *they may not intrude merely because they are relatives.*"[6] The mass of studies is acknowledged which, through demonstration of visiting and help patterns, invalidates Parsons' "isolated nuclear unit" hypothesis, but the basic point remains that in general, the extended or blood kin no longer provide the main source of values, beliefs, goals, and norms which structure the nuclear family.[7]

FAMILY INTEGRATION

Drawing on Williams, it is possible to conceptualize this change as a difference in degree of integration. He defines "integration" as the extent to which ". . . interests, values, norms, beliefs, symbols . . . are shared."[8] Integration between groups may be conceived of as the extent to which they possess a common culture and social organization. Before Western society became highly industrialized, the nuclear family was integrated into the extended family to a much larger degree than is the case as industrialization progresses. While the current nuclear family is by no means "isolated," it is, to a much larger extent than ever before, free from the "determinations" of the blood kin.

[5] See Panos D. Bardis, "Family Forms and Variations Historically Considered," in *Handbook of Marriage and the Family*, ed. by Harold T. Christensen, Chicago: Rand McNally Co., 1964, pp. 403–461. Also William J. Goode, *World Revolution and Family Patterns*, Glencoe, Ill.: Free Press, 1963, Chaps. 1 and 2.

[6] Goode, *Ibid.*, 1963, p. 76.

[7] An excellent representative article from the "visiting" and "help" literature is Marvin B. Sussman, "The Isolated Nuclear Family: Fact or Fiction," *Social Problems*, 6 (Spring 1959), pp. 333–340.

[8] Robin M. Williams, *American Society*, New York: Alfred A. Knopf, 1959, p. 543.

The second notion, which is also well known, is that divorce rates (i.e., an index of conflict resolution that ends in dissolution), or the incidence of marriages which become disorganized, have increased during this same period in which the integration of the nuclear unit into the blood kin has decreased. In the U.S. in 1900, the rate of divorces per thousand marriages was 75.3; in 1960, it was 259.0. In Germany during the same period and using the same base, the rate jumped from 17.6 to 88.7; in Norway, from 12.6 to 88.5; in England, from less than 2.2 to 69.5; and in other Western lands, the change is in the same direction.[9] It was Durkheim, of course, who first suggested that integration and disorganization in terms of suicide may somehow be related. The difficulties and problems with Durkheim's early formulations have been summarized by Gibbs and Martin, but nonetheless, they acknowledge their debt to his pioneer insight and empirical work.[10] To carry out their research, they defined "integration" as role compatibility, or the absence of role conflict, and they hypothesized that degree of integration and rate of suicide are inversely related.[11]

This recent work demonstrates that Durkheim's integration-disorganization hypothesis is still viable for modern sociology, and there seems to be no reason why it might not have even wider and more general scope in terms of family disorganization. In other words, previous to mature industrialization, the blood kin exercised considerable influence and control over the nuclear unit. They provided a cultural framework, structural reinforcement, as well

as "significant others" to maintain these strong relations. What is more, the nuclear unit tended to accept this high degree of integration with the blood kin as legitimate. A serious problem in family sociology has been the failure to recognize the nuclear family as a small group which shares much in common with other types of small groups. One of these common characteristics is the sociological truism that extensive and intensive relations with external groups will affect the culture and structure of the group. It may be suggested that the effect of strong integration of the nuclear unit into the blood kin in a predominantly agricultural society was to provide cultural and structural elements which resulted in relatively low rates of marital disorganization.

In a recent report, which has *not* overlooked the structural determinants of marital organization, Ackerman, from a study of 62 primitive societies, concludes that "when the spouses maintain predominantly common affiliations, the incidence of divorce is low; that, when the spouses maintain predominantly separate affiliations, the incidence of divorce is high."[12] In an attempt to test Gluckman's hypothesis that "the divorce rate is a reflex of the kinship structure itself,"[13] he used measures of community endogamy, consanguine endogamy, and also a combination of both measures. Significantly, he also raises the cross-cultural implications of his findings. He cites Burgess and Cottrell, and Goode on the importance of the relationship between "homogeneity in the background and interests of the spouses."[14] He then

[9] Goode, *op. cit.*, 1963, p. 82 ff.

[10] Jack P. Gibbs and Walter T. Martin, *Status Integration and Suicide*, Eugene: U. of Oregon Press, 1964, pp. 5–13.

[11] *Ibid.*, Chaps. 2 and 3.

[12] Charles Ackerman, "Affiliations: Structural Determinants of Differential Divorce Rates," *American Journal of Sociology*, 69 (July 1963), p. 13.

[13] *Ibid.*

[14] *Ibid.*, p. 14; Ernest W. Burgess and Leonard S. Cottrell, *Predicting Success or*

compares Zimmerman's "family-friend groupings," i.e., relationships of the nuclear unit with external collectivities, to "disjunctive" and "conjunctive" relations of the nuclear units in his sample.[15] Ackerman suggests that in our society, as well as in primitive societies, mutual membership of both spouses in the same (i.e., conjunctive) external collectivities leads to the same "norm and value sets" within the nuclear unit. Conversely, individual membership in disjunctive collectivities results in conflicting "norm and value sets."[16] (What Zimmerman and Ackerman call "homogeneity" between the nuclear unit and external affiliations, we have chosen to call "integration.") He then raises the question as to whether or not the degree of consensus of norms and values is related to the degree of divorce, and whether or not this consensus is in large part determined by conjunctive or disjunctive affiliations (i.e., degree of integration) of spouses with external affiliations.[17] It is this question which he has tested in several primitive cultures. The schema which follows suggests means to test these ideas now in American society.

PREINDUSTRIAL AMERICAN FAMILY

First, we shall attempt to isolate four variables which may have been significant in terms of nuclear unit conflict resolution when the United States was predominantly an agricultural,

or perhaps an early industrial society. Next, we shall seek to explore their relevance with regard to conflict resolution within current family situations. In effect, we are saying at one level of abstraction that degree of integration with certain external groups or networks is related to family disorganization. At a lower level of abstraction—at the level of operational research—we hope to isolate four independent variables which are related to the aforementioned three categories of the dependent variable.

First, there is the variable of control of mate selection by the extended kin. While apparently there was greater freedom of choice in the colonies and in early America than there had been in Europe, ". . . parents and masters . . . often influenced mate selection extensively."[18] It is possible to assume that one consequence of this control of mate selection was to raise the probability that the marriage would possess a common universe of values and goals. It does not appear likely that the kin would mate partners who did not possess value consensus or who at least did not appear likely to be able to establish such a consensus. It would seem that the greater is the control of mate selection, the less is value consensus a matter of chance, and more the result of somewhat systematic planning. Consequently, value consensus in itself means less conflict over the bonds which hold the marriage together. The basic principles or goals which maintain the marriage-group are less likely to be challenged. In addition, sharing of basic goals provides a framework within which normative conflict may be resolved by means other than dissolution, i.e., by change or institutionalization.

Second, the nuclear family was related to the blood kin in terms of structural *interdependence*, or mutual participation of both partners in the

Failure in Marriage, New York: Prentice-Hall, 1939; Goode, *op. cit.*, 1956.

[15]Carle Zimmerman, "The Present Crisis," in *Marriage and the Family*, ed. by Carle Zimmerman and Fr. Cervantes, S. J., Chicago: Henry Regnery Co., 1956, pp. 111 ff.

[16]Ackerman, *op. cit.*, p. 14.

[17]*Ibid.*

[18]Bardis, *op. cit.*, p. 452.

same external groups. "Interdependence," suggests Coser, is "a check against the breaking of consensual agreement." [19] In the traditional family system, the chances were high that both partners would participate mutually in the same external group or groups in terms of economic behaviors, friendship behaviors, religious behaviors, and so on. The fact that this was so increased the probability that the marital partners would possess a common universe of values and goals by which to structure their own interaction. In essence, both partners tended to belong to the same reference group and to interact with the same "significant others." The possibility that conjugal conflict might result from membership in competing kin groups was lessened by the peculiar economic conditions of a predominantly agricultural society. Whichever kin group provided the greatest economic opportunities usually obtained the maximum amount of participation from the nuclear unit. In practical terms, this often meant geographical proximity to the kin with whom the nuclear unit maintained the strongest economic interdependence. If conflict did arise between kin groups over the behaviors of the nuclear family, the latter was likely to conform to the expectations of the kin group with whom economic interdependence was most vital for its own maintenance. Therefore, in a fashion similar to that of controlled mate selection, interdependence provided a common set of values and, consequently, a framework within which normative conflict may be resolved by means other than marital dissolution.

Third, there was the existence of the "patriarchal ideology," or belief in ultimate male dominance. In Western preindustrial society, this cultural factor was an integral part of the extended family

19 Coser, *op. cit.*, pp. 76 ff.

system. Greatest authority was vested in the older male members of the family, least authority in the younger women. While this factor differs from the first two factors in that it did not serve primarily to *establish* nuclear unit goals, it did function as a means to *resolve* any conflict which might arise over these goals or the means to attain them. In effect, the wife was not free to reject the norms and behaviors established by her husband as being legitimate. She was free only to conform to his authority. This says nothing about psychological hostilities and frustrations that the wife might experience if she did not desire to conform. However, as a result of her own socialization process and her participation with her husband in the kin group, i.e., the group which legitimates this ideology, the chances are good that she tended to accept this belief as an acceptable mode to resolve marital conflict.

Finally, nuclear family-blood kin ties were marked by the ideal of "permanence." Marriage was for life, and more desirable than divorce no matter how much personal dissatisfaction or unresolved conflict existed. Adultery was in some cases a legitimate ground for divorce, but by no means was this qualification to permanency universally accepted. Since both nuclear unit partners were members of a group that held this belief (i.e., the same blood kin), the probability was good that they accepted this ideology, and thus either made great effort to resolve conflicts, or else maintained an organized marriage in spite of the conflicts. In addition, their economic interdependence with the kin made divorce impractical, particularly in the case of the woman. Similar to the "patriarchal ideology," this factor does not establish common goals within the nuclear unit, but it does serve to bring about resolution of conflict by means other than divorce.

CONTEMPORARY AMERICAN FAMILY

Thus far, we have suggested that marital disorganization is only one of three possible outcomes of conjugal conflict. We have examined blood kin-nuclear unit relations historically, in an attempt to discover certain variables which might affect the outcome of conflict. It was further suggested that the lower rates of dissolution which existed historically were due to the relatively high degree of integration of the nuclear unit into the blood kin. What remains now is to show the pertinence of this schema for the current empirical scene.

First, let us explore the available studies of blood kin-nuclear unit relations, in order to probe what implications may be present for family disorganization. Cohen and Hodges, on the basis of data collected in the Far West, report on the differences between middle-class and lower-class extended kinship networks:

> In short, the essential contrast is perhaps not so much one of lower class extended kinship system *versus* a middle class structurally isolated nuclear family, as it is one of tenacity, in the lower class, of *individual* kinship networks, overlapping but not identical, and relatively resistant to change *versus*, in the middle class, reorganization of the networks of both spouses in the interest of the solidarity and primacy of the conjugal unit.[20]

In other words, they are suggesting that lower-class nuclear families tend to become polarized as a result of each spouse identifying with and participating in his or her blood kin group. This was the same point that Ackerman made with regard to nuclear units in his sample of

[20] Albert K. Cohen and Harold M. Hodges, Jr., "Characteristics of the Lower-Blue-Collar Class," *Social Problems*, 10 (Spring 1963), p. 309.

primitive societies. Participation of spouses in conjunctive external networks results in less conflict and lower divorce rates. Individual participation in disjunctive networks leads to more conflict and higher divorce rates.[21]

It will be recalled that in an American agricultural setting, the probability of the above type of polarization was lessened as a result of mutual participation with the particular kin which offered the greatest economic rewards. Since economic participation of this sort is increasingly less common in an industrial society, particularistic, ascribed loyalties of both partners emerge to divide the marriage, especially in the lower class. In the middle class, there appears to be more of a tendency for the partners to act in a solidary fashion to manipulate kin networks (rather than *be* manipulated) so that they contribute to the "primacy" of the conjugal unit instead of its polarization. (Why the middle-class family should be able to act in this solidary fashion, in contrast with the lower-class unit, is discussed below.)

Cohen and Hodges report that they would expect to find greater dissensus between spouses in the lower class because (1) kin are geographically closer, (2) they tend to press their "claims" more than do middle-class kin, (3) more effort is spent in honoring these claims because the uncertainty of life at this level makes the need for reciprocality ever present. The husband tends to exercise behaviors and utilize resources that will benefit his kin, the wife attempts the same for hers, and the probability of conflict over these divergent interdependencies rises sharply.[22] Their data indicate that lower-class individuals know more families that have become disorganized or are experiencing severe marital conflict, than do those at higher-

[21] Ackerman, *op. cit.*

[22] Cohen and Hodges, *op. cit.*

class levels.[23] At the same time that they maintain strong individual participation in divergent kin networks, their "family life is more unstable and strife-ridden."[24]

The same kinds of conclusions were reported by Young and Willmott in England. They write that among working class families, ". . . marital insecurity and kinship were inextricably bound together."[25] They discovered a definite relationship between high levels of unresolved conflict and a tendency for both partners to seek the support of their respective kin networks. Another consequence of the wife's seeking support from her kin was to drive the husband to seek support and solace at the local pub. Likewise, in England, Bott discovered that lower-class families tend to have close-knit kin networks which "interfere with conjugal solidarity."[26] The same phenomenon emerged in her work as noted by the above authors, viz., that this divergent involvement with one's own kin tended to polarize partners and raise the incidence of unresolved conflict. In a very recent study in the East, Komarovsky reports this identical pattern:

> The prevalence of in-law problems among the less-educated workers is caused not only by an excess of conflict-producing situations but also by the inability to escape them once they arise. The mode of life and the social norms of these workers create close dependence upon relatives . . .[27] . . . in-law problems . . . are created by continued interdependence of the married couple and their parental families.[28]

In addition to the increased conflict at lower-class levels as a result of the polarization caused by opposing kin, Komarovsky reports that her working class respondents felt deep dissatisfaction with their marriages, and that this was a crucial factor in the high rates of disorganization found at this class level.[29]

In other words, what these several reports appear to indicate is that in lower-class families, there is an absence of integration of both partners into the same blood kin and a tendency to identify with one's own kin, with the result that mates tend to become polarized. Significantly, the rates of divorce and desertion in Western society tend to increase with decreasing class level. Marital dissolution is correlated with most of the variables related to lower-class position such as lower income, lower status, younger age at marriage, lower education, and so on.[30] It may be that *part* of the explanation for these correlations is due to the failure of many lower-class nuclear units to be highly integrated to one dominant set of kin. This lack of integration results in the absence of a common universe of values and goals which in itself means dissensus, and which also gives rise to normative conflict which cannot easily be resolved without shared goals. Individual involvement with one's own kin apparently leads to a polarization of values and norms.

However, this would be only *part* of the explanation for higher rates of lower-class disorganization, and it does not go far enough to explain higher rates of middle-class marital organization. In this regard, several sources may be of further help. For example, Bott dis-

[23] *Ibid.*

[24] *Ibid.*

[25] Michael Young and Peter Willmott, *Family and Kinship in East London*, New York: Free Press of Glencoe, 1957, pp. 158 ff.

[26] Elizabeth Bott, *Family and Social Network*, London: Tavistock Publications, 1957, p. 94.

[27] Mirra Komarovsky, *Blue-Collar Marriage*, New York: Random House, 1964, p. 279.

[28] *Ibid.*, p. 333.

[29] *Ibid.*, p. 342.

[30] Jacobson, *op. cit., passim.*

covered that lower-class families who became socially mobile tended to establish friendship networks with new friends at their same class level. This mutual participation of both partners in the *same* external network resulted in increased solidarity between partners, reduced the threat of competing external groups, and enabled the partners to present a "united front to the world."[31] She goes on to make the point that since a modern, industrial society results in the "differentiation" of the nuclear family from the extended kin, the former has more freedom to choose its external networks and to "govern its own affairs."[32] In other words, there appears to be some relationship between middle-class position, freedom from kin control, freedom to participate voluntarily and mutually in external networks, and marital solidarity.

Rainwater and Handel report that as families in their sample move from lower class to the upper-working class, they tend to experience attenuation of divergent kinship ties and a greater solidarity between mates.[33] Movement to the lower-middle class results in a greater and more significant change, for it is here that participation in external interests by the couple tend to multiply and "are seen as enriching the conjugal relationship."[34] In other words, participation in these interests and networks tends to draw the couple together. Komarovsky makes a large point of the fact that working class families in her sample experience very little participation in external networks, and that this factor is, in part, related to

their high levels of unresolved conflict and marital dissatisfaction.[35]

> For the great majority life is narrowly circumscribed . . . the relatives, a few friends, the boss and some work-mates, the tavern keeper, the church and the union . . . top movie stars . . . athletes, TV performers and top national office holders . . . Beyond that circle extends a vast darkness. These . . . persons do not enjoy full membership in their society. . . . A proportion of Glenton's children will grow up to live as do their parents, on the fringes of their society.[36]

The fact that lower-class families participate only minimally in external networks and interests is well known.[37] The implication that this may somehow be related to marital disorganization has not been quite as evident. In terms of the integration-disorganization schema discussed above, the explanation of this relationship may fall along the following lines. It has already been noted that lower-class families tend to be polarized due to competing kin interests. Adding to this situation the fact that they possess few external networks from which they might derive a set of common goals to reduce dissensus and to resolve normative conflict, there exists a situation in which conflict is compounded and the mode of its resolution uncertain. These nuclear families lack integration with meaningful external networks which might possibly provide for them the source of stable organization. Conversely, while middle-class families have by no means cut themselves off from the kin, it is not these types of ascriptive relationships which tend to supply their basic cultural and structural elements.

[31] Bott, *op. cit.*, p. 95.

[32] *Ibid.*, p. 1000.

[33] Lee Rainwater and Gerald Handel, "Changing Family Roles in the Working Class," in *Blue-Collar World*, ed. by Arthur B. Shostak and William Gomberg, Englewood Cliffs, N.J.: Prentice-Hall, 1964, pp. 71–72.

[34] *Ibid.*, p. 73.

[35] Komarovsky, *op. cit.*, pp. 342–334.

[36] *Ibid.*, p. 344

[37] Goode, *op. cit.*, 1963, p. 76.

MIDDLE CLASS INTEGRATION

In contrast to the "social debt" idea which governs mutual help patterns in the lower class,[38] Litwak suggests that when middle-class nuclear units draw on the kin to achieve certain kinds of social goals, this "does not involve burdensome obligations which interfere with the democratic industrial order of our society."[39] Consequently, to accept aid from kin on either side in no way means that one or both partners are compelled to conform to the values and norms held by the kin. In essence, the middle-class nuclear unit becomes the focus of aid from the blood kin, but not a focus of their control. In this way, the pattern of lower-class polarization is avoided.

The middle-class nuclear unit is thus free to relate itself to whatever external networks or clusters of interests which it deems best, and indeed, in the middle class, rates of social participation are high. To the extent that marriage partners are mutually involved in these external relations, they will be influenced by the cultural elements of these networks, i.e., be integrated with them, and thus share a common universe of values and norms. Presumably, this will result in resolution of conflict by means other than dissolution. Farber has coined the term "quasi kin" to describe these kinds of external networks, and to convey the idea that they are in a sense the functional equivalent of the blood kin due to their influence over conjugal values and norms.[40] If this expression is conceived of in terms of its broadest meaning, it then becomes useful in discussing these external networks. In other words, *it would appear that in a universalistic-achievement type society, it seems as valid to hypothesize that integration and family disorganization are inversely related, as they were in a particularistic-ascriptive society.* However, in keeping with the complexities that accompany the change from one type of society to the other, the possibilities for meaningful integration have greatly expanded. Concomitantly, the possibilities for frequent polarization have also expanded. Not only may the blood kin perform this latter function in the lower class, but the quasi-kin may do this also for middle-class marriages. The wide range of external participation possible to husbands and wives can easily result in polarization, and hence dissensus over values and norms. It is not at all uncommon for the family researcher to be told, "I live in my world, he lives in his."

FUTURE RESEARCH

The actual validity of this approach to family organization and disorganization must await the results of an empirical test which is currently being planned. For comparative purposes, the sample will consist of both organized and disorganized marriages. After quantifying the seven independent and dependent variables, attempts will be made to discover their interrelationships. For example, do marriages which rank high in terms of parental and peer approval and also interdependence, experience resolution of conflict by *change* of norms,

[38] Donald E. Muir and Eugene A. Weinstein, "The Social Debt: An Investigation of Lower Class and Middle Class Norms of Social Obligation," *American Sociological Review*, 27 (August 1962), p. 532.

[39] Eugene Litwak, "The Use of Extended Family Groups in the Achievement of Social Goals," *Social Problems*, 7 (Winter 1959), p. 179.

[40] Farber, *op. cit.*, p. 220 ff.

rather than by *dissolution?* Conversely, do marriages which rank low on these factors tend to experience dissolution rather than change?

For current research purposes, the patriarchal ideology is reconceptualized into a continuum of *compromise-commitment.* "Commitment" refers to the strength with which one or both partners adhere to particular values or norms. It carries with it the idea of being unwilling to yield in a certain conflict area because of this commitment. "Compromise" refers to the willingness to yield, change, or alter values or norms in any particular conflict situation. It can readily be seen that commitment by both partners to divergent sets of goals or values precludes a high probability of change, whereas an ideology of compromise toward certain goals would probably lead to change. It should be noted that since we are not treating this as a personality variable, but as a structural variable, incidences of compromise or commitment may vary. For example, a wife may be strongly committed to certain goals regarding leisure and yet be willing to compromise in the area of religion. Thus the question to be investigated is whether high levels of commitment by each partner to divergent sets of values and norms are related to dissolution, and whether high levels of compromise by each partner are related to normative change and marital organization.

It is likewise necessary to sharpen the concept of permanence into a continuum of "permanence-pragmatism." It will be recalled that Farber and others have argued that the older belief is being replaced by one in which the chief end of marriage is believed to be personal benefit. If this pragmatic (and, to the respondent, tangible) goal is not achieved, then it is legitimate to end the marriage and seek this "personal benefit" else-where. To our knowledge, the actual extent and strength of this ideology has never been empirically tested. However, in connection with the schema presented above, the question arises as to whether those near the "permanence" end of the continuum tend to resolve conflict by change and institutionalization, while those near the "pragmatic" end tend to resolve it by dissolution. In other words, in the empirical world, is it actually the case that those holding the former view are more apt than those holding the latter view to avoid dissolution in spite of conflict over values and/or norms? Conversely, are those with a pragmatic view more apt to choose dissolution as an acceptable means of conjugal conflict resolution?

SUMMARY

The issue of marital disorganization and organization has been approached from the standpoint of integration with external networks. In a predominantly agricultural setting, the nuclear unit was highly integrated into the blood kin, i.e., the latter was a strong determinant of the culture and structure of the former. The exact nature of this influence was spelled out in terms of four independent variables and their relationships to three categories of the dependent variable, conflict resolution. In a mature industrial setting, several studies seem to indicate that lower-class marriages tend to be polarized by competing kin interests. In the absence of participation in nonkin external networks or interests, the lower-class family tends to experience a high incidence of marital conflict and dissatisfaction. It is also true that rates of disorganization increase with lower class level. In other words, it appears that many lower-class families tend to be only minimally integrated with the kinds of external networks which might supply a common universe of values and norms. Lacking this integration, they tend to experience greater polarization and disorganization.

On the other hand, middle-class families, who tend to experience fewer divorces, maintain extensive "quasi-kin" networks along with blood kin relations. These latter kinds of 'relations do not appear to polarize the middle-class nuclear unit, nor do they often supply the values and norms which govern it. Consensus over goals and means comes chiefly through voluntary, mutual participation in external networks and interests. To the extent that the couple is mutually integrated into these external networks, it will share common values and norms, hence resolve conflict by means other than dissolution, and thus remain organized. Two of the four independent variables were reconceptualized to account for presumed cultural changes which have occurred both in family authority and permanence. Finally, the four independent variables were linked to the dependent variables in terms of research questions which are soon to be tested.

19

RESPONSES TO MARITAL DISSOLUTION:
MARITAL DISORGANIZATION AND RE-ORGANIZATION

William J. Goode's essay on the structural importance of divorce points to the ambiguous expectations that surround post-divorce behavior in the United States. To a large extent this ambiguity is equally characteristic of widowhood. When a marriage is dissolved, the formerly married encounter difficulties in returning to their premarital "single" standing. Goode describes society's reluctance to forget the divorcee's marital history and its corresponding failure to provide clear norms for postmarital life.

Finally, the question frequently arises as to the outlook for remarriages. Thomas Monahan remarks that our literature seems to hold two conflicting views—that remarriages tend to be less stable than first marriages and that they tend to be equally stable. Using records for a three-year period in Iowa, he shows that remarriages of divorced persons are much more likely to end in divorce than are first marriages, but remarriages of widowed persons are less likely than first marriages to lead to divorce.

The Anomic Social Position of the Divorcee*

William J. Goode

Whether or not we judge this segment of the population or this rate to be large, it seems at least likely that in our society the group impact of divorce is much greater than in most others. . . . some of the behavioral indices of this concern . . . may be summarized as follows: (1) A widespread condemnation of the extent of divorce and of its increase; (2) the emotional difficulties suffered by the individuals in the divorce; (3) the number of panaceas offered as general solutions for the problem; (4) its frequency as an object of clinical research; and (5) the development of organizations and experts whose aim is to ameliorate this distress.[1]

The kinship structure fails to define

*Adapted from William J. Goode, After Divorce. New York: The Free Press, 1955, pp. 12–15.

[1] For a series of reports on various aspects of this "social problem," see the November, 1950 issue of the Annals, 272, especially William J. Goode, "Social Engineering and the Divorce Problem," pp. 86–94.

clearly an acceptable behavior pattern for this experience in the life history of a substantial segment of the population. The kinship system fails to furnish unambiguous arrangements for the following kinds of problems.

1. There are no ethical imperatives for relatives or friends that would make them feel constrained to furnish material support during the crisis and afterwards to the divorcees *as* divorcees. This is a period of dissolution of certain household arrangements. Most often, the two spouses separate from one another, and at least one of them must set up a new abode. There are new problems of purchasing food and housing, and, of course, there are various legal fees. These costs cannot usually come out of existing income. There is no room for such added expenses. In addition, of course, one or both spouses may lose their jobs, and there is only rarely enough money for both to continue their usual activities without need for added funds.

2. Similarly, there are no ethical imperatives for friends and relatives to furnish *emotional* support during this period. There is a general ethical imperative to furnish support to close friends during any kind of crisis, and to some extent this is applicable to the divorce situation. It is not comparable, however, to the kind of crisis created by an emergency operation or sudden illness, death, loss of job, etc. In the event of divorce, the friend must make an adjustment among several other imperatives, such as whether he *should* support the break-up of a family, whether he approves his friend's conduct, or how friendly he is to the other spouse. What we are distinguishing here is the difference between a crisis situation in which the imperatives are clear and one in which they are not clear. As we shall show later, friends and relatives actually do help in this situation, but this is not the crucial point at issue. Whether a given individual gives such support is

the resultant of many factors, but he cannot, in our society, base his action upon a simple rule of the kinship or friendship structure. The most striking contrast, of course, is with death of the spouse, for in this case the relative or friend who is unwilling to provide economic or emotional support is viewed with disapproval by all within the group.

3. A further point of ambiguity centers around the *readmission* of participants into their former kinship structure or into a new one. The importance of this ambiguity is not to be underestimated, and it is indeed the base on which other ambiguities rest. By contrast, among the Zuñi, for example, the kinship is matrilineal, divorce is relatively common, and it is accompanied by little public concern and attention. This is the case generally, as it happens, for merely private matters of marital conflict and even marriage. In this society the property in land is owned by the woman's side of the family and descends through her line. In one sense, divorce means that the man is "dismissed." We are not, however, concerned with the personal impact of this situation, but with the fact that in the case of a divorce, all the parties concerned know what they are supposed to do. The man returns to his mother's household, where there is a known place for him. He is part of her family line, and marriage has not changed that fact. He does not carry away the corn he has raised, and there is no argument about the ownership of real property, for that remains in the possession of his wife's lineage. There can be no argument about the children, since the children belong to his wife's line. Whether she herself rears the children or they are given to one of her male relatives to rear, the children are nevertheless part of her family, and it is the right of her family to make decisions about the children's welfare. There is no alimony and no child support, since both sides are simply reabsorbed into an existing and

usually extended familial network. These provisions exist whether or not either family approves the behavior of either spouse. There may, of course, be some deviations from these rough rules laid down here, for in no society does everyone live up to the ideal. Nevertheless, these are the general moral imperatives, and the individual or family who failed to live by them would be criticized.

In our own society, by contrast, we are not at all clear as to where the members of the divorcing family ought to go. Indeed, in our society the emphasis is so much on the single family unit, the nuclear family, with only rather tenuous and increasingly vague connections with the older generation or with collateral relatives, that often there is almost no other family cell to which the members of the divorced family *can* go. This is a somewhat exaggerated statement, but it does describe the *norms*. The husband's original family has no moral imperative to take him back. He has made a claim to adulthood and independence, having founded his new family. He has left the family nest. There is no room for him, not alone spatially as is so often the situation in our time, but in kinship terms. It is assumed that if he divorces he will continue to work and support himself, together with perhaps his divorced spouse and children, but this is not a necessary concern of the family from which he originally came. Again, we must emphasize that, concretely, his original family may help him and be friendly to him, but there is no moral injunction that *as divorcee* he has such rights.

The wife is in an even more ambiguous position. Our own society is patrilineal, and patriarchal to a degree. By the Judeo-Christian traditions of the Western world, the wife leaves her original family and becomes a member of the husband's family. Actually, because of the pattern of small nuclear families in our generation, husband and wife simply form a new family unit. In any event, she is considered to be part of that new unit, and no longer part of her family of orientation. This is emphasized by the fact that she takes her husband's name and, if she has children, usually keeps her husband's name even after the divorce. The children also have her husband's name, so that even if she returns with her children to her own family's home, her name and kinship designation lie with the family of her husband. To this degree, then, the divorce asserts a legal cleavage which is only partially carried out in institutional fact.

In any event, for all the family members involved in the divorce, there is some ambiguity about the family status and role to which each must *return* when a divorce is made final. Neither of the two families of orientation is given clear definitions of the approved kinship status to be reassumed by the two married children.

4. As an almost necessary consequence of these ambiguities, the kinship structure does not point out avenues for the *formation of new families*. In some strata, after what is considered an appropriate period of emotional recovery, the divorced wife gradually forms new male friendships. In others, this behavior is considered vaguely or definitely improper. What is certain, however, is that the family's obligation to help her form a new family is not clear. This is in contrast with the moral imperatives families feel for helping the younger generation find a first husband or wife. Daughters are admonished by both parents that they must look for the right kind of husband, and parents usually make at least token gestures toward helping in this process.[2] Even the most protective mother gives at

---

[2] Of course, due to various emotional involvements one or both parents may also sabotage their own child's efforts by destructive criticism and similar behavior.

least lip service to the notion that she must help her son find a wife. The push toward marriage is strong in our culture, and it affects both generations. The family has, however, discharged its obligations when the child is married. The unhappiness and disorganization of the divorced spouse may lead in time to the parent family offering help in moving toward a second marriage. However, this is a result of the personal affection of family members for one another and the distress caused by the other's suffering, and is not so much due to a socially recognized obligation to offer this type of aid to a divorced child.

5. Correlative with these gaps is a further ambiguity concerning the proper behavior and emotional attitudes of the spouses most directly concerned. We have just noted the failure to specify the proper behavior for various activities which might be carried out by relatives or even friends. However, the other side of all such sets of definitions is a specification of the appropriate role behavior of the two spouses. There is no clear definition as to whether they should be grieved or relieved. They are in some sense now "single," but the role behavior of the never married is much more definitely specified. Having *once* been defined as adult and married, a status which is in turn defined as being chronologically *later* than the status of "never married," neither the spouses nor their families have a simple definition of an in-between state: they are neither old nor young, adult nor child, married nor single. Lacking such a specification, the divorced spouse is subject to criticism by some, no matter what she or he does. Behavior and emotion may seem inappropriate to some members of the family or to some friends. In particular, the proper relationship *between the divorced spouses* is not clearly defined.

These ambiguities do not necessarily create great emotional distress and . . . many women may adjust to divorce with relatively little anguish. However, social behavior is simplified in all societies by role definitions, accepted and known to almost all participants, and morally approved. When these definitions are lacking, the necessary decisions must be made on a more individual basis, and the people concerned can not count on general social approval, whether or not their previous behavior has been proper.

The Changing Nature and Instability of Remarriages *

Thomas P. Monahan

CHANGES IN REMARRIAGE

. . . Until recently, although there are no reliable statistics on the subject in this country, it had been the consensus that most divorcees did not remarry. Many well-known writers subscribed to the guess that only about one-third remarried, while some others estimated it to be about 50 per cent and as high as 88 per cent.[1] Available statistics do not easily lend themselves to an exact determination of the proportion of the divorced or widowed who ultimately remarry, now or in the past. In spite of the uncertainty of the information on "divorce," the data we do have, however, give considerable support to the new pronouncements that a large proportion of the divorcees remarry, perhaps as high as three-fourths.

In contrast to colonial times when widowhood accounted for nearly all remarriages, in the last few generations a new element has interposed itself into the American marital pattern—namely, the gradually swelling tide of remarrying divorcees. This drastic change is illustrated in the charts showing the nature of remarriages in the contiguous states of New York and Connecticut.[2] Data from a number of other states and cities extend-

°Adapted from Eugenics Quarterly, 1958, 5:2: 73–85.

[1] Alfred Cahen, Statistical Analysis of American Divorce (New York: Columbia University Press, 1932), pp. 98–109; Popenoe, Paul, Modern Marriage, New York, Macmillan, 1943, p. 118; Willard Waller, The Family, A Dynamic Interpretation (New York: The Cordon Co., 1938), p. 531; E. R. Groves and W. F. Ogburn, American Marriage and Family Relationships (New York: Henry Holt and Co., 1928), pp. 363–64; Ray E. Baber, Marriage and the Family (New York: McGraw-Hill Book Co., 1939), pp. 475–79; Paul C. Glick, "First Marriages and Remarriages," American Sociological Review, XIV (December, 1949), 730, and American Families (New York: John Wiley and Sons, 1957), p. 139; and United States Bureau of the Census, Population—Special Reports, P-46, No. 4, June 1, 1946.

[2] Census of the State of New York for 1855 (and for 1865), Secretary of State, Albany, New York, 1865, p. xcv, and Annual Reports of the Division of Vital Statistics, State Department of Health, Albany, New York; Annual Registration Reports, Division of Vital Statistics, Connecticut State Department of Health, Hartford, Connecticut. According to some data in the early 1900's, New York City, with its large Catholic and Jewish population, seems to have lagged behind up-state New York in the extent of divorce among persons remarrying. However, by 1940 the two jurisdictions were not far apart (cf., National Office of Vital Statistics, Vital Statistics— Special Reports, Vol. 15, No. 19, and Vol. 17, Nos. 9 and 13). New York City currently publishes no statistics. Because of migratory-marriage effects state data cannot be accepted as being precisely definitive.

TABLE 1   Persons married during January 1950 to April 1953 by number of times married, percent distribution*

HUSBAND	*Wife*		
	TOTAL	ONCE ONLY	TWICE OR MORE
Total	100.0	77.7	22.3
Once Only	79.6	70.1	9.5
Twice or more	20.4	7.6	12.8
	Previous Marital Status of Remarried		
	TOTAL	DIVORCED	WIDOWED
Grooms	100.0	74.6	25.4
Brides	100.0	69.9	30.1

* National Office of Vital Statistics, *Vital Statistics-Special Reports,* Vol. 39, Nos. 3 and 5, pp. 108, 210. Compare to Glick, *op. cit.,* 1957, pp. 141 and 144.

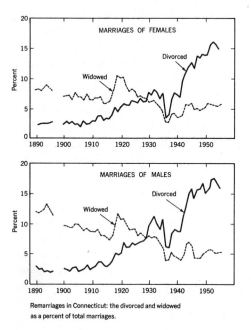

Remarriages in Connecticut: the divorced and widowed as a percent of total marriages.

FIG. 1. Remarriages in Connecticut: The divorced and widowed as a percent of total marriages.

ing over a period of years further substantiate the pattern of change.[3]

[3] For example, Maine, New Hampshire, Rhode Island (and Providence), Wisconsin (and Milwaukee), and others. See Ruby Jo Reeves, *Marriage in New Haven Since 1870,* unpublished Ph.D. thesis, Yale University, 1938, pp. 1–17, IV—1 to 13.

Some *population* survey data on marriages in all of the United States gathered in 1953 disclosed that 30 per cent of all marriages from January 1950 to April 1953 were remarriages for either party and in 13 per cent of all marriages both parties had been married before. Seventy-five per cent of the remarrying males and 70 per cent of the remarrying females had been *previously* divorced (Table 1).

A compilation of statistics from *marriage* records in 21 reporting states for the year 1954 indicated the same thing: about three out of four persons who remarried had been divorced, and in a higher proportion of cases at least one of the parties had been divorced (Table 2).

Explanation for the change in the nature of remarriage is two-fold. With the increase in life expectancy widowhood has been occurring at older ages when eventual remarriage is less likely and, at the same time, divorce has been becoming more common for American couples at the younger marriageable ages. As a result divorcees predominate among those who remarry. Actually, if it had not been for the rise in divorce in the earlier years of life, the over-all proportion of remarriages would have been on the de-

TABLE 2 Marriages in 21 reporting states by previous marital status, 1954, percentage distribution*

HUSBAND	Wife			
	TOTAL	SINGLE	WIDOWED	DIVORCED
Total	100.0	75.9	7.0	17.1
Single	77.1	·68.4	1.8	6.9
Widowed	6.2	1.4	3.1	1.7
Divorced	16.7	6.1	2.1	8.5

* Eliminating cases of marital status not reported by one or both spouses.
SOURCE: National Office of Vital Statistics, *Vital Statistics–Special Reports,* Vol. 44, No. 6, p. 130. Approximately the same relationship holds for 23 states in 1955.

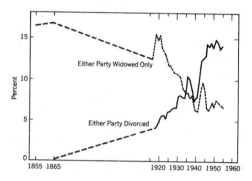

FIG. 2. Remarriages in New York State (excluding New York City)°: Divorced and widowed combinations as a percent of total marriages.

° Includes New York City in 1855 and 1865 only.

cline in the past 50 years in the United States.[4]

THE SUCCESS OF REMARRIAGES

Present Interest

Americans are not merely interested in achieving the state of marriage; they are also eager to be successfully married, with divorce being an unintentional and unpremeditated outcome. The allegation that the prospects of a successful or a happy marriage for divorcees were poor

[4] Paul H. Jacobson, "Differentials in Divorce by Duration of Marriage and Size of Family," *American Sociological Review,* XV (April, 1950), 235–44.

(according to some cogent reasoning and selected case studies) was an acceptable conclusion in sociological and popular literature at one time—when divorces were fewer and held in low esteem.[5] In view of the swelling tide of remarriages of divorcees and the apparent success of many of them, and the more tolerant public attitude nowadays, sociologists are reporting more favorably upon this class of remarriages, in support of which viewpoint some rather selected kinds of data are offered in evidence. The push to make divorce acceptable is growing, but, as yet, there is no espousal of the novel idea expressed years ago (1924) by a judge who averred that "Every divorce makes four people happy."[6] One authority on divorce, however, was recently credited with the statement, "There is no question now that second marriages are happier than first marriages . . . (and) the percentage of failures is less among all second marriages than among all first marriages."[7] This conclusion is shared by

[5] W. Waller, *The Old Love and the New* (New York: Horace Liveright, Inc., 1930), pp. 157–58, and *op. cit.,* 1938, p. 566.

[6] R. L. Hartt, "The Habit of Getting Divorces," *World's Work,* XLVIII (August, 1924), 407. Cf., A. Q. Maisel, "What Divorce Crisis?", *McCall's,* LXXV (August, 1948). 18ff.

[7] William J. Goode cited in E. M. Duvall and R. Hill, *When You Marry* (New York: Association Press, 1953), p. 291—a

others but is in direct opposition to certain facts and needs careful evaluation . . .

IOWA DATA

Only two or three states gather records showing the marital background of couples entering into marriage or being divorced. In Iowa a rather full marital history of the parties is asked for on the new (1953) marriage and divorce forms for state registration. With the help of Mr. L. E. Chancellor, the Iowa State Director of Vital Statistics, it was possible to obtain tabulation sheets on both marriages and divorces according to prior marital history of the couples. Whereas, heretofore, we have been limited in our analysis to remarriages by the number of the marriage without regard to type, now we have for the *first time* information detailed according to widowhood or divorce. In the period 1953–1955 Iowa marriages totaled 70,901; divorces, 15,502.

Representativeness

Iowa is a fairly representative area in the mid-Western United States, with a strong agricultural base and a small-industry economy. An outward migration state, its population is over 95 per cent white, about one-fifth Catholic and less than one per cent Jewish; and Des Moines, with a population of 178,000 in 1950, is the only city with over 100,000 inhabitants. There seems to be a liberal

---

widely used pre-college text. Cf., Bernard, Goode, Monahan, Popenoe, cited herein; J. H. S. Bossard, *Parent and Child* (Philadelphia: University of Pennsylvania Press, 1953), pp. 149–50; and M. F. Nimkoff in *Conference on Divorce* (Chicago: University of Chicago Law School, 1952), Conference Series No. 9, p. 61.

attitude toward divorce and no special legal impediments are imposed against it, although remarriage within a year without court permission is technically prohibited by law. In spite of Iowa's agricultural emphasis and non-urban nature, the divorce rate per 1,000 population in 1954 was 8.7 compared to the national figure of 9.2. In 1954 the duration-specific divorce rates indicated the marriage fatality rate in Iowa to be about 21 per cent of all marriages.[8] All in all, even though it may not represent the condition prevailing in highly urbanized, industrial areas, or in other places characterized by a large nonwhite population, in its geographic region Iowa may be taken as a typical middle-American state.

The nature and accuracy of all data on marriage and divorce (and marital status) need careful appraisal, and familiarity with registration records gives one reason to be most cautious about small differences in findings. This matter and other methodological perplexities are variously discussed in the literature cited. . . .

DIVORCE STABILITY
BY MARITAL BACKGROUND

Ratio of Divorces per 100 Marriages by Marital Type. The overall ratio of divorces per 100 marriages in the 3-year period was 21.9.

Primary marriages (a first marriage for both parties) show a ratio of only 16.6 divorces per 100 marriages in that category, but where both parties had been divorced *once* before the figure doubles to 34.9, and where both parties had been divorced *twice or more* times before the ratio climbs to 79.4. Not all marital com-

[8]See, Iowa State Department of Health, *Annual Report of the Division of Vital Statistics, 1951* (Des Moines, Iowa), pp. 83–86.

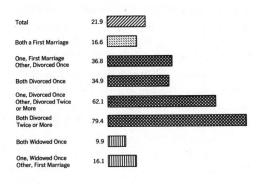

Total	21.9
Both a First Marriage	16.6
One, First Marriage Other, Divorced Once	36.8
Both Divorced Once	34.9
One, Divorced Once Other, Divorced Twice or More	62.1
Both Divorced Twice or More	79.4
Both Widowed Once	9.9
One, Widowed Once Other, First Marriage	16.1

FIG. 3. Ration of divorces per 100 marriages of selected type of marital background° Iowa, 1953–1955.

° Divorced-widowed combinations excluded.

binations are shown in the chart; some have too few cases per cell. One of the ratios obtained (a first-married bride with a twice-or-more divorced husband) appears extremely high. In this regard it must be remembered that marital types which are relatively infrequent may not be accurately gauged in this 3-year compilation; and also, in view of the nature of the information and the method, the ratios can only be accepted as approximate. A certain variability appears in the set of figures, but one must hesitate about drawing any inference from them regarding any unequal fragility on the male or female sides which have a similar prior marital history. Allowances for a later age at marriage for divorcees as compared to first marriages (and mortality reduction before divorce could occur) would only accentuate the divorce ratios found. The duration of these remarriages before divorce takes place a second time is shorter than for the first marriages, and this would tend to exaggerate their "rate" of failure. Nevertheless, everything considered, the differences in the "divorce ratios" obtained need not be disqualified to any appreciable extent on these scores.

As to the widowed, they show abnormally low ratios: 9.9 for the both widowed *once* only, and 2.0 for the both widowed *twice or more* only. One very important element, which it is not yet possible to eliminate from the results for the widowed classes, is their much older age at remarriage. In a group of 14 reporting states in 1954, divorced grooms (last or prior status) remarried at about age 36, whereas widowed males remarried at age 57—and brides of corresponding classes about 5 to 9 years earlier, respectively. [9] The low divorce ratios of the widowed may be due largely to the effect of joint-mortality, such that previously *widowed* couples do not survive as a unit to endure the rigors of divorce or make it necessary. The divorce ratio of first-married with widowed spouses bears out this surmise of age bias, as witnessed by the ratios of 15.1 for the widower with a first-married wife, and 16.8 for the widow with a first married husband. . . .

CONCLUSION

Marriages which are successful must certainly survive the social storms of life. Those which do not can hardly be called a "success." One author in this field, who compared a divorced and a happily married group in great detail, based his thesis squarely on the point that "divorce is a criterion of marital adjustment." [10] However, he and others have produced results which purport to show that remarried divorcees "on the whole are happy and adjusted in second marriages," [11]

[9] Supra, *Vital Statistics—Special Reports*, Vol. 44, No. 6, p. 108.

[10] H. J. Locke, *Predicting Adjustment in Marriage* (New York: Holt, 1951), p. 3.

[11] See feature article on the Goode study (*supra*) in *This Week* newspaper magazine, January 8, 1956, p. 8, which states, "Nine out of 10 divorcees who remarry claim that their

and a new school of thought seems to be developing around this belief. Whatever the reason for it, there is a fundamental contradiction between the two viewpoints: that remarriages of the divorced are more likely to end in divorce *and* that divorced persons are as successful in their remarriages as once-married persons.

For the first time in the United States we have been able to gather data on a broad basis to show the incidence of divorce among remarrying classes. According to this information for one state, Iowa, as for marriage survival alone, it seems that the widowed who remarry fare as well as do the *primary* marriages, after making considerable allowance for the differential mortality effects upon the widowed group. With the divorced it is the opposite story: a divorce for one party weakens the strength of the marriage bond, and a second divorce experience greatly lessens the chances of survival of the marriage. It may well be that the twice-second marriages are better."

divorced, who are sometimes referred to as the "neurotics," [12] have only about 20 to 25 chances in 100 for a lasting marriage.

Such are the hard demographic facts for the general population of Iowa, at least. Incidental information from a few other cities confirms this finding. The qualifications to the Iowa data given above should not be overlooked, however; and similar studies should be made to test the general or special validity of these findings.

All this is not to deny that there are other elements to a truly happy marriage; and the fact of mere legal endurance is not enough. Some marriages are indeed an endless round of tensions and conflict, until "death do them part." On the other hand some divorced persons do achieve a successful remarriage, and perhaps for the 50 per cent or so which manage to survive there is a high level of happiness.

[12] Waller, *op. cit.*, 1930, p. 140; Edmund Bergler, *Unhappy Marriage and Divorce* (New York: International Universities Press, 1947); Shirley Raines, "Personality Traits of Persons Who Divorced and Remarried," MA. Thesis, University of Southern California, 1949, as reported in *Family Life* X (June, 1950), 1–2; Kingsley Davis in M. Fishbein and R. Kennedy, eds., *Modern Marriage and Family Living* (New York: Oxford University Press, 1957), p. 111 (1947 edition, p. 467); and Rev. H. Loomis, "Divorce Legislation in Connecticut," *New Englander and Yale Review*, XXV (July, 1866), 450–51.

NAME INDEX

Italicized page references indicate selections contained in this volume.

SUBJECT INDEX

Abortion, in Taiwan, 224 (*tables*) 225, 226, 227–30
Abstraction, process of, 8–9
Achievement, and values and family interaction, 364–80
Achievement-vicariousness, 536
Adolescence: in American society, 383–95; choices open in, 386–87; conservative treatment in, 387–88; normative regulations on, 387; parents, peers, and culture, 381–95; psychological preparation for maturity, 385–86; relationship to family, 389–90; sociological definition of, 381–82
Adult control, see *Parental control*
Adult noninterference, 311
Affectional function of family, 59
Africa, and social control of youth, 479
Age: at childbearing, 167; at marriage, 167–68; and mate-selection, 489 (*table*) 489
Aged persons: in China, 410; and community life, 411; and Eskimo culture, 410; and group memberships, 413; and health, 415; and income, 414–15; in Ireland, 409; and kinship, 411; in London, 431–32; major social roles of, 413–14; marital status of, 414; among Masai (African tribe), 410; mutual dependence of, 411–12; post-retirement stages of, 428–29; problems of in U.S., 412; and productivity, 411; property and power of, 413; and property ownership, 410–11, 413; and religion, 411; and separate households, 131; solutions posed for, 415–16; strategic knowledge of, 411; welfare of, 409–16; and work, 414
Allport-Vernon-Lindzey Study of Values, 283
Anaclitic love, 519
Animal psychology: findings of, 268–73; and "imprinting" process, 269–70
Anomie, and American youth, 387, 392, 393
Armenians, 85
Ashanti kingdom, Ghana, matrilineally structured family in, 25–28, 31
Assistance, and reciprocity, 147–48
Assortive mating, 517
Atomistic family, 127, 129–30, 137

Authoritarian control, and permissive non-control, 314–15
Authoritarian personality syndrome, 299, 311–12
Authoritarianism, 302
Authoritative parental control, 299–317, (*table*) 304–306
Authoritativeness, 302–303

"Baby boom," 235, 236
Bilateral family, 28–29
Bilateral kindred, and nuclear family, 397
Birth cohorts, 167–68
Black see *Negro*
Brahmin problem, and sororities, 514–15
Brazil, 46
British Guiana, 49–50, 52, 53, 54

Caribbean countries, illegitimacy in, 203
Catholics: and extended familism, 83–84, 135; interethnic and intra-ethnic marriages, (*table*) 492; and mate-selection, 490–91, (*tables*) 490, 494, 495; Polish, 85; use of contraceptives, 237–38
Central America, 46
Child (first): birth of, (*table*) 169; median age of mother, 168; median spacing of, 168
Child (last): age of mothers at birth of, (*table*) 171; birth of, (*table*) 169; first marriage of, 170, (*table*) 169
Child behavior: and disciplinary techniques, 303–13; effects of authoritative parental control on, 299–317, (*table*) 304–306
Child bethrothal, 466, 475–76
Child psychologists, 243
Child rearing: advice on, 254–59; effects of communication on, 257–58; information-seeking behavior, 256–58; patterns of, 312–13; permissiveness in, 300–301
Childbearing, 168
Children: concern for, 247; of divorced couples, 567–68; in feudal Japanese family, 463; firm control and creative thrust, 312; lower-class, and education, 339–48; rebelliousness in, 308–309; of working mothers, 277–80